# Augustus

# JOCHEN BLEICKEN

# Augustus

## *The Biography*

Translated by Anthea Bell

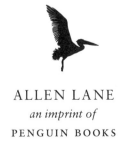

ALLEN LANE
*an imprint of*
PENGUIN BOOKS

ALLEN LANE

UK | USA | Canada | Ireland | Australia
India | New Zealand | South Africa

Allen Lane is part of the Penguin Random House group of companies
whose addresses can be found at global.penguinrandomhouse.com.

First published in German by Alexander Fest Verlag, Berlin 1998
This translation published in Allen Lane 2015

001

Copyright © Alexander Fest Verlag, Berlin, 1998

Translation copyright © Anthea Bell, 2015

The moral right of the author and translator has been asserted

Grateful acknowledgement is given to the following for permission to reproduce
copyrighted illustrations: p. 260 Sammlung Walter Niggeler; pp. 458–9 Vatican Museum,
Rome; p 535 Kunsthistorisches Museum, Vienna

Set in 10.2/13.87 pt Sabon LT Std
Typeset by Jouve (UK), Milton Keynes
Printed in Great Britain by Clays Ltd, St Ives plc

A CIP catalogue record for this book is available from the British Library

ISBN: 978–0–713–99477–3

# Contents

# I

# The Ides of March

Rome was on the alert. Gaius Julius Caesar, who had been appointed dictator for life at the end of the previous year, was planning to set out in a few days' time to wage war on the Parthians, who had been threatening the Roman province of Syria since the crushing defeat of Marcus Licinius Crassus at Carrhae in the year 53 BC. It was clear that this would be a difficult venture, comparable in its extent to the Gallic War, the campaign of several years in which Caesar had conquered those parts of Gaul that still remained free and subjected them to Roman rule. No one knew whether Caesar's aim this time was simply to exact revenge for the defeat of Crassus or whether he wanted to acquire more territory. The only certainty was that he would be absent from Rome for some time.

The dictator had called a meeting of the Senate for the Ides of March, to be held in the Curia of Pompey, an assembly hall built by Pompey the Great adjoining the theatre that also bore his name. Caesar shrugged off warnings of an assassination attempt, just as he dismissed the idea of surrounding himself with a bodyguard, trusting that his policy of reconciliation with the representatives of the old aristocracy and his own political position, so far uncontested in public, would stand him in good stead. He had dismissed his Spanish guards from his service some time earlier. It is possible that, at the height of his power and in view of his age and his failing health, he felt a certain indifference to the future. In fact we are told that he said, at this time, that his well-being was of importance primarily to the state; he had gained power and fame in abundance long before, and if anything were to happen to him now, then unrest and civil wars far worse than any seen before would threaten Rome.

Caesar could not, therefore, be dissuaded from attending the scheduled Senate meeting. As soon as he was seated in his gilded chair of office, the conspirators surrounded him on the pretext of supporting a petition presented by one of their number. Then, at an agreed signal, they stabbed him. Struck by many dagger thrusts, Caesar resisted only briefly and then fell to the ground at the foot of the statue of Pompey, his old adversary in the struggle for power and influence in the state. The assassins had agreed that every one of them must stab him, so that they would all be equally complicit in their violent act, but in their fury and agitation they had delivered their blows so indiscriminately that of all the twenty-three wounds (or, according to another account, thirty-five) a doctor later established that only one was mortal. After the deed was done Marcus Brutus raised his bloodstained dagger in the air, called out the name of Cicero and congratulated him on Rome's return to freedom.

Now that the tyrant had been eliminated, the assassins thought that the republican order he had toppled would come into its own again. But the conspirators' cries of liberty rang unheard through the Senate as its members scattered, horrified by the murder. Only two senators, the praetors Lucius Marcius Censorinus and Gaius Calvisius Sabinus, had tried to stand by the dictator, but the conspirators had pushed them out of the way. The people of Rome themselves were dismayed by the assassination and incapable of any political reaction. Shops and businesses closed, some of those eager for news ran to the Forum, many others barricaded themselves into their houses, and only a few spoke of freedom.

The conspirators were a very mixed bunch. Hardly any of them could claim never to have served the dictator; many, including their leaders, had even held high rank in the army and the administration, and still did at the time of Caesar's assassination. Even if they kept at a certain distance from the new regime, they were what would be called fellow travellers today. The real, uncompromising opponents of Caesar had taken up arms to defend the old order, had perished in its cause or were now wandering around the vast empire in search of a centre of resistance somewhere. Many of the conspirators, including Marcus Brutus and Cassius, had originally fought on the side of the Senate and Pompey against the dictator, but after being defeated had sought pardon and

THE IDES OF MARCH

political promotion, which were generously granted. Not a few of the assassins belonged to the dictator's intimate circle, including several experienced generals (legates) and others who were personally very close to him. It is not always easy to discern a clear motive for these men's participation in the plot. In fact there has been no discussion of the motives behind the murder in general, either in antiquity or today; it seemed unnecessary, since few have doubted that at least the great majority of the conspirators were motivated by the idea of restoring the old order of the state, which they associated with political freedom. Whether they had fought with Caesar in the civil war or had opposed him and been pardoned after the defeat of Pompey, they might approve, or at least tolerate, his securing of his exceptional position by violent means, but they were not ready to go along with the increasingly obvious transformation of the old aristocratic order into a monarchy.

The uncompromising traditionalists numbered among them not only Brutus and Cassius, but also some conspirators who had not yet held high office in the state, for instance Publius Servilius Casca and Lucius Pontius Aquila, who as tribune of the people in the year 45 had been the only man in the college of tribunes to show the dictator his republican sympathies. Personal motives may have played a part for some of the conspirators; Servius Sulpicius Galba, for instance, must surely have joined their ranks not least because he had been passed over for promotion by Caesar. All the conspirators, however, whether 'republicans' or opportunists, had lived for years under the dictator's rule or even worked in his administration, so there was a great gulf dividing them from those who had remained steadfast in opposing him by armed force. It was only natural that after the Ides of March such men expected the conspirators to explain their readiness to be reconciled with the tyrant, or even work for him. At first, many who had been associated with the dictator for so long might not have fully understood the political consequences of the civil war waged by Caesar in 49, allegedly solely to retrieve his personal political status, although later, once their general had risen to the position of a monarch, they withdrew their allegiance. They incurred the hostility of Caesar's supporters, who were bound to regard participation in the plot by those who had been his colleagues, generals and even friends as treachery.

Only a few of the circle of assassins could consider themselves members of the old aristocracy, the *nobilitas*, which had guided the state in past centuries and built the Roman empire, but those few were the men who mattered. They included Gaius Cassius Longinus, who was regarded as the instigator of the conspiracy and was the most logical thinker in the group, a man of uncompromising principles who urged action. He had followed Pompey in the civil war, was pardoned by Caesar after the defeat of the Pompeians at Pharsalos and had been appointed praetor for the year 44, thus becoming a holder of one of the highest offices of the state. A considerably more illustrious name was borne by the Bruti, descendants of one of the two first consuls of the republic, Lucius Junius Brutus, who according to tradition had driven out the last tyrannical king, Tarquinius Superbus, in 509 and transferred government of the state to the heads of the noble families of Rome. His name was linked to the very idea of liberty. It meant first and foremost the freedom of the nobility, since, although the people took part in many political decisions, the members of the influential old families who sat in the Senate in fact controlled the state.

One of the Bruti, Marcus Junius Brutus, was related through his mother Servilia to Marcus Porcius Cato, the man who had been at the heart of the old nobility's resistance to Caesar in the civil war and had taken his own life in Utica when he found himself in a hopeless position after the defeat at Thapsus in 46 BC. As Servilia's half-brother, Cato was an uncle of Marcus Brutus, who after Cato's suicide married his only daughter Porcia in the year 45. In his youth Brutus had had himself adopted by the old noble family of the Servilii Caepiones, but because of his famous ancestor Lucius Junius Brutus he had kept his old surname of Brutus; his adoptive father seems to have been his mother's brother. Before his real father could embark on an official career, he had been executed by Pompey in 77 as the supporter of a consul who had tried to carry out a coup against the Senate. As a result Brutus felt deep hostility to Pompey and suspended it after the outbreak of the civil war solely for the sake of opposing Caesar. Caesar pardoned Brutus too, and in 47/45 BC, as he still had no particular career, appointed him to the governorship (proconsulate) of what was then the most important Roman province, Gallia Cisalpina (Upper Italy). This was a particular mark of favour, since it would normally have been essential for the man holding that post to have been a consul or at least a praetor already. After his governorship he, like Cassius, was appointed praetor for the year 44. Caesar valued him above all as a man of letters, for Brutus was one of the outstanding intellectuals of his time; hence also his close relationship with Cicero, who found his ideas stimulating and dedicated a number of writings to him. After the disaster of Pharsalos, which sealed the fate of the old order, Brutus was bold enough to write a eulogy of his uncle, Caesar's great adversary, which he entitled 'Cato' and in which he also studied the old republic, which had been the bone of contention. Caesar did not ban this work but responded with an 'Anti-Cato' of his own.

The other Brutus, Decimus Junius Brutus Albinus, came from a noble family very active in the last years of the republic; both his father and his grandfather had been consuls. He himself, at the age of only twenty-three, joined Caesar when the Gallic War began and became an outstanding commander, distinguishing himself both in Gaul and during the civil war at the siege of Massilia (Marseille), particularly at sea. Later he became governor of the newly conquered parts of Gaul (Gallia Comata) and finally praetor. Personally he was very close to Caesar, much closer than Marcus Brutus or any of the other conspirators. Caesar even named him substitute heir in his will should his main designated heir refuse the inheritance or die suddenly. Gaius Trebonius was another of the conspirators who had made his name in Caesar's service. As tribune of the people he had worked in the year 55 for the three powerful figures of Caesar, Pompey and Crassus, without gaining much of a political profile for himself; but he then proved his worth as a general in Gaul and in the civil war and in 48 was appointed to the most distinguished of the praetorships, the office known as *praetor urbanus*, praetor of the city, where he was responsible for trials arising from disputes between citizens. After acting as governor for southern Spain (Hispania Ulterior), he was the first member of his family to be appointed consul, in this case for the last months of the year 45 as a replacement for Caesar, who retired from the consulate early. Servius Sulpicius Galba, the scion of an old noble family, had also been a general under Caesar. As early as the year 54, before the outbreak of the civil war, he became praetor, and he fought in the first two years of the Gallic War as Caesar's second in command, although without much success. Since Caesar did not promote him to any very high office, and at the age of fifty-one he was among the older commanders, one of his reasons for joining the conspirators was disappointment.

We do not know exactly when the conspiracy took shape. The idea of eliminating the dictator emerged gradually within a small circle of men, assuming concrete form only the year before the assassination itself. In all, about sixty people were involved. Cicero was not among them, for good reasons. His age – Cicero was already over sixty at the time – will have been immaterial, but the conspirators feared his political unreliability. Members of the ruling families accused him, particularly in the last decade before the outbreak of the civil war, of vacillating between the political camps – Pompey and Caesar on one side and the hard core of defenders of the old order, known as the *optimates*, the 'best men', on the other – out of personal inclination, weakness or even the desire for personal profit. Some may have seen him as an opportunist, and it is a fact that Cicero quite often had to defend himself against such accusations, both publicly and in his private correspondence. An important motive for his friendship with powerful men will have been a wish not to see them excluded from the political game played within the old leadership class, but to see that game further prolonged. Cicero had also repeatedly advised making peace with Caesar before the outbreak of the civil war and during its first months, well knowing that the state itself would be severely damaged by conflict, even if the traditionalists won it. He was thus equally suspect to the radical proponents of war and Caesar's adherents: he had placed himself between all their camps. Hence the paradoxical situation that Cicero, who was certainly no Caesarian and could even be said to symbolize the old republic in his writings on the theory of statesmanship, had no access to the circle of the conspirators. However, no one doubted his republican leanings: when Marcus Brutus called out the name of Cicero to the Senate just after the assassination, as if it were a key to what had happened, all who heard it recognized it as a synonym for liberty. Mark Antony himself could later say that Cicero had known about the conspiracy and was even behind it and he did not trust him. But Cicero knew nothing of the plot to murder Caesar until he saw the assassination carried out at the Senate meeting of 15 March.

At the time of his conflict with Caesar's political heirs, Octavian and Antony, Brutus had coins minted with the reverse side showing the freedman's cap, the *pileus*, between two daggers as the symbol of a man released from slavery into freedom, with the legend 'To the Ides of March' below it. With the design of this coin, Brutus claimed that the assassination had been committed for the sake of freedom, and just as the tyrant Caesar had been killed on the Ides of March, the same fate was to meet all who considered themselves his political heirs. Brutus had, after all, called on the name of freedom directly after the assassination. The deed had been tyrannicide. Its justification arose from the distaste then felt throughout the political systems of the Graeco-Roman world for autocratic rule founded on no legal or moral order. History offered plenty of examples of this unpleasant form of government, and Greek thinkers had used philosophical arguments to underpin the abhorrence felt for it. Tyrannicide was a favourite subject for declamations in the schools of rhetoric, the most commonly cited example being that of the friends Harmodios and Aristogeiton, who had killed Hipparchos, one of the tyrants of Athens, in 514 and lost their own lives in so doing. They were regarded as the liberators of their city, for their act had helped the Athenians to a system of government based on political equality, a democracy. Every educated Greek and Roman could conjure up a mental image of the statue of the two of them holding their swords.

To members of the ruling aristocracy of Rome, the nobility, anyone who tried to set himself up as their master was a tyrant. In the terminology of political conflict, anyone even suspected of planning anything of the kind was branded an autocrat, a king or indeed a tyrant, no matter exactly how far his intentions went – and as far as we know, hardly any member of the nobility before Caesar seriously thought of striving for sole rule. When Brutus struck that rhetorical note, he could count on being generally understood. And for the sake of the purity of the idea, he had persuaded his fellow conspirators that only the tyrant should be killed, and not any of his followers such as Mark Antony and Marcus Aemilius Lepidus. Cassius disagreed but was unable to carry his point. So what exactly did 'freedom' mean to Marcus Brutus and the other conspirators at the time? Did they have in mind the same freedom for which the nobility had fought at the time of the Gracchi and in the decades before the last civil war?

In the last decades of the republic, the freedom (*libertas*) for the sake of which the dictator had been murdered related largely to the nobility, the group of ruling families. Ordinary Romans were indeed included in the process of political decision through the assemblies of the people, but since only the Roman magistracy, whose members as a rule were nobles, had the right to petition for laws to be passed, the people of Rome remained subject to whatever laws the nobility imposed on them through the magistrates, and whatever candidates for office were presented for election. And even the extremely limited participation of the common people in the formulation of political objectives was in great danger, for since the right to Roman citizenship had been extended to all Rome's Italian allies in the years 91–89 BC, the citizenship area now covered all Italy, but few men living at any distance from Rome could travel to the assemblies held there. Consequently those who voted in the assembly of the people were increasingly only those citizens who actually lived in Rome, the people of the city themselves (*plebs urbana*). The sometimes anarchic conditions in the last decades before the civil war meant that the people of the city were also increasingly dependent on individual politicians who gained their support through bribery or by exerting physical pressure. The great majority of citizens who lived in central and southern Italy might hear of what went on in Rome but took little part in events there. Yet as a mainly rural population, they felt more strongly bound to the old tradition of the state and to the aristocratic families than many, even most of the progressive, urban Romans who were open to new ideas and hoped to gain material advantage by them. If individual aristocrats, robbed of the plebeians as a pliable legislative instrument, turned longing eyes on Italy, where the people of the country towns and villages were still the same and appeared to look kindly on the ruling aristocracy, that did not do them much good, for the great majority of Romans could not be included in the old order. Rome was a city state and retained that character; all the state institutions as well as the ruling social class were concentrated in the capital. Any change would have been accompanied by the abolition of the city-state regime, and no one had yet seriously entertained such a notion.

Whereas the people took part in political decision-making only through those citizens who lived in Rome itself, the nobility functioned as a social group until the last decades of the republic. Since time immemorial the same families had filled posts in the magistracy, generally after discussion between themselves, and above all they held the highest offices. It was very rare for a man outside this circle to rise to the highest office of all, the consulate, and thus gain access to the governing elite. A 'new man' (*homo novus*) founded the nobility of his whole family when he attained such success, but he did so usually only with the help of those who were already noble, and even then only for very specific political reasons. Cicero was a 'new man' of this sort, but throughout his life he had to fight for recognition by the old-established nobility of his newly won status. He often felt that he had been slighted, and such experiences nourished his sense of his own inequality of birth.

From their own point of view, the old families had every reason to be proud of their nobility. Their forebears had been active in the state for centuries, sometimes since the beginnings of the republic itself over 400 years earlier; they had defended the city and extended its territory, finally subduing all Italy and making it a federal system, then reaching further out and bringing large parts of the Mediterranean region under Roman rule. The nobles were masters of the world and when they travelled the areas governed by Rome as holders of office, or simply as senators, the inhabitants of the provinces greeted them like kings. The Cornelians and Fabians, Claudians and Aemilians, the Fulvians and Sempronians, Licinians and Domitians could look back on many famous members of their clans, the *gentes* or extended families. The wax masks of such men were carried at every funeral of an important family member, so that they were ever-present in all minds. The pride and reputation of this society, however, were not founded on its origins alone, but were always linked to achievements on behalf of the state. Only the noble holding office who later entered the Senate took part in decision-making, and when a man called on the names of his ancestors he was always referring to their deeds as consuls, praetors and provincial governors. Cicero had good reason to praise his own achievements to the point of tedium: he had no noble ancestors whose deeds might vouch for him, but must rely on himself.

Brutus and his fellow conspirators were closely connected to this society, to the Senate as the assembly of the nobility and to senators who were close to them, men who had held only minor offices in the magistracy but in political life closed ranks with individual noble families for the sake of their own protection and promotion. However, where were the leaders of government when the dictator who had raised himself to rule over them all fell? There were few noblemen sitting in the Senate meeting when the murder was committed; the representation there of the very highest class had shrunk considerably. That class consisted of former consuls (consulars), and it had a crucial influence on all decisions as the group with the greatest achievements to its credit. In practice it was the consulars who controlled the 'council of the world', as Cicero calls the Senate. Only a handful of them, however, including Cicero himself, actually witnessed the murder.

At this time the nobility was only a relatively small group. The episodes of civil war and civil unrest that had periodically plagued the republic since the tribunate of Tiberius Sempronius Gracchus in 133 BC had taken its toll on the nobility. Lucius Cornelius Sulla, who saved the supremacy of the Senate once again, had made the murder of all political opponents into a sort of political mission. At that time, when Caesar and Cicero were young, he published lists of the names of his enemies (*proscribere*) with a view to allowing anyone to eliminate them violently. The systematic removal of opponents by proscription made the nature of the political crisis in the republic glaringly obvious. World domination, with its material and political opportunities, had long ago begun thinning out the nobility as a self-contained society defined by its political intentions and ethical stance. The disintegration of the ruling group went on apace. Sulla's attempt to restore the old conditions had been only a delaying tactic, for the internal dissolution of the nobility was added to their physical attrition. After some decades of peace, Caesar's civil war against the Senate left new gaps in its ranks. Who was still left? And was the little group of survivors in the Senate capable of exerting control over the nobles in office who, as consuls, praetors and governors (proconsuls and propraetors, men who had been consul or praetor and still held the power of those offices), administered the many provinces of the empire. For centuries it had been the political task of the nobility to supervise the powerful magistrates who were sent as executives to hold office outside Rome and Italy for a year like kings, and sometimes commanded great armies. How many noblemen were in the Senate at home now? How many were holding office in the empire?

When the tyrant fell under the blows of his assassins, and Brutus, bloodstained dagger in hand, called on the name of Cicero, the idea was to remind the Senate of its past glories. There were good reasons, however, why no one responded. Instead, they all scattered: the few nobles among them could not revive the Senate, which Caesar had turned into a body of senators willing to do as he wished, and they did not even try to. The nobility was a spent force, incapable of action. Those nobles who were left had mainly attached themselves to powerful men, most recently Caesar. There were few noblemen among the conspirators, and not one of them had been consul at a time when the office must be gained by dint of the candidate's own powers. Those of them who had in fact held high office – like the two Bruti and Cassius, who had been praetors, and Trebonius, who had been consul – had owed their positions to the dictator. Only Servius Sulpicius Galba had been praetor before the outbreak of the civil war, but it seems that he himself had joined the conspirators for extremely self-interested reasons, which is probably why, even among them, he played no outstanding part.

The republic, in effect the nobility, did not spring to life again after the murder. It had been the conspirators' fatal error to believe that with the death of the tyrant whom they hated government of the kind once in force would spontaneously enter into its own again, and liberty, removed from the clutches of the dictator who stole it, would be back in the right hands. As it soon turned out, however, Caesar was not the only robber. Others came on the scene after him. But however many stepped on to the political stage, there was no reaction from the nobility. The conspirators remained a self-contained group. Formally, they had indeed restored the old order, but the old political powers were no longer in place. What kind of state structure did contemporary Romans now face? Had the aristocracy no more say in public affairs? If not, the only alternative was a purely military dictatorship such as the state was supposed to have left behind on the Ides of March.

In fact the outlines of the government destroyed by Caesar did at first seem to reappear after the Ides of March. In the political vacuum left by the assassination of the dictator, the Senate gathered when summoned by the consul, as it had of old, the praetors dispensed justice, and the people's assembly met by order of the tribunes of the people and the consuls, although these measures were neither controlled nor supervised by any central authority. The dictatorship was gone, that was clear; it was equally clear to all Roman citizens that the important offices of state were still held by men of high social prestige, even if the old aristocrats among them were now in the minority. The inherent flaw here was not immediately obvious; it was true that the nobility was being replaced mainly by men who had risen under Caesar, but their military achievements in his service meant that they could not be denied the recognition and respect paid for centuries to men of the old nobility. In future, however, the vital question was who would take over control of the machinery of state from the aristocracy. They had held in their hands the entire administration of both the Roman state itself and the regions of the vast empire ruled by Rome. The experience of centuries was concentrated in them, and they had carried out administrative business with the aid of members of their own families, and in particular of freedmen and slaves. Those concerned about government under the new order must seek people able to fill such posts. The future of the state, whatever it was like, could not dispense with a class of eminent men.

The question of the future aristocracy was not yet on the agenda directly after the Ides of March, particularly as several members of the old nobility held the highest offices and were at the centre of political activity. More important and pressing, at this point, was another problem, and it chiefly confronted those who intended to take up the dictator's political inheritance. These men, who had supported Caesar and had almost all held public office, had to consider what political aims to pursue now that he was dead, and how to address their own past, when they had served him as their master. The conspirators were of course spared such considerations. What they had done formed the background for all they would now do; they did have an idea of the political future, however idealistic or Utopian it might be. But what did their adversaries, the dictator's former supporters, think of the dictatorship? It had been legally rescinded for ever soon after the assassination; Mark Antony himself had petitioned for its abolition. But what did that mean? The question would have to be answered some time. Just now the political manoeuvring and military operations with which the Caesarians tried to assert their claims among themselves and against the conspirators were to the fore. But sooner or later a solution for the future must be found on the basis of what was known of the character of Caesar's rule and what he had set aside. So exactly what had his rule been like, and to what had it put an end?

The removal of the tyrant by no means consigned the form his rule had taken to the past. Caesar had been the first monarch of Rome, and although at first it might look as if Rome were now returning to the political conditions of the time before him, the future was to belong to the monarchy. How, then, did Caesar's monarchy relate to the rule of those monarchs who, since the time of Augustus, have been known as emperors, and who held that title for half a millennium, and in the east even a millennium and a half? The imperial empire as set up by

Augustus was a durable institution that weathered many storms. What made it so strong, and why did Caesar's own rule fail? I shall try to answer the first question later. Here we must understand Caesar's monarchy as a form of rule that Augustus, architect of the imperial Roman empire, found in place and had to confront.

Caesar had not regarded sole rule as one of his political aims before the civil war broke out. As a member of a distinguished family with the ambition to emulate the best of his own rank, he sought to vie with his peers to acquire an office with extraordinary powers of military command. In this he resembled Sulla, Pompey and Crassus. He intended his political and social influence within society, the quality called *dignitas* by the Romans, to outshine that of all others: he wanted to be the most powerful man in Rome. After successfully gaining that extraordinary command, he conquered those parts of the Celtic lands that were still free and presented himself to the Roman public as the most capable and indeed the best military commander of his time. By the time he had held power over all the north-western provinces of the empire for ten years, those who were of equal rank with him began to fear for the equilibrium of the ruling group. Caesar seemed to be displacing them, threatening the normal aristocratic equality. They asked him to step down, but he refused, reckoning that, as a private citizen, he would inevitably fall victim to enemies who hated and envied him. As he saw it, therefore, he had to make war on the Senate as a man who had declared war on all his equals and who was opposed by the state as represented by the Senate. He tried to justify himself to the Roman public by suggesting that his *dignitas* had been at stake in this quarrel and he would not and could not surrender it at any price. Since *dignitas* was a political value recognized by all the Romans, something for which every member of the nobility strove and that was respected by every Roman, even the simplest members of society, most of them undoubtedly understood Caesar's attitude. None the less, they were unable and unwilling to allow him to give his own *dignitas* an absolute value above that of all other noblemen.

Caesar appears to have accepted the situation in which he was thus placed, as all his subsequent actions show. When he crossed the Rubicon dividing his Upper Italian province from Italy itself, he left the traditional state behind him for ever. He had become sole ruler, and that was what he now wanted. His sole present concern was to place his rule on a firm footing. Caesar initially used a conciliatory policy to win over as many of the nobility as possible to his side, but he was only partially successful. Some of them immediately realized that the *clementia Caesaris*, the clemency of Caesar, whereby he pardoned many men who in themselves were guilty, was already an instrument of the new monarchy. Mercy overruled the law; but mercy, a royal quality, is granted by the ruler. Yet although Caesar could not by any means win all the nobility over, he did not need to concern himself about the part that remained hostile to him. Many members of the old nobility had died in the civil war, others had committed suicide, others again had retired into private life. The nobility had been disintegrating for a hundred years, a process that had worn down the group and severely reduced its numbers. Caesar obviously did not feel threatened from that quarter.

So, having initially gained power at the point of his soldiers' swords, how did he set about ruling?

The state from which Caesar's rule distanced itself is known to us as the republic. The word derives from the Latin *res publica*, 'the public matter'. The *res publica*, then, the republic, merely means the affairs of state. The Romans had lived under such a government for 450 years, and in itself it needed no further description. Only when Caesar created a different kind of state, a monarchy, was the old order sometimes additionally described as 'free' (*libera*) in order to convey the fact that the nobility ruled it, and ordinary Romans – within certain limits – had a voice in government through the assembly of the people. Caesar introduced the change from the republic to rule by a single man on three levels that all impinge on each other.

First, he wanted to destroy the most important republican institutions. Here his most striking act was to abolish the consulate, which as the supreme official authority had carried out the decisions of the Senate and thus of the ruling nobility for centuries. Caesar himself had been consul four times between 49 and 44, which in itself was a break with tradition, for a man was normally barred from being consul again until ten years had passed. Even worse was the fact that in the year 45 he initially held it alone, without a colleague, only to resign suddenly in October and appoint two other men consuls for the rest of the year. It was unprecedented for someone in perfect health to give up the consulate; hitherto there had been by-elections only if a consul died during his term of office. By overturning the official order, Caesar was demonstrating that the office of consul was not as important to the administration of the state as it had been, and that it no longer represented supreme office but had been more or less downgraded to an honorary position, bestowed by the ruler on those men who had distinguished themselves by their loyalty and devotion to him. But he did not stop at that. When one of these two substitute consuls, Quintus Fabius Maximus, died suddenly around midday on 31 December 45, the last day of his term of office, Caesar swiftly appointed Gaius Caninius Rebilus consul in his place for the last few hours of the year. Rebilus, sad to say, thus became famous because no one ever ate breakfast during his consulate, and there were many similar jokes at his expense in circulation. When the leading figures of Roman society solemnly performed the usual custom of accompanying the newly elected consul to his home Cicero, who was among the escort as one of the most distinguished senators, remarked caustically that they had better hurry in case the consulate of Caninius ended before they reached his house. This by-election showed a cynical disdain for the essence of republican authority. The formal observation of the proprieties, which in this case were comically inappropriate to the result of the election, represented a deliberate and intentional degradation of the highest office of the republic.

The Senate had been at the very heart of the republic, and comprised all the men who had formerly held high office (the magistrates). The senators were arranged in order of rank according to the offices they had held, and they decided all affairs of state. From time immemorial the nobility, more particularly those among them who had held consular office, had tipped the scale in decision-making. The Senate was thus Caesar's real opponent when he went to war with the republic, and it was the Senate above all, forming as it did the administrative centre of the state and uniting all political power in itself, that he must deprive of its independence. His demolition work was facilitated by the fact that the Senate had not been unaffected by the republic's 100 years of crisis. The highest and most influential class in Rome consisted of only a few men. The former consuls who sat in the Senate at the time could be counted on the fingers of one hand, and many of those supported the dictator.

Weakened as the Senate was, however, it still had to be made incapable of carrying out its task of governing the state. Caesar achieved this aim by greatly increasing the number of senators. The existing prerequisite for senators – to have held office as a magistrate as a precursor to entering the Senate – was retained in principle, but Caesar increased the number of magistracies, which meant that the incumbents naturally owed their office to him, and thus, as the number of senators grew, so did the number of Caesar's own supporters in the Senate. In addition, through his dictatorial authority Caesar appointed many senators who had never held any office at all. Cicero remarked sarcastically that it was easier to become a councillor in Rome than in Pompeii. The Senate, which had never before had more than 600 members, soon increased its numbers to 900.

However, it was not only the number of senators that made the Senate an organization incapable of working on its own and compliant to the will of the ruler; another contributory factor was its new social composition. The humble origins of many of the new senators caused particular offence. Several men from the middle and lower ranks of army officers, including centurions, and even sons of freedmen, were admitted to the Senate, along with many Romans from the western provinces, drawn from the ranks of Italians or men from formerly non-Roman families, for instance in Spain. It is easy to understand the harsh criticism of this development by Cicero and other influential politicians, as well as the mockery and derision that they turned on the young senators, who were quite often ill at ease in these unfamiliar surroundings. But ultimately these senators who would never before have met the essential minimum conditions of family or fortune were not the telling factor; the real cause of the Senate's demise lay in the loss of individual influence. Nine hundred senators had to be controlled, and the numbers of men from southern and northern Italy, from the Adriatic coast and Etruria, were now equal to those of their colleagues from Latium, Campania and the Sabine country, from which most senators had previously come. By comparison with what it had once been, the new Senate, as no one could fail to see, had declined into a mere tool of Caesar and in future would be the instrument of whoever presided over it. For how could motions be discussed and different opinions put forward in such a huge assembly? No debate worthy of the name could be held any more. From here on, everything put before the Senate had already been decided by the man who had convened it; the activity of the senators could consist only of giving their blessing to the will of its head. Caesar was anxious to expand the Senate in order to dissolve the structures that had evolved in the old governing class. The new assembly that would take over affairs of state under the dictator was to have no independent reason for existence but must depend on the grace and favour of its ruler.

The third institution beside the magistracy and the Senate, the assembly of the people, had carried almost no political weight in the decades before the civil war. It did epitomize the idea of participation by the Roman people (*populus Romanus*) in political decision-making, but apart from representing this and offering a guarantee of the continuing public nature of politics, it had little actual function. All the same, the dictator did not leave even this institution unscathed. He was concerned not so much with legislation as with election to the magistracy. He could pass laws himself by virtue of his dictatorial powers; the results of elections, on the other hand, could not be decreed. However, elections to the upper ranks of the magistracy were extremely significant politically, for they were linked to tenure of the highest offices in the administration and entry to the Senate. Even in the republic, therefore, and in so far as their results had not already been negotiated in advance in the houses of the noble families, they had sometimes led to ferocious competition between the nobles. What significance Caesar attached to elections is shown by the fact that so far as he could he presided over them himself, since then he could control the voting process. By the time the Parthian War was imminent he had also chosen most of the magistrates, in particular the consuls, for the next few years in advance. Of course, a permanent presidency as well as the advance selection of magistrates contravened all the rules of the republican age, when the ruling group had repeatedly secured and determined its influence in the state through those elections. In a process probably comprising several stages – the records are not perfectly clear here – Caesar finally obtained the right to make a binding recommendation (*commendatio*) for half of all the higher magistrates apart from the consuls; that is to say, all the praetors and curule aediles. It is hard to imagine that the assembly of the people voted to any effect in elections of this kind, for the results were already decided, and it had thus been downgraded to the status of an authority that had nothing to do but acclaim elected candidates.

A hundred paths lead from Caesar the dictator to the Roman emperors. If there is much in the history of those emperors that began under

Caesar, it is because of the way he used the republic to further his own monarchy. He did not rescind the norms of public law, but transformed them into a set of rules that made monarchical power visible without depriving it of a republican background. The monarchy made its garment, so to speak, out of republican cloth. To that extent, Caesar had already given the Roman empire of the future its shape. What remained of the Caesarian state when Augustus took it over, however, was in many ways not its outer, institutional form, and often not the legal details either; the imperial empire of Augustus went its own way. However, the idea of monarchical power as the legal power continued. For however much Caesar bent the old state rules to construct the form of his new monarchical state, he still related it to the law of the old republic, at least to the public law, which alone was concerned here.

In this process of the appropriation of legal forms by the monarch, however, the internal structure of the law was altered. In the hands of the ruler, as he remodelled it, the law became deformed and was to retain that shape for centuries in the imperial empire. A particularly clear illustration is provided in the way Caesar dealt with the tribunate of the people. At the time of what is known as the 'struggle between the orders', the tribunate had been the protection and refuge of the rising plebeians against the old patricians, and after the end of that struggle, when the orders of society were reconciled, it was conformed as a full office of state with full authority. From then on, it had many ways of taking a hand in public business, and thus, when the quarrel was resumed under the Gracchi, it once again became a focus of internal confrontation. The dictator, as a patrician, could not hold an office which from the beginning of its history had been tailored to the needs of the plebeians. In addition, a man might hold only a single office, and as dictator Caesar was already a magistrate. But since he did not want to give up the opportunities offered by the tribunate of the people, he sought and found a way to get control of it all the same: he divided the office itself (*tribunus plebis*) from the power of the office (*tribunicia potestas*), claiming only the latter for himself. This hair-splitting gave him the authority linked with the office of tribune of the people, while he could still observe the ban on his taking that office itself. The dictator also divided the office from its sacred nature – the tribune of the people was *sacrosanctus* and inviolable – and assigned that 'sanctity' separately to himself, thus obtaining the religious aspect that had protected the tribune of the people from attack by patrician magistrates during the 'struggle between the orders'. Caesar dealt with many other institutions in the same way. As one example, we may look at the dictator's mandatory electoral arrangements, which did away with the chief electoral officer's right to present candidates for office, leaving the dictator's official power the only rule in force. Sooner or later, the nonsensical isolation of the separate powers of office was bound to distort and ultimately destroy the office itself. In republican times bending the public law in such a way would have been unthinkable. The institutions and legal rules of the constitution as it had developed historically had indeed undergone much change in their sense and significance, but there had been no tension between past and present law in the minds of the people, so the traditional order had always been seen as a coherent whole. It was all the easier to regard Caesar's manoeuvring as an expression of contempt for the public law of the republic, or even a desire to do away with it.

In fact the dictator appeared to his critics, more particularly the conspirators, as a figure who despised and intended to destroy the republic, that is to say the state itself, and who thus symbolized a bad form of government, a tyranny. On the other hand, if we look back at his measures from the viewpoint of what was to be the monarchical future, we have to admit that in his approach to republican law, problematic as his methods may have been, he did in a certain way respect it. Its internal logic, however, was certainly changed, for it would now relate to the monarchs and not to the aristocratic society that had set it up and developed it as its instrument of rule over the centuries. Public law had been in the hands of the nobility, who had maintained it, changing and expanding it to preserve their rule. The collective nobility had thus also been its guarantor; without one, no law could be valid either then or now. When Caesar's dictatorship eliminated the political relevance of the old society, the public law of the republic lost its guarantors. If he did not wish to rule thereafter solely through his supreme command of the army, that is to say by force of autocratic omnipotence, but wanted to disguise his powers behind the legal system of the defunct republic, he did so to give his rule some kind of due form, implying that it also had its limits, and to connect it to the centuries-old experience of the republic. He was showing that he did not intend to abandon the basis of tradition. At the same time, however, it was clear that from now on the law related to him alone: the dictator had become both its point of reference and its guarantor. His critics might object that everything was done in line with his will, and he was indifferent to the law, since it was his to use as he wished and could be bent accordingly; he is reported to have remarked that the state (*res publica*) in itself meant nothing but was a mere concept without physical shape and form. If Caesar really did say this, it must have been an irate reaction to criticism of his approach to the public law of the republic. However, his actions showed that the old law did indeed matter to him, although where the change in his point of reference was concerned his critics were right. The precarious character of the new, monarchical law, apparently subject only to its master's will, must have made them especially anxious. The sense that the new order was temporary and insecure sometimes troubled even Caesar's supporters, particularly because in the few months that he spent in Rome between the outbreak of civil war and his assassination – in all less than a year and a half; his longest stay there from September 45 BC to the Ides of March was about six months – the dictator's reforms advanced at a frenetic pace, and the torrent of new regulations was hardly likely to convey a sense of durability and legal security. In spite of all his efforts to give his rule some kind of structure, then, Caesar seems in retrospect more a destroyer of the old than a builder of something new.

Caesar was awarded many honours, some of them new. They were either pressed upon him or were his own idea. At first moderate in number and nature, they proliferated ever further after the battle of Thapsus, when the republican party was finally beaten, and after the defeat of the last major resistance to him at Munda they went beyond all the bounds of tradition and decency. The aim of all these honours was glorification of the dictator's person verging on worship, although his actual divinity was not directly postulated. We need not regard this as the empty expression of servility; the dictator's own guiding hand can frequently be seen in the apparently chaotic shower of honours. As he put his own ideas into practice, and accepted or rejected the suggestions of others, he was crafting an aura of sanctity for himself. Much of this emerges in the subsequent imperial period and can to a great extent be seen as fundamental to the empire itself.

Some of these honours had particularly far-reaching consequences and referred to specifically Roman ideas. The assumption of the title *imperator* as part of Caesar's name was of central importance; he jetti-soned his *praenomen* of Gaius and thereafter called himself Imperator Julius Caesar. Initially, any Roman official holding a military command that allowed him to give orders in the field had been able to call himself *imperator*. Under the late republic, however, the title was mainly employed in a narrower sense, as an honorific for a victorious com-mander who had been hailed as *imperator* by his soldiers on the battlefield and could thus claim a triumph in Rome. When Caesar joined the title to his name (*nomen*), he was firmly identifying himself as an individual with the quality indicated by the term *imperator* and was now the very personification of the victorious military commander. The title gave him the aura of a divinely gifted, charismatic and invincible army leader, and since invincibility was really an attribute of the gods, it showed him in a sacral light. This was emphasized by a privilege that allowed him to wear – at first on special occasions, but later all the time – the purple sequin-embroidered toga and laurel wreath of a man who had won a triumph. Finally, special games, the Victoria Caesaris, were held in his honour.

The title of 'father of the fatherland', *parens (pater) patriae*, which Caesar received shortly before his death, also originated in old Roman ideas. Its holder was to be seen as the caring patron and protector who, like the father of a family (*pater familias*) presiding over his household staff and clients, watched over all the citizens of Rome and the state as a whole. He was the *pater patriae*.

It is impossible to overlook the sacral character of many of these honours. To the Roman way of thinking, Caesar as *triumphator*, a leader who had been awarded a triumph, incarnated the highest of the gods, as his outer appearance and clothes indicated. He stood beside Jupiter, and his face, when painted with red lead, was regarded as a depiction of one of the divine statues that in ancient times had been made of terracotta. Many statues of Caesar standing in public places and temples reinforced the impression that he was unique and elect. Statues in honour of living Romans had quite often been erected in the preceding decades, but never in such numbers or placed in such prom-inent positions as the statues of Caesar. When an ivory statue of him was set up in the temple of the Capitoline Jupiter, it finally became clear to everyone that, besides simply honouring Caesar, such figures symbol-ized his proximity to the gods. On certain occasions, beginning with the games of 45 BC in honour of the Victoria Caesaris, this statue and other divine figures were carried in procession on the sacred chariot known as the *tensa*, which was really for gods alone. Another statue of Caesar, this time in bronze, stood in the temple of Quirinus, an ancient Roman war god, and if the wording (which has come down to us only via an ancient Greek source) has been accurately reported, it abandoned all restraint with its inscription 'To the Invincible Deity'. Especially provocative was the statue of Caesar placed on the Capitol among the statues of the kings of Rome and the first consul Lucius Brutus, although, as it stood next to Brutus, it could be taken to signify the saving of the citizens of Rome from distress and danger.

If we see a carefully manipulated policy in all this, then the last step in the deliberate deification of his person was the dictator's decision to build a temple for himself and his clemency, which was personified as the *clementia Caesaris*, and to appoint a special priest of the cult, a *flamen Julius*. Mark Antony had been chosen for the post of priest. The cult does not seem to have been up and running at the time of Caesar's murder; perhaps he himself had intended it to be introduced immediately after his death and not before. But merely planning such a thing went beyond anything previously thought possible. In antiquity, of course, the distance between the divine and the human was not so great that divinity, in some form or other, seemed beyond human reach. The Greek myths in particular revered human beings who were close to the sphere of the gods or even dwelt in it. Since the fourth century, historical figures had been raised to the rank of deities who were worshipped in line with their supernatural status, and since the time of Alexander so had the kings of Hellenistic realms. Many Roman governors, who in a way were following in the footsteps of the former Greek kings, also received divine honours, for instance in Asia or Bithynia. But worship of this kind was Greek rather than Roman, and it was considerably more difficult for Romans to understand giving a man divine honours or actually deifying him.

The religion of ancient Rome was essentially a nature religion; the relationship of man to the powers of nature was one of preventive magic, taboos and rituals of atonement, rather than any idea of personal closeness. Although the Romans did distinguish between a number of gods, a deity's personal character derived from his or her specific field of action, and such a divine aura was known as the *numen*. No path led from this imaginative world to any identification of man and god. How-ever, acceptance of Greek religious thought gradually changed the Roman view of the divine, and the personal characters of deities took on a more distinct outline. Myths were even adapted to manufacture divine origins, especially in the houses of such great families as the Julians and Antonians. So if Caesar intended to raise his own person to divine or near-divine status, he was thinking like the Greeks. However, he was not aiming at any clear, generally evident goal, and a policy of religious glorification so foreign to the Romans would certainly have repelled or baffled them. Only the large number of tentative moves of an obviously exploratory nature gradually showed that Caesar's aim was to clothe outright military dictatorship in a religious form. The change in the name of the fifth month of the year – the Romans counted their months from 1 March, which had once been the New Year – from Quintilis to Julius also shows that he was thinking along Greek lines; such ideas were traditional in the Greek East. Did he intend create a Hellenistic-style Roman monarchy, including the deification of his per-son, on the model of Alexander the Great? Alexander had pursued just such a policy in the last years of his life, although Caesar did not take him as a point of reference in other respects.

Augustus and his successors at the head of the Roman state aspired to legitimize their rule by the religious glorification of their persons and achieved that aim. They went about it very cautiously, particularly with respect to the circles to which they appealed in any given case. Augustus was well aware that a policy of religious legitimization too vigorously pursued could alienate the Romans; he therefore proceeded with care and forethought, and proved to be a master of the art of getting other people to involve themselves in his political aims and put his own ideas into practice. By comparison, Caesar seems to have been more insistent, but his precise intentions remain unclear, not least because his brief five years of rule, which were largely spent campaigning against his oppon-ents at home, left him no time to give final form to his political ideas. However, the obstacle deciding the matter was not just lack of time but also the lack of readiness among the Romans to accept or even contem-plate a monarchical state at this point, and that fact stood in the way of any open discussion.

What was rule over the Romans to be like anyway? They had acknowledged no ruler of the political constitution since the expulsion of the last king 450 years before. What *could* it be like? Few of the distinguished men of Rome, or indeed the leading figures in the countless Italian towns and cities, could even imagine such a thing. But if the old state was gone for ever, what form of sole rule was acceptable? Through his victory in the civil war, Caesar had become ruler by means of brute military force. If he wanted to establish his power on a formal basis, whether legal, religious or simply charismatic, he needed the consent of his 'subjects'. Without the assent of those he ruled he would remain what he was: a military potentate. His various tentative initiatives, in particular the honours given to him, show that Caesar was looking for a monarchical regime that the Romans would find acceptable. But for the very reason that he had to conceal his intentions we do not know what direction his mind was taking. Perhaps he attempted various methods, and we can no longer distinguish between them because the records are fragmentary. The sources present no homogeneous picture, partly because much of what they describe as his own will consists of insinuations made by his opponents.

Modern scholars differ widely on the question of the form that Caesar wanted his regime to take. Some believe that he wished to be king (*rex*) and was thus aiming for kingship (*regnum*) on the Greek or Roman model. But that is very unlikely, because to all Romans, particularly the upper classes to whom Caesar had turned as potential aides in administering affairs of state, kingship meant tyranny. By assuming the title of king, Caesar would have shown himself a tyrant without gaining any support at all from the Romans for the idea of a monarchy. On the contrary, as a ruler with the title of king, whether or not he had kingship of the Greek or ancient Roman type in mind, he would have represented the quintessence of illegitimacy, deeply offending all Romans. And there can be no doubt that Caesar retained his ability to reason to the last; he was no Caligula, whose character could be deformed by the pressure of power. Caesar's desire to be king was therefore probably an invention of his enemies. For centuries, such accusations were among the tools used by those opposed to any member of the nobility who looked like breaking away from the group. Such a maverick character might be described as a tyrant, master (*dominus*) or king, and his influence was equated with royal rule. That was naturally the line taken by Caesar's opponents, especially Cicero, although he once, more accurately, called Caesar's rule 'power of the royal kind', meaning power exceeding dictatorship.

Caesar had obviously chosen another way. The only form of sole rule that could ever be considered within the old order was dictatorship. Introduced during the republican period as 'temporary rule' to deal with a situation of extreme emergency, it was limited to a certain period, generally six months. Rome also resorted to it in certain political crises, for instance in the choice of consuls if those holding the consulship had both fallen in fighting or were absent. A generation earlier, Lucius Cornelius Sulla had even used dictatorship to reform the state as a whole, and he held the office for three years. When he thought his task was completed, he had resigned this extraordinary dictatorship, introduced for a specific purpose, and retired into private life, true to the republican principle that all offices were only temporary.

During his first period in Rome after his return, Caesar had held a short-term elected dictatorship, getting himself declared dictator for a year after the battle of Pharsalos. This year of office was clearly a case of emergency dictatorship. It was not especially conspicuous in itself because of the civil war. Caesar liked to consider that he was fighting it to save the citizens of Rome, and there was no suggestion that he had any intention of making this emergency dictatorship into a monarchy. Even when Caesar assumed dictatorship for ten years after the final defeat of the 'republicans' at Thapsus in the year 46 BC, the announcement of a time limit could be seen as reassuring, and perhaps some even hoped that the dictatorship would come to an end before the ten years were up. Even the yearly renewal of the dictatorship had a republican ring to it, as all offices were traditionally held for one year only. At the end of the year 45, however, before the ten-year period ran out, Caesar had the dictatorship made permanent (*dictator perpetuus* or *perpetuo*), meaning for his lifetime. He took up his new office in the middle of February 44. This was unusual, and likely to attract the attention of all his contemporaries, who would suspect some particular intention behind such an extraordinary move. The step seems to have been taken to underline his monarchical position. Well knowing that the soldiers would recognize him as permanent dictator if need be, Caesar was still disguising his special political role with a Roman title. In appointing himself dictator for life, he might have hoped that the Parthian campaign, which called for the concentration of all the forces of the state, would help him to win wider backing. And as the ten-year dictatorship period would have covered the Parthian War, Caesar might have intended the change to draw the line under his efforts to create a monarchical form that, after the various attempts at religious glorification of his person, would return to the sober Roman principle of a magistracy. It is reasonable to assume that, since the sometimes shocking proliferation of honours heaped on him had made for much bad feeling in Rome, Caesar was led to see that he had to stop at being dictator. With the dictatorship, he was declaring that what had arisen in a state of republican emergency was now a permanent solution. It is true that a situation of permanent national emergency cannot be seen as a form of rule or simply a form of government, and equally certainly it is not a political idea deserving of the name; it is no less than a declaration of political bankruptcy. Caesar had failed in his attempt to give his de facto rule a form acceptable to Roman society. Until the leading group had agreed to the idea, no Roman monarch could hope for recognition. So Caesar was taking refuge by going off to the Parthian War, and then, in their own way, the events of the Ides of March solved the problem that he himself had found insoluble.

The dictator had written the final version of his will in September of the year 45. It was not the will of a monarch, because there was not yet any institutionalized monarchy in Rome. Caesar had drawn it up as a private person. But since, as a private person, he was not just a member of the nobility but also the most powerful man of his time, appointed to the office of dictator, of course his will had political implications. In it Caesar made his great-nephew Gaius Octavius, his sister Julia's grandson and the son of Gaius Octavius and Atia, heir to three-quarters of his property, while his two nephews (or great-nephews) Quintus Pedius and Lucius Pinarius, the sons (or grandsons) of another sister called Julia, inherited one-eighth each. If they were to decline the inheritance or predecease him, then Decimus Junius Brutus and Mark Antony were named as substitute heirs. Caesar left his garden on the opposite bank of the Tiber to the people of Rome, and the sum of 300 sesterces (= 75 denarii) to every citizen. This was about one-third of a soldier's annual pay. If a son should be born to him posthumously, he named several persons as guardians. At the end of the will he adopted Gaius Octavius into his family and gave him his name. The position in the will of his decision to adopt the young man, who was then eighteen, shows that it was made late in the day. In addition, since we know from a reliable source that he did not inform Octavius himself of it, it could be concluded that at the time when he drew it up he still hoped for a son of his own.

In its form, the adoption of Gaius Octavius was unusual. Normal adoption in Roman law was of minors, and occurred when both parties concerned were alive; Octavius, however, was adopted by will, that is to say by virtue of someone's death, and as a man who had attained his majority (a man 'of his own law', *sui iuris*). This, as well as the unique expression stating that Octavius was to be adopted 'into the family and name' of Caesar, as our main extant source cites the text of the will (not itself preserved verbatim), raises the question of what it meant to the testator. Did he aim to equate it with testamentary adoption by a living person, making Octavius his son, or did he simply want to transfer his name to him? In the latter case, how did the transfer of a name differ from adoption? Modern scholars also ask whether an adoption such as Caesar's posthumous adoption of Octavius was legally valid.

Octavius himself did not make the search for an answer to that question any easier. He started calling himself Gaius Julius Caesar immediately after the terms of the will were made known, but later had his adoption placed before the long-obsolete people's assembly divided into *curiae* (the divisions of the Roman state) and also had it confirmed by the *plebiscitum* or people's law. Was that because he did not think his testamentary adoption legally adequate? There can have been no doubt of the validity of the will, for it had been legally established through its official acceptance by the heir before the praetor of the city, a process that Octavius set in motion as soon as he arrived in Rome. What did he intend to achieve by the involved procedure of legal confirmation if there was no doubt that the will was indeed valid and if, in claiming to bear the name of Caesar, Octavius had met with no resistance from either the army or his own peers? It is worth lingering on this question for a little while. For if Octavius or Gaius Julius Caesar (Octavianus), the name he assumed as Caesar's adoptive son, bore his adoptive name illegally then he was a political nobody; a Gaius Octavius might hope for a career in public office, but could not compete for the dictator's inheritance. As Octavius successfully established himself as Gaius Julius Caesar, son of the deified dictator, and became the founder of the later Roman empire, then if his adoption had not been legally valid he would have been a kind of false Caesar. His own contemporaries said, deliberately and often, that he owed all he was in political life to his adoptive name of Gaius Julius Caesar. 'You owe everything to your name, boy,' was a taunt flung at him by Mark Antony.

In assessing the adoption, our prime consideration must be what the testator intended. The will itself, over and above the adoption clause, gives us an important clue. Caesar, as mentioned above, had left a legacy of 300 sesterces to every citizen of Rome. Assuming that there were 300,000 adult male citizens in Rome, then 90 million sesterces had to be made available for these payments. The almost incredible magnitude of this sum can be gauged by the fact that it would have paid the wages of ten whole legions for a good two years. There can be no doubt that the legacy should be seen in a political context, and whoever paid it out therefore had to be publicly regarded as Caesar's political heir, or at least the man who was politically closest to him. Unlike his two cousins, Octavius was therefore not just a private heir, and Caesar had made it clear at an early date that he planned to give his great-nephew a prominent public position.

Even before the outbreak of the civil war Octavius, then only twelve years old, had been chosen to deputize for Caesar, otherwise engaged in Gaul at the time, in mounting the speaker's rostrum in the Forum to make the funeral oration for his grandmother Julia, Caesar's sister, who died in the year 51. He thus made his first public appearance before he had even put on the toga of a grown man, which was not until October of the year 49, when he was fourteen. After introducing him on this occasion as a noteworthy member of the Julian family, the dictator Caesar promoted the public career of Octavius above other members of the family by ensuring that his great-nephew was elected to the politically significant priestly college of the *pontifices*. The significance of this priestly office is clear when we remember that Octavius replaced Lucius Domitius Ahenobarbus, a resolute enemy of the dictator who had been consul in the year 54 and had recently fallen in the battle of Pharsalos. Also significant is the break with tradition whereby a young man of only fifteen, not yet known for any public achievement, succeeded a military commander who also had consular experience. In addition, the dictator had made the Senate raise Octavius to the patriciate, the old nobility among the aristocracy, and appointed him an aide and a cavalry commander in the forthcoming Parthian campaign. Caesar also took care to further the young man's political education by taking him on his Spanish campaign, or rather making sure that he followed later.

He had probably planned to do the same in the African campaign, but the latter plan came to nothing because of Octavius' youth, and similarly the young man's poor health prevented him from acting as an organizer of public games. Even apart from his testamentary provisions, then, the dictator had given clear indications that, of his three nephews, this one was destined for a political career and was being specially put forward for it. So no one could be surprised that he explicitly adopted Octavius in the last clause of his will, whether that clause was already part of the last version drawn up or added later. He had already said publicly more than once in his lifetime that he wanted Octavius recognized as his, the all-powerful dictator's, choice. In the aristocratic world of Rome, that made him the man to offer the sacred sacrifices to ancestors of the Julian family.

We may, however, wonder what the dictator's desire to promote him politically meant in concrete terms, over and above his family duties. It certainly did not make Gaius Octavius heir to the monarchical rule virtually usurped by Caesar, for the dictator had not set himself up as a king with an institutionalized succession. Instead, Octavius was his political heir, just as traditionally all sons of noble families of high reputation had an unwritten but none the less acknowledged claim to a political career when they came of age. That had been as much as the dictator could do for Octavius, well knowing that his adoptive son could now assert a special right to a political position above all other aristocrats, and he himself would undoubtedly have created one for him if he had lived longer and still had no son of his own. Now that Caesar could not make that claim, his son and heir must do it for himself.

If this appears to clear up the question of Caesar's intentions in making his will and adopting Octavius, the problem of the legal basis of the testamentary adoption remains open because of the testator's death. Modern scholarship has offered various explanations, but in my view the records make the matter clear. First, there is general agreement that, although the legal sources of the time provided only for adoption by living persons, testamentary adoptions were definitely practised in Cicero's time. The first such adoption known to us is that of one Lucius Licinius Crassus (Scipio or Cornelianus) in the early first century BC; he was adopted as a child and died young. Obviously adoptions made in wills were recognized by custom if the child's birth father did not go before the praetor to oppose the adoption. That stipulation was necessary, however, because these adoptions were usually of children who were still under the guardianship of their birth fathers, not of adults who had attained their majority. The question of the validity of Octavius' adoption, quite apart from the fact that it occurred because of the testator's death, is all the more difficult to clarify because Octavius was a grown man and as such no longer subject to the decisions of a *pater familias*. But examples of such adoptions are known to us from the late republic. For instance, Marcus Junius Brutus (Caesar's assassin), Titus Pomponius Atticus, Cicero's friend, and the knight Gaius Rabirius Postumus were adopted at a comparatively late age, and in the case of Atticus at least it was a testamentary adoption. Unusual as such adoptions might be, they were practised and were obviously recognized by society.

To us, then, the crucial point is how the contemporaries of Octavius regarded his adoption. Since this was an important political affair, if the process was unknown or at least unusual in legal practice, then it might have been expected that not only his political opponents but also all those members of the nobility not closely connected with Octavius himself would reject outright a claim based on Caesar's will, or at least show a certain reserve. However, there was no such reaction. In his letters up to May 44 BC Cicero does speak constantly of 'Gaius Octavius', and Octavius' own stepfather, Marcius Philippus, still uses that name in April – unlike, for instance, the companions with whom Octavius had set out from Brundisium. However, that was no doubt because the will had not yet been officially accepted by Octavius himself. In addition Philippus certainly avoided the adoptive name because he had expressly advised Octavius *against* accepting the will. In view of both men's attitude to the acceptance of the will and its political implications, recognition of the name in advance was not to be expected. From the middle of June onwards – Octavius had accepted the will in front of the praetor of the city at the beginning of May – Cicero calls him Octavianus, which presupposes recognition of his adoption as Gaius Julius Caesar (Octavianus). If he did not, like those in the immediate circle of Octavius' friends, address him as 'Caesar', and if Mark Antony also avoided doing so on their initial contact in Rome, they had their reasons: at the time the name of Caesar suggested a political programme, and neither Cicero nor Antony – least of all Antony – was going to admit in public to the political significance it conveyed. However, for all their rivalry Antony never questioned the adoption, and indeed expressly assented to it by the agreement of 17 March, since recognition of the will was to be seen as one of Caesar's decrees (*acta*), and thus as the business of the Caesarians. It was an admission with political consequences that he certainly cannot have entirely failed to see at the time. If, as was claimed later, he had once said that Octavian had obtained the adoption by engaging in unnatural sexual practices with his great-uncle – which was little more than a rhetorical device to discredit an opponent – that presupposes that in principle he recognized the adoption itself. Brutus, on the other hand, persisted in calling the young man Octavius, presumably because he was not ready to allow him a political role at any time, so he simply ignored the adoption. It is unlikely that he considered it illegal, for he himself had been adopted as an adult, although his was not a testamentary adoption.

It remains for us to see what curiate law and confirmation of the adoption by the *curiae*, that outmoded and by then rarely used form of the assembly of the people, actually meant. It has often been said that Octavius finally became Caesar's heir only by virtue of curiate law, but that seems unlikely. Antony prevented his first attempt to apply for confirmation of his adoption early in the summer, so it was not until well over a year later, in the summer of 43, when Octavius was consul and in possession of power, that he was able to get the adoption confirmed and could thus control the constitutional apparatus of the city of Rome. As we can see from all this, both he and Antony ascribed some significance to curiate law, but he had long ago been recognized by the soldiers and most members of the nobility as Caesar's son, and not just for reasons of power politics. Some time before Cicero became an ally of Octavius, for instance, he was using the young man's adoptive name in private correspondence with his friend Atticus. Curiate law thus did not influence official recognition of the adoption.

The fact that Octavius resorted to this ancient form of confirmation of his adoption at all had to do with one of its areas of competence: the admission of an adult in place of a son, called arrogation in legal sources. In its context in the early Roman period, it presumably gave official status as Roman citizens to men who had come from outside to join a group of Romans, for instance a distinguished family like the Claudians. In Cicero's time, however, it was no longer used for that purpose, as the then degenerate form of the curiate committees shows. Octavian seems to have thought of this very old-fashioned legal instrument in order to present himself *publicly* as the dictator's political heir by raising the act of adoption to the level of a popular decision. At an earlier date, in the year 59 and in an entirely different case, Publius Clodius Pulcher, something of a rough diamond despite being a member of the patrician nobility, had misused this now obsolete popular assembly by having himself adopted by a plebeian so that he could be elected a tribune of the people, because tribunes of the people had to be of plebeian birth.

Consequently, the curiate law served Octavius/Octavian only as political validation of an adoption that was already generally accepted. Some time earlier, the Roman public had already accepted this new Gaius Julius Caesar as the all-powerful dictator's son, and since there was no distinction drawn between sons by birth and sons by adoption in Roman law or in public perception no one ever accused him of being 'only' an adoptive son.

One final consideration is the question of the significance to Octavian of Caesar's testamentary dispositions in case a son was born to him after his death – *postumus* would have been the Roman name given to the child. In his will, Caesar had appointed guardians (*tutores*) in the event of such a son's birth, and our authoritative source on this point mentions the fact that they had included several of his later assassins, although only Decimus Junius Brutus is named. In the law of the time the birth of a posthumous son invalidated arrangements made for the substitute heirs unless otherwise laid down in the will: for instance, if it said that those named as substitute heirs were to be regarded as co-heirs with the posthumous son from the first. The appointment of guardians presupposes, first, that Caesar wanted any posthumous son to be regarded as his heir, while the others (Octavius, Pinarius and Pedius) were to be regarded as substitute heirs. Their status as heirs was thus conditional. If Caesar said nothing in his will about provisions for the substitute heirs if he had a posthumous son – and our sources do not suggest that he did – then Octavian and his two co-heirs could consider themselves to be inheriting only conditionally. It is obvious that when he expressed himself willing to accept the will, Octavius/Octavian was ignoring the question of any posthumous son who might yet be born to Caesar, and indeed the situation never arose.

# 2

# The Dictator's Heir

News of the dictator Gaius Julius Caesar's murder reached young Gaius Octavius in the Greek city of Apollonia on the Adriatic coast, several kilometres south of Dyrrhachium (Durazzo) at the end of the great military road from Thessalonika (Saloniki). His mother had sent a messenger riding post-haste from Rome to Apollonia with the shocking news directly after the event. Octavius had been born on 23 September 63 BC, the son of Gaius Octavius and Atia, daughter of one of Caesar's sisters. As the dictator's great-nephew, he and two grandsons of another sister were among the closest male relations of Caesar, who had never had any legitimate male offspring himself. At this point Octavius did not know that his great-uncle had left a will specifically marking him out, but if only because of his close relationship to the murdered man he considered it only natural for him to go to Rome to deal with any business that might arise from Caesar's estate. He therefore set off without delay, taking only a few companions.

Octavius had spent a good three months in Apollonia, completing his studies and taking part in military exercises under officers of Caesar's troops stationed in the province of Macedonia. The army had been assembled for the great Parthian war that was imminent, and the dictator had been about to lay before the Senate his final arrangements for organizing the war on the Ides of March, the very day of his assassination. There were already several legions standing ready in Macedonia at the time, and Octavius himself was to go with Caesar as his master of the horse, the title traditionally assigned to a dictator's deputy. He had not yet taken up this office, but formal permission had been granted for him to do so as soon as the present incumbent, Marcus Aemilius Lepidus, went to his take up his post as a provincial governor.

33

At the age of only eighteen, Octavius had no experience at all in the political or the administrative sphere, and despite his great-uncle's many attempts to encourage his military capabilities – an essential prerequisite for a man of good birth embarking on a political career – he had no practical experience of leading troops either. Hence the idea of familiarizing him first with cavalry formations. In the aristocracy that made up the ruling class of Rome and its empire, it was not unusual for high command to be given to an inexperienced young man like Octavius. It was simply assumed that anyone chosen for a position entailing the leadership of troops would be capable of doing so. And such a command could be given to a young man without any great risk, for every legion had a large number of officers who had proved themselves in long years of service and would back up their commander in councils of war and in battle. In addition, over the centuries the Roman legion had become a unit held together by rigorous discipline which enabled it to survive even serious mistakes on the part of its leaders. In fact Octavius lacked not just a solid military training but any inclination for a soldier's life. At least, for a Roman – a true Roman of the old school, as he was to proclaim himself so often later – he kept any enthusiasm for the military life well within bounds. The role intended for him in the Parthian campaign, then, was principally of a political nature; his military function took second place to his great-uncle's wish to make him better known to the army as a member of his, Caesar's, family. Octavius himself may well have found his studies of literature more important at the time, and he was pursuing them in the Greek city of Apollonia with his tutor Apollodoros of Pergamon, one of his retinue. As well as Apollodoros, two friends returned to Rome with him: Marcus Vipsanius Agrippa, a young man of his own age, and Quintus Salvidienus Rufus, who was only a little older.

Octavius did not choose the direct route by way of Brundisium (Brindisi), usually the point of departure for all travellers coming from the eastern provinces, passing through Greece on their way to Italy and intending to journey on to Campania and Rome. Instead he took the shorter way across the Adriatic Sea to the Apuleian coast and landed in Italy near the town of Lupiae (Lecce), which he then approached on foot. Octavius had decided on this unusual route for fear of any pursuit, for after the murder of the dictator the situation in Italy was very confused, indeed completely unpredictable. Caesar's great-nephew had to bear in mind that the conspirators might want to get rid of the dictator's family and friends as well. More news from Rome reached him in Lupiae. Here he learned of the tumultuous scenes beside Caesar's funeral pyre in the Forum Romanum, and most important of all he heard about his great-uncle's will, the sums of money left to him and his adoption by the dictator. Since the will had been officially recognized as valid by both the Senate and the Caesarians, Octavius could now consider himself the testator's son even though he had yet to declare his readiness to accept the provisions of the will before the praetor of the city in Rome. Once further letters had reassured him that no immediate danger threatened him in Rome, and there were no personal enemies waiting in Brundisium, the nearest city of any size, he went there at the end of March and then travelled straight on to Campania, where his mother and her second husband, the consular Marcius Philippus, were staying at their country house near Puteoli (Pozzuoli).

He arrived in Naples on 18 April and left at once for Puteoli. Of course he discussed the question of his inheritance with his parents. Both his mother and his stepfather advised him earnestly to decline it. They realized that, although the inheritance might officially be merely the acceptance of a private legacy, it could not fail to have political connotations, and they had good reason to fear that in the struggle for Caesar's succession the young and inexperienced Octavius would be eliminated by the dictator's generals and his assassins. Octavius himself was well aware of that, but he saw more clearly than his parents that he had no choice in the matter: the civil war had been going on for more than five years, it was not over yet and might continue with renewed ferocity because of Caesar's murder, and in view of those facts he would certainly have fallen victim to whichever side eventually won. He himself acted in exactly that way later, in the year 30, when as the victor over Antony he had the innocent Caesarion executed because the sixteen-year-old youth was the putative son of Caesar and Cleopatra, and thus a potential rival for power.

While he was staying at his stepfather's country house Octavius visited Cicero, who owned a property nearby and happened to be staying there at the time. Cicero wrote to his friend Atticus about this meeting, telling him that while Octavius was in Naples he had met a close friend of the murdered dictator, Lucius Cornelius Balbus, and had been extremely friendly and respectful to him, Cicero. However, said Cicero, he had not liked Octavius' companion, who was sycophantic and very obviously hostile to Caesar's assassins. He sums up his uneasiness at this meeting with 'the boy' by doubting whether he can become a citizen who is really true to the constitution (*bonus civis*). Octavius did not conceal from Cicero – and indeed this was a somewhat explosive political move – that he intended to accept his inheritance. He may have made his decision already, but it was here in Campania that he first made it publicly known to both the Caesarians and those who sympathized with the assassins. His course was set; from now on there was no going back for Octavius.

Campania, one of the most fertile parts of Italy, was in turmoil at the time because of the settlement of army veterans there and the resulting changes in property ownership. It was particularly important for Octavius to find out the mood among those old soldiers who had fought under Caesar, and also to discover how members of the governing political class – the nobility, or rather those of them who did not belong to the close circle of the assassins – saw the political future. Here in Campania he could feel relatively safe among Caesar's veterans, battle-hardened men who fiercely respected their general and hated his murderers, and in view of his present almost complete political isolation that was something he desperately needed. While he was still in Brundisium, Octavius had set aside as much of the money collected for the Parthian War and the taxes of the Asian province as he thought was due to him by the will and was now available – undoubtedly very large sums – used some of it to pay Caesar's bequests and sent the rest to Rome. That too made it clear that he was going to accept his inheritance.

He had had little choice over the decision to accept, but in his position it took great courage to approach the inevitable with vigour. It might almost be said that it called for the courage of despair, if we did not know of the energy, subtlety and ruthlessness with which nature had endowed this apparently nondescript young man. His acceptance of the role assigned to him in the will brought Octavius no immediate political credit in the eyes of almost all members of the upper classes. His appearance on the political stage of Rome, therefore, led at first to no shift of power, let alone any reversal of the existing positions, even though the will itself was not contested, and Octavius was related by blood to the dictator through his maternal grandmother Julia. What made him appear so weak in other people's eyes was not even primarily his youth, or his inexperience of holding any kind of office that might have given him a firm foundation on which to rise, although of course both did make a difference. Above all, he had no recourse to what at the time was a crucial factor: he had no army, or initially even a small military division for his personal protection, and he could not point to military achievements or indeed any experience worth mentioning in that sphere to raise his reputation among the soldiers and their officers. Nor, in spite of his relationship with the dictator, were his origins exactly spectacular for a man setting out to play a political role in Rome.

His birth father, the late Gaius Octavius, had been one of the upper class in the small Latin town of Velitrae (Velletri) on the southern slopes of the Alban mountains, originally a Volscian rather than ancient Latin settlement. Gaius Octavius had been praetor in the year 61, and governor of the province of Macedonia, but any further political rise was abruptly halted by his early death in the spring of 59, when his small son was not yet four years old. Only the remarriage of Octavius' mother to Lucius Marcius Philippus, a former consul and member of a distinguished family, gave the boy a noble household to grow up in. His mother's own background was in small-town society. Her father, Marcus Atius Balbus, was from Aricia, which at least was an old Latin town. Some of Balbus' ancestors had sat in the Senate, and he himself rose to be praetor. Both the Octavians and the Atians were certainly highly regarded families of equestrian (knightly) and ultimately senatorial rank but until now they had been active solely in the small towns from which they came, and even after their rise to the Senate in Rome those towns were still their political homeland. Their rise in the world had not brought them noble status, and the attempts of later genealogists to give the Octavians a higher rank in the annals of the early history of Rome than was really theirs have proved to be forgeries. Other attempts to denigrate some of Octavius' forebears as freedmen – the sons of slaves – or to claim that they had pursued demeaning professions turned out, similarly, to be political slanders.

Octavius himself did not disown his small-town origins even long after he had received the title of Augustus, and indeed admitted openly that while he came from an old and wealthy family of equestrian rank, his father was the first of its members to have become a senator. This honesty might do credit to the established ruler of the empire, but in his early political activities his comparatively undistinguished background was an obstacle to him in searching for support in his political career. There were slighting mentions of his less than noble origin; there were attempts to humiliate the man who had assumed the name of Caesar by maliciously circulating stories, either true or invented, about individual members of his family; and he was even teased about his rather puzzling nickname Thurinus (perhaps 'from the town of Thurii, in southern Italy), although he seems to have borne it only as a boy. He and his friends might dismiss such talk as merely the inflated rhetoric used by someone wanting to disparage a political opponent, signifying nothing. But at a time when Cicero was already one of Octavius' allies and officially called him Caesar's son, he felt it necessary to defend him against such accusations and sought to have all this dirty linen washed in the Senate – or rather, to show that it was in fact spotlessly clean – which is evidence, if not of the truth of all the claims made, at least of the politically perilous nature of the question of Octavius' origin. His opponents wanted everyone to know that Caesar's son was a young man from the rural, and perhaps rather insecure, aristocracy. It is true that when Caesar himself ruled Rome such origins, even among very influential Romans, had been not uncommon, and many such men, some of whom had rather dubious reputations, continued to be active in political life even after his assassination. And the dictator had given many high positions in the army and the administration of the state to men from small towns in central Italy. But for Octavius to enter into his political inheritance, more was needed than the mere official declaration that in accepting the dictator's will Gaius Octavius had become Gaius Julius Caesar. Caesar's adopted son was not to be equated with a Vatinius or Caninius, creatures of Caesar who, thanks to their master, strutted proudly on the political stage as consuls and for whom that was enough.

The first steps taken by Octavius as a major political player determined not only his own future but, as no one could have guessed at the time, the future of Rome. In assessing what followed, both the general and the specific background of Octavius' apparently risky decision are important: what was the political situation in which the young man presented himself to the world as heir to the great Caesar, and how could he gain a political base?

The events of the Ides of March created a political situation entirely different from the one the conspirators had expected and hoped for. The old order which their 'tyrannicide' was to restore had been disintegrating even before the civil war, and during Caesar's five years of sole rule he had eliminated or adapted for his own purposes much of what was left of it. It soon turned out that the leading group, the nobility, could not raise it again from the ruins left behind by Caesar; it had been breaking up for over a hundred years, and in the last civil war had lost many of its leaders, who either died or went over to Caesar's side. The consequences were obvious immediately after his assassination. The assembled senators before whose eyes the murder had taken place scattered in horror. Brutus had a stirring speech ready to deliver, but found no audience in the Senate; the old central organ of government was no longer capable of making political decisions, and the clarion call to freedom also echoed unheard outside the Senate house. The assassins, shaken, finally entrenched themselves on the Capitol and called on the protection of gladiators who were not even Roman citizens.

Caesar's adherents had been taken by surprise just as much as those senators who were not in on the secret. Their horror was soon mingled with bewilderment, and uncertainty about the extent of the conspiracy. Ignorance of the political background of the murder and the possible reactions of the people of Rome paralysed the will of the Caesarians, which explains their wish for a breathing space in which they could get a clearer picture of the situation and the next steps to be taken. That is the only way to account for the fact that, on 17 March, two days after the Ides, Mark Antony, the consul left in office after Caesar's death and so chosen as spokesman for all the Caesarians, decided on a kind of truce with the conspirators. This was agreed at a Senate meeting in the temple of Tellus and it secured an amnesty for the murderers and recognition of Caesar's dispositions (*acta Caesaris*) for the Caesarians. Among these *acta* was the will deposited with the dictator's father-in-law, Lucius Calpurnius Piso, and although Piso met with some opposition he had it officially opened and read. The will was read in Antony's house, and thus in public to all the nobility.

The agreement of 17 March could not be a real political settlement but must be seen as a compromise born of the necessity of the hour, tiding the opposing parties over their inability to take any action after the dictator's death and allowing them, they hoped, to clarify the situation and establish their own political positions. For the agreement was extremely humiliating and basically unacceptable to both sides; indeed, it was like a declaration of political bankruptcy on the part of all involved. It meant that the conspirators had given up their former hopes of the political consequences of their action, and the Caesarians had abandoned the idea of revenge for the murder of their much-honoured military commander and patron. The general mood of uncertainty was evident, for instance, in the fact that the two leading Caesarians of the time, Antony and Lepidus (the dictator's last master of the horse and already appointed governor of southern Gaul and Citerior Spain), received the chief conspirators, Cassius and Marcus Brutus, in their own houses.

The subsequent course of events very soon showed what a political hiatus Caesar's death had left. The shock of the murder paralysed everyone at first; the compromise of the 17 March agreement was only a consequence of that paralysis. People waited to see what would happen, sounding out the political ground. Italy was a hotbed of rumours, assumptions about the future, and deliberate distortion of what was being planned and discussed. It was a climate in which political adventurers could thrive. For instance, a man appeared in Rome after Caesar's murder claiming to be Marius, grandson of the great conqueror of the German tribes, and he was recognized as such by many, although others, including the mother of Gaius Octavius, rejected his claim. The alleged Marius had caused something of a sensation in Spain the previous year, and had contrived to assemble a considerable following in Rome; at this time he was even bold enough to make overtures to Cicero and the young Gaius Octavius. Neither of them could think of anything to do but refer him to the dictator, who instantly banished him. The false Marius, whose name was probably Amatius and who may have come from the slave class, returned from exile after the dictator's murder and won considerable influence over the people of Rome, many of them now ready to believe what had previously been dismissed as mere gossip. As the dictator had been related through his aunt to the real Marius, the false bearer of the name counted on gaining advantage from this 'relationship', and he even had an altar built on the place where the dictator had been burned. In the middle of April Antony put a swift end to the man's nuisance value by having him arrested and unceremoniously strangled. But the charlatan's wiles were a sign of the times. Everything was in flux: the whole situation was confused, and no one could yet see any future solution.

In this chaotic state of affairs, it quickly became clear that the assassination of the Ides of March had been a total political failure. Some might wonder whether that was mainly because the conspirators had been obliged to avoid any contact with those who knew nothing about the murder plans, so that it had been almost impossible to prepare for the aftermath, or whether the reason was that the conspirators had simply misjudged the political situation, expecting that the majority of the nobility and other senators would spontaneously restore the traditional order. In any case the appeal to freedom, meaning mainly the freedom of the nobles, had not stirred hearts, and it was nothing short of naive to ignore the many new faces among the nobility and those who had risen to senatorial rank only through Caesar. Also ignored were the very many soldiers and veterans who, as had been well known for two generations, were alienated from the state and relied on their own commanders. So the conspirators' action misfired, failing to have the expected effect, and as no successor to Caesar appeared on the scene – and in view of the situation no such successor could appear, because the dictator's power had been *sui generis* – there was nothing they could do but adjust to whatever seemed politically possible as matters now stood. But just what *was* possible? Since the old tradition could not be revived for lack of the men who had formerly represented it, and Caesar, as a great figure with whom men could identify, was also gone, there was no clear point from which bearings could be taken. All that happened, therefore, was that those who held good cards for the coming political game, or thought they did, tried to improve their initial position through various intrigues and initiatives. However, the game had begun from a point of departure previously unknown to all the players, the cards had been shuffled more or less by the chance of the moment, and as a result the players were a rather motley collection. Anyone in high office at the time of Caesar's death, or who was actually in command of an army on which he could rely for support, held a trump card. Many were surprised by the way chance played into their hands, others were simply unable to exploit the advantage that had been thrown into their laps.

Antony, who was in the best position at the start, was the man who acted most consistently in this situation. However, he did not stage Caesar's funeral, so widely and forcefully presented in classical and modern literature as a political platform for the elimination of Caesar's assassins, exactly in the way that has been assumed. As consul and Cae-sar's close companion in arms, and in the absence of a direct heir, he was the natural choice to deliver the traditional funeral oration (*laudatio funebris*). The frequently cited episode when, after praising the dead man, he showed the assembled citizens either Caesar's toga, shredded by the assassins' daggers and drenched with blood, or a wax reproduc-tion of his body bearing the marks of the stab wounds, may well be accurate. But there was no need for him to get the people of the city of Rome worked up into a state of indignation. Caesar had shown them extraordinary favour since his early political life, particularly when he was aedile and held lavish games, and he continued to do so during his period of sole rule. They could well have hoped for further advantages from him, especially of a material nature, so it was predictable that the funeral would lead to uproar and acts of violence against the conspir-ators. And what political use would an indignant populace ready for anything have been to Antony? The people of Rome offered little help to an ambitious man in his situation. The false Marius might act on such a platform, but Antony had better means of agitation at his com-mand and he now employed them. To start with, he was very well placed legally. He was consul, and his two younger brothers also held high office in the city of Rome that year. The elder, Gaius, was praetor; as such he had the power of military command, and in April he took over the post of city judge (*praetor urbanus*). The younger, Lucius, was trib-une of the people, an office that made it eminently suitable for him to carry out a number of initiatives.

Antony built on the compromise negotiated with Caesar's murderers on 17 March in the Senate. It granted the assassins an amnesty, and unlike the Caesarians themselves it recognized the validity of Caesar's decrees. To take that as a stroke of political genius on Antony's part, as it is often presented in the light of later developments, would be a mis-take. The laws and decrees of Caesar could not be set aside without the threat of chaos; many of them, relating to the settlement of veterans, were now taken for granted and had already been implemented in part. The really remarkable feature of the compromise, in fact, was the concession allowing all who took part in the murder to go unpunished. Antony and Caesar's other friends and companions had let themselves be persuaded to grant it, although there was something deeply repellent to all Caesarians in refraining to punish the murderers of a commander who had been loved and revered by all his soldiers. A subsequent series of decisions in the Senate was calculated to strengthen the assassins' position yet further. Among other measures, there was to be a committee to investigate Caesar's official acts, but, most important of all, dictatorship was abolished for ever, a decision legally confirmed. The fact that Antony himself brought this petition before the assembly of the people says little for the strength of his position at the time; he was disowning the dictator in a manner that placed him side by side with Caesar's murderers, and Cicero did not refrain from holding that against him later in his First and Second Philippics. There is no doubt that, when confronting a Senate rather inclined to favour the murderers of Caesar, Antony was the weaker party. None the less, the political circumstances gave him a chance to consolidate his position on the basis of the resolution of 17 March.

His basis for his further activities was the consulate, through which he controlled official affairs of state in Rome, and his personal closeness to the house of Caesar. Both helped him to obtain large sums of money, for instance from the state treasury deposited in the temple of Ops, goddess of plenty. In addition, and even more important, he was able to lay hands on all the dictator's documents concerning the current and future business of state. In her initial state of shock, Caesar's widow, Calpurnia, is said to have given him all the papers in the house. Antony made the most of what these papers offered him, and naturally he was anxious to broaden his political base. With the help of Caesar's private secretary, Faberius, he manipulated those papers from Caesar's estate that dealt with legal projects, expanded them or even invented other projects allegedly for laws that Caesar intended to introduce. His idea was to make them legally binding as the dictator's own dispositions, thus logically interpreting the senatorial decision of 17 March. A flood of resolutions concerning the recall of exiled persons, the granting of offices, grants of land to veterans and the gift of civic rights poured out of the consul's office. Even the inhabitants of Sicily, a province without a single Roman city or even a sizeable proportion of Romans among the population as a whole, received Roman civic rights. This gift – for such it was – was so monstrous that it is almost tempting to think of it as a mistake in the records. In both his Philippics and his letters, Cicero never tired of denouncing Antony's legal wire-pulling and castigating it as a violation of the law. 'Legal writings are publicly contravened, freedom from taxes is granted, large sums of money are distributed, exiles are recalled, and false senatorial decisions announced,' he writes indignantly to Cassius in early May. His indignation was understandable, for there was no means at all of checking that the proposed laws really derived from Caesar's own plans. But what counted was the de facto recognition of Caesar's actual or alleged projects, and with it the enormous expansion of the political base from which Antony operated. Now his principal concern was to win over the soldiers, especially the veterans.

His growing influence also gave Antony the chance of acquiring military power. As consul and Caesar's former general in Gaul and in the civil war, the commander who had led the left wing of the Caesarian army against Pompey in the decisive battle of Pharsalos in the year 48, he was undoubtedly seen by the veterans as the man best qualified for future military command. To Antony such a command was the most desirable aim of all, for it would extract him from the demeaning position in which he found himself after the Ides of March. His own military past was discredited by the moral condemnation of the dictator implied in the amnesty allowed to Caesar's murderers. Turning to the army was like declaring his support for the dictator Caesar and distancing himself from Caesar's murderers, as well as the section of the Senate that supported them. He was clearly about to break with the assassins; the compromise of 17 March had been only a makeshift reconciliation. The new political front lines had Antony with Caesar's soldiers on one side, facing the conspirators on the other.

Antony now set energetically to work to increase his influence. As soon as March or early April, he had important provincial governorships transferred by law to him and his fellow consul, Publius Cornelius Dolabella, appointed suffect (substitute) consul to fill Caesar's now vacant place. Once their consulate was over he proposed himself as governor of Macedonia, while Dolabella would go to the province of Syria, which had probably already been promised to him by Caesar. At the time there were six legions standing ready under arms in Macedonia, a force intended by Caesar to fight in his Parthian war. They were to march along the great army road, the Via Egnatia, to Thessalonika and go on from there to Syria. This placed two important provinces in the hands of the Caesarians, and it also made a large army available to Antony. The success of this move was all the more remarkable because

Caesar had intended the governorships of these provinces for Brutus and Cassius when their praetorships were over, and it can probably be explained only by the special situation in the second half of March, when a majority of senators, fearing the outbreak of open conflict and in a state of perplexity about the future, wanted to see the opposing sides reconciled at any cost and might even still have thought a genuine reconciliation possible. In April, to secure his position further, Antony, acting with Dolabella, proposed a law for the settlement of Caesar's veterans; among other sites to be used for this purpose was the extensive terrain of the Pontine Marshes, part of which Caesar had already had drained, particularly where they bordered the Appian Way, the great main road to the south. Then, at the end of April, Antony went to Campania, allegedly to supervise the implementation of this law, but in fact to present himself to the veterans as a future leader of the Caesarian party.

New legions could, if necessary, be formed from the ranks of the veterans. In the weeks and months after Caesar's death, however, the focus was on those legions still under arms and the political attitude of the officials commanding them, as a rule the governors of the provinces where they were stationed. There were many legions stationed on a war footing in the provinces of the empire – in contrast to Italy, which had been a demilitarized area for over a generation – and they had not yet been demobilized, because military operations were still in progress. For if Caesar's political enemies at home could also be regarded as defeated in military terms, there were still stubborn areas of resistance in various parts of the empire, in Spain and in Syria. In addition, preparations for the Parthian War had been in full swing at the time of the Ides of March. It had to be assumed that the war might be as far-reaching and last as long as the Gallic War, and it therefore called for powerful armaments. Consequently Caesar had concentrated large bodies of troops in the provinces of Macedonia and Syria.

The Macedonian legions were commanded by Quintus Hortensius, a son of the famous orator and rival of Cicero, and Antony was to take the province over from him after the end of March to 1 January of the year 43, as decreed by the Senate. Much to the displeasure of Cicero, Hortensius had allied himself with the dictator during the civil war, and not only he but the officers of the Macedonian army naturally thought along Caesarian lines. There were also strong Roman forces in Syria, where the war was to begin, because of the threat of Parthian incursions, which had been a considerable nuisance to the province ever since the heavy Roman defeat at Carrhae in the year 53. The three legions under the command of the governor Lucius Staius Murcus, dispatched to Syria by Caesar, had been joined in the year 44 by the three legions of the governor of the province of Bithynia with Pontus, Quintus Marcius Crispus. He had marched to Syria to support Murcus against the adventurer Quintus Caecilius Bassus, who had contrived to take command of two legions during Caesar's lifetime by exploiting the confusions of the civil war. In addition, the four legions stationed in Egypt, ordered to Syria by Dolabella under the command of Aulus Allienus, had now joined these strong forces in Syria, so that ten legions in all were finally assembled there. Since Dolabella was to govern Syria in the coming year the initial position of the Caesarians, and more particularly of Antony and Dolabella, was not unpromising in the eastern half of the gigantic empire – always assuming that the provinces and legions legally transferred to the consuls actually were handed over to them by the governors currently in place.

Nor did the situation look bad for the Caesarians in the west of the empire. Marcus Aemilius Lepidus had been given southern Gaul (Gallia Narbonensis) and the northern Spanish province (Hispania Citerior) by Caesar. Lepidus was regarded by both parties as rather unreliable and he did in fact very soon come to terms with the 'republicans' left in Spain after the civil war. In the part of Gaul conquered by Caesar, Gallia Comata ('Gaul of the long hair' – the Celts differed most noticeably from the Romans and Greeks in the way they let their hair grow), prospects looked better. Here Lucius Munatius Plancus was in command of three legions and raised further troops; he could be considered a Caesarian. Decimus Brutus, who was among Caesar's murderers and governed the province of Upper Italy (Gallia Cisalpina), was not. At the time of Caesar's murder these three men were still in Rome; Decimus Brutus and Lepidus went to their provinces a few weeks after the assassination; Munatius Plancus stayed in Rome until the summer. Two more important provinces were administered by able men who had been Caesar's generals and remained his supporters even after his death: Illyricum was in the hands of Publius Vatinius with three legions, although they were busy dealing with provincial uprisings, and the newly constituted

province of Africa Nova (the former Numidian kingdom) was administered by Titus Sextius with an equally strong force.

During the weeks he spent in Campania Antony could feel secure in his
position. Not only was he the leader of the Caesarians, he also held a
major command that would make him the leading man in the state, like
all military potentates of the now failing republic before him. The conspirators and their sympathizers began to see Antony as the new tyrant,
the 'heir to the throne', as Cicero puts it. Cicero's letters tell us something about the atmosphere in those weeks. Traditionalists bemoaned
the fact that, although the tyrant had gone, tyranny remained, and
people began to fear violence against those who had revealed their
private approval of the tyrant's murder. There were also frequent complaints about, and criticisms of, the inadequate planning and execution
of the assassination, with suggestions that those closest to Caesar, first
and foremost Antony, ought to have gone as well. 'What a magnificent
but senseless act,' remarked Cicero to Atticus in the second half of April.
'It was carried out with the courage of men but the understanding of
boys.' And two weeks later, writing to the same correspondent, he says:
'The tree was felled, but the roots were not torn out.' Antony's dynamism paralysed his opponents, and by now many of them considered
the republican cause lost. Cicero himself resigned, retiring in early April
to one of his villas in Campania, where he intended to await further
developments.

Octavius had arrived in Campania from Brundisium about the same
time as Antony, perhaps a few days earlier. Their paths crossed, although
they did not meet. Octavius still had too low a profile for the now con-
fident Antony to feel that he needed to take much notice of him, and
Caesar's will could not yet create a political base for Octavius, for
although its contents were generally known it was not legally in force
until he had accepted the inheritance in due form. And he could not
expect anything useful to come of any discussion with Antony; indeed,
the outcome was more likely to be humiliating. On the political stage of
Rome Octavius was still a nobody; so far, the only political fronts to
open up had been between the murderers and Caesar's generals. Those
fronts might shift, at the most, as a result of rivalry among the latter, for
instance between Lepidus, who had been particularly close to Caesar
during the dictator's period of sole rule, and Antony as consul. Octavius

still had no place in the struggle, and it remained doubtful whether he would ever play a part on the political scene. His youth, his inexperience and his lack of military followers seemed to restrict him severely. The cards in the new political game had already been dealt, and although Octavius had not exactly gone away empty-handed, he was not among those to be taken into account. Did he have any chance at all in the struggle for political power? What were the inclinations of those striving for influence and those on whom it depended? Before we look at the further events that were finally to clarify the fronts, it will be worth dwelling briefly on those questions.

Every noble who had a good political position at the time of the dictator's murder, or was reckoning on his chances of acquiring one, tried to recruit supporters. He sought them among those who traditionally exerted influence in the state: first the nobility, then the rest of the senators and the equestrian order, after that the people of the city of Rome, who decided on the petitions of the magistrates in the assemblies of the people, and finally the veterans and the soldiers still under arms. They had been the prop and stay of Caesar's rule; with him they had conquered first Gaul and then, as it seemed, the entire empire during the civil war. It may be easy to understand the exceptional commitment that all parties devoted to their recruitment campaigns, but the essential factor seems to be not their eagerness but the difficulty of predicting their success. Why did one man make few gains, despite making great efforts, while everything fell into another man's lap? Were there no established political factors to act as a guide, at least up to a point, in predicting success?

In fact any calculable political factors had lost a good deal of their force with the outbreak of civil war, but they had not entirely disappeared. The rules and norms of government by a firmly established aristocratic society that had been in force for centuries still existed. The structure of legal criteria erected over a long period and the customs relating to them meant that in fact the state was dominated by the nobility, but the idea of the integration of the people as a whole into government had not yet been overthrown. A guiding principle for political action was the devotion of the masses to their aristocratic patrons – as a clientele, they were divided among the distinguished families – as well as the obedience of the soldiers to the magistracy, and a general respect for tradition. Were these not sufficient guidelines? But it now turned out that the norms of community life in the state obviously no longer had the same binding force as before; they had been shattered over long decades of political crisis in the republic. It might be something that every Roman had sensed, even before the outbreak of the civil war in the year 49, but the war itself had been preceded by over thirty years not of peace at home but of conditions that were at least largely free of bloody confrontations. The last civil war and the monarchy set up by Caesar had changed the general political climate; soldiers who for two generations had looked to their commanders rather than to the government in Rome were even further alienated from the state. The potential for decisive political action no longer seemed as firmly established as it had been. There was more latitude, although greater political mobility was not available to everyone in the same way. This last is an important point and demands special consideration. Here we must distinguish in principle between the soldiers and other Roman social groups.

On the whole the civil war and Caesar's rule ranged the soldiers on the side of the state. Recruited without exception from men who owned little or nothing, they expected their commander – and rightly so by the ideas of the time – to treat them fairly after their military service was ended. He would pay them off with a farm and a considerable lump sum of money. Some time earlier Caesar had begun providing for those of his soldiers whose units he was about to demobilize. However, since the flames of the civil war were not yet entirely extinguished, and Caesar was preparing for the great Parthian war, the demobilization had not yet gone very far, so in the months after the Ides of March both Italy and the provinces were teeming with legions and soldiers who, already or about to be demobilized, were waiting to know what provision was being made for them.

This situation meant that the generals had to shoulder the dictator's commitments to the soldiers. The general to whom the soldiers could turn first in this matter was certainly Antony, particularly as his consulate gave him the means of obtaining land and money. Nothing, therefore, can have annoyed the soldiers more than his agreement to an amnesty for Caesar's murderers. They were bound to ask themselves just where this general stood. It was certainly clear to all the soldiers that he was not about to throw in his lot with the murderers, but his wheeling and dealing must have undermined their sense of security. The fact that Octavius was now presenting himself as Gaius Julius Caesar, the dictator's son, may have appealed to a number of the soldiers, but Octavius was not a general, had little idea of military life and knew nothing about the efforts that they, the soldiers, had made over the course of many years under their general Caesar. And would he be able to assert himself?

On the other hand, those who continued to support the generals might come up against one of Caesar's murderers. Decimus Brutus had been one of Caesar's most successful commanders. When he went to his province of Cisalpine Gaul in April the two legions stationed there, one of them consisting of veterans, gave him a friendly reception. As this showed, common experiences shared by the soldiers and their general, as well as respect for military ability, might loosen their ties with former army patrons and in any case were still valued so highly that, in spite of the part played by Decimus Brutus in the conspiracy against Caesar, the soldiers of the two Upper Italian legions could recognize him as their commander and thus the man guaranteeing the provision to be made for them later. Recognition of Munatius Plancus and Aemilius Lepidus, who had distanced themselves from the assassination, naturally gave the soldiers less difficulty, but even so it could not be entirely taken for granted. For under Caesar there were many generals, and this new situation opened up an opportunity to choose between them. In certain circumstances a general who presented himself to the soldiers as the rival to a commander already in place might profit by that opportunity. The really new aspect of this time was that the soldiers suddenly had their own political significance. Events now depended above all on them, not just on what the leaders of the nobility thought.

It was even more difficult to foresee where the nobles would turn. There was no choice for the conspirators, of course: they had to back the restoration of rule by the Senate whatever it turned out to be like. They might be joined by many who, without having taken part in the conspiracy themselves, believed it possible to return to the status quo. Such men included Cicero, who was ultimately to emerge as a champion of the old order. But not all who sympathized with the conspirators had to adopt such an uncompromising attitude as Cicero in his opposition to Antony. If the political situation were to change, a fellow traveller of the conspirators, unlike the conspirators themselves, had the option of retiring from political life, or alternatively – as the safer course – of allying himself with a successful general.

It was not just the supporters of the old order or those who sympathized with it who found it hard to choose a political direction from the outset; it was the same for distinguished followers of Caesar and their clientele of soldiers. Where were the Caesarians? And above all: what did they represent as a political group? Caesar had been a unique personality, and his political aim of ruling the Roman state must not only have appeared out of the reach of every noble, it had also been a thorn in the flesh of the great majority of Romans. In the opinion of many, the rupture that Caesar's rule had created could not be reversed, and a new master must be sought; but then who was going to put himself forward to the nobility and the soldiers as that man? The Caesarians obviously had greater difficulties finding political alternatives to Caesar than the conspirators and their sympathizers, who could, after all, call on tradition. But on what did a Caesarian with influence and supporters have his eye? Did he not want, as perhaps Caesar had intended in his last years of life, to try entirely new forms of political fulfilment, or could he aim only for a major military command like the powerful nobles before the civil war? Ultimately, those men had brought down the old republic. He might think of the extraordinary military commands of men like Gnaeus Pompeius and Caesar himself, especially Caesar's command of the campaign in Gaul. Any ambitious Caesarian had to look to the soldiers for protection, for the sake of his own security and his political influence. But who was in the running for such a major military command? Of the many generals, to whom would the others as well as the officers and men allow such military rank? Every aspirant naturally sought first to gain a good position in the hierarchy of public office, and to recruit as many supporters as possible among the soldiers, aiming for the consulate or a governorship with good prospects and courting the favour of the soldiers and the veterans. As consul and Caesar's former legate, Antony undoubtedly started from the best position but, although he made the running, even he was not to be regarded from the first as the most capable, efficient and radical candidate, the one who must necessarily emerge the victor.

For all concerned, whether sympathizers of the conspirators or supporters of Caesar in the widest sense, the structure of the republic increasingly became increasingly irrelevant in the search for a political standpoint. The constitution as it had grown up over the centuries, and the strong influence of the nobility, were still acknowledged as political quantities, and at first, directly after the dictator's murder, they came to the fore again. But the political mood was less and less inclined to take them as guidelines, instead paying more attention to individuals, whether those individuals were strong supporters of the old order or were only lukewarm about it. The state, shaken by internal crises for the previous 100 years, had after all been more or less dissolved by the rule of Caesar, who had systematically destroyed its framework of norms, and the nobility, after many losses in the various civil wars, was now a spent force. The Caesarians backed individuals rather than political programmes, and those to whom they looked – and to whom they could also look up – were increasingly men of less distinguished descent who had risen to prominence only under Caesar.

A sign of the new mood, in which old and new ideas mingled, is the correspondence of Cicero in August 44 (only a few days before he launched his major attack on Antony) with the highly cultured Gaius Matius, who had been very close to Caesar and also a friend of Cicero from their youth. Cicero lays emphasis on the personal relationship between them, and between Caesar and Matius, to gloss over their actual political differences; he dismisses the discrepancies as misunder-standings and contents himself with a brief expression of his opinion, in a single but clear statement to the effect that correct political conduct consists in placing the freedom of the fatherland above the life of one's own friend. Matius, in reply, speaks plainly, and frankly asks how useful Caesar's murder really was. He also points to the ambivalence of the so-called republicans, droves of whom were courting Antony even as he wrote. For both correspondents, the old state forms the political background – what possible alternative was there? – but their attempt to formulate a stance in the post-Caesarian era shows that in the changed political world there were various possible answers to the question of how to defend the fatherland.

Octavius made his way from Campania to Rome to build himself a pol-itical base before Antony returned. He arrived in the first days of May. Later it would be said that as he entered the city a circle had been visible around the sun in a clear sky, an omen that could be interpreted as the wreath of future fame, and that lightning sent by Jupiter had struck the tomb of Caesar's daughter Julia. Whether these portents were really observed at the time or invented later, Octavius immediately succeeded in gaining the support of two extremely important recruits: Mark Antony's brothers Gaius Antonius, as *praetor urbanus*, praetor of the city, responsible for legislation among the citizens of Rome, including the acceptance of wills, and Lucius Antonius as his assistant, the tribune of the people.

Only a few days after his arrival in Rome, Octavius officially and publicly declared before Gaius Antonius that he accepted the legacy set out in the will and his adoption by Caesar, and in emphasizing the father–son relationship made it clear that nothing would deter him from a son's duty of avenging the murder of his adoptive father. Lucius Antonius enabled Octavius to address an informal assembly of the people – known as the *contio* to distinguish it from the voting assembly – at which he publicly introduced himself to the Roman capital as Caesar's son. Gaius Octavius was now officially known as Gaius Julius Caesar. He deliberately did not take the additional name usual for those who had been adopted, alluding to the family of a man's birth father – in his case, as a former Octavian, 'Octavianus' – but called himself Gaius Julius Caesar like his adoptive father. However, he will be referred to in what follows as Octavian to make it easier to distinguish him from his adoptive father. Mark Antony's two younger brothers, particularly Lucius, had been rather rash, as it would soon appear, in helping Octavian to chalk up this success, which to him meant no less than the political basis of all his future actions. However, they might be excused on the grounds that the young man appeared innocuous: for the time being he was merely accepting the will already recognized by both the Senate and Mark Antony on 17 March, making a formal declaration before the praetor and thus presenting himself as Caesar's legal private heir.

In the middle of May the consul Mark Antony returned from Campania, accompanied by a considerable force of veterans recalled to military service; they were there not only to protect him but also to demonstrate his authority as the leader of Caesar's soldiers. Antony, who unlike his brothers had a position to defend, immediately scented the potential danger in Caesar's heir. He made use of a courtesy visit by Octavian, who formally introduced himself as such, to humiliate the young man; he kept him waiting and made it clear to everyone what he thought of the appearance of this 'boy' on the political stage. At this time Antony was living in Pompey the Great's confiscated house above the Velia, the slight rise between the Forum and the low-lying area later to be occupied by the Colosseum, in one of the residential districts favoured by the rich and distinguished. The house also served Antony as a suitable venue for grand occasions.

Now that Octavian was in Rome, Antony tried to consolidate his position among the Caesarians. Only a few days after his return he came to an understanding with Marcus Aemilius Lepidus, who after Antony himself was the most influential man among the Caesarians in Rome and Italy. Lepidus, as Caesar's master of the horse, had held a position that could be described as deputy dictator and had received the governorship of two provinces from Caesar himself before the Ides of March. They were southern Gaul (Gallia Narbonensis) and Citerior Spain, which was administered for him by legates. Antony now appointed him to the office of high priest, *pontifex maximus*, which had fallen vacant on the dictator's death, and he was voted into the post on 20 May by the assembly of the people responsible for such things; in addition, Antony betrothed one of his daughters to the son of Lepidus. Thus strengthened as effectively first among both the dictator's generals and the holders of public office, he could oppose Octavian energetically if necessary. When Octavian tried backing up his testamentary adoption with a law to be passed by that outmoded voting assembly the *curiae*, associations of family representatives which no longer had any real social standing, Antony used his official powers to prevent it. It looked as if Octavian had not after all furthered his political ambitions. Did he have any chance? How is his political situation at the time to be judged?

It is easy to regard Antony's conduct towards Octavian as disproportionate and to see his arrogance as the outcome of pride and envy, with Octavian playing the part of the young challenger demanding his rightful inheritance. Of course, that is also the opinion of our sources, which focus on the situation from the viewpoint of Octavian/Augustus, and we are usually only too willing to go along with them. But like everyone who fought for Caesar's cause with him, Antony could assume that, as there was no son or grandson in a direct line of descent from the dictator, the political successor to Caesar could come only from the ranks of his tried and trusted generals. What that successor's function would be like, of course, no one could say exactly. He could not inherit Caesar's unique political position, he could only recommend himself as a patron to the soldiers who expected leadership and to have provision made for them. Of all Caesar's generals, Antony could feel predestined for such a position, not only because of his consulship in the important year 44 and his military abilities, which he had repeatedly shown during the civil war, but because of personal gestures on the part of the dictator. For instance, on his return from his last Spanish campaign Caesar had given Antony a place in his own travelling carriage – Octavian, still Gaius Octavius at the time, had to sit with Decimus Brutus in the second carriage – but most important of all, he had named Antony in his will as secondary heir, with Decimus Brutus, if Octavius declined his inheritance. Since Decimus Brutus was among the murderers, that left Antony as the sole secondary heir, and his conduct after the assassination on the Ides of March, particularly in taking charge of the entire archives of the chancellery, was based on that fact. In addition, there were no rivals to Antony at this point among the other generals who had been loyal to the dictator. Antony seems to have satisfied the man who had been promoted to particular distinction by Caesar at the end of his life, Marcus Aemilius Lepidus, with the position of *pontifex maximus*, for the time being anyway. At least, Lepidus went off to his province without protest. Other generals or supporters of Caesar who had already held the post of consul, and thus enjoyed a high reputation, fell into line, for instance Quintus Fufius Calenus, Gaius Caninius Rebilus and above all Lucius Calpurnius Piso and Gnaeus Domitius Calvinus, who had been consuls in the republican period. Antony was thus in a secure political position without having had to fight for it; it had come to him naturally, and he therefore regarded his future task as expanding his power base by gaining the support of Caesar's veterans, and as many as possible of the army still on active service. He did not consider Octavian a serious rival. Antony probably assumed that this inexperienced young man – described not just by Cicero but by Antony himself as a boy – from a not very well-known family would decline the will, as his mother and stepfather had indeed advised him to do. His acceptance must have seemed positively absurd, since it could not be regarded as a purely private matter but had obvious political implications. The story that, when the news of Caesar's murder came, Octavian's friends of his student days, Marcus Vipsanius Agrippa and Quintus Salvidienus Rufus, as well as several officers, tried to persuade him to march to Rome with the army assembled in Macedonia for the Parthian campaign as his great-uncle's avenger, conveys quite the wrong idea of the situation in which Octavian, or Octavius as he still was, found himself: a man without an army or a great reputation. It was certainly invented at a later date. If Octavius did accept the will, political ambitions of his own were not to be ruled out, but his scope for political action had to be regarded as extremely limited. The role of political heir (or heirs) was already taken.

Antony was acting in the context of the political opportunities available to him on the grounds of his origins and his own achievements, and in exploiting those opportunities to the full he could count on understanding if not always approval from the senators and other generals of Caesar, but Octavian was in a much more difficult situation. His claim to be the dictator's adoptive son might be allowed as valid – and so, as we have seen, it was – but at first the taint of youth and inexperience in public and particularly in military life clung to him. It was natural for it to be regarded as a disadvantage by all members of the old ruling class and those of the dictator's cronies who had risen by their own achievements. *Dignitas*, influence in official life, had from time immemorial been the quality only of those who could point to their achievements for the state. The hierarchy in the Senate speaks for itself: former consuls set the tone, while the praetors might contribute to discussion, and all other senators merely supported the views of those superior to them. As Octavian was not crown prince of a hereditary monarchy, but only the adoptive son of a noble, he too must prove his ability by holding office before he could gain a hearing in the Senate. A young man of distinction could count on the support of his own family, other friendly noble families and the many men of equestrian rank and other clients bound to it by friendship or dependency, but until he could point to deeds of his own on behalf of the state he was a political nonentity. After his adoption Octavian did bear a distinguished name, but so far he had not held a single office. Thanks to the dictator's favour, he had merely carried out a few political errands, which were to be regarded as more of an honour than anything else, and even those he had not performed particularly brilliantly. Nor was Octavian able to convince his opponents and rivals in Rome that he had the personal contacts that a rising man needed for his reputation and ability to assert himself. Who were the people with whom he mixed and on whose support he could count? Because of what a noble would regard as his relatively undistinguished background, there was an attempt to present Octavian as an adventurer and gambler. That may seem an exaggeration, yet we can see how such opinions might have been formed. Octavian's close family, the Atians and Octavians, came from the upper classes of small country towns in Latium. Although membership of the nobility could gloss over such origins, they were often cited in evidence by opponents in the cut and thrust of daily political life, for descent was an important part of a man's rank; Cicero, who came from Arpinum in central Italy, could have told the young man something about that. Octavian's reputation depended solely on the name he had inherited from Caesar. But that counted for a good deal, because the Julians were an ancient patrician family which recently, even leaving aside the dictator himself, had made a name for itself through active participation in politics. An uncle of the dictator, for instance, had been consul; his father had been praetor; and as a family of the ancient nobility the Julians had excellent connections within their social class. Many contacts had been broken during Caesar's dictatorship, but a sister of Octavian was married to Gaius Claudius Marcellus, one of the famous family of the Claudii Marcelli, and he had been consul himself in the year 50. Octavian's stepfather, Lucius Marcius Philippus, also belonged to an important noble family: he was the son of a highly regarded consul and had himself been consul in the year 56. Neither Octavian's brother-in-law nor his stepfather, however, was universally respected. Marcellus, in spite of his relationship by marriage to Caesar, had been a radical opponent of his while consul, only to bow submissively to the victorious general; everyone ignored him, from Caesar himself down. Marcius Philippus was regarded as a colourless and not very reliable politician, apt to change sides both in the decisive years before the civil war and under Caesar's rule, and he seemed content to be left alone. The only other name to be mentioned as a supporter of Octavian is that of Gnaeus Domitius Calvinus. He had been consul in 53 and had gone over to Caesar just before the outbreak of the civil war; after the Ides of March, however, when the dictator was at his house early in the morning, we hear no more of him until autumn of the year 42, when he was going to send troops to Octavian and Antony.

Octavian could hardly make a very impressive display with only these three nobles on his side. The others with whom he had links were still unknown quantities. No one on the political stage of Rome knew the families of Marcus Vipsanius Agrippa and Quintus Salvidienus

Rufus, his student friends from Apollonia, and nor was Gaius Maecenas well known. He came from an extremely prosperous family of equestrian rank which could trace its descent back to Etruscan royalty, and we find him in Campania as an adviser to Octavian. Men like Maecenas or Agrippa seemed to appear from nowhere – not just to us, but to those active in politics at the time. Their contemporaries were rather better acquainted with Lucius Cornelius Balbus, who appeared in Octavian's company soon after his departure from Apollonia. Balbus, of Spanish origin, had gained Roman citizenship as a young man and at an early date joined Caesar, under whom he carried out several administrative tasks. However, he seems to have been chiefly useful to Caesar as a kind of *éminence grise* in various affairs, without any official function. His knowledge and his wealth made him an important aide to Octavian, to whom Balbus offered his services early, while he was still in Campania, but because of his origin he could be no more than that. Octavian's advisers and financial administrators also included Gaius Rabirius Postumus, a man of equestrian origin, who had inherited an enormous fortune from his father and did business deals all over the known world, lending money to various states. Earlier he had been accused of malpractice because of such dealings, and was defended by Cicero. Although the dictator had turned to him as an adviser and promoted him to the dignity of office, he was far from being respected by either the citizens or the nobility.

However, the fact that Octavian had gathered more unknowns than men of high reputation around him did not by any means make him a political adventurer. He was the son of the famous Caesar: that was his capital. In view of the instances revealed during the civil war of cruelty, avarice and corruption among Caesar's entourage, particularly men holding office, he may even have seemed to many innocence personified, and thus perhaps a hope for the future. The dictator, it might be thought, had left all the ills of the time for his cronies to deal with. Who, then, were those followers of his whom Octavian must fear as rivals?

Mark Antony, whom we have already encountered, clearly towered above the rest. He was not yet forty at the time, and all things considered had a normal career behind him: after being quaestor and tribune of the people, he rose to be consul in the year 44 without ever having held the office of praetor, and as Caesar's general he enjoyed a high reputation as a soldier and an officer in the last years of the Gallic

War and during the civil war. His father and his grandfather had also been consuls, and the latter was regarded as one of the most famous orators of the time; his mother, a member of the Julian family, was of very high descent. Like the Julians, the Antonians traced their family tree back to divine origin, regarding Anton, a son of Hercules, as their ancestor. Few men of noble rank could compete with Mark Antony. However, his sometimes impetuous and uncouth behaviour and his rather dissolute way of life had led to a tense relationship with Caesar and also made him a number of enemies among his equals in rank as well as many ordinary citizens of Rome. What the population of the city held most against him was his violent reaction to the attempt in 47 BC by Publius Cornelius Dolabella, then tribune of the people – and later his fellow consul in the year 44 – to pass a law on the remission of debts during Caesar's long absence in Egypt. At the time Antony, in his capacity as the dictator's master of the horse, had prevented a vote on it being taken in the Forum by bringing in the troops – whether because he was a political rival of Dolabella or out of revenge for the latter's adultery with his wife we do not know. The clash between these two hot-headed characters had cost the lives of many citizens, and the Romans – or at least those who would have profited by the law – had not forgotten what Antony had done. In addition, he had lost the respect of quite a number of soldiers and officers by what they thought his mystifying attitude towards Caesar's murderers. None the less, all the nobles, whether they supported Caesar or his opponents, regarded Antony as a man to be reckoned with in the scramble for influence.

By comparison, Marcus Aemilius Lepidus had less political weight than Antony. He too was of distinguished origin as the member of a family of the old nobility which had come to prominence in recent decades for its services to the state; his father had been consul in the year 78, although his memory was overshadowed by his attempt to carry out a coup against the Senate after his consulate. Lepidus the Younger had already followed the career appropriate to a nobleman of his family before the civil war, in what might be called normal circumstances. He had been aedile and praetor, and after the outbreak of the civil war he had immediately joined Caesar, under whom he was governor of Citerior Spain. He became consul in 46 and then rose to be the dictator's master of the horse. In this post he had held a central position in the management of affairs in the capital during Caesar's absence in Africa and Spain. Lepidus, who still had a great political career ahead of him, does not enjoy a good reputation among modern scholars. His military abilities were in fact limited, and above all he lacked a gift for leadership, which in view of the growing influence of the army on politics had fateful consequences for him. On the other hand, he was a skilful diplomat, which must have made him a useful aide to the dictator in managing the daily business of Rome.

Another possible rival to Octavian was Dolabella, also descended from a highly regarded family, though one which had not held the consulate during the late republican period. His marriage to the daughter of Cicero, who did not like him (the marriage ended in divorce in 46), had served the purpose of furthering his career and repairing his finances, and his political astuteness became even clearer when, casting aside these family links, he immediately allied himself with Caesar at the beginning of the civil war. As tribune of the people he had already tried to give himself a broader political platform by introducing the law to remit debts mentioned above but had failed when he came up against Mark Antony. When he replaced Caesar as consul and became Antony's colleague, Dolabella, who was still a young man – he was only just twenty-five at the time – found himself in a position offering unlimited opportunities over and beyond the power of his office. In fact, as part of a political team with Antony, who needed him at this point, he was soon offered the province of Syria and thus the conduct of the Parthian campaign. But for the fact that his career had been, so to speak, planned for him from the cradle as the scion of a noble family, he could be seen as the type of parvenu to be found in an embryonic monarchy.

These three Caesarians, then, members of the old nobility, were the really dangerous rivals whom Octavian must take into account. In addition there was the large number of men who had risen to high office through Caesar, 'new men' by the old criteria, who had yet to find a place among the old nobility. Octavian had to solicit their support too: they were not necessarily to be feared as competitors, but their friendship and backing for him as Caesar's son was not to be taken for granted. Finally, there were the conspirators against the dictator. They represented, or claimed to represent, the old tradition. Could there be men among them more highly regarded than the Caesarians? Let us take a brief look at them before we follow events further.

Apart from the two Bruti, the conspirators were not notable for the brilliance of their noble origins, and only a few of them had made their mark in the service of the state. The Bruti, however, both of them in the prime of life, were highly regarded members of society, and could trace their family tree back to the first consul of the republic. The immediate family of Decimus Junius Brutus Albinus was particularly active in the last years of the republic; the father and grandfather of this Brutus had both been consuls, and so had his adoptive father, from whom he took his second cognomen Albinus, and he was related by marriage to several noble families. At the age of barely twenty he followed Caesar as a general to the Gallic War, in which he distinguished himself several times. The family of his fellow member of the gens, Marcus Junius Brutus, could not boast any consuls in recent times, but through his mother Servilia he was the nephew of Cato the Younger, the most prominent adherent of the old republic, and he had excellent connections among the nobility. Although he had initially neglected to follow the traditional 'course of honour' by successively holding the various offices of state, Caesar encouraged his political career by giving him the governorship of Cisalpine Gaul, then the most important of the Roman provinces, and the praetorship for the year 44. Beside the two Bruti, Gaius Cassius Longinus appeared less brilliant, although he was a man of blameless character and a very capable soldier and he too was from a distinguished family and presumably the son of a consul. Also a member of the nobility was Servius Sulpicius Galba, who had served as a general in the first two years of the Gallic War and held the praetorship, although Caesar did not promote him further. Apart from Gaius Trebonius, who had committed himself to Caesar as tribune of the people and later served him as a successful general, the other conspirators had a lower profile. However, we may mention Lucius Tillius Cimber, who became praetor by favour of Caesar in the year 45 and then governor of Bithynia and Pontus, although he was more of a zealous assistant than an independent personality. Octavian could therefore assume that he would meet with no dangerous competition from among the conspirators who had served as generals under Caesar and, in the eyes of the Caesarians and more particularly the soldiers, had shamefully betrayed him. This assumption was to turn out wrong, at least in the case of Decimus Brutus.

However we assess the balance of power between the various groups striving for influence, Octavian's chances, then, were not bad. The general public as well as the soldiers had been accustomed for centuries to leaving power and political responsibility to members of the noble families. To Octavian's advantage was not only his own adoptive noble descent but the lack of prominent leaders among his opponents, both those who were his father's murderers and his rivals in the Caesarian party. The misfortune of the already tottering republic – and Octavian's good fortune – was that there were no men of political experience committed to tradition who, as representatives of the nobility who could have slowed its decline, were able to halt the advance of men of their own class now breaking away from the old code. The few who might perhaps have been in a position to do so, for instance Marcus Tullius Cicero or Servius Sulpicius Rufus, could not as men of consular rank create opposition in the Senate to the ambition of the Caesarians. There were no men left like Marcus Porcius Cato, who took his own life in Utica, or Marcus Claudius Marcellus and Lucius Domitius Ahenobarbus, the consuls of 51 and 54, whose rank in society and uncompromising support for the old order had made them authoritative figures highly regarded by all Romans, including the soldiers. However, they and many other distinguished nobles had perished in the civil war. There was a lack of men with similarly high reputations among both the conspirators and the Caesarians, who for all the noble birth of some among them had been merely aides to the dictator and must now show their independence. A man spared by the civil war, however young or inexperienced he might be, now had the chance to make a name for himself if he had links with the old order to which the citizens, and among them the soldiers, still looked up.

After Octavian's good start, he might seem to be going nowhere once Mark Antony, consul and as things stood leader of the Caesarians, returned to Rome. But with his next step on the political stage he showed not only courage but imagination in confronting his all-powerful adversary. Equally important, he gave evidence of good judgement in assessing his political opportunities. Universally recognized as the dictator's private heir, he now also appeared in Rome, the metropolis of the empire, as his adoptive father's *political* heir; he thus presented himself as a man with political ambitions – not, of course, for the same position of power as the dictator had held, but at least for a part of that power.

The path that Octavian took in his efforts to acquire influence showed all his rivals that he knew where to look for the base of future political power and that he was someone to be reckoned with. He publicly declared that he would pay the legacy left to the citizens of Rome by Caesar in his will and he immediately set about distributing the money. As Antony, understandably enough, contributed nothing from the dictator's property that he had seized, Octavian had the part of his own property over which he had control put up for auction, requested and received their part of Caesar's inheritance from his co-heirs Pedius and Pinarius and, since the proceeds from the sale of his goods still did not make the sum nearly enough, also borrowed large sums from friends and relations. As soon as the money came in he had it passed on to the citizens of Rome district by local district on the *tribus* system. A wave of sympathy came his way, and the distribution process gave him repeated opportunities to present himself as a dutiful son of his father, lament Caesar's death and marginalize the conspirators and their political sympathizers. He deliberately did not conceal the fact that he considered it his duty to avenge Caesar, murdered by his own friends, and the more often he repeated that, the more closely was the idea of revenge linked with his person, while the other Caesarians, Mark Antony included, who had sat at the negotiating table with the murderers, were forced ever further into the background.

Very soon it was clear to everyone that Octavian was a match for Antony on the political scene. He staged his appearances with skill and he could exploit his opponents' political mistakes. He chalked up a particularly notable success in his search for money to pay the dictator's legacy to the Roman people. Antony, in a not very clever political move, refused to hand over many of the dictator's goods that should have been sold to meet the terms of the legacy, basing his stance on the fact that legal possession of those of them that the dictator had confiscated in 49 as the property of enemies of the state was still at dispute between Caesar on the one hand and the state or their original owners on the other. This was certainly a valid legal standpoint, but not that of a Caesarian, and, most crucially of all, the subsequent legal cases regarding property rights gave Octavian a chance to present himself publicly, in many ways and in front of an ever-growing audience, as the dictator's heir and benefactor of the citizens of Rome. Antony was thus on the defensive, at least in the political arena, while Octavian had still not by any means played all his trump cards. The weeks and months after Antony's return from Campania were filled by each of the rivals' efforts to present himself to the Roman public as the political kingpin of the Caesarians. In the middle of May, not long after Antony's arrival, Octavian tried to have Caesar's gilded chair, granted to him for all public appearances during his lifetime, set up for the games then taking place, and thus to make a ritual to his memory. The aedile organizing the games prevented it, and the consul Antony, when Octavian turned to him for support as a man ostensibly of his own way of thinking, rejected the idea.

Antony was in control for the time being. He even began a new political offensive to reinforce his legal position and consolidate and extend his following. Above all, in early June he succeeded in exchanging his Macedonian province for Upper Italy and Transalpine Gaul, where Aemilius Lepidus was stationed. In fact this was more than an exchange, since the two provinces that he received in return for his were far more important where their governor's political and military position was concerned, and in addition they were granted to him for five years. This was no longer governorship but an extraordinary command, to be compared with Caesar's governorship of Gallia Cisalpina, Gallia Narbonensis and Illyricum, granted to him in the year 59 for a period of five years which was then extended to ten and which had led to the conquest of the free part of Gaul. The true nature of Antony's new function could also be seen in the fact that he was able to take to his new provinces four of the legions assembled for the Parthian campaign in his previous province of Macedonia. Antony had achieved his political aim: he had a larger command than any of the other generals, and on the very ground where the dictator too had held command. Octavian supported him in this political move, but certainly not gladly. The deciding factor for him may have been that Antony would soon be out of Rome. The other consul, Dolabella, also agreed, since the legal decision meant that Antony would be no rival to him in the Parthian campaign, for which the dictator had prepared both the Macedonian army and other forces, so that when Dolabella went to his Syrian province at the end of his consulship he could consider that he held the most authoritative military command in the east.

In Italy the Caesarians had now consolidated their position, and the sterner tone they adopted after the beginning of June made that clear to everyone who hoped for the restoration of the old order. They seldom went to the Senate to take part in political decision-making. The consuls in particular might have feared the influence of senators of a republican way of thinking less than a revival of the Senate itself as the organ of government. It therefore seemed to them more correct and convenient to implement their plans and wishes through the assembly of the people, which was tractable and, should there be unexpected opposition from magistrates with a will of their own, could be forcibly brought to see reason. Several new laws from the inexhaustible source of Caesar's archives were again laid before the people for acceptance, including another law on the settlement of veterans, which was intended to gain Antony their support, and a law to change the criminal code. The Senate was not usually asked for approval, and any attempt by magistrates or priests loyal to it to prevent application to the people for ratification by legal means was brutally halted, in disregard of all the rules of public and religious law. Here all the Caesarians, Octavian included, formed a closed front which the Senate was powerless to oppose. To its further humiliation, it even had to approve a petition adding a day in honour of Caesar to all the usual festivals of thanksgiving to the gods.

Caesar's murderers and their adherents were visibly losing ground, but they could not yet be entirely discounted. Above all, they profited by the rivalries that kept flaring up between their opponents. Several weeks later, at the end of July, Octavian began a new round in the struggle for political influence over the organization of the games already dedicated during the dictator's lifetime to Venus, the founding mother of the Julian gens. With the support of many friends, he had been occupied with their preparation since May. When the priesthood responsible refused by a majority to organize the games, Octavian took over the task himself and also financed them, a move that won him more friends (including Gaius Matius). With the backing of these friends he once again tried to have the dictator's gilded chair set up to preside over the games and to use the laurel wreath that the Senate had granted as a symbol of his presence. Antony dared not forbid the games, but he yet again prevented the setting up of the gilded chair, threatening sanctions. In the tussle of these two disparate opponents as they struggled for influence and power, Octavian consolidated his position as Caesar's political heir, while Antony was forced into a role that separated him from the Caesarians, which he cannot have liked. Octavian was seen as the son of Caesar by the people, including the soldiers, and his mourning for the murdered man and desire for revenge made him more than just one Caesarian among others; people were already beginning to see him as mystically close to the dictator, whom they honoured as a godlike figure. As early as May, when he first entered Rome, many claimed to have seen a corona around the sun, as mentioned above, the sign of a ruler. A comet appeared in the sky for several days during the games for Venus and was said to be the soul of Caesar which had risen to the gods. Octavian fostered these popular beliefs and a little later had a statue of Caesar with the heavenly body described as the 'Julian star' placed in the newly built Forum of Caesar. Even in the context of his later skill in exploiting religious or superstitious fantasies for his political ends, we must not assume that Octavian invented this omen himself and guided its interpretation. At this time he did not yet have the reputation and the means to influence or convince people in that way. But there can be no doubt that he recognized the political value of the dictator's religious elevation for his own purposes and consistently used it to support his position.

The distribution of the legacies to the people of the city of Rome took some time because of the legal cases about the rightful ownership of goods declared to be Caesar's, and indeed it dragged on for months. At some point – we do not know the exact details – Antony seems to have been driven to lose his self-control. One day, when he was presiding over the law-courts, he fell into such a rage that he had Octavian taken away by his officials, the lictors. Octavian countered by playing the part of a man in danger, shut himself up in his house and, as he intended, aroused great indignation not only among the citizens of Rome, who were to profit by the sale of the goods, but also among many supporters of Caesar, who, correctly, saw the delay as a threat to the agreement of 17 March by which no decision of the late dictator was to be rescinded. When the situation caused by the quarrel over the exhibition of Caesar's chair at the games became critical at the end of July, not a few Caesarians, some of them officers and soldiers, began to fear for the future of their cause, meaning their share in what the dictator had left. Finally, still in July, all this culminated in a public reconciliation between Antony and Octavian, leading to a notable success on the part of the latter, because it was forced upon the disputants by the soldiers of Antony's bodyguard, Caesar's old veterans. Antony would not have taken much notice of the ordinary civilians of Rome. Octavian, who had shut himself up in his house because of the consul's apparent or real hostility, made sure the soldiers asked his permission for the meeting and escorted him to the Capitol, where he was to see Antony. The solemn reconciliation ceremony took place in the most sacred place in all Rome, the temple of Jupiter Optimus Maximus. It was of the utmost political significance for Octavian, since it set him alongside Antony in the military arena, making him Antony's partner in the soldiers' eyes. Nothing could have been less opportune for Antony. For the first time Octavian was recognized publicly – and by the Caesarian army – as a man to be reckoned with.

The reconciliation of the Caesarians brought about a fundamental change in the political and military situation in Italy; the fronts now seemed to be clearly drawn. Antony, as consul, would set off for his large provincial area in the north with the legions that had been intended for the Parthian campaign, and it looked as if he would stay there for some time, because the incumbent governor, Decimus Brutus, was not going to leave the field clear for him of his own free will. In this way Octavian, not exactly an ally of Antony's but now not his opponent either, had more of a free hand in Rome and Italy, which, in line with his political platform, could be useful in his opposition to those of the dictator's murderers who were still in Italy. For a moment it looked as if the Caesarians, who now all, including Octavian, formed a common front, were going to go on the offensive against the assassins and their supporters, whose situation had rapidly deteriorated. However, they were not yet out of contention.

There was very soon to be a major change in the balance of power and it took many by surprise, Antony included. It came about not least through the conduct of the republican party, particularly its two leaders, Marcus Brutus and Gaius Cassius, who as praetors for the year 44 had official authority and were thus natural points around which resistance to the Caesarians could gather. So let us now look once again at the 'republicans', whom we left on one side after the agreement of 17 March.

Even after the March compromise, the conspirators did not feel entirely secure in Rome. After the tumultuous events of Caesar's funeral they had even left the city for a short time, but they soon came back. The effect of what they had done still resonated among the population of Rome. Initially Brutus and Cassius, who with Decimus Brutus were the recognized leaders of the republicans, could continue their official business as praetors. Marcus Brutus was still pursuing a consistent policy of reconciliation with the Caesarians. As he saw it, the old order had been legally restored by the murder, and he insisted that a peaceful settlement with Antony, as the consul, was necessary for the sake of peace at home. The quarrel, in his view, must be fought by legal means. From the first, this viewpoint excluded Octavian's potential as a figure of political importance, for he had neither the power of office nor the qualities of a noble whose achievements and experience must be taken into account. Only by looking at these months in retrospect can we see this view as pure idealism or an empty attempt at legitimization. The murder is impossible to understand without the belief that the republic still lived, and in addition it was entirely unthinkable to any Roman that the state and the social tradition that had made Rome a world power for 400 years could simply come to an end.

It was not just in Rome that Brutus and Cassius had sympathizers at this time. They also had many supporters in the cities of Italy and could fall back on them at any time, for instance as followers when they appeared in Rome. At least those conspirators who had served under Caesar as generals could, as Decimus Brutus showed, rely on the support of veterans. Not all were as optimistic as Marcus Brutus. Cassius was more sceptical, and so was Cicero, who now increasingly emerged from the political reserve that he had maintained during the dictator's lifetime and in the first few months after Caesar's murder. In June he complained to Atticus that the liberators, whom he calls 'our men', had only as much hope of staying alive as Antony would grant them. In fact the situation was difficult, and scepticism was an appropriate response. For while the conspirators might enjoy great sympathy in Rome and Italy, the question remained of how it could be made politically relevant. It was not first and foremost the resistance of Antony and Octavian that caused them concern but the passivity of the Senate. Among the population of the capital, however, they could on occasion expect broad agreement, and in July, when Brutus arranged official games in his capacity as praetor, he had even hoped for a reversal in the general mood. That was an illusion, due to the fact that he himself could not be present – but he was also wrong in thinking that public opinion in Rome at this time was any substitute for official or legal decision-making.

Only the Senate, the ancient centre of government, and not the people of the city of Rome could give the conspirators support. Antony did not rule the Senate, but in his official capacity he could convene it, present petitions and exert pressure if necessary. In view of the Senate's loss of individuality after Caesar made it an amorphous gathering of almost 900 men, not to mention its lack of leaders – the authoritative group of former consuls had shrunk to only a few – it was unlikely to make any independent decision that would be supported by the upper classes. The Senate needed leadership, and anyone who had official power and the requisite lack of scruples in using it could do as he liked. Antony was at the head of the apparatus; the second consul, Dolabella, went along with him in the certainty that he had already taken care of his own interests, and the other holders of office, particularly the praetors, were legally subordinate to him. Those who believed in the republic and its order had to follow the consul's lead in Rome. If something went wrong, if any holders of office or tribunes of the people ventured to oppose the consul, then Antony, like Caesar before him, did not scruple to proceed against them without regard for tradition or the law. When something had to be carried in the Forum, he was determined to break any resistance, even legal opposition, brutally and if necessary by military force. Brutus was not, which in view of the force exerted against him may well seem very idealistic. Cicero, for his part, thought and acted differently, as we shall soon see.

It was obvious that Antony did not mean the reconciliation seriously when he sought to expel the two praetors Brutus and Cassius from Rome and Italy. For that was the real import of his general assent to their wish to be allowed absence from Rome as praetors for longer than ten days – the legal term – and it was also behind his efforts to keep the praetors away from the Senate meeting of 1 June, when important decisions were to be made on the allocation of provinces and other matters. His strategy became even clearer when, a few days later, he managed to get the Senate to give Brutus and Cassius the task of bringing grain in from the provinces of Asia and Sicily. What was that if not an order to leave Italy? As the activity of the legal officers, who naturally included the praetors, was confined to Rome and Italy during their term of office, and they could leave for their provinces with promagistral status only after that term was up, that is to say after 1 January of the next year, this 'demand' made to the two praetors meant in practice the withdrawal of the praetorship from them: it was both a humiliation and a declaration of war.

On 8 June there was a meeting in Antium between those whom

Antony had thus put under pressure, to discuss the crisis. Besides the two praetors, their wives and Brutus' mother Servilia were present; it was as if these dignified matrons were compensating for the gaps in the republican ranks. Cicero was also present. The debate was heated. Once again there was talk of missed opportunity – meaning first and foremost sparing Antony's life on the Ides of March, which Cassius in particular deplored. For the rest, they discussed their future course of action. Servilia was the calming influence and energetic centre of the meeting, showing what influence women of the time could have behind the scenes of political power. There were no concrete results, but it was here that Brutus and Cassius finally decided to leave Italy. In view of their lack of military protection, something that had not previously troubled the conspirators, and Antony's growing determination, there was no other real option open to them.

Brutus and Cassius, who had de facto been expelled from the centre of power where they ought to have stood by virtue of their office, were now in touch with the consul only in writing, through edicts. Their last official communication from Italy dates from 4 August. In it they both repudiate the threatening tone adopted by Antony in his last letters to them and emphasize how little such threats impress them. But even at this point they did not want to give up entirely the policy they had so far followed, and called Antony a 'great and highly regarded man'. However, the heart of this missive to the consul, written prior to the two praetors leaving Italy, is their acknowledgement of their action on the Ides of March and a threat to terminate their political friendship with him should freedom be at stake – a freedom which, they write, Antony himself had regained only through them. 'We wish to see you great and respected in a free state, and we are no enemies to you, but we value our freedom more than [political] friendship with you.' In the second half of August, Brutus and Cassius left Italy. Antony sent another humiliation after them: he caused the Senate to allocate them the posts of governors of Crete and Cyrene, and they were to take up their duties there when their praetorship ran out on 1 January 43. Less important provinces in military, political and economic terms could hardly be found in the entire empire.

Antony might see the retreat of the heads of the conspiracy from Rome as the culmination of his political hopes. He now seemed to enjoy an uncontested position of power, for he had a military command assured by law, guaranteeing him influence in the west of the empire and enabling him to put pressure on the capital. In addition, he was consul until the end of the year, and after the retirement of his colleague Dolabella, which was to be expected soon, he would thus be legally the leading man in Rome and Italy. Caesar's boots were certainly too large for him to fill, but it was doubtful anyway whether there could be any real successor to that unique man. No one dared to follow in Caesar's footsteps. The extent of his power had shaped the decade before the civil war, in which the great men of the nobility had struggled with one another for influence. As it now seemed, Antony had achieved all that was possible in this respect. He had only to drive Decimus Brutus out of Upper Italy, but Antony was sure he could do that. Octavian was no more than a disruptive political factor, a man without office and without an army.

# 3

# Cicero and Octavian against Antony

Italy belonged to the Caesarians, and Antony was their leader. He was the rightful consul and Caesar's most highly regarded general; who could stand in his way? Even Cicero gave up the cause of tradition as lost and set off for Greece. He was planning to seek refuge from what he foresaw would be Antony's tyranny in the east, using the influence of his former son-in-law Dolabella, the other consul, who held an official position as legate. The terrible vision of a bloodbath among the leading men of Rome such as had been seen a generation earlier under the dictator Sulla gave him no peace. His aim was to get out of Antony's trap, not to escape entirely – for where could he go? – but in the hope of a better death. His decision to leave had been made after the inconclusive conference with the conspirators at Antium. On 1 July 44 he left his villa in Tusculum. At first he planned to accompany Brutus to the east, but then he went alone to a harbour in the south of the Italian peninsula and put to sea. He did not get far. Adverse winds near Syracuse drove his ship back to the coast of Italy, where he received rather better news of the political situation; after Octavian's appearance on the scene, many supporters of the conspirators were hoping for a split in the Caesarian camp. On hearing this, Cicero decided to stay in Italy after all for the time being. In the south, he happened to meet Marcus Brutus, who reproached him bitterly for what he saw as his flight and blamed him for abandoning the res publica. Although the good news received by Cicero was not in the end confirmed, he gave up his plans to travel, allowed Brutus to revive his desire for action, and in late August returned to Rome and the lion's den. He had not been there since early April, and despite his private sympathies he had kept well out of all that was going on in the capital. His nervousness and indecision, prompting him to wait on the sidelines, had forced him to the periphery of events. No one saw him as the man who, only a few days later, made up his mind to act as the figurehead of the old republic, the *princeps civitatis*.

On 31 August Cicero arrived back in Rome. Antony had called a meeting of the Senate at the temple of Concordia on the slopes of the Capitol for the next day. Cicero failed to turn up, which Antony saw as an affront: he now very obviously had his sights set on Cicero as leader of the anti-Caesarian faction, while Cicero had his own eye on Antony as the tyrant's heir. It was not until the following day that Cicero came to the Senate, where the other consul, Dolabella, was presiding, and made his first speech against Antony (the First Philippic). In form it was an attack on the two consuls which Cicero framed as a friendly dispute between noblemen. He presented his criticism as a warning to change tack, but he also clearly condemned what Antony had done in Rome since 17 March, especially the laws brought in since June, for which it was claimed plans had been found in Caesar's archives. The speech was the opening of his anti-Antonian campaign, and he was to continue it until the end. Cicero's point was his sincere conviction that the republic must be saved, and he regarded himself as its champion. He had not been at the centre of political life since he went to Cilicia as its governor in the year 51, but now he symbolized resistance to tyranny in succession, as it were, to Cato. How did Cicero, who for years had been politically passive, cautious and indeed a mere spectator of events, now come to be leader of the 'republicans'? Who appointed him to that position? Did he feel himself obliged to take such a role, or was it his own decision? And why, after always recommending peace, did he now head the opposition to Antony?

Whatever the relationship between Cicero and the Antonians had been before 63, it was in that year, when Cicero was consul, that the foundations of lasting political discord between them were laid. At that time Cicero had Publius Cornelius Lentulus Sura executed as a fellow conspirator of Catiline. He was stepfather of the three Antonian brothers and had been consul in the year 71 and officiated as praetor in 63. After the decision to execute him had been made in the Senate, Cicero himself had even had Sura, certainly the most distinguished member of the circle of conspirators, removed from his provisional house arrest in the home of a highly regarded nobleman and taken to the state prison, the Carcer Tullianus, where he was strangled. Mark Antony, as his stepson, might have been expected to feel more hostility to Cicero than vice versa. But while Cicero, quite apart from the events of December 63, might always have held back from forming any close connection with Antony because he did not care for his rather boisterous and boastful manner, his feelings of real enmity towards him post-dated the Ides of March and had been sparked off by Antony's increasingly obvious efforts to be recognized as first among Caesar's generals. Cicero saw him as Caesar's heir and thus someone to be put out of action. However, Antony did not have Caesar's stature, and would never simply have been conceded the position that Caesar himself had occupied at the end of his life. Why, then, did Cicero grant him that position by implication now? Did Antony even have any ambitions such as Cicero assumed?

Antony had created a large extraordinary command for himself, extending over several provinces and including the leadership of an army of considerable size. That had been nothing unusual before the civil war broke out. Caesar, Pompey and Crassus had held such commands, and usually the reason on which they were based was not – or was only superficially – a threat to Rome from some outside enemy. As every Roman of the time well knew, they were rather to do with the attempts by powerful individual nobles to gain authority and influence in the state. Cicero had several times had a hand in granting public support to men for such extraordinary military powers. What was so different now? It might indeed be assumed that once Antony held a great command he would not readily give it up and instead would try to extend it. But although the ghost of Caesar might be seen looming behind him, why did Cicero want to begin a war on that account? Before the civil war, he had been steadfast in urging peace, although he found little understanding among most of his equals, men who went to war with Pompey against Caesar, and it was because of his peace policy that he had not been considered a central figure among the supporters of republican aims during Caesar's rule. What was so different about Antony and the circumstances of the time that Cicero now positively urged war? Was another civil war really necessary? Even his political friends did not entirely understand his hostility to Antony, least of all Brutus, who considered Octavian far more dangerous.

It was obvious in advance that conflict with Antony would lead to another civil war, with hostilities as harsh and cruel as the war waged by Caesar and Pompey. In view of such fears, would it not have been right to consider the consequences of war for the state and for society? Cicero had seen them very clearly during the civil war with Caesar, for when he, with Brutus, Cassius and many others, had been cleared of blame by Caesar after the disaster of Pharsalos in the year 48, he justified his political U-turn to the like-minded Cassius by saying that if a state fell he saw nothing left to hope for, whereas if something of that state remained – and under Caesar it did – then confidence might be felt. Cicero knew very well that to decide on a military solution meant chancing everything and said so to Brutus in the year 43: 'Of all the civil wars waged in our state in my time, there was none in which, regardless of which side won or lost, some form of state (*aliqua forma . . . rei publicae*) did not remain. I cannot say what kind of state we shall have if we are the winners, but if we are the losers then there will be no state at all.' He wrote this in July 43, only a few weeks before the end of all his hopes. He knew what was at stake.

Once the assassins of Caesar had left Italy, Cicero was the most highly regarded man in the Senate. Among the few consulars who were of the old nobility, rather than owing their rank to Caesar, was Lucius Julius Caesar, consul in the year 64, a member of a collateral branch of the family quite remote from the dictator. He was widely respected, and was an undaunted supporter of the old order; even his close relationship with Antony, whose maternal uncle he was, had not deterred him. However, he was in poor health and seldom put in an appearance at the Senate. Servius Sulpicius Rufus, the most famous lawyer of his time, was the same age as Lucius Julius Caesar and Cicero. His own desire for peace was probably more strongly rooted in his anxious nature than in political calculation, so his well-known liking for compromise could easily be interpreted as opportunism. That ruled him out too for the role of leader.

Two other former consuls were more likely prospects. They were Lucius Calpurnius Piso Caesoninus, consul in the year 58 and the dictator's father-in-law, and Publius Servilius Isauricus. The former was an enemy of Cicero, who did not forget that the orator had not supported his own attempt to avoid exile, but he was an honest man who inclined to a policy of rapprochement. Isauricus, a member of an ancient patrician family, had also begun his career before the civil war, but it was Caesar who had appointed him consul. Through his wife Junia, he was related by marriage to Brutus and Cassius. However, for all their readiness to compromise and promote reconciliation, both Piso and Isauricus were handicapped by their connections with the dictator, and they did not hide their political leanings; they might criticize the Caesarian cause, but they were still associated with it. It was solely for lack of alternatives, then, that Cicero became leader of the 'republicans'. Indeed, if the consulars are regarded as the embodiment of the republic – and who else could have represented it? – we might say that Cicero *was* the republic. Destiny laid the burden of this role on him, and he did not resist. But just why, having shrunk from such situations earlier, he now assumed this very dangerous political responsibility in an Italy dominated by the Caesarians must ultimately remain a mystery. Did he want, after all the humiliations of the past fifteen years, to be praised and shown honour at last by all the supporters of the old order, including those who, in the pride of their noble rank, had regarded him as a social climber? Those of his own rank knew about this weakness of his. Had his ambition brought him to see Antony as a second Caesar? A decision to wait and see how events developed might have shown him who the new Caesar really was.

So Cicero became head of the republic. But it was a republic of Caesarians; the armed conflict that threatened to break out would be a war for the republic in which no republicans took part. Apart from Lucius Julius Caesar, there was no one of consular standing in the Senate who could definitely be called a republican. By comparison with the year 50, when conflict with the dictator loomed large, the general political situation had changed entirely. At that time the nobles had still been a strong group, and in Gnaeus Pompey they had a well-respected leader to oppose Caesar. Pompey was a military potentate himself, but not as radical as his rival. Now there was no such group. In so far as there were still any members of the old leadership elite, then with only a few exceptions they had either become army leaders themselves or had joined such leaders. Italy had become a Caesarian army camp. Caesarians held almost all the western provinces, and the two consuls for the coming year were also Caesarians. The *res publica* had dissolved into *partes*, factions. Indeed, in an official letter to the Senate of March 43 Antony himself no longer speaks of the *res publica* but of the *partes*: on one side the Caesarians, whose leader he felt himself to be, on the other the Pompeians, who had fought against Caesar in the civil war and whom the 'republicans' of the time had joined. When Cicero speaks of the *res publica* he means the 'party of Pompey'; he does not recognize a *res publica* comprising all the Romans and indeed no longer takes the existence of such a republic for granted. In fact the *partes*, which had no discernible joint basis, were more different from each other at the time than Antony was prepared to admit in his endeavour to become leader of the Caesarians. The 'party' of Caesar had existed only during the dictator's lifetime. Now there were several Caesarian groupings. As well as Antony's there were the factions of Octavian, Lepidus, Plancus and a number of other men with ambitions for political power. Cicero rejects Antony's phrasing in his letter to the Senate sharply, indeed with horror. Parties, he tells Antony, are names for the political associations of Romans, particularly the leading men of Rome, who engage in peaceful dispute in the Forum and the Senate house on the occasion of elections held by the Senate or the people, they are not armies attacking the Senate. Antony, who makes war on the *res publica*, he adds, is not the leader of a party but a man guilty of high treason. This quarrel about the concepts behind the deep rift splitting the state and its citizens casts light on the political situation as a whole and in particular shows that there was now hardly any hope for a political consensus in Italy.

Anyone who imagined that republican ideals were to be found among those who had actively opposed, and still did oppose, their oppressors – the dictator Caesar and his heirs – must pin his hopes on the two Bruti, in particular Decimus Brutus, who was closest to Italy and commanded an army, and in addition on Cassius, Trebonius and all who had accompanied them to the east. What did Cicero aim to achieve in Italy? When he launched his attack on Antony, he had obviously mistaken the political situation entirely. From whom could support be expected? Decimus Brutus, in Upper Italy, was not helpless, but he was surrounded by former generals of Caesar whose hostility was at best merely concealed. In the Senate, Cicero could hope for backing from the more politically independent Piso, the dictator's father-in-law, who was not well disposed to Antony, and from Isauricus, who had supported him at the beginning of his anti-Antonian campaign, but ultimately both belonged to the Caesarian party. The local notables of the Italian cities outside Rome, and a large part of the urban population, might well show sympathy for Cicero. But what use was sympathy when war loomed? A majority in the Senate was needed, and above all soldiers, an army.

There was a brief respite before hostilities broke out, but not because fear of what was to come had made many men anxious for reconciliation. On the contrary: the general mood was in favour of war. A good two weeks after Cicero's attack on him in the Senate, Antony made a speech imbued with personal spite in which he sought to represent Cicero as a failed politician and a troublemaker, and Cicero hit back with an extensive pamphlet, the Second Philippic, not published until after his death. This exchange burned all the bridges between them; they had now officially declared themselves enemies. But the war that threatened, at least at this point, was certainly not the one that Cicero had wanted, for it was not to be between the republic and the new tyrants. Instead, Caesar's heirs were confronting each other: it would be a war between generals for the leadership of the enormous military force that Caesar had left behind. They had already staked their claims in the provinces. In the coming year, 43 BC, Antony would be governor of the part of Gaul conquered by Caesar and of Upper Italy, Lepidus would be governor of Citerior Spain and Gallia Narbonensis, Plancus governor of Gaul until Antony arrived, and Asinius Pollio governor of Ulterior Spain. Pollio had not yet made up his mind what course to follow, but he too could hardly be described as a 'republican'.

And all eyes turned at first not to Cicero and his so far invisible 'republican front', but to the anticipated struggle for control in Italy, which so far had no clear leader in the west. The combatants here were Antony, Decimus Brutus and Octavian, all three with very different political aims and different points of departure. Of the three, Octavian was the weakest in the power struggle and at the same time the most enigmatic. Did he want to govern a province or gain a major military command? It is likely that at the time no one thought he had any greater ambition. But the name he bore was good reason to suppose that he would not be so easily satisfied.

The departure of Brutus and Cassius from Italy had not defused the political situation, but that was not because of increased activity among their supporters. While Cicero's attack on Antony had been well received in many quarters, now that there seemed to be no more danger to the dictator's supporters in Rome and Italy matters depended on the relationship of the Caesarians to each other. And with less pressure at this point from supporters of the old order, rivalries showed ever more clearly. Octavian in particular, having profited from the sense of threat felt by the Caesarians, was bound to feel isolated once he was no longer protected by the solidarity between them, however weak and fragile that solidarity had been. He had neither high office nor supporters among the soldiers. His reconciliation with Antony was only a few weeks in the past, but in view of the change in the political situation as a whole it had lost any binding force. Octavian had to look around for a base that was worth more than approving murmurs from the people in the market place of Rome. He now saw very clearly that he needed what his rivals already had: high office or soldiers, preferably both.

In September he thought he had an unexpected chance. An election was to be held to find a successor to Gaius Helvius Cinna, tribune of the people, who had died at the time of the Ides of March, torn to pieces by a raging mob after Caesar's funeral, when he was mistaken for the praetor and conspirator Lucius Cornelius Cinna. Octavian offered himself as a candidate. As tribune of the people he would have had a good position, at least in Rome, and in particular an opportunity to propose laws in the assembly of the people and present petitions in the Senate. However, his application to succeed Cinna was too audacious, or perhaps merely showed his lack of political experience. Octavian had become a patrician through his adoption by Caesar and was thus not qualified to stand for election to a post reserved for plebeians. Antony rejected his candidature on those grounds and threatened reprisals for any contravention of his decision. Nothing came of Octavian's attempt.

There remained the soldiers. There were plenty of them in Italy, and Octavian was not alone in hoping to gain their support. Of course he had not the faintest legal basis for recruiting soldiers, but that did not deter him. The race for power that led to the war in Italy began in October, and in its first phase it consisted of competition between Antony and Octavian for the favour of the veterans and Caesar's soldiers. They did not in fact begin the race at the same time; Octavian, a man without an army who was outside the group of competing generals, began it when he suddenly set about forming an armed troop of his own. So far it had been unquestioningly assumed that the soldiers and veterans in Italy (and Macedonia) were at the disposal of Caesar's experienced generals. When Octavian began recruiting on his own behalf this assumption was, so to speak, suspended. The question of whom the soldiers 'belonged to' suddenly arose.

Octavian began his recruiting campaign with secret intrigues among the Macedonian legions who had been promised to Antony and were to be transferred by him to his new northern province. Early in October, Antony accused Octavian of instigating an attempt to assassinate him; this was probably in reaction to his unforeseen activities among the soldiers and veterans. Although many took the accusation at face value it was rather foolish and indeed unworthy of Antony. Would a man with no soldiers of his own plan to murder such a well-guarded consul? A suspicion the other way around might have sounded more likely. The accusation was probably no more than a shot across Octavian's bows to keep him in check during the consul's absence from Rome. On 9 October, Antony set out to take command of his legions in Brundisium. Not much later, Octavian went to Campania and recruited a troop of his own from the veterans who had settled there (they had belonged to Caesar's Seventh and Eighth Legions). He paid them a bounty of a year's double wages, i.e. 2,000 sesterces, an amount for which a soldier might have followed any adventurer at the time, and by this means quickly assembled 3,000 men. But Octavian did not succeed with all the colonists, for Antony's own standing among the veterans was high, both as one of Caesar's generals, bound to them by many campaigns together, and as the patron of those whom he had helped to acquire their small properties by the settlement laws he had introduced. In view of the enormous bounty offered, many of the common soldiers might have overlooked the dubious nature of Octavian's recruiting campaign (which also seemed to be directed against Antony as the rightful consul), allowing the name he bore to overcome any reservations they might feel. However, many of the centurions who formed the backbone of the army, the men who trained and led the soldiers, held back, even issuing warnings, and so did many of the leading civilians in the Campanian towns and cities. For the troop recruited by Octavian was a private army: there was no legal basis for its formation. Such conduct amounted to high treason – or would have done in normal times. Cicero, as guardian of the constitution, very soon showed how far from normal these times were.

Cicero himself had left Rome in October, retiring to one of his estates on the Campanian coast, and Octavian now sought to win his support. From early November onwards, he positively bombarded him with letters. He asked Cicero's advice, tried to arrange a meeting, attempted to persuade him to go to Rome and call the Senate together. He also clearly said what he wanted the senators to decide: he wanted war against Antony under Cicero's leadership. Cicero felt flattered but remained cautious. He saw the obstacles in Rome and feared for his personal safety in an Italy in warlike mood. Above all, however, he was suspicious. 'Remember his name, remember his age!' he wrote to his friend Atticus. It troubled him that he was not sure of 'the boy's' attitude, and he finally conceded that if Octavian won a victory, the dictator's political plans would be carried out even more ruthlessly, but he immediately added that after a victory by Antony he, Antony, would become intolerable. He still saw Antony as the more dangerous opponent. Cicero found himself and the political trend he represented faced with a choice between two evils. He kept a cool head and rid himself of Octavian's attentions by advising him to go to Rome alone. But whatever Cicero's own attitude when he saw Octavian recruiting men, it is clear that not he but Octavian was really stirring up hostility to Antony.

Around 10 November, Octavian did indeed go to Rome with the troop he had recruited, less in obedience to Cicero, who had in fact been reluctant to advise him to march to Rome, than by his own decision. It was a bad mistake, although he led his soldiers into the city not in military array but as guards and hired supporters – with daggers hidden under their clothing, of course. Was he after all just a thoughtless 'boy' who knew no moderation? Did he hope to seize power in Rome in Antony's absence? If so, how? What were his political calculations in this venture? He knew that Antony was marching to Rome with the Fifth Legion, known as the Crested Larks. If he wanted to make sure of Rome before Antony arrived, he could count on support from many of the plebeians in the capital to whom he had promised Caesar's legacy. But what good would that do him? He needed to win the goodwill of the Senate, and as a matter of urgency he must ask it to give him a military office to counterbalance the consul's. Octavian probably had his eye on the Senate when he asked Cicero, who had been its leader as a consular, to support his march to Rome. If that was his calculation, then his small troop would have been intended to deter any hostilities on Antony's part, merely as flanking support for the enterprise.

Once in Rome, however, Octavian did not turn first to the Senate but to an assembly of the people of the city of Rome. A tribune of the people who was hostile to Antony summoned them to the Forum near the temple of the Dioscuri, Castor and Pollux. Here Octavian presented himself as a man who would come to the Senate's aid against Antony – even though he himself was not a senator and thus could not even set foot in the Senate, and that body had not called him to its aid! For the Senate had not declared Antony an enemy of the state, nor had Cicero at this point presented himself publicly as leader of the anti-Antonian faction. Over and beyond announcing his support for the Senate against Antony, Octavian openly told the people that he wished to gain his father's honours (*honores*), even reinforcing his words by pointing to a statue of Caesar, either one of the two standing on the former speaker's rostrum or the statue erected on the site of Caesar's funeral pyre: all three were visible from the steps of the temple of the Dioscuri. Another mistake. Whom did he expect to impress with this undisguised declaration of his aims, making a public show of his boundless ambition? Did he really think that the plebs, so often and not entirely unjustly reviled by Cicero, could do anything to further it? And would not the Senate, to which he was offering his services in his speech as a political or even military ally, and to which he had hoped to turn with Cicero at his side, be greatly alarmed by such vainglorious talk, wholly inappropriate in so young a man without either office or great deeds to his name? In addition, every Roman in Italy knew that the ambitious remark about his wish to succeed to his father's honours – and the term honour (*honos*) could be understood as including the offices held by the dictator – was meant not just for the dictator's assassins but above all for the rightful consul. Could Octavian really assume that Antony, who at the time had the strongest military force in all Italy at his disposal, would stand by and watch such a challenge without retaliating? For a challenge was what Octavian's march to Rome amounted to.

Even his own soldiers, if the veterans he had bought can be called that, were horrified by Octavian's behaviour. They might feel that they were clients of the dictator and had followed his son, but they did not want to be sent into war against Caesarians, particularly not against the consul. And Antony was now advancing, making a forced march with an elite legion to oppose Octavian, whom he correctly saw as guilty of high treason. He was sending his other three legions, those he had taken over in Brundisium, north along the coastal road. Most of Octavian's soldiers thereupon quickly made off, and he was left with only a small troop of about a thousand men. Octavian seemed to have lost the ability to assess the political situation and its possibilities correctly. Having manoeuvred so skilfully up to this point, and after creating himself a strong position in the scramble for the favour of the Romans, he was staking everything on this coup, if such a poorly managed venture may be so described. Obviously he had not understood that the struggle was not yet being carried out on the basis of a free-for-all without any rules, or reduced to a mere display of muscle. There were rules of conduct, and in the chaos of the power struggle after the Ides of March they had come to the fore more clearly again. And the rules were still those of the old order: it was necessary for a man to have official authority, to use the machinery of the law as it affected the distribution of power and above all to make sure of the Senate. Antony had understood that. Octavian's ignorance, or perhaps it should be called arrogance, almost cost him his political life – which at this time would have meant his physical life too. His career nearly ended here and now. But he was clever enough to admit to failure and call an immediate halt to his venture. He did not blame the soldiers who wanted to leave him; indeed he even gave them gifts and withdrew first to Ravenna and then to Arretium (Arezzo), where Maecenas had great influence.

Only a few days after Octavian's retreat, Antony arrived in Rome. If Octavian had not already left the city a clash would have been inevitable. There might even have been much bloody fighting, and considering Antony's strong position there can be no doubt what the outcome would then have been. As it was, he had to content himself, once Octavian had withdrawn in haste, with sending a furious answer to his address to the people after him. He delivered a tirade of abuse. But his military superiority in Italy was not quite so strong as before; the seed sown by Octavian had begun to take root in the legions that landed in Brundisium. The soldiers considered Antony's offer very tight-fisted: it was one-fifth of the bounty that Octavian's agents were ready to pay. Many of the legionaries were indignant, and when an actual mutiny finally broke out Antony was forced to restore discipline through executions for dereliction of duty. Old soldier that he was, he could not summon up any sympathy for the men's insubordination to the consul; but perhaps for that very reason he had no alternative to harsh measures, because his financial means were running out. What had happened to the enormous sums he had taken from the dictator's funds?

In Rome, Antony received news that one of his legions, the Martian Legion, which was on its way north along the Adriatic coastal road, had declared allegiance to Octavian, or rather, in view of the hostile course on which the two had now engaged, had gone over to him. Antony swiftly went to the legion's base, but his efforts to win back the soldiers met with nothing but contempt. There seemed to be no end to the bad news. Back in Rome at the end of November, he heard that more troops had defected; the Fourth Legion, another legion of veterans, and some smaller units had all gone over to Octavian. The soldiers also resented the consul's rigorous suppression of the Brundisium mutiny. Octavian exploited their mood, took an oath of allegiance from the men of the Martian Legion, which was encamped at Alba Fucentia only about 100 kilometres from Rome (one wonders how they got there, since the marching route led from Brundisium north along the Adriatic coastal road), and paid the soldiers another 2,000 sesterces. He promised that on the day of victory there would be a further 20,000 – such a large sum, more than twenty years' pay, that one is tempted to regard it as a mistake in the records. And on the day of victory over whom? Mark Antony?

At any rate, Octavian had learned a lesson from his disastrous march to Rome; he gave more and better thought to any future steps he took. For when the soldiers, intoxicated by the prospect of money, urged him simply to claim the military command (*imperium*) of a propraetor, he referred them to the Senate and prevented them from marching to Rome to force that body to make the decision they wanted – although he was to do exactly that nine months later, if in different political and military circumstances. His soldiers' demands again showed Octavian clearly that he had no proper official standing. A number of them might even have felt more uneasy than their leader himself to think that he, as a private person, had recruited them. They had never known or heard of such a thing, and the soldiers were bound to wonder what an oath to a self-proclaimed military commander was worth. But at least now, rather late in the day, Octavian knew how he must proceed. Legally, he was still a usurper, no less now than during his march on Rome, but he had extricated himself from that debacle. However, it was not primarily his own skill that had helped him to reach this unexpectedly good position but Antony's lack of it, or at least his lack of foresight. Many unearned strokes of luck were to help Octavian to reach the pinnacle of his career.

Antony now gave up the game in Italy as lost. To save the troops he still had, he left Rome in haste at the end of November and marched with his remaining soldiers to his province of Upper Italy. First, however, he had to take it over from Decimus Brutus. Antony still had four or five legions; his brother Lucius brought another to Upper Italy for him. Octavian had a fighting force of about the same size; as well as the two legions that had gone over to him, by January of the next year he had formed three more from the veterans whose allegiance he had gained and from new recruits. A page had turned. Octavian had become a rival to be taken seriously.

And now came Cicero's hour. Octavian's offer to have him appointed by the Senate to command the forces opposing Antony was still open, and Gaius Oppius, whom Octavian had taken over from Caesar as his personal aide, along with Balbus, went to see Cicero to seal the alliance. Even now Cicero did not entirely abandon his suspicions and he also had to deal with reservations on the part of his political friends, Caesar's assassins. He asked for guarantees of Octavian's intentions, suggesting that he should treat the 'murderers of the tyrant' (*tyrannoctoni*) not only without hostility but in a friendly manner. He regarded consent to the coming election to the office of tribune of the people of Caesar's first assassin, Publius Servilius Casca – the man who had struck the first blow with his dagger – as the touchstone of Octavian's sincerity, saying that, 'The election of Casca is the dividing line on which opinions differ.' On behalf of Octavian, Oppius agreed to everything. They had come to terms. Octavian was now ranged with Caesar's murderers against the Caesarians. The reward for this betrayal of the dictator, his adoptive father, was power. Octavian's political about-turn brought him a new father figure in Cicero, whom he addressed as his father in letters. It was Octavian who made the alliance; Cicero was only the ally he had acquired, although naturally Cicero himself did not see it like that.

Now Cicero set to work to strengthen the coalition and introduce it to the public. On 9 December, he arrived back in Rome from his home town of Arpinum. The tribunes of the people, representing the absent consuls Antony and Dolabella, called a meeting of the Senate at which Cicero sketched the outlines of his 'republican front': its leaders would be Decimus Brutus, Octavian and the new consuls Hirtius and Pansa. The order in which he mentions these members of his 'front' indicates his agenda. But since the front bore the stigma of illegality, it had to be legalized or at least justified first: Brutus, whose province was lawfully allotted to him, the troops who had defected to Octavian and Octavian himself had to be praised, their conduct to the state declared meritorious and correct, and finally the new consuls, due to take office in fourteen days' time, were requested to apply for the men thus named to be honoured (Third Philippic). All this was approved, except that Cicero wanted Antony declared an enemy of the state (*hostis publicus*), while the Senate was unwilling to burn all its bridges. Once again it proved itself the compliant apparatus it had been ever since Caesar's time, ready to go along with everyone who was at its head or could make himself its speaker. Cicero had not assured the senators of the legitimacy of the new front's actions; instead he dwelt on the intentions of those carrying them out. A private citizen, in this view of matters, stood above a consul if he wanted what was right. And how good, said Cicero, that the state still had someone to ensure a right way of thinking! On the same day he informed the people of the decisions that had been taken (Fourth Philippic). Now the coalition of republican forces, as Cicero saw them, had to be given a solid (meaning a legal) foundation by the Senate. Cicero's 'republican front' must be the Senate's armed fist.

It was arranged that all this was to be established under the presidency of the new consuls in the Senate on 1 January 43 BC, meeting in the temple of Jupiter on the Capitol. But Cicero encountered unexpected opposition in the person of Quintus Fufius Calenus, consul in the year 47 and a supporter of Antony. Calenus spoke in favour of a reconciliation with Antony and suggested sending a delegation to him requiring him to cease hostilities. The Senate met over a period of several days, and in the end Cicero carried his wishes through (Fifth Philippic). Decimus Brutus was praised for defending Cisalpine Gaul against Antony (although by law it was not his province any more), and Lepidus was granted a gilded equestrian statue in the Forum for bringing about a settlement with Sextus Pompey, whom Cicero classed with the republicans. Above all, however, Cicero presented Octavian, whom he calls Gaius Caesar, as the saviour sent by the gods in the republic's hour of need. 'Who sent him to us, who sent the Roman people this godlike young man, what god sent him? Who suddenly appeared against all expectations, when all lay open for our destruction to that bringer of ruin, and raised an army to oppose Mark Antony in his rage before anyone could suspect that he planned to do so?' Cicero compared young Octavian to the young Gnaeus Pompey – forgetting how hard he himself and those who thought like him had tried to keep Pompey's ambition within bounds – he compared him with Scipio the Elder, conqueror of Hannibal, he even compared him with Alexander the Great. He heaped praise on Octavian that would be excessive even for an established military commander, calling him 'saviour of the state', and saying that the nineteen-year-old was worthier to bear the title of Father of the Fatherland than his adoptive father, on whom it had been officially bestowed. Above all, however, he was anxious to allay the senators' distrust of Caesar's son. He presented the son as a paragon of virtues by comparison with the father, who had not complied with the Senate and had followed the path of violence: 'His son is of a different nature, one who is highly esteemed by all citizens of Rome, particularly the best of them. Our hope of freedom rests on him, we have been saved by him once, and the highest honours are sought for him and await him.' Finally he petitioned for Octavian to be granted propraetorial command of the troops he had with him, as well as the privilege of applying for any office as if he had already been quaestor, and finally for his appointment as a senator with the right to speak in the Senate as one who had held praetorial rank. All this was agreed, and there were even additional petitions, made by Octavian's stepfather Philippus, Isauricus and the lawyer Sulpicius Rufus. The privilege was extended by granting him permission to apply for office ten years earlier than legally permitted, and the senatorial rank of a praetor was raised to that of a consular. As the crowning touch, it was decided to grant Octavian – who could boast not a single achievement on behalf of the state – a gilded equestrian statue, indicating the value of such a monument at the time.

Cicero's rhetorical effusion could not have blinded anyone to the fact that monstrous demands had been made and granted. They legalized the conduct of a man who had assembled an army without any official mission to do so, who in addition was praised for his actions in glowing terms. Even more incomprehensible was his appointment as senator. No one had ever been *appointed* senator in Rome before. Since time immemorial, the people had conferred the dignity of senatorial rank. The elections, with their ritual campaigning between candidates, had always ensured that there was equilibrium within the ruling class, and their legitimacy had been confirmed again and again, although holders of the franchise represented only a section of Roman citizens as a whole. If the Senate rather than the people was now appointing a senator, and more-over promoting him to high senatorial rank, it was controlling its own constitution by co-opting him. The people of Rome had been replaced as the source of the magistracy by the Senate, which was now deciding on its own composition without the introduction of any new legal or social mechanism as a substitute for the franchise of the people – some device whereby in future a man could be appointed senator or pro-moted to a higher rank. It seemed that now an arbitrary proposal and the Senate's willingness to go along with it decided who would be a senator. Cicero's other petitions were dubious enough as things were, but on occasion, in times of outside threat or internal political difficulty, a military command had been given in an unusual way, or a man had been appointed to a position before his time, so it was possible to over-look the legalizing of the young man's action in recruiting an army on his own and the privileges of office granted to him. But the idea that the Senate could add a new member to its ranks ran counter to the repub-lican idea.

The price Cicero paid for incorporating Octavian into the republican front was a high one, and he met with resistance in the following days. Those who did not want to see young Octavian elevated to the status of a true son of Caesar now joined the genuine adherents of Antony. They were thus supporting Calenus' policy of reconciliation: their idea was to send a delegation to Antony, which of course would mean negotiating with him. He was to be required to desist from acts of war in Upper Italy. As it must have been clear to everyone that he would do nothing of the kind, this demand was to be seen as providing a breathing space for further negotiations. The Senate did indeed decide to send a delega-tion of three men, and even made sure it was well balanced – consisting of Caesar's father-in-law Piso, Philippus and Sulpicius Rufus – and sent them off to Antony. Cicero never tired of raging against this policy of reconciliation. As soon as the decision to send the delegation had been taken he spoke against it in front of the people (Sixth Philippic) and just two weeks later in the Senate (Seventh Philippic).

As was only to be expected, Antony rejected the Senate's demand to cease hostilities, as delivered by the envoys; he naturally wanted to feel sure of the tenure of his province for the five years granted to him by law, that is to say until the end of 39. He pointed out in his answer that he intended to keep his province until Marcus Brutus and Cassius had held the consular posts granted them for the year 41 by Caesar himself and had also completed the following proconsular year. This recognition of the offices intended for the two assassins of Caesar also shows his readiness to negotiate with them. Even if Antony saw the two men's proconsular year only as a negotiating counter, it meant that all bridges to the murderers of Caesar were not yet burned. Naturally Cicero studiously ignored all signs of Antony's willingness to negotiate and pointed only to his rejection of the vital point: withdrawal from Upper Italy and submission to the Senate. Cicero had predicted as much, so he could now brand Antony a lawbreaker and an enemy of the state. After the return of two of the envoys – Sulpicius Rufus, the third, had died on the journey – to make their report, the Senate found itself in a very awkward position and not sure what to do next, caught as it now was between the war party, led by Cicero, and the peace party, led by Calenus, who wanted to send another delegation. The opposition of two groups of more or less equal strength but with different aims gave the Senate another opportunity to make a decision of its own, but it never came to that point. There was probably general relief when it had its present unusual role in affairs of state taken away by Lucius Julius Caesar, Antony's uncle and an extremely independent man – independent of his nephew as well as others. He suggested opting for neither of two alternatives, but pointed out that uproar (*tumultus*) prevailed, and the senators had better arm themselves. For all the military clamour that this decision might set off, it was not at all binding, since it neither declared war nor labelled Antony as an enemy.

Early in February, Cicero tried to put an end to the state of uncertainty between peace and war by making a speech in the Senate (Eighth Philippic), in which he identified the enemy by his name. And now at last he achieved partial success: at his petition, the Senate decided that all men in arms under Antony must leave him by 15 March and report to one of the commanders in the Senate, that is to say to the consuls, to Decimus Brutus or to Octavian. Anyone remaining with Antony after the announcement of the senatorial decision was to be regarded as an enemy of the state. This was as good as a declaration of war, and it was Cicero who had brought the Senate to make it. The coalition against Antony was first and foremost his work, and it was Cicero too who in no uncertain terms put those in favour of compromise in their place, presenting Antony as the new tyrant, leader of a militia that would reward itself for victory by looting the senators' own fine villas and other properties.

So far the war against Antony had not really started, although early in January the Senate had confirmed Decimus Brutus and Octavian in their positions, which had not been legally confirmed before, and promoted them to full military commanders. The praetorian command that Octavian had received gave him, as an official with military power (*imperium*), the opportunity and the right to ask the gods formally to approve any official action (*auspicium*), and on 7 January he made use of that right for the first time. It was from that day, the *dies imperii*, that he was to date his entire reign, the longest of any Roman ruler, lasting fifty-seven and a half years until his death in AD 14.

However, legalizing his usurped powers did not lead to any immediate activity on the part of the Senate's army. Octavian had indeed moved north in January, and so had Hirtius, one of the two consuls, but the troops they commanded remained inactive in winter quarters. No one seemed particularly interested in fighting, Octavian because he did not want to fight side by side with one of Caesar's murderers, and the consuls because the fighting on both sides would be largely waged by Caesarian veterans. The soldiers themselves cannot have felt particularly keen to take up arms against their comrades. In addition, the Senate was still wavering.

Now Antony took the initiative. In December he marched from Ariminum (Rimini) into the province of Upper Italy. When, in the face of Antony's superior forces, Decimus Brutus withdrew to the fortified town of Mutina (Modena), Antony advanced on the town and began laying siege to it. The war had begun. It was called the 'Mutina War' (*bellum Mutinense*) because Mutina was at the centre of military operations. However, hostilities outside the besieged town almost came to a halt. It seemed as if everyone but Cicero and Decimus Brutus was waiting for matters to be resolved by some sign of an understanding. Cicero tirelessly sought to strengthen the senators' will for war. Early in February, when the question of a second delegation was raised again, he appeared in the Forum ostentatiously wearing a *sagum*, the woollen cloak regarded as a military garment – the only senator to do so. In these weeks he did not cut a very impressive figure; his radical stance increased the distance between him and the influential men in the Senate, even those who in principle were prepared to back his policy. Everyone could see that the cause of the 'republicans' – now meaning Caesar's assassins – rested entirely on him and Decimus Brutus, and the coalition with the Caesarians against Antony was on a very weak footing.

In this stalemate, movement came from the east. In February the Senate received an official letter from Marcus Brutus, informing the senators that instead of going to his province of Crete he had seized Macedonia, Greece and Illyricum. Publius Vatinius, governor of Illyricum, driven into a corner by his mutinous troops, had handed the province and the army over to him, and he had surrounded Gaius Antonius, brother of Mark Antony and governor of Macedonia, in Apollonia. There was still no certain news of Cassius; even at the beginning of May no message from him had yet reached Rome. He had reached an understanding with Trebonius, governor of Asia, and had gone on to Syria. Although it was not yet known in Rome, he had succeeded in taking over the six legions stationed there, and in March he also gained control of the four Egyptian legions. He too, so much at least was clear in Rome, was intent on building himself a power base in the east.

Marcus Brutus' letter made Cicero hope for success, but he now had something else to justify to the Senate, conduct that flew in the face of all legal tradition: Brutus and Cassius had marched into provinces which were not theirs and had simply seized them and the legions stationed there. Again, Cicero defended their actions with what by now had become almost his stock argument: in times of emergency, when an enemy of the state gave its defenders no time or opportunity to set up properly organized resistance, a right way of thinking must supersede the law (Tenth and Eleventh Philippics). In the emergency of the hour, Brutus and Cassius could not wait for a decision by the Senate, 'for Brutus and Cassius have already acted as the Senate themselves on many occasions'. Yes, Cassius had made his own decision not to go from Italy to the province of Cyrene allotted to him, and went to Syria instead, but it was in obedience to a higher law. For, said Cicero, he was acting 'on the basis of the law established by Jupiter himself, whereby all that means safety for the state is regarded as right and lawful. For the law is nothing but the rules of right behaviour derived from divine authority, ordaining what is good and preventing the opposite. Cassius, then, was obeying this law when he marched to Syria, a province not his by the written laws of men, but those laws give way to the law of nature in her own province.' He could hardly have said more clearly that the rules of public law must bow to political beliefs. And many people agreed with Cicero. For if the enemies of the state had the machinery of state in their hands, as was the case under Caesar as dictator and as (it was claimed) was the case with Antony as consul, true republicans must determine to put themselves above the law and act according to the old order, as if law backed it up. The only question was whether there were still any 'true republicans' and, if so, where they were to be found. Did they exist outside the small circle of the murderers of Caesar and those who sympathized with them? The leaders of the 'republic' and their world of traditional political rules and social norms had increasingly retreated into the background, and their place had been taken by those whose power and personal aura could cover up for any kind of political attitude. That was evident in the legalization of the powers usurped by Marcus Brutus and Cassius. The Senate passed Cicero's petition on behalf of Brutus, but not Cassius. Only rather later was he at least confirmed in the proconsulate of Syria. Cassius might appear to many who wanted reconciliation the more radical of the two, but Brutus, at least in retrospect, was no less consistent in his approach to the central political question.

In the east, matters had taken a different turn as a result of the seizure of all the eastern provinces by Brutus and Cassius. But there had been a hitch. When the proconsul Dolabella was crossing the western part of Asia Minor on his way to Syria in early January of the new year 43, he met Gaius Trebonius and had him killed. With Trebonius, one of the most able men among the conspirators, Caesar's assassins lost an important member of their group, and in view of that fact the Senate's immediate declaration that Dolabella was an enemy of the state was little use. Cassius was at least able to avert the military consequences of this setback by intercepting Dolabella when he marched into Syria in May and surrounding him in Laodicea (Laodikeia). Manoeuvred into a hopeless situation, Dolabella ordered one of his men to kill him.

The success of the 'republicans' in the east was bound to have immediate repercussions on the situation in Italy. Cicero's jubilation could not veil the fact that all the Caesarians, including those who were members of the front opposing Antony, regarded developments in Macedonia and Syria with great concern. In view of events in the east, they felt increasingly uneasy to be allied to one of Caesar's murderers, who was thus a comrade of the new lords of the east, against one of themselves, as Antony ultimately was. Octavian in particular, although he seldom missed an opportunity to present himself as his father's avenger, will have seen more and more clearly that with Decimus Brutus as his colleague in the alliance he was in the wrong camp, and his position would gradually become untenable. He still wanted to feel bound to the coalition, which, after all, he himself had brought into being – or perhaps by now he preferred to feel he had been forced into it – but as yet he saw no new partner to whom he could turn. He was too far committed to his enmity with Antony, and had built up his position in Italy on it. However, events in the east were changing the political situation as a whole to such an extent that the collapse of the 'republican front' seemed possible. Cicero, buoyed up by his mission as a freedom fighter, refused to see that. He was fixated on his hatred of Antony as a new tyrant.

So in February Cicero opposed the idea of another delegation to Antony, one that was again proposed by Quintus Fufius Calenus, but this time also by Lucius Calpurnius Piso, and once again he carried the day (Twelfth Philippic). Nor would he have anything to do with the appeal that Marcus Aemilius Lepidus had made to the Senate for peace – not a wise reaction in view of the influence of a man who had at his disposal two provinces (Gallia Narbonensis and Citerior Spain) and a large army. Diplomacy was called for here; Cicero should have tried, cautiously, to restrain Lepidus, whose appeal seemed to bring him closer to Antony, instead of offending him and thus positively forcing him to side with Antony. In the same speech in which he rebuffed Lepidus' idea (Thirteenth Philippic), Cicero criticized a letter from Antony to the consuls setting out and justifying his political standpoint. The outcome might have been sympathy for Cicero's point, especially as in his political analysis Antony spoke only of Caesarian factions (*partes*) and would have no truck with the idea of a central *res publica* or a party of 'republicans'. As matters had turned out – or, rather, as Octavian and Cicero had manipulated them – he was now the enemy of the Senate, and an attack on him was, so to speak, part of the political repertory of the time. Consequently Cicero's harsh reaction to the contents of the letter is not as surprising as his purely polemical manner, for the part of his address attacking Antony is markedly inferior to his earlier speeches. Seen as a whole, Cicero's unyielding attitude, inflexible as he was in reacting to changes within the Caesarian camp, can be understood in view of the new situation, in which Brutus and Cassius had gained ground for the 'republican' camp.

Everything in Italy, for Cicero and his followers, depended on Octavian. Cicero never entirely lost his distrust of him; ultimately he could not simply forget that Octavian, like Antony, was a Caesarian, even if ambition had made them political opponents. Since October of the year 44, the rivalry between Octavian and Antony had been raised to a military level, at first only in a minor way, with the recruiting and dismissal of soldiers, but after the beginning of the year armies were on the march. The quarrel over who was to succeed the dictator had become militarized, and at the same time it concentrated on the two protagonists. Octavian had wanted a fight; Cicero had merely given him the legal framework for it and got the consuls on his side. If Octavian were now to leave the existing coalition without a fight, he would lose face. Whatever happened, he must try to weaken Antony before he rejoined his proper place, the front against the murderers of Caesar. At some point that time would come. But it had not come yet, and so the war in Italy slowly gathered pace as the days of the year 43 grew warmer.

The consul Hirtius and Octavian, now an officially appointed propraetor, had gone into winter quarters on the Via Aemilia, the road running from Ariminum (Rimini) through the wide plain between the Apennines and the Po, and linking the towns of Bononia (Bologna), Mutina, Parma and Placentia (Piacenza). In the middle of March they began advancing towards Mutina along the Via Aemilia to relieve Decimus Brutus, besieged there by Antony. Octavian had to leave supreme command of their forces to Hirtius, who was higher than he was in rank, but he led some of the troops under Hirtius' command. Hirtius was not a dynamic or imaginative military commander, but he was a reliable officer and a good tactician. They approached Mutina by way of Bononia, without encountering much resistance at first. Now that the Senate's troops were advancing, Antony had to fight on two fronts: against Brutus, whom he had penned up inside Mutina, and now against Hirtius too, so he was in the same situation as Caesar during the siege of Alesia in the year 52, when he had to fight both Vercingetorix, whom he had surrounded, and an army of Gauls coming to relieve their leader. Above all, Antony had to try to keep open the link to the south somehow or other, even though it was now blocked by the advancing army of Hirtius, since it was from there and the Picenum region on the Adriatic that he expected Publius Ventidius Bassus to come with an army of new recruits.

Hirtius too was expecting reinforcements. His colleague Pansa was to bring four new legions, also exclusively consisting of new recruits, a considerable fighting force and one that would mean the senatorial army would vastly outnumber Antony's, which even now was numerically weaker. It was not easy to assess the military position, in view of the interlocking fronts and the two advancing relief forces; great circumspection was required by the commanders on both sides, and then decisive action at the right time. Hirtius, who was still in charge of the strategic opportunities and necessities of the situation, proved his worth here. He sent the experienced Martian Legion and his and Octavian's bodyguard (*cohors praetoria*) down the Via Aemilia to meet Pansa's legions of raw recruits, and the troops did indeed join forces in the area of Forum Gallorum. But Antony, learning of these movements, led some of his troops, including two legions of veterans, along side roads – since the main army road was barred to him – to meet the enemy. He lay in wait on both sides of the main road for Pansa's fighting force, now reinforced by Hirtius' auxiliaries. On 14 or 15 April, there was a bloody battle in which Antony, an experienced tactician, inflicted a heavy defeat on his opponents' united army. There was terrible slaughter among the recruits, Octavian's bodyguard was wiped out, and the consul Pansa himself was badly wounded in the turmoil of battle. Most of his army scattered, and only the fact that the tried and tested Martian Legion held the camp averted catastrophe. But although there was no denying that they had suffered a severe setback, Hirtius saved the military situation as a whole – so far it had been extremely favourable to the Senate's troops – and he also laid the foundations for the final victory. On hearing news of the battle, he immediately left the ring of besiegers outside Mutina, set off on a forced march to the battlefield with his core troops, including the Fourth Legion of veterans, and once there he immediately attacked Antony's weary army. After a short fight, Antony was defeated and had to withdraw. The victory was due above all to the decisive and swift actions of Hirtius and to the Martian Legion. The report on the battle written for Cicero by Servius Sulpicius Galba, who himself had been a general under Caesar and then joined the conspiracy against him, shows how much the outcome had depended on battle-hardened veterans and how little on young recruits. Galba's report also makes it clear that the veterans would listen only to proven, recognized generals, which made it difficult for an inexperienced man like Pansa to lead them.

Octavian had not taken part in the battle. His task had been to hold the camp at Mutina, which most of the troops had left, and a day after the battle of Forum Gallorum he repelled an attack by Lucius Antonius, Mark Antony's brother, when Lucius tried to exploit the now denuded ring of besiegers. Octavian did well, or at least well enough for his soldiers to hail him after the battle as *imperator*, meaning victorious general, the first of a long series of what in the end amounted to twenty-one such acclamations. Antony withdrew to his camp at Mutina, pursued by Hirtius and Octavian. He had clearly not achieved the strategic aim of his campaign in Upper Italy, and the weakened state of his troops after their defeat, together with the presence of the Senate's army outside Mutina, now made it unlikely that the siege would succeed. It was undoubtedly a bad mistake for him not to withdraw now, for his victorious opponents were not, of course, going to remain inactive. On 21 April, only a few days after the battle of Forum Gallorum, Hirtius and Octavian attacked, and even got inside the enemy camp, but Antony managed to save it thanks mainly to one of his legions of veterans, the famous Crested Larks Legion (Legio V Alaudae). During the fighting in the camp Hirtius, in overall command after the wounding of Pansa, was killed. Although he had recaptured the camp Antony was still on the defensive, and his position soon became untenable. He made the logical decision that he should have taken after the first battle: he left the camp next day and retreated westward.

The Senate had won, but both consuls were dead, for Pansa too, severely wounded at Forum Gallorum, died of his injuries in Bononia only two days after the second battle. The death in particular of Hirtius, who had proved himself a tactically capable and on occasion an energetic military commander, was a severe loss to the Senate and the 'republican front'. But not to Octavian. Command of the Senate's entire army now fell to him, as the next highest in military rank after the consuls. With their death, Fortune made him one of the most powerful of the many army commanders now making their way through the Roman empire with their legions, and his success in the War of Mutina had at last won him recognition by the soldiers and his 'colleagues'. The twin battles for Mutina, leading to his supreme command of the senatorial troops, were to form the foundations of his further rise.

In view of the importance of the victory to Octavian, there were many stories about him and his conduct in circulation. As usual they are evidence less of what actually happened, or of what Antony and Octavian thought about each other at the time, than of the tensions between them in their later bitter enmity. Antony is said to have claimed that Octavian fled in the first battle of Forum Gallorum, reappearing only two days later without his horse or cloak. He had thus, the story implied, proved himself a coward, a man who, as the Greeks would say, had 'thrown away his shield'. Antony knew perfectly well that Octavian had not even been present at the battle, but had been defending the camp outside Mutina, so his invention of this tale must have been a downright lie. But even as a lampoon it does not bear examination. Octavian's side came up with the touching tale of how, in the midst of the battle, he took the legion's standard from a severely wounded standard-bearer and carried it himself for some time. No doubt that is how Octavian would have liked to see himself, but for that very reason there is unlikely to be much truth in the story. Then there is the outrageous insinuation that Octavian had the two consuls poisoned so that he could take over their army. There were thousands of witnesses to refute this gross slander, but more than anything else, it is evidence of the wide range of what was thought and even believed possible.

With Antony's defeat, the political situation was to take new shape within only a few months. In the aftermath of victory, and with perceptible pressure from the east, the Caesarians moved closer together. Paradoxically, it was the success of the 'republicans' that broke Cicero's coalition. The new wind blowing showed itself directly after the withdrawal of the defeated Antony because Octavian, the victor, did not pursue him. The political calculation behind that fact was not immediately clear in Rome, or alternatively was suppressed, just as no one was able to recognize and assess the real situation. In the weeks before the battle Rome had been a hotbed of rumours, the most ridiculous of which, some of them perhaps spread by agents of Antony, fell on fertile

ground. It was even said that on the Parilia, 21 April, the day when the
founding of Rome was celebrated, Cicero intended to have himself
acclaimed as dictator. In this gloomy and depressed atmosphere, news
of the victory in the first battle came as a great relief, sending popular
opinion to the opposite extreme. Cicero's party and their sympathizers
were jubilant; in the belief that the republicans had won at Forum Gallorum, they indulged in the illusion that they had at last restored the old
order.

When news of the victory arrived on the Parilia, the Senate met, and
Cicero made a speech asking for a festival of thanksgiving to last fifty
days, and for honours to be awarded to the commanders and the fallen
soldiers (Fourteenth Philippic). His proposal, naturally, was adopted,
but it shows a total lack of any sense of reality that Cicero, apparently
relieved of any immediate threat, once again saw himself at the centre
of aristocratic wrangling over rank and influence. In his speech he spoke
disparagingly of the disfavour of many former consuls who, he alleged,
envied his merits in the struggle for the leading position in the state
(*principatus*). Considering the current situation, he devoted an excessive
amount of space to this criticism. His audience might have thought they
were hearing the Cicero who, just fifteen years earlier and back from
exile, had attacked many of his own rank for their lack of support. Even
if there was any foundation for his suspicion that the consulars did not
look kindly on him, did that matter in the present situation? Surely it
would have been better to blame the rumours on Antony's subversive
activities? And whom did he mean by the consulars? As he well knew,
not many of them were still alive. Cicero was in closer touch with reality when he singled out for mention Decimus Brutus, who had not been
sufficiently honoured in the senatorial debate, and noted that the war
could not be considered over while Brutus was still under siege. But also
absent from this speech is any mention of another man who had played
his part in the victory, Octavian. He is named last among the military
commanders to be honoured.

In these days and weeks a witty remark by Cicero was in circulation
and was sure to hurt Octavian's feelings: 'This young man is to be
praised, decorated, and eliminated' ('laudandum adulescentem, ornan-
dum, tollendum'), he said, playing on the double meaning of the verb
*tollere*, which can mean both 'elevated' and 'removed'. Often Cicero
could not check his sharp tongue even when failing to do so might

injure him or the position he was defending. Even Decimus Brutus, certainly no friend to Octavian, reproached Cicero for his comment, which had come to his ears too, for he understood its politically explosive nature. Octavian had heard of it himself and he had replied, wrote Brutus, that he would not let matters come to the point of 'elevation' (or 'elimination').

When, shortly after news of the victory at Forum Gallorum, word of Antony's defeat in the second battle reached Rome, triumph was complete. Now, on 26 April, Antony was finally declared an enemy of the state, as Cicero had so often urged. Cicero saw himself reaching the aim of his political wishes. For the second time he was the saviour of the state, but this time he had saved it not from a miserable political gambler in the shape of Catiline, but as he thought from a new tyrant in Antony – and thus also from the shade of the great dictator that Cicero had seen looming behind him. 'Let us remember,' he said in the Senate on 21 April, 'that on 20 December [44] freedom was demanded again on my initiative (*me principem*), that I have kept watch for the state from 1 January [43] to this hour, my house and my ears have been open day and night for suggestions and admonishments from one and all; that letters, messages and admonitions from me have called upon all, wherever they were, to come to the defence of the fatherland; that in my propositions in the Senate since 1 January I never spoke of envoys to Antony, but always considered him an enemy of the state, regarding the fight against him as war . . .' Cicero felt that he was the real victor in the war against the enemy of the state. On the same day, he told Marcus Brutus proudly how, when news of the first victory at Forum Gallorum came, the people first accompanied him to the Capitol and then made him mount the speaker's rostrum at the Forum. He believed, he said, that he had restored the unity of all classes of society, and thanks for it are due to him alone. He was basking in the wonderful feeling that the tyrant had been conquered, and he was the man who had shown the way.

But Antony was not finished yet, and nor was tyranny. That many-headed monster was very soon to swallow up what was still left of the republic.

# 4

## The Fall of the Old Order

Only now had the old political order been restored. The Ides of March had been merely the prelude to the liberation from tyranny now experienced by Italy after the defeat and shameful flight of Antony. The Senate, not the military camp or the tyrant's court, was the centre of the state once again, as in the past: an assembly of leading politicians, and the central government of both Rome and its empire. That was Cicero's view, and he was not alone in it. Once again a majority of senators seemed to be forming to control policy, independently of the power cartel of military barons. All that now remained was to exclude Antony entirely and bring Brutus and Cassius, the liberators in the east, back to Rome. They had already built up a considerable fighting force and had the east largely in their hands. In addition, the concessions that had been made in the political and military emergency of the year 44 had to be pruned back to suitable proportions. There can have been no hurry about that, particularly since the still confused situation in Italy made it actually dangerous to move too fast there, alienating the man whose aid they had used against Antony. But success blurred the senators' vision. Upper Italy in the power of Decimus Brutus, all Italy free, the east under Brutus and Cassius at the Senate's disposal: what more could they want? However, there were still opponents, and some of the generals were not reliable. There was Antony, weakened and in flight, but still at the head of a large army; there was Lepidus in Spain and Gallia Narbonensis; there was Plancus in that part of Gaul conquered by Caesar. They all commanded large military forces.

And there was Octavian. But he did not really belong to the Caesarians, he was a victorious 'military commander of the Senate', as Cicero thought. All the same, it was not Octavian whom Cicero and his friends in the Senate, and indeed most of the senators, now wished to see in authority as leader of the republican military forces. The man they wanted was Decimus Brutus. Although there was no disputing the contribution that Octavian had made during the republican war with Antony, they regarded him as a young parvenu. He had to be awarded honours, but in view of his youth and lack of experience the Senate was not prepared to recognize him as a leading figure. Now that the danger seemed to be over, the personal and political reservations about Octavian felt by many who had previously suppressed them or discounted their significance came to the fore again, and concern over his political aims grew. What did he want? He did not fit into old-established political society, and even among the Caesarians he was out of place. He did command an army now, indeed a victorious army, but he was not in the military tradition that had moulded all the Caesarians. Could he be considered a Caesarian at all? The club of Caesar's generals had been closed to new entrants since the dictator's death. But in any case, after victory in the north there were weeks and months of relative leisure in which to try getting a clearer view of the situation. In the process Cicero and his friends grew careless, overestimated their own forces and underestimated those of others, and above all they assumed that after victory over Antony the Caesarians would allow themselves to become part of senatorial policy.

The death of the consuls was a heavy loss. They would have been a conciliatory influence in the forthcoming negotiations, for although they were Caesarians themselves they had stood loyally by the Senate in the last few months. They had been honourable men, not over-ambitious or dismissive of others; they had done their duty. But the cause for concern in the present situation was not so much the unavailability of two holders of high office who might quite probably have helped to reconcile opposites. Far more alarming was the gap that their death had left in the political organization of Rome. The highest offices were now vacant and attracted the greedy eyes of men who, if they became consuls, would bring strife rather than reconciliation. Decimus Brutus, as a commander who had in effect been defeated under siege, and whose army was debilitated and partly demoralized, could not fill that gap. In fact, in so far as any of the victors was to be honoured with the consulate, Octavian had to take the post. After the death of the two previous consuls, he was the only victor in the battle still left. He looked like their

heir. Not only did Octavian's own legionaries think so, the men whom the consuls had commanded agreed with them, and, accordingly, Octavian, the only remaining commander of the Senate's former army of relief troops, took supreme command with the goodwill of all the soldiers. It was not an act of usurpation, it was in the natural order of things. He now expected to be appointed consul by the *placet* of the Senate but he waited for it in vain. He knew only too well that he had to do something about it himself.

At this point the Senate and Cicero, as its leading figure, made a bad mistake. In the elation of victory, and given what they supposed was their new-found ability to act freely, they sought to weaken Octavian politically. They did not exclude him entirely from public affairs; that would have been impossible in view of the power he now represented. But they wanted to keep the fruits of victory from him. The Senate's troops in Upper Italy were assigned not to the command of the victorious Octavian, who as propraetor had been specifically appointed general of the Senate's army, but to Decimus Brutus, who was officially only a provincial governor and had played no part at all in the victory. Did they really expect to separate Octavian from his soldiers so easily? To his political demotion was added humiliation. Cicero proposed to grant Decimus Brutus a triumph. But over whom? Besieged in Mutina, Brutus had been more a spectator than a participant in the conflict. Octavian was to be fobbed off with the 'lesser triumph' (the *ovatio*, ovation), a ceremony granted by the Senate at its own discretion for less spectacular achievements than those warranting a full triumph, and regarded as a second-class honour. In an *ovatio* the victorious commander did not drive through Rome to the Capitol in a chariot, but went on foot or horseback. The absurdity of this graduation of honours granted to the victors lay in the fact that they were for the same event, thus making Octavian's political humiliation immediately obvious. Cicero cannot have been unaware of the potential consequences of his proposition. He must have acted under pressure from the assassins of Caesar, who did not want to see Octavian honoured in any way, and when he writes to Marcus Brutus saying that he considers himself particularly astute in distinguishing thus between triumphal honours it merely illustrates his difficulty. Because of the conspirators in the east, he could not allow Octavian a full triumph, but nor could he exclude him entirely from the celebrations. In Marcus Brutus' opinion, the mistake that forced him into these political moves, or rather contortions, lay further back, in the fact that Cicero had ever made use of Octavian to help him at all.

The slight to Octavian was even more obvious when an attempt was made to separate him from his army. The Senate wanted him to resign supreme command to Decimus Brutus. But to the discomfiture of Cicero and his now numerically large body of adherents, matters did not turn out as they expected. The military balance of power could no longer be simply regulated by decree of the Senate; not only the commanders but the soldiers themselves had a say in it. The belief that Octavian's legions of veterans could be simply separated from their commander shows a lack of any grasp of reality. Octavian did let Brutus have three of Pansa's four legions of new recruits, but Brutus asked for the fourth in vain. However, the Senate continued to exert pressure. In a very unusual move, Octavian was excluded from a ten-man committee formed to settle soldiers on their new properties – most of them, of course, veterans about to be demobilized – on the grounds that by senatorial decree no commanding general should be part of it. When a senatorial delegation turned up at the camp of the Fourth Legion and the Martian Legion, the first two to have been assigned to Octavian, to pay the soldiers the 5,000 denarii promised by the Senate, without including Octavian in the discussions, it was the last straw for the men. The envoys even promised the veterans a higher sum if they would agree to be commanded by Decimus Brutus. This was incredible: the legionaries had been separated from their own commander and treated as if they already *were* under the command of Decimus Brutus, in line with the wishes of the Senate. They told the envoys that they would negotiate only through their patron, and he was their general. Soldiers were no longer at the disposal en masse of the Senate or its representatives; it was only through their generals that they could be approached. The army had won wider political latitude, and taught the senators a lesson that they should have learned long before.

It had all been so well planned. Decimus Brutus and Octavian were to go in hot pursuit of the fleeing Antony, while the supposedly reliable Plancus put pressure on the fugitives from the north; then Lepidus, who had gone from Spain to Gallia Narbonensis and was considered a loose cannon, would have no alternative but to join the pack. Furthermore, the Senate expected to see Brutus and Cassius in Italy with their huge armies in the foreseeable future, and the senators also thought that the politically rather neutral Sextus Pompey, who could hardly claim the reflected glory of his father Pompey the Great but was becoming more and more of a corsair, could then be included in the great coalition against Antony. Even during the siege of Mutina, a delegation had gone to see him and try to persuade him to join the witch-hunt.

The Senate soon realized that events would not turn out as they had expected, and indeed were about to pass right out of their control. For what followed was no less than a complete *renversement des alliances*.

It began when Decimus Brutus took up the pursuit of Antony alone, without Octavian. Octavian's absence was not the outcome of the humiliations inflicted on him, but a political calculation that he had been considering for some time; in fact his political background and that of his soldiers positively forced it on him. Octavian might at times have thought of doing away with Antony, who stood in the way of his attempts to gain an influential position in Rome, but he had to ensure that his political capital – which lay in his name alone – was not impaired. Forced by circumstances, and not least at the urging of his soldiers, he had needed at first to shore up the foundations of his political position, and in that an alliance with the legal powers of the state had been useful to him. Now, after victory over Antony and the death of the consuls, he was in a very different situation. His real opponents, Caesar's assassins, had clearly gained military ground, and it was clear that the elimination of Antony would put the Caesarians on the defensive.

So Octavian waited. He stayed in Upper Italy, parrying the Senate's humiliation of him with a demand for a full triumph – and for the office of consul. The 'republicans', however, saw that as an affront – a young man of nineteen as candidate for the consulate! There was no precedent for granting his wish in any of the previous examples of early appointment to that office, which in law could not be granted until a man was forty-three and had worked his way through the usual offices leading up to it. But the consulate was now essential to Octavian. With a single decree, the Senate could deprive him of his propraetorial command – it could decide how long he held it – and the Senate had just shown what it thought of him. In his struggle to achieve power and influence in the face of his competitors, who governed provinces, Octavian urgently needed a better legal basis, and naturally his soldiers felt the same. The consulates vacant after the deaths of Hirtius and Pansa offered him the chance of gaining the highest office of all. In May, still only a short time after the victory over Antony at Mutina, Octavian's demand had become generally known, and he stood firmly by it.

The main thing for Octavian now was to release himself from his dependency on the Senate. He could no longer contemplate *whether* he should do so, only *how* to do it. His claim to the consulate had been one means of gaining greater independence; another was to detach himself from Decimus Brutus. Octavian had an interview with him in which he refused outright to agree to Brutus' demand that he should join in the pursuit of Antony or cross the Apennines to cut off his supplies. Brutus needed help, for although he had ten units at his disposal after taking over Pansa's legions of recruits, only a part of his forces were battle-ready. The recruits were inexperienced by comparison with Antony's veterans, Brutus' old legions were debilitated after the siege, and he was also short of money, food and horses, so he could not pursue Antony very fast. Antony, on the other hand, was getting extensive reinforcements from Publius Ventidius Bassus. Bassus, coming from the east coast of Italy, had managed to join Antony as the latter made for the coast of Gallia Narbonensis. He and the three legions recruited in Picenum, taking a route south of the Apennines in a forced march, had reached the vicinity of Genoa, where he met Antony. Among the many men of humble origin who rose to influential positions at that time through military service, Bassus was a special case. He had been a muleteer, had won Caesar's favour in the Gallic War and under the dictator's rule had been tribune of the people. Later he became a capable general, and he still had a fine career in the service of Antony ahead of him. Once he had arrived, Antony was in command of seven legions again, several of them made up of veterans.

And that was not all. Antony also succeeded in joining Lepidus, who had pitched camp beside a small river not far from Forum Julii (Fréjus). When Antony arrived he camped on the other bank of the river and ordered no barriers to be set up – with the full consent of the soldiers of both armies; those of them who were veterans and former soldiers of the dictator had no desire to fight their old comrades. The two camps were soon fraternizing. The soldiers built a bridge over the river to ease communications, and finally Antony himself, with a large retinue, crossed this bridge to the centre of Lepidus' tented camp. Lepidus, not a born leader of soldiers or a military tactician, was taken by surprise and had no alternative but to make the best of it with good grace. Antony left him command of four of his seven legions – the legionaries who followed Lepidus, a Caesarian, would hardly have tolerated any other arrangement – but took supreme command of their united forces himself. In all, he now had an army of fourteen legions, the strongest in the empire. And the Senate had lost another ally, albeit one always regarded as unreliable. When the Senate now declared Lepidus an enemy of the state and took down the equestrian statue erected in his honour only that year, at Cicero's petition, it was merely a gesture of impotence.

Antony and Lepidus had joined forces on 29 May. It was only with difficulty that Plancus, who had come from his province of Gallia Comata to meet Lepidus and was only thirty kilometres away from him, managed to avoid the fall-out from fraternization between their soldiers. At this time Plancus regarded himself and his troops as part of the Senate's army; he and Lepidus had indeed made a joint appeal to the Senate for peace, but in a letter to it at the end of March he had declared his allegiance to the republic. In refusing to join Antony now, Plancus was showing publicly that he still backed the cause of the republic and the Senate, and after he had retreated across the Isère at Cularo in early June he also emphasized his political position by joining Decimus Brutus, who had made his way there with some difficulty. They spent two months encamped together, Plancus with about five legions, three of them battle-hardened veterans. Brutus had ten, but only one of those was made up of veterans. Even together, they were thus clearly inferior to Antony's men as a fighting force. The morale of the generals, Decimus Brutus in particular, was low. They were hoping for Octavian's two legions of veterans to arrive and were in touch with him by letter, but Plancus did not believe the young Caesar would support them. In July, he openly expressed his opinion of Octavian's now obvious change of mind to Cicero: Octavian, he said, had no intention of joining them now, but had turned to 'other plans'. In no uncertain terms, Plancus blamed Octavian for the fact that Antony was still alive and had been able to join Lepidus.

The army of the two generals Decimus Brutus and Plancus, now stationed in the border area of the two provinces of Gaul, was the republic's only hope in the entire west of the empire. It represented a considerable fighting force and was commanded by two able men who had once been generals of the dictator; as governor of Gallia Comata, Plancus had proved his military capabilities only recently in battle against the Rhaetians north of Lake Constance. As seen from Rome, the indecisive behaviour of this senatorial army was bound to seem strange. Meanwhile, in spite of its numerical size it was still no match for the joint army of Antony and Lepidus, and Plancus rightly shrank from direct confrontation – not only because of his military inferiority in numbers but because he feared suffering the same fate as Lepidus. His soldiers were battle-weary, and the veterans in particular did not want to fight former comrades. Even Antony, when he moved from Mutina over the Alps into Gallia Narbonensis, discovered how much political latitude the soldiers now had, and how difficult it therefore was for many commanders to deal with them. At a parade his soldiers, fearing involvement with the other army nearby, had called out that they would either die or win a victory in Italy, and Antony could control them only by appearing to give way. So Plancus held back, and Decimus Brutus had to follow suit. However, Plancus did not break his links either with the Senate and Cicero or with Antony. He was a cautious man, but as the Caesarians united in the west he ultimately had no option but to be reconciled with 'comrades' from the time of the dictator.

The union of the Caesarians against the disaster threatening them from the east was proceeding apace. Now it was legions that mattered, above all legions of veterans; there was no more talk of liberty and the law. Many a man who, on the endless marches through Italy and the western provinces, had seen liberty before him as the aim of all their labours had to acknowledge that he had been chasing a mirage. Marcus Iuventius Laterensis, a legate in Lepidus' army, committed suicide after the armies joined forces. As a nobleman and an implacable opponent of both Caesar and the Caesarians, one who, as Cicero said, would not deviate one jot from the path along which he had set out, he saw no chance left for the republic and gave its cause up for lost. The Senate still had enough power to honour him by decree with a public funeral.

The summer of the year 43 saw Rome seething with political activity. These were the last months of a free Rome, as might have been guessed after the defection of Lepidus. The north of Italy was one massive

Caesarian army. The hopes of the republicans now rested entirely on Plancus and the weakened Decimus Brutus. They still did not trust Octavian, who was closest to Rome. However, he had not broken with the Senate, nor had he joined Antony. He wanted to be consul. The Senate considered it an unreasonable demand, but Octavian knew how to moderate his presumption skilfully by proposing to Cicero that they should share the consulate, and he meekly assured his old ally that he himself would be content with the role of junior partner. For all his reservations about the young man, Cicero was flattered and did not immediately turn the idea down. Nor was Octavian entirely without support in the Senate. In particular, Publius Servilius Isauricus, to whose daughter he became betrothed that summer, came to his aid. Isauricus was not, however, in tune with Cicero's way of thinking; they had sometimes engaged in vigorous verbal fencing in the Senate, and Cicero had been known to call him a firebrand. And the overwhelming majority of the Senate where Octavian's wish for the consulate had to be discussed, if only because he needed exceptional permission to be granted, rejected the idea. The Senate felt it still controlled the situation, but with wise forethought it had ordered two of the three legions stationed in the second African province, recently established by Caesar (Africa Nova or Numidia), back to Rome to protect the capital. The governor of the province, Titus Sextius, did indeed send them to Rome, although he was a loyal Caesarian, but they were legions of veterans, and it was easy to see that they were not likely to march against their comrades under Octavian simply on the Senate's orders.

If these orders ignored reality, other political manoeuvres in those weeks just before the freedom of Rome became a thing of the past seem positively outlandish. Many men, among them leading politicians, who should have known better, acted as if they were living in a smoothly functioning, peaceful republic. For instance, Marcus Brutus entered the general free-for-all over filling the vacancies for official and priestly positions created by the consuls' death by proposing Lucius Calpurnius Bibulus as a member of the college of augurs, in which Pansa's death had left a gap. This young man was no older than Octavian and could claim no merit apart from his distinguished family; his candidature would also have created bad feeling among all the Caesarians, because his father, Marcus Calpurnius Bibulus, had been Caesar's fellow consul and rival in the year 59. How could anyone be bold enough to put the son forward in the present situation? Almost as remote from reality was a letter of recommendation written by Cicero to Decimus Brutus in the summer of 43 (Brutus was encamped far to the north at the time), asking for support for Lucius Aelius Lamia's application for the praetorship, and yet more absurd was his letter to Decimus of early July 43, asking him to put in a good word with Marcus Brutus for a young nobleman, Appius Claudius Pulcher, a supporter of Antony at present in his, Marcus Brutus', power. How was Decimus Brutus supposed to correspond with his namesake when they were divided by the whole region under the control of Antony and Octavian?

Octavian finally came to a decision. Time was short. He was clearly weaker than Antony in the Caesarian camp, having only eight legions at his disposal, although four of those consisted of experienced soldiers. After the Senate had twice turned down his request for the consulate, he determined to take it by force. He began by sending a deputation of 400 centurions to Rome at the end of July, to ask for Octavian's entire army to get the pay already allocated to the two legions of veterans and to demand the consulate for their commander himself. When the Senate showed its reluctance, the spokesman for the centurions indicated his sword and said, 'This will do it if you don't.'

As soon as the centurions returned, Octavian and all his legions marched on Rome. Officially, he said that the soldiers had forced him to take that course, and given the situation it even sounded credible. This was the second time he had marched on Rome, but he was better prepared than on the first occasion, in October of the previous year, and hence more successful. The Senate tried in vain to stop him outside the city boundaries by making concessions, including a promise to pay all the legions the sum already granted to the two legions of veterans and giving permission for Octavian to apply for the consulate in his absence. In a brief display of bravado, the Senate even put the city on a defensive footing and ordered Octavian to stop at a certain distance from Rome. Hope revived when news came that the two African legions ordered to Rome by the Senate had landed. The Senate also planned to seize Octavian's mother and sister as hostages, but the two women could not be found (they had taken refuge with the Vestal Virgins). However, it was all too late. Octavian and his soldiers did not care what the Senate said now. As the army column came closer, the Senate's will to resist collapsed, and concurrently all independent political activity in the city ceased.

This military coup – for such it was – put an abrupt and permanent end to the republican activity of the preceding few months. Octavian, who had come from the north along the 'salt road' (*via salaria*), appeared on the Quirinal Hill and camped with his troops outside the Colline Gate (near the present Stazione Termini), well knowing that the legions from Africa would not attack him. In fact they went over to him at once. The people of Rome streamed out of the gates en masse to greet him as their new master. He entered the city the next day. There he met Cicero, to whom he addressed the enigmatic remark that he was the last of his friends to greet him. Without waiting to be elected consul and thus have a legal basis for his actions, he appropriated the state treasury and paid his soldiers half the sum of money promised by the Senate, which now came from *him* rather than the Senate itself, so what had been intended as payment for victory in battle against the enemies of the Senate now became a reward for the conquest of Rome. Then he left the city in order not to influence the consular election by his presence, a move that, in the present situation, was something of a mockery of the entire election. It was held in haste, following an extraordinary procedure in place of the usual one conducted when both consulate positions were vacant, because that would have dragged on too long, and, given the pressure of the situation, Octavian and his cousin Quintus Pedius were elected consuls without much discussion. The date was 19 August. Octavian was still in his twentieth year, and for the rest of his life he took pride in this ultimately farcical show of force, including a meek offering of thanks to the Senate for freeing him from the old-established legal requirements for candidature for the consulate.

After Octavian had re-entered the city, now as its elected consul, twelve vultures were seen. They were interpreted as a sign of divine favour for the new consul, but they reminded the Romans of a similar sight seen by Romulus, the founder and first king of Rome, when he asked the gods if they would look kindly on the city to be called Rome that he was going to build. Did this augury, which seemed to show the gods repeating their promise to Romulus, point to Octavian as the new architect of Rome? Whether any vultures were really seen did not matter much to either Octavian's contemporaries or posterity; what counted was the validation by the augury of the link between Octavian and the divine founder of Rome. On his first appearance in Rome, Octavian had begun to influence public opinion by symbols and images, myths and legends, and he was to do so for many decades to come. At any rate, Rome had its new Romulus. Octavian was not, like Romulus, king of Rome, but as consul and commander of the legions he was no less master of the city. The real head of state, who by republican law was the praetor of the city in the absence or death of the consuls, took his own life in shame at the inglorious end of the republic. With his death the praetor Marcus Caecilius Cornutus invested that end with a final hint of the republic's former liberty.

And now the new master of Rome began to rule. All the measures that he caused the Senate or the people to approve in the time that followed served to establish his political position and prepare for his next major scenario: reconciliation with the Caesarians and the distribution of roles among their leaders. First, since his own funds would not have covered the dictator's legacy in his will to the people of Rome, Octavian had the money taken from the city treasury and made his fellow consul Pedius pass a law condemning the murderers of Caesar. This Pedian Law ordered a special tribunal to be set up for all who took part in the assassination and decreed the death penalty for those found guilty, as well as the confiscation of their property and rewards for any who helped to track them down. Octavian headed the tribunal himself and on a single day he had all the murderers condemned to death in their absence. Agrippa was the prosecutor of Cassius, taking the opportunity to deliver a eulogy of the dictator; Lucius Cornificius, one of Octavian's officers, prosecuted Marcus Brutus. Few judges dared to find any of the accused not guilty. A single judge was brave enough to say openly that Marcus Brutus was innocent: to maintain the appearance of liberty and because of time pressure on the part of the new ruler, he escaped unscathed – although not permanently, because a few weeks later he was back on the list of proscribed men whom the military potentates wished to see eliminated.

Since it had not yet been possible actually to lay hands on the assassins of Caesar, they were declared outlaws; however, Octavian had the sentence passed on Dolabella for having killed Caesar's assassin Trebonius annulled. The outlawing of Antony and Lepidus pronounced by the Senate could not be rescinded so easily, for Octavian himself, although he did not hate them nearly as much as Cicero did, had been an opponent of Antony at least. So he put off this tricky move until he was absent and then had the business done by the consul Pedius, who stayed in Rome and at whose petition the now compliant Senate finally rescinded the sentence of outlawry on both men. The way was clear for reconciliation between the Caesarian generals.

Cicero had seen the end coming. His suspicions were first aroused when Octavian did not go in pursuit of Antony and they grew when the young man forcefully and persistently set about demanding the consulship. 'Caesar,' writes Cicero, meaning Octavian, in a letter to Marcus Brutus as early as June, 'who until now has been guided by my advice, has set certain hopes on the consulate, and although he is of excellent disposition and admirable steadfastness has been induced to do so by dishonest writings and messages bearing false news ... if he should stand by his word and continue listening to me, then we will have sufficient protection. But if he prefers to follow the ideas of the villains rather than mine, and if his youthful inexperience is not up to the gravity of the situation, then all our hopes rest on you.' A month later, in July, his suspicions become certainty. In a long letter, he evidently feels required to justify himself against Marcus Brutus' repeated accusation that he has encouraged Octavian too much, building him up into a dangerous enemy by legalizing his position. He points out that he is in an exposed situation in Rome, one that cannot be adequately appreciated from the security of the east, and indicates the danger represented by Antony. But Brutus, who from the first had reservations about Cicero's deep dislike of Antony, was not much impressed. In his view the main enemy had always been not Antony but Octavian, despite his youth, and it would be impossible to come to an understanding with Octavian because of his role as Caesar's successor. Brutus had also brusquely rejected Cicero's idea, sent to him of course before Octavian's march on Rome, of trying to get some kind of guarantee from Octavian of the safety of Caesar's assassins in the east. After the defeat of Antony, Cicero had obviously been toying with the possibility of an association uniting Octavian with Brutus and Cassius, on condition, naturally, that Octavian undertook to refrain from pursuing Caesar's murderers. However, it was unreasonable to expect Octavian to protect Brutus and become the champion of a free *res publica*. In a reply imbued by a strong wish for unlimited freedom of action, Brutus confronted Cicero and 'his Cae-sar', as he put it, with the basic convictions of a true republican, which ruled out any pact with Caesar's son. Octavian, he continued, was a danger to freedom; they could not expect anything from him. For some time to come, however, Brutus still thought it would be possible to come to an understanding with Caesar's generals, in particular Antony.

Only when he was faced with the end of a free Rome did Cicero see his mistake. In a letter to Brutus on 27 July, the last of his writings to have come down to us, he says he sees no chance now of any successful resistance in Italy; he is staking everything on the swift arrival of Brutus, who is now the only hope. Whether this letter was written before the centurions came to the Senate is not clear, but it shows that Cicero was aware of the extreme danger that, as he now recognized, Octavian could represent. For the first time Cicero acknowledges that he may have been mistaken in him. 'As I wrote this I felt great pain, because after vouching to the state for the young man, I might almost say boy, I shall hardly be able to keep my promise. What is more important and urgent, however, is to have incurred an obligation with regard to the state of mind and opinions of someone else – particularly when it hinges on more import-ant matters than money. For a monetary debt can be paid, and means only a tolerable loss of funds. But how can one pay a debt to the state if the man for whom one vouched simply allows it to be paid for him; that is to say, suffers one's promise to be broken, leaving one to pay for what was promised on his behalf?' After expressing a vague hope that it may after all be possible to restrain Octavian, Cicero ends this excursus by adjuring himself to hold Octavian pledged to the republican cause, lest he should get a name for ill-considered action. Here, in the last sign of life we have from Cicero, it is clear that he sees his links to Octavian as a potential mistake. Indeed, their erroneous nature was probably obvi-ous to him even before Octavian marched to Rome. As a result, the other mainstay of his policy after the Ides of March, implacable hostil-ity to Antony, could not hold either. His hatred of Antony, or his ambition to gain the leading position in the state through opposing him, had blinded Cicero to the facts.

Octavian's about-turn had excluded the Senate from active politics, cre-ating the conditions for fraternization between all the Caesarians. All that now remained was to win over Asinius Pollio and Plancus to the new political front, and also, of course, to eliminate Decimus Brutus, who was still encamped in Gaul with Plancus, inactive. Antony and Octavian now made closer contact, and Pollio and Plancus did not hesitate to go over to the stronger side when news of the coup in Rome reached them. It seems that Pollio, coming from Ulterior Spain, joined Antony willingly ahead of Plancus. He brought two legions of veterans to the Caesarian camp and left a third legion consisting of recruits behind in Spain. Plancus had no alternative but to join Pollio, which meant parting from Decimus Brutus. He handed his five legions over to Antony and Lepidus, but remained a general.

Decimus Brutus was now hard pressed. Surrounded by enemies, he had to try to get through to Marcus Brutus in the east. But the way led through Upper Italy, which was teeming with hostile legions. The six legions of recruits that he had taken over after the battle of Mutina were the first to leave him. Since Octavian was geographically closer to Brutus at this point he was able to receive them as part of his forces, considerably improving his position for the forthcoming negotiations. The other four legions – those that had been besieged in Mutina – did not stand out much longer but went over to Antony, who at this time was closer to them. Octavian now had seventeen legions available to him, while all his rivals together – including those still in the provinces – had twenty-six, although Antony could really consider only eleven of them his own.

Left to his own devices, Decimus Brutus tried to reach the east. With a small and swiftly dwindling band of companions, he obviously hoped to escape by a route north of the Alps. Some time in September a Celtic chieftain finally captured him and sent word to Antony. Antony did not want him alive and simply asked for his head. He got it. Thereupon Marcus Brutus had his prisoner Gaius, Mark Antony's younger brother, killed, although in principle he was against taking vengeance on members of a man's family in his place – in this thinking more humanely and justly than Cicero.

With Decimus Brutus, one of the three pillars of the conspiracy had fallen. Although several letters from him have been preserved in Cicero's correspondence, we know very little about him personally, and what little we are told is inconsistent. No doubt some of it was distorted in accounts by his enemies – probably including the story that he died a coward's death. There was no need to single out any of his actions for praise, since in the midst of a sea of Caesarians there was only one verdict to be passed on Caesar's murderers. It was only under Caesar that Decimus Brutus had been a really good general; in fighting Antony he had been rather indecisive and hesitant. What marked him out from the other conspirators was his unusually close relationship with the dictator, who had named him substitute heir and tutor of any posthumous son who might be born to him, appointments that went down badly with many writers of that time.

The great act of fraternization between all Caesarians finally took place under the aegis of the strongest generals. Antony had marched back with the major part of the united army to Upper Italy, where Octavian too had his military camp. At the end of October they met near the Roman colony of Bononia (Bologna); the place chosen as the site of the negotiations was a small, flat and thus easily surveyed island in the river Lavinius. The meeting was one of the great spectacles of Roman history, and at the same time it is a classic example of the solution of political problems by the physical elimination of enemies and their political system. It was also one of the most lavishly staged scenes of mass assembly known to classical antiquity. The soldiers appeared neither as part of an entertainment nor to fight, but exclusively in a demonstration of brute power. The armies were commanded by five generals, although only two of them, Antony and Octavian, really counted, because only they had come together of their own free will, and they also had the largest armies. The other three, Lepidus, Pollio and Plancus, were peripheral figures who had been forced more or less willingly into the alliance, but of those three Lepidus stood out on account of his large army and presumably also because of his personal friendship with the dictator. The dependency of these three on Antony, and their equally strong inward reservations about Octavian, meant that they stood closer to Antony, and as a result the entire assembly could be roughly divided into two camps. Octavian's was the weaker, but they had not come to fight. If anyone had tried it, the soldiers themselves would have intervened. What they wanted was to set bounds to the political scope of the military leaders, and all the generals knew it.

The generals had been rivals, so basic suspicion was the prevailing mood when they met. In the advance negotiations, it had been agreed that Octavian and Antony were to come with an equal number of legions, five each. The fact that ten legions, some 50,000 men, attended the meeting indicates the logic behind the assembly: division of power on the grounds of the strength of the army commanded by each individual general. However, the presence of the legions is also evidence of the bias in the political thinking behind the occasion: nothing counted except the 'capital' of the individual leaders. Finally it illustrated the political role of the armies. No negotiations could be conducted over their heads, or not in anything that concerned the soldiers closely. It had also been agreed in advance discussions that the two armies would be stationed on opposite sides of the river, and the two leaders would then go to the bridges built from the two banks to the island with exactly 300 bodyguards each, they would leave their guards on the banks and cross to the island alone. It was clearly visible from the banks of the river, but none the less Lepidus, allowed to join the main negotiations as the strongest of the 'minor generals', was to inspect the terrain before the march to the bridges and if he found everything correct to give a signal that no danger threatened with his war cloak, the *paludamentum*. And so Antony, Octavian and Lepidus found themselves on the island together. One historian says that even once they were there, they searched the place for hidden weapons, but in view of the entire scenario, dictated as it was by outright distrust, he might simply have assumed this detail, which is hardly relevant. The three men negotiated for two days on the island. They had to make decisions, roughly speaking, on two major and complex subjects: the division of power in the state, and the destruction of their enemies. There was bargaining on both subjects, but the three men came to an agreement.

They decided nothing less than to take over formal rule of the state, dividing between them the entire area then at their disposal, that is to say Italy and the west of the empire. They created a special magistracy, the triumvirate (meaning a college of three men), for the formal assumption of rule. The term dictator was avoided, and indeed at Mark Antony's petition had just been abolished. All the same, the special magistracy was in fact a power taking precedence over all other offices of state, and was thus essentially a plural dictatorship. To disguise what the triumvirate actually was, at least on the surface, they went to a certain amount of trouble (although not too much) to construct it as a legal entity. The three triumvirs, colleagues of equal rank, received legal powers for the city of Rome whereby they could decree any measures they liked, frustrating the activities of all other holders of office within that restricted area. Outside Rome itself, in the provincial regions, they took over all the provinces of the western part of the empire and divided them between themselves. As a result there were now no independent governors, and the Senate was formally excluded from government of the empire, its influence being restricted to the interior of Rome. Even there it depended entirely on the triumvirs. This order of precedence was emphatically expressed in the formal terminology, where the three called themselves 'triumvirs for the restoration of the state', implying that they intended to save the state from its crisis or, in concrete terms, purge it of Caesar's murderers. The terminology referred back to Sulla, who, forty years earlier, had made use of a similar explanatory rider to the terms of his office but had been a dictator all the same. The trium-virate also set a period of five years as the duration of their extraordinary command of the late republic. On petition by the tribune of the people, Publius Titius, a law known as the Titian Law was formally passed on 27 November 43 by the assembly of the people. The triumvirate was not to end until 31 December 38.

Since a triumvir was to be seen in practice, if not formally, as a magistrate superior to the consuls, the consulate that Octavian had taken more or less by force no longer had any political value. It was agreed that he should resign it. He could do so with an easy mind, because it had fulfilled its purpose and indeed had been replaced by a considerably better office. Since his colleague Pedius had died during his term of office, both positions were once again vacant, so two new consuls were appointed by the rulers for the rest of the year – one adherent of each of the two main actors in events, Gaius Carrinas as an Octavian supporter, Publius Ventidius Bassus as an Antonian. Carrinas was praetor at the time, but what did that matter? The old public order had to yield to the will of those in power, not the other way around, so he swiftly resigned the praetorship, was immediately appointed consul and thus climbed two rungs up the ladder of office in a single year. Ventidius, on the other hand, held no public office, so he was available and had now risen from muleteer to consul – a career that the Romans did not fail to lampoon.

However, matters did not stop at the establishment by the three generals of their military rule as a legal power. Now they had to share out their tasks, and in particular to divide up the huge part of the empire that they ruled. Antony received, or rather took, the best part: Upper

Italy (Gallia Cisalpina) and the part of Gaul conquered by Caesar (Gallia Comata). Lepidus too came off well, getting the two Spanish provinces and Gallia Narbonenis. Octavian had to content himself with the meagre scraps: the two African provinces and the large islands of Sicily, Sardinia and Corsica. In addition, any pleasure he might take in his share was tempered by the fact that one of the two African provinces was under the administration of Quintus Cornificius, a loyal republican, and thus had yet to be conquered, while the islands of Sicily, Sardinia and Corsica were part-occupied, part-threatened by Sextus Pompey. The triumvirs had left Italy out of the distribution process, as the area inhabited by Roman citizens and a reservoir of recruits. It was regarded as a common district of administrative authority, or more correctly a joint possession, for the state and the empire were being sliced up like the cake at a birthday party.

They still had to bear the future in mind. The 'restoration of the state' was an aim directed mainly against the murderers of Caesar in the east – the state would not be restored until it was no longer divided. It was taken for granted that the two main rivals in the triumvirate would take over as joint leaders in this war. Neither could relinquish command of the army as a whole or a share in the expected victory without giving up his political and military position. So Antony and Octavian agreed that each of them would take twenty legions and, forming them into an army of invasion, go to meet the armies of Brutus and Cassius in the east. Lepidus was to stay in Rome with three legions to keep the capital safe for the triumvirate. This agreement was written down, sealed and read out to the assembled soldiers.

The soldiers thought dynastically. Just as Caesar's daughter Julia had been married to Gnaeus Pompey, thus forming the pledge of their union, a family tie was now to be created between Antony and Octavian, the two leading figures in the present agreement. Octavian agreed to marry Clodia, Antony's stepdaughter and the daughter of his wife Fulvia by her first marriage to Publius Clodius Pulcher, the famous (or infamous) tribune of the people in the year 58. It was true that a few months earlier Octavian had been betrothed to Servilia, the daughter of Publius Servilius Isauricus, but that, of course, was no obstacle; the betrothal was simply terminated. The armies happily welcomed the announcement of the marriage. There was peace again – or more correctly, as the parties to the agreement were the armies rather than groups of the

Roman people represented by them, the army as successor to Caesar was at peace again.

And then the triumvirs marched into Rome, although their entrance was more like an occupation. They entered the city on three successive days, each of them with a special bodyguard and a legion. The streets rang to the sound of marching feet. It must have been like this, many Romans may have thought, when the city was conquered by the Celts 350 years earlier. At first the law was invoked to set up the triumvirate. But since all concerned were in a hurry – the war against Caesar's assassins was imminent – they did not let themselves be held up by the regulations stating, among other things, that a legal text on the new agreement must be published three weeks before it came into force. The triumvirs also filled various offices easily enough. Imitating measures taken by the dictator, who had appointed holders of these posts for three years in advance of his planned departure for the east, they appointed men to hold office in advance for the whole period of their triumvirate as established by the Titian Law, i.e. for five years. We do not know whether the people's assembly, traditionally responsible for electing officers of state, was even consulted.

Consuls for the coming year were to be Lucius Munatius Plancus, whom the dictator had already agreed to appoint, and the triumvir Marcus Aemilius Lepidus – the latter because of his task of protecting Rome and Italy during the absence of the other two triumvirs in the east. Provision was made for Lucius Antonius, Mark Antony's brother, and Publius Servilius Isauricus to be consuls in the year 41. They and other men were both rewarded by these appointments, which meant a rise in rank, and pledged to the cause of the triumvirate. A state mentality whose ethos had united the members of society for centuries was now replaced by personal connections to those in power, resting solely on a man's standing in the military hierarchy and on material reward.

The triumvirs had come to another important agreement, one not officially divulged to the soldiers. They had agreed to settle accounts with their political opponents by eliminating or eradicating them, verbs more suited to the project than 'execute', since no provision was made for any prosecutions. The enemies of the triumvirs were simply to be tracked down, captured and then killed. The only formal part of this act of mass slaughter was the publication of an edict indiscriminately justifying it and the announcement of the names of those condemned to death in lists that were publicly displayed. The process was called proscription (*proscriptio*), from the verb *proscribere*, to publish in writing.

Ever since the time of the Gracchi barely a hundred years earlier, Rome had been shaken by internal unrest on a scale often resembling civil war, and there had been bloody street fighting and persecutions. The customary method of destroying internal enemies – physically as well as metaphorically – did not differ much from the usual practice among the Greeks or indeed later. There was indiscriminate violence, and the defenceless were massacred. Afterwards, any surviving opponents were eliminated by the due process of law, or what was presented as that process. Thousands had died in Rome over the previous ninety years. What the triumvirs intended was something different but not without precedent. Forty years earlier, at the end of the civil war of that time, when Lucius Cornelius Sulla restored the shattered structure of the state and had to safeguard it from enemies within, he had devised the idea of the physical elimination of any opposing factions; the legal or pseudo-legal basis for this first round of proscriptions was contained in Sulla's dictatorial edict. At that time nearly 5,000 people had perished within about two years, including 40 senators and 1,600 men of equestrian rank.

The triumvirs followed Sulla's example. They enacted an edict announcing and accounting for the removal of their opponents, arranging for the confiscation of their property and in addition promising rewards and anonymity to those who killed or accused the condemned men, but threatening with death any who hid them or helped them to escape. They published the edict along with lists of their victims. They were merciful enough to let the widows of executed men keep the dowries they had brought to the marriage, and sons could keep one-tenth and daughters one-twentieth of their fathers' property, although they did not always observe their own rules in this respect. Unlike Sulla, who as sole dictator had made all the decisions on who was to die, the three triumvirs had to agree on the names among themselves. Since they did not all have exactly the same enemies, and in certain circumstances some of one triumvir's enemies could be friends of one of the other two, negotiations were difficult, particularly when a triumvir was asked to agree to the death of a close friend or even a family member. At times there was a barter transaction in which the friends or relatives concerned were weighed up against each other. There were long bargaining sessions, but even in this grisly business the triumvirs were united.

A first list of seventeen names, including Cicero's, was immediately sent to Rome. Further lists were issued only after the three men had entered the city. Several of the first seventeen persons named were killed by agents sent ahead even before the list was officially published. If the Romans had previously just felt anxious about what was to come, terrible memories of Sulla's proscriptions were now aroused, and scenes that everyone had heard of came vividly to mind. Panic broke out, for no one knew whose turn would come next. Not only the hard core of 'republicans', but a number of Caesarians too had an uneasy conscience when they looked back on the events of the previous months, in which many had sought safety between the fronts. The consul Quintus Pedius obviously found the task given him by the triumvirs too much for him, particularly as he had heard nothing definite about their arrangements. All the same, he tried to calm anxious minds and, contrary to the intentions of the triumvirs, published the list of seventeen names as if they were the only men who were to die. Pedius did not have his cousin's strong nerves; he suffered a breakdown over the murders he had to supervise and died very suddenly the following year. That, of course, did not bring the coldly planned project to a halt; far from it, the massacre was now in full swing.

Rome and all Italy became a hunting-ground where victims were tracked down. Magistrates and private citizens alike were slaughtered. In the city itself, a tribune of the people and a praetor who had just held an assembly of the people were both killed. For these two and many others, death came entirely unexpectedly; those who brought notice of their doom carried out the executions at once. Once news of the murders spread there were terrible scenes. Most of the proscribed tried to escape, but few succeeded. Many resigned themselves to their fate, others defended themselves desperately. Very many of them were betrayed for the reward offered or out of a personal grudge. Not a few committed suicide, either fearing the cruelty of the executions or at least to protect their families by dying first. Many stories circulated about the heroic courage of relations, friends and slaves who, in spite of the death threats, had fled with the outlaws or hidden them, and there were as many stories again about the treachery, disloyalty and avarice of which not just friends and slaves but sometimes relations and even wives stood accused. Ties between friends and relatives were often loosened, but in other cases they were reinforced by readiness to help a man in need. The triumvirs and their soldiers seemed to be in a murderous frenzy; there was no end to the slaughter. The Romans were made equally anxious by uncertainty over who would escape in the end, for new lists were drawn up and old ones altered. When the bloodbath finally approached its end after the battle of Philippi, about 300 senators and 2,000 equestrians had been killed. The heads of those who had been captured in flight and murdered were sent to Rome as evidence of their execution, to adorn the speaker's rostrum in the Forum.

Proscription removed those of the old nobility who remained, if they had not fled east or, like the triumvirs themselves, joined the victorious army. Naturally Cicero was at the top of Antony's list, and Octavian, whom Cicero had built up into a political power, had to agree willy-nilly. Cicero's brother Quintus was also killed, along with his son of the same name. The son of Marcus Cicero, also called Marcus, was on the list as well, but escaped death because he was in the east with Brutus. Other names high on the list were those of the brother of the triumvir Lepidus, Lucius Aemilius Lepidus Paullus, and of Antony's uncle Lucius Julius Caesar, as well as Lucius Plautius Plancus, brother of the general Munatius Plancus and in office as praetor. The last two in particular were staunch republicans. Plautius Plancus was killed, the other two escaped: Paullus because the soldiers sent to arrest him refused to kill him, knowing of his close relationship to the triumvir, and Caesar because his sister Julia, Antony's mother, told the soldiers when they came that they would reach her brother only over her dead body. Saved by his sister's courage, the former consul, who had been in poor health for some time, later died a natural death. Cicero was thus the only consular to be murdered – not because of any clemency on the part of the triumvirs but because there were so few former consuls left.

No leniency was shown to Gaius Toranius, who had been aedile along with Octavian's birth father in the year 64 and after his death had been tutor to the boy, then four years old. He shared Cicero's political convictions and so, like Cicero, had been unable to support the dictator; after the Ides of March he had shown his sympathy for the assassins of Caesar. Perhaps Antony had wanted him on the list so that Octavian would have to sacrifice him. At any rate it was Antony who put Marcus

Terentius Varro, the foremost scholar of his time and now an old man, on the death list. As Pompey the Great's legate, Varro had surrendered to the dictator Caesar in Ulterior Spain and was not only pardoned by him but also shown great favour, and appointed to organize a great library that Caesar was planning. However, even in the dictator's lifetime Varro had earned the hostility of Antony, who had his eye on Varro's properties, particular the villa in Casinum (Cassino) on the Via Latina that he called his study (*deversorium studiorum*). Fortunately for Varro, he was protected by another Caesarian general, Quintus Fufius Calenus, and so escaped death. As Varro's proscription shows, the triumvirs were sometimes guided not just by personal enmity in choosing those they condemned to death but also by greed. That was undoubtedly the reason for putting Gaius Verres, the former governor of Sicily so successfully prosecuted by Cicero, on the list of the proscribed. He had lived in exile for twenty-six years and thus could hardly be the target of politically motivated revenge. He was to die for refusing to give Antony his valuable Corinthian vases.

The historians of antiquity, whether they were forced to do so or not, played down Octavian's share of responsibility for the proscriptions. In particular, they tried to absolve him of the murder of Cicero, his patron. It is said that Octavian protested against his condemnation and only gave way after three days. Later, touching tales were told about his veneration for the great orator and philosopher – among others, that he found one of his grandsons reading a Ciceronian text and did not punish him but only took the text, looked at it and gave it back, saying that Cicero had been a master of oratory and a patriot. His patronage of Cicero's rather insignificant son, who became consul with Octavian's backing, shows that he felt some guilt for his death. In the year 43, however, he will have had no choice and probably very few scruples in the matter. After all, he very well knew that, to Cicero, he had been only a tool in the struggle against Antony and after the victory over Antony had been discarded without another thought.

Cicero must have known what to expect after the failure of his political plans. When Octavian had marched into Rome he withdrew from the city, and we hear no more of him for three months, although he must have gone on writing to his friends, especially Atticus. Not exactly a hero at times of personal difficulty, he will have been in a bad mental state, and possibly his friends destroyed any letters written in these final months. He seems to have been suffering an inner crisis, as if paralysed. Instead of setting out for the east at once, while there was still time, he stayed on his estates. Only when news of the proscription came did he make haste to the coast from his villa, the Tusculanum, in the Alban Hills, where he had been staying with his brother Quintus. He went to Circei. However, he did not sail on from there, but took the land route north back towards Rome and then turned south again, finally reaching his estate at Formianum, where he met his fate. When a troop of soldiers was announced on 7 December, his servants tried to take Cicero to the safety of the sea in a litter, but the executioners reached him first. A tribune of war cut off his head and hands and sent that grisly evidence of the act to Rome, where they were displayed, with the remains of other victims, on the rostrum from which he had so often spoken.

Cicero was no war hero, and in times of personal crisis had been rather hesitant and timid; in elated mood after a success he showed excessive exuberance and was inclined to petty acts of revenge. Much criticism of his character and policies has been expressed by both his contemporaries and modern scholars, if not always as brusquely as Theodor Mommsen, who dismissed him out of hand as a 'statesman without insight, opinions or useful intentions'. Mommsen did not even respect Cicero as a writer, considering him merely a 'stylist'. One can see how Mommsen came to make this harsh judgement, but there can be no doubt that he was wrong. Cicero's vacillations were a result of the complete change in the political situation within Rome after Caesar's consulate in the year 59: since then the holders of great military commands had controlled policy, and, in so far as the leaders of the old nobility, among them Cicero, could hold their own at all beside their equals in rank who were armed with special powers, they were forced into a policy of manoeuvring and conciliation. At least theirs was a policy not ignoring the real opportunities of the time, while radical rejection of the new political factor in the shape of the great military potentates, itself undoubtedly the result of new conditions in the empire, drove the state to confrontation with Caesar and thus into civil war. The policies that the old nobility wanted to maintain were ideas unrelated to political reality, so that a man like Marcus Porcius Cato, praised to the skies by Mommsen and many other historians for his honour and courage, was something of a fantasist, or at least had no deep insight into the causes of events. Cato, Cicero once said, came to the Senate with propositions that sounded as if he were living in Plato's ideal republic and not the deep mire of Romulus (meaning everyday Roman politics), a remark that shows more political understanding than Cato ever had. In Rome as it now was, a policy of insisting on pure idealism was bound to lead to catastrophe. While despite his understanding of the political realities Cicero lacked the courage of a truly upright man, the superiority of a wise one and stamina in pursuing what he thought right, we must allow that in a very difficult position he offered himself as leader of a collapsing and indeed ruinous republic. Ambition and perhaps vanity may have induced him to accept the political leadership that he thought due to him, and that had been denied him by the proud old nobility, but what politician is free of ambition and a desire for lasting recognition? Seen in this light his death, unheroic as it was, becomes a kind of symbol, setting the seal on the extinction of the republic.

The proscribed men were supporters of Caesar's assassins and, like Cicero, supported the maintenance or restoration of the old *res publica*. Characteristic is the high number among them of equestrians, the social class who came second only to the senators in political esteem. They were wealthy merchants and tax collectors, closely involved in high politics; most of them lived in Rome or Campania or were leading figures in the Italian cities and among the hereditary clientele of many noble families. Cicero was not the only one to have called frequently on their support; so did Brutus and Cassius after the murder of Caesar.

All three triumvirs were responsible for the murders; they were burying the political past. It is true that outside the circle of those who did these monstrous deeds no one had any sympathy for them, let alone understanding, but it was at least possible to find an excuse or even an explanation for Antony's participation. During his consulate he had made no secret of his hostility to the murderers of Caesar and their sympathizers, even his hatred for them, and he himself had been outlawed for it. But Octavian, who had risen with the support of a Senate controlled by the anti-Caesarian party and could not claim to have done the state any service, could not expect to meet with anything but hatred, contempt or at the very least dislike after betraying men who had furthered his career. Of his own achievements, victory in the War of Mutina was hardly worth mentioning, for it was linked to the names of the consuls and Antony. Still less glorious was his march on Rome, which had been more of a brutal military occupation of the city accompanied by the violation of its venerable institutions. He was bound to feature as the man who first stepped on to the political stage by committing mass murder, his first noteworthy act so far: a man who killed out of cold calculation without a trace of humanity, in short a run-of-the mill terrorist.

None the less, all three powerful men were agreed on the implementation of their plan and merciless in carrying it out. Each of them was very careful that neither of the other two should win the favour of some person or group or even the public as a whole by showing leniency. The infamous aspect of their actions was the absence of any flaw in the implementation of their plan, the kind of flaw that marks, or can mark, the actions of a single dictator such as Sulla. In the present case nothing was overlooked: six eyes were watching all the time. Since the close attention of his colleagues prevented any one of them from showing leniency in any given case – or at least, his freedom of action was severely limited – the business of killing went on pitilessly and with mechanical precision. A proscribed man could be spared only if all three were indifferent to his fate. Rule by a single tyrant could not be worse than the furious frenzy of three at once.

Among many other honours awarded to the triumvirs at the time, they received as a special distinction the citizen's crown (*corona civica*), a wreath of oak leaves bestowed on a citizen who had saved another man's life in battle, placed on his head by the man he had rescued, the award being vouched for by his military commander. If the concept of life-saving were considerably extended, this high honour could be given to those who, like Cicero in the year 63, had preserved the state from an enemy within it. Many might now ask from what the triumvirs had saved the Romans. The assassins of Caesar, or the nobility who still believed in the old republic? Was the award perhaps merely shameless flattery on the part of the now cowed Senate? It is difficult to imagine that the triumvirs themselves felt they had saved the state, but we hear no hint of their declining the wreath. Those they had 'saved', on the other hand, might see the honour as derisive; perhaps they coped with it by regarding it as a joke, taking it as a celebration of the fact that even more people had not been killed.

Although the triumvirs had not told their soldiers anything about the proscriptions when the solemn proclamation was made, they could assume that there would be no protest against the elimination of their enemies, who as matters stood were the enemies of their troops too. They could certainly take the soldiers' approval for granted in another and no less cruel project, the expropriation of eighteen Italian towns. It seemed a necessary measure if they were to have enough land on which to settle the veterans. The great majority of this huge number of soldiers had no property of their own, and according to the custom of the time they expected their commanders to provide them with a farm that would keep their future family when they left the army. Many of the soldiers were not due for demobilization until after the murderers of Caesar had been overthrown and as they almost all came from Italy their preferred place of settlement was their homeland. There had been land problems with earlier settlements of veterans, and ruthless measures had sometimes been adopted then too. During Caesar's consulate in the year 59, he had settled the veterans of his ally Pompey in Campania, simply expelling the farmers who already lived in this fertile part of the country. As dictator, however, he spared Italy for the most part, resorting mainly to areas outside the country to provide for his soldiers.

The triumvirs had fewer scruples. To avoid dispossessions, they would have had to seek out free parcels of land and buy them up, a laborious process. It would also have been time-consuming, and even so they would have found only a little land, certainly nothing like as much as was needed. The practical measures they took made it much easier for them. They expelled the entire population of certain towns and distributed the land within their boundaries to their soldiers. In this operation they sought out places that had been more or less openly committed to the enemy, including such large and flourishing towns as Ariminum (Rimini), Cremona, Capua, Venusia, Beneventum and Rhegium (Reggio Calabria). While proscription had affected the upper classes, and the seizure of property had upset the inhabitants of large tracts of land, the farmers and domestic servants living on their estates did not always suffer. But the expulsions from those eighteen towns had literally turned at least a hundred thousand people out into the street. It is likely that only a minority could find shelter with friends or family; most roamed Italy with a life of hunger and poverty ahead of them. The sources say little about the wretched plight of these people; the common folk were not at the centre of historians' interest or even on its periphery. Only now and then do we get a faint idea of the general wretchedness, for instance when Virgil, in his *Eclogues*, written at the end of the forties, speaks of *misera Cremona*, the misery of Cremona, not far from his own home town of Mantua.

The proscriptions, as well as the formation of the triumvirate as a completely new form of rule, marked a decisive turning point in the political life of the Romans, signalling the end of an epoch, and appeared to the people of the time themselves a break with tradition. The unusual feature here, however, was that no one could recognize or even guess at the nature of the new regime. However, it was more than clear that the old order had ended. The Romans felt that they were living in sombre times, with an uncertain future ahead, and an aura of cold cruelty emanated from the trio, who, supported by an army of over forty legions, had trampled down the old world.

There was no wide-ranging discussion of the motive for the proscriptions, but it seemed obvious enough: elimination of the triumvirs' political opponents. If those opponents had won they would have acted in the same way. The edicts of outlawry passed by the Senate show that this was extremely likely, as did the remarks of Cicero, leader of the opposing party, who had always urged the killing of all three Antonian brothers. But was it merely an escalation of hatred that had led to murder? One is inclined to suggest a further motive: the systematic annihilation of the old leadership class. Such an assumption, however, may well go too far, for apart from the fact that the three men in power themselves belonged to the oldest families of Rome, the traditional elite had shrunk a good deal even before the proscriptions, which merely further thinned out what little remained of it. It is significant that there was only one former consul among the proscribed, and he was Cicero. More probably, we should assume that the acquisition of land and money was a motive, or at least one among others. For, as it was to turn out during the preparation for the war against the assassins of Caesar, the triumvirs were short of ready cash, which was not only inconvenient but extremely dangerous to them. They had to supply the army on which their power depended with money and property. About 250,000 soldiers had to be fed, paid, given gifts and provided with plots of land.

The triumvirate thus meant military rule by three men, both over Italy as the territory inhabited by Roman citizens and over the provinces. Of the three triumvirs, however, only two had real power – that is to say, military power. They merely tolerated the third. Why did Antony and Octavian take a third man into their power cartel at all? When his army was commandeered, Lepidus, who had been an intimate friend of the dictator, became dependent on Antony. It must therefore have been Antony, to whom Lepidus was closer than to Octavian, who included him in the college of three, and the reason should be obvious: together with Lepidus, he created a power superior to Octavian's, for Lepidus strengthened the Caesarian, that is to say those who had served and become great men under Caesar – unlike a man who was not strictly speaking a Caesarians at all and, as Antony and Lepidus saw it, had made his way into their ranks only through his family relationship to the dictator. Octavian was indeed the weakest of the three triumvirs, a fact that became evident when the west was divided up between them. Since the islands he received were occupied or at least threatened by Sextus Pompey, he did not even have a force at home; even Lepidus had done better out of the deal. Octavian had no territory to fall back on, only his legions, and he now went east with them. His sole if considerable success was that he was one of the cartel of military despots, and for that he could thank not his now powerful army but the threat represented by the Caesarians in the east. There was no denying that at this time, in spite of all he had achieved, Octavian's situation was precarious. For him, everything depended on how he did in the campaign against the murderers of Caesar.

The fact that there were three men in power had one unintended but very useful side effect: it drew a veil over the difference between the two main competitors. Antony and Octavian were rivals in the struggle for Caesar's inheritance, and when we consider the nature of their power bases their rivalry was bound to be a life-and-death struggle. There is no lasting bond between military despots, and as a result the annihilation of the power-sharers was programmed into the arrangement from the first. Lepidus himself was probably well aware that his was a subsidiary role, but he had to gain a high profile as a triumvir, and no doubt the considerable provincial area he now had under him added to his new sense of self-worth. As the third man in the alliance he had more consequence, a fact that promised the relationship between Antony and Octavian a certain amount of stability. If he went, the opposition between them was bound to show more clearly.

What had once been the state, the *res publica*, was now reduced to sheer military might. Once Rome had been a state ruled by law and custom, and over the centuries an order had grown up that was moulded and led by a large number of distinguished families. The nobility had already been weakened in the long decades of internal crisis, then the dictator Caesar had placed it in a situation of crisis, and now the triumvirs' proscriptions concluded the process. The old families had ceased to exist, at least as a group, and with them went the network of connections that they had made with other important members of society, in particular the equestrians and the leading men in the Italian towns. With their fall, the system set up by the nobility for the group exercise of their power was broken too: the rules of public law no longer meant anything. They were still there, because even rule by force needs a formal structure in order to consolidate itself. But that structure could be changed at any time, depending on circumstances, and was entirely subject to the will of the men who held power, as the triumvirs made very clear to the general public. Holders of office were appointed and dismissed, their number and their areas of competence altered, just as the three wished. Their will alone was the real law.

History has not seen many instances of purely military rule; even when generals have seized ruling power they are usually kept within bounds, guided or even led by traditional forces, whether elites or a civil service. The triumvirate, on the other hand, set itself up after the traditional forms of political co-existence had been eliminated, and those parts of society that had made up those forms were reduced to no more than the regulating of a military way of life. The ruins from which they rose no longer even showed what they had once been.

Preparations for hostilities against Brutus and Cassius began even in the last month of the year 43. There was no need, of course, to recruit and form legions; they were ready for battle. Supplying provisions for the army was more difficult; above all, money to pay and equip the soldiers was scarce. Profits from the sale of confiscated estates were not enough, and the flow of taxes was sparse. For the Romans paid no direct taxes, and those that came in from several of the western provinces were irregular because of the activities of Sextus Pompey. In so far as any payments were made, little was left after the deduction of expenses for those troops left in the provinces and Italy. A cash flow in Italy could be expected only from tolls and a few other lucrative indirect taxes. There was no income from the rich eastern provinces; the enemy was getting the benefit of them instead. In the past, the authorities in Italy used to resort to an extraordinary tax, the *tributum*, at times of crisis. They did so now. An income tax was levied on the more prosperous Romans, as well as a two per cent property tax on a credit basis. Imaginative ideas for new taxes were thought up. The taxation of rich women attracted much attention; presumably these women were mainly widows no longer subject to a man, a father or husband and thus, in Roman terminology, 'emancipated'. Protests from the most influential of these ladies did not lead to abolition of the tax, but to a drop in the numbers of those due to pay it.

The war could begin. As it would take Caesar's assassins time to arm themselves, there was no need to fear an invasion of Italy. The military situation was not unlike that of the winter of 49/48. At that time, after putting down resistance in Italy and Spain, Caesar had marched east, where Pompey and his republican friends had retreated to arm for battle against the dictator. The combatant based in the west, in that earlier case Caesar, had the stronger and above all better-trained army, and like the triumvirs now he faced an enemy who was expecting invasion from the west. And now, once again, the first problem was to get the troops across the straits of Brundisium to Dyrrhachium or the other harbours of the west coast of Greece, without maritime supremacy in the Adriatic and Ionian Seas.

From August 44 to the autumn of 42, Brutus and Cassius had time to establish a footing in the east and build up an army. It was an enormous and almost impossible task for them, given that they had first travelled east as propraetors to administer two minor provinces. The fact that they did it shows that they were energetic politicians, careful administrators, and good leaders of their troops. But other qualities were required too: a tough approach to challenges, and when necessary ruthlessness and brutality. They proved that they did not shrink even from extreme measures, and once again Cassius was the more energetic of the two.

A ruler of the eastern empire could rely on the more prosperous part of the Mediterranean area for support. In economic terms, there was a clear difference between east and west. The seven eastern provinces comprised the richest countries of the time. Macedonia, from which the rest of Greece was administered, was the most strategically important but certainly not the strongest area economically. More prosperous was the province of Asia in western Asia Minor, and in addition Cilicia, with the present Plain of Adana at its heart, to which Cyprus also belonged along with large parts of south-west Asia Minor roughly as far as the river Meander (Menderes). Considerable income flowed into Rome from the province of Bithynia and Pontus on the coast of the Black Sea, and even more significantly from Syria. Large tracts of the interior of Asia Minor, particularly Cappadocia and Galatia as well as Syria, were ruled by local princes who were none the less dependent on Rome, and in case of war had to supply troops and money. Only Egypt had remained independent; the one surviving major Hellenistic state was still firmly in the hands of Cleopatra, and in view of her earlier relationship with the dictator, who she claimed was the father of her son – although the paternity of the boy, born in 47, was disputed even in antiquity – she favoured the Caesarians. Obviously her aim, with the aid of Caesar's alleged son, whom she had proclaimed Ptolemy XV Caesar (he was generally known as Caesarion, 'little Caesar') in the year 44, making him co-regent with her, was to assert her independence of the Romans, and she had already clearly emphasized her preference by establishing links with Dolabella. For decades Cyrenaica, west of Egypt, which had been set up by an Egyptian secondary line, and the island of Crete – probably not united with Cyrenaica yet – had also been Roman provinces. They were in the sphere of influence of Caesar's murderers.

The sole importance to Brutus and Cassius of the Greek-speaking east at this point was to serve them in forming a large army as fast as possible. The purely utilitarian attitude of the Romans to the regions they ruled was nothing new to the local inhabitants. The provinces had hardly ever enjoyed the attention of the Roman administration, whose officials usually followed only the interests of the Roman state – as well, of course, as their own – and there were few governors who found any room for the welfare of the provincials in their administrative plans. But despite the sometimes systematic plundering of the towns and cities by governors, tax collectors and Roman merchants, most of them had managed to maintain a certain degree of prosperity.

For the last few decades, however, the entire east of the empire had also been plagued by many wars. First Mithradates, king of Pontus, had

THE FALL OF THE OLD ORDER

attacked Asia Minor. Then Sulla and subsequently Lucullus and Pompey had marched through Asia Minor and Syria with their armies to drive Mithradates out again. The civil war fought by Caesar and Pompey followed, and with it a redoubling of misery, for the sides fighting the war demanded their dues ruthlessly, rigorously punishing anyone who failed to pay up in whole or in part, or who actually backed the wrong side. Pompey had begun by seizing everything he could lay hands on, and he was followed by Caesar, who similarly expected his men to live off the country. After Caesar, Trebonius and Dolabella appeared, and once Trebonius was removed Cassius marched against Dolabella. Every change of master was accompanied by expropriations and the punishment of towns or the client princes that had supported the other side. You had to know the situation very well to guess who would emerge victorious. Hardly a town, a tribe or a kingdom went unscathed; many had been pillaged repeatedly.

Brutus and Cassius were no better than their predecessors, if anything worse because they were in a hurry and could neither tolerate opposition nor allow any payments to be delayed. For instance, Caesar had levied a very high tax on Laodicea and Tarsos for supporting Dolabella. The same thing happened to the unfortunate island of Rhodes after it had been besieged and taken; the city had to hand over all the precious metals in it, including all the temple treasures, not excepting the chariot of the sun god Helios, the patron of Rhodes, regarded as the masterpiece of its maker Lycippus. Although Xanthos in Lycia defended itself tenaciously, it suffered even worse and was laid waste. Patara in Lycia, which gave in, got off with a monetary fine. The princes who were vassals of Rome were treated in the same way; anyone who did not obey the Romans was severely punished. Deiotarus, the powerful ruler of the Galatians, who had supported Pompey against Caesar, joined Brutus. On the other hand, King Ariobarzanes of Cappadocia, another of Pompey's party, paid for his refusal to follow Cassius with his life. All the cities and princes of the east also had to pay taxes at an extortionate rate. There was no escape; a city could not even complain that it had been unjustly treated, for every official who came making demands did so as the rightful representative of the Roman state, calling for help in its time of greatest need. It was useless for a city to suggest applying to the Senate for adjudication in disputes about money and allegiance; the answer was that tyrants sat in the Senate, and the rightful authority was now in the east. And if an official from the other party came a little later, demanding the same sum or, in view of the city's previous support of the enemy, even more, he too represented Rome as well as Roman rule and Roman order.

For Brutus and Cassius, everything depended on how many soldiers and warships they could get together. Cassius had contrived to take over the dictator's legions in Syria, as well as acquiring the four that had gone to Syria from Egypt. With Dolabella's two legions, which he took over after the latter's death, that made twelve legions in all – troops of intact units, a vital point, made up of battle-hardened legionaries. The Parthian expeditionary force assembled by the dictator in Macedonia had been largely withdrawn to Italy by Antony. In Brutus' legions, some of which had to be reconstituted, there were thus many inexperienced soldiers, including Romans who were temporarily in the east or had lived there for a long time, along with local men who were simply pressed into service and drilled in Roman warfare. The cavalry was in better condition, and the naval forces were better still. Brutus had built up a considerable fleet and had a capable admiral in Lucius Staius Murcus, who despite his former loyalty to the dictator had joined Cassius in Syria. When the armies of the two commanders united at Sardes in the summer of 42, they amounted to a considerable fighting force. They were led across the Hellespont for a parade in Sardes, because by now the triumvirs' armies had crossed the Ionian Sea and were stationed in Macedonia.

Brutus and Cassius represented the republic, and the leading group was the nobility. In the west all leaders who did not obey the triumvirs had fallen victim to proscription. Any of the old upper class who still supported the republic were in the army of Brutus and Cassius, unless they had sought refuge with Sextus Pompey. Recruits to the republican army were mainly young noblemen who had not yet held any office because of their youth and had stayed on in the east partly for purposes of study. Among them was the son of Marcus Cicero, who bore the same name as his father, as well as Lucius Calpurnius Piso, son of the consul of 58, and Publius Cornelius Lentulus Spinther and Marcus Valerius Messalla Corvinus, sons of the consuls of 57 and 61 respectively. Spinther had been Trebonius' quaestor, and at the time was about thirty years old; the others were considerably younger. Gnaeus Domitius Ahenobarbus, son of the consul of 54 and a relative of Brutus on the maternal side, was just over thirty, and so was Lucius Licinius Lucullus, son of the famous consul of 74 and commander in the second war with Mithradates. Marcus Favonius, a stern republican who venerated Cato Uticensis, had held office as a praetor. But impressive as this list may be, the nobility was mainly represented by young men who had not yet begun on the official course of honour at all, nor could they have done so, because of the unfavourable political circumstances. Besides the proconsuls Brutus and Cassius themselves, only Favonius had held office. Not a single nobleman of consular rank was to be found in the army. So who, if they won a victory, was expected to fill the offices of the magistracy in Rome, as well as the many governorships and other provincial posts? Men of lower rank, who joined the proconsuls in large numbers, could not step into the gap, enthusiastic as many were in wishing to fight for the good cause. Among the young Romans who joined the fighting, incidentally, was Horace, the son of a freedman from Venusia.

The triumvirs were also contending with considerable difficulties as they prepared for armed confrontation. They had to take over the government in Italy, solve their supply problems, and before setting off for the east they must try to weaken Sextus Pompey at least enough to prevent him from keeping Sicilian grain away from Rome and Italy and hindering their crossing to Greece. This last task was given to Octavian, who entrusted the military operations to his friend of their student days, Quintus Salvidienus Rufus from Apollonia, who immediately proved himself a capable and courageous commander and successfully repelled an attack on Rhegium. Although he then failed to win a naval battle, he retreated without losing face and without suffering casualties worth mentioning.

Further activities in southern Italy were prevented by a call for aid from Antony, who could reach the high seas from Brundisium only at great risk because of the strong naval forces of his opponents. Staius Murcus, who had gone over to Cassius, thwarted all his attempts to leave harbour for the open sea. Octavian and his fleet at last gave Antony a breathing space, and the great expeditionary force successfully crossed to Dyrrhachium. But Murcus brought reinforcements to Gnaeus Domitius Ahenobarbus, the second-ranking admiral of the republican party, and when their united fleet had grown to some 130 warships supplies for the army that had crossed from Italy were almost completely cut off. A large part of an auxiliary fleet from Cleopatra, who had already supported Dolabella and was now expected to extricate the triumvirs from their difficulties, was destroyed in a storm. Again, the situation was not unlike the position in which Caesar had found himself on his way east in 49/48, when, largely cut off from Italy by enemy ships and short of supplies, he finally had to march to Thessaly and try to give battle. In the year 42 the Caesarians were not completely cut off from Italy, but the blockade was so effective that Antony and Octavian, like Caesar before them, could get out of their awkward situation only by fighting. Some time later, and on the very day when the first battle against the assassins of Caesar was fought, Staius Murcus even managed to intercept a squadron of enemy troop transports, escorted by warships and under the command of Gnaeus Domitius Calvinus, bringing two full legions, a bodyguard and many cavalrymen to reinforce the main army. Most of it was destroyed in probably the greatest catastrophe to befall a convoy since the First Punic War. The famous Martian Legion was also on board the transport vessels. Most of its men died on the ships or drowned in the sea.

On arriving in Macedonia, Antony immediately made haste east along the Via Egnatia. A strong advance party of about half the entire army had already reached the Nestos, crossed the river and occupied the coastal passes. The triumvirs brought twenty-one or twenty-two legions into action in all, as well as cavalry and auxiliaries. Nineteen of those legions were present at the first battle against Brutus and Cassius. Octavian had fallen ill from the stress of the campaign soon after it began. He stayed behind in Dyrrhachium and could only hope to rejoin his army in time for the deciding battle.

In expectation of the enemy army, Brutus and Cassius had massed their troops in western Asia Minor. When news came that the enemy had landed on the west coast of Greece and was in Macedonia, they had set off westward with seventeen of their total of twenty-three legions, a strong cavalry force and many auxiliary troops and, after crossing the Hellespont, had finally reached the passes on the north coast of the Aegean that were already occupied by their opponents. Under Lucius Tillius Cimber, himself one of the assassins and now governor of Bithynia and Pontus, the fleet followed the army along the coast. Deceiving the enemy, the main force made a detour around the passes over the mountainous land to the north and reached Philippi, a city founded by

King Philip II of Macedonia, father of Alexander the Great, and named after him. Antony's advance guard thereupon withdrew to Amphipolis. Brutus and Cassius let it. Well aware that their enemies were in considerable difficulties over getting supplies, they wanted to avoid them for the time being and erected fortifications at Philippi, behind which they felt safe from enemy attacks and which could also prevent the enemy from marching on.

Philippi lay on a southern spur of the mountain range bordering the plain to the north. This rocky spur was closed off about three kilometres further south by almost impassable marshland, and south of that again mountainous terrain rose to about 500 metres. The line of fortifications erected by Brutus and Cassius reached across the entire land area between Philippi and the marshes, barring the way east. It could not be skirted either from the north, where the heights rose to 700 metres and were densely wooded, or, so it was thought, from the south by going around the marshes. As the land also fell away west of the fortified line, a further problem was that any attacker would have to approach an enemy well established behind fortifications on rising ground.

Two permanent camps were set up behind the barricade, with Brutus to the north and Cassius to the south. The camps were on each side of the Via Egnatia, the great Macedonian army road leading south over the plain from Philippi. From this secure position, they could feel easy as the enemy approached. Supplies could be quickly and easily obtained from the island of Thasos and the harbour of Neapolis opposite it; small rivers and the forest north of Philippi provided the army in the immediate vicinity with plenty of water, and timber for use both as fuel and in erecting fortifications.

When Antony finally arrived with the rest of the triumvirs' troops, there was nothing he could do but camp on the open plain opposite the barricade. He set up a single camp for the entire army. Supplies were his main problem, for, apart from the fact that he had none or only very few coming up behind, there was a shortage of anything useful on the ground. There was hardly any timber and little water where the army was encamped; the soldiers had to dig wells and search the marshes for wood that could be used as fuel and building material. Octavian appeared just in time for the beginning of the battle. However, he still felt too weak to lead his legions on horseback, so he had himself carried to the lines in a litter.

Two formidable massed armies faced each other; measured by the number of combatants, the coming battle was to be the greatest yet known in the Old World. The legions of Brutus and Cassius confronted the nineteen legions under the triumvirs. But only Antony and Octavian's legions were at full battle strength, and in addition only they consisted mainly of experienced soldiers, whereas less than half of the legionaries led by Brutus and Cassius, but including in particular the Caesarian legions that had gone over to Cassius in Syria, could be called really battle-hardened men. The assassins of Caesar were clearly superior in cavalry, which the Romans usually formed from contingents provided by their allies, and in allied infantry. The Caesarians had over 100,000 legionaries and about 13,000 cavalry, while their opponents had about 80,000 legionaries and just under 20,000 cavalry, and in addition a considerable number of allied infantry. In all, there were well over 200,000 soldiers present. Everyone knew the importance of the battle, and many divine signs (*omina*, omens) and oracular sayings were reported or perhaps invented in retrospect, foretelling what was to come, more particularly victory or defeat. There was talk of strange apparitions in the sky, nocturnal sounds and lights, the birth of monstrosities, even rivers drying up. It was said that the statue of Jupiter on the Alban Mount had sweated blood, and a boy carrying a statuette of Victory had fallen to the ground during a ritual parade in Cassius' camp.

Antony was bent on fighting. His position on the plain, which was untenable in the long term, and the increasingly pressing problem of supplies left him no other option. It was also near the end of October, and winter was coming. Rain fell, softening the ground even beyond the marshes, and cold weather would give the army more problems because of the need for more fuel. Antony faced Cassius on the right wing, Octavian faced Brutus. As the more experienced general and strategist, Antony had in effect taken supreme command. Since the rampart of fortifications could be breached from in front only at the price of heavy casualties, and even then without very much chance of success, Antony wanted to make a detour around the enemy. That was impossible to the north, near Philippi on its high-lying site. So he tried to reach the enemy's southern flank with his wing of the army over the marshy area. He secretly had a dam built, and after crossing the marshes south of the enemy lines occupied as much firm ground as possible. When Cassius

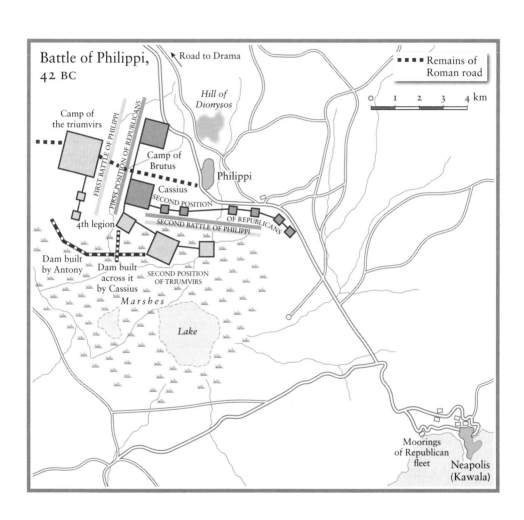

Battle of Philippi,
42 BC

↗ Road to Drama

Remains of
Roman road

0   1   2   3   4 km

*Hill of
Dionysos*

Camp of
the triumvirs

FIRST BATTLE OF PHILIPPI

FIRST POSITION OF REPUBLICANS

Camp of
Brutus

*Philippi*

Cassius

SECOND POSITION

OF REPUBLICANS

SECOND BATTLE OF PHILIPPI

4th legion

Dam built
by Antony

Dam built
across it
by Cassius

SECOND POSITION
OF TRIUMVIRS

*Marshes*

*Lake*

Moorings
of Republican
fleet

Neapolis
(Kawala)

finally understood his manoeuvre it was too late, but he still tried to halt or cut off those of Antony's men who had made their way into the marshes by building a dam running the other way. The first battle developed from these operations.

Antony saw that the only way of improving his army's difficult position was to make a bold advance with his main fighting force across the dam and into Cassius' south flank. There was bitter hand-to-hand fighting. Losses on Antony's side were high, but he managed to reach Cassius' camp. At the same time, to take the pressure off Cassius, Brutus ordered his legions to storm the enemy's left wing, commanded by Octavian, and he succeeded in throwing the enemy forces back and taking the camp shared by Antony and Octavian. Octavian would certainly have died there if he had not been in the soldiers' lines in his litter. An expert in exploiting such situations for ulterior purposes, he claimed in his memoirs that a dream of his doctor had warned him. In fact he was missing for some time after the battle and was even assumed to be dead; several of Brutus' soldiers claimed to have killed him. Later it would be said that he had hidden in the marshes and reappeared only three days later. Unlikely as that sounds, we can draw two conclusions from this story: first that the real leadership of the troops under Octavian was not in his hands, but in those of experienced legates, so he was not actually needed; second, that he was not especially popular in the army, and perhaps was even hated or despised in some quarters. As a general, Antony was the criterion against whom all others were assessed. Whatever the truth of the matter, Octavian did not win renown that day; the defeat of the wing under his command was clear to everyone. But although the camp was taken, and Octavian's legions had suffered heavy losses, the entire left wing was not destroyed; he had managed to come through after a fashion. However, the enemy's very success entailed a severe loss, for because of the impetuous advance of the right wing under Brutus, communications with Cassius seemed to have been broken. After the storming of his camp Cassius for one assumed that the battle was lost, obviously because he no longer had an overall view, and he ordered one of his men to kill him. With him the more gifted of the two republican commanders died.

After Antony's success and the defeat of Cassius, the military situation stabilized to much what it had been before the battle. But Antony took advantage of Cassius' defeat by leading the main body of his army south around the enemy, thus surrounding his opponents from west and south. Although this manoeuvre put Brutus in danger, he refused to engage in open conflict on the battlefield. He knew the advantage of his good fortifications and the fact that his supply routes were being kept open for him by his fleet. In contrast, the supply problems in Antony and Octavian's army would soon reach a critical point: the soldiers were suffering from hunger and increasingly cold temperatures. But Brutus also had to deal with his men's discontent, and, even worse, with criticism of his hesitant conduct of the war from his officers; they thought they had a good chance of victory against an exhausted opponent. In addition the breathing space caused the leaders of some of the auxiliaries to defect. Amyntas, commanding the troops of Deiotarus, king of the Galatians, changed sides, and Rhescuporis, a Thracian prince whose brother was fighting for the triumvirs, set off for home. Brutus did not have Cassius' decisive temperament and finally gave way to his officers. The fear that his men, particularly those who were Caesarian veterans, might go over to the enemy could have influenced his decision. Our classical source for the history of the battle, Appian, himself made this suggestion.

In the middle of November, then, twenty days after the first battle, fighting broke out again. After a bloodbath, the left wing commanded by Octavian drove the triumvirs' enemies as far back as their own camp. At this point Octavian had the gates of the enemy camp occupied and closed. Brutus' soldiers were thus unable to retreat. They fled in increasing disorder past the camp to the northern heights of the surrounding country. Brutus himself escaped uphill with several soldiers to a fortified position, but at this time he still did not think of surrendering; he hoped to withdraw to his camp. Next day, however, when his officers refused to return to the camp, he gave up and, like Cassius, had himself killed by a loyal follower. Fourteen thousand legionaries immediately surrendered to Antony and Octavian, and so did the fleet stationed at Thasos. Its commanders, Marcus Valerius Messalla Corvinus and Lucius Calpurnius Bibulus, asked and received pardon from Antony and entered his service. Many republican survivors of the battle were picked up by the fleet under Staius Murcus and Domitius Ahenobarbus, who as yet did not intend to surrender; others, like the legions pressed into service in Macedonia, dispersed to their homes. The battle left many thousands dead and even more wounded, many of them scarred for life. As it had been a battle between citizens of Rome, the dead and wounded on both sides were Romans. The losses of the two sides were equally balanced, with about 40,000 dead alone.

When Octavian took the body of Brutus, he had the head cut off and sent to Rome, so that it could be laid at the feet of the statue of Caesar. However, the ship that was to take it there encountered a storm, in which this grisly item of loot went overboard. The mutilation of the mortal remains of Octavian's defeated enemy was probably intended to compensate for his obvious lack of experience, achievement and military talent by emphasizing that he was Caesar's son, and so he – not Antony – was closer to the dictator who had been venerated by all his soldiers. The sources of classical antiquity speak not just of the desecration of the corpse of Brutus but of other instances of Octavian's cruelty to captured opponents; it is hard to explain them all, let alone justify them, as compensation of this kind. Antony, on the other hand, showed magnanimity and gained sympathy among many soldiers as well as republican supporters in Italy from the contrast with his colleague. He had what was left of Brutus' body burned, and the ashes sent to his mother Servilia.

With Brutus a number of supporters of the old order also died, by their own hand or in battle. They included the son of Cato Uticensis, who bore the same name as his father, as well as Pacuvius Antistius Labeo, one of the assassins of Caesar and father of the great lawyer Marcus Antistius Labeo. Marcus Livius Drusus, adoptive son of the famous tribune of the people in the year 91 and the father of Livia, later to be Octavian's wife, took his own life in his tent after the battle, and so did Sextus Quinctilius Varus, a quaestor in the year 49 and father of the commander and consul who perished in the battle of the Teutoburg Forest in the year AD 9. We hear no more of Lucius Tillius Cimber, who had belonged to the circle of the conspirators and whom we last met commanding the fleet of Brutus and Cassius, and similarly no more is heard of Publius Servilius Casca, who had fought in Brutus' army. They will both have died in the battle. We may assume the same of Quintus Ligarius, whom Cicero had defended before the dictator in the year 46. To the long list of the dead from the nobility of the Senate were added the names of the murderers of Caesar and their sympathizers who fell into the hands of the triumvirs as prisoners and were executed, including Marcus Favonius and Quintus Hortensius, son of the famous orator and a former proconsul of Macedonia, who had joined Brutus and handed the province over to him. Antony had him executed beside the grave of his own brother, Gaius Antonius, whom Hortensius had had killed on the orders of Brutus in revenge for the killing of Decimus Brutus. The blood-letting among the members of the old noble families was extensive.

Philippi seems to stand for the end of an epoch, and many historians have indeed seen it in that light. Even in antiquity, people would say that such and such an event marked the end of something and a new beginning. The historian Cassius Dio, writing in the reign of the Emperor Severus over 250 years later and certainly quoting older sources, thought that at Philippi the monarchical system had taken over from freedom and democracy, as he described the aristocratic order of the republic. He presents Brutus as the incarnation of the republic, and it is clear, from the watchword of 'Liberty' that he gave his soldiers before the battle, that Brutus indeed saw himself in that light. But he could no longer symbolize the republic, because it no longer existed at the time of Philippi, nor had the triumvirs destroyed it in that conflict. The battle does not, therefore, mark a real turning point, any more than the triumvirs' earlier proscriptions did; even the outbreak of the civil war in the year 49 was a turning point only to a very limited degree. It would be very difficult for anyone to pin down the end of the republic as a political system to a definite point in time, for its end coincided with the disappearance of the ruling class of the nobility, which had controlled the republic and its formal structure, and the nobility did not vanish overnight. But it certainly no longer existed at the time of the battle of Philippi, and even the proscriptions destroyed only remnants of it.

The republic as a working political structure, however, presupposes the nobility as a numerically strong group of active politicians qualified by sheer numbers to control those of its own rank who held office. Without a balanced relationship between the nobles in charge and those in office, the old ship of state could not be steered. Perhaps we can say with some reason that there was still a noble class of society capable of functioning before the civil war broke out in 49. But even here reservations must be made, for the disintegration of the nobility took place over a long period. At least it can be said with certainty just when its full ability to function no longer existed. The process began with the unrest accompanying the death in 133 BC of Tiberius Sempronius Gracchus, tribune of the people. Political wrangling led to terrible bloodshed that year, and the following years of crisis added to both disunity and the bloodletting of the nobility that was linked to it. It is very doubtful whether Caesar faced an elite still able to function in the year 49. When so many nobles had died in the civil war, and others had taken service under the dictator and were thus lost to the old order of society, it is reasonable to doubt whether the conspirators against Caesar and their sympathizers would have been able to run the state at all. There can certainly be no question of it after the proscriptions and the renewed outbreak of civil war.

The political aims of Brutus and Cassius must therefore remain a mystery. Who could have run the state in the traditional way after a victory over the Caesarians in which yet more men of the old ruling class had been eliminated? The children of the noblemen who had fallen in battle, or had been executed or died? They were still in their minority or only just grown men. Or was it thought that a new elite could be produced out of thin air? That would have been to think along the same lines as the Caesarians, who were constantly recruiting new men and putting them in positions of leadership. But this new elite did not care about the old order that the assassins of Caesar had wanted to maintain. Who was to apply the thousands of rules whereby the state had been governed for centuries if there was hardly anyone left who had learned them from childhood? Any revival of the old traditions of the state was bound to fail because the regulations of political conduct had been largely forgotten, or were remembered only by a few. Which of the nobles would have been left after a victory over Octavian and Antony? Who apart from Brutus and Cassius, who themselves had not even held consular rank? And how would the two of them, as victors in Rome, have got the machinery of state working again? As dictators, or as lawgivers above the law creating a new society by decree? They were fighting, it seems, for nothing but an idea. But do leaders fight battles and cause so many deaths for such a reason? In the east, at the latest, the pointlessness of their struggle must have dawned on them. However, they continued on their course. Were they fighting simply for their lives? They took the answer to the grave with them.

So Brutus, Cassius and their political friends were really left only with the purity of their wishes and their boldness of action in relation to the ideal of maintaining the old state, with the opportunities it offered the nobles for political development, and it is true that no one extolled the 'republic' as the wellspring of freedom and praised its defence as a fight against servitude more eloquently than Brutus. He was certainly sincere when he acknowledged his part in tyrannicide on the Ides of March and gave assurances that his political reputation (*dignitas*) and liberty itself (*libertas*) were worth more to him than his life. Brutus and Cassius appear more as the defenders of a good constitution, for which they gave their lives, than as noblemen lamenting the past and merely wanting to avenge themselves on those who had destroyed its tradition. Modern historians and those of antiquity alike have been very ready to endow them with an aura of nobility and the love of freedom and have been more generous to Brutus than to Cassius. Consequently the latter appears to us to have been more of a realist than the former. But such a view of the situation has mainly come about because Brutus wanted only Caesar to be killed on the Ides of March, thus realizing the idea of tyrannicide in its pure form, while Cassius had also wished to eliminate those who stood closest to the dictator. We also see Cassius as a military commander who had proved his abilities as quaestor after the catastrophe of Carrhae.

Thanks to his literary talent and philosophical education, Brutus is sometimes seen by posterity in a rather improbable light, as the symbol of virtue, and one historian of antiquity puts the words of Heracles in his mouth before his death, to the effect that he had acted virtuously, but virtue had proved to be merely a name that served Chance. The fact that he was firmly anchored in the aristocratic world, including its darker aspects, is evident, among other things, in his financial activities: he lent money at 48 per cent interest, an excessive rate even then, in pursuit of his private efforts to get armed forces from a provincial governor. He was neither a dreamer nor an ineffectual idealist and he showed a realistic grasp of politics. He knew better than Cicero that it would be useless to make common cause with Caesar's son and would have preferred Antony to Octavian as an ally in Italy. He could sum up the political values of his time more trenchantly than most and hold them up to the hated enemy, his equals in rank striving for supreme military power. He even recognized the danger that came from the ranks of the nobility themselves. But his preference for Antony rather than Octavian shows a weakness that he shared with Cicero, and indeed with many, perhaps most, of the nobility. He still believed in the principle of an aristocratic society capable of functioning. How else could he have considered Antony as a possible ally? In his mind, the network of relationships within the leadership group, with its political friendships, hostilities and coalitions, was still valid, and there was no place in it for any link with soldiers and the military tradition. He had not seriously understood the changes in the political world of the Romans, seeing them merely as distortions of reality that must be removed. The murder of the tyrant, however, had not set the Roman world to rights.

As military commander in the east, Brutus had coins struck bearing his head on the front, with the inscription 'Brutus imperator', and on the reverse a picture of a freedman's cap (*pileus*), the symbol of personal and political freedom, lying between two daggers, as well as the words 'Eidibus Martiis' ('To the Ides of March'). The message was clear to one and all: on the Ides of March, Marcus Brutus had killed the tyrant for the sake of freedom. Coins bearing the portrait of his ancestor Lucius Junius Brutus, traditionally regarded as one of the two first consuls of the republic and the man who drove out the last tyrannical king, Tarquinius Superbus, were also intended as symbols of the freedom for which Marcus Brutus was fighting. But the more significant series of coins, departing from the Roman tradition, is the one showing the head of Marcus Brutus himself, for the portrait of a living man did not belong on the Roman coinage; it was the sign of rule. The dictator Caesar – the tyrant, as Brutus saw him – had been the first to break with that principle. The coins that Brutus had struck in the east were intended not for the provincials, who would have seen nothing unusual in the portrait of a living man on them – it was normal practice for their former kings; rather, as the Latin inscription shows, they were for Romans, in particular the soldiers whose wages were paid with this currency. No one else could have made Brutus put his portrait on the coins; it was the work of his nobleman's pride and his wish to assert his claims. Cassius, minting coins at the same time, put no such portrait on them. The coins struck by Brutus show the ambivalence of a situation in which a nobleman was fighting for the republic against the usurpers but in the course of the struggle appeared a usurper himself.

It is easier to understand the political aim of the triumvirs. They were Caesar's successors and for their own safety they had to do away with those who had murdered Caesar. They, therefore, were the new military potentates. But their point of departure was not the same as that of the man they claimed to be following. For Caesar had begun his military career within the network of relationships of the old society when on the whole it was still functioning. His military rule of the Roman state was a result of the civil war and, as he saw it, had been forced upon him. The triumvirs did not have the same background; they began their political careers already holding military power – as generals or, in Octavian's case, as Caesar's adopted son. They were fighting, with their soldiers, for something that, whatever they themselves or their successors called it, was in point of fact a military despotism. Their purpose, therefore, was nothing but to maintain their power; their actions presupposed the sweeping militarization of politics. So they were not revolutionaries, as has sometimes been claimed. What would they have been revolting against? A naked power struggle is not a revolution. They cannot even be described as the men who buried the republic, for that would be to assume that there was still some of it left to be buried at Philippi.

Consideration of the political aim of the triumvirs immediately brings up the question of how the political future looked after their victory over the old state system. The answer is both simple and shocking. No new state was set up, nor did they have any new state in view. The result of Philippi was to establish unconcealed military rule. The triumvirate and the traditional offices and legal rules of the old state that still existed were merely disguises. In so far as the concept of a 'state' is linked to the idea of order resting on consensus by the citizens of that state, there was no Roman state any more.

# 5

# Rome under the Despotism of the Generals

Caesar's generals had won, exacting bloody vengeance on his and their enemies. Just as the Roman world had belonged to Caesar before the Ides of March, it now belonged to the generals as his political heirs. The triumvirs made that clear on 1 January of the year 42, when they themselves swore, and had all other holders of office swear, that they would not tamper with the dictator's measures (*acta Caesaris*). The oath was to be renewed annually. At the same time a decree of the Senate and people of Rome elevated Caesar to divine status; as Divus Julius he was to be honoured with a cult in Rome and all the other towns and cities of Italy. His deified figure was to have a temple on the east side of the Forum, at the place where his body had been burned, and those who fled to it could find asylum there. It was not completed and dedicated until the year 29; for the time being a column bearing the inscription 'To the Father of the Fatherland' (*parenti patriae*) marked the spot as sacred. The temple to Mars Ultor, 'Mars the Avenger', which before the war against Caesar's assassins Octavian had vowed to build if he overcame them, was finished only forty years after the battle of Philippi. As a monument to the revenge that had been taken, its purpose was also to underline the legitimacy of Octavian's political role.

The spirit of Caesar seemed to have revived again in the generals, as if he once again controlled the destiny of the world. But it was now a very different world from the one that Caesar had left. In the last years of his life he had been determined to establish his power within the structure of formal government and had already made tentative moves in that direction, but his plans never came to fruition. However, it could be seen from his fragmentary measures that he did not want to break entirely with tradition or exclude the society associated with that tradition wholly from the state system. Caesar was still too firmly rooted in the world of the nobility to want to burn all his bridges with the past. Matters were different now. The nobility no longer existed as an exclusive group, and its shattered remains could not resist the new spirit of the times; whether they were on the side of the triumvirs or of Sextus Pompey, the nobles had become either impotent spectators or participants in military rule. The world was now under the control of generals and generals alone. They might call themselves officers of state and use the old state system to support them, but public law held good only so far as they tolerated it.

The new masters were faced with the task of creating order out of Italy and the provinces of the empire once more, full as they now were of fear, misery and unrest. To do that they first had to decide among themselves on their responsibilities, above all their local areas of competence. While they were still in the east Antony and Octavian agreed to redivide the empire, and the new areas of power reflected the changes that had taken place since the previous year. Lepidus was almost excluded, and for a while the other two may even have contemplated leaving him out of account entirely. In any case, it was provisionally agreed that Octavian should hold the two African provinces for which Lepidus had previously been responsible. But Lepidus was not knuckling under of his own accord, and Octavian and Antony shrank from turning the triumvirate into a duumvirate (rule by two men), particularly because such a change could probably be made only by force, and they might risk alienating the soldiers, so in the end Lepidus held North Africa without Cyrene. As one of the victors of Philippi, Octavian could make sure that he now had a better position in the triumvirate. He waived the islands – there was not in fact much he could have done with them anyway – and instead the two parts of Spain, taken from Lepidus, fell to his share. He chalked up a particular success by ensuring that Cisalpine Gaul, in effect Upper Italy, was now merged with Italy in line with a plan of the dictator. The geographical area of the country where Rome stood was now the same as that of modern Italy without the islands. In the rearrangement Antony lost this important province, which dominated Italy, but instead he received Gallia Narbonensis, which Lepidus also had to give up. Taken together with the Celtic lands conquered by Caesar, Gallia Comata, which had already been under his control since the previous year, Antony now ruled the largest and most important provincial area in the west. Of all three triumvirs, he had the strongest position.

Antony's status as the first man of the empire showed not only in the distribution of the triumvirs' areas of power in the western provinces but also in the division of tasks between them. Lepidus received nothing at all here, which was indicative of his role as a bit-part player in the triumvirate. Octavian had the difficult and indeed dangerous job of supervising the settlement in Italy, as planned the previous year, of those soldiers who wanted to leave the army at the end of the war, sometimes after many years of service, and expected to be appropriately provided for. Antony was to raise the necessary financial means in the east. The entire east itself, certainly the more prosperous part of the empire, was excluded from the redistribution of their spheres of influence among the men in power, but in effect it was Antony's through his mission to raise money there.

These agreements, like all the others between Antony and Octavian, were written down again just like the previous Bononia agreements and sealed before witnesses; they thus took the form of a contract, but the nature of the contract was very different from the one that they and Lepidus had concluded in Bononia. At that time they had been generals, and as such were formally under the command of the central government of the state, namely the Senate and the principal magistrates in Rome. The Bononia agreement had thus had only the character of a private arrangement (*coitio*), of the kind that had often been made by the nobility to achieve political aims, for instance the one between Pompey, Caesar and Crassus in the year 60. The contract after Philippi, by way of contrast, made it clear that they were triumvirs, that is to say formally the ultimate authority in Rome. Despite its origin in the world of aristocratic communication, the agreement was thus valid in Roman law, and the partition of the empire set out in it was legally binding on all Romans.

The contract yet again emphasizes Antony's domination of the triumvirate. But it would be wrong to assess the balance of power between the men who now ruled Rome, or their political intentions, solely by what the ultimate outcome was. Antony was no more master of the east than Octavian was master of the west and the representative of Roman Italy. The two of them had again agreed that Italy was their joint possession, and they meant that to be taken seriously. The Roman homeland as a recruiting ground was an essential part of Antony's powerful position in the triumvirate. As for his political plans, they did not aim exclusively at the east, and certainly not at setting up separate rule there. With Octavian, he had established himself as a military despot just a year before, and both he and his colleagues in the triumvirate naturally had to adjust their aims to the political experience they now had behind them – all the more so because, in the vacuum left after the disappearance of the leading social class and the form of state that it had governed, there was no sign of a new order to give them guidelines.

Octavian, who controlled both parts of Spain but of course stayed on in Italy, was bound to see himself as successor to Pompey the Great, who had administered Spain from Rome in the years 55 to 49, just as Octavian did now. And Antony, already in possession in the west of Gallia Comata, the Celtic lands conquered by Caesar, had acquired Gallia Narbonensis as well and thus had the extraordinary command he wanted as successor to Caesar. He must have seen it as a base for his political future. Both men had considerable powers of command in the west, controlling as they did groups of provinces with strong armies. With his powers in the east, Antony had a second great command, and as things stood he would be following in the great dictator's footsteps here too. For in the east, although not in Gaul, he had a definite military mission: he was going to lead his army into action against the Parthians, a campaign enabling him to wage a war that he could be said to have inherited from the dictator. As a result Antony was not just the strongest member of the triumvirate but also the man entrusted with the future defence of the empire – its military arm – a situation that suited him perfectly, for, unlike his two colleagues, he was an experienced general.

By comparison Octavian had no particular military task in the division of future duties between the triumvirs. His was the job of winding up the campaign now concluded by settling the soldiers on their plots of land. It must have been clear to him when the agreements were made that this would be a difficult business, more likely to win him enemies and even hatred than renown. Not only did he know about the problems of acquiring land, he was also aware that in Italy he had to act in full view of his rivals, for the place was teeming with Antony's legions and generals. Octavian was not alone in Italy. Perhaps he imagined that in settling the soldiers he would come closer to them, even gain authority among them, and he may have had in mind the example of Sulla, who a generation earlier had provided land for an army of about the same size after the civil war. The veterans settled by Sulla had then supported him in power. Octavian did not lag behind Sulla in the ruthlessness required for such a task. But one thing had changed fundamentally since Sulla's time, and it was the factor that was sure to make difficulties for Octavian: the soldiers were no longer clients gratefully accepting the gift of their commander, but had risen to become political partners.

The distribution of tasks that year, therefore, should not be understood as a long-term division of the empire between the two triumvirs, or a final establishment of responsibilities, particularly as the east was not assigned to anyone as a province: the only thing that had been defined there was the mission to be accomplished. For all three triumvirs, Italy was still the political centre, however they might act, and later events show that Antony's followers expected their patron to be back.

The number of demobilized soldiers who must have plots of land provided for them was large. The civil war had raged from the first days of 49 to the battle of Philippi, a full eight years, and at times there had been forty to fifty legions on the move in Italy and the provinces – not to mention the troops of cavalry and contingents of allied forces who had no long-term claim on Rome to provide for them. Many of the men who had fought with Caesar in Gaul had been in arms since 59/58. Mass demobilization had been impossible in the civil war, and many of those who had been granted a plot of land in the interim by the dictator or by Antony, in Italy or the provinces, had been called up again. Since Rome had no official standing army yet, now that the enemy was conquered and peace reigned, except in a few trouble spots in the empire, most of the soldiers would have had to return to civilian life. The fact that they did not was only to a limited extent because scattered remnants of the enemy still held out in various parts of the empire; Sextus Pompey in particular, a general still independent of the triumvirs, had not given up and had even gained ground. Nor did Antony's punitive operations in the east against cities and dependent princes who had supported the enemy affect the situation much. Small military units of the kind available to every governor at the time would have sufficed for that purpose. The real reason for the necessity of continuing to keep large bodies of men under arms was the rivalry between the generals; it made the presence of armed force essential even if the empire had been entirely at peace. Nothing shows more clearly that the structure of the state had changed entirely since the civil war broke out in the year 49. The fact might have been obscured by the presence of a strong enemy during the period of armed warfare, but with the advent of peace it was more clear: a standing army had become a constituent part of the state. Not all contemporaries might yet be aware of it, and the imminent necessity of dealing with such tasks as putting the east in order or confronting Sextus Pompey helped to blur the changes. But ultimately they could not be ignored, and then it would be necessary to face the question of how to treat a standing army and keep it occupied in peacetime.

Antony and Octavian had agreed that between them they would keep on eleven legions and 14,000 cavalry: men from their own armies who had fought in the battle of Philippi and other Roman soldiers who had come over to them. Antony had six legions and 10,000 cavalry, Octavian the remaining five legions and 4,000 cavalry. In addition, Octavian was to let Antony have two of his legions and in return receive replacements from Antony's units stationed in Italy. Then they set about the missions on which they had decided. Octavian went to Italy to settle the veterans and oppose Sextus Pompey; Antony went to the east to raise the capital necessary for the settlements and sort out the confusion caused by the civil war in the provinces and the kingdoms dependent on Rome.

At the beginning of the year 41 the Roman world still echoed to the marching footsteps of countless soldiers; never before had so many Romans been under arms at the same time. Besides Antony and Octavian's eleven legions with their 55,000 men, and the 14,000 cavalry, we must add the soldiers due to be demobilized, 50,000 to 60,000 of them, who were on their way to Italy or already there and waiting to be settled on their land. In addition, when the triumvirs had set out to confront the assassins of Caesar, they had left twenty-four legions, including the three legions under Lepidus, behind in the west; these amounted to well over 100,000 men. There were also large bands of troops under Sextus Pompey, who was still operating in the western part of the empire, and the many remnants of the defeated 'republican' army, including soldiers and sailors from the fleets commanded by various admirals, particularly Lucius Staius Murcus, Gnaeus Domitius Ahenobarbus – a nephew of Cato Uticensis and one of those proscribed by the triumvirs – as well as Gaius Cassius of Parma, one of Caesar's assassins. These commanders had gathered their remaining men together and joined Sextus Pompey. Thus even after the heavy losses suffered in the battle of Philippi there were well over 250,000 Romans in arms, perhaps as many as 300,000. The great majority would continue to be soldiers, but even the 50,000 or 60,000 men whom Octavian had to settle threatened to be a huge burden on Italy, where they wanted to live.

On the crossing back to Italy Octavian fell sick and he lay so seriously ill in Brundisium that news of his death was rather prematurely announced in Rome. He faced his hardest test so far, since everything he did and must do in Italy in the immediate future would arouse hostility. Octavian could rely on understanding from hardly anyone: the Romans saw him as a bloodthirsty executioner, and he had no outstanding military achievement to his credit to compensate for this negative image. All the soldiers knew that Antony was the real victor of Philippi, and through them so did the rest of the Romans.

At the time of Octavian's arrival in Brundisium, Italy was full of unrest such as the country had hardly ever known before – and it had seen much trouble in preceding centuries. It tore the entire population apart. Thousands upon thousands of small property owners were dispossessed, and thousands of large estates changed hands or were parcelled out. From the Alps to the southern tip of the peninsula, misery and want prevailed. Hundreds of thousands of people were on the roads in search of somewhere to stay, camping as best they could in the towns, or if they were lucky finding accommodation with friends and relations. Insecurity reigned everywhere; the outlook was gloomy. Even those who were not driven from their homes had good reason to fear for them, since at that time there was no guarantee of property rights unless you happened to be on the side of the victorious soldiers. In addition there were widespread food shortages because Sextus Pompey and his new recruits, men from the defeated army of Caesar's assassins who had taken refuge with him, blockaded the Italian harbours and intercepted ships at sea. The search for food and the hope of charitable donations drove many to the towns and cities.

The unusual mobility of the population typical of these years was not just the result of violent expulsions or the people's sheer fear for their lives. Many of the soldiers who had been settled by the dictator Caesar and later by Antony, well over 100,000 of them, had left the property allotted to them, lured by the new prospects on offer, and quite a large number of them did not yet have adult heirs to tend their land while they were gone. Many reasons had led them to give up the homes they had looked forward so much to owning when they were first recruited, and during long years of fighting and marching. After years of military service, many of the new settlers must have been unused to the existence of a farmer and indeed civilian life in general and would have found it difficult to settle into a new role, others had fallen for the exaggerated promises of recruiting officers. It is no coincidence that within a few months or even weeks a general, or a man like Octavian who made himself out a general, could assemble a large army consisting of veterans who left the land where they had been settled, their sons and unsuspecting young men who were entirely unfamiliar with the military life. That was what Octavian and Mark Antony had done in the years 44/43, particularly in Campania. Ventidius Bassus and Pansa had done the same in Picenum and central Italy respectively, and soon Lucius Antonius would do so too in the year 41. The long list of newly recruited legions at that time speaks for itself.

The Italy that Octavian entered was not under his sole authority; it was the joint possession of the triumvirs, and large bands of Mark Antony's men were stationed both there and in Upper Italy, which had not yet been cleared of troops despite its unification with Italy on the decision of the triumvirs. Lucius Antonius, the youngest of the three brothers, commanded six of the Antonian legions, and another eighteen were commanded by his brother Mark Antony's generals in Upper Italy, eleven under Calenus, seven under Asinius Pollio. In contrast, Octavian had only ten legions at his disposal in Italy, and six of those had gone to Spain, the region assigned to Octavian's authority, under the command of Salvidienus. His already difficult position was not improved by the fact that the two consuls were not among his supporters. One was Lucius Antonius, the other Isauricus, who had wavered between Antony and the Senate party in the year 43 but after the cancellation of his daughter's betrothal to Octavian could not be considered friendly. As a triumvir, Octavian stood above the entire hierarchy of office-holders and thus above the consuls, but he had to take account of Lucius' brother, his colleague Mark Antony. The third in the triumvirate, Lepidus, stayed in Italy with his three legions; he did support Octavian at first, but he was indecisive and unreliable.

The year 41 began with a triumph arranged in Rome by the consul

Lucius Antonius, celebrating victory over the Alpine tribes. It was an unprecedented degradation of that ceremony, since no one could say exactly when and where any Alpine tribes had been defeated, but obviously military operations of some kind carried out in the aftermath of the War of Mutina served as a pretext.

The planned settlement of the veterans led to severe complications that were to plague Italy that year and the next. No unoccupied land was available. The basis for the allocation of plots must therefore be on the one hand the estates of proscribed men, although the intention had been to sell them and use the proceeds to defray the expenses of the settlements, and on the other hand the land of the towns and cities marked out for expropriation. Octavian received a flood of petitions, pleas for clemency and demands, and naturally the representatives of the towns and cities due to lose their land made it their main argument that the burden should be equably distributed between all the Italian communities. At first Octavian tried taking a conciliatory line, granting many requests, and even before the campaign against Brutus and Cassius he had exempted from the expropriation process Rhegium and Vibo, two coastal towns of importance in the campaign against Sextus Pompey at sea. But his measures were thwarted by agitation on the part of the consul Lucius Antonius, and Mark Antony's wife Fulvia, who had stayed behind in Italy, associated herself with him. Her purpose was obviously less to put obstacles in the way of the settlements – after all, Mark Antony's soldiers were to receive land too – than to force Octavian out of the political game as far as possible. However, her motives are not always clear, all the more so because the historians of antiquity, some of them particularly well disposed to Lucius Antonius, others simply hostile to Fulvia, drew a veil over them.

Antony was certainly not aware of the intrigues against Octavian from the first and later he prudently kept out of the dispute as far as he could for some time. On the one hand, he did not wish to strengthen Octavian's position against his brother; on the other, it made no sense for him to sabotage the settlement of the soldiers. And he could not tolerate having his supreme power as a triumvir weakened by magistrates subordinate to him. He remained inactive, presumably because he was happy to see Octavian in difficulties and did not want to involve his own supporters in Italy. Consequently he gave no outright answer when

Octavian asked him to intervene as a colleague in the triumvirate. His brother and his wife went on appealing to him, but in their eagerness to broaden their political base they very soon found themselves politically offside. As consul, Lucius Antonius began presenting himself to the Senate and the people as a lawful power, thus slighting the triumvirate and enhancing the status of the old political order that had just been destroyed. The word 'liberty' circulated again; it had last been heard as the battle-cry of the men around Brutus and Cassius. Attempting to manipulate public opinion with political slogans of the past shows little sense of reality, but it is not clear how seriously we should take the consul's political intentions. The citizens of municipalities, many of them notable men, thought in traditional terms and were undoubtedly more loyal to the old order than the soldiers who were now free from all constraints. We see evidence of that at the time when the civil war broke out again, as it soon did, and the inhabitants of the town of Nursia in Umbria, besieged by Octavian and handed over to him, wrote on the funeral stelae of their fallen citizens that they had died for liberty. Octavian inflicted harsh punishment for this. If Lucius Antonius' praise of the old order was directed chiefly at Octavian, he was also attacking his brother, which was certain to upset Mark Antony.

In their attempts to rouse public opinion against Octavian, Lucius Antonius and Fulvia finally took sides with the dispossessed, holding out the prospect of hope to the farmers driven from their land who asked them for protection and denouncing Octavian as the representative of a ruthless policy of expropriation. To avoid alienating the soldiers demanding land and money, they did not dispute their claims but backed the idea of postponing the settlements until Mark Antony arrived in Italy. The agreements between the triumvirs had stipulated that he was to gather the requisite funds in the east. On finding that the soldiers did not accept their reasoning, they tried to safeguard themselves by claiming that there was enough property available from the estates of proscribed men for land to be distributed at once. By saying that it was for Antony's officers and not Octavian to settle the soldiers, they also tried to sow discord among the veterans.

On this last point, the question of the veterans, Octavian gave way, and also showed himself ready to make further concessions to dispossessed landowners. For instance, he excluded from the amount of land for distribution all landed property of a size less than the area to be allotted to a single soldier, as well as senators' estates and women's dowries. But he could not satisfy both sides, and as the man responsible for the settlements he soon brought the wrath of the soldiers down on his head. To mollify them, he returned all plots of land or refrained from distributing them if they belonged to soldiers who had fallen in battle, or veterans settled by the dictator Caesar. But that was to be taken for granted anyway. And still the considerable number of exceptions forced him to expropriate land not previously marked out for distribution. To avoid settling the soldiers in too many different districts, he turned mainly to land in the vicinity of the towns and cities that had had their property confiscated. The poet Virgil lost his estate at Mantua because it was close to Cremona. Octavian, whose past did not make him popular with the people as a whole anyway, was soon the most hated man in Italy. To the widespread indignation was added the famine suffered by Italy because Sextus Pompey in the Tyrrhenian Sea and Domitius Ahenobarbus in the Ionian Sea were cutting off all supplies.

The quarrel escalated. In his anger at the actions of the Antonians, Octavian had already divorced his wife Clodia, Fulvia's daughter by her first marriage to Publius Clodius Pulcher. He had married her after the conference at Bononia as a pledge of his loyalty to the future triumvirate, for reasons of state or alternatively, since there was no longer any state, out of a clear vision of the logic of maintaining power. Now, when he sent Clodia back to her mother with a declaration made on oath that the marriage had not been consummated, since she was not of marriageable age at the time, this entirely uncalled-for remark was bound to give the impression that he wanted to rid himself of an unwelcome encumbrance. And when Octavian's six legions, on their way to Spain, found obstacles on their route through Upper Italy and Gaul, where large bands of Mark Antony's men were stationed, and in addition Octavian did not receive the two legions intended for him by the triumvirs' agreement, it looked as if a new civil war was about to break out, this time on the home ground of the Romans themselves. At this point Lucius Antonius and Fulvia went to Praeneste (Palestrina), a secure place because of its geographical position, as if they needed special protection.

The confrontation between the supporters of Antony and Octavian particularly concerned the soldiers, and they showed the rulers yet again that they had become a political power in themselves. Their ability to assert themselves grew with the discord between the generals, for the old public and legal order still held good only in those areas where the new masters would allow it; in any dispute, chaos threatened. It was the rank and file of the soldiers who had the greatest interest in preventing trouble, since their future material welfare depended on peace within the army. Again, the belief that all Roman soldiers, or at least the legionaries, formed a single unit was more current among them than among the generals, who were driven to confrontation by personal ambition and rivalry. The soldiers, on the other hand, saw each other first and foremost as comrades and so could easily change fronts. The sense of unity among them was such that they even had to overcome an internal barrier when they had to follow *their* general into battle against comrades. They could feel an attachment to their general, formed by long years of campaigning with him, as well as proven military achievements and a willingness to engage with them on his part, but as a rule the soldiers could be persuaded to fight against their own comrades only if disobedience would endanger their material aspirations. Every soldier thought himself an independent man, and this feeling was reinforced by the awareness that most of them had not been called up because they were on the lists of those fit for military service but had joined the army as volunteers.

In his dispute with Lucius Antonius and Fulvia, Octavian was soon made aware of the independence and even audacity of his soldiers, who feared for their future in the general confusion, reacting with hostility to every concession to the farmers and the leading townsmen. Typical of their edgy mood was the way they could sometimes react angrily to reprimands from their commanding officers. At a theatrical performance, when for lack of space a soldier simply sat down on one of the benches reserved for men of equestrian rank, and Octavian ordered him to vacate the seat again, the man's comrades ganged up together and threatened him. If they could take the liberty of quarrelling with their general in the manner of a tavern brawl, then it was possible that they might put their feelings into action some time. Such a situation occurred at an assembly of soldiers summoned by Octavian on the Field of Mars in Rome for the purposes of land distribution. Several soldiers expressed loud indignation when he was slightly late, and when a centurion gave them a dressing-down they were so angry that after a violent exchange of words they killed the officer and left his corpse lying where Octavian was bound to see it as he passed. This kind of thing was unheard of. Only a few years earlier, far less serious infringements of military discipline would have led to the instant execution of the culprits. And such cases of insubordination were not rare. But even beyond such incidents, every general, and in particular Lucius Antonius and Octavian, sensed the increase in the soldiers' independence. Their greater scope for action loosened the old, strict rules of the military life, and the duty of obedience above all suffered. A warning sign was the mutiny of Octavian's soldiers in Placentia, which was settled not by commands or punishment on the part of the generals; instead, the soldiers ended it themselves by extorting from the townsfolk the money that was the reason for the mutiny and dividing it up between them. The military leadership knew what to expect if the sums promised to the legions did not materialize.

At this period the soldiers and officers did not just play an indirect part in decisions taken by the generals, say by occasional acts of indiscipline, but above all through direct demands with a concrete outcome in view. These incidents were regularly caused by rifts between the commanders which soldiers and officers from the various camps felt it was their business to settle. The first immediate intervention in the decisions of the military leadership was in the dispute over the closing of the Alpine passes, which prevented Octavian's legions from marching into his Spanish area of command. The controversy had become more acute as a result of Mark Antony's refusal to find Octavian a substitute for the two legions he had handed over to Antony. The soldiers wanted reconciliation and arranged a meeting of the generals at Teanum in Campania at which other disputed points were also to be settled, including the question of the relationship between the triumvirs and the consuls, and the problem of how to limit the number of soldiers with a justified claim to a settlement. It was agreed that only those who had fought at the battle of Philippi should be given land, and the others would receive monetary compensation. Here the policy of the triumvirs was actually decided for them, and their legal freedom of action was restricted, as it also was in the question of their conduct towards the consuls. Even though he consented, Octavian did not stick to these agreements. At least he had managed to get the Alpine passes opened again.

A little later, when armed confrontation seemed imminent, the veterans of two of Antony's legions settled in the Ancona area felt it was incumbent on them to bring about a reconciliation. They insisted forcefully that Octavian and Lucius Antonius should submit to an arbitration tribunal. First, after having the earlier agreements between the triumvirs laid before them in Rome, they confirmed them; then they put their own resolutions to disputed points down in writing; and finally they decided on Gabii in Latium as the place for negotiations. They even had rostrums for the speakers of both parties erected in a hall in the town. In itself, the outer framework of these events made it clear that the soldiers and officers regarded their arbitration as legal, but in showing the audacity to confirm the triumvirs' treaty they had already set themselves above their rulers. However, the military tribunal never sat. Lucius Antonius stayed away on the pretext that he feared an assassination attempt and even after he was assured of safe conduct he would not change his mind. Much against his own interests, as it was to turn out, he felt free to be offhand towards the soldiers. With derision, he called the arbitration tribunal at Gabii a 'Senate in soldiers' boots' (*senatus caligatus*), a cogent description of a committee which, in line with the spirit of the times, made a mockery of all civil and military tradition. So the Gabii meeting ended with the soldiers condemning Lucius Antonius and Fulvia. The two of them were accused of breaking the law. What law, however, had they broken, the one passed by the triumvirs or another passed by the soldiers?

Octavian grew more cautious. As the victorious general of Philippi that he made himself out to be, he knew that ultimately his place was with the soldiers. He soon began supporting their demands more emphatically, great as the misery of the Italian population might be. He thus gradually gained ground, which was particularly important when matters came to a head in an armed confrontation. After the failure of the first attempt at reconciliation in Teanum, supporters of the consul Lucius Antonius and Fulvia had followed them to Praeneste. In Rome, Octavian was backed by Lepidus at this time, but Lepidus was still a very unreliable ally; he wavered between camps as the mood took him. When Lucius finally boycotted the reconciliation tribunal arranged at Gabii by the veterans, which among other matters was to try to settle the allocation of land, a storm began brewing. But Octavian presented himself as a friend to peace and turned to the senators with a request for further negotiations. It bore no fruit, and the bridges were burned.

For Octavian, whose benevolent attitude to the soldiers at the time of the attempted negotiations had bound others besides his own men more closely to him, this had been a good start, and he needed one, because where the military balance of power was concerned his situation was far from good. He had only ten legions, six of which, under the command of the friend of his youth Quintus Salvidienus Rufus, had not yet left Upper Italy to march to Spain, and they were now immediately called back, while the others were stationed in Campania. Lucius Antonius, on the other hand, could rely not only on his own six legions but on another eleven of his brother's still stationed in Italy, and in addition, as he thought, on the contingents under his brother's generals in Antony's provincial area in the west. There were also thirteen legions commanded by Gaius Asinius Pollio, who on Mark Antony's behalf was in charge of land settlements on the other side of the river Po (Transpadana), by Publius Ventidius Bassus in Transalpine Gaul and by other subsidiary commanders. As a result, the troops of the Antonians vastly outnumbered those supporting Octavian but they had no unified leadership. As consul, Lucius Antonius commanded only his own six legions, and the other leaders of the Antonian soldiers acted as proconsuls and proxies for Mark Antony, still away in the east. Octavian was also under pressure in the south from Sextus Pompey's admiral, Domitius Ahenobarbus, who was laying siege to Brundisium, and in his Spanish provinces from a general of Antony's who was threatening the Pyrenean peninsula from Africa. But that counted for little in a war which depended on the legions available in Italy.

From time to time as many as forty legions were involved in the civil war now breaking out. They might not all be at full fighting strength, but the total number of combatants, including cavalry, lightly armed units and the soldiers with the fleets still came to 200,000 men, and with few exceptions they were all Romans. The inhabitants of the Italian peninsula, already hard pressed by proscriptions, dispossession and famine, now had to endure the further hardship of seeing their country become a theatre of war.

The war was waged in central Italy, and was called the Perusian War (*bellum Perusinum*) after its final act, the siege of Perusia (Perugia). Octavian began it by surrounding two towns in the Sabine country and in Umbria, although he was unable to capture them. At about the same time Lucius Antonius occupied Rome and inaugurated a form of government that must have looked to the Romans like a revival of the republic. He bluntly declared the triumvirate a tyranny and claimed that his brother Mark Antony was about to resign his office of triumvir and content himself with the consulate. He announced that the other two triumvirs would be indicted for their despotic rule by the Senate, which was willing to go along with him. The people were intoxicated by all this, thinking they detected behind the words not just the imminent relief of their desperate situation but also the return of their old importance. Had it not been for the war, one might have thought a political farce in the manner of Cola di Rienzo was being acted out. Consequently the Antonians in Italy took no notice of Lucius Antonius. He had been foolish enough to alienate not just the triumvirs but also the soldiers, whose material welfare depended on the agreements of the triumvirate.

The commanders were deeply personal in their conduct of hostilities, indulging in savage abuse, slanders and even vicious tirades. All the same, apart from the misery that the war brought to Italy, it is notable that, for all the acrimony and hatred, military operations were not pursued to the bitter end and as a result they effected no far-reaching political changes. Individual operations sometimes dragged on for a long time, and because of the large number of generals it was difficult to form a clear view of what was going on, as was obvious even in the opening phase.

Lucius Antonius and his troops had marched north to block the way south to Salvidienus, who was advancing with his six legions, and take him in a pincer movement with the help of his brother's generals as they pursued Salvidienus from Upper Italy. But being commanders of Antony's armies in the north, the generals were not accountable to the consul Lucius Antonius, only to his brother, the triumvir Mark Antony, and they did not want to be involved in destroying another triumvir without explicit orders from their supreme commander – who was far away, keeping a low profile whenever news did reach him. In addition the situation of the Antonian generals in the west meant that they did not form a single unit, for they had been appointed governors and generals in various areas by Mark Antony himself and they all commanded legions that were in part bound to them personally. Finally, discord between them was promoted by the fact that the individual generals had very different temperaments. All this meant that nothing came of the attempt to surround Salvidienus. Octavian – or more precisely his

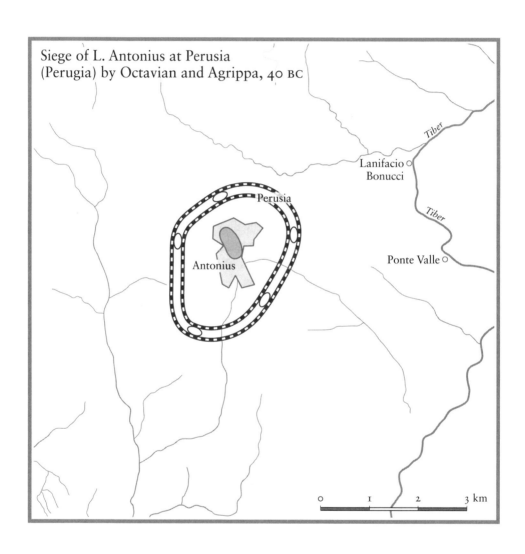

Siege of L. Antonius at Perusia
(Perugia) by Octavian and Agrippa, 40 BC

Tiber

Lanifacio
Bonucci

Tiber

Perusia

Ponte Valle

Antonius

0    1    2    3 km

second-in-command Agrippa – now stepped in, coming from the south to wedge Lucius Antonius between himself and Salvidienus. Agrippa occupied Sutrium in south Etruria, thereby cutting off Lucius Antonius' retreat. Pressed hard from north and south at the same time, and before Agrippa could carry out any further operations, Lucius Antonius went to the safety of Perusia, which lay several hundred metres above the Tiber valley and was easy to defend. Octavian and his generals Agrippa and Salvidienus immediately moved in and took up their position outside the city with all their troops.

The fighting for Perusia was the climax of the war, and at the same time one of the most remarkable sieges in Roman history. Here was an instance of a Roman army besieged in a Roman city by another Roman army. And the grim determination with which both sides fought marks the conduct of the war out distinctly from the usually intensive efforts of the soldiers to stick together. Although it might have been expected that a siege at such close quarters would make reconciliation by negotiation easier, the opposite occurred. Competition between the soldiers certainly played a part. In the course of warfare which had already lasted eight years – in the case of those who had fought in Caesar's Gallic campaign as long as eighteen years – many legions had won renown, and some had even become military institutions of a kind. As a result, an *esprit de corps* had formed among the men of the individual units concerned and could now be seen, by the wider soldiery, manifested in the rivalry between the generals, who encouraged the relentless bitterness of the confrontation. They all gave vent to their mutual fury outside Perusia. We know this from the graffiti on slingshots found near the city, which bear not only the names of individual commanders but also crude abuse: mockery of Lucius Antonius for his bald head is certainly the most harmless of such quips. The leaders could not control themselves either; a lampoon by Octavian has come down to us, and Fulvia delivered inflammatory tirades to the soldiers with a sword slung around her.

Octavian cast defences covering a good ten kilometres around the city: a ditch, a rampart and a line of palisades, later to be reinforced by a wall acting as a parapet and 1,500 wooden towers. These fortifications were further secured by another defensive structure going all the way down to the Tiber. Lucius Antonius countered with similar defensive works. There was fierce fighting for parts of this defensive ring for months, and of course those besieged inside were always trying to break out. Soon those of Mark Antony's generals who had been summoned to help arrived, Ventidius Bassus and Asinius Pollio from the north, Plancus from the south, and once again the siege resembled the situation that Caesar had known as the attacker at Alesia, and Mark Antony as the besieged party in Mutina. As the main army of the Antonians advanced from the north to within 30 kilometres of Perusia – their fiery signals could be seen from inside the city – Octavian used his inner defensive line to hold off the attackers. Soon the famine in the city was barely tolerable – the 'Perusian famine', *Perusina fames*, became a standard phrase – and the will of the besieged to break through the ring of their besiegers grew in proportion.

However, the outcome of the war was decided by the hesitancy of the relieving armies; they advanced no further, which was not entirely due to the ability of Octavian's generals, Agrippa in particular, but also the outcome of differences of opinion between Mark Antony's generals. Clearly they shrank from the crucial step, which called for determination to destroy Octavian completely; faced with the question of how far to go, the very different natures of the commanders came to light. Gaius Asinius Pollio, a highly gifted, well-read man, with clear powers of judgement and an independent mind in the political sphere, could not stand Munatius Plancus, who had no backbone and who in his own turn despised Ventidius Bassus as a former muleteer. Asinius Pollio was inclined to like Mark Antony as the most straightforward and capable of the Caesarians, and although he had venerated the dictator Caesar, showing the courage to praise him at a time when the Senate seemed to have the upper hand, he kept his distance from Octavian, in particular for his part in the proscriptions. He himself did not feel at ease with the intrigues between the generals into which he had been drawn and he later retired. But he knew that the republic, which he would have preferred to any military despot, even the dictator, had ended, and somehow he must come to terms with the present situation.

The outcome of the struggle became clear when the besieged soldiers, tormented by hunger, began going over to the other side in large numbers. Lucius Antonius had to surrender at the end of February, and as things stood Octavian could only put clemency above justice. It was impossible for him to execute his fellow triumvir's brother, and equally unthinkable to punish his soldiers. Consideration for his own men ruled that out, since despite the fierce fighting they still saw their opponents as comrades. None of them could be guilty of high treason, because all the soldiers, whichever side they were on, had been Caesarians and would thus consider such a man one of themselves. Was Octavian to treat his adversary's men as traitors because they had obeyed not him but their commander Lucius Antonius? Octavian as victor pardoned Lucius and even treated him with great respect. Only a few senators and knights from the army of Lucius Antonius were sentenced to death. The inhabitants of Perusia did not fare so well, but paid the penalty instead of Lucius Antonius and his men. With only one exception the town councillors were executed and the city burned down, no one could be sure whether it was a result of arson or the unintentional consequence of an ordinary fire. The report that Octavian slaughtered hundreds of senators and knights on the altar of his deified father is a slander but was convincing enough to be believed. A remark ascribed to Octavian, that he replied to the pleas of those condemned to death with the verdict 'You must die', repeated many times, sounds more authentic. It conveys something of the merciless animosity of the civil war, and also of the cold mind that controlled Octavian in such situations, or so at least it could be credibly reported by his contemporaries.

After the fall of the city, Asinius Pollio and Ventidius Bassus finally went north. The former was consul that year with Gnaeus Domitius Calvinus but did not take up his office in Rome until later. Munatius Plancus disappeared from the scene too; hesitant as he was, he simply left his army and travelled east with Fulvia to join Mark Antony. In a magnanimous gesture, Octavian gave Lucius Antonius, no longer consul, a post as legate in the Spanish army, but he died in Spain towards the end of the year.

Fulvia had not stayed in Perusia, although she continued to support those besieged there from outside. She now considered the game in Italy lost, and with her two sons by Antony she set out, unharmed by the enemy, to join her husband in Athens. However, she was very ill and could not return to Italy with him; she died in Sicyon in the summer of the same year. She had played a part in the outbreak of the war and fed the ferocity with which it was fought. Whether she believed that her intervention might induce her husband to leave Cleopatra, as both modern and ancient historians have surmised, we do not know, but it is not very likely, for Antony had only just met the queen of Egypt at the time. In view of their later close relationship, this motive must therefore have been a retrospective conjecture. Fulvia had not acted the part of a true Roman matron in the war; the mere notion of a woman wearing a sword and delivering inflammatory speeches to the soldiers is likely to arouse horror, or at least incomprehension, in every reader of the annals of Rome both then and now. She was not yet forty in the year 41 but she had a chequered career behind her, although we should not see her through the eyes of Cicero, to whose arch-enemy Clodius she had been happily married before her marriage to Antony. Like many aristocratic women of her time, she felt personally independent and took an interest in politics. According to Plutarch, she wanted 'to rule a ruler and command a commander'. But the reason why she acted as she did in the Perusian War need not be sought in herself so much as in the fact that her audience, in this case a military one, accepted and even clearly approved of her conduct. The armies were already thinking in dynastic terms, and the commander they respected most, by a very long way, was Mark Antony. Fulvia was therefore the wife of a highly respected dynast. With Fulvia, the signs of nascent monarchy were visible in women for the first time, and the monarch's family appears on the horizon of public life with him.

After the relieving armies had withdrawn in the spring of 40, many hoped that lasting peace would develop from the parting of the hostile forces. Italy, above all Etruria, had been a theatre of war. The ferocity of the fighting had meant many losses, and in a moving little poem Propertius, who was born in Asisium (Assisi) in Umbria, only a few kilometres from Perusia, and was only sixteen years old at the time of the Perusian War, lamented the death of a member of his family during the internecine strife. However, Sextus Pompey, threatening the Romans of Italy with his sea blockade and raiding the coasts, was not the only obstacle in the way of peace. Another was the still uncertain relationship between Octavian and Mark Antony after the Perusian War. Antony was now on his way to the west, meaning to raise troops for his military ventures in the east, and, although he was not close to his brother, to represent the rights of Lucius Antonius now that the turmoil of war was over. Octavian must have felt caught between Sextus Pompey in the west and the south, Mark Antony's generals in the north, and Antony himself in the east. He was in fact in an extremely dangerous situation, for not only was he threatened by superior military forces, but the people of Italy were hostile to him too. They admired Sextus Pompey and Antony not exactly out of personal devotion, but because they hoped the two of them would bring relief from famine, and both men were enemies of Octavian. From the viewpoint of Pompey and Antony, there could have been no better time to do away with him. And as if that was in fact their intention, Quintus Fufius Calenus, who had taken over from Ventidius Bassus as governor of the provinces of Transalpine Gaul, now marched south with a strong army.

Since Antony had not yet arrived, Octavian's priority must be to get rid of the danger from the north. Before he could do that, however, he had to put down a small uprising in Campania, instigated by an Antonian from Perusia, Tiberius Claudius Nero. Nero fled to seek refuge with Sextus Pompey, taking with him his young wife Livia and their son Tiberius, who was not yet two. Before marching north, Octavian also secured himself against Lepidus, his colleague in the triumvirate. He did not want the vacillating Lepidus at his back so he forced him out of Italy by giving him six of the legions he had taken on after the surrender of Perusia – troops that he had some reason to consider unreliable – and let him lead this strong force to Africa, where he was to take over the two provinces allotted to him in the agreements between the triumvirs. The governor of Africa, a strong-minded man and a supporter of Antony, dared not refuse to hand the provinces over to Lepidus. Once that was done, Octavian set out for Gaul.

As soon as he had arrived in Upper Italy the goddess Fortuna, by pure chance taking a hand in events, helped him out of a dangerous predicament. It was not the first time she had come to his aid; she now swiftly broke the ring encircling Octavian and cutting him off on all sides and even doubled his power base: Calenus, the commander of eleven legions, died suddenly and unexpectedly, and his young son handed his army and his provinces to Octavian. It seems barely credible that this son, who had held no office yet and was acting without any authority from Antony, could do such a thing and have it accepted by the legates of the legions and the soldiers themselves, but it is consistently reported by sources in classical antiquity, and modern historians do not demur. Any general with a large army was far more than just a general by now; he had the aura of a dynast about him, even a man like Calenus who had risen only through Caesar. But in this case we can probably discount the possibility that Calenus' inexperienced young son made the decision to hand over the army by himself, if indeed he played any important part in it. The surprising change of sides by the army of Calenus is certainly based on the fact that Antony was far away and Octavian was close, and immediately after Perusia the soldiers shrank from more warfare and longed for the peace that would guarantee their material rewards.

Whatever the facts of the matter, as a result Octavian was now master of Antony's army in Gaul and Antony's western provinces, and contrary to the agreements after Philippi he was not going to hand back either. He was seizing what rightfully belonged to Mark Antony, with whom he was not at present on a war footing. But he had not closed the door to an understanding with his colleagues in the triumvirate: he had made Mark Antony's brother Lucius his second-in-command in Spain, something that Antony was bound to see as the overture to a reconciliation. Hoping to break through the sea blockade, with its devastating effect on Italy, Octavian also tried to come to an understanding with Sextus Pompey; he sent him his mother Mucia, who was in his, Octavian's, sphere of command at the time. Moreover, he decided that he himself would marry Scribonia, whose niece was married to Pompey. Scribonia was considerably older than Octavian. Twice married already, to members of the Cornelian family, she had several children by those marriages, and this seems to have been a purely political union. However, Pompey did not take the proffered hand. He saw better chances with Antony.

And Antony duly arrived in autumn of the year 40, bringing an army to Italy. As a triumvir he had the right to stay there, to preside in Rome beside Octavian and to raise troops. At present, however, his intentions did not look peaceful. The problems arising from Octavian's hostilities against Antony's brother Lucius and Fulvia were not the only ones still awaiting a solution; in fact they might not carry much weight because Mark Antony himself had kept aloof from the conflict, and he was generally known to be critical of Fulvia's conduct. The main bone of contention was the provinces and legions that should have been Antony's according to the agreement between the triumvirs; Octavian had simply appropriated them. As a result Antony first made contact with Sextus Pompey, offering him a rapprochement with the college of triumvirs or, if Octavian objected, help in opposing him. The idea of support from Antony against Octavian was indeed welcome to Pompey, and as a sign of goodwill he sent Antony his (Antony's) mother Julia, who had fled to Pompey during the Perusian War. In these months, probably through the agency of Asinius Pollio, Antony also succeeded in winning over Gnaeus Domitius Ahenobarbus, who was operating in the Ionian Sea, and with his own fleet and the naval forces of Ahenobarbus he set sail from the Greek coast to Italy. Much to his annoyance, however, the troops in Brundisium kept him out of the harbour, and as the city was secured by five legions and had strong fortifications, storming it was out of the question. Thereupon he cut it off from the sea, and the isthmus – it lay at the end of a peninsula – and soon afterwards, having taken the town of Sipontum a little further to the north, he had a harbour and was even able to defeat bands of Octavian's men in a cavalry battle. At the same time Sextus Pompey took Sardinia and Corsica and landed in the south-west of Italy, where he laid siege to Thurii and Cosentia.

The war between the triumvirs was now in full swing. Octavian advanced from the north, but for a while illness kept him in Canusium (Canosa). He will have found the delay welcome, since he could wish for nothing better than reconciliation with Antony. It would allow him to consolidate his now well-established situation further and above all would lead to either solidarity or to conflict with Sextus Pompey. He also knew very well that it would be difficult to induce his soldiers, quite a number of whom he had led only since the Perusian War, to fight the man who was the military hero of the Romans. He had first felt their self-confidence, indeed their defiance and obstinacy, during the Perusian War, and now he felt it again. When Agrippa, marching to southern Italy, called on the veterans who had settled along his route to rally to the standards, a good many initially joined him, but when they realized that they would be fighting Antony, most of their support crumbled again. So Octavian had to be ready to yield to the soldiers' wish for reconciliation and indeed he may even have been calculating on their desire for peace. The latitude he had won for himself proved extremely useful now. He could build on the fact that Antony too was ready to negotiate, not least because he had few legions to set against the forty now under Octavian. He had enough ships, and his cavalry too was strong and experienced in war, but he was short of infantry. In addition, at this inopportune moment bad news reached him from the Parthian front. The Parthians had overrun the entire province of Syria, and even Cilicia and Asia were endangered. Antony needed legionaries, which he could find only in Italy, and then he would have to return to the east as soon as possible. There was nothing he wanted less at the moment than armed conflict with Octavian, and he knew how unreliable an ally Sextus Pompey was.

It was Octavian's soldiers in particular who urged reconciliation, and Antony showed his readiness to comply by transferring the governorship of Bithynia to Domitius Ahenobarbus, who as a proscribed man and an enemy of Octavian was a bone of contention, and sending him east. In contrast to the time of the Perusian War, the soldiers did not venture to set themselves up as arbitrators of the triumvirs' decisions, and in Antony they would have been tackling the wrong man. All the soldiers also remembered how heads had rolled in the autumn of 44, when the legions mutinied in Brundisium, the same city to which he was now laying siege. One did not disobey Antony with impunity. With the consent of the soldiers, therefore, a delegation from both camps went to negotiate with the triumvirs. Octavian's side was represented by Maecenas, Antony's by Gaius Asinius Pollio, and the third member was Lucius Cocceius Nerva, who was on good terms with both parties. With their aid the two powerful triumvirs did indeed come to an agreement at Brundisium, the third alliance they had made after Bononia and Philippi. However, there were only two of them involved, for at the time the third triumvir, Lepidus, was in his province of Africa and was at best a sleeping partner in the triumvirate. The entire world, or at least the Roman world, was partitioned out by this treaty.

They agreed that Antony was to command the entire east as far as the river Euphrates, and Octavian the entire west as far as the ocean. Lepidus could keep his African provinces. The border agreed between east and west was the city of Scodra (Scutari) in Dalmatia. This borderline roughly coincided with the linguistic border between the areas dominated by the Greek and Latin languages respectively. For the first time, the entire territory ruled by Rome was thus divided between the potentates. They ruled over all the provinces; the Senate was now excluded from the government of Rome in theory as well as practice. Naturally Rome and Italy still remained the central point for all three triumvirs, and each was explicitly granted the right to raise troops there. However, as before, that depended in real terms on the goodwill of the triumvir who happened to be there, and he was Octavian. They agreed on their missions in the immediate future: for Antony the Parthian War, for Octavian reconciliation with Sextus Pompey or, failing that, conflict with him.

Once again, the treaty was to be sealed by a family alliance; the armies in particular expected it. Gaius Claudius Marcellus, the husband of Octavian's sister, had opportunely died at the beginning of the year, leaving Octavia free. We have met Marcellus before: he was the consul in the year 50 who, although one of those who urged war against Caesar, had rather ignominiously changed sides after the defeat of the 'republicans'. Octavia had two daughters by him, Marcella the Elder and Marcella the Younger, as well as a son, who was now two years old. At the age of just under thirty, she was now married off to Mark Antony, who was a good ten years her senior. Whether she liked the idea of the marriage or not made no difference. Women of marriageable age in the families of the despots were at the disposal of politics, and had been even when the nobility still ruled. Octavia could not even be allowed her ten-month period of mourning; the triumvirs were in a hurry. The marriage was officially celebrated in Rome, and the army greeted it with great jubilation. In Roman society, split as it had been since the civil war broke out in 49, the monarchy had long been a *fait accompli* in the soldiers' minds.

A sour note was struck for Octavian in their reconciliation: Antony revealed that Quintus Salvidienus Rufus, Octavian's friend since his stay in Apollonia in the year 44, and with Agrippa his most capable general, had been secretly corresponding with him, Antony, about changing sides. Salvidienus had obviously sought this connection and cannot have done so until after Antony had landed in Italy, in the belief that Octavian had little chance. He did so even though, despite the fact that he had never yet held any office, when Octavian took over the army of Calenus he had made him governor of Gaul and even designated him for the consulate. At a time when the law served only the needs of military despots this was admittedly only one outrageous departure from custom among others, but it should still be mentioned. Without letting Salvidienus know what he now knew, Octavian lured him to Rome, detained him when he arrived and accused him of high treason in the Senate. Salvidienus was declared an enemy of the state, and Octavian forced him to commit suicide. What Salvidienus had done was not a crime (or rather an attempted crime) according to the old criminal law of Rome. To change from supporting one holder of office to another, for such were the facts of the matter from the purely legal angle, was no more than terminating a friendship, but at this time of military despotism it was a mortal offence, particularly for a general in command of a large army. Antony's conduct in the matter did not meet with unanimous approval, although he was less to blame than Octavian, having intended only to help the colleague to whom he was newly reconciled, or in the worst case to put one of Octavian's two really good generals out of action. Even though the charge against Salvidienus was true, it seems strange that Octavian could find no better way to deal with a man who had been extraordinarily useful to him than to eliminate him and in addition to let the state give public thanks for the discovery of attempted treachery. A hint would have been enough to prevent that at least.

Thereupon the two powerful triumvirs entered Rome. On this occasion the Senate had to grant them the lesser triumph, the *ovatio*, but, as they had not defeated enemies of Rome, even that was really excessive. But the entry of the rulers into their capital city was more important than a victory celebration. This was a foretaste of the ceremonial arrival of the monarch (*adventus*) as we would come to know it in imperial times. The two triumvirs wanted above all to show Rome how they stood in relation to Sextus Pompey. By their agreements in Brundisium, Pompey was to keep Sicily but give up the other two islands. However, Menodorus the freedman, Pompey's admiral (also known by the shorter form of his name as Menas), had taken Sardinia, which had changed owners several times, back from Octavian. The entire Tyrrhenian Sea, including the Etrurian coast, thus became an operational area for Menodoros and Menecrates, the commanders of Sextus Pompey's fleet, and the blockade was particularly hard on Italy and Rome.

It was not just the famine; the imposition of new taxes depressed the Romans and inflamed feelings. The people of the city itself, who had so often demonstrated their strength to the ruling nobility in the late republic, thought their political role was not yet over. In fact the tension between the men who held power gave them some latitude, and they exploited it. The people wanted a reconciliation with Pompey because it would put an end to the famine. In their agitated state, they saw the triumvirs who were there in Rome as tyrants, while the absent pirate Pompey seemed to be the liberator for whom they longed. Suddenly they had a vivid picture of him as the son of Pompey the Great, who had defended the republic against the dictator Caesar, Octavian's father, and lost his life in the attempt. His son Sextus too had always laid great emphasis on his filial love (*pietas*) for his father, even linking it with his name; he called himself Sextus Pompeius Magnus Pius. In his respect and love for his father he also appeared to the Romans the opposite of Octavian, whom they hated, and who presented himself to them rather too often as the son of Caesar, *divi filius* – the son of a tyrant and, as scornful voices now said, a tyrant himself. So young Pompey's stock rose in Rome, and the people not only acknowledged the close relationship he claimed with the gods but publicly paid homage to it. At games in the Circus, the people loudly acclaimed the statue of Neptune, which was carried in procession at the start with statues of the other deities, because Sextus Pompey, in his position as ruler of the seas, was regarded as the son of Neptune. When the triumvirs next issued an edict levying taxes – an inheritance tax and a poll tax on slaves – many Roman citizens banded together, tore the edict down, heaped abuse on the two triumvirs and overturned their statues. They even threw stones at Octavian, whom they particularly disliked, and he might have perished in one of these incidents, wedged where he was in the crowd, if Antony had not brought soldiers in to cut a way through to him. Antony showed no mercy; there were many dead and wounded. He had the bodies thrown into the Tiber. Once again the triumvirs had shown their real nature as despots, and when peace was restored it was the peace of a graveyard.

The official business carried out by the triumvirs at this time was, as always, notable for its striking disregard of tradition. All the same, the carelessness with which they misused the Roman offices of state to give their own followers high office and seats in the Senate deserves special mention. Their measures outdid any of the dictator's. The consuls in office retired to let two other men succeed to that honour. One of them was Lucius Cornelius Balbus, an intimate friend of the dictator, who came from Gades (Cádiz) in Spain and had been granted citizenship by Pompey the Great; he was the first consul to come from outside Italy rather than being Roman-born. His appointment once again showed what had become of tradition; the magistracy now served the purposes of the potentates alone. When an aedile died on the last day of the year and a successor was quickly found to hold office for the few remaining hours, it also showed disregard for the old order of public law, but those who still valued tradition were the most offended. There were material reasons for the triumvirs to act in this way. Their adherents must be given honours and titles, and two measures served that purpose: first, the expansion of the magistracy of the city of Rome by the creation of new offices not actually required for the amount of work and variety of affairs to be dealt with, and second, the appointment of several men to the same annual offices by dint of retiring a holder of office before his time and giving his post to the successor favoured by the triumvirs. It is said that in the year 38 there were not sixteen but sixty-seven praetors in all. This disregard of tradition culminated in the year 39, when Octavian's old tutor Sphairos, a freedman, was given a state funeral.

Finally, Sextus Pompey let himself be persuaded to approach the triumvirs after all; following their agreement in Brundisium, a confrontation may not have seemed advisable to him. Negotiations were entrusted to Lucius Scribonius Libo, one of Pompey's admirals and for the last year Octavian's brother-in-law. Mucia, Pompey's mother, apparently wanted a reconciliation too. The discussions took place in the summer of 39 near Cape Misenum, not far from Baiae. As in Bononia, the meeting was also a demonstration of military might, and again it was attended by the utmost suspicion. Sextus Pompey, coming from the island of Aenaria (Ischia), entered the Bay of Puteoli (Pozzuoli); the triumvirs approached with their legions from the land. Two platforms made of planks resting on piles had been erected only a little way from each other in the waters of the harbour, and Pompey approached one from the sea, Antony and Octavian the other from the land.

The following points were agreed: Pompey was now to keep all three large islands, not just Sicily but also Sardinia and Corsica, as well as all the other islands already in his hands. Since Octavian wanted Antony too a little further from his sphere of influence, Pompey also received the Peloponnese as his command. In return he had to leave the positions he had occupied in Italy, give his word to take in no more runaway slaves, raise the sea blockade and guarantee the delivery of the usual amounts of grain from the area he controlled. Antony and Octavian also agreed to Pompey's long-standing demand to be compensated for the confiscation of his father's property. His freeing of slaves who had already entered his service should be recognized, and his soldiers, if they were free men, placed on a par with the soldiers of the triumvirs. The proscribed men who had taken refuge with him, except for those of Caesar's murderers who were formally condemned to death, were reinstated and were to get a quarter of their property back. In addition, Pompey was to be an augur, and he was promised the consulship in some future year. He was, of course, free to return to Rome. The agreement was to be valid for five years, and Pompey was also promised the consulate within that time.

The agreements were written down, sealed and later deposited with the highly regarded priestly college of the Vestal Virgins. As usual, the contents of the treaty were also made known to the armies and fleets, and the whole Bay of Baiae echoed to the jubilation of the soldiers. The announcement that the alliance was yet again to be confirmed by a family link between the two main parties to it, in this case Octavian and Pompey, was greeted with particular delight. Octavia's son by her marriage to Claudius Marcellus, who was also Octavian's nephew and now Antony's stepson, was betrothed to Pompey's daughter. Marcellus and Pompeia were just three years old at the time and were never in fact married, but the betrothal was effective as a political demonstration. Then the men in power invited each other to banquets, the sequence being decided by lot. The first was given by Pompey on his flagship, a magnificent galley with six banks of oars moored beside the pier, then by Antony and Octavian in tents erected on the pier itself. They all feared an assassination attempt, so the place was teeming with armed bodyguards and concealed daggers, but all went smoothly. Antony stayed in Italy until autumn, and he and Octavian had a friendly meeting. He was also formally appointed a priest of the deified Caesar (*flamen Caesaris*), a post for which he had been marked out even in the dictator's lifetime. While she was still in Rome Octavia bore her first daughter, Antonia the Elder, who was to be the grandmother of the later Emperor Nero.

Pompey had not been taken into the triumvirate by the treaty of Misenum. None the less, his position had been officially recognized by the legal triumvirs. He might not be a triumvir and thus not one of the magistrates, but nor, like those appointed by the magistrates to carry out their mandates, did he depend on a member of the magistracy. As an independent commander with a clearly defined area of responsibility, he certainly bore some form of title, but probably not that of proconsul, as has sometimes been assumed, since that was a rank in Rome subordinate to both the triumvirs and the traditional Roman magistrates. He had placed on his coins the title 'Commander of the Fleet and the Shores of the Sea' (*praefectus classis et orae maritimae*), bestowed on him by the Senate at Antony's urging in the year 43, and would have seen it as the formal description of his power. It was not the title of a traditional Roman office but expressed what Pompey in fact represented, and in concept it reveals once again the small importance in these years of public law, on which the actual power relationships and personal agreements by the potentates were superimposed.

With the two treaties of Brundisium and Misenum, the danger of the civil war between the 'republicans' and Caesarians developing into internecine strife among the Caesarians seemed to have been banished. After all their experience of war during the past decade there was a longing for peace, in particular among the Romans of Italy, for all these wars had been between Roman citizens. Italy had suffered not just from the fury of war but also from proscriptions, the seizure of property for the settlement of veterans and the famine caused by Sextus Pompey's blockade. And in addition there was the fact that individual Romans no longer had the security of an intact legal and social order. The old order of Roman law had become a plaything for the powerful. Its guarantee of the security of a citizen's person and property was only conditional, and since many of the connections of the past had now been destroyed, even a man's personal circumstances were often inadequate protection. Everything depended on the favour of the new masters. The people of Rome therefore longed not just for peace, but also for a new order in which a man's life, property and livelihood were secure, or at least at his own disposition.

There is evidence of this state of mind in Virgil's Fourth Eclogue, probably the best-known and certainly the most influential. It is dedicated to Asinius Pollio, consul in the year 40, and was written that year, perhaps in the autumn; if so, it could be seen as an immediate reaction to the reconciliation of the triumvirs. In it Virgil describes the birth of a divine boy during the consulate of Asinius Pollio, a child with whom the Golden Age would dawn. Free of the terrors of the past, men and beasts would live at peace together, having everything they needed in abundance, and after a brief interlude in which traces of 'the former wrong' would be seen again, all would be well once the child was a grown man.

The god Apollo would reign over this wonderful age. The poem expresses the longing of Virgil's contemporaries for peace, and its poetic form still touches readers today, allowing us to feel the emotions of a generation that had seen nothing but war, hunger and misery.

In the year 39 there was to be a new marriage for Octavian. He met Livia Drusilla. She was nineteen years old at the time and married to Tiberius Claudius Nero; her husband belonged to one of the most distinguished patrician families of the old nobility, and Livia herself was of the Claudian gens. Her father was one of the Claudii Pulchri, but had changed to the Livian gens by adoption; his adoptive father, and thus the adoptive grandfather of Livia, was Marcus Livius Drusus, the famous tribune of the people of the year 91 whose policies had led to the outbreak of the war between Rome and her Italian allies. After his adoption, Livia's father took the name of Marcus Livius Drusus Claudianus. He was probably praetor in the year 50, but he kept his political ambitions within bounds. Political pressure by the powerful, especially the dictator, had perhaps kept him from being more active, for after the Ides of March he joined the 'republicans'. He was therefore on the triumvirs' list of proscribed men and he went with Brutus and Cassius to the east, where he killed himself after the defeat at Philippi. Livia, then, was on the other side of the political barrier, and her husband Claudius Nero was not a supporter of Octavian. He had chopped and changed between the parties. Although initially an adherent of the dictator, he seemed to sympathize with the assassins after Caesar's murder and then switched his allegiance to the triumvirs, under whom he held the praetorship in the year 42. He was on the side of Lucius Antonius in the Perusian War. After its end he wanted to go on fighting Octavian in Campania, where he called for an uprising, and finally he took refuge with Sextus Pompey, taking his wife and his son Tiberius, who was only just two at the time. He stayed for only a few months and then, presumably feeling that his merits were insufficiently recognized, he fled with his family from Sicily to join Mark Antony in the east. When the triumvirs were reconciled at Brundisium he returned to Rome with Antony.

No sooner did Octavian meet Livia in Rome than he fell passionately in love. He immediately began an affair with her, even though his marriage to Scribonia had lasted only a year and she was pregnant by him. Octavian's ethical standards were a good deal lower in affairs of the heart than those of most of his contemporaries and equals, and all his life he ruthlessly exploited his position of power to satisfy his sexual needs. He did not stop short at other men's wives. Unlike many of his contemporaries, he was not drawn to his own sex, or at least hardly at all, but he uninhibitedly expressed his urges, even when he began preaching morality. In Livia's case, he was firmly determined to marry her and to sweep aside the various obstacles in his path. His break with Scribonia might have caused him few guilt feelings – if the concept of guilt can be applied to him at all – for his marriage to her was probably of a purely political nature. However, she protested, and Octavian paid her back in his memoirs by accusing her of immorality. The circumstances of his divorce and remarriage were scandalous. Scribonia was heavily pregnant by him when he met Livia, and he disowned her immediately after the birth of their daughter Julia. Livia herself was pregnant, but despite her condition her husband, Claudius Nero, had to agree to a divorce, so that she could marry Octavian at once. Octavian was at least cautious enough to ask the priests who ruled on such matters, the *pontifices*, whether Livia's pregnancy was any obstacle to the marriage. They naturally said it was not.

The wedding took place on 17 January 38, just before Livia's twentieth birthday. Three months later she gave birth to a boy, who was given the first name of Decimus or Nero and later, better known by his epithet of Drusus, was to be the great conqueror of the German tribes. Octavian had him handed over to Claudius Nero after his birth, to avoid any rumour that the child was his by his own adulterous relationship with Livia. All the same, the event was naturally a gift to the gossips of the city of Rome, and many sayings are recorded, one of which, to the effect that 'babies are granted to the fortunate after three months of pregnancy', became proverbial. Claudius Nero was sufficiently lacking in dignity to give the bride away at the wedding of Octavian and Livia, as if he were her father, conduct that is not excused by the suggestion that it can be seen as penance for his opposition in the Perusian War. In his will, he named Octavian guardian of his children if he should die, and when he did indeed die not much later his two boys, Tiberius and Drusus, moved into Octavian's household.

Such a hasty marriage is unthinkable, of course, unless Livia herself had felt drawn to Octavian. But even if we hold Antony the man responsible for her father's proscription and take her own infatuation into account, her behaviour is still difficult to understand. Octavian's marriage to Livia, despite his desire for a son, remained childless. A prematurely born baby died very soon or was born dead. Julia, his daughter by his marriage to Scribonia, was Octavian's only living child, and as a result Livia's sons by her marriage to Claudius Nero had a great future ahead of them, in particular the elder, Tiberius, who was to succeed Augustus. The gods took a late revenge, but Octavian (or by then Augustus) was not the only one to suffer. Two generations of Romans had to pay his successors the price for the childlessness of his marriage.

The peace with Sextus Pompey did not last long, and indeed the people of Italy did not notice any interruption in the fighting. It is not easy to work out who was mainly responsible for resuming military operations. Pompey complained that Antony thought he should pay the taxes owed by the Peloponnese in return for taking the region over, and we hear that in Italy Octavian was indignant because occupying forces were not after all withdrawn from the coastal areas. However much Pompey might have been to blame, he was the more passive partner in the deal. Octavian seems to have understood the treaty of Misenum as merely a breathing space to let him re-arm against Pompey, as supplies to Italy could not be allowed to depend on his goodwill alone. Not everyone was prepared to see the necessity of renewed hostilities, for with the treaties of Brundisium and Misenum only just concluded the people were justified in hoping for peace at last. Horace, not yet one of Octavian's close circle, was one of those who felt bitterly disappointed, and he expressed his feelings in two poems denouncing the civil war to his readers. 'Where, where are you monstrous men going? Why do you draw your swords again? / Has not enough Roman blood yet been shed on the fields and the seas?'

Open conflict began in the new year of 38, when Pompey's admiral Menodoros went over to Octavian. With Menecrates, also a freedman, he was the most able naval commander in the Pompeian fleet after Pompey had had his admiral Lucius Staius Murcus killed the previous year. Menodoros brought with him the islands of Sardinia and Corsica as well as three legions, whereupon Pompey at once resumed his blockade. Octavian reacted by stepping up the building of new warships and brought in legionaries from Illyricum to guard the coast more efficiently and win back areas occupied by Pompey. Then he brought his fleets into action. He ordered the Tyrrhenian squadrons to sail south and sent the fleet equipped in Ravenna to Tarentum (Tarento); he himself took supreme command of this fleet and sailed into the Straits of Messene (Messina) with it. The torrid phase of the war at sea had begun.

At Cumae, the northern fleet under Gaius Calvisius Sabinus and Menodoros met a Pompeian fleet under Menecrates, who was a personal enemy of Menodoros. The battle entailed losses on both sides but proved the superiority of the Pompeians. However, Menecrates was killed, and after the death of their outstanding commander, the Pompeians withdrew to Sicily. Octavian was in command in the south, demonstrating how little idea he had of naval warfare. It is no excuse that he was only one in a long line of Roman generals who thought they could fight at sea just as they fought on land. He sailed into the straits – probably to prepare for a landing in Sicily – and when the enemy met him at Skyllaion opposite Messene, as was only to be expected, he withdrew to the Italian coast, anchored his ships and tried to maintain a defensive strategy until the northern fleet arrived. Pinned down just off the coast, however, his ships were attacked by the enemy, and since they could not move many were destroyed. Only the appearance of what remained of his northern fleet saved Octavian's remaining ships from complete annihilation. When a violent storm broke next day, raging particularly furiously in the straits, Menodoros, who knew what to do in a storm and was now operating with Octavian, took his ships out to the open sea, roped them loosely together and had them rowed against the wind. By those means he survived the storm, whereas Octavian, still hugging the coast, lost over half his vessels and suffered considerable losses among his men. Only Pompey's passivity allowed any remnants of his fleet to be salvaged from this disaster. It was not just a defeat but an embarrassment, far from likely to raise Octavian's reputation as a military despot where it mattered most, among the soldiers.

But Sextus Pompey did not exploit his success, and so Octavian was given time to pacify the starving country of Italy, demand more sacrifices from his friends and build a new fleet. He left the construction of the fleet to his friend and best general Agrippa. Agrippa had taken over the governorship of Transalpine Gaul in the year 39 and once again proved his abilities as a military commander there. He had put down unrest in Aquitania and crossed the northern Rhine at a place where

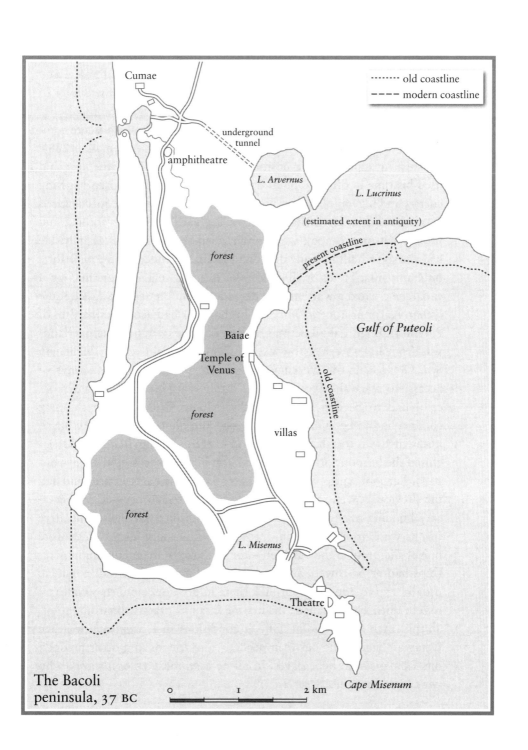

Cumae

underground
tunnel

amphitheatre

········ old coastline
– – – – modern coastline

*L. Arvernus*

*L. Lucrinus*

(estimated extent in antiquity)

present coastline

*forest*

*Gulf of Puteoli*

Baiae

Temple of
Venus

old coastline

*forest*

villas

*forest*

*L. Misenus*

Theatre

Cape Misenum

The Bacoli
peninsula, 37 BC

0          1          2 km

many of the Ubian tribe had crossed the river in search of land where they could settle in the fertile area once inhabited by the Eburones, whom Caesar had destroyed. Agrippa settled the Ubians on the left bank of the Rhine, thus relieving the Rhine border of the burden, and founded the first Ubian town there (*oppidum Ubiorum*). It was later to become the city of Cologne.

On 1 January of the year 37, Agrippa and an otherwise obscure commander called Lucius Caninius Gallus, probably an Antonian, became consuls. Agrippa held the position of consul all through the year and used his time in office to build up another strong naval force, showing energy and ingenuity almost unparalleled in his time. The job he faced was a hard one, for he had to create a great fleet out of nothing and protect it from Pompey, who commanded the west coast of Italy. He had the ships built in many different places, but concentrated his efforts on Campania. Here, by linking Lake Avernus to Lake Lucrinus by a canal, he created a war harbour defended from the sea and called it the 'Julian Harbour' (*portus Iulius*). This harbour had access to the Gulf of Puteoli through Lake Lucrinus, and another way out (going overland) was from Lake Avernus by way of Cumae straight to the Tyrrhenian Sea. Great feats of civil engineering were required for both ways of access. To reach the Tyrrhenian Sea a tunnel (today the Grotta di Cocceio) had to be dug through rocks (Monte Grillo), and a shipping channel had to be built for the way out into the Gulf from Lake Lucrinus, which was too shallow. The road to Herculaneum (*via Herculanea*) closed the harbour off from the Gulf, and bridges crossed the ways out of the harbour. Agrippa built wharves all over the harbour area and had the previously well-forested land almost cleared to provide the necessary building materials. Since he still did not have enough timber, tree trunks were brought in from further afield. As soon as the ships were finished he trained the oarsmen – for the sake of manoeuvrability warships had to be rowed, and each ship had a strong team of oarsmen, usually 170 to 200 men – drilling them in dry dock until they could all row in time. Then he made the marine infantry practise boarding ships, all this often at sea and in difficult conditions such as stormy weather. Octavian begged the oarsmen needed from friends and other prosperous Romans who kept slaves. In all he assembled 20,000 slaves, who were freed for military service.

*

Although Octavian was now in a better military situation than he had been during the Perusian War, Mark Antony's attitude to him was still crucial. If Antony did not put much pressure on the west at this time it was mainly due to his problems in ruling the east, but also due to to his personal inclinations: after the trials of the previous few years, he wanted to enjoy life and his position as commander. He had set up a new system of government in the east after Philippi, rewarding his supporters and penalizing friends of Caesar's murderers. Always short of money, like his colleagues, he asked the cities of Asia Minor for large sums, but since they were hardly able to pay more than they were already providing, he confined himself in the end to demanding nine years' worth of tribute over the following two years. Even so, he plunged most of the cities deep in debt because of the loans they had to take out. The client kings and princes also had to pay up; Antony readjusted their relationship to Rome as well. During these financial discussions the Egyptian queen Cleopatra met him in Tarsos, to which he invited a number of princes in the year 41. As representative of one of the mighty empires that had formed after the time of Alexander, she towered above the many other princes and minor kings of the east. She wanted to regulate her connection with the new masters, whose cause she had backed, if rather inadequately, at the time of the war against the assassins of Caesar. She claimed to have made haste to the aid of the triumvirs with a fleet at the time, but the vessels had sailed into a storm off the coast of Libya and had had to turn back. Her alleged attempt to render aid did not accord with the fact that she had supported Cassius against Dolabella, by sending him ships through the agency of her powerful councillor and general Serapion – something that Antony was bound to regard as a hostile act.

Cleopatra came with a magnificent ship and a retinue displaying both the material and intellectual culture of the oriental Hellenistic world and its ability to stage a splendid political spectacle. Everything Roman paled and looked outmoded by comparison. There is no doubt that Antony, who enjoyed the pleasures of life, was impressed – not just by the queen's physical charms but also by her lifestyle and her intellectual gifts, including fluency in several languages, her conversational skills and her leadership abilities. The love affair between them obviously began in Tarsos and was continued in Alexandria, where Antony spent the winter of 41/40. Historians deduced that even then he was enslaved to her and had forgotten all else around him from the fact that, after the Parthian invasion of the province of Syria that winter, he took no action, but after putting in briefly on the Syrian coast took the fleet to the west, where his brother Lucius and wife Fulvia were at war with Octavian. The war was inconvenient to him, and the radical approach taken by his brother and wife troubled him – that is as clear as the fact that he made the right decision in going to Italy instead of fighting the Parthians. His one rival of any importance was Octavian. In addition, he needed troops, more particularly legionaries from Italy, in order to oppose the Parthians. So Antony first made his peace with Octavian in Brundisium, stayed for some time in Rome, which was his city too, and travelled back to the east only in the autumn of 39 with his new wife Octavia, going first to Greece.

The Parthians had already made deep incursions into Syria in the year 40, even reaching Cilicia and the west of Asia Minor. Their forces were commanded by Pacorus, son of the great king of Parthia, and Quintus Labienus, a son of Titus Labienus. Titus Labienus had been Caesar's most able general but had not wanted to join him in opposing the Senate and consequently had gone over to Pompey and fell at Munda in 45. His son Quintus had also joined the 'republicans' but escaped the disastrous defeat at Philippi because he had been sent by Caesar's assassins to negotiate with Parthia. He stayed there, now styling himself 'Imperator Parthicus', 'Parthian commander', and was able to recruit many legionaries for the conquest of Syria, most of them from the legions that followed Caesar's murderers. He was a capable man and responsible for the Parthian success. When Antony's general Lucius Decidius Saxa was forced out of Syria and back to Cilicia, where he lost his life, and finally Lucius Munatius Plancus, proconsul of the province of Asia, fled to the islands – the only place where he could feel safe, since there was no Parthian fleet – the Parthians felt that they were masters of all the country east of the Hellespont. However, while he was still in Rome Antony had sent a gifted military commander against them in the person of Publius Ventidius Bassus.

In the year 39 Bassus, who had already been very helpful to Antony after the War of Mutina, quickly put an end to the Parthians' activities in Asia Minor and pushed the enemy back over the Taurus mountains to Syria. Labienus died in the fighting. In the autumn of 39, after a victory over another Parthian army, Bassus even managed to open the passes through the Amanus mountains, which joined Cilicia to Syria, whereupon the Parthians withdrew to the other bank of the Euphrates. In the following year, 38, he repulsed another attack on Syria, led by the king's son Pacorus, in a great battle in which Pacorus died.

When Antony finally arrived in Syria that summer the war was over. He was now contemplating a campaign against the Parthians such as the dictator Caesar had planned. For the time being, however, nothing concrete came of this idea. Ventidius Bassus was dismissed from his command; perhaps he had been too successful. However, he was granted a triumph in Rome in November 38. He had risen from being a muleteer to the status of a general who had earned a triumph, a career that would have been impossible in republican times, but it was not to be typical of the immediate future either. Bassus was a product of the time of upheaval in which the old network of society had dissolved and no new social links had yet been made. After his triumph we hear no more of him, and he presumably died not long afterwards. Antony at least had no use for him any more.

Gaius Sosius replaced Bassus as governor of Syria. Among other things, he brought Herod, who had been king of the Jews as a client prince of Rome, back to Jerusalem, from which he had been driven out by the Maccabaean Antigonus during the turmoil of the Parthian conquests. After heavy fighting and a five-month siege of Jerusalem, Herod was finally able to enter his city again in the summer of 37, and Antigonus, the last king of the Hasmonaean clan, was executed.

In spite of the tension in the east since the year 40 – for even after their withdrawal the Parthians still represented a threat – Antony was in no hurry to leave Greece. He lingered for a long time in Athens, where he was hailed as 'the new Dionysos'. Antony was happy to go along with the Greek tendency to elevate powerful men to the divine sphere. In fact there had been several examples of eastern rulers taking the name of Dionysos in quite recent times, but Antony will not have wanted to be associated with Mithradates Eupator, king of Pontus and a fierce enemy of Rome, or with Ptolemy XII, Cleopatra's father, both of whom had called themselves 'Dionysos' or 'Neos Dionysos'; the latter, in line with Egyptian thinking, would no doubt have seen himself as the reincarnation of Dionysos/Osiris. Antony might simply have sought to be associated with the god in taking the name, popular as Dionysos was with the people of Greece and Asia Minor. He had already been hailed as Dionysos during his visit to Ephesos in the year 41, and when the citizens of Athens, proud of having this mighty man within their walls, offered him (as the new or young Dionysos, Neos Dionysos) marriage to the goddess Athena, patron of the city, he agreed. A magnificent wedding was arranged, but Antony wanted a thousand talents from the Athenians as the goddess's dowry. Although they were acting as 'parents of the bride', they had not thought of that, but of course they had to pay up. It was all very enjoyable for Antony, who delighted in good living. He dressed like the Greeks, listened to lectures on philosophy and joined in wrestling bouts. War and politics were not the be-all and end-all of life.

When Antony at last made ready for war in the new year 38 and prepared to sail to Syria, he was held up for a while by Octavian's request for him to come to Brundisium for a meeting, since conflict with Sextus Pompey looked imminent. Antony set off but soon left again on the grounds that Octavian had not turned up at the appointed time, and his presence in the east was required to deal with the Parthians. In that case, why did he start out at all? Perhaps he did not want to help Octavian out of his difficulties, but he might have thought of that before, in Athens. He now showed little sense of purpose; indeed, it was difficult to say what a military potentate should consider his political task. If he had no rivals to oppose, he was, so to speak, unemployed. But a military commander had to show off his soldiers, who were his political capital. It is true that Antony needed to do that less than his rivals, but now that a subsidiary commander had fought the Parthians so successfully, perhaps he too felt he must present himself to the army.

In the summer of 38, then, Antony finally went to Syria. He arrived when everything was over, so he sailed back to Athens and spent the winter of 38/37 in that city. By now Octavian had been outmanoeuvred at sea by Sextus Pompey, and Antony correctly scented a good opportunity to recruit men from his colleagues for the Parthian War. In the spring of 37 he sailed for Brundisium, but his large fleet – he had 300 warships with him, and one wonders why he wanted to take so many vessels to the west – found entrance to the harbour barred. Thereupon he set course for Tarentum. The two powerful triumvirs had no interest in a war against each other, which would do neither Antony nor Octavian any good; each had his own problems, in Octavian's case Pompey and in Antony's the Parthians. One of them needed ships, the other legionaries. But Octavian kept Antony waiting and ignored his envoys. It was Octavia who finally got negotiations going – as Octavian probably ultimately wanted. Not far from Tarentum, at the mouth of the river that gives the city its name, Antony and Octavian concluded another treaty, the fourth since Bononia. As a sign of good faith they issued invitations to each other, but since a sense of personal danger never entirely left them, these visits were more in the nature of perilous adventures than heartfelt social encounters.

This time the definition of areas of authority was not at stake. The distribution of those areas remained as before. Instead, each equipped the other with the armaments he needed for his coming campaign. Antony asked for 20,000 legionaries, Octavian for 120 warships. Antony immediately left the ships behind in Italy, and Octavian was going to send the soldiers after him, but they never arrived. They gave Octavia 20 ships and 1,000 soldiers as recompense for her negotiations, but she immediately handed them back again. This 'negotiation fee' is interesting, since it expresses an awareness of sovereign power over the troops; the potentates obviously regarded them as material possessions that could be given away, and for that very reason could be transferred even to female members of their families. In addition, Antony and Octavian agreed to extend the duration of the triumvirate, which had already run out in December of the previous year, for another five years, from 1 January 37 to 31 December 33. No confirmation of the extension by a people's law corresponding to the Titian Law which had founded the triumvirate in November 43 was anticipated. They already thought themselves so far above the law that such a confirmation would be an unnecessary nuisance. Finally they once again sealed the restoration of harmony with family ties. Octavian's daughter Julia, two years old at the time, was betrothed to Antony's son from his marriage to Fulvia, not yet ten, whom the Greeks called 'little Antony' (Antyllus).

Lepidus had no part at all in this treaty. This can be explained by the fact that in the main the subject of the discussions affected only Antony and Octavian, but still, the duration of the triumvirate had been extended without consulting him. The omission of Lepidus from the talks probably meant more: it seems to indicate his loss of political weight between the agreements. When the triumvirate was founded in the year 43, there was still a use for Lepidus. He was not just the man who, in the absence of the other triumvirs, had the task of protecting

Rome and Italy; he had also helped to hold the balance in the tension between Octavian and Antony, and at that time he could also be presented as the most important of Caesar's generals, after Antony, to all Caesarians who had not explicitly shown themselves ready to follow Antony himself. In the five years of the triumvirate's first period of office, however, all the Romans, in particular the leadership elite and the soldiers, had looked only to Octavian and Antony, whether they themselves considered each other colleagues or rivals, and the dual power available to them now had a firm geographical basis. Although Lepidus' position in the triumvirate was unaffected, because his two colleagues could not afford a military confrontation at the moment, they merely tolerated him. Perhaps Octavian had a special interest in maintaining the status quo for that very reason: he thought he needed the support of Lepidus in the expected fight against Sextus Pompey. Antony, as his lack of reaction a year later when Octavian ousted Lepidus shows, does not seem to have felt that he ought to remain a member of the triumvirate. Lepidus himself, a sensitive politician, was aware of the decline of his power in the triumvirate and, as subsequent events were to show, tried to counter it and get himself back into the power play between the three of them.

The treaty of Tarentum was the last between the two military commanders. Antony soon left Italy again and set sail for Cercyra (Corfu), from where he travelled on to the east. He never saw Italy again. The Romans had been spared a fratricidal war; they had their peace, and the two triumvirs had their wars. The world of the military potentates was back in order.

The wars waged by the two triumvirs in the following year, 36, were defensive, and as such they were justified and necessary for the security of the empire. That was certainly true of the Parthian war that Antony intended to fight. The Parthians were at present defeated and had been forced back over the frontiers of the empire, but a Parthian attack in the years 41/40, when the enemy had finally made its way into the province of Asia, must be punished in the interests of the long-term coexistence of the two great empires, and the Parthian king had to be deterred from further revival of his policy of expansion by a decisive demonstration of military power. The fact that the war of conquest twenty years earlier had been started by the Roman side in the person of Crassus was immaterial. Now at least it was the Romans who were under attack. And the war with Sextus Pompey was like defence against an enemy of the empire, for he was no longer an opponent in home politics. He had abandoned law and order and had long ago become a freebooter whose motley followers were a reflection of what he himself had become. Even as a military potentate, in which character he liked to feel he stood beside the triumvirs, he was a special case. Totally unpredictable, he would not be tied down to any agreement even in a provisional form. It is questionable whether he had really been in control of his undisciplined bands of seamen and legionaries, among whom there were many who can hardly be called soldiers.

Octavian now resumed the war against Pompey. It was no longer just a case of getting rid of a serious disruptive factor, but also of ensuring supplies of provisions to Italy, for without grain coming in from outside the people would starve. Sextus Pompey had his military base on the island of Sicily, and the coming struggle would be for possession of it. The 'Sicilian War' began in early July 36 and lasted for only about two months. Both sides were to suffer unusually high losses. Despite many setbacks, however, it ended with the total destruction of Pompey's forces by Octavian. Octavian's strategic task was to bring his superior infantry into battle against Pompey, and that meant that he had to start by creating bridgeheads for his legionaries on the island, which was defended like a fortress.

Octavian prepared his operations carefully. A northern fleet under Agrippa was to sail for the north coast of Sicily from the Liparian (Aeolian) Islands, particularly from the most southerly of the islands, Vulcanus/Hiera (Vulcano), which served as a base for the fleet. Octavian was to advance from the straits to Sicily from the east, supported by the squadrons from Tarentum under Titus Statilius Taurus, while Lepidus was to come from Africa to occupy the west of the island. The world had never before seen such great numbers of warships and transport vessels. The Roman military machine acquired a new dimension in this war. Lepidus alone came with seventy warships and over 1,000 transport ships, carrying twelve legions. Even if those legions were nowhere near full fighting strength, it was an impressive armed force. Lepidus clearly wanted to use this war to rejoin the game played by the really strong men.

The large-scale invasion almost entirely failed in its early stages, not through any military weakness but because of the vagaries of nature. In the middle of summer – the invasion began in early July – a fierce storm arose, with a wind blowing first from the south and then veering to the south-west. It capsized many of Lepidus' transport ships, thousands of men were drowned, and Octavian was held powerless in the Bay of Elea, where he had fled from the storm. As he ran for harbour he lost a considerable number of his ships, some of them smashed to pieces on the coast, some through collisions with each other. Only Lepidus succeeded in landing, on the west of the island at Lilybaeum (Marsala) with his main forces. The invasion of the island from the east had failed, and a new attempt at landing could not be made immediately because of the necessity of repairing damaged vessels and building replacements for the lost ships. In spite of the advanced season of the year, when the much-feared autumn storms had to be borne in mind, and although famine threatened in Italy, which meant that Octavian had to reckon with unrest at home, he dared not put the venture off until the following year.

Before the second attempt at landing, Menodoros, who felt he was insufficiently appreciated by Agrippa and Octavian and had thus changed sides again, successfully disrupted the repairing of ships and building of new vessels by making rapid attacks on the coast, but then he went over to Octavian for the second time. The attempt by Lepidus to bring another four legions over to Sicily from Africa ended in disaster. The fleet was attacked by the Pompeians, some of the ships were sunk, and the rest forced back to Africa. The soldiers of two legions died. In this interim phase Octavian proved his worth if not as a military commander, at least as organizer of the war. The old plan of attacking the island from the north, west and east was retained. So far only the landing in the west had succeeded.

In August Octavian prepared another attempt. Coming from the north, as planned, Agrippa was to attack the north-east coast of the island. He himself would land on the east coast, again from the straits, and Lepidus, who had already gained a foothold in the west, was to keep up the siege of Lilybaeum, the main Pompeian bastion there. On the second attempt Agrippa above all was successful. Four legions were brought from the Liparian Islands as a landing party. To force their landing on Sicily, Agrippa approached the north-east coast of the island, met a strong Pompeian fleet and defeated it at Mylae. Some 300 ships took part in this battle between forces of equal strength. Agrippa's ships, which had higher sides than the lighter but more manoeuvrable ships of Pompey, won the day, reinforced as they were by tower-like superstructures from which they could rake the enemy decks with missiles. The Pompeians, however, were able to withdraw in good order thanks to the mobility of their ships, and as they did not have such a deep draught as Agrippa's they were able to get to safety in shallower waters. Agrippa took his fleet back to the island only briefly and then immediately turned and exploited his success to land with his legions at Tyndaris. He was unable to take the city itself, but meanwhile he occupied many local areas and thus had a foothold on Sicily.

Meanwhile Octavian was trying to land at Tauromenium (Taormina), and he did indeed land three legions. But as the city would not surrender to him, he tried to secure himself with a well-established camp a little further south, near Naxos. Here, however, he was dismayed to come under attack from both land and sea. He had fully expected the Pompeians' naval forces to be held back by Agrippa in the north. But now Sextus Pompey himself came on the scene, threatening the entire venture on land. Octavian made the sensible decision not to hug the coast with his fleet but to give battle, to protect the link with Italy for his landing party. There was a fierce battle, and Pompey won it. Octavian lost half his ships and, thinking that he was in a hopeless situation, he even contemplated suicide. He asked his friend Gaius Proculeius to kill him, but Proculeius declined – fortunately for Octavian, since he finally succeeded in fleeing to the Italian coast, where he was taken in, exhausted and downcast, by Marcus Valerius Messalla Corvinus and his troops. Corvinus, one of the men who kept changing sides at this time – he had been a member of the Senate party and a friend of Caesar's assassins when he was just under thirty, had then served Antony and finally changed to Octavian – thus committed himself very firmly.

It was a terrible defeat; worst of all, Octavian had lost touch with the legions which had landed at Naxos, and they were now thrown entirely on their own resources, without supplies and surrounded by enemies. However, Lucius Cornificius, commander of the expeditionary corps, was not giving up. Pursued by his enemies and short of water, he took his soldiers right across the north-east of Sicily and finally, in a forced march of several days, he reached the troops that Agrippa had landed in the north of the island. It was this brilliant achievement on the part of the men and their leader, not least, that encouraged all Octavian's followers and thus ultimately contributed to his victory in the war. Agrippa had just taken Tyndaris, where Octavian went with further units. Without the troops under Lepidus, Octavian finally had over twenty-one legions at his disposal on the island, even if hardly any were at their full battle strength of 5,000 or even 6,000 men – a mighty fighting force. The tables were turned.

In these battles, Sextus Pompey showed a sometimes barely comprehensible restraint. He had not secured himself sufficiently to the north, thereby giving Agrippa the chance to create a first base on the island of Vulcanus/Hiera. In addition he had failed to oppose Cornificius vigorously enough when the latter was entirely isolated in Sicily, and it is hard to understand why, when his enemies had suffered heavy losses in storms during the first phase of the conflict, he did not at least destroy one of their established bases with a determined attack from the sea. Instead, he exchanged his red commander's cloak for a blue one in a theatrical gesture demonstrating his closeness to Neptune, to ensure that his ships' crews and legionaries saw the lord of the seas as his helper. After the battle of Mylae and the taking of Tyndaris, he became even more cautious and hesitant. Leaving aside Lilybaeum, his base in the west, he and all his land troops and ships had now been forced back to the north-east tip of the island and his main base at Messene (Messina), and when he saw Agrippa's fleet operating off Cape Pelorias, the north-east tip of Sicily, he simply lost his nerve, gave up Mylae and the passes there and tried to barricade himself into the north-east corner.

Pompey's situation had deteriorated badly. He was finding it very difficult to supply his troops with provisions, and defeat not just on the island but also at sea was imminent. To strengthen his position, he withdrew troops from the west of Sicily and ordered them to join him without actually giving up Lilybaeum. Lepidus, who was keeping watch on the Pompeian forces in and around Lilybaeum, thereupon pursued the Pompeian relief troops to north-east Sicily with his own main force. He did not wish to miss the final battle, his position in the triumvirate was now a good one because he had so many legions, and he hoped to improve it even further. He camped near Octavian, and tensions instantly arose between them over who had supreme command.

The deciding moment came quite suddenly. But even more remarkable than the surprisingly early prospect of an end to the war was the very unusual way in which the battle was officially announced. Although Octavian undoubtedly had more men and was in a considerably better strategic position than he had been a few weeks earlier, he and Pompey agreed on a battle as if the two of them were equal in fighting power and in the situation in general: they decided not only on the time and the place, but also on the number of ships each of the combatants was to bring into action. The time was to be 3 September, the place an area on the north-east coast of Sicily outside the small harbour of Naulochus, so that the troops of both sides could watch. Each party was to bring 300 ships into battle, their crews and equipment being left to the commanders to decide. Who proposed this agreement, the hesitant Pompey or more likely Octavian, intent on getting the outcome decided quickly, our sources do not say. Pompey must have had more interest than Octavian in a sea battle under conditions equal for both sides, because he was numerically inferior on land and his motley assortment of legions was not a strong fighting force. But only the stronger party, in this case Octavian, could allow him the opportunity of a naval battle. Obviously the rivalry breaking out between Octavian and Lepidus, particularly the increasing weight brought to it by Lepidus' legions, induced him to wish for a swift decision at sea, so that he could present himself as the victor here in the main theatre of the war. So Pompey had an unearned chance. Had they agreed on the prize of victory too? Hardly, for if Octavian had lost he would not have withdrawn from the island. Never in the history of Rome had a battle been fought in such circumstances. The speeches made before the battle evoked old themes. It was as if two Homeric heroes were about to measure their strength against each other, although the potentates lacked the Homeric ethic. The same factor prevents us from comparing this engagement with the battles of Hellenic hoplites in the late archaic and classical periods, although agreements of this kind had sometimes been made on those occasions.

The battle did indeed take place under the agreed conditions. However, the heroes themselves did not fight on the ships but watched from the shore, just as they had watched the battle of Mylae. Octavian's forces were commanded by Agrippa, the Pompeians by the freedmen Apollophanes and Demochares, two capable Pompeian admirals who had been instrumental in the devastating defeat of Octavian in the

Straits of Messene in the year 38 and had commanded the fleet in the battle of Mylae.

The two fleets took up their positions and, as if at some sporting event, attacked each other when a trumpet was sounded. No tactics of any kind had been worked out in advance, although such tactical considerations generally determine the outcome of a battle either on land or at sea. The two sides simply made for each other, and everything depended on the energy, training and courage of the soldiers, as well as the ships and their equipment. A milling crowd of vessels swiftly formed, and soon even the leaders no longer had a clear view of what was going on – indeed, that was seldom possible in the naval battles of classical antiquity after the opening phase, if only because problems of communication made any central command so difficult. Agrippa seems to have managed to break through the enemy lines – an important manoeuvre in sea battles, since after the ships had broken through and turned they could advance on what remained of the enemy line from behind. In addition his ships, which were much larger and higher-built than the enemy's, had been well prepared for battle and they used an improved grappling iron known as a 'gripper'. It had a wooden arm about 2.25 metres long, with a barbed iron hook fixed to the end. This hook was fired from ballistas to land on the enemy ship and fasten on and was then winched in on cables attached to the end of the wooden arm. The harpoon-like device thus brought the enemy ship close enough to be boarded. Since the ballistas could be installed only on quite large ships, Agrippa's grappling irons gave him a special advantage, not to mention the fact that the higher sides of his ships made boarding very much easier, and the enemy could be harassed with spears and arrows from the tower-like superstructures much more efficiently than from the Pompeians' smaller ships.

Agrippa's victory was overwhelming; he lost only three ships in the battle, while his enemy lost twenty-eight, and almost the whole Pompeian fleet was destroyed as it fled. Those vessels that did not burn or capsize were left beached or surrendered to the victor. Great rejoicing broke out among Octavian's army, which had been watching the show, and conversely the Pompeians were downcast. Octavian honoured Agrippa as the victor with a sea-blue banner and a golden crown never awarded to a naval commander before, adorned with representations of the prows of ships (the *corona rostrata*).

Only seventeen of Pompey's ships survived the slaughter. Pompey himself fled to Messene on one of them without troubling himself any further about his troops at Naulochus. Left without a leader, they went over to Octavian. Pompey's other measures also betray a total inability to plan ahead sensibly and indeed are evidence of panic. He ordered the eight legions stationed at Lilybaeum under the command of the legate Lucius Plinius Rufus to go to Messene but before they arrived he continued his flight eastwards with those ships he still had left. Plinius did reach Messene, after a cross-country march right through Sicily, but found Pompey gone and was immediately surrounded in the city, which was still under siege by Lepidus and Agrippa, while Octavian remained with his army.

The war against Sextus Pompey ended with a quarrel between Octavian and Lepidus. The latter wanted to derive political advantage from his part in the war and with a clever coup he succeeded in considerably improving his point of departure for negotiations with Octavian. He started negotiating with the Pompeians encircled in Messene, and although Agrippa kept out of the affair and advised waiting for Octavian to arrive, Lepidus received the surrender of the city and took Plinius' eight legions into his own army. He now commanded twenty-two legions as well as a strong body of cavalry and was no longer numerically inferior to his rival. When Octavian arrived with the fleet, he reprimanded Lepidus severely, but Lepidus insisted on retaining the full dignity of a triumvir and demanded Sicily as the reward for what he had done in the war and as compensation for what he had lost when the empire was divided up after Philippi. However, Octavian was in a good negotiating position. He could rely on the core troops of his army and on his fleet, for while his legions had usually been led by other men, by now he was recognized as a successful military commander, and his reputation as such was established among the soldiers.

In the elation of his new-found authority, he now thought he could emulate Antony's actions when he entered Lepidus' camp in the year 43 to take the army from him. Accompanied by only a few men, Octavian planned to show Lepidus who was master of Sicily. His attempt to put on a show of courage and distinction before the soldiers failed miserably and almost cost him his life. Many men did acclaim him as *imperator*, particularly those whom he had just taken over from Pompey and whom he had not yet recognized as soldiers serving the triumvirate, but there were a number who, probably angry at having been prevented from looting Messene, abused Octavian and crowded close around him. One of his bodyguard was even killed. Octavian had to face about in a hurry, amidst derision. He came back with his entire army and laid siege to Lepidus' men, not to start a fight but to use his army to demonstrate to his rival's soldiers the superiority that he personally lacked. In fact many soldiers did go over to him, either individually or in troops. Even some centurions of Lepidus' bodyguard changed sides, and finally there was a general exodus to Octavian's camp.

Lepidus was a general without authority. The soldiers saw none of the qualities in him that, to their way of thinking, made a military commander: daring, courage in battle, a soldierly spirit, persistence in carrying out a plan. He owed all he was to the nobility of his family and the generosity of Caesar, who had recognized and exploited his diplomatic skill. And so his huge army, some 70,000 men in all, left him in isolation, not a tragic but more of a comic figure. He now had to fear that the irate Octavian would execute him and, lacking the courage to be a hero, he begged instead. He took off his commander's cloak and appeared before Octavian in mourning garb. Octavian was clever enough to receive him when he came to plead and even prevent him from kneeling, not of course out of consideration for the man – Octavian had driven his best friend to his death when he was accused of treason – but for the sake of the army that was now his.

Lepidus had to give up his army, his part in the empire, even the dignity of his title as a triumvir. Except for the post of *pontifex maximus*, which he had received as a legacy from the dictator after the Ides of March, he was deprived of everything, and his freedom was restricted. Octavian gave him a country house near Circei where he could live, but he must not leave it. When his eldest son ventured to rebel against Octavian a few years later and was executed, Octavian made the father move to Rome so that he could keep a closer eye on him. Lepidus lived on, punished by Octavian's contempt, until early in the year 12 BC. He owed his long life as much to his personal insignificance as to the fact that Octavian, after achieving undisputed rule in the west, decided to appear to the outside world as a changed man, the representative of law and order, mercy and cultured behaviour.

Octavian was now master of the entire west. He had won Sicily and

the two African provinces in military victories and he did not intend to
let his colleague Antony share the booty. Immediately after the end of
the war, he put his newly won provinces in order. The economic prosperity of Sicily, where the cities had known a last flowering of relative
independence during the rule of Sextus Pompey, came to an abrupt end
with the harsh levies imposed by Octavian. The province was to recover
only when veterans were settled there after the battle of Actium, but
even then it remained only a kind of agrarian appendage of the Italian
economy. As governor of the African provinces, Octavian appointed his
trusted general Titus Statilius Taurus, a man who, as if emerging from
nowhere, quickly proved himself capable and reliable in both the administrative and the military areas and had already been consul the previous
year.

Octavian now had over forty-five legions in all at his disposal,
25,000 cavalry and many thousands of lightly armed auxiliaries, together with 600 warships and their crews. Undoubtedly hardly a single
legion was at full strength, and among the Pompeians there will have
been a number of former slaves and freedmen of non-Roman origin
whose service was now at an end, and not all of whom by any means
could expect proper remuneration and provision for the future. Without the oarsmen, the majority of whom were freedmen, the regular
army of legionaries at the time would not have been much more than
100,000 to 120,000 men.

Like every military potentate in these years, Octavian was faced with
the problem of demobilizing the army after the end of the war, and
simultaneously with the question of the amount of pay and the extent
of provision made for the soldiers to be disbanded. He no longer had
the means for that: the war, particularly the building of ships, had swallowed up huge sums of money. A levy raised in Sicily brought in only
the most necessary funds. Attempts to satisfy the soldiers with only a
small sum now by holding out future prospects of more and placating
them with honours failed. One tribune of war shouted angrily at Octavian that the bestowal of such items as wreaths and garments was like
giving toys to children; soldiers had to be rewarded with land and
money. The tribune disappeared from view and was never seen again,
but the problem was not so easily eliminated. The older soldiers wanted
a peaceful retirement, with treatment as much on a par as possible with
the veterans of Mutina and Philippi. Octavian had to give way and he

managed somehow. He must have cut back on payments to several units of troops, in particular the Pompeians and many Antonians, but otherwise he paid the bounty of 2,000 sesterces that he himself had introduced in the year 44, and which had now become almost a norm. Above all, he granted men who had fought at Mutina and Philippi, about 20,000 in all, as well as those who had served ten or more years, retirement and settlement on a farm. To provide the farms, he drew on all the publicly held land still available in Italy, probably most of it confiscated estates, and since this was nowhere near enough, further land was bought from private owners. Octavian promised the centurions that he would ensure that they were made councillors in their home towns. These and other concessions, known to us from the chance find of an Egyptian papyrus, show how much Octavian depended on the goodwill of the soldiers at the time. The document concerned is the statement of a veteran made before a court of law and contains parts of an edict of Octavian from the time of the triumvirate, in which veterans are granted full freedom from taxation (*immunitas*) for themselves, their parents and their children, as well as exemption from military service and the privilege of being registered in any urban district of their choice.

The star of Sextus Pompey had set. On his way east he showed himself as unsteady and aimless as ever, sometimes effervescent, full of vigour and new plans, then rejecting them all again; now a commander with grand aims, next day a desperate petitioner. From Messene, he fled first to the west coast of Greece, stopping off in true corsair style on his way to plunder the time-honoured temple of Juno in the Lacinian foothills south of Kroton (Crotone), the shrine to which another general in flight, Hannibal, had affixed an account of his deeds in Greek and Phoenician before he left Italy. On the island of Cephalonia he surprisingly drew up an official document stating his military rank, in so far as he could still be said to have any, dismissing the men who had fought with him up to this point and saying they must all now fend for themselves. Then he went on, with only a few companions, to Lesbos. His father had once fled there from Caesar, and the son of Pompey the Great was well received too. Did he intend to settle down on Lesbos? He was still too young to go into retirement, and above all he had many enemies who were hardly likely to let him live there in peace. When he heard, while on the island, of the failures of Antony and his Parthian campaign, he immediately reversed his decision. He put the cloak of a commander on again, made contact with the Parthians and assembled his own supporters and desperadoes of all shades of opinion. At the beginning of the year 35 he even got a footing on the south bank of the Propontis (the Sea of Marmara) with a considerable fighting force. We may wonder how many adventurers were on the roads of the east at the time, ready to follow even a man like Pompey when he switched to recruiting infantry – and how it was that a governor had to fight men whom the enemy had recruited in his own province. Social and family ties had become loosened in the cities of the east too, plagued as they were by wars and financial levies, and for many Romans who lived here, or were temporarily in the region, both sides must have seemed as Roman as each other. After all, the corsair – or highway robber – did bear the name of Pompey the Great. Antony's generals finally trapped Pompey as he vacillated between armed conflict and his constantly expressed wish for discussion with Antony and took him prisoner. Not long before this, the last of his loyal friends had left him, including some proscribed men like the now elderly Quintus Minucius Thermus, who under the old republic had been praetor and governor of this same province of Asia where he was now at odds with his master. These defectors from Pompey found clemency and a welcome from Antony. Pompey himself, having tried to get in touch with the Parthians, could not count on any such thing.

The incumbent governor of Asia, Marcus Titius, had the captured Pompey taken to Miletus and executed there – whether on Antony's orders or by his own decision was a question debated even in the ancient world. At least Antony did not protest against the execution. Sextus Pompey died at the age of almost forty; he had been in flight for fifteen years of his life. He came from a famous gens, but none the less had been no one's ally in the civil war. The fact that he was condemned to play the part of an outsider was probably not just because of his personal disposition and the fact that he had found refuge with the fleet, but also because of his relationship to his father, Pompey the Great, which kept him from the Caesarians without winning him any real friends among the 'republicans'. In spite of his unpredictability and his affectations of oriental grandeur, a number of his contemporaries, among them some historians of classical antiquity, thought it to his credit that he had sheltered many proscribed men. The idea of asylum was linked to his name in these confused times of change by many, those proscribed as well as runaway slaves, deserters and men who lived dangerously.

Without any change in official terminology, the rule of the triumvirate, which had been constructed as a three-man office to govern the entire empire, had now become rule by two men, a duumvirate. In contrast to what had been anticipated at the founding of the triumvirate, the duumvirate rested on the principle of clear spatial separation, although the two parts of the empire did not become separate states. Instead, they had the character of military districts, in exactly the same way as the Roman provinces of the old days under their respective governors. The governorships of many provinces had, so to speak, come together in the persons of the two potentates. That made them heirs to the holders of extraordinary military commands in the last days of the republic, men who, like Pompey and Caesar, had commanded a whole series of provinces, except that, unlike them, the two triumvirs commanded not just several but all the provinces of the *imperium* between them. And as with the former holders of extraordinary military powers, a time limit was set to their authority, but the extension of their office of the triumvirate depended exclusively on them, since there was no longer any state power above them. Rome and Italy might be formally exempted from this military system, but the triumvirs (or in practice Octavian alone) were the dominating power here too. As that power in Rome was a legal one, and the consuls and Senate still existed as central institutions of state beside or under the triumvirs, from a purely formal viewpoint the triumvirate could be regarded as a special authority set up only to end the civil war and for a limited period of time, while the Senate and the consuls might be seen as the true heads of the state, as they had once been. But it would have been impossible for the people of the time to see it like that. In fact, the consuls were appointed by the triumvirs, and as they filled the other offices qualifying a man to enter the Senate in the same way – that is to say, just as they liked – the Senate too was an authority entirely dependent on them. In this system of government the old *res publica* had gone. Even the society on which the old state rested had been eliminated; its meagre remains served the triumvirs. Rome had become a naked military dictatorship divided between two men.

Public life in the huge empire had been reduced to the acceptance of orders from the two potentates. In accordance with the character of the regime, a militaristic spirit prevailed. Politics followed the marching footsteps of the legions, not the other way around. It is no coincidence that historians both in classical antiquity and today have dwelt so much on the numbers of legions in describing this period. The potentates themselves had to listen to those marching steps; they themselves depended entirely on the soldiers. Since there were Roman citizens on both sides in the civil war, the number of active soldiers reached previously unknown heights, and those who had already been demobilized rejoined the troops when they were needed. The financial requirements too were high, both because of the large number of those who had to be paid, rewarded and provided for and because of the unusually high payments. Formerly wars had brought money into the coffers of Rome; now the vast sums needed for the equipment and pay of the armies had to be extorted from the Romans themselves and their subject peoples. To the terror of the slaughter of thousands in the opposing camps of the civil war, with all its terrible consequences, and the misery of a military dictatorship stifling all public life was added the impoverishment of millions. Italy suffered severely under the expropriations and huge tax burdens, and it was even worse in the provinces. The eastern provinces had received new Roman masters four times between the years 49 and 37, and each of those masters had set about punishing or executing provincials and confiscating their property.

At no time had the misery of the Roman state been greater. No worse could come. It was like the aftermath of a great fire: new buildings had to be erected from the very foundations. But as yet, in the year 35, there was no architect in sight.

# 6

# The Generals in Contention
# for Sole Rule

With the annihilation of the forces of Sextus Pompey, the civil war could be considered over, as Octavian had said publicly in Sicily in front of his soldiers. All Romans, indeed the entire population of the empire, drew from that statement the reasonable hope that a new time of peace was dawning. The Golden Age proclaimed with such longing in Virgil's Fourth Eclogue seemed within reach at last, and it was felt that the blessings of peace, justice and prosperity were not far off. Many linked their hopes to the expectation that, with the end of internal strife, the triumvirate itself would yield to the old order in which the consuls and Senate had ruled the city and the empire. After all, the triumvirate had been founded in the first place out of the necessity to end the civil war.

Octavian did not resign his office, but he did announce that new days of peace lay ahead. And when he returned in the autumn of 36 as victor of the Sicilian War, he displayed the intuitive sense of how to make an impact that he was to demonstrate all his life by turning his arrival in Rome into an impressive spectacle. He received the Senate and the people not in the city itself but outside its walls, justifying this unusual scenario by saying that, as holder of a military command, he could not cross the *pomerium*, the sacrosanct boundary of the city, until the day of his triumph. In fact his reasoning showed little understanding of the rules of public law; in itself, the justification cited by Octavian applied only to the promagistracy, the holders of office active only in the provinces, not for those holding office in the centre of the city. A triumvir, uniting in himself authority over both areas, could have crossed the *pomerium* at any time without losing the dignity of his *imperium*. But the finely defined norms of republican constitutional law, which not so long ago had determined the balance of power between rival families, were certainly no longer in place in Rome at this time. If Octavian now referred back to the old order, showing it all due respect, it was done only to make a display of the most meticulous eagerness to observe the law.

The real point at issue, however, was to set a new tone. After all the lawlessness of the past, his announcement caught the attention of those who heard it and indeed astonished them. It was like an echo from another world. Did they know what to make of it? All that the Romans had learned in the last few decades was to obey the generals' orders and, knowing the murderous ferocity and greed of those generals as they did, they had indeed obeyed them without trusting anything they said. If one of these tyrants was now waxing eloquent about the coming Golden Age and the rule of law, it could be taken that he said so just for show. And so he did. At this time no one saw that this might also hint at the beginning of a still-distant reality. However, it became increasingly clear that Octavian was developing a remarkable ability for leadership. One of his principles was to outline his political intentions in various ways, finally giving them credibility by dint of almost incessant repetition. The most ferocious bloodhound of the civil war was now staging a new show under the banner of peace, order and justice. At the end of this year and the beginning of the next, many of his measures did suggest a new era to come.

In September 36, when Octavian won his war against Pompey, he had celebrated his twenty-seventh birthday. Now he addressed the Senate and people of Rome, assembled around him outside the city gates, to announce the end of the civil war and the restoration of the old order, which would be ushered in as soon as Antony returned from the Parthian campaign. He did not shrink from speaking of the horrors of the past few years, explaining and in the same breath apologizing for them. The last thing the people expected was to see one of the tyrants standing before them all and asking for pardon, or at least for understanding of what had happened. But that was not all: Octavian wanted his new ideas to reach everyone and he had them written down, copied and widely distributed.

His words were followed by actions that could be taken as indicating a new policy, a new spirit in the air. Octavian paid the debts of private citizens from the state coffers and rescinded many of the emergency taxes that the triumvirs had levied in the previous few years. He also showed his concern for law and order in Rome and Italy by giving his trusted general Gaius Calvisius Sabinus the title of prefect, with instructions to track down and eliminate the roving bands of criminals and highway robbers who had been so disruptive during the recent turmoil. Sabinus completed his mission within twelve months to his master's complete satisfaction, once again showing what the Roman administration could do.

To the surprise and approbation of the Romans, Octavian also provided settlements for almost all the freedmen who had served as soldiers, sailors or oarsmen in Sextus Pompey's army, quite a number of whom had formerly been slaves in Lower Italy and Sicily. These were men who had run away from their masters in the chaotic conditions of the civil war and had then been granted their freedom so that they could serve as soldiers. Octavian had recognized their situation in the agreements between the triumvirs and Pompey at Misenum. Those he had taken prisoner, however, he treated as runaway slaves (*fugitivi*) and returned them – about 36,000 of them in all – to their former masters or the heirs of those masters. And 6,000 of them, whose masters could not be found, were crucified: a shocking breach of the law on a large scale, since most of the delinquents had not tried to conceal their status. But Octavian was not concerned with that. He had more of an eye to the effect his measures would have on the masses, and for them law and justice stopped short where slavery began. If he expected that this particular measure would get him regarded in future as the right man to put the tottering social order on a firm footing again, his expectations were soon confirmed. The message had been understood, and the Romans were very happy to find him reviving something that had seemed gone for ever. Octavian's calculations were correct, and the terrible outcome was so important to him that, half a century later, in the memoir that he himself wrote, he still wanted it immortalized as a brilliant act on his part.

As the victor and bringer of peace he was showered with honours. Many may have remembered the humiliating way in which the docile Senate had once heaped such honours on the dictator Caesar. And, like Caesar, Octavian did not accept all the tributes offered to him: as in the dictator's time, the Senate merely laid a kind of selection of potential honours before him, and Octavian chose the most appropriate. In effect, he made his own decisions, but obviously no one even noticed the implied belittling of the Senate. Octavian accepted his triumph, as well as an annual celebration of his victories and the honour of a statue in the Forum. This gilded statue was to stand on a plinth adorned with the prows of ships, with an inscription under it stating that he had restored the peace so long disturbed by the civil war. On 13 November 36, Octavian celebrated his triumph over Sextus Pompey in the more modest form of an ovation. The inscription describing his victory as 'over Sicily' was only a thin disguise for the fact that he had triumphed over Roman citizens.

And now, so the Romans were supposed to think, they had only to await the appearance of Antony. Then they would be back where they had been before Caesar crossed the Rubicon. Few probably really believed that, but considering what they had suffered even the official announcement of such a state of affairs as a long-term aim, and perhaps not so distant a possibility after all, was satisfying and allowed them to hope for a secure future.

The year 36 saw Octavian's first important measure in the field of religious policy, and it too goes hand in hand with anticipation of a better future. Octavian lived on the Palatine Hill (mons Palatinus), close to the slopes that fell to the Forum and to what had once been the marshy plain at the foot of the Palatine, Esquiline and Caelian hills, residential areas favoured by distinguished citizens. Octavian, who had been born on the Palatine, owned the house of the orator Quintus Hortensius, famous as Cicero's rival, and he extended the property by adding other plots of land close to it. When the house was struck by lightning in the year 36, he declared the area sacred, dedicated it to Apollo and immediately had a temple built next to it. He had access to the temple along a ramp from his private apartments. Although the site of the temple had been transferred to public ownership and henceforth was the property of the god, clearly separate from his private rooms, Octavian now seemed so closely connected with Apollo that he could almost be regarded as a fellow occupant (*synnaos*) of the divine dwelling – exactly as he had intended.

In this his aim of approaching the sphere of the immortals is as significant as the choice of Apollo in particular. The physical proximity of the ruler's residence and the temple looks back to Hellenistic models; it was meant to emphasize rather than play down Octavian's commanding position. Building work on the temple lasted for eight years, and the importance that Octavian ascribed to it was evident, not least in purely visual terms. It was unusually magnificent; hardly a temple in the city could rival it for beauty. The building itself was very handsome, constructed entirely of pale marble quarried in Luna (Carrara); there was also a series of equally attractive subsidiary buildings, including libraries and a pillared hall with statues of the Danaids, and the furnishings were equally fine. Octavian adorned the temple with works by famous Greek sculptors. The cult statue of Apollo was by Skopas, and it was surrounded by four bronze bulls, the work of Myron.

Such elevation of a man or his extended family (*gens*) by association with supernatural powers was by no means a natural element in the religious tradition of the Romans. Divinity was perceived first as a direct image of natural phenomena such as lightning, thunder, wind and storms; its numinous power (*numen*) had no personal character and was thus in principle as various as the way in which nature expresses itself. It was encountered through propitiatory magic and ritualized expiation, highly formalized questions and answers, and taboos to ward off bad luck. Only in a long and complex process, under Etruscan and Greek influence, did anthropomorphic ideas of divinity and the association of certain distinct powers with individual gods develop in Rome – a development largely disregarded by the upper classes in the late republic. And yet the old ideas lived on here and there, not just in rural areas but also in the official religion of the city, and the barrier between the human and the divine still existed, at least to the extent that, even if in Rome a kind of divine aura surrounded powerful men such as rulers, it was not in quite the same way as in the eastern and particularly Hellenistic concept of the numinous. None the less, it had become possible for distinguished men to find something like an approach to the immortals. Individual clans had long boasted of their descent from ancestors of a mythical prehistoric period, heroes or even gods. Octavian himself, as a member of the Julian *gens,* entered the supernatural world through his ancestress Venus, and through the descendants of Aeneas, the son of Venus, he was also connected with Romulus, the founder of Rome, who as the son of Mars added yet another god to the Julian family tree. Then there was the apotheosis of his adoptive father; he was the son of the dictator who had been elevated to divinity, *divi filius.*

But all of this had come to him by inheritance. Consequently he looked outside his family and clan for a god who would be his own and would help him personally. This was not Octavian's own idea; his rivals had long preceded him in the religious elevation of their persons: Sextus Pompey as the favourite of Neptune, Antony as Dionysos himself, for in the east a powerful man was associated with divinity as a matter of course. The only strange thing was Octavian's choice of Apollo, even though that god had a secure position in the official state religion. We can trace his worship in Rome back to the fifth century BC, and at the end of the third century games had even been instituted in his honour (*ludi Apollinares*). They were held in July and probably owed their origin to an epidemic: the god was honoured for dealing with it. To the Romans, Apollo was first the god who sent diseases, then the deity who cured them again (Apollo medicus); he was linked more closely to the Greek world than any of the other immortals and therefore had no specific Roman name. In addition, the Romans honoured him as the god of oracles. They had had a close connection with Delphi since the late third century, and Roman poets had celebrated Apollo as the god of the Delphic oracle long before Octavian discovered his uses. He enjoyed particular importance in that function through being linked to the oracular sibyl of Cumae in Campania. Either at the same time as the temple was dedicated or directly afterwards, Octavian had the collection of Sibylline oracles, which according to old tradition contained predictions of the future of Rome, placed inside the plinth of the cult statue.

From time immemorial the god had had an altar in Rome (the Apollinare) on the site of which a temple was built in the early republican period, not far from the banks of the Tiber on the Field of Mars, and several years after the dedication of the new temple on the Palatine it was thoroughly renovated by Gaius Sosius, victor over the Jews and consul in the year 32. Sosius gave the temple some fine statues, among them, as well as a statue of Apollo in cedar wood, the famous Niobid group by Praxiteles or Skopas, which as one of Antony's generals he had appropriated from Seleukeia (now Silifke) in Cilicia. The Apollo of this temple was primarily the god of healing. After the building of the second temple to Apollo on the Palatine he was known as Apollo Sosianus, after his renovator, while the god of the new cult was Apollo Palatinus. Apollo's sister Diana (Artemis) and their mother Latona (Leto) were also worshipped in the Palatine temple. Octavian had established a close connection with Diana through his victory over Sextus Pompey at Naulochus, for she had a temple on the coast not far from the battlefield and could be cited retrospectively for helping Octavian in the conflict.

Octavian did not merely declare that he was close to Apollo, like Sextus Pompey proclaiming his relationship with Neptune. The connection was institutionalized in the worship of the god on the Palatine: in fact Palatine Apollo existed only through Octavian. However, at this early date it is not very likely that he intended this association as a prototype of the religious elevation that he later gave to his position. In the year 36 he needed to stand out in strong contrast from his rival for power. The way in which he put his intentions into practice is typical of what could be expected from him in future: a simple declaration was not enough; he created a framework in which his plans were clearly set out and established on a permanent basis.

There is further evidence of that in another measure of the same year closely connected with the Palatine cult. Octavian made the Senate transfer the 'sanctity' (sacrosanctitas) of the tribune of the people to him. A good 400 years earlier, the tribuneship of the people had been a revolutionary institution, endowed with religious force by the common people, the plebeians who strove for social and political recognition, to allow them to stand up to the established magistracy of the patrician holders of office. The sanctity of the tribune meant that he must not be approached with any intent to threaten him, and any obstacle placed in the way of his activities was punished as sacrilege deserving death. That was still the case after the plebeians had achieved their aim and made the tribuneship of the people an office like all the others. Sanctity still surrounded every tribune, and Caesar had already used that fact to acquire a sacred aura and personal inviolability of his own. Since only a man of plebeian origin could become tribune of the people, and he was a patrician, he was unable to hold the office himself, and he had simply separated the 'sanctity' from the office and had it transferred to him – disregarding the fact that this was an outright violation of republican law.

In the year 36 Octavian resorted to the same measure as his adoptive father. By now the ruthless exploitation of public law to the benefit of their own power base had become almost customary among the triumvirs, and in addition this new transgression of the law seemed to be mitigated by the dictator's previous example. Octavian thus surrounded himself with that aura of inviolability that his close association with Apollo also gave him, at the same time emphasizing yet again his role as Caesar's political heir.

The years after the victory over Sextus Pompey brought the Romans in Italy and the provincials of the empire the peace they had wanted so long. Conscription, the billeting of soldiers on civilians, expropriation of property, pillage and burning, punishments inflicted for siding with the wrong party and a heavy burden of taxation were now things of the past. The old order was gone along with the society it had served; nothing was left but the bare bones of the regulation of public affairs. Admittedly that regulation was no longer left to itself; the triumvirs intervened as they liked, but there was still a framework providing a sense of direction for the time being. For the provincials, hardly anything had changed anyway, and the Romans adapted as best they could to the tyranny of the generals. At first, the rejoicing at the restoration of peace and the security it brought veiled over all misgivings.

The triumvirs, on the other hand, were now at a standstill. The triumvirate had been formed to end the civil war, or in precise terms to get rid of the assassins of Caesar. That had been done long ago, and the period of unrest associated with Sextus Pompey, the reason why they had continued in their specially created office, was over too. The duration of the triumvirate had been extended to the year 33, but in the present year 36 Octavian himself had publicly held out the prospect of an end to it. The Romans knew that he could conclude it only jointly with Antony, and that Antony would have to come to Rome for that purpose and would certainly keep everyone waiting. So the prospect was still some way off. What was to be done until the time came to end the triumvirate?

As a military dictatorship, the triumvirate was in the tradition of the extraordinary powers of military command in the late republic, which meant that the army raised under that command for a specific purpose had to carry out its mission. But the mission was now completed, and as the Roman system did not provide for a standing army the soldiers had to be demobilized. However, by now this kind of political logic had lost its force: the two potentates, eyeing one another suspiciously, each waiting for any sign of weakness in the other to attack his rival, would have been surrendering power by giving up their legions. Consequently both huge armies remained under arms. As they could not be accommodated in barracks, they had to be brought into the field. And so they were: the triumvirs presented themselves to their armies as those with the power of command and marched against the enemy. The only question was, where *was* he? For the operation was not the result of danger from outside, but was based on the necessity of keeping the legions on the move, so it was left to the two triumvirs to decide where to lead their men. A state of war still prevailed, but the enemy had yet to be found.

The search for an enemy was simpler for Antony than for his rival, since there was a war on his doorstep, one that, so to speak, he could inherit. The Parthians had indeed been defeated and thrown back over the frontiers of the empire, but a security problem could be constructed on the basis of the Parthian attack of the years 41/40, and by looking back to the defeat of Crassus in the year 53. The dictator Caesar, whom all generals aspired to emulate, had planned much the same thing, although in his time it was still to be a campaign of actual vengeance for the defeat at Carrhae.

So, in the summer of 36, Antony opened up a new theatre of war in the east. The campaign was carefully prepared in advance, and a large army of invasion was equipped with everything it would need, including a large artillery section. With the auxiliaries, their strongest troop being the cavalry of King Artavasdes of Armenia, an ally of Rome, Antony's forces numbered about 100,000 men, including 60,000 Roman legionaries. However, the strategic plan for this mighty army's march does not seem to be entirely clear. Evidently Antony did not want to attack the Parthian heartlands of Mesopotamia and Persis directly by crossing the Euphrates from the Syrian side. Instead, he advanced from the river without crossing it in Syria and then marched through the mountainous country of Armenia, by way of what is now Erzurum, and north of Lake Van to the river Araxes (Araks). From there in the north, he invaded the north-west of Media, a district called Atropatene (Media Atropatene: Media Minor, today Azerbaijan on the borders of Iran), at the time ruled by a client prince of the king of Parthia. Here Antony camped outside the capital, Phraaspa (Phraata), and it looked as if he would have to take it before marching any further. Only then could he have gone south, whether into the old central provinces of the Persians,

Medians and Susians, or – more probably – to the capital of Ctesiphon in Mesopotamia.

What was the strategic idea behind this huge detour? Perhaps Antony was thinking of the fate of Crassus, harassed by the Parthian cavalry, and therefore wanted to avoid the plains. It turned out to have been the right decision. Although the army had its own large body of mounted men, it was to suffer severe losses later under attack by the Parthian cavalry, both those men who rode in armour and were known as cataphracts and the riders lightly armed with bows and arrows. The detour also seems to have been part of a feint: the appearance of Antony at Zeugma on the Euphrates was probably meant to make the enemy believe he planned to take the usual way to Ctesiphon, and indeed the Parthians with their main army did at first camp in the great bend of the Euphrates. That may also explain the haste of Antony's march through Armenia and Media Atropatene. At the same time, we may wonder whether the dangers of taking the detour were not bound to outweigh the advantages of avoiding the plains. Should not the difficulty of such a great march through sometimes almost impassable terrain, and of supplying provisions for such a huge number of men and animals in bleak and unfamiliar country, have made Antony stop and think?

There were also bad mistakes from the start in the timing of the campaign. Antony did not set out until summer, and by the time he arrived in the northern mountains winter was already imminent. But, as the wide detour he had intended to take was justified only by the advantage of surprise, when he appeared on the borders of the Parthian heartlands he gave the army no respite in friendly Armenia. To make up for lost time, he hounded his soldiers on to the Araxes, even leaving behind the artillery, slow and clumsy as it was to transport, so that he could go on even faster towards Mesopotamia and arrived outside Phraaspa without it. He had clearly been taking the war engines with him to besiege Ctesiphon, but he could have done with them now. He could not storm the city without them, and no new engines could be built for want of suitable timber in the surrounding countryside. Meanwhile the Parthians had had time to go to Phraaspa by the shorter route from the bend of the Euphrates. Now their mobile formations attacked, falling first on the baggage train marching on a separate route south of Lake Urmia. They destroyed the siege engines it had been bringing and killed the guard of 10,000 men. Artavasdes of Armenia, who had been with the baggage train, fled. And although the Parthians had immediately gone on the attack here, where the enemy proved weak, they subsequently declined to give battle to the main Roman force, well knowing that the enemy was in a hopeless position. They could expect to defeat it without too much trouble.

Antony, whose military and strategic abilities were always at their best in an emergency, did the only thing he could in the circumstances: he began to withdraw. But the retreat almost ended in disaster. Pursued by the enemy, who were almost constantly advancing and then withdrawing again, tormented by hunger and terrible thirst, the army dragged itself back over the mountains and valleys of Media to the Araxes and on to Armenia, where wintry weather made life particularly hard for the soldiers. Although while he was still outside Phraaspa Antony, infuriated by his defeat, had had several units decimated – every tenth man, chosen by lot, was executed – on the retreat he now showed himself a cautious general who was concerned for his troops, and whose authority remained uncontested even in the greatest hardships. No less

Parthian campaign of Antony in 36 BC

admirable was the conduct of the soldiers themselves. For all their hunger, thirst and exhaustion, they seldom fell out of line, and even now showed the world what tough and well-trained fighting men they were. Under the present circumstances they were still able, as historians of antiquity record, to form a 'tortoise' (*testudo*) when a single command was given in an emergency; in that formation all the soldiers held their large rectangular shields above their heads, the men in front kneeling, the men behind them standing, and thus created a solid roof that would resist attack, since any hail of spears and arrows bounced back off it. Yet in spite of the great achievements of this retreat, undoubtedly one of the outstanding deeds of any Roman army, the end of the campaign was depressing. Antony had lost 20,000 men and 4,000 cavalry in Media itself, and on the march back he lost another 8,000 men.

The power of Rome, none the less, could not be considered destroyed by this defeat as it had been at Carrhae, only impaired. However, the political implications of an operation planned on such a large scale were devastating. Antony had achieved nothing, and on the retreat had not even managed to wrest from the Parthians his minimum demand: the return of the Romans captured at Carrhae and the standards taken there. The Parthian empire, which since the taking of Syria by Pompey the Great had formed the eastern border of the Roman *imperium* and in Roman eyes had to be annihilated, had once again defied the masters of the world. It had asserted itself as an independent empire to match the realms of Rome. As Augustus, Octavian was quick to draw the political conclusions arising from the year 36, and no Roman ruler after him tried invading Parthia again.

Back in Syria, Antony gave himself up to leisure. Cleopatra brought him equipment and money, but he dropped his original plan for another Parthian expedition and in the years 35 and 34 waged only a not very glorious campaign against Artavasdes, king of Armenia, whom he blamed for his failure. The king was tricked into coming to a meeting and was taken prisoner and led in triumph by Antony through Alexandria. In Rome, however, considerable distaste was felt for this 'triumph', more particularly because of its location. All previous triumphs had been held in Rome, and there was also the question of whom exactly he had triumphed over. The Romans had indeed won a number of minor skirmishes with the Parthians on the march out and back again, but

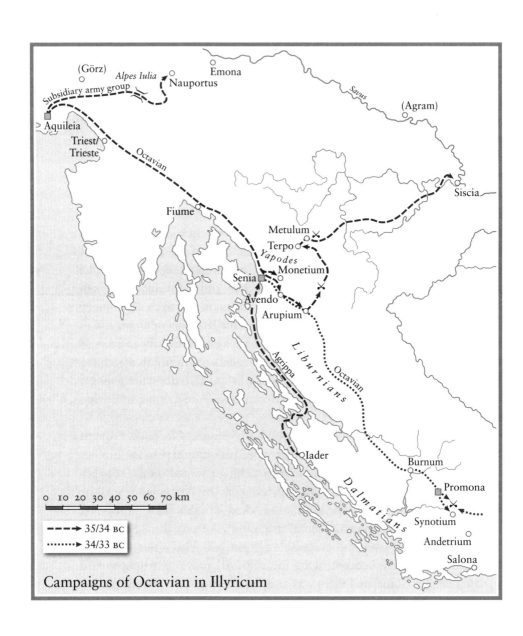

(Görz)    *Alpes Iulia*    Emona

Subsidiary army group    Nauportus

Aquileia

Triest/
Trieste    Octavian    Savus

(Agram)

Fiume    Siscia

Metulum

Terpo
*Yapodes*
Senia    Monetium
Avendo
Arupium

Agrippa    *L i b u r n i a n s*    Octavian

Iader    Burnum

Promona

*D a l m a t i a n s*    Synotium

Andetrium

Salona

o  10 20 30 40 50 60 70 km

- - - ▶ 35/34 BC
········▶ 34/33 BC

Campaigns of Octavian in Illyricum

they had lost the war, although Antony boasted of victory in his report to the Senate. No Roman, however, could doubt that the great man had lost authority in his own provinces. Octavian, who had defeated Sextus Pompey, was no longer just the junior partner. In fact he gained in stature through Antony's setback, although he owed his own victories, or at least the more important of them, to his generals. Nor did he have his rival's plain, straightforward nature or his frankness and geniality, all of them qualities that Antony's men valued highly, such that even in the utmost need they not only obeyed his orders but felt they were his devoted comrades.

Meanwhile Octavian too had found an enemy against whom he could pit his army and present himself as a general. He had his eye on the tribes of Dalmatia and its hinterland, people of partly Celtic and partly Illyrian origin. Their ancestors had interbred freely during centuries of conflict for land and supremacy. They had never been any real danger to the towns and tribes of the plain of the river Po, let alone Italy as a whole; only at the end of the second century BC did there seem to be a threat from Germanic tribes approaching from that direction, and with it the possibility of invasion. At the time (109 BC) Rome had suffered a severe defeat against Cimbrian Germans at Noreia in the eastern Alps. But the Cimbrians had withdrawn again, to invade the Roman empire by other routes through Gaul. Since then the Romans of the north-east of Italy had had to deal only with occasional incursions, which could be troublesome and sometimes went as far as the north-eastern Roman colony of Aquileia but had never been any serious threat. Danger did not come that way.

The wide expanse of land involved, still not entirely explored in depth but none the less closely linked to Roman history for 200 years, and the question of how a clear land route could be created from there to the province of Macedonia in the south of the Balkan peninsula, seemed to offer itself on a plate to a general in search of a military task. In addition, Illyria was next door to Italy, and although the Romans did not really know much about the land mass lying beyond the coastal area of Dalmatia, so that strategic aims at the beginning of the campaign could not be very clearly outlined, an expedition to restore peace and good order on that particular frontier could be made to sound plausible to the public. When Caesar looked around for an extraordinary military command in the year of his consulate (59), so that he could recruit an army devoted to him and use it to further his ambition to be the first man in Rome, he had Upper Italy, still known as Cisalpine Gaul, and Illyricum, the coastal area of Dalmatia ruled by Rome, assigned to him by popular decree for the period immediately following his time of office. He obviously had an Illyrian campaign in mind, but then news of movements in central Gaul made him give up the idea in favour of a war against the Celts in the north of the Roman province of Gallia Narbonensis (the south of France). He induced the Senate to grant him that province too, and the Illyrian War became the Gallic War instead.

Octavian took up the idea. An Illyrian campaign had the advantage that, in contrast to Antony with his operations in the east, he could make it look as if he were going to war to protect Italy. In addition, Octavian could return quickly to nearby Rome at any time. Finally, the action was no more than the fulfilment of a plan which, so it seemed, had already been made by his adoptive father Caesar.

First, in the year 35, Octavian set off for Sicily again. He really wanted to cross from there to Africa, to visit the provinces that he had taken over from Lepidus and put them in order. But he suddenly abandoned that plan – presumably mainly because of the bad weather that kept him too long in Sicily and made a crossing to Africa seem inadvisable. Instead he planned his Illyrian campaign, although no one could have said that there was any serious threat to the border in view of the contingents of troops encamped in Italy at this time. Even Burebista, king of Dacia, who had built up considerable domination of the Danube area decades before and may well have meant to advance against Caesar in the year 59, could no longer serve as the pretext for a campaign, since he had been assassinated in the year 44. If Dalmatia was the object of attack none the less, it was because Octavian wanted, not to contain a genuine danger, but to show off his gifts as a commander and form closer bonds with the army. A general subordinate to Octavian was to march against the Alpine tribes, who were less suitable to feature as the enemy in a war that would make a real impression on the soldiers and citizens of Rome.

Before setting out, Octavian had to face the discontented veterans of the Sicilian army again. They had not yet all received compensation, many wanted to rejoin the army, and sometimes the general dissatisfaction led to an outright refusal to obey orders. The demobilization planned after the Sicilian War had not yet finished, and in this phase of change, marked by demobilization on the one hand and the retention of strong units to protect the military barons on the other, various possibilities opened up to the soldiers, indicating the already problematical nature of a standing army. The recalcitrance of the soldiers was due to several factors: the consequences of their growing self-confidence and their long inactivity, as well as their disinclination for a future as farmers that lay ahead of them. What were these battle-hardened veterans to think about, in their poor lodgings, if not a future of material security and their special political position? It was only with great difficulty that Octavian managed to carry the day. He succeeded in the end by punishing some of the protesting or even mutinous groups, rewarding others or breaking them up by removing particularly subversive men. It was not to be the last time that he felt the power wielded by the army.

The Illyrian War began, or rather was started, in the spring of 35, and dragged on with long interruptions until the year 33. Octavian and Agrippa set out from Senia (Senj) on the Adriatic coast, where the army and the fleet had gathered, to invade the land of the Iapodes, a mixed Celtic-Illyrian people in the hinterland of the north Dalmatian coast (today western Croatia). Like all the larger tribal federations in the area, the Iapodes consisted of many subsidiary tribes, and at least in part already owed tribute to Rome. They were easy prey for the legions. The invaders met with more determined resistance outside the town of Metulum, which capitulated only after a siege of some length. The Romans tried to take it by throwing up ramparts to the height of the walls and laying wooden bridges across them. But the bridges kept collapsing under the weight of the men on them, and when Octavian and Agrippa, followed by many soldiers, hurried on ahead the bridge they were crossing fell. Octavian was slightly injured on the right thigh and both arms. However, because of his participation in close-quarter combat and his injuries the soldiers saw him as one of them; he could have wished for nothing better. As he had neither the temperament of a fighting man nor the qualities of a commander, his 'wounds' might suffice as evidence of what was expected of him as a soldier.

After the defeat of the Iapodes, in summer, Octavian went on to the Save, where the Pannonians, another Celtic-Illyrian mixed people, lived on both sides of the river. His destination was the town of Siscia, which had great strategic importance because of its situation. Octavian seems to have seen it as the point of departure for enterprises that would take him as far as the Danube and then across the river to fight the Dacians. The attack was therefore not a reaction to any threat from the Pannonians; its justification lay in itself – or rather, in the fact that Octavian wanted to win military fame and had enough legions to make the attempt. The Pannonians are described by the historian Cassius Dio, who administered the provinces of Dalmatia and Upper Pannonia 250 years later under the emperor Severus Alexander, as simple peasants who grew hardly any olive trees or vines and ate barley and oats instead of wheat – a wretched existence in the eyes of the people of the Mediterranean region. It was usual in classical times to describe such people as brave but bloodthirsty, with modest needs but passionate, and Dio does exactly that. Octavian was soon able to subdue the town and the surrounding countryside. In a naval battle on the Save, incidentally, Menodorus, the gifted admiral who had changed sides several times, found a fitting death in Octavian's service. Octavian brought twenty-five cohorts to Siscia as a garrison, the strength of which in itself indicated that he did not mean to give up the land he had conquered. By the late summer of 35 the country of the Iapodes and Pannonians could be considered subdued.

Next, Octavian turned to the conquest of the Dalmatians who had settled in the coastal area of central Dalmatia. A restless people, in the winter of 48/47 they had even lured a Roman unit of 2,000 men under Aulus Gabinius into an ambush and cut them to pieces. They went on giving the Romans trouble, so their subjugation was in fact necessary to secure the coast and the land route to Macedonia. Octavian spent the summer, and the following winter of 34/33, 'taming' them, especially by conquering towns and small fortified positions on difficult terrain. He received another injury in this fighting, from a sling stone that struck his right knee. However, he won through, and when the last town surrendered in the winter and he also won back the prize of the standard that had been lost in the defeat of Gabinius, the war could be considered over. Only those who see the Illyrian campaign as a struggle for a definite border can claim that he interrupted it because of the confrontation with Antony that was looming and with it abandoned the idea of going on perhaps as far as the Danube. But Rome was not on the defensive. Indeed, with the total militarization of politics, it had just entered a very dynamic phase of its foreign policy. The potentate had to give his army some practice, and securing the Dalmatian region, which had been full of unrest in the previous few decades, offered a means to that end. It made an advance into the interior of the Balkans necessary, but not a campaign all the way to the Danube, the precise situation of which would still have been largely unknown to the Romans at this time. With the pacification of the Dalmatians and the conquest of Siscia, the establishment of the Save as a borderline – after advancing to the river from several directions – and the securing of the route south from Dalmatia, these achievements could be presented as the purpose of a strategic plan and intended from the start. The strong garrison left occupying Siscia shows that Octavian wanted to claim that he had done what he set out to do. Another advance into the depths of the Balkans, however, would be a new enterprise needing new prerequisites. Later, Octavian had the standard that had been recovered set up in the pillared hall called after Gnaeus Octavius (porticus Octavia) on the Flaminian Circus, which he probably began to renovate that year, 33.

In fact it was high time to cut short his military commitment in Illyricum: the two men who held power over Rome were already arming for the final battle. In retrospect it seemed inevitable. Was that really so? The republic and its society were gone; Rome and the *imperium* were led by two potentates who were rulers in all but name. Did this situation mean there could be no established duumvirate? At least the triumvirate as set up in the year 43 could no longer be the vessel of the new system of government, for it had been founded as a by-product of the civil war with the sole aim of restoring peace on a military basis. But the civil war was over, and the period of the triumvirate ran out at the end of 33. It would have had to be re-formed to become a permanent institution as a duumvirate. But that was unthinkable, for the relationship between the two men was marked by mutual distrust.

Only one thing still linked the triumvirs: Antony's marriage to Octavia, which had produced two daughters but no son. Octavia stood loyally by her husband and his supporters. Her house in Rome was a kind of gathering point for the Antonians, and after the unfortunate Parthian campaign she immediately set out for the east with a guard of 2,000 soldiers as well as money and armaments, to demonstrate personal as well as political solidarity. Perhaps Octavian gave her the means to do it, or perhaps he was at least glad to see her leave, more for the sake of a public display of untroubled relations with his rival than because he seriously believed in the political future of the duumvirate. As a wily tactician, he probably guessed what awaited his sister: as soon as Octavia reached Athens, Antony sent a message telling her that she could send the soldiers and money to Syria for him, but she herself must return to Rome. This was the final break. When Octavian embarked on his first campaign against Antony soon afterwards, he instantly exploited this insult to Antony's widely respected, faithful and now shamefully abandoned wife. The blame lay fairly and squarely on his rival's side.

However, there were also other reasons for the loosening of the bond between Antony and Octavian over the last few years. They concerned the difference between the two halves of the empire and Antony's policy of government in the east. Something should be said about that here.

After his last meeting with Octavian, Antony had set off from Tarentum in the spring of 37 for the east, to begin the Parthian campaign. While in Syria he had made several important decisions on the organization of the eastern half of the empire, and Cleopatra played a significant part in them. In the year 40 she had borne him twins, Alexandros Helios and Cleopatra Selene. After that their affair seems to have lapsed for three years, but now Antony took it up again, linking the resumption of the relationship to a new political order of the entire Syrian-Asiatic area. Whether he married Cleopatra formally later is not clear, and indeed it is rather improbable. If he had done so it would hardly have troubled anyone in the east, whereas the Romans, in particular Octavian, might have felt injured, despite the fact that such a marriage would not have been recognized in Roman law.

More important than this close personal relationship, however, was the transfer by Antony of considerable parts of the provincial Roman area to the queen of Egypt. She received that part of Syria known as 'hollow Syria' (Koile Syria), comprising all the land between Lebanon and the desert, and part of the Phoenician coast, from the province of Cilicia to the island of Cyprus with what was called 'rough or rugged Cilicia' (Cilicia Aspera, the mountainous western part of the coastline). Until now the Roman system had rested above all on two factors: direct (i.e. military) rule over the provinces, and indirect rule over the dependent or client kings and princes whose lands lay partly inside and partly outside provincial areas. That was now changed in favour of other client rulers as well as Cleopatra. In 40/39, during an extensive reorganization of the clientele system in Asia Minor and Syria, Antony had already installed several petty kings, as a rule, with the exception of Herod and Polemon, preferring members of established royal houses. In the year 37 he had also reorganized the system by promoting those who were not descended from any royal family but over the last few years had proved themselves loyal supporters of the Romans or of Antony personally. Four men in particular had been helpful to him in his plans: Herod the Idumaean, whom he had expressly confirmed as king of Judaea after the elimination of the last legitimate Hasmonaean successor to the throne; Polemon, who received the realm of Pontos on the Black Sea coast, to which eastern parts of the Roman province of Bithynia and Pontus were later added; Archelaos, who was set up as king in Cappadocia; and finally Amyntas, to whom Antony gave Galatia and Pisidia as well as parts of Lycaonia and Pamphylia. What role was intended for the queen of Egypt within this clientele system was not at first clear. Was she to be regarded as a client princess like the others, or was she to have an independent function? In any case, Antony's measures had considerably reduced the extent of the Roman provincial area east of the Hellespont, as created by Pompey and taken over wholesale by the dictator. After the year 34 the province of Cilicia had disappeared, and Bithynia and Pontus was now about half as large as it had been. From now on there were only three Roman provinces east of the Dardanelles: Asia, Bithynia and Syria.

The next stage in the reorganization of the east came three years later – at a time when the failure of the Parthian campaign, rearmament and the capture of the king of Armenia were all in the past. And although Antony's relations with Cleopatra in that period had hardly been notable for constancy and deep intimacy, politically they reached a new zenith with the celebration of 'victory' over the Armenians in the year 34. After his magnificent triumph, Antony organized an official ceremony in the Gymnasium of Alexandria, in which, in the presence of Roman officers, client princes and the great men of the Ptolemaic kingdom, he enthroned the queen of Egypt and their three children in new dignity (the third, Ptolemaios Philadelphos, had been born in the year 36). Even the outward show emphasized the importance of the proceedings: Antony and Cleopatra sat on golden chairs on a raised dais covered with silver. Then the Roman declared his lover 'queen of kings' over

Egypt, Cyprus and Libya (Cyrenaica) as well as Koile Syria and appointed the thirteen-year-old Caesarion, allegedly the dictator's son, king of kings and her co-ruler. Of their own children he gave Alexandros Helios Armenia, Media and the Parthian empire (if and when he conquered it), while the youngest, Ptolemaios Philadelphos, was to have Koile Syria as well as the plains of Cilicia with Tarsos, and his daughter Cleopatra Selene received the province of Libya – this last area undoubtedly under Cleopatra as supreme ruler. At the ceremony Alexandros wore Median and Ptolemaios Macedonian costume. At the same time, Cleopatra was proclaimed 'the new Isis', an unusual identification even for the Egyptians. They did not doubt the divinity of their rulers, but no mortal had yet seen the goddess in human form. So the 'new Dionysos' now had his companion in the 'new Isis'.

One cannot help noticing that the districts so solemnly transferred to her had already, in principle, been granted to her in 37, and the occasion was mainly about titles and the confirmation of the transfer, besides involving the children. When Alexandros Helios was granted the dignity of great king of Parthia and the Parthian empire in this theatrical ceremony, while Ptolemaios Philadelphos had the area between the Euphrates and the Hellespont bestowed on him, these were theoretical titles and not a real transfer of power, for the existing administration continued as before. It is not out of the question that the 'gift' to Ptolemaios was a piece of propaganda circulated by Octavian and was never actually announced. Antony celebrated thousands of festivals of all kinds in the east, particularly Alexandria, and always enjoyed himself hugely. He appreciated good living to the full, a characteristic censured by modern historians in disparaging terms such as 'debauched conduct'. He saw no reason for a ruler to abstain from the pleasures of life. But the solemn ceremony in the Gymnasium in Alexandria was no joke. If Antony had not lost all touch with reality – and we have no reason to suppose so, or to see him as the Roman hero blinded by love sometimes helpfully presented to us by historians both ancient and modern – there must have been some political sense in his reorganization of the east.

We can see at once that Antony had not abandoned his hopes of conquering the Parthian empire; the appointment of Alexandros Helios (in Median costume) as great king of Parthia shows that clearly. But at the centre of the ceremony was a reorganization of the areas that he actually did control. What did Antony intend by it? His preference for indirect rule through client princes or members of the Ptolemaic royal house is clear and was certainly founded on the basis of geographically defined provinces which were a burden on the direct military administration. Antony's grants of provincial areas as kingdoms to his children will have been understood and accepted by his Roman followers as the announcement of a dynastic inheritance, and such ideas had become familiar to many Romans during the period of military rule. In addition, the change of political order is easier to understand as a reinforcement of existing rule by client princes if we think of the difficulty Antony had in administering huge areas. He had neither enough Roman administrators nor enough Roman tax collectors, two groups of officials indispensable for direct Roman administration, and in addition he was short of Roman soldiers who could secure his sphere of military influence. It looks as if client kings were to fill that gap.

We may be able to follow Antony's thinking here, but the role occupied in his mind by Egypt, the last and most powerful of the Hellenistic kingdoms, is much harder to understand. It is also noticeable that Antony was excluding from the system of 'dynastic rule' his daughters by Octavia – not to mention his two sons by his marriage to Fulvia. We might accept that dependent princes were now to have greater weight in the process of provincialization; we might even justify all this by pointing out that the inclusion of Egypt in the Roman clientele system increased the entire sphere of Roman rule and influence. In fact, however, Egypt had been a client kingdom of Rome for a long time, and now, by way of contrast, it seemed to have achieved a certain independence, for in her political ranking the Egyptian queen rated a place beside rather than below Antony. The minting in the year 32 of denarii – Roman, not Egyptian currency – with her head on the reverse of the coin that bore Antony's head on the obverse could be taken as confirming her rise in rank. And how exactly did the eastern client princes, how above all did Cleopatra, stand in relation to Antony in this system? Even after the triumvirate had run its course at the end of 33, Antony still called himself a triumvir and featured as patron of all the rulers enthroned by him. But was not 'triumvir' an empty title after the year 33? And what did 'patronage' mean? What would happen if he died? Would the political arrangements that had now been made put Cleopatra and Caesarion in his place?

There is no overlooking the fact that for all his efforts to create a structure of government suitable for the east by linking the clientele principalities with the Roman provinces, it ultimately depended solely on Antony's power over the Roman part of his army. Moreover, the political system of the east would not keep going of its own accord, and apart from a few cities founded by the dictator with no tradition of their own, some still under construction, Rome had a presence here only in the form of Antony's not very numerous legionaries and the rather mixed society of his 'court'. But a military despot here in the east could not become either a Roman or a Hellenistic ruler.

Whatever Antony intended by his reorganization, we have to distinguish it clearly from what Octavian's propaganda made of it in describing him as 'squandering Roman provinces on his oriental concubine'. Antony's policies do seem to have laid him open to such slanders. In 33, however, when he asked the Senate in Rome to recognize the measures he had taken, he must at least have supposed that many Romans would understand and accept them. So was the criticism purely a product of the tension that now existed between the two camps, or was there a kernel of truth in it?

In the various meetings of the triumvirs, Antony had realized that he would get no support from Octavian and more particularly could expect no replacement of his Roman legions. Even the 20,000 legionaries promised to him in Tarentum had been withheld. Of the 120 ships that he had lent Octavian in the year 37, only the seventy still intact were returned, with no replacements for those lost in the Sicilian War. It is strange, however, that he adopted such a passive attitude to a man who let slip no opportunity to damage him, having himself received so many concessions from him, Antony. Indeed, in retrospect we can only marvel at it. In the year 40, Antony had accepted the annexation of his Gallic provinces; he had also tolerated the fact that Sextus Pompey, who could have been useful to him to counterbalance his rival, was brought down by Octavian; he had not even protested with any vigour at the dismissal of Lepidus, and Octavian's annexation of the latter's African province and his army. And that is not by a long way all that Antony let his rival get away with.

He was passive, however, only in his relations with Octavian, not in his activities in his own sphere of influence. Here he had both to carry his plans through and make preparations for a possible confrontation.

He did so with an energy that is illustrated not least by his installation of the system of client princes. The dependent princes, above all those kings who were personally devoted to him because, to the Greek way of thinking, they were not 'legitimate', served to reinforce Roman rule and at the same time to some extent made up for his lack of fresh supplies of Roman soldiers from the west. And although the Egyptian kingdom was clearly first among the others in this order of things, the general framework of its expansion had some precedence in older traditions of power politics: Cyprus and Cyrenaica now went 'back' to the royal house of Egypt, as former Egyptian possessions on the secundogeniture principle, and the extensions of the Syrian area were also within the old Ptolemaic area, or what the Ptolemies themselves claimed to be that area. All these regions were now linked with Antony, admittedly not directly, but indirectly through Cleopatra's children, who were also his.

However, hard as we may try to explain and justify the reorganization of the system in the east, we cannot fail to see that Ptolemaic Egypt, which in the century before the dictator's time had increasingly been a mere plaything tossed hither and thither in Roman internal politics, and thus had lost any independence, had now been politically upgraded by Antony. In her political ambitions, which were bent on linking the home territory of Egypt with Syrian and Cilician possessions, Cleopatra obviously took her guidelines from her great ancestor Ptolemaios II Philadelphos (r. 285–246), whose name she had given to her youngest son. It was significant that with the first major transfers of territory she ordained a new numbering of the years of her reign, beginning with the year 37/36 as the first. Nor could anyone fail to see that through the expansion of her territory in the Syrian and Cyprian area she now controlled the most important suppliers of timber for ship-building and thus represented naval power in the new system. There was no overlooking the fact that this considerably increased the importance of Egypt, and Octavian's propaganda deliberately made it central to its slander campaign against Antony. Whether or not an inclination to Cleopatra that we cannot now assess played a part in the preferential treatment of Egypt in the reorganization of government in the east, there is no disputing that with its financial power and its fleet this particular country was a great support to Antony, one that should not be underestimated. Perhaps, swayed by personal relationships, he did not fully perceive the political dependency that had been created in this way, any more than he understood the problem of succession by inheritance in the Roman sense. But in this last respect it was the same for Octavian. In both cases, military despotism was seeking permanent establishment.

The coexistence of two military potentates did not cause friction as long as they still had a joint task. After the end of the civil war their rivalry showed more clearly, finally turning to outright hostility. In the end nothing was left of their former common interests, and the naked military power that replaced those interests urged each to destroy his rival, who was now his enemy. Rivalry and resentment, writes a historian living at that time, were bound to dominate the two men, 'for each of them desired to be the first man (*princeps*) not only in the city of Rome but in the whole world'.

Of the two, Antony was undoubtedly less inclined to settle their differences by military means. He had established himself in the east and he was more magnanimous than Octavian. Even at the beginning of the year 33, he was obviously still not thinking of armed conflict between them, for in the spring he set out for Armenia again. Certain political changes in the east at the time seem to have induced him to take up the failed campaign of the year 36 again, under better political auspices. In the intervening time, the prince of Media, who had then defeated Antony, had fallen out with the king of Parthia. He now wanted to ally himself to Antony, and an agreement was indeed reached, sealed by the betrothal of Alexandros Helios to one of the king of Media's daughters. For Antony, this opened up a chance to attack the central provinces of Parthia from the north once more, with better prospects of success. But if he had really made any extensive plans, he broke them off and ordered his general Publius Canidius Crassus to lead his troops to the west of Asia Minor, where he and Cleopatra later went themselves. The now intolerable tension between the military camps had shown him the wisdom of taking a closer look at what was going on in Italy.

Since the year 36 Octavian had established himself there more firmly. By now he had a clear political line of his own and he worked tirelessly to build it up. He constantly emphasized and consolidated his position as the dictator's son and thus the leader of the Caesarians. After the

Sicilian War, when he was already being offered many honours, he had granted himself the right to wear a laurel wreath at any time, thus reminding everyone that he personally had earned a triumph. In addition, in these years (and perhaps even earlier, in the years 40 or 38) he had associated the title *imperator* with his own name, as the dictator had done before him, using it instead of his own praenomen and subsequently calling himself Imperator Caesar. Not the least important feature here was that the military term, the right to which he had now won in warfare either himself or through his generals, was so associated with his own name that it became almost a part of himself.

Over and beyond such consolidation of his position, Octavian energetically continued the peacetime activities on which he had embarked after the war with Pompey. In this way he could both show his concern for Rome and Italy and secure his position in relation to Antony in the homelands of Rome. Agrippa in particular distinguished himself here. The year before, he had begun repairing the Marcian aqueduct (aqua Marcia), the longest of the many aqueducts of Rome at over 90 kilometres and famous for its good water, which came from the valley of the Anio. Although Agrippa was already consul, he had himself elected to the post of aedile for the next year so that he could carry out extensive civil engineering work in Rome. Besides repairing many public buildings and streets, he also turned to the cleansing of the sewage system (*cloaca maxima*) and constructed some works of his own. Among them the most important was a small aqueduct called after Octavian (the aqua Iulia) that brought excellent water from the Alban Hills. Such measures not only provided for the increased population of Rome, but also ushered in the major rebuilding that, at the time of the death of Augustus, already showed what Rome would be like as an imperial city.

At the same time, the year 33 was notable for a social welfare policy which was aimed at striking a chord with the wider population. Oil and salt were distributed; at theatrical performances, vouchers to claim money, clothes and other goods sometimes rained down on the audience; and the use of the baths was to be free in future. Agrippa also expelled astrologers and magicians, whose arts were believed by many to serve criminal activity and in any case did not accord with traditional religion and were deeply disliked by those who represented it, first and foremost Octavian himself. Here again, something was emerging that was to become official policy in important areas of religious thinking in the empire.

If these measures were calculated to please the population of Italy, and Rome in particular, and win support for Octavian, the real preparation for war began with manipulation of public opinion on a grand scale. The enemy's reputation must be damaged. Both sides worked to do so, but Octavian was more active in this than Antony. Never before had the Romans been so extensively exposed to propaganda directed from the centre of government; never before had slanders and denigration been so ruthlessly and officially employed.

The war of words began at the end of the year 34, at first in the form of letters, in which Octavian poured scorn on Antony's new arrangements in the east. It continued with the sending of delegations back and forth and culminated in public announcements. Friends of the rivals also joined in the exchange of true or invented accusations: on Octavian's side, for instance, one was Marcus Valerius Messalla Corvinus, who wrote several pamphlets attacking Antony. Octavian, with the institutions of the republican constitution available to him in Rome, was able to appear before the Senate and the people to good effect. But Antony himself did not lack for supporters in both Rome and Italy. All the old arguments used in the past to discredit the two men were dredged up once more. No rhetorical flourish seemed too banal to be used, no argument too despicable or unlikely, and those people open to such things absorbed them all without believing everything. Accounts of Antony's alcoholic excesses, his lustfulness and craving for pleasure found a ready audience, as did stories of Octavian's cruelty, his wandering eye for other men's wives and his humble origins. Many of these diatribes were made accessible in writing to a wider audience in the form of small treatises or pamphlets. Antony himself wrote one in defence of intoxication just before the battle of Actium. More dangerous because more effective was the politicization of what in themselves were ordinary human weaknesses. For instance, when Seneca says that Antony gave himself up to foreign customs and non-Roman vices out of drunkenness and his love for Cleopatra, he speaks in line with a campaign constructing a front between Octavian and Italy on one side and Antony and Egypt on the other. But there were also concrete accusations linked to particular political or personal incidents. The suggestion that in raising no objection to the name of Cleopatra's eldest son, Cae-sarion, 'little Caesar', Antony thereby recognized him as the dictator's offspring reflects certain anxieties of Octavian. Caesarion was indeed particularly dangerous to him and for that very reason had been distin-guished by Antony within the Ptolemaic family. He was a threat to Octavian's claim to be the dictator's sole heir. The unfortunate boy had become a political issue.

To the accusation of lustfulness, Antony retorted that as a young man Octavian had yielded to the sexual desires of the dictator Caesar, later his adoptive father, and of course the old story already circulated by Lucius Antonius, Antony's brother, during the Perusian War was brought up once more: the rumour that on the Spanish campaign of 45 Octavian had prostituted himself for the sum of 300,000 sesterces to Aulus Hirtius, Caesar's legate and later consul. In addition, Antony brought up a kind of counterpart to his much-criticized relationship with the queen of Egypt by accusing Octavian of betrothing his daugh-ter, who was promised to Antony's son, to Cotiso, king of Dacia, and in return asking for one of Cotiso's daughters for himself. In addition, as was only to be expected, he mentioned the demotion of Lepidus and the quashing of his claim to be administrator of part of the empire, and the fact that Octavian had taken over Lepidus' army, a breach of the trium-virs' agreement in that it took no account of Antony. He brought up the same accusation over the islands and legions that Octavian had taken from Sextus Pompey and kept for himself. That hit the mark, but such complaints came rather late in the day: the events concerned were now over three years in the past. Octavian responded by demanding half the loot taken by Antony and in doing so was thinking in particular of Egypt and Armenia. As for Sextus Pompey, he brazenly claimed to have spared him deliberately, which was a lie, whereas Antony had had him murdered, which at the most was a half-truth. Some of the mutual accu-sations and demands were simply conjured up out of thin air and indeed were in the realm of improbability. Antony, for instance, complained that Octavian had settled few but his own veterans on Italian land and demanded half of all those soldiers who had been recruited in their joint possession of Italy. Octavian in turn rejected the claim about the settle-ments and scornfully suggested Media and Parthia, allegedly conquered by Antony in his glorious campaign, as a possible settlement area.

As in all propaganda campaigns, truth was not the point. The point was what would please the people and have a chance of being believed, what things would arouse indignation or at least induce laughter. It remains Octavian's own secret what his aim was in accusing Antony of injuring the good name of the Roman people with his cunning deception and capture of Artavasdes, king of Armenia. More effective was a measure introduced in the same year, and intended to show the Romans an example of the correct policy towards subjects, with obvious reference to the dispositions in the east. On the death of Bocchus, king of Mauretania (roughly equivalent to Morocco and western Algeria today) and a long-standing ally of the dictator and then of his son, Octavian made his territory into a new Roman province: an unwise and over-hasty decision that can be explained only by the tension between him and Antony. The area was not ready to be taken directly into Roman provincial rule, if only because it had so few cities, and in fact Octavian revoked the decree making it a province only a few years later and transferred Bocchus' kingdom to an indigenous prince. Just now, however, increasing the extent of the empire looked good, particularly in the context of the 'squandering' of Roman provinces in the east. The triumph generously awarded by Octavian to two governors who had won victories during their time of office in Africa and Spain was also evidence of the power of Roman rule. At the same time it seemed to cast a faint reflection of republican glory on the system practised in the west.

Octavian had a wider audience: the senators and knights, the soldiers and citizens of Rome and the Italian cities listened to him. But Antony did not have to content himself solely with legionaries and his personal entourage. Many in Italy were ready to hear what he had to say, and among both the veterans of his legions now settled there and the upper classes he had willing supporters; his publicity campaign was chiefly aimed at them. As usual, his arguments served both to consolidate his own bases and to denigrate the opposing camp. But all this was only the smokescreen behind which preparations for war were going on. It was not to be long now before the differences between the two camps were expressed in violent action.

Antony spent the remaining months of the year 33 with Cleopatra in Ephesos and he also assembled his forces in Asia Minor. When the new year began he went to Samos, again with the queen. The triumvirate had not been in force since the end of the year 33, but he continued to call himself a triumvir. No one in the east contradicted him. Who was going to tell him what to do?

Octavian's position was much more difficult, for two reasons. He was in Italy, the land of the Romans; more precisely he was in Rome, the centre of constitutional law and order, and he had to keep that in mind. In addition, he had also consolidated his political base, not least through his invective against Antony: he had constantly emphasized the value of Roman land and the Roman way of life by comparison with the favours shown to foreign realms and the 'giving away' of the provinces. He could not simply disregard all that now, especially as he had made promises to the upper classes in particular and he wanted to make his position of power acceptable to them and reconcile it with the republican past. For that very reason, unlike Antony, he could no longer call himself a triumvir. The outlook for Octavian was not good. He had had no constitutional basis for any official measures and decisions since 1 January 32 and in view of his new political line he could not get the legal basis he needed by using force, as he had done without a second thought earlier. According to the agreements he had formerly made with Antony, he was not a consul in this new year and indeed held no office at all, unless his 'sacrosanctity' as tribune of the people, with the right to sit on the tribunes' bench in the Senate, were taken as a part, if a very small one, of the tribune's office.

His difficulty was illustrated by the central problem of the time: the old order had gone, and the triumvirate, which as an extraordinary office legally constituted to restore peace at home had lasted for ten years, could not be extended yet again. Peace had indeed been restored, and the alliance could not be renewed for the very reason that the two potentates were now bitter enemies. Fundamentally, there was no legally binding order in the state any more, only a skeletal framework of institutions and rules that the former triumvirs used as they thought fit. What had once been the *res publica* was now in their hands.

The citizens had so far been either more or less aware of all this; now it was revealed to all eyes. And at once the question of political order in the future arose – what was it to be like? Those who held real power had to find the answer, Octavian even more so than Antony. As commander of the eastern provinces and armies, as well as the patron of a series of dependent princes, the latter could feel that he was the legal holder of an *imperium* in the Roman sense, in spite of the fact that the triumvirate had lapsed, but only until the Senate sent a successor. Until then, he continued in office 'in the place of a magistrate' (Latin, *pro magistratu*), and it did not matter so much if, interpreting the old custom in its broadest sense, he still called himself a triumvir after that office had formally ended. In any case he could say he had been legally exerting his command even after 31 December 33. As for the question of a successor to it, he need have no anxiety. For the decision was in the hands of the former triumvirs, in fact with Octavian, and if he were to induce the Senate to send a man to take over Antony's command in the east it would mean war, an entirely different situation.

Matters were not so simple for Octavian. He too, of course, had a large provincial area under him and by Roman custom could feel that in practice he had the power of command over it, and he certainly need not fear that the impotent Senate would appoint a successor to him. But in Italy he was confronted with the Romans and in Rome with the traditional institutions of the old order, which he must not disown by cancelling Antony's policies. So it was not surprising that the Antonians made full use of the new and to Octavian awkward situation as soon as 1 January 32 came. He now held no office, and the two new consuls, Gnaeus Domitius Ahenobarbus and Gaius Sosius, were supporters of Antony. The former, a member of one of the most distinguished families in Rome, had not been among the assassins of Caesar himself but had served first their party as admiral, then Antony as a general, and he was even related to Antony through the betrothal of his son Lucius to the elder of Octavia's two daughters (Antonia the Elder), while the latter, whose family was not distinguished, had risen under Antony and had proved himself a good commander.

In the very first meeting of the Senate in the new year, Sosius opened hostilities with a vigorous attack on Octavian. However, although Antony had written telling him to ask for formal confirmation of the new order set up in the eastern part of the empire, he did not venture to do so. But Antony's offer, which meant that both sides would lay down their power, was still on the table. Sosius addressed it, and for a brief moment the senators may have had the impression that a gateway to the old freedom was opening again. But that was an illusion. Speaking on Octavian's behalf, a tribune of the people prevented any decision from being taken.

Octavian himself had stayed away from this first meeting of the

Senate, probably not wanting to expose himself to the attack that might be expected. However, he returned to Rome a few days later and had another meeting called in order to reply to the accusations made against him. He entered the Senate with friends carrying weapons concealed under their togas, simply sat down between the consuls, although he no longer held any office, and spoke in defence of his position, making accusations against Sosius and Antony. When no one ventured to oppose him he had the meeting adjourned: next time, he announced, he would bring written proof of Antony's guilt. But before the appointed day came the consuls secretly fled to Antony in Ephesos. Some 300 senators, one-third of the entire Senate, fled to the east with them.

Octavian let them go. He had lost face by their exodus but he was now rid of his enemies and could feel that he was master of Rome and Italy. At the beginning of the year he had weathered the situation, which was not without its dangers for him, had outplayed his opponents move by move and had shown courage and imagination in the process. At the same time these events made the final break between the two men who held power clear to everyone. Their mutual recriminations had poisoned the atmosphere, and reconciliation was now unthinkable, particularly since Octavian obviously wanted no such thing.

War had not yet been declared. None the less, the situation cried out for resolution and those distinguished and influential men who were still wavering were forced to align themselves with one or other of the two rivals. By leaving Rome many senators had acknowledged their support for Antony, but even among them there were still many doubts, and much hesitation and indecision: the Antonians were a very heterogeneous group. Men of the old nobility associated with generals who had risen to prominence in Antony's service, Caesarians of very varied origin with adherents of the old order, and even a few of the murderers of Caesar who were still alive; the group included Canidius Crassus, a self-made man, as well as the nobleman Domitius Ahenobarbus, Munatius Plancus and also Caesar's assassin Cassius of Parma. And many bearers of famous names who had never held office themselves joined Antony's camp, not so much representing as decorating it.

By contrast, Octavian's entourage had grown in stature. Clever tactician that he was, he had two members of the oldest families in Rome appointed consuls to replace the two who had fled: Marcus Valerius Messalla (not Octavian's similarly named friend Marcus Valerius

Messalla Corvinus, who was consul the next year), and Lucius Cornelius Cinna, both rather insignificant but of distinguished origin. In addition, there was the fact that those who had fled Rome and Italy were a mixed blessing to Antony. They strengthened his camp but also sowed discord, because, having listened to Octavian's arguments for months, they now urged the removal of Cleopatra from the centre of power in the east. But Antony paid so little attention to them that in the spring he took the queen with him to his new headquarters, now moved from Samos to Athens, and sent his wife Octavia a letter of divorce. She had always been loyal to him in word and deed; now she was asked, at his express wish, to move out of their joint house in Rome. He did not simply cut his connection with Octavian through this step, he also alienated the sympathies of many in Rome and Italy whose support he would need if he intended to return to the west victorious one day. Would not every Roman say that his conduct could be explained only by his relationship with the queen of Egypt, just as Octavian's slanderous campaign had always said? The idea that the queen was an enchantress and had bewitched Antony was now readily believed, and the belief was further nourished by the fact that the goddess Isis, in whose person Cleopatra had appeared for the last year, was regarded as a kind of Egyptian equivalent to the moon goddess Selene, patroness of witches and magicians. The Egyptian world itself, which was difficult for Romans to understand, helped to convince them that the queen had power over Antony.

Meanwhile, Antony's refusal to change, or at least show discretion in, his conduct with Cleopatra led to the first manifestations of discontent in his own ranks. In the autumn, Lucius Munatius Plancus, a man who had always had flexible links with both camps so that he could change sides at any time, appeared in Rome with his nephew Marcus Titius, son of one of the men proscribed by the triumvirs. These famous names were good recruits to Octavian's camp, and their knowledge of his enemy's state of mind and intentions also came in useful to him, for Plancus had been on excellent terms with the queen of Egypt. Most importantly of all, however, Antony had made both men witnesses of his will, which was deposited with the Vestal Virgins, and they knew about several compromising provisions made in it. Octavian immediately did his utmost to get possession of the will. When the revered priestesses refused to hand it over he simply arrived in person and took it, subsequently reading out extracts in the Senate and to the assembly of the people. Octavian drew attention not only to the declaration that Caesarion was indeed Caesar's son, and to certain 'gifts' made to Cleopatra and her children, but also to a passage in which Antony stated his wish, even if he died in Rome or elsewhere in the west, to be buried beside the queen of Egypt in Alexandria. This disposition, in itself not very strange in the man who governed the eastern half of the empire, was deliberately publicized by Octavian because it immediately led to rumours for which there was no real foundation in the will. If Antony won the victory, it was said, he was going to give Rome to Cleopatra and move his capital to Egypt. A remark by the Egyptian queen was also in circulation: allegedly she added to every oath she took, as if to give it additional force: 'as truly as I will administer justice on the Capitol one day'.

'They could not bring the best wine from the cellar,' Horace wrote later in his famous ode on the victory at the battle of Actium, 'as long as the queen threatened the Capitol and the whole *imperium* with disaster and downfall' – and that was certainly not cheap court propaganda, but a view to which Antony's own conduct lent credence. The queen of Egypt as mistress of Rome: it was grist to Octavian's mill, and he did his utmost with it by causing Gaius Calvisius Sabinus, who had already been a loyal servant of the dictator, to spread further slanderous statements about the queen, in particular her alleged contempt for all that was Roman, her relationship with Antony and his subjection, or indeed enslavement, to her. However much or little of all this was believed, the will was definitely thought genuine. Very few objected to the way Octavian had got his hands on it, or to the fact that he was challenging a living man to account for dispositions he had made that were to come into force only after his death. Furthermore, there were plenty of men who had come over from Antony's camp and could be presented as respectable witnesses. The sole idea was to make it felt that the eastern government had been to some extent discredited. In that Octavian undoubtedly succeeded.

By now Rome and Italy were ready for the last step, a declaration of war. The Senate and the Fetial college of priests, responsible for so doing according to ancient custom, finally made it in due form, but war was declared only on Cleopatra. Antony merely had his promagistral power of command in the east withdrawn, on the grounds that he had lost his reason under the influence of the queen and her entourage. In addition, the assurance of his consulship for the year 31, promised in earlier treaties by the triumvirs, was rescinded.

After the declaration of war, the Senate no doubt also formally gave Octavian the mission to carry out military operations, but although he had no office at the time, and in particular was not consul, he intended to consolidate his political position by becoming warlord of Italy and the entire west. Every man able to bear arms voluntarily swore an oath to Octavian, pledging obedience to him in the war against the east. Every man in the west was thus now behind him not as a holder of office but as himself, Octavian as Imperator Caesar, son of the deified Caesar. This oath made Italy a community of Roman citizens in the struggle to prevent the east from taking over Rome, and Octavian was its leader (*dux*). A broad elite stood shoulder to shoulder with him: over 700 senators and eighty-three men who had held the post of consul before this time or did so after it, as he proudly wrote in his account of his deeds. At their head, as he wished all the Romans to see it, he was going to war together with the entire Roman people and all their gods against a barbarian woman. The threat from Egypt seemed to unite Italy as a nation, and Octavian may have hoped that the coming 'national war' would make them forget the sufferings and humiliations of the past – not least those for which he himself was responsible.

At the same time he exploited this new unanimity as a kind of cover for raising the urgently needed financial means. Every inhabitant of Italy had to pay a quarter of his annual income, and the freedmen were also burdened with a capital levy. Small rebellions in a Rome that was full of rumours, party dissidents and discontent were easily put down, and fires lit by arsonists with malicious intent were extinguished. None the less, parts of the great Circus, and the temples of Ceres and Spes, fell victim to the flames.

In the new year 31, Octavian became consul for the third time, as agreed in the days when the triumvirs were in harmony with each other, and so held official power once more. Instead of Antony, from whom the consulate had been withdrawn, the man appointed as his fellow consul was Marcus Valerius Messalla Corvinus, a man of about his own age, who after several years of indecision had proved a loyal supporter of Octavian since the year 40.

The deployment of the fighting forces had been largely completed the previous year. Antony had assembled a large part of his thirty legions in the west of Asia Minor, as well as 12,000 cavalry and the auxiliary contingents provided by many client princes, among them, from the Syrian area, those sent by Kings Polemon, Amyntas and Herod. Even his recent ally the prince of Media had sent troops. In addition Antony had over 500 warships, including several in which each oar in the three banks of oars was manned by eight or ten oarsmen. These were mammoth galleys whose fighting power did not, as with smaller ships, depend on speed, manoeuvrability and forcefulness when ramming another vessel, but on the soldiers operating from the deck and the catapults stationed there. Octavian's forces were smaller. He brought only 80,000 legionaries and 12,000 cavalry, with a complement of no more than 250 warships.

While the armies were forming there was yet another verbal skirmish, although this was no more than a final flourish in the fierce political argument with which both rivals had been working on the public since the year 33. This time they were merely boasting in an attempt to encourage themselves and their followers. Antony announced that two months after the battle he would restore political power to the Senate and people of Rome; he said nothing about what was to happen next. In addition, he swore on oath that there would be no more negotiating with Octavian. Octavian himself offered to give battle in Italy, promising to draw back from the coast until Antony had landed; if his opponent preferred, however, the arrangement could be reversed and Greece chosen as the battlefield. Antony exposed this rather feeble swashbuckling on Octavian's part by asking who was to be arbiter if such an agreement was broken. His suggestion of single combat between him and Octavian, however, was not to be taken seriously either.

Antony brought his troops together in Greece, and for reasons of supplying the men divided them between several camps in Greece and the Peloponnese. He drew up his fleet in the sound on the west coast that divides Epirus and Acarnania and leads into the Ambracian Gulf. The promontory, a good ten kilometres long and bordered by the Actian mountains to the south, offered the huge fleet plenty of sheltered anchorage, especially as Antony had the access to it guarded against enemy

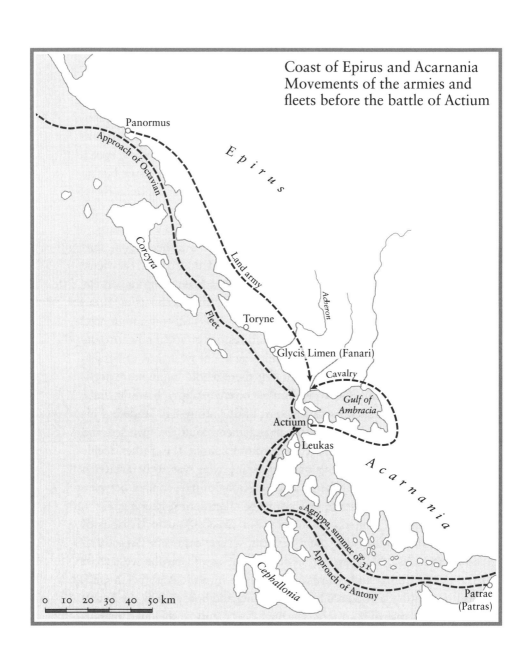

Coast of Epirus and Acarnania
Movements of the armies and
fleets before the battle of Actium

Panormus

*Epirus*

Approach of Octavian

*Corcyra*

Land army

Fleet

Toryne

*Acheron*

Glycis Limen (Fanari)

Cavalry

*Gulf of Ambracia*

Actium

Leukas

*Acarnania*

Agrippa, summer of 31

Approach of Antony

*Cephallonia*

Patrae
(Patras)

o  10  20  30  40  50 km

attacks. He had probably decided not to use more northerly bases such as Dyrrhachium, which would have been better for marching on into Italy later, because of the longer supply routes or less favourable anchorage available. The choice of location certainly also fell on Actium, however, because in a small naval expedition during autumn of the previous year the Antonians had come into contact with the enemy near Cercyra (Corfu). They therefore expected to find them already present in large numbers in this area. Of Antony's thirty legions, nineteen formed the real army of operations under the command of the capable Publius Canidius Crassus. The others had been left behind in Cyrenaica, Egypt, Syria and Macedonia to secure those provinces against attack. Antony does not seem to have planned an invasion of Italy at first, or at least the naval expedition into the Ionian Sea was not a failed attempt to cross to the Italian shore. Everything suggests, rather, that he intended all along to wait for Octavian in his own sphere of power. He himself went into winter quarters in Patrae (Patras), again accompanied by the queen of Egypt.

Octavian assembled the army and his fleet in Tarentum and Brundisium. A direct attack in the winter of 32/31 on Antony's ships lying off Actium failed because of bad weather, and his forces had to turn back with the loss of several units. After that, Octavian abandoned the idea of a direct attack. In the spring he landed his army, keeping a respectful distance from the enemy ships, near the Ceraunian mountains in northern Epirus. From there, he had to make a difficult march south of more than 200 kilometres to reach the Ambracian Gulf. The fleet occupied Toryne on the coast of Epirus, and then Cercyra itself, driving out an enemy garrison. Meanwhile Agrippa set about disrupting the enemy's supply routes all along the west coast of Greece and even took the Peloponnese town of Methone.

The leisurely way in which Antony approached the war is clear from the fact that he was still in Patrai when news of Octavian's landing reached him. Only then did he set off for Actium with his troops. But by this time his situation had deteriorated. Octavian's ships were operating in the entire Ionian Sea, and it was getting more difficult to provide supplies; the soldiers were soon suffering from lack of food, which now had to be brought through sometimes difficult terrain from the interior of the country. His strategy of playing a waiting game, which in a better situation would have allowed him to attack the enemy at a place of his own choice, was turning more and more into one that forced him to go on the defensive. It became impossible for the Antonians to move.

The rapid deterioration of the military situation immediately raises the question of why, even if Antony intended to let the enemy approach, he allowed matters to reach this stage. Why did he fail to harass the invaders while they were still at sea, particularly as over the last few decades the Romans had had plenty of experience in crossing the Ionian Sea to land large bodies of men? After the outbreak of the civil war in early 48, first the dictator Caesar and then, in the autumn of 42, Antony himself and Octavian had crossed from Italy to northern Greece. In both operations the side in the civil war stationed in the east had asserted its mastery of the seas and had disrupted the enemy crossing from Italy, in particular its troop transports, sometimes even preventing them from landing. Did Antony not remember his own difficulties as second-in-command to Caesar when he had to take troops from Brundisium to the coast of Epirus after the enemy's superior naval force had control of the sea? Did he fail to recall the losses that, as one of the triumvirs, he had suffered from the republican fleet in the year 42? An entire elite unit, the Martian Legion, had been lost then beneath the waves. Now he was the one expecting an invasion from the sea, and his strategic aim, if only because of those earlier experiences, should therefore have been to make himself master of the Ionian Sea. And he had the means to do it, just as Pompey the Great and later Brutus and Cassius did: he had a far larger fleet than Octavian.

But Antony seemed to be in no hurry. Without harassing or repelling the invaders, he waited where he was, in a position which he clearly did not intend to give up. In the end he even brought all his troops together in Actium. He made his main camp on the peninsula, closing off the sound in the south, where there was a temple to Apollo, and secured it with fortifications all the way down to the sea so as to keep his way to the water open. When the enemy land troops finally appeared at the foot of the northern peninsula, he erected a camp there just a few kilometres from the enemy's entrenchments, while Octavian concentrated his fleet in the width of the bay, also building walls to link it to his camp lying above it. The roadstead where the fleet lay did not, however, offer full protection from dangerous south-westerly storm winds.

The fleets and armies faced each other all summer, most of the time inactive, Antony in the better position but now unable to move, Octavian in a situation where he had more freedom of movement, but his fleet was at risk. He several times offered battle at sea, but there was no reaction from his enemy, and when conversely, after the arrival of Octavian's army, Antony offered to give battle on land on the northern peninsula, that too was declined. They eyed one another for months. Apart from minor scuffling, there was only one larger skirmish, at Actium itself, and the outcome did not favour Antony. He had sent his superior force of cavalry around the Gulf to attack the enemy's flank and if possible cut off Octavian's supplies but suffered a considerable defeat himself. Agrippa then succeeded in improving the general strategic position of Octavian's forces by occupying the nearby island of Leucas, as well as Patrae and Corinth. Antony was now cut off from the Peloponnese.

His soldiers were in increasingly poor condition, and so were the crews of the ships at sea. Disease was rife. Morale was at a low ebb. Many men deserted; those who were left fervently hoped that there would soon be a change for the better. Finally Antony could no longer avoid making a decision, but his situation, which was now worse in military terms, did not make it any easier. Many of his advisers, notably Canidius, suggested marching to Macedonia or Thrace to force a decisive land battle, just as Caesar had done against Pompey and the triumvirs against Brutus and Cassius. But that seemed too much like a retreat and begged the question of what the fleet was there for. Was it to be abandoned? On the other hand, a land battle, under the leadership of Antony with all his experience of conflict, might seem to many almost to guarantee victory. Our sources claim that Cleopatra prevented it, wanting the decisive battle to be fought at sea because of her large share in the fleet, and wishing them to return to Egypt after it. In fact there may have been other reasons why Antony decided against a land battle. Above all, he will no longer have had confidence in many of the legions and other units of his fighting force because they were weakened by hunger and sickness. In addition, the ranks of many of the army units had been swelled by comparatively inexperienced men from the provinces who would not be worth much in the field. It was years since he had been able to recruit more soldiers in Italy. On the other hand, his fleet was stronger than Octavian's, or at least it had been at first, and if even so he did not take the initiative by starting a naval battle – he could, for instance, have attacked his opponent's ships in their more vulnerable position – that was presumably also to do with the poor condition of his crews. Moreover, Antony knew all about the experience of battle gained by Octavian's soldiers and oarsmen in the war against Pompey, as well as Agrippa's abilities in a naval battle. In spite of all this, however, it is hard to explain Antony's hesitation solely by his soldiers' and oarsmen's exhaustion and lack of training, or by his increasingly poor tactical and strategic position. There must also have been a psychological factor that made him uncertain, and that uncertainty was finally transmitted to others among his military leadership. Several high-ranking men defected and went over to Octavian, among them the mortally sick Gnaeus Domitius Ahenobarbus, consul in the previous year and one of Cleopatra's sharpest critics, as well as the client princes Amyntas of Galatia and Deiotarus of Paphlagonia.

It was already late summer by the time Gaius Sosius, one of the admirals in command of Antony's fleet, suddenly confronted Octavian with his squadron. Tired of the long wait, Sosius attacked at once and even put the enemy to flight. But the able Agrippa came to his commander's aid and himself inflicted considerable losses on Sosius. Now, at long last, Antony decided on battle, partly because the advanced season positively forced him to make up his mind. It was the end of August. He could not afford to wait through another winter, in view of the difficulty of getting supplies and the defections among his own immediate entourage. He chose to fight at sea. What exactly, however, was his strategic concept?

The anti-Cleopatra literature of the time speaks of his breaking out of the sound of Actium, where he was now encircled. It was alleged that the queen had urged him to give up his positions in Greece and go back to the south, and there were also rumours of the queen's flight and betrayal. Betrayal of whom? It is certain that Antony wanted or more precisely had to force a way out of his now untenable position by winning a victory. However, in view of the present balance of power, which was now much worse from his point of view, he could not hope to destroy the enemy in such a victory, only to weaken him. His aim, in any case, was to break through the enemy lines, a classic manoeuvre in fighting at sea, and then, having reached clear water, to take the fleet south. Breaking through the enemy lines was thus the tactical aim of the battle, free passage in the open sea its strategic purpose. Naturally a successful breakthrough, with the enemy suffering as many losses as possible, would also be the signal for the legions to set off for Macedonia and Thrace and take up winter quarters there. Since Octavian's camp had cut off the northern peninsula, the decision to break through the lines of ships was logically linked to a withdrawal of the Antonian army from that peninsula, where it had been opposing Octavian. We can see that Antony was not, thus, concerned with winning a decisive victory in his struggle against his rival, but with striking a kind of blow for freedom, which he might hope would give him a better military base for the next battle. A clear sign that he intended to go south directly after the battle was his order to burn all the ships that could not sail – because of the shortage of oarsmen and sailors, Antony had had to break up many of his crews – and to bring the sails of the others and stow them in the hulls. As ships were powered exclusively by oars in a naval battle, the sails and rigging, which would only impede fighting, were normally left on land. Octavian's ships did just that. Antony also ordered all valuable items to be loaded into the ships.

His originally superior fleet had been weakened by the shortage of crews and by losses, and encircled as the ships were it had been impossible to build any more or have relief vessels brought in from outside. Antony still had 230 battle-ready ships, including the queen's sixty galleys. Octavian, on the other hand, stationed in the outer position, had received reinforcements with the arrival of more ships, and now had about 400 vessels. They were mostly small, many of them triremes, of the kind that had proved their worth over the centuries as fast, easily manoeuvred warships, or liburnians, fast, narrow-built, not very large and with only two banks of oars. They could travel an entire ship's length with one stroke from their oarsmen. Such ships came from the eastern side of the Adriatic Sea, and Octavian had already used them in the Sicilian War. Antony had some smaller vessels too, but he was particularly strong in very large warships. Their size enabled them to take on board many soldiers, archers and spearmen, and catapults and ballistas for firing stones and arrows. As their high sides towered above those of the smaller ships, boarding them was not easy, and their fighting power was reinforced by strong towers on deck. Antony ordered 10,000 of his best soldiers and 2,000 archers to go on board the fleet, and in the same way Octavian manned his with legionaries and lightly armed men, in all a stronger force than Antony's because of his much greater number of ships. As it would be difficult for Octavian's smaller ships to sink the large galleys, even by ramming them, both sides in this battle would have to fight mainly with soldiers. The land armies watched from shore – Octavian's army under Statilius Taurus from the northern peninsula, the Antonians under Canidius Crassus from the southern.

Heavy seas prevented the two sides from joining battle for several days. Octavian was well informed about his enemy's plans by men who had come over from Antony's camp, among them Quintus Dellius, the legate and historian, said to have been a favourite of Antony in his youth, who appeared just before the battle. The burning of the ships that Antony was leaving behind removed any last doubts in Octavian's army that the enemy's strategic aim was to break through and sail away. At first the battle-shy Octavian had wanted to let the enemy fleet through and then set off in pursuit, but Agrippa persuaded him to give battle, and in fact his situation when the fighting began could hardly have been better.

When the storms finally died down on 2 September, and a north-west wind that would help Antony to break through the enemy line rose, he formed his fleet into a large arc at the western exit from the sound. He commanded the right wing himself, and put Sosius in command of the left wing, and Cleopatra with her sixty ships took up a position behind their line. The Antonian galleys were stationed along the coastline, close together to prevent any breakthrough. Octavian – or more properly Agrippa, who in fact was the military leader here – stationed his ships in a slightly crescent-shaped line and himself, with Marcus Lurius, took command of the right wing, while Agrippa on the left wing faced Antony.

They lay opposite each other like that for several hours, barely 1.5 kilometres apart. Antony did not want to manoeuvre in a way that would break up his line ahead or on the flanks, and thus give up the advantage of his well-fortified position. Only towards noon, when the hot-blooded Sosius, unwilling to wait any longer, moved forward did some movement come into both fleets. What caused the attack? Perhaps the fact that Agrippa had extended the line of his galleys sideways, to make the most of their superior numbers and perhaps surround the enemy. Now Antony could hesitate no longer; he brought his entire fleet into battle. The two lines were instantly wedged together. Opposing ships engaged each other in small clusters; usually several of Octavian's smaller ships were gathered around one of Antony's large war galleys,

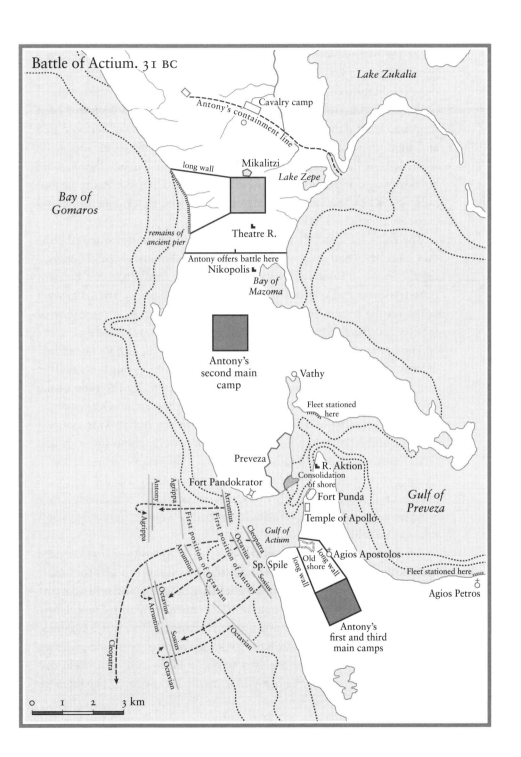

Battle of Actium. 31 BC

*Lake Zukalia*

Cavalry camp

Antony's containment line

long wall

Mikalitzi

*Lake Zepe*

*Bay of Gomaros*

*remains of ancient pier*

Theatre R.

Antony offers battle here

Nikopolis

*Bay of Mazoma*

Antony's second main camp

Vathy

Fleet stationed here

Preveza

R. Aktion

Consolidation of shore

Fort Pandokrator

Fort Punda

*Gulf of Preveza*

Temple of Apollo

Antony

Agrippa

Arruntius

Agrippa

First position of Octavian

First position of Antony

Octavius

Cleopatra

*Gulf of Actium*

Sp. Spile

Sosius

Old shore

long wall

Agios Apostolos

long wall

Fleet stationed here

Agios Petros

Arruntius

Octavius

Arruntius

Sosius

Octavian

Octavian

Antony's first and third main camps

Cleopatra

0    1    2    3 km

trying to subdue it by ramming it and firing missiles, and if possible storm it, while a hail of shots rained down from the decks and tall towers of the galley. None the less, the mobility of Octavian's ships easily gave them an advantage, although there was no decisive outcome in sight yet. In the middle of the battle – and not, it appears, only in its final phase – Cleopatra made her way with her sixty galleys, which had been stationed behind the others, through the fighting vessels of her own side and then through Octavian's, and, hoisting full sail, the galleys made south with a favouring breeze. Only she had carried out the planned breakthrough. When Antony saw this, he boarded a quinquireme and sailed after her. Several of his ships followed him as soon as they could extricate themselves from the battle.

The ships left behind went on fighting. Indeed, jammed together as they were, they had no option. The courage of Antony's men in continuing the battle did not fail them until Octavian finally had fire brought from the coast and sent a dense hail of torches and fiery arrows raining down on the enemy. Soon many ships were in flames, and the fate of that part of the Antonian fleet which had not fled was sealed.

The battle had lasted a good four hours, and in the end Octavian had destroyed or captured all of the other side's remaining ships. Years later, in his memoirs, he claimed to have taken 300. But by the time of the battle Antony did not have as many vessels as that left, so Octavian was probably including all the vessels involved in the Actian War, not just those destroyed or taken in the battle itself. Twelve thousand men had fallen on Antony's side and about 5,000 on Octavian's, either killed in fighting at close quarters or burned or drowned. Only a few ships set off in pursuit of those in flight, but as Octavian's entire fleet had left its sails on shore and was relying on oars to propel the vessels, only a brief pursuit was possible.

Antony's army had watched the disaster from land. At first they did not know that their commander had followed Cleopatra and they must certainly have thought it beyond belief that the great victor in so many battles was simply going to abandon his entire army to its fate. It still numbered nineteen legions and many thousands of cavalry. Canidius dared not give battle but declined all suggestions of surrender. Clearly, he soon lost authority in the eyes of the soldiers. Some of them dispersed, and the part of the army that finally set off for Macedonia, in line with their original orders, was persuaded to surrender during their march.

At this time Canidius had already left the army and set off for Alexandria. While still in Greece, Antony is said to have ordered Canidius to march through Macedonia to Asia Minor, but those instructions will hardly have reached him. Surely, however, such an order was to be taken for granted. Ever since Antony had made his decision to try breaking through the enemy lines with his fleet, whether he was victorious or not, there must have been some clear idea of the movements of the army on land – and it would very likely have been along the lines of the order that Antony allegedly gave only after his flight.

After leaving Actium, Antony himself reached the foothills of Tainaron in the south of the Peloponnese and went on from there to Egypt. His enemy was now master of Macedonia, and with it all the land west of the straits. The way over the straits to Asia Minor, Syria and Egypt was now open to him. Who or what could still stop him? The eleven legions left behind by Antony in those regions?

We are told that, after abandoning his fleet, Antony went on board Cleopatra's galley and spent three days there alone in the foreship, as if numbed, before going to visit the queen again. This naturally expresses the shock of defeat, but his reluctance to look Cleopatra in the face after the disaster says something about the closeness of their relationship. Cleopatra is also central to the theories of ancient sources on the causes of the catastrophe. According to them, Antony was dependent on her and was no longer master of his own decisions; they present him as driven by Cleopatra's wishes, so that he left his army in order not to abandon her, the betrayer of his own forces (*desertor exercitus sui*). But did Cleopatra wish for his downfall? Would a woman who was both clever and calculating not have known that it meant her own end too? She had only to listen to the note being struck in the west to know what her fate would be after a defeat. So there are many inconsistencies which leave the defeat itself, and the decisions that went before it, still shrouded in mystery. Some of what has been said may derive from propaganda, for the victor covered up or distorted a good deal. But that still does not explain everything.

Why, we may ask, did Antony, with all his experience of land battles, rely so heavily on his fleet at Actium, well knowing that Octavian's men had a great deal of experience in fighting at sea and fine qualities of seamanship? And how could that wily tactician have let himself be caught in the sound of Actium as if in a trap? Why, once he had lost his freedom of movement, did he not take the initiative and offer battle on land? And, if Octavian declined such a battle, as indeed he had, why did Antony not set off again with his army in good time, while it was still summer? Octavian would have had to follow him, and Antony could have forced a battle elsewhere. Finally, was it really a good idea to try breaking through the line of enemy ships? If the attempt had been successful, it could not have been an end in itself for him to reach Egypt and wait there for Octavian's army and death. So why try it? Could the fleet in the sound of Actium not have held out for another winter, thus making an attempt to break out of the sound, now only a trap, absolutely necessary? Even then, such an experienced and successful military commander as Antony should not have tried to save ships at the price of losing his entire army on land. And even if his soldiers had been so weakened and demoralized that they could have retreated only with difficulty, should he not have rejoined his legions after the naval battle, whether or not he emerged from it victorious, to offer Octavian battle on land again, or make his way through to the east with his own army?

In view of all these questions Antony's conduct can be explained only by suppositions. It might be, for instance, that the naval battle took a turn for the worse against his expectations, and the queen, on seeing it, broke through the enemy lines on her own initiative to save their remaining ships (particularly hers), whereupon a demoralized commander gave up his intention of leading the land army to Macedonia after the battle. If that was the case, a contributory factor might have been that Antony had taken his best soldiers on board the fleet for close fighting, thus weakening the army as a whole. When the unfortunate outcome of the battle made it impossible to reunite the soldiers with the fleet and those still on land, Antony might no longer have trusted his legions to make a forced march through country occupied by the enemy. But why – and the question then becomes all the more crucial – did he prefer a naval battle anyway? Why leave his army to fight on board ship? Perhaps the queen and the strong contingent of ships she brought to the fleet were instrumental after all. And still, before any of these events, we have to wonder about those months of inactivity which left Octavian free to improve his position.

The battle of Actium brought the war to an end. Octavian ordered a city to be built on the site of the victory and called it Nicopolis, 'city of victory'. He dedicated some of the captured ships to Actian Apollo, and where his tent as commander had stood he had a magnificent monument erected in memory of the battle, adorned with the prows of many ships. The monument was ready for dedication in early summer of the year 29, when Octavian stopped in Actium when returning to Italy from the east. The dedicatory inscription spoke of a victory 'for the state', and peace restored on land and sea.

After his victory, Octavian's sole concern was to inspect the loot and remove the now almost defenceless leaders of Antony's party. Before that could be done, however, and as always in wars between military potentates, there was the question of paying the soldiers. Octavian had no money, so he had to send the part of his army that he wanted to demobilize home without pay for the time being. The outcome could not be good, but Octavian obviously thought he had time to settle matters properly. So he set off for Egypt, travelling by way of Athens, and went into winter quarters on Samos.

News soon reached him there of riots and insubordination among the discontented veterans. In the middle of winter, and in sometimes stormy weather, Octavian made haste back to Italy. From Brundisium, where he spent just under a month, he was at least able to placate the soldiers for the time being. He distributed money that he had raised in the east, made presents of the land at his disposal in Italy and the eastern provinces, and in general practised the art of prevarication.

Back in Asia Minor, Octavian went to Syria by way of Rhodes, and from there crossed the desert separating Syria from Cleopatra's territory. The Egyptian border fort of Pelusium immediately opened its gates to him. Princes came from all sides to meet him proffering apologies and speeches promising loyalty, among them Herod of Judaea, who instantly made himself useful to Octavian as he had done before to Antony. Octavian's legions were also marching to Egypt from the west by way of Cyrenaica. Soon Antony's legate – Lucius Pinarius Scarpus, Octavian's cousin – surrendered with his four legions to Gaius Cornelius Gallus, who was advancing from the African provinces.

When Antony left Greece he had first gone to Paraetonium (Marsa Matruh), on the western border of Egypt. Obviously he intended to go to meet his legions stationed in Cyrenaica, the largest contingent of troops still left to him. But instead of energetically taking command of them, he fell into a lethargic mood for several days. When, soon afterwards, he heard that his legions had surrendered, he even tried to commit suicide, but failed. Then he went to Alexandria. The queen had already hurried there ahead of him.

The mood of the couple at this point alternated between fierce determination and deep despair. Sometimes they appeared ready to make a last stand, sometimes they positively seemed anxious to receive the victor's humiliating demands. Octavian, however, still convinced that the war was to be seen as a campaign against Egypt, ignored Antony's letters and held out to the queen the prospect of being taken to Rome to be led in his triumphal procession some day. The actual content of the defeated couple's offers has obviously been toned down in transmission. But even their most modest and realistic expectations had no chance of being fulfilled. Cleopatra's hopes of retaining her kingdom were vain – she sent Octavian the insignia of her royal dignity and asked him to keep the Ptolemaic royal house in trust for her children (who were also Antony's). Equally hopeless was Antony's idea that by offering to commit suicide he could still salvage something for the queen. An attempt by Cleopatra to seek refuge in the south with her fleet failed; the ships taken from the Mediterranean to the Red Sea were burned in the Gulf of Aqaba by Arabs at the instigation of Octavian's governor of Syria. Egypt was bound to fall to Octavian as the spoils of war – a country that had been, as it were, available for two generations and had not been annexed by Rome long ago only because the great men of the *imperium* could not agree on how to divide it up. For Antony, the only way out now was death. Was he, the great commander and warlord, to beg Octavian for mercy? His own fate as well as the queen's had been decided at Actium.

The end came quickly. Antony had spent the last few months in Alexandria partly in apathetic withdrawal, partly in wild feasting and carousing. The club of those who 'followed an inimitable way of life' that he and his boon companions had founded in happier days was now a company bound together in death. They were, so to speak, dancing on the volcano. When the armies finally appeared outside the city Antony roused himself once more, and for one last time fortune in war was kind to him: in a cavalry skirmish he managed to defeat Octavian's men. Then followed the final battle, fought with army and fleet. It ended miserably. His fleet surrendered to Octavian without a struggle, whereupon the cavalry changed sides too, and the remaining land forces were defeated easily on 1 August. The city too immediately surrendered.

On hearing false news that Cleopatra had killed herself, Antony had thrust his sword into his own breast, but the blow was not instantly mortal. When he was told the queen was still alive, he had himself carried to her mausoleum, built within the palace complex on the great harbour, where she had withdrawn with her treasures. The ground-level access was barricaded, but there was an opening in the roof of the building, which was not quite finished. The severely wounded Antony was let down through this gap by ropes into the interior, and died there in the queen's arms.

In spite of her hopeless situation, Cleopatra made one last attempt to salvage something from it for herself or her country. Since Octavian intended to lead the queen, whom he had publicly described as the real enemy, in his triumphal procession in Rome, he did not brusquely reject her first approaches, but negotiated with her several times through members of her immediate entourage and even came to the mausoleum for a conversation with her himself. Perhaps he was simply curious to have a personal meeting with the woman who had conducted passionate love affairs with the two greatest military commanders of the time. Now almost forty years old, the queen was unable to beguile Octavian, although she ran the whole gamut of her arts, in particular recalling the memory of the dictator and citing evidence of their mutual love. The fact that Octavian reacted with nothing but cool reserve robbed her of her last hopes of any political future, and when he finally took her captive in her mausoleum through a ruse, and the assiduity of her prison warders in trying to prevent her from committing suicide showed her that she was indeed destined for the triumphal procession in Rome, she took her life. How she did it was a mystery even in antiquity. Apart from a few small puncture marks on her arm, no clue to the manner of her death could be found on her body. It is not improbable that, as contemporary accounts claimed, she died of a poisoned needle or the bite of a viper smuggled in to her in secret. Her corpse was buried according to the Egyptian funeral rite, next to Antony's.

The Ptolemaic royal line, which had ruled the most important of Alexander the Great's successor states for almost 300 years, ended with Cleopatra. Her death was attended, if not with glory, at least with a certain dignity that has attracted the attention of posterity into our own times. Even Horace paid tribute to her in his victory ode on Actium, in calling her, a moment after he has described her as a terrible monster (*fatale monstrum*), a proud queen who preferred suicide to the humiliation of walking in the triumphal procession. She was, says Horace, 'a not ignoble woman' (*non humilis mulier*).

The victor showed unaccustomed clemency. The soldiers had expected to plunder Alexandria, but Octavian spared the city and even paid the soldiers 1,000 sesterces each for their restraint. He had shown mercy to Alexandria, as he made it known, for three reasons: first for the sake of its main god, Serapis, which was a lie; second for the sake of its philosopher Arius, which was mere flattery; and third for its founder Alexander, which was at least credible. The real reason was that he was going to need the city in future as an administrative centre for an Egypt that was now Roman again. For the same reason Alexandria had to give up its city council, its central organ of self-administration; it appeared necessary to rescind the ancient constitution of the council so that the Alexandrians, who were intellectually open and inclined to be rebellious, could draw no support from it in future. The weakening of Alexandria also allowed Octavian to found a new city on the site of the last battle with Antony, only a few kilometres to the east. Like its counterpart at Actium, it was called Nicopolis, and it grew fast, but it was first and foremost a garrison town and could not compete with Alexandria as a second urban metropolis.

Many hard-line followers of Antony were also shown clemency, although some of them only after others had interceded energetically on their behalf. One such was Gaius Sosius, who had fought fearlessly on Antony's side at the battle of Actium; another was Sextus Pompey's half-brother, Marcus Aemilius Scaurus, for whom his mother Mucia, formerly the wife of Pompey the Great, pleaded. Gnaeus Cornelius Cinna, a grandson of the popular politician, was saved by his origins. Octavian had a few men executed. There was no pardon for the two last surviving assassins of Caesar, Turullius, whom Antony himself had handed over, and Cassius of Parma. Others to die were the devoted and capable Canidius Crassus, whose own loyalty was his downfall, and the seventeen-year-old Caesarion, allegedly the son of the dictator and co-regent with Cleopatra, as well as Antony's eldest son by Fulvia, Antyllus, who like Caesarion had already assumed the toga of a grown man. Both made a final desperate attempt to escape their fate. Antyllus sought safety in the temple of the deified Caesar, and Caesarion tried to run for it. They died for reasons of state, especially Caesarion, whether or not he was really the dictator's son. As the Ptolemaic king that his co-regency with Cleopatra made him, he was doomed. Octavian spared the three small children of Antony and Cleopatra, but they were put on show at his triumph the next year. After that their stepmother Octavia took them into her household and had them brought up by excellent tutors. Except for the girl, Cleopatra Selene, who was later married to the younger Juba of Mauretania, no more is heard of them.

Antony himself, although not formally an enemy in war, came off badly even in death. His statues were overturned, his name removed from official documents. It was the first time in Roman history that a ruler had suffered, by decree, the destruction even of his memory (*damnatio memoriae*), although the ban seems to have been lifted later. On hearing of Antony's suicide, Octavian is said to have withdrawn into his tent and wept, apologizing and justifying himself to friends and calling to mind his moderate conduct towards his opponent and Antony's arrogant responses. If anything it had been the other way around, but the struggle between the rivals, which in fact was a war to the death for the possession of supreme power, required no justification. Octavian's show of grief does him no credit, and his tears were no more than the cheap addition of a historian with an eye for touching effects.

For Octavian, who was always in financial straits, the precious metals were the most important part of the huge amount of loot taken. He minted coins with almost all the gold and silver that he found in the royal Ptolemaic treasury, or that came to him from other sources. Fines and a special tax imposed on the inhabitants of Egypt brought in further sums, and the client princes who had guilty consciences, especially those of the Syrian region, also made large contributions. Octavian was able to settle all his debts and in addition make presents to his loyal supporters among the senators and knights and to pay off all the soldiers. In fact the amount of money flowing into Italy from Egypt was so large that property prices suddenly rose considerably, while the rate of interest sank to a level never before known: one-third of the previous amount, dropping from twelve to four per cent. Octavian could even afford to decline financial gifts celebrating his victory offered to him by the cities of Italy in the form of gold wreaths. In the euphoria engendered by all this wealth, the pressure of taxation in previous years was soon forgotten.

Egypt and the entire east now had to be reorganized. The kingdom became a Roman province, and Octavian appointed Gaius Cornelius Gallus its first governor. He belonged to the second rank in society, the knights or members of the equestrian order, and was thus the only governor in the entire empire not to be a senator. This fact reveals the problem inherent in making a province of Egypt: the huge riches of the country produced by its centralized economy could not be entrusted to the hands of any potential rival, and Octavian even forbade senators to set foot in Egypt without his permission. These measures show that the land was regarded as a province under the direct control of the ruler, for Egypt was a power base. And in so far as it now stood beside the other provinces and had also been withdrawn from the control of the Senate, which was still officially regarded as the administrative centre of the empire, the old Ptolemaic royal power was now invested in Octavian.

For the rest, Octavian made few changes to the system set up by Antony, which had juxtaposed provinces and client princes – a sign that it could not have been entirely inappropriate to the political conditions of the east. The core, however, as represented by Egypt, was removed from the system and now, conversely, reinforced the provincial part of the power structure in the east. Octavian confirmed Herod, Amyntas, Archelaos and Polemon in their control of Syria and Asia Minor, with some slight modifications, and sometimes even extended their powers: for instance, not only were the regions of Herod's country that had fallen to Cleopatra returned to him, he also received access to the coast, which was very desirable, as well as Samaria. At the same time turmoil over the succession in the Parthian empire meant that settling the Parthian question could be postponed for the time being. Consequently no Roman policy of reconciliation or renunciation towards that powerful land in the east is yet discernible at this time, and in view of the unresolved situation in Parthia no preconditions for one existed.

The land of marvels on the Nile, however, exercised great powers of attraction on the usually rather sober Octavian. He even went to

Memphis, the administrative centre of ancient Egypt and also the home of the famous Serapeum, the place where the sacred Apis bull was worshipped. But Octavian, who like most of the people of Italy found Egyptian beliefs alien to him, did not want to see that. Instead, he expressed a wish to view the body of Alexander the Great, who was buried in Alexandria. The sarcophagus was opened for him, and Octavian paid tribute to the great king by placing a golden wreath on him and strewing flowers on the body. He also touched Alexander's face, perhaps in the expectation that the laying on of hands would create a kind of supernatural link between them. He was showing that he had not gone down into the tomb out of the pure curiosity of a tourist but wished to associate himself with the long line of rulers who had sought physical proximity to Alexander before him. His visit, however, did not have any concrete results of a political nature. In touching the face of the dead Alexander, Octavian, or so a chronicler either ill-disposed to him or simply indignant tells us, accidentally broke off a part of the nose. He rejected the suggestion that he might also visit the tombs of the Ptolemaic kings by remarking that he had wished to see a king (i.e. Alexander), not corpses.

The end of Antony's career, particularly in relation to his love for Cleopatra, is often perceived as a tragedy demanding pity and understanding. All readers of history are free to see it in that way if they wish. But the political evaluation of Antony is another matter, and here it must first be said that he was a military potentate and as such no more nor less than a rival of Octavian. The power of both men rested on military dictatorship, validated only formally in the triumvirate, and in the practical use of that power there is nothing to choose between them in their lack of scruples and the wish of both to assert themselves. Octavian's cruelty was probably more obvious because he was the younger man, but he lacked the frankness, ease and charm of youth, while a striking feature in Antony, the more experienced of the two, was his sometimes obvious passivity and indecision. But these are facets of different characters affecting neither the political position of the rivals nor the means with which they chose to impose their will. Antony, as it turned out, had made the worse choice. He opted for the east, although he had first set up his power base in Upper Italy and the Gallic territory conquered by Caesar, and as the more powerful man when the Roman world was divided up he had a free choice of the area of the empire where he could lay the foundations of his future rule. In spite of the failure of his Parthian campaign, and his obviously preferential treatment of Egypt, he had succeeded earlier in making something of the east, but no efforts on his part could compensate for the fact that he did not control Roman territory, and indeed it looked as if he had quite unnecessarily left it to Octavian. Presumably he had underestimated his rival, who succeeded in the almost impossible mission of overcoming Sextus Pompey and uniting Italy behind him. In fact Octavian was undoubtedly the better statesman, even if he owed his success to a number of coincidences. His fate had often been balanced on a knife-edge.

Both Antony and Octavian are to be seen in the context of their political origins and their power bases. No political assessments of them should be made if they cannot be explained in that light. Antony, a member of one of the most highly regarded families in the nobility, felt that he was an aristocrat and could present himself as such on occasion by making a show of magnanimity and clemency and demonstrating geniality. And he also knew that there is a place in life for cheerfulness as well as politics. But in spite of his origins he was never, as has sometimes been claimed, a 'republican'. Nor should Octavian be seen as an 'adventurer', distinct from Antony, who was so firmly anchored in the nobility. His personal background might not be very distinguished, but he had been a part of noble society since the dictator's death, and neither he nor his rival can be seen as higher or lower in status than the other. In all his ventures after Philippi, Antony largely lost sight of the west, and that was his worst mistake: for one thing, it derived from a mistaken judgement of the situation as a whole, and for another it showed a mortally dangerous *laisser faire* attitude. Nor can we overlook the fact that in the end his military talent forsook him. The commander of the year 32/31 was no longer what he had been in the year 42.

Octavian left Egypt in the year 30 and went on by way of Syria and Asia Minor to Samos, where he spent the winter. It was there that he entered upon his fifth consulate on 1 January 29, which was also his third in succession.

# 7
# Establishing the Monarchy as a Principate

The Roman empire now had a sole ruler again. The nature of his rule, however, in the present and the future, remained an open question. Octavian was no longer a triumvir, nor did he call himself by that title. He held the consulate, but what did that mean? Nothing was left of the old state but the bare bones of its governmental system; Octavian was consul, but that said nothing about the power he really held.

The victory that had given him control over Rome and the empire had removed his rival for power. But Octavian had no intention of letting it appear in that light. He did not want the Romans seeing his rule as the outcome of unbounded political ambition that had removed all competitors, ending with his last remaining rival, nor that it had simply emerged from rivalry between military potentates, each intent on eliminating his opposite number by force. Octavian did not even wish the power and renown that had come his way at Actium to be seen as founded primarily on what he himself had achieved for the state, however much emphasis he laid on his military success. It had been a god who gave them to him: victory had been won for him by Apollo, the god whose temple stood so close to his own residence, and on whose particular solicitude he could now rely. It was no coincidence that Apollo had a temple on the foothills of the Actian mountains, high above the scene of the fighting. From there, he had intervened in the naval battles, which had been not simply a conflict between two rival Roman generals, but a confrontation between Romans and barbarians, Italy and Egypt, the Roman leader (*dux*) and the Egyptian enchantress. He wanted everyone to acknowledge that victory over the oriental witch had saved Rome and the Roman way of life from foreign rule and barbarian customs. The gods, meaning Apollo, had preserved the fatherland

Denarius of Octavian, 29/27 BC. From the east. Obverse: winged Victory striding over a ship's prow, with palm branch and laurel wreath in her outstretched right hand. Reverse: triumphal chariot with Octavian as triumphator holding a laurel wreath, in section below IMP(erator) CAESAR.

Denarius of Octavian, 31/29 BC, from the east. Octavian, Victory standing on the globe with a laurel wreath in her right hand and a palm branch; inscription CAESAR DIVI F(ilius).

Octavian, tetradrachm, 28 BC, Ephesos. Obverse: Augustus with laurel wreath, inscription: IMP(erator) CAESAR DIVI F(ilius) CO(n)S(UL) VI LIBERTATIS P(opuli) R(omani) VINDEX '(Imperator Caesar, son of the deified one, consul for the sixth time, saviour of the liberty of the Roman people.' Reverse: the goddess Peace with caduceus (the staff of the herald of the gods), standing on a sword, behind her the *cista mystica* wirh a snake – the basket containing the sacred objects used in the Mysteries of Eleusis, and at the same time symbolizing them. Inscription: PAX, also inside the laurel wreath.

from shame and humiliation, and Octavian had been their instrument. Thanks were therefore due to the god Apollo.

Actium became a bright political symbol. It sent out various different messages. Above all, it surrounded the victor of Actium with the aura of divine assistance: Apollo was ever-present in Octavian. However many victories he had won before this one, especially since the Sicilian War, and however closely victory (*victoria*) and peace (*pax*) therefore seemed to be connected with his own person, the triumph at Actium meant more, and at the same time it meant something else: it had preserved liberty for the Romans, and the man who won it had saved them from the threat of servitude. Every Roman who did not already know that fact now learned it from the many symbols he encountered in public images and reliefs, in official declarations and inscriptions, and above all in works of literature. While Octavian had been shown with Victoria and Pax personified before, for instance on the coinage, after the battle he now also appeared as guarantor of the freedom of the Roman people: *vindex libertatis populi Romani*. He had saved the citizens of Rome from the danger of foreign oppression and enslavement to tyranny, and on the great arch in the Forum Romanum that the Senate and people of Rome donated at the time of his triumph in the year 29, the dedication did not refer to his victory over Cleopatra or to the name of the battle, but stated that it was built 'because he has saved the state' (*re publica conservata*). In this instance the state (*res publica*) was, naturally, to be understood as the only form of state imaginable for Romans at the time, the republic.

Octavian was not back in Rome yet. Reorganizing the east took time. On the way home from Egypt he went into winter quarters again on Samos, the island that Antony before him had favoured in the cold season. In Rome, meanwhile, the Senate was awarding him a variety of honours. Since Octavian was now increasingly distinct from other Roman citizens, indeed to some extent from ordinary mortals in general, and appeared to be near the gods, he was cautious in accepting such honours in case they prejudiced his future status, which he had only just begun to outline. Among the other decisions taken was that all his measures should be ratified under oath on 1 January of the new year, 29. Until this point holders of office taking up their new appointments had sworn on the first day of every year to observe the law of Rome; now the new ruler's decrees stood beside that law. Here again Octavian was in the line of succession of the dictator Caesar, whose measures had also been ratified at the beginning of every year. It was yet to be seen how far that similarity was deliberate. For the moment, at any rate, the new order had not yet taken shape; all else was obscured by Rome's desire to honour the victor.

The highest honour accorded to Octavian was an indirect one, and it too was bestowed just before his arrival. On 11 January, by decree of the Senate and as a symbol of the peace now reigning throughout the empire, the Arch of Janus, god of the city gates, was closed, and with it entry to and exit from Rome. This arch, which was also the sanctuary of the god, stood very close to the new Senate building, the Curia Julia, and bridged the major road known as the Argiletum, leading north-east from the Forum to the Subura, the most populous district of the city. Later, in his account of his own deeds, Augustus is still priding himself on the fact that in the year 29 the Arch of Janus was closed for only the third time in the history of Rome – it was closed twice more after that during his own reign. A number of minor battles in the north-west of Spain, on the Middle Rhine and in Egypt were magnanimously glossed over, so that the homecoming victor could be hailed as a prince bringing peace. For the end of the war, to which the closing of the gate related, of course meant the end of the civil war itself, not just some kind of skirmishing in a distant province, and the civil war really was over. Also dedicated to the victor were a triumphal arch in Brundisium, where Octavian landed in Italy, and another in the Forum Romanum rising above the Sacred Road, the Via Sacra. These were the first stone arches to be erected as monuments to victory over foreign enemies, and had a broad cornice (*attica*) suitable for an inscription, with a rostrum to accommodate statues. Many more such arches were to follow in both Rome and the provinces.

It was already summer when Octavian landed in Brundisium. From there, he travelled on to Campania, where after negotiations with the city of Naples he exchanged the island of Capri for Ischia, which was under his control. After visiting Capri, he was prevented from travelling further by illness; this time a heavy cold and a sore throat. In Atella he made use of his involuntary inactivity to have the whole of Virgil's great poem on country life (the *Georgics*) read to him over four consecutive days. In the guise of a manual on farming, this work encompasses the entire life of mankind in a then unusual poetically ambitious form. Virgil himself and Maecenas took turns reading it aloud.

The Romans welcomed the returning victor with great pomp. The undisputed high point of the festivities, which even the fact that Octavian was ill again could not dampen, was the three-day triumphal procession on 13, 14 and 15 August. On the first day Octavian celebrated his victory over the Dalmatian tribes, on the second his victory at Actium, and on the third his victory over Egypt. The last procession in particular outdid anything ever seen before. Setting out from the Field of Mars, it traversed the Flaminian Road and the Circus Maximus and then passed through the triumphal arch of the Servian Wall, which lay between the Capitol and the Tiber. It now entered the city, went on eastward around the Palatine to the Via Sacra, and so reached the entrance of the Capitol, which the triumphator ascended in order to dedicate his laurel wreath to the principal god of the city, Jupiter Optimus Maximus. The loot and the prisoners were at the head of the procession, the magistrates usually came behind them, just before the triumphator, behind whom the soldiers were posted. Octavian, who incidentally was celebrating his triumph not in a chariot but on horseback, made what to outward appearance was only a slight alteration to the order of the procession: he had the magistrates walking behind rather than in front of him. Although they were formally holders of the highest offices in Rome, they were thus no longer presenting the triumphator to the city as representatives of the state, but walking behind him at the head of the soldiers. This meant that any observer would, to some extent, see Octavian as the sum of all state power (which in fact he was), with the magistrates merely taking orders from him. The relationship between the holders of high office and the trimphator had been reversed. Did that indicate the nature of the future state, or was it only an unfortunate error that had slipped in during all the intoxication of the celebrations? There was no one now to keep an eye on of the old political rules that included the granting of triumphs and the form they took. The society that could have prevented such a state of affairs, the nobility, had stepped down.

Only a few days after this final triumph, on 18 August, the temple that Octavian had been building for the last decade in honour of his divine father, the deified Julius, was dedicated in the Forum Romanum.

It marked the border of the narrow south-east side of the square and made it a self-contained complex. The cult statue of Caesar was depicted with the 'Julian star' (*sidus Iulium*) above its head, and as the interior of the temple was quite short, it could be seen from the square when the doors were open. The temple itself had been adorned with a picture by Apelles, the great painter of the time of Alexander the Great, showing Venus rising from the sea and thus alluding to Caesar's divine descent. The altar stood in front of the temple, in a niche in the recently erected second rostrum of the Forum, in the very place where the body of the dictator had been cremated. The new rostrum stood on the eastern side of the Forum, facing the old one, and both its situation and its façade, which was decorated with the prows of ships in reference to the victory at Actium, were intended to suggest that a new political beginning had been secured by divine aid.

At almost the same time the new Senate building (*curia*) was completed, to replace the building burned down in the year 52. Begun by the dictator and named after him, this structure, the Curia Julia, stood not far from the site of the old building in the Forum. As reconstructed by the Emperor Diocletian after another fire, it has been preserved to the present day. Octavian gave it an altar to Victoria, and a statue of the goddess of victory hovering on the vault of the firmament (*globus*). The Romans had taken this as war booty from Tarentum in the year 209, and although Victoria was now more or less synonymous with Actium, and was thus connected with Octavian as the victor of that battle, the goddess donated to the Curia was not meant to refer primarily to him, but to the Senate representing the triumph of Rome as the central government of the empire, which it formally still was. As in the past, when the Senate and people of Rome had subdued the world, the solemn sacrifice made in the Senate house before every meeting would continue to link it with that idea. The recognition of the Senate as the highest organ of state, which the gift of this Victoria implied, is one of many signs at the time that the way was being prepared for Octavian's great reform of the constitution of the state.

Providing for the soldiers now about to be discharged was still a difficult problem. With the units taken over from Lepidus and Antony, the number of legions after the end of hostilities had grown to nearly seventy, and that did not include formations of lightly armed soldiers, the Roman cavalry and the naval crews. It was true that not all the legions were at full fighting strength, but the number of soldiers must have been in all above a quarter of a million. Octavian had already begun demobilization and preparations for settling them in retirement before Actium, and the work had been energetically pursued both while he was away and after his return. In this, on principle, he treated the legions of Lepidus and Antony as equal with his own.

However, the main difficulty, yet again, was the land question. Most of the men due for discharge, and the number must have been at least 80,000, were settled in Italy, undoubtedly in line with their own wishes, and a number of others – although not an excessively large number at this time – in the provinces. Octavian's Egyptian booty enabled him to provide large sums of money for the purchase of land in Italy. Generally speaking, the demobilization was a more orderly procedure than after the battle of Philippi, especially as, at the time of his triumph, the commander gave soldiers settled in Italian towns a triumphal gift of 1,000 sesterces each.

Not all the legions were dissolved: dangers threatening the borders of the empire called for strong military forces in areas at particular risk. The question of the military safeguarding of the empire, which the republican state had been unable to achieve, and had even deliberately neglected because a large army fired the ambition of certain individual aristocrats and endangered the balance of political powers at home, could be satisfactorily solved now that the military potentate had taken power. The price was a standing army. How Octavian was to deal with that was still an open question; rules of conduct between soldiers stationed in barracks and their general had yet to be drawn up. It is not quite certain how many legions Octavian kept on after the end of the war; they numbered at least twenty-three, but more probably there were twenty-eight.

After the victory celebrations and the generosity that went with them, Rome and its politics had to return to everyday life. What was ordinary life like now, under the rule of the all-powerful lord over the Roman armies and provinces? Was the victory that had been celebrated so enthusiastically really a victory of the Romans over their enemies, or was it not really the triumph of Octavian and his soldiers over his rivals for power? Many might have been wondering what Roman citizens, the state and its organs had to do with that victory. It was true that the framework of the old constitution was still in place; there were consuls and praetors; the Senate met to take decisions, and so, on occasion, did the people. Octavian, who had been consul every year since 31 – and had held the office all through the year, not just for a few months – seemed to be formally only a link in the constitutional order. But the very fact that he had already occupied the consulate for three years running – although holding that office was legally permissible only once every ten years – made the unfortunate state of affairs plain: the commander of the army was not subject to the constitution. He took what he needed from the various offices and regulations and he took it when he needed it. The constitution had become an empty shell. The society that had once filled its offices and guaranteed its existence – the nobles as a ruling class of aristocrats, then the rest of the senators and the men of equestrian rank, and the mass of citizens qualified to vote in the people's assemblies – no longer stood behind the constitution as its guarantor. Instead, the new military potentate, through his patronage of the soldiers, united all power in his own person. He, that is to say Octavian, was now the guarantor of security and the law, which he could now bend to whatever form he pleased. In fact his adoptive father, Caesar the dictator, had treated the old state in an equally cavalier fashion. Would his son follow in his political footsteps in future? Did he want to be dictator himself? After Caesar's murder, the dictatorship had been officially abolished, but what did that mean to a man who had power to change everything? A word from Octavian would be enough to make him dictator. But by saying that word he would, at the same time, have torn off the mask that he had worn, or attempted to wear, for the previous few years, a mask that had already seemed to take clearer shape during his war of words with Antony. The features of that mask were sharply delineated – and at this point, undoubtedly, it was still seen by everyone as a mask and not yet his true face. Already, however, concepts irreconcilable with a dictatorship were being linked with it: concepts such as the nature of Rome, Roman tradition, respect for the ancestors and the gods, respect for the once firmly established rules of political life. If all that Octavian claimed to the Romans to personify was not just to be empty words, he had to make it political reality.

Octavian's situation was not simple. He carried a huge burden of expectation. However, that expectation did not come to the same extent from all groups of Roman society. The common soldiers were not in

contention as the most important group: they had no political prospects, their expectations were purely material, and Octavian had fulfilled
those expectations, so he had only to take care never to disappoint
them. The majority of Roman citizens did not expect any new political
beginning either, at least not in the immediate future. To the average
citizen, what mattered most was the restoration of peace and the security of his economic livelihood, and here the situation was not as bad as
it had been a few years earlier, so it was possible to look to the future
with confidence. For several generations, the only citizens to have had
real political ambition were those living in Rome or its surroundings,
men who took an interest in what went on in society and could play an
active part, for instance in the assemblies of the people. However, those
who lived in Upper Italy or the plain of the Po, or even in Campania or
the Sabine country, could not participate in the political life of the city
because of the great distances involved, and the character of the city
state of the political world at that time meant that nothing could be
done about that. No one even considered changing the Roman city
state, which took it for granted that politicians would be there in the
city, into an Italian territorial state with a representative constitution.
Even the idea of enabling those living far from the city to take part in
the assemblies of the people by sending written votes to Rome, thus
making the political rights of all citizens a reality, was an idea that
Augustus considered only once, and then only to a restricted extent. Of
the great mass of ordinary citizens, then, only the people of the city
(*plebs urbana*) were really affected by the future political order.

The main result was that even if the people of the city of Rome as a
whole were not unimportant, as those to whom policies were addressed,
the attitude of the more distinguished and prosperous men among them
was what mattered. The administration of the Roman state and the vast
areas over which it ruled was in their hands. There were countless posts
to be filled, and, for the very reason that there was no specialist administrative organization, only men of property with experience in business
could be considered for them, men who personally had all that a modern bureaucracy makes available to the holders of high office – money
and staff – and who were also willing to spend their money for the sake
of their reputation in society. That was exactly what the old nobility
had done, and so, under their direction, had the senators of middle rank
and many of the knights. The nobles and other senators had occupied

the magistracy, the knights had been tax farmers, collecting the huge amounts of taxation due from the provinces through the companies (*societates*) that they managed. However, while the circle of persons from which officials to run the administration of the state must come might be obvious, there was still the question of how to find men among them who were willing and able to do so. The old society from which such officials had been drawn, until the outbreak of the civil war in the year 49, had been thinning out ever since the unrest at the time of the Gracchi brothers about a hundred years earlier, dwindling steadily until at last it had been largely physically eradicated in the previous two decades. Only a few families still remained, like monuments to a long-gone past, in the present age as it sought a new beginning. Most of those whose names had the ring of the good old days, however, were young men, novices who had done little or nothing so far – for instance Lucius Cornelius Cinna, consul in the year 32 – or who were nonentities tolerated by the new ruler merely for the lustre of their origins, such as Marcus Tullius Cicero, son of the great orator and consul in the year 30.

Octavian's huge, all but impossible task consisted of assembling around him a considerable circle of men who were able and willing to take on the organization of the state and its government. However, finding such people was not the end of it. Octavian was no longer living in the midst of civil war, and the days were over when he could give men whom he knew to be able and loyal to him posts as generals or governors, rewarding them for taking over the business of administration with high rank and, naturally, material profit in the form of money and land. In the safe haven of peace, a general or official who had achieved a post of honour no longer looked just to the next month or the next year to establish him in his position, but to the coming decade and indeed his whole future life, which he certainly did not intend to devote entirely to the function he had taken on. He wanted to see the reputation he had won established in the long term, not only for himself but for his descendants, so now the secure social position of whole families was at stake. The noblemen of the old days knew that their rank was secured by the reputation of their families and their own fortunes and network of personal relationships, which extended to the nobility as a whole, indeed the whole of Roman society, and even to the subjects in the provinces, where their situation was safe. This network, however, had been largely destroyed, and only a few men could still fall back on their old connections.

Most of those who had gained a high reputation in the past decades, in the service of the ruling powers, and had been lucky enough to be on the side of the victor at the end of the civil war, or had received clemency from him, were from obscure families. And the majority no longer came from Rome or its surroundings, but from many different parts of Italy. This was a very mixed society, and the names of quite a number of parvenus succeeded each other fairly quickly. Many of the 'new men' might not pass on their recently acquired social rank to their descendants, and their names disappeared again from the lists of holders of high office. One such was the famous general Publius Ventidius Bassus, from the Picene district on the Adriatic. Many social climbers, on the other hand, were able to acquire official positions for their sons as well, thus passing on their own higher social rank to the next generation. No longer content with honours and rewards, they sought models to emulate as they strove to preserve an elevated position and looked back at the society that had done so much in the past. Although the present pathetic remnants of the once proud and mighty nobility, a class that they had before their mind's eye and to which they looked up, did not enable them to form much of an idea of its former glories, they still took their guidelines from the accounts of men who had lived and governed the state in what was not, after all, such a very distant past. Of Octavian's immediate circle of close friends, those generals and officials who were possible candidates for political activity in the future, very few were descended from the old nobility. Gnaeus Domitius Calvinus, one of the dictator's most able generals, a man who was also among Octavian's most loyal supporters, was now very old – if indeed he was still alive at this time. Other highly respected families had simply died out during the civil wars, and not a few of those who remained had backed Sextus Pompey and Antony. After the battle of Actium, moreover, Octavian had had few opportunities of granting pardons to the descendants of such families. One of those was Marcus Junius Silanus, who, after changing sides several times, had gone over from Antony to Octavian before the Actian War and was rewarded for it with the consulate in the year 25. Another was Gnaeus Domitius Ahenobarbus, consul in the year 32, but he died directly after being pardoned. All the same, it was possible for Octavian to grant a pardon to Marcus Licinius Crassus, grandson of the Crassus who had twice been consul and was a 'colleague' of Caesar's in the so-called First Triumvirate. Crassus the Younger had followed first Sextus Pompey and then Antony. His noble rank was beyond question, for he was not only a Licinian but through his mother, Caecilia Metella, daughter of one of the consuls of the year 69, was related to another extremely powerful and influential late republican *gens*.

When Octavian, bypassing his own tried and trusted followers, appointed Crassus his fellow consul the year after Actium, he showed how anxious he was to surround himself with the lustre of ancient names. In the following year, the consul picked by Octavian was a member of the distinguished Apuleian family and, as his half-sister Octavia the Elder's son, was related to him. Also descended from an old clan was Marcus Valerius Messalla, mentioned several times above. After wavering for some time, he had joined Octavian in the year 37, proved himself a good commander in the Sicilian and Dalmatian wars and was appointed consul with Octavian to replace Antony in the year 31. Similarly, Gaius Carrinas, of Octavian's party from the first, and Gaius Norbanus both belonged to families that had played a part in the noble society of the republic. Their forebears had been supporters of Gaius Marius, and thus closely connected with Caesar the dictator's political life. Carrinas and Norbanus in turn had proved their worth as generals in Octavian's service and had been rewarded with the consulate in the years 43 and 38. They had even been granted a triumph for the successful campaigns they had fought in the provinces they administered. Lucius Antonius Paetus, who featured as one of the many consuls in the year 33, also came from a family highly regarded in late republican Rome.

All these were joined by the 'new men', some of whom had first risen to prominence under the dictator or even Octavian himself, including some very able generals. First among them, undoubtedly, was Octavian's outstanding general and admiral Marcus Vipsanius Agrippa, one of the most loyal and capable of his supporters, and there were a good many others, in particular Titus Statilius Taurus, who had come over from Antony to Octavian after the Sicilian War and proved his worth by his military achievements and his loyalty. The new men also included Gaius Calvisius Sabinus and Quintus Laronius, who had both commanded fleets or legions during the Sicilian War, if not very successfully, and others who had defected to Octavian, such as the former Pompey supporter Lucius Arruntius, who served Octavian as an admiral at Actium. Finally Antony's former adherent Gaius Furnius should also be mentioned; he was a political friend of Cicero and one of the tribunes of the people in the year 50. Thereafter he had been first a Caesarian and then an Antonian, until in the year 30, at the request of his son, who was an Octavian, he was one of the last to be pardoned by Octavian. Although he had never been consul himself, he was allowed to sit with those of consular rank in the Senate. In addition, Octavian also had a whole series of able and knowledgeable men who, although already of mature years, had never yet achieved eminence, or of whose previous activities the records tell us little. However, we can trace their successful careers over the next two decades. To mention only two of them, Marcus Lollius was a close personal friend of Octavian whose first major task was to integrate the kingdom of Galatia into the empire as a Roman province in the year 25, and Marcus Vinicius, who, after a career difficult for us to trace today, made his mark more clearly only after his consulate in the year 19. After a great career in the administration, he was to be one of the closest table companions of the ageing Augustus.

One could write at length about the motley ranks of the Octavians. In particular, those who had been on the side of the eventual victor even before the war broke out made up a group of some size who could be relied on, and who stood high in public esteem. Did they already represent the foundations of a new administrative aristocracy? Hardly, and Octavian knew it. The times in which these men had risen to prominence and gained their reputations could not have merged them into a unit, for the very reason that their origins, characters and party allegiances differed widely. Success alone did not create political morale. Octavian could rely on most of his adherents who came from the old nobility, but he had to be wary of them, particularly when they had been successful as generals, because their families had a long tradition and considerable influence in Rome and Italy, and many of them might think poorly of the dictator's nephew. Octavian faced two of these immediately. Marcus Aemilius Lepidus, son of the triumvir, seemed a risk because of his illustrious descent: through his mother Junia he was a nephew of Marcus Brutus, and through his wife Servilia he was related to another noble family. She was the same Servilia to whom Octavian

had once been betrothed, before rejecting her after the treaty of Bononia in favour of a relationship by marriage with Antony. Young Lepidus
could expect a good chance of a political future because of his father's
former position and his family contacts. So he risked entering into a
conspiracy. It was obviously poorly planned, and was uncovered by
Maecenas during Octavian's absence at Actium before it could come to
anything, whereupon Octavian had young Lepidus instantly executed.
However, if a man of such slight political weight, indeed a man whose
political capital consisted chiefly of his origins, would venture on a plot
of that kind, how much more caution was advisable in dealing with the
publicly recognized generals who were of ancient noble families! And
indeed, as soon as Octavian returned to Rome a potential rival from a
very old family did arise. This was Marcus Licinius Crassus, mentioned
above, grandson of the consul of the years 70 and 55.

Crassus, promoted by Octavian to the office of consul with himself
in the year 30 purely for the sake of his name, had not until now been
one of his adherents, instead supporting first Sextus Pompey and then
Antony. Only at Actium had he gone over to the winning side, probably
in advance of the battle. He was given Macedonia as his province, along
with a good-sized army of some four to five legions. Why Octavian
favoured a man who was evidently not of his own political colour in
this way is not entirely clear from our sources. It has been suspected
that, evidently being keen to forge a bond with a man of distinguished
family, he was paying Crassus with the consulate and a governorship in
return for his change of sides. But he hardly needed to do that after the
battle. It seems more likely that the privileges granted to Crassus were
part of a general policy of reconciliation after Actium, just as Octavian
also showed extraordinary clemency after his victory, emphasizing it by
ensuring that his own soldiers and those of his opponents were treated
in the same way. Even if Octavian was thinking along the lines of a fair
bargain, his calculations did not work out, at least so far as Crassus was
concerned. Crassus did not by any means show meek obedience in
return for the preferential treatment he was given. And in his battles
with the peoples on the northern border of his province he proved himself a talented commander over the following two to three years, very
energetic and above all independent.

After stepping down from the consulate at the end of June in the year
30, Crassus will have gone to his Macedonian province the same year.

In the following year he made an attack by the Bastarnae in the area south of the Danube his excuse to cross the northern border of his province. The Bastarnae were of Germanic origin; they had settled in the area north of the Lower Danube and had only recently seceded from the mighty tribe of the Dacians, thus gaining freedom of movement. In the winter of 30 to 29, they advanced south, crossed the frozen Danube and poured into the Thracian area inhabited by the Moesians, who lived north of the Balkan mountains between the Magus (Morava) and the Black Sea. As they were making their way through the high passes, engaging in conflict with Thracian tribes in the northern approaches to Macedonia, Crassus took the initiative. He crossed the border of the province with his legions. Although the Bastarnae immediately retreated into the area between the Balkans and the Danube, Crassus now crossed the mountain range from the south, began subduing the Moesians settled to the north of it and finally attacked the Bastarnae too on the Danube. Since they could not cross the river, where the ice had now melted, their whole army was stationed on the banks of the Danube and was largely wiped out in a bloody battle in which Crassus killed their king with his own hands. Crassus went on to conquer the entire country of the Moesians, showing harsh cruelty at times, before withdrawing to his province again at the onset of winter. Only at the beginning of the following year, 28, did he advance on the Danube once more. The Bastarnae had crossed the river again, but Crassus forced them to retreat and then turned to fight the Thracians in the eastern part of what is now Bulgaria. At the end of 28 all the country lying between the Danube and the northern border of the province of Macedonia and east of the Magus could be regarded as conquered. The huge area comprising modern Bulgaria and the eastern part of Serbia included what were later the two provinces of Lower and Upper Moesia, but at first they were not made into provinces. Instead, divided between princes dependent on Rome, they were annexed to the province of Macedonia.

The operation was a huge success. And yet, although in the year 29 the Senate had already decided to award Crassus a festival of thanksgiving and a triumph, he was now at the centre of interest not primarily for his military prowess but for its possible political consequences. He had, after all, done exactly what all military potentates since Caesar had wanted and striven for: to gain political influence in the state by holding a military command and conducting a large-scale campaign. Just as

Octavian felt that he was following in the footsteps of Caesar, and indeed had planned his Illyrian expedition with that in mind, to legitimize his status as military commander to the Romans, Crassus too could now claim that he was acting in the tradition of his grandfather, who had fought the Parthians and was on a par with the other mighty generals. Since after Actium there was only one of those left, he was on the same footing as that remaining general. If it was bold to regard himself as equal to Octavian or even Agrippa, he might well feel that after those two he was among the most highly regarded military leaders of his time. In any case, it was clear to all Romans, the common soldiers and veterans as well as the present and former generals and holders of office, that Crassus had acted not as Octavian's subordinate, but as a governor responsible only to himself who had boldly seized his chance to act and whose success seemed to justify his actions.

Not only were his qualities as a commander and his energy remarkable; so above all was his bold if also unconsidered move out of his province (which Roman foreign policy did not justify) and the sheer size of the territory that he had finally won for Rome. As a governor, Crassus seemed to have taken his guidelines not from the political situation, which would have confined him to the defence of his province, but from political aims such as those of the powerful holders of extraordinary commands, men like Pompey, Caesar and his own grandfather Crassus, or indeed the commands of Octavian and Antony. They had used their huge armies to consolidate and extend their political influence (*dignitas*) among the Romans, rather than simply to defend the empire against invading tribes from outside or rebellious provincials. One might think that Crassus wanted to measure himself and his objectives by these men, not by the objective demands of his governorship. It was hardly possible not to compare his deeds with those of Octavian, who had sought to prove his military talent in the same part of the country only a few years before. He too had been successful, but he had not brought nearly so much territory under Roman control. Was there perhaps an alternative to Octavian after all?

Octavian was familiar with conditions in the north of the province of Macedonia from his own operations in Dalmatia and Pannonia. He might at first have welcomed the activities of Crassus, might even have prompted them, but he was not prepared for such a great success. He immediately saw the danger that it presented, or could present, and tried to limit the damage. No objection could very well be made to the fact that his soldiers in the province had hailed Crassus as *imperator*, an honour that had been shown to far less successful generals in past years, and which Octavian himself had accepted without demur. More dangerous, because in the eyes of the general public it conferred more prestige, was another honour to which Crassus could now lay claim. He had killed the chief of the Bastarnae: if a Roman military leader killed the commander of the opposing army with his own hands in battle, he could dedicate the dead leader's armour – 'glorious armour', as it was called, *spolia opima* – to Jupiter Feretrius in a solemn ceremony on the Capitol. Tradition said that this honour had first been awarded to Romulus, founder of the city, and to only two other Roman military leaders since him: Crassus would be the fourth. Of course, after the battle with the Bastarnae the matter was a subject of lively and sometimes malicious discussion in the summer of 29 among senators who did not much like Octavian, perhaps even hated him. He had to be all the firmer in preventing Crassus from entering Rome as a 'new Romulus'. As a result, he did not even let matters come to that point. Whether he gave Crassus an unmistakable hint, or whether Crassus himself anticipated the opposition to be expected and avoided it, we do not know, but at any rate Crassus refrained from applying to the Senate to be allowed to dedicate the armour he had taken as the spoils of war and contented himself with the triumph, which was not refused him, and indeed many of Octavian's generals had been allowed their triumphs before.

We can tell that the affair created a great sensation at the time from the fact that Octavian later tried to justify his preventing the dedication. He found, probably during the restoration of the temple of Jupiter Feretrius, an inscription into which, as we are told by the historian Livy, a contemporary and friend of Augustus, he read confirmation of what in his opinion was the proper prerequisite for that honour: according to the inscription the dedication of such armour was granted only to a general who had fought as a magistrate with independent powers of command. Crassus, the public was expected to conclude from this, held no independent command and thus had no claim to dedicate the 'glorious armour'. This late justification, however, was put forward at a time when most of the provinces (but not Macedonia) were under the control of legates dependent on Octavian (by then Augustus), and therefore, strictly speaking, the problem in the year 28 was not in the same category. It came *before* the division of the provinces between Octavian and the Senate, and also before the formal appointment of a governor dependent on Octavian (*legatus Augusti*). At the time, Crassus could have said that, even if the Senate had not expressly appointed him proconsul (which we can be fairly sure it had), he had been a proconsul in accordance with the rules and thus an independent magistrate, particularly as he was also officially thus described. Anyway, the question was not really whether a general who had killed an enemy general was an independent magistrate. The situation was simpler: had he acted as leader of the Roman troops when he killed the leader of the enemy in battle, or had he not? Never before, in the matter of the right to dedicate armour, had the nature of the victorious general's official position been called into question.

In the year 28 Octavian, on the other hand, was solely concerned to maintain and consolidate his power in the face of a potential rival, and only in retrospect did he raise his actions where Crassus was concerned to the legal level. He simply recognized the potential danger to him of Crassus' success, and had to assert himself, for his power, extensive as it might seem, was still on very shaky legal ground at the time. It was true that he was consul in Rome, but he commanded his provinces and armies only in so far as the Senate had not appointed anyone to succeed him after the end of the triumvirate and similarly had not yet come to a decision on Antony's provinces, which he had occupied in accordance with the laws of war and which included Macedonia. So before the year 27 he held no legal power by the normal rules in force in his provincial territory. If a third party now had the audacity to exploit this grey zone between power held in fact and power legally held, and challenged the military potentate in his own heartland, the provinces, then at all costs he must show him where he had to stop short.

Crassus had represented a possible rival in the struggle for power. Reminded by this confrontation of the temporary nature of his own position, Octavian had to act even more firmly after this incident to transform his power base, which was largely ill-defined in form, as soon as possible into a final official position that conformed to the law, was firmly established legally and at the same time would in future avert dangers such as those conjured up by Crassus. For the moment, however, he made sure that Crassus disappeared from public view. Although he was a man in the prime of life, after his triumph we hear no more of him.

The Roman state, termed by the Romans themselves *res publica*, 'the public matter', no longer existed. Octavian, now in sole command of the army, had done much to give a sense of security and peace to the Romans, particularly men of distinction, and of those in turn particularly men who had achieved honours through himself, and he had also made it clear that he was ready to negotiate, to respect the old order and bring its traditions back into high esteem. But courteous respect and goodwill alone were not enough. Whatever innovations he had introduced, they did not suggest to anyone that a political order other than that of the military potentate existed in its own right, nor could what Octavian and his alleged 'colleagues' had done during their decade in power be forgotten. The days of autocratic proscription still sent a shudder down the spine – and that was not all. Even now it was clear to everyone, from personal experience, that the legal structure on which the state had once been based could be ignored as the ruler saw fit. Consuls were appointed to office as he wished, or conversely were made to resign it to create a vacancy for someone else from the ranks of his followers. If the Senate or even the assembly of the people was called in, as the ultimate authority, it was clear to everyone that it too did as the ruler wanted.

Octavian could not disappoint the expectations of a change of political course; they were also felt in his own close circle. His frequent promises that the special powers granted to the triumvirs would be rescinded once the civil war was over must now at last be honoured if he was not to lose face as a military commander. Although it was not publicly expressed, there had always been a perceptible desire for a 'return' to the old ways – whatever form exactly the old ways might take in the minds of those who wanted them back without having known them personally. All this ran counter to Octavian's efforts to consolidate his own position. Crassus had shown what dangers the unresolved political and legal situation might yet throw up. By using the framework of the state organization, now sunk to the level of a mere mechanism, a successful general could perhaps give himself a position from which he might compete with Octavian. Crassus had not been the cause of what now began to happen, but he did set it off.

If Octavian did not want to present himself to the people and the Senate of Rome merely as the holder of power, but as the representative of the state lawfully chosen by the Romans, something for which he had striven since the year 36, and with redoubled efforts since his quarrel with Mark Antony, he was in a very awkward situation. It was true that he had been consul since the year 31 without a break and consequently held, together with one colleague, the highest power in Rome; it was true that in that capacity he had the right to propose laws and lay them before the Senate; and although it might be objected that the continuous prolongation of his consulate was against the principle, now 400 years old, of 'annuity', whereby all the high offices of state were held for the term of a year, yet his actions at the centre of power in Rome were covered by the law and not acts of pure autocracy. In the empire, however, his situation looked much worse. The triumvirate, through which he had taken over governorship of all the western provinces since the years 42–36, had long ago run its course, and his rule over the eastern provinces, which he had assumed under martial law in 31–30, could not be regarded as different in any way from his rule over his own provinces. In fact he ruled everywhere in the empire solely by virtue of the fact that a Roman governor could not be relieved of his position until the Senate or people had appointed a successor. Octavian's rule over the entire empire must thus be regarded as provisional, a state of affairs that would last only until it was properly regulated by the central authorities of state, the Senate and people of Rome.

Even all the honours and special privileges that Octavian had acquired over the preceding few years could not conceal the provisional nature of his political position, let alone eliminate it. In fact they appeared rather strange against the background of the past and might even strike many as a violation of tradition. Octavian's adorning himself with the 'sacrosanctity' of a tribune of the people, an office that had been, as it were, tailored to fit him as successor to the dictator in the tribuneship, might be allowed as an honour to his person. However, the right to appoint patricians, which he had assumed since the year 30, was harder to accept. Men were patricians by birth, by virtue of the fact that they belonged to one of the ancient noble families that, for 500 years, had been considered qualified to rule. How, in the circumstances, could someone be 'elevated' to the rank of patrician? The dictator had done exactly the same thing before him, but that might make the matter even more suspect. And if Octavian had tried to counter such objections by arguing that, now that the old aristocracy had almost entirely died out, certain religious offices reserved for patricians since time immemorial could not be filled without the creation of a new nobility, that was no excuse nor even an acceptable explanation for his assumption of those special powers.

Clarification of the constitutional situation was urgently needed. It must fulfil the expectations of those who had helped Octavian and also correspond to his own needs, and naturally it had to be done by means of a public act abolishing the special powers associated with the name of the triumvirate. Those powers had to be given up, and at the same time the position that Octavian still held must be redefined. Most important was the first of those two points, his relinquishing, so often announced, of special military powers. But to whom were they going to be relinquished?

Discretionary full powers could be handed back only to the central organ of government, the Senate. The Senate, however, like the assembly of the people and the magistracy, initially represented only one of the institutions that were entirely at Octavian's disposal. It was an automaton at its master's service for passing resolutions; it merely took his orders and for the last two decades it had been unable to make a single independent decision. Now, however, he needed not an institution but a society, a group of men to fill the institutions of the Senate and the other organs of government, and here again the prospects were poor. In the days of the republic, even in the year 50 before the outbreak of the great civil war, the nobility had guided the Senate and with it the entire state. It had been the guarantee of public law, and all knowledge of the way in which the state functioned had been collectively stored in it. But none of that existed any more, and the remnants of the once numerous aristocratic families were entirely unable to form the nucleus of a new nobility, particularly as Octavian, who had contributed so much to the demolition of the system, was not prepared to revive it. The group could therefore only be one whose members enjoyed the confidence of Octavian, men who had risen in his service and whom he had promoted, so that at least its core could consist only of the close circle of those around the ruler. In so far as the circle was wider than Octavian's own assistants and close friends, the men concerned must not oppose him, and in so far

as they belonged to the old noble families who had been in other political camps, they must at least have made their peace with him. We may
leave aside the question of whether at this point, the year 29, the 'new
society' could be seen as a set of distinguished and influential men ready
to take over – under the protection of the holder of power, of course – as
a group capable of running the government. It was to such a group, in
any case, that he intended to relinquish his powers.

The men who mattered to Octavian already occupied the higher
ranks of the Senate. At the time, however, that venerable institution was
merely a committee entirely without form or influence. Inflated into an
institution of about a thousand members, it could not be considered
capable of the serious work of administration, simply by virtue of its
numbers. In addition, by now there were many men who, since the year
49, had been promoted to the minor or major offices of state on the
whim of one or another of those in power and then had entered the Senate, but who were wholly unfit for the work of government and were
often even unwilling to undertake it. Consequently the dignity of the
Senate must first be restored and its voice heard if the extraordinary
powers of authority were to be given up to it, and at the same time any
change of circumstances must meet with a positive response from both
distinguished men and the common people of Rome. At stake was what
had once been called *auctoritas senatus*, the authority of the Senate,
which had been synonymous with the will of the state.

Octavian's first task, then, was to reform the Senate. In practice that
meant nothing less than subjecting its present composition to a stern
examination, and Octavian prepared carefully for the forthcoming
'cleansing' of the Senate. In view of the importance that the committee
and its members still had, this was a difficult, perhaps even dangerous
and certainly unpleasant undertaking, since it might sometimes involve
the humiliation of individual senators. Who was to go? Many were
fairly obvious candidates for removal from office; with others there
could be some doubt; there were others again, men who were among
Octavian's more or less open opponents, or whose character and actions
made it intolerable to think of keeping them but who, it was to be
feared, had influence on other important persons. The 'cleansing', as
could be seen in advance, would affect not only the unworthy and
incapable, but also those who had thrown in their lot with the wrong
party and neglected to ask forgiveness or failed to obtain it. Not a few

of the 300 senators who had followed the consuls to Antony's camp in the year 32 might expect to pay for it now.

In the year 28, not long after his return from the east, correctly seeing the Senate as the body to which the full powers granted to him should be returned, Octavian began placing it on a new foundation. Acting together with Agrippa, he began by having the power of the censor transferred to him. That allowed him to undertake a personal check on the senators. There had always been two censors, chosen every five years, whose job was, among other things, to record information on all Roman citizens and estimate their fortunes, since the basis on which they were deemed capable of filling certain state functions depended on the wealth they owned. At the same time they had to check the list of senators, that is to say enter those officials who had been active in the years since the last census was taken in the classes appropriate to their rank, and in some circumstances remove from the list of senators those whom, on the grounds of some incident or other, they did not consider men of integrity. They might also add to the list persons who had not yet held any office, but whom they thought worthy to do so. This last power had been exercised very rarely in the last two centuries, and indeed, because of the general crisis, it was a long time since any censors had been chosen. After all, the office of censor, by virtue of the power invested in it, could in some circumstances question a man's entire political existence, so that it had always been offered only to trustworthy men of great distinction. For over a generation, in a society hopelessly riven by conflict, it had been impossible to agree on those who would be approved by everyone as fit to hold it.

First Octavian set about checking the list of senators. This process was called the 'reading of the Senate' (*lectio senatus*). The censor, in this case Octavian with the extraordinary powers of censorship granted to him, read out the list of members according to their class and rank. Anyone whose name was omitted was de facto removed from the list; anyone whose name was added became a senator. Octavian went to great pains to settle this difficult business without discourteous personal detraction from a senator's character. He did not simply read out the list of men who, he thought, should remain in the Senate, but held personal conversations beforehand with those whom he meant to remove, trying to persuade them to retire voluntarily. This method succeeded with fifty senators and failed with another 140. He did not simply throw the latter out, but let all 190 continue to hold their old rank. They could go on calling themselves senators and holding titles (for instance praetorian) in accordance with the last office they had held. The only penalty he inflicted on those who were not retiring of their own accord was to make their names public. In addition, he brought a number of new men into the Senate, including two of his former opponents who had been designated for the consulate by Antony but were not considered for that office after the outbreak of hostilities. This was undoubtedly a measure intended to create the broad consensus that Octavian so badly needed for his forthcoming settlement. When he finally appointed some senators patricians, members of the old families will not have been pleased.

He also took the opportunity of this 'reading' to have himself appointed 'First in the Senate', *princeps senatus*. That title had once denoted the man whose name stood at the head of the list of senators, that is to say, the oldest former censor of patrician origin. The list of the Senate then not only followed the class of the former censors (censorians) and consuls (consulars) and so on but also acknowledged the antiquity of the office within the separate classes of rank, as well as a man's plebeian or patrician origin. Later, the *princeps* was chosen from among former censors of patrician origin, and finally he was only the consular whose name was first called, according to his rank and influence, by the magistrate presiding over the Senate. With the appointment of Octavian to the title it was fixed from now on and could not be bestowed at random in future.

But, although at first the title *princeps senatus* stated merely that Octavian stood at the head of the list of senators, the term *princeps* had also always been associated with the idea of high social standing, so that it was linked only with the most highly esteemed men of the nobility. These men, the *principes viri*, had been swallowed up by the civil war, but the title could still be given in Octavian's time to men who enjoyed high esteem in general. His election as *princeps* of the Senate was thus Octavian's point of departure in reserving the term more and more for his own use, and indeed in his account of his life he even dates certain events as occurring during his 'principate' by writing *me principe*, 'when I was *princeps*', meaning 'during my reign'. He was thus giving new meaning to the linking of the term with his person, using it as a title, as if he alone could call himself *princeps*. However, the expression did not become an official title. That was impossible, because it did not exactly denote formal leadership, only rank and position compared to that of other, also distinguished citizens. It was not a legal concept, but related to the idea of the social hierarchy behind formal order, and its function was to link reality – which naturally enough was at odds with that order – to social assumptions. Ultimately, the term could sum up the entire new order that claimed, according to its ideals, to be not a monarchy but a principate, the ruling power of an oligarchic society.

The second act in the restoration of constitutional conditions referring back to the political past followed the next year. In that year Octavian and Agrippa were consuls, and both remained in office for the full period of the consulate. That office, which since the year 45 had often – and since the year 40 regularly – been divided between several pairs of consuls a year, seemed to have recovered its former glory when once again both consuls stood at the head of the state for the whole year, and the consulate was not a cheap institution for bestowing titles on good friends. In 27 both were also consuls again for the whole year, and from now on it remained usual, over quite a long period, for no substitute consul to replace one of those taking office at the beginning of a year except in cases of emergency. This measure was intended to appear as if it showed the way that Octavian intended to take in future. Tradition was the criterion. He and Agrippa therefore set about the second task of censorship, taking a census: an assessment of all Roman citizens. It was the first census for forty-two years, and came up with a total figure of 4,063,000 adult male citizens.

The previous year, Octavian had already made the Romans another handsome gift of 400 sesterces each, thus helping the once mighty people of Rome to accept what was to follow. He also went ahead energetically with his plans for the reconstruction and expansion of the state. Besides providing work for the people of Rome, his wide-ranging measures once again pointed to the political direction that he was taking. He decreed that the many ruinous temples in the city should be restored, either shouldering responsibility for the restoration himself or, if a temple had been built by private citizens, suggesting to the descendants of its original builders that they should get the necessary repairs done. In his account of his own achievements, he boasts of having restored eighty-two temples at this time. The majority of these were small shrines with religious purposes that were no longer always understood. They tended to have fallen into disuse or neglect, and their restoration also meant a revival of their former purpose. These measures introduced a religious policy in which the old religion of Rome was rediscovered and revived, and, if Octavian's policy also aimed at old Rome and old Italy in other respects, he hammered the point home by simultaneously banning from the inner mile of the city the celebration of Egyptian cults; their strange deities and rites and the loud noise they made aroused distaste in many quarters. That autumn, the temple of Apollo on the Palatine was re-consecrated, and its extensive artistic and sculptural ornamentation followed, to a great extent, a political programme celebrating Actium as a victory over the barbarians on the one hand, and a symbol of peace and Roman rule on the other.

But two measures, one dating from the beginning of the year 28 and the other from the end of it, formed Octavian's real prelude to his settlement of January 27. At the beginning of 28, he left the regular management of affairs of state to his colleague in the consulate, who thus received, in line with tradition, the lictors, a consul's official attendants and guards, who always walked ahead of him carrying bundles of rods. Until now, whenever Octavian was consul he seems to have claimed the management of the state solely for himself – perhaps as a relic left over from the days of the triumvirate. But in any case, he intended this gesture to show that the collegiality of the consuls was now restored, and he himself was to be regarded as part of the old order of offices. Roman society liked such demonstrations of restraint and modesty and no doubt understood the meaning of the gesture.

The second measure was more important and caught the attention of all Romans. Towards the end of the consulate, only weeks before the settlement, Octavian issued an edict to come into effect at the end of the current year, rescinding all measures taken in the triumvirate period that had been regarded as illegal and unjust. This did not, of course, mean that all actions introduced on the grounds of triumviral decrees or laws, for instance through the edict on proscription or the laws for use in settling the veterans, were declared invalid, only that their effective period was to end on 31 December 28. Even that, however, was more than had been expected, and it was done entirely to show that Octavian was publicly and expressly distancing himself from all the brutality, injustice and autocracy that had accompanied the triumvirate. People were to think that only now was the time of terror really over, and at the same time to expect that they would enter into a new age with the coming year. When Octavian finally took his oath in public in December, like every outgoing official, swearing that he had fulfilled the duties of his office according to the law, he wanted the Romans to see it as something like the return of normal conditions. The only question was what exactly could be considered 'normal' in the state at this time. The new consuls were the same as the consuls of the previous year: Octavian, in his seventh consulate, his fifth in unbroken succession, and Agrippa, entering on his third. On 13 January 27 the announcement of the constitutional settlement began. It went on for several days and had been well prepared in advance, but since there could always be unplanned incidents the occasion was not entirely free from anxiety. On the first day Octavian resigned all his powers, including command over the army and control of the state's financial means. This resignation affected only the provinces, not the consulate with its privileges and honours. When he laid down his provincial powers of command, they 'reverted' to the Senate, which was thus identified as the source of all official power, both civil and military, just as if it were now getting back what it had given away at some point in time. The settlement made it clear that the Senate was formally declared to be the sole source of public law while, as the result of developments that had begun as early as the second century, the people and the assembly of the people remained very much in the background. With the reversion of these powers to it, the republic was now formally restored: *res publica restituta*. However, it could certainly not be revived in its old form of the year 49. All participants in the ceremony knew that they were not witnessing the rebirth of the old republic, only that the state was distancing itself from the political practice of the previous twenty years, in which the old order had been autocratically abused, and Romans citizens had lived in lawlessness, subject to the whims of tyrannical despots.

If a line had been drawn under the past in this way, then the future position of the military potentate also had to be regulated at once, indissolubly linked as it was with the return of power. As a political factor, of course, the potentate could not now be removed. After all, this 'return' to the conditions of the past was bound to integrate the commander of the army into a new constitutional structure, and that very idea, for all the talk of tradition and liberty, was at the heart of the ceremony on 13 January 27. It was a question of the form in which Octavian was to become part of the 'restored state': that was the crucial factor, not the actual power relationships, which hardly changed at all. The form, however, made the all-powerful commander a predictable factor, creating the sense of legal security so much desired by everyone in public life.

A partition of the provinces was agreed and had of course been fixed, or negotiated, in advance of the settlement. Octavian immediately received back half of the twenty Roman provinces of the time, several of which, for instance the part of Gaul conquered by Caesar and the Spanish provinces, were subdivided this year or were to be subdivided in the foreseeable future. The other half came under the direct administration of the Senate. Governors were to be appointed by the authorities responsible, that is to say by the Senate and by Octavian, and in so far as the Senate made future appointments, they were chosen by lot from among the former consuls (consulars) and praetors (praetorians) in a selection procedure of which no details have come down to us. These governors were called proconsuls, irrespective of whether they had ever held the office of consul or not, and formally held the position of magistrates. They were responsible solely to the Senate, and as a sign of their independence in their capacity as magistrates each was allotted twelve lictors, or six if he had been only a praetor. The Senate now recovered its own area of command, in contrast to the triumvirate period. Octavian would be governor of the other ten provinces, and in this way he united ten proconsulates in his own person. But as his power of command extended to many provinces, it was summed up not under the title of proconsul, which was reserved for the governor of a particular area, but was known by the abstract term of *imperium proconsulare*, proconsular *imperium*. As holder of that title, Octavian appointed all his governors – or rather, as a governor was an independent official, he appointed proconsuls to represent him in the post of governor. As they were under his command, and were thus only his deputies, they bore the old title of legates, a term used for the subordinate of a high military official. But as the legates also had to have a certain administrative and military independence, since Octavian, the real holder of the power of command, was usually absent, they received an 'imperium' which, although derived from the *imperium* of Octavian, had an added quality bringing it close to the independence of the magistracy: they bore the double title of legates with propraetorian powers (*legati pro praetore*) and had not twelve or six but five lictors to precede them.

At the same time, the selection of provinces that Octavian was to administer explained to the public why an extraordinary military command was still needed at all, and why in that respect the 'full republic' had not been restored. Octavian was allotted the endangered provinces, especially those with restless neighbours on their borders. Most of the legions were stationed here. In detail, he took over the two northern Spanish provinces of Tarraconensis and Lusitania, all the provinces of the greater Gallic area (Narbonensis, Aquitania, Lugdunensis and Belgica) and the south-east Mediterranean area (Syria, Cilicia, Cyprus and Aegyptus). The Senate received the south of Spain (Baetica), the large islands (Sicilia, Sardinia et Corsica), Macedonia, Illyricum, Achaea (that is to say, Greece, which now became a province in itself), as well as Asia, Bithynia et Pontus (the Black Sea coast), Creta et Cyrene and Africa. Octavian promised that when his provinces were fully pacified he would hand them over to the Senate, or rather, in the spirit of the agreement that had just been made, 'return them' to that body, which since time immemorial had run the administration of the entire empire. And in the year 22 the southern province of Gaul (Narbonensis) and Cyprus did in fact pass into the hands of the Senate. Apart from that, however, a term was set to Octavian's time in complete command. A period of ten years was agreed, double the time limit that had been usual for this type of command in the republican era.

Although Octavian's main aim with his ruling of January 27 was to show that he was forging a link with the republican past, and with that end in view he emphasized the fact that he was giving up parts of his previous military power, the outcome was also good for him personally. From now on his own provincial district was administered by legates whom he could remove from office at any time, or alternatively could allow to remain in office longer than anticipated. Above all, however, the administrative circumstances were now perfectly clear. In his own district, he could manage his affairs just as he pleased, particularly as he had undisputed command of the army there. It is true that in some of the Senate's provinces, for instance Macedonia and Africa, there were considerable contingents of troops – in all there may have been as many as five legions, a generous relinquishment of military potential intended to illustrate the new amity of Octavian and the Senate. But the overwhelming majority of units were stationed in Octavian's provinces, and through the officers and many of the lower ranks the influence of the all-powerful military potentate may well also have extended to the troops in the Senate's provinces from the first.

Octavian could not be denied the right to decide on war or peace with those who lived near the borders, on his own responsibility, another reason why he was taking over the endangered border provinces. In the old republic the Senate, together with the people, had been responsible for such decisions and indeed for all matters of foreign policy. In major conflicts Octavian will not, therefore, have failed to get the Senate's agreement.

Even Octavian's contemporaries regarded the settlement of 13 January 27 as a great event, one that re-established the state after the turmoil of the civil war with recourse to republican conditions, giving the senators (and the people) a new part in political life. For them, therefore, the 'revival' of the old state was not just an empty slogan. Of course everyone knew that there could be no real return to the days when the nobility had collectively determined the fate of Rome. Nevertheless, something very similar to the decades immediately preceding the outbreak of the civil war in the year 49 could be found in the new rulings. Then, too, from time to time individual men holding a special military command (*imperium extraordinarium*) were able to exert political influence, their claim to such authority being based on the Senate's and provincial governors' inability to deal with the issues of the day. And, although there were times when the Senate could not entirely dismiss the necessity of such a special military command, it was clearly alarmed at the powerful dynamic of those of its own social class who did not hesitate, should the occasion arise, simply to incite a crisis in foreign policy in order to create the rationale for extraordinary measures. These special commands were never without their problems, but they were widely accepted, and now the settlement of 13 January 27 seemed to take up that old idea. People thought, perhaps, of Pompey's great military commands against the pirates and against Mithradates, which had also involved several provinces, great armies and a generous allowance of time for the task to be carried out. The powers granted to Caesar, Pompey and Crassus in the year 55 were even more similar to the present measures. At that time the three generals had received the Gallic and Spanish provinces as well as Syria, together with large military forces and a series of special rights, while the remaining provinces remained under the administration of the Senate. A possible objection to this comparison is that the republic was already in decline in the fifties, for the very reason that such extraordinary commands had existed. None the less, it seemed undeniable that a bridge had now been built from the year 27 to the late republican period. What lay in between – the tyrannical rule first of Caesar and then of the triumvirs – was to be dismissed from the mind as a period of terror. The way to look at it was to say that the extraordinary commands of the late republic had been a part of the order of the state, and the connection with the republic seemed even closer if you remembered that Octavian, like the late republican special magistrates, had been given his provinces only for a certain length of time, and in respect of a certain task, namely their final pacification.

Yet the rulings of January 27 differed in some not inconsiderable details from those of the year 55, and these details show that here we are dealing not with a return to the old ways, but with the construction of something new: a monarchy. For one thing, it was clear that, judging by the experience of the triumvirate period, setting a term to the holding of power was to be regarded as a pure formality. Extension of the term – already twice as long as it was during the republic – was certainly not an option. Nor was the army the same kind of institution as the armies of Pompey or Caesar, and not just because it was much larger – indeed, almost three times the size of the mighty army with which the dictator had conquered Gaul. More crucially, unlike all the armies of the republican era, it did not first have to be raised. It was standing ready in the provinces, particularly the provinces under Octavian's command, waiting to go into action. In addition, and despite Octavian's claim to be taking over only those provinces where there was unrest, military duties were not the same everywhere. The provinces of northern Gaul and the Parthian front did present security problems, but as a rule the troops were involved in crisis areas where there was no war or open rebellion at the moment, where the danger was only latent. The particular difference, and a fundamental one by comparison with the general rule in the republic, also lay in the fact that such questions would not really be at issue in the future. There was a standing army and it obeyed the man who commanded half of all the provinces. That institution, never known before, immediately raised the question of the function of such an army:

were not soldiers, most of whom were stationed in their camps without employment, not there to support the old (and new) military potentate, holding off any possible rivals, and must not those circumstances be regarded as evidence that a monarchy existed? After all, there was a third factor distinguishing the new rulings from the extraordinary commands of the late republic, namely the idea of *dividing* the entire provincial area between the Senate and the new military commander, as opposed to the latter commanding a particular provincial area that might, in some circumstances, be in particular danger. Instead, the whole empire was being divided as if between *partners*, just as the triumvirs had divided up its entire area between them.

Thus the division of roles between the Senate and the holder of extraordinary military power was different from what it had been before the year 49, and even setting aside Octavian's potential to intervene in the Senate's provinces, a matter not entirely clear at first, it would be difficult to argue that, with a few slight reservations, the circumstances prevailing before the year 49 had been restored. The rulings of January 27 did not aim to restore the republic in essence (rather than formal appearance); they clearly signified the establishment of a monarchy. That was not the same as a dictatorship. Octavian was expressly not master of everything, nor did he aim to be. Rather, what he *was* master of had received an established legal guise, making it clear where the limits of his power lay and thus creating a sense of security and distinguishing the new regime from the tyranny of the triumvirate. Legally tamed in this way, Octavian's monarchy is still called today, as it was at the time, a principate, 'rule by the first citizen', because the holder of actual power neither held nor claimed any formally pre-eminent position.

However, the settlement of January 27 was not confined to the new regulation of the order of the state. Over and above the legal constitution of the principate, Octavian's power rested on social connections as they existed between him and countless senators, knights, soldiers and ordinary Romans as well as 'peregrines' (subjects who were not natives of Rome) in the other cities of the Roman world. This is made particularly evident in the honours that he had received earlier, and that were now given to him in close connection with the new legal regulation of the state administration: in fact they were to become a constituent part of the character of his regime as it was now gradually developing. On the last day of the great settlement, 16 January, at the petition of Lucius Munatius Plancus, the Senate bestowed the honorific Augustus on Octavian. The term means something like 'sublime, holy' but is also close to the idea of 'increase', and was used for gods and sacred places. In addition, it carried connotations of the mythical history of Rome. When Romulus wished to found a city on the Tiber and made a ritual request to the gods for their approval, he was the first to take on the role of 'questioner' (*augur*) for the new state; he was therefore acting as the first questioner (*primus augur*), and that first request was generally termed, because of its importance, a 'sublime questioning' (*augurium augustum*). The religious allusion in the name of Augustus is also emphasized by the fact that its bestowal expressly implied the approval of the highest-ranking college of priests, the *pontifices*.

The term 'Augustus' had been entirely unknown as an honorific before. It appears so unusual that we must consider it the result of a compromise. In fact Octavian is said to have wished, first, for 'Romulus', but the name of the first king of Rome had been politically exploited during the last days of the republic and was thus compromised. However, as 'Augustus' also referred to the founding of the city, it could denote the divine favour that surrounded Romulus. Once Octavian had replaced his first name Gaius by Imperator, and abandoned his gens name Julius, which was often no longer used at his time, he was not known, as before, as Gaius Julius Caesar, but as Imperator Caesar Augustus. It was his own name, but its structural alteration had already made it a title. In what follows Octavian will be called by his new name of Augustus.

A few days earlier, on the first day of the constitutional settlement, Augustus had been given the citizen's crown (*corona civica*), which he could hang over the door of his house. This wreath, made of oak leaves and thus also called the 'Crown of Oak' (*corona quercea*), was originally awarded to a soldier who had saved the life of a comrade in battle but was also later bestowed on a man who preserved and saved his fatherland. As a further honour, the Senate allowed Augustus to hang garlands of laurel on the doorposts of his house. All three honours, the name, the crown of oak leaves and the laurels, placed him above other citizens, raising him from their ranks and, so to speak, elevating him to the world of the gods. 'Augustus' linked him to the mythical history of Rome, the laurel was the tree of Apollo, the oak the tree of Jupiter. In addition, he was given a golden shield on which the virtues ascribed to him were listed: manly courage (*virtus*), mercy (*clementia*), justice (*iustitia*) and piety to the gods and the fatherland (*pietas erga deos patriamque*). This catalogue of virtues referred to the republican ethos of nobility, and the place where the shield was hung, the Senate house, was undoubtedly meant to show the world that Augustus was to be connected with the new aristocracy which was gradually forming and took its guidelines from the old society.

The settlement of January 27, as every Roman could see, implied a change of direction towards tradition. The dictatorships of Caesar and the triumvirate were to be relegated *ad acta*, and at the same time the former state, thought to be extinct, was to be called back to life with such expressions as 'restoration of the state' (*res publica restituta*), 'return of the state' to the Senate and people (*res publica reddita*), or 'to bring freedom to the state' (*rem publicum in libertatem vindicare*). Historians and poets, and even Augustus himself, praised the event in these and similar words. However, by *res publica* no one meant the old order that had existed before the year 49. Every Roman knew that it was gone for ever. But there was a passing resemblance in so far as the arbitrary wielding of power was rejected, and security was established on the pattern of the old order. If this did not bring the old 'republic' back to life, the direction which the new order was taking, or seemed to be taking, was at least the right one.

Yet conversely, it could also be said that here, in January 27, the settlement ushered in rule by one man, that is to say a monarchy. For the legal powers that, after the rule of the triumvirate, commonly regarded as a tyranny, had been given by the Senate to the commander of the army were now granted to him covering half of all the provinces, and like the de facto concession of permanent consulship, which also gave the potentate all the necessary means to govern from the centre, it could be understood as formalized rule. The Senate might have a set time limit, but everyone knew that the time limit would be extended again and again. So the sense of regained political freedom of movement went hand in hand with an awareness that Rome now also had a ruler in the formal sense. No one could fail to see that the events of January 27 were ambivalent, and the ruler who had staged the whole thing certainly did not want to conceal that fact either. Indeed, ambiguity was a constituent part of his great settlement, and the same was true of the new order as a whole that it aimed to create, the principate that had its beginnings here.

However, the permanent establishment of monarchical rule within the order of the Roman state was unthinkable without reference to the past, the days when the Roman empire had grown and reached its enormous size. It was also unthinkable without reference to the society that had created it all, the nobility. Augustus had to take that into consideration and he knew it. Taking it into consideration, however, meant two things in this instance: one, that the formal framework indispensable to every form of rule if it hopes to rise above ephemeral usurpation and military dictatorship could be derived only from the past; and second, that it had to address itself to the new society, because the members of that society would be treading in the footsteps of their predecessors as administrators, generals and senators. However much the formal legal framework had changed, it must inspire confidence in the permanence of the government among the new elite, and a sense of security in society in general.

But this sense of security was not to be established so easily or so fast. The new regime had to be combined on the one hand with legal security, and on the other with the permanent assurance of social status, that is to say, with what could still be called liberty (*libertas*) but now meant above all security (*securitas*). Yet in view of what the dictator, the triumvirs and in particular Augustus himself had done in the past few decades, that very thing might be seen as a contradiction in terms. Suspicion, or at least reserve, therefore seemed appropriate. It had to be made clear to everyone that the new order was guaranteed only by the man who had brought it in – Augustus himself. He alone was the guarantor of the restored state.

For all Romans, the great tradition of their city was also an indispensable part of their present existence. They took their guidelines from it; it was the touchstone of all that they did. The names of famous families were indissolubly linked with it, and so was the structure of the state, which went back to the earliest days of its history. In the actions of the magistrates, of the legionaries, indeed of the entire people, made evident in countless examples (*exempla*), the moral integrity of a Roman was ever-present, his virtue and his courage, qualities that had led to the creation of a powerful empire unparalleled in the history of the world. The success of Rome rested on the achievement of the people as a whole and its ruling class, although the members of that class, for all their special status in society, never presented themselves as masters in the political sphere but always as the most distinguished citizens of a society depending in principle on equality. Some foreboding of the fact that Rome must now break with the political past may already have occurred to most Romans during the dictatorship and autocratic rule of first Caesar and then the triumvirs, and the reiterated announcements of the triumvirs that once the civil war was over everything would go back to normal would have done little to allay such fears. However, people were only too willing not to accept the facts immediately, visible though they were. Instead, they were led to believe in the possibility of a return to the old ways, although the society that could have vouched for it no longer existed.

After January 27, at the latest, eyes could no longer be closed to the political future, for the great settlement symbolized the return to normality that had been desired for so long. Neither the members of the new elite nor the people of the city of Rome could accustom themselves immediately to the idea that by now 'normality' included special military powers that looked like supplanting all others and indeed shattering the structure of the state. Although in fact integrated in the official order of the state since the time of Pompey and Caesar, the extraordinary power that had always been a subject of political controversy was still regarded and officially declared to be a temporary measure, and many could consider it part of the structure of the state only with great difficulty. Only now did it become clear to a number of people that the exceptional state of affairs maintained in the form of extraordinary power for so many years was a permanency, and had thus itself become normality. It even alarmed many of those who had profited by the new regime as supporters of Augustus. Suddenly it was realized that Rome had a new master, and with him its own political freedom of action was finally lost. It had to be conceded that Augustus took care not to show that this state of affairs existed but sought to disguise it behind a form of governmental control that took into consideration the sensitivities of many distinguished men and large parts of the general population, and it was obvious that he wanted the traditions of the state to be seen as behind the new order, even restoring them to their old validity within a certain framework. At the same time, however, it had to be accepted that the military potentate whom everyone had previously been obliged to recognize as ruler of Rome – many called him its tyrant – was now its ruler in a form supported by the law. The Romans might now be even more likely to see a paradox in the linking of the new rulings with the old traditions as Augustus so emphatically presented them. In fact even with the settlement of January 27, seen from the point of view of Augustus, everything was not yet done. There were further steps to be taken to reinforce tradition and integrate the ruler into it yet more clearly. Although the experience of twenty years of civil war had prepared the way, the transition from the old to the new order, from the rule of the nobility during the republic to the monarchy of Augustus, required further measures and also, in particular, called for time in which not only those who had always opposed the new system, but many of Augustus' own supporters, who did not form a self-contained 'party', could come to terms with it.

It was not that Augustus had failed to see the political consequences of the settlement in advance. We can gather that from his cautious, tentative attempts along the way to a final establishment of his legal power, which could be foreseen from the end of the triumvirate onward and was not uncontroversial, as well as from his policy immediately after January 27. Correctly realizing that the new establishment of his rule, declared to be a 'return' of power to the state, had made him many enemies even among his own adherents, he was counting on the army to secure his new state structure. First, he had the pay of his bodyguard doubled by the Senate, providing official confirmation of the status of the unit declared to be the Praetorian Guard – the guard of the military commander – and at the same time setting out its special military position. The republic had given its generals bodyguards, but only the triumvirs had made them into an established and permanent body of soldiers. The rise in their pay was thus in the tradition of the triumvirs, and Augustus was incorporating a triumviral element into the structure of the state.

He also decided to go to his provinces now, in order to observe and control further developments from the power base that he had secured for himself. He decided to mount an expedition to Britain that would bring him further glory in the footsteps of the divine Julius, also reinforcing his public position. However, nothing came of that. He fell ill on the way north, had to stop in Narbo (Narbonne) until he was better and then determined to gather the laurels of war in Spain, an easier place to reach. It looked as if he could also consolidate the close connection between the army and its commander there – as he had already done during his Illyrian campaign – and at the same time show the Romans the necessity of a military presence in the empire.

Admittedly, there was no obvious military problem in Spain at the time. It was true that the Cantabrians and Asturians in the north-west of the country, against whom Augustus finally marched, were seething with discontent. For over ten years the Roman governors had been skirmishing with them and other tribes, particularly the Pyrenaeans. But in the year 27 at least, the Asturians and Cantabrians do not seem to have been in revolt. So Augustus initially concerned himself with administrative matters in Spain. War did not begin until the year 26, and it then went on into the next year. At first Augustus accompanied the army, and during a night march he was almost struck by a lightning bolt that fell beside his litter, killing a torchbearer. Then he was laid low by severe illness, so he left the conduct of the war mainly to his legates and had to content himself with directing its course from his sickbed in the provincial capital of Tarraco (now Tarragona). It was in this war, incidentally, that Augustus' fifteen-year-old stepson Tiberius did his first military service as a tribune of war.

Although the campaign involved large numbers of troops and correspondingly large amounts of money – in all, there were seven legions in action – there were no great successes, either for the new commander himself, who had watched operations only from a distance, or for the security of northern Spain. This last great military campaign led by Augustus in person was purely political in its nature and was intended to impress the Roman public. Before Augustus set off for home at the end of the year 25, he saw the soldiers who were due to be discharged settled in the new veterans' colony of Augusta Emerita (today Mérida). There was no more talk of Britain. The Spanish campaign had brought hardly any results, or anyway far fewer than the Illyrian campaign ten years earlier, and even before Augustus was back in Rome the allegedly defeated tribes of north-west Spain rose in revolt again. It was not until years later that the area was finally pacified.

Theatrical effects compensated for the lack of glory. Once again the clever manipulator of public opinion had the gate of the Arch of Janus closed, as if the campaign had restored peace to the world, and had even brought victory and fame. Pax and Victoria were stereotypical concepts used to form public opinion, with little reference to real events, but showed those events in images prefigured and shaped to achieve the desired effect. A writer was also on hand to hail the hero returning from the coasts of the Ocean as the victor guiding the world itself. Whether they had to be asked to write or not, poets were usually ready and willing to praise the Julian house. Another poet, Virgil, who was busy in these years working on his epic account of the deeds of Aeneas, ancestor of Augustus, did not comply with his ruler's request to send him a draft or a completed part of the great poem. However, that was certainly not to be understood as resistance to the spirit of the times.

Military success in northern Italy at the time was gained not by Augustus but by Aulus Terentius Varro Murena, who was related to Maecenas by marriage. In the year 25 he defeated the Salassians, who had long been restless, in the central western area of the Alps (the Graian Alps) and almost wiped them out. Varro had those of their men who were still alive and capable of bearing arms rounded up and sold in the slave market. Resistance in the region that Rome regarded as a safety zone was considered a crime, and failure to understand the blessings of the Pax Romana as arrogance that had to be broken. That made the Salassians guilty twice over, if unintentionally. However, no Roman was troubled by a sense of injustice at the time. On the contrary, poets hailed the punishment of the 'arrogant' tribe. Their annihilation brought a great strategic gain: the Alpine passes leading from south-east Gaul to Italy (the Great and the Little St Bernard) were now open. Later, Augustus founded a city on the place where Varro had pitched his main camp, and it was given the name of Augusta Praetoria (now Aosta).

In the same year, at the other end of the empire, Aelius Gallus, the governor of Egypt (*praefectus Aegypto*), set off, on Augustus' orders, with a large fleet and 10,000 men on a campaign to the south-west corner of the Arabian peninsula, which to distinguish it from the desert (Arabia Deserta) was called 'happy Arabia' (Arabia Felix, today Yemen). Aelius Gallus put out to sea with his fleet from a harbour somewhere near today's Suez, suffered the wreck of several ships but landed on the north-east coast of the Red Sea, and in the next year, going overland, reached Arabia Felix after a march lasting six months. He took several towns and finally reached, although he did not capture, the capital of the Sabaeans, who lived in this area, Mariba (near the present Yemeni capital of Sana'a). Because of the heavy losses suffered by the army in a climate to which the men were not accustomed, the campaign had no further success. Gallus was obliged to turn and retreat and was lucky to get back to Egypt. The venture was certainly intended to be more of a journey of exploration to discover the extent of the land mass to the east of Egypt and Syria than a war of expansion. Its spatial extent indicates increased imperial self-awareness since the end of the civil war, and at the same time a growing interest in the geography and peoples outside, and indeed far beyond, the frontiers of the empire.

It had been a clever move for Augustus to leave Rome and Italy for a while after the great settlement of the year 27, so that later he could return to the capital with his reputation enhanced by new military achievements. The two years of his absence gave the Romans time to think, and during that period many of them understood for the first time that the republican past, the object of such nostalgia, was not going to come back. The new situation, where there were no rivals for power and thus no scope for 'little generals' to make their mark, may have brought a more sober mood even to the close circle of Augustus' friends and supporters. There was nowhere in Rome now for a man like young Crassus, the sight of whose triumph Augustus had spared himself by setting off for Spain. Not everyone was content with a subordinate role, particularly as the second rung on the ladder of the hierarchy was already occupied by two men whose insight and inclinations left them content with it: Agrippa and Maecenas.

Augustus' frail health certainly gave cause for concern; everyone knew about his illnesses. Augustus himself provided further material for discussion when, in the year 25 and while he was in Spain, he pressed ahead with the marriage of his daughter Julia, who was only fourteen, to her cousin Marcus Claudius Marcellus, then seventeen years old, his sister Octavia's son. He was in such haste to see his only child married that he did not even wait until he was back in Rome himself, but asked Agrippa to step in for him as proxy to give the bride away. Understandable as his wish for an heir was, however, this hastily arranged child marriage, in which both partners were of Julian origin, made the general public doubly familiar with those of their ruler's ideas that touched directly on the political arena. For one thing, as was now obvious, Augustus was anxious to have an heir of his own blood. In the same way as himself, the adopted son of the dictator, that heir must also be regarded as his political successor and could not be ignored by any Roman when the question of the succession arose. Accordingly, his closest private and political heir would be Marcellus. But as the marriage of Marcellus to Julia showed, he was to be regarded only as keeping the place warm for a son of that marriage who, as Augustus' grandson, would be a suitable substitute for the son of his own that he had longed for in vain. Moreover, that the marriage was arranged in such haste showed that Augustus was seriously concerned for his health and did not expect to have a long life ahead of him. As soon as he was back from Spain, he made it known officially that Marcellus was his potential successor by bestowing privileges on him. The youth now became a senator, could sit among former praetors in the Senate and was allowed to apply for the consulship ten years earlier than the usual rule. In addition, he was made aedile. The fact that all this elevated not only the person of Marcellus but the whole house of Augustus to a rank above all other families was also obvious in the granting, at the same time, of the privilege of eligibility for all public office five years earlier than the legal age to Tiberius, Augustus' stepson. Although he was not yet eighteen, Tiberius was appointed to the office of quaestor for the year 23. For all the grandiose words expended on the subject, it could not be concealed from anyone – and was not meant to be concealed – that the ruler of Rome and his house were placing themselves on a par with the old state, or even above it. That fact was part of the revival of the structure of the state in January 27.

The construction, not long before, of the huge mausoleum that Octavian had ordered to be built for himself on the banks of the Tiber directly after his return from Alexandria had shown where the path was leading. Planned on the model of Alexander's tomb, it was a mighty circular building (a tumulus) 87 metres in diameter and 40 metres high and was crowned by a larger-than-life bronze statue of Augustus in armour. The building was finished in quite a short time, even before Augustus went to Spain, and by its sheer size alone the mausoleum was bound to make even the least realistic aware that the end of the triumvirate did not affect the master of it. The sight of the building showed the marriage of Julia to Marcellus to the people of Rome in a special light. It was to ensure the succession in a monarchy that, for all the quiet manner of its staging, was already clearly apparent in the year 27. It could not yet be considered firmly established, but, rather than doing away with the problem, that only made it more acute.

The uncertainty about Augustus' political scope that even friends felt was soon to be revealed by the disastrous case of Gaius Cornelius Gallus, for which the way was already being paved in the year 27. Like Salvidienus, executed in the year 40, Gallus had been raised by Augustus from very humble origins to the world of high politics. He was one of Augustus' oldest friends and even before the battle of Philippi was an influential and prosperous man who rescued Virgil, among others, from the economic difficulties of the time. In addition, he was known to the Roman public as a gifted writer of elegies and minor epics and enjoyed considerable esteem among the contemporary men of letters. Appointed by Augustus to the post of first prefect of Egypt – the viceroy, so to speak, of that country – he had proved a capable and successful administrator. Even in the ancient world, no one knew exactly what his offence had been, although he was accused not of treachery, like Salvidienus, but of 'ingratitude' and 'malice' towards Augustus. Gallus seems to have talked too freely. Perhaps he had not appreciated the difference between a poet and a politician. In any event, Augustus officially withdrew his friendship from Gallus (*renuntiatio amicitiae*), meaning that Gallus was forbidden to enter his house or set foot in his provinces. Thus deprived of his post in Egypt, Gallus was banished by an official decision of the Senate passed in a spirit of excessive zeal and lost his fortune at the same time, whereupon he committed suicide. Augustus, in tears, bewailed the cruel fate that did not allow him, Augustus, and him alone, to chide his friends only so far as he himself would wish. So it was not Augustus but reasons of state that had killed Gallus. However, his crime as described before the Senate – and the wording is unknown – was undoubtedly not covered by traditional law, but was a political offence of the new monarchical period. The way was being prepared for the claims to majesty made later under the emperors.

Augustus had made sure that during his absence his co-consuls were from the old families, or those whose own achievements had brought them to prominence more recently. Such men could not therefore offend the feelings of traditionalists. For the years 26 and 25, they were the loyal Titus Statilius Taurus and Marcus Junius Silanus, a member of a noble family who had served under Lepidus and Antony and defected to Octavian just before Actium. However, general uneasiness about the now apparently established head of state was aired over the question of his deputies. Who was to stand in for Augustus in Rome while he was away? Probably with effect from 1 January 26, he had nominated the faithful Messalla Corvinus as his deputy, giving him the title of *praefectus urbi* (prefect of the city). In very ancient times, that title had been in use for those who deputized for the consuls, but it was no longer granted except to the man who received it for the occasion of the *feriae latinae*, the 'Latin Festival', a holiday calling the Latin cities to mind. Over a long period, if both consuls were absent from Rome then the praetor of the city had deputized for them, and in any case there was no point in having a deputy if one of the consuls, as now, was still in Rome and therefore available. In the matter of his deputy, Augustus had obviously acted as he did at the time of his triumvirate and the Actian War, when he appointed Maecenas as his representative (prefect) and gave him the power of command over Rome and Italy – that is to say, appointed him military potentate. The city prefect Messalla Corvinus, accordingly, was the deputy of a monarch rather than of a consul, and in this way Augustus himself seemed to be disavowing the settlement of January 27, although it was supposed to be restoring the old institutions, particularly the Senate and the consulate, to their former high status and influence. At any rate, after a few days Corvinus resigned the office, stating that it was contrary to the constitution. He was certainly not distancing himself from Augustus, but yielding prudently to a Senate in which the majority felt indignant about this return to the times of tyranny. Augustus had not yet achieved his later perfect command of the manipulation of public opinion when he depicted his rule, at every opportunity, as the resumption of tradition.

Augustus accompanied the political measures to consolidate his power with a huge building programme that outdid even the architectural ambitions of the triumvirate period. In grateful recognition of the bolt of lightning that missed him during the Spanish campaign, he himself had a small but unusually magnificent temple built to Jupiter the Thunderer (Jupiter Tonans) on the Capitoline Hill, towering above the other hills of Rome and the place where the father of the gods resided. The first any visitor to the Capitol now saw would be this building, and the god to whom it was dedicated therefore received the additional epithet Janitor (doorkeeper), which was also given to make it clear that he was not in competition with Jupiter Optimus Maximus. Built entirely of marble, the temple, which was not consecrated until the year 22, was adorned with a wealth of works by Greek artists of the classical period – in effect, art that had been looted. The cult statue of Jupiter Tonans with his sceptre and lightning bolts was by the famous sculptor Leochares, the two equestrian statues of the Dioscuri at the entrance were the work of the rather less well-known Hagias.

Once again Agrippa distinguished himself in architectural planning. He had acquired a large area on the Field of Mars (the Campus Martius), which was no longer used by the army as a place of assembly, and was being offered for sale to private interests by the Senate. In the year 27 he began building on this site. Previously, the Field of Mars could boast one large building, erected in its southern part by Pompey the Great and accommodating the first stone-built theatre in Rome, as well as a meeting place for the Senate, which in fact had been the scene of the meeting on the Ides of March in the year 44, and a large pillared hall (*porticus*). The semicircular outline of this extensive complex can still be made out today in the general design of the city, and it served both public and private purposes; it was a place of meeting and edification for the population of those parts of the city close to it, and as such the beginning of a large architectural ensemble for both public and private use, unequalled at the time for the size and variety of its buildings and the magnificence of their furnishings. Only a few years earlier one of Octavian's successful generals, Titus Statilius Taurus, had erected an amphitheatre on the Field of Mars, the first stone amphitheatre in Rome and primarily meant for gladiatorial games. Its position – it was destroyed in the great fire of Rome in Nero's time – is not known exactly, but it was probably to the west of the Capitoline hill. This was where Agrippa began work, erecting three large buildings on a linked site.

Outstanding among Agrippa's buildings was the Saepta Julia (the 'Julian Enclosure'), which Caesar had begun at the time of his campaign in Gaul. Only now was it finished and named for him by his adopted son. It was completed in the year 26. The complex consisted of a hall with a covering over it (probably sun awnings) for the assembly of the people when it met to take a ballot, and a building for the counting of the votes cast (*diribitorium*, from *diribere*, 'to divide the votes'). In the huge hall, which was just under 300 metres long and over 100 metres wide and built of marble, the various sections of votes could be quickly and easily processed. The *diribitorium* (begun by Agrippa but not completed until a few years after his death) was notable for the mighty span of its roof, about 30 metres. So, although the people no longer had any effective part in political decision-making, they did have a fine, large and magnificently constructed building, probably designed to hide the fact that in future what went on there would mean nothing: a kind of farewell present to the increasingly marginalized people of the city. However, not only the building itself but the use of the site for all kinds of amusements might have seemed reassuring.

The baths, the second great building erected on this site by Agrippa, would have helped to soothe any indignant minds. Both buildings have vanished today, although the third in the complex, built to the west of the Saepta Julia, has been preserved. This is the Pantheon. Agrippa may have built it as a rotunda, but its present form dates from the time of the Emperor Hadrian, who rebuilt the whole thing from the ground up. The temple was indeed planned as a pantheon, a place for the worship of all the gods, or in point of fact of the twelve Olympians, and clearly it was to be on the Hellenistic model, in which the ruler was also venerated as one who lived in the pantheon with the gods. Agrippa seems to have conceived the building as a place of worship for the new ruler of Rome and his family, and indeed his evident intention of setting up a statue of Augustus there would have brought the Hellenistic cult of the king to Rome, and with it the divine elevation of the ruler. The idea was not politically tactful. Augustus immediately ordered a change to the programme concerning statues: he forbade any cult dedicated to his own person and made Agrippa concentrate on the worship of the twelve Olympian gods, more particularly the divine ancestors of the Julians, Venus and Mars, with the addition of the deified dictator. None the less, Agrippa was not to be deterred from putting up statues of Augustus and himself in the outer hall, to the left and right of the entrance.

Most of this building work, as well as that on several other official buildings, was finished while Augustus was absent from Rome, at the same time as the Italian road network was improved. However, Augustus himself undertook the extension of the great army road (the Via Flaminia) leading through the Sabine country into the plain of the river Po. In recognition of that achievement, and of his merits in road-building, the Senate put up an arch to him where the Via Flaminia ended at Arimimum (Rimini). A few years later, in 20 BC, Augustus had a pillar clad in gilded bronze erected in front of the temple of Saturn in the Forum, to mark the ideal centre of the Italian and indeed world road network. It was called the Golden Milestone (*miliarum aureum*) and bore on it the distances from the city to the most important cities in the empire.

The absence of Augustus had at best muted the uneasiness felt over the settlement of the year 27, but had not been able to obliterate it. Many Romans might have accepted the new state of affairs in a spirit of resignation; others, entirely failing to grasp the situation as a whole, took it as an opportunity to try to extend the political room to manoeuvre as it had previously existed. On 1 January 23, Augustus began his eleventh consulate in Rome, his ninth in unbroken succession. In this year he was to be confronted by severe conflicts, including a conspiracy even involving his own close circle.

First, and obviously on the initiative of Augustus himself, Marcus Primus, governor of the province of Macedonia, one of the provinces in the hands of the Senate, was charged with having attacked the Odrysians, a Thracian tribe settled around the river Hebros (Maritza), without authorization. He did claim to have obtained the agreement of the *princeps* himself and of young Marcellus, but the latter's word did not yet count for much, and more importantly Augustus, who appeared before the tribunal without being summoned, expressly denied the governor's statement. The embarrassing and indeed strange aspect of the affair was the fact that his fellow consul that year, Aulus Terentius Varro Murena, who came from a noble family and whose sister was married to Maecenas, not only appeared publicly as the lawyer defending Primus but also mounted a sharp attack on the *princeps* himself during the trial. Primus was found guilty, but several of the judges, in a move that might well give Augustus cause for concern, acquitted him. It is difficult to make out exactly what conflict lay behind this affair. However, the reforms in the power of the principate carried through the same year, reinforcing the influence of the *princeps* in the provinces administered by the Senate, indicate that Primus, as governor of a province equipped with a large army, had acted independently and perhaps even against the instructions of Augustus. Augustus was bound to feel that he was under pressure in his central area of influence, the command of the army, in the same way as he had felt Crassus exerting pressure on him in the same province a few years earlier. This affected his standing with the legions stationed in the Senate's provinces, where he did not want to and indeed could not give up his influence, in spite of their formal incorporation into the area under the administration of the Senate.

The tension arising from this conflict also seems to have been the reason why Augustus reacted ferociously to the second dangerous confrontation of that year. We are told that there had been a plot against him in which the consul Terentius Varro was involved, along with one Fannius Caepio. When the plot was discovered, the conspirators fled. Thereupon a court condemned them both to death in their absence, and once they had been arrested they were immediately executed. It was particularly embarrassing that Terentia, when informed of the discovery of the plot by hints from her husband Maecenas, had warned her brother and thus brought the trail of possible suspects into the circles of Augustus' closest friends. We cannot now tell what was behind the accusation of conspiracy. Had remarks by Varro, who was known to be blunt and forthright, been taken too seriously? Or was there really a plot against the life of Augustus? Varro and Caepio on their own could hardly have hoped to stage a successful coup. This affair caused great uneasiness. The memory of Salvidienus and Gallus, both of them friends of Augustus, one executed and the other driven to take his own life, was revived. Augustus himself ascribed weight to the incident and indeed emphasized its significance by harshly criticizing some of the judges who pled for an acquittal, although they had not delivered their opinions publicly. But judges too had to learn what freedom might mean in the new political circumstances.

The pressure on Augustus grew when his closest friend and supreme general, Agrippa, was alienated from him. For all his great achievements, Agrippa had never tried to step out of the shadow of his master but now he felt humiliated by the obvious preference of the *princeps* for young Marcellus as his successor. Finally, Augustus, who had been in frail health ever since the Spanish campaign, suffered a severe physical breakdown. Close to death, he himself hardly believed he could yet recover. But even now that he faced the necessity of making provision for the future in the event of his death, his sure sense of what was politically feasible did not desert him. He had his signet ring sent to Agrippa, thus showing that if need be the general was to be considered as his successor. No mention was made of Marcellus. He gave a list of all the troops under his command to his co-consul Gnaeus Calpurnius Piso, who had replaced Varro, along with an account of the income from his provinces. They thus went to the man who, as consul, represented the old order of the state and the Senate. Both dispositions clearly show that at this point Augustus still saw no future for an overtly monarchical solution.

His illness passed. Antonius Musa, his doctor, saved his life with a course of compresses and cold baths and as recompense received, among other rewards, a statue put up to him beside that of the god of healing, Aesculapius. Augustus also managed to restore Agrippa to good humour. Once he was better, he publicly distanced himself from the rumours that – like the dictator in the past – he was going to adopt Marcellus in a statement in his will, thereby designating him his successor. He even intended to read out his testamentary dispositions in the Senate. He was prevented from doing so, but the incident shows what importance he ascribed to the affair. In this year of crises at home, it could not be in his interests or those of his friends to risk his good relationship with his best general, and so once the political implications of the marriage of Marcellus and Julia became clear, Augustus put the requirements of the state before his private wishes. After all, quite apart from their long friendship, Agrippa was irreplaceable as a general and an administrative expert. Augustus showed the world that they were still friends by sending him on a special mission to the east in the same year. Agrippa received an extraordinary command over the eastern provinces for a period of five years and was thus, regardless of the higher standing of Augustus, not beneath but alongside the *princeps* in rank. Once again, Augustus was demonstrating that, for all the power he held, the state was still founded in traditional law by the provisions made in the year 27 and would not recognize any hereditary succession to the *princeps*.

All the discussion set off by the marriage of Marcellus to Julia was to end towards the close of that same year, and in a way that Augustus certainly did not want. Marcellus, not yet twenty, died in Baiae of an epidemic illness that killed many people in Italy at the time. It is said that the doctors tried to cure him in the same way as his uncle, but without success. The grief that Augustus felt for the death of his beloved nephew knew no bounds. He had the body brought back to Rome in state, like that of a prince's son, and Marcellus was buried in a magnificent ceremony in his own mausoleum by the Tiber. Augustus himself delivered the funeral oration, and we hear an echo of his grief in Virgil's lines, when Marcellus is conjured up among the Roman heroes whom Anchises shows his son Aeneas in the underworld, as a pledge of the future glories of Rome. A Roman hero, in the mind of Augustus, was what the young man would have been.

The political pressure had increased; Augustus felt it and tried to defuse it. Whatever had really been behind Varro's conspiracy, on that occasion the *princeps* had shown that he was determined to suppress any factions. He could counter hidden resistance, mainly expressed in passivity and veiled words and actions, only by demonstrating his honest goodwill. He had to prove that the rulings in the settlement of January 27 were not to be seen as a cheap way of touching up the façade of the state, or the monarchical transformation of the *res publica*, as which they might well be, and indeed were bound to be, understood. It had to be made clear that the settlement illustrated the elevation of the old and new families in the Senate as participants in the government of the empire. To make the senators aware of that, he now showed that he was ready to be reconciled, not least, with families who as members of the old ruling class had so far rejected him or kept their distance from him, even former adherents of the murderer of his father. He had Gnaeus Calpurnius Piso, now sixty years old, appointed his fellow consul to replace the executed Varro. Piso had once fought with Pompey against the dictator, then with the Pompeians in Africa, and even with the murderers of Caesar against him. He was not particularly keen to be exploited by the *princeps* in a gesture of reconciliation and had to be persuaded to accept. But reconciliation alone would not do what Augustus wanted. The new order had to be made credible.

Here the bone of contention, despite the problems that the trial of Primus had shown up, was not really in the rulings affecting the provinces. They had obviously been approved by a large majority and they did in fact contain a slight suggestion of restoring the independence of the old institutions. The position that Augustus held at the centre of the capital was a different matter. His occupation of the consulate without interruption since the year 31 contravened the centuries-old tenet whereby the office was held for only a year, so that in principle the highest offices of state were held in turn by the most distinguished men of the city. As a 'permanent' consul, Augustus was keeping the highest office of all occupied. He was thus able to do or prevent everything, and together with his proconsular office in many of the provinces and his power over the army, as well as many other minor offices, priesthoods and privileges, the permanent consulate was bound to look rather like another name for dictatorship. In addition the highest office had by no means lost its attraction for other prominent men, particularly the generals who had fought under Octavian. It was still the visible summit of the hierarchical pyramid of the empire, and to hold it ensured the consul and his family the highest social rank. It was no coincidence that the triumvirs had increased the annual number of consuls so much by forcing men to resign from the office before their time was up. The high honour of the consulate had to be provided for a great many men at the time.

Fundamentally, however, Augustus could not dispense with the office of consul. After all, it represented his only claim to legal authority over all the magistrates and what they did, and thus the opportunity to take the initiative at the centre of Rome at any time. So he hit upon the clever and yet, as it turned out, rather imprudent idea of suggesting to the Senate that in future, whenever he was consul – which meant every year – another consul, so to speak a third consul, should also be appointed. The suggestion clearly shows how difficult it was for him to part with an office that was obviously vital to him, and how little, for all his efforts to give his power a legal basis, he really knew about the republican idea of the state. He was treating the venerable institutions in as cavalier a manner as in the time of the triumvirate of evil memory, and the reaction was what he might have expected. Three consuls! Even the worst tyrants of the past had never contemplated such a thing. Furthermore, that was no way to get rid of the real problem, which was the permanent consulate held by Augustus. The Senate was at liberty to reject the proposal, but ingeniously disguised its rejection by suggesting that one colleague in the consulate already diminished his sovereignty enough; with two he would seem even more humiliated.

Augustus gave way. As he was not to hold the consulate without interruption, but he did not want to dispense with the legal power that had given him that office in the capital, he sought a substitute of equal value elsewhere. What emerged was an artificial product, amounting to the sum of various legal privileges, and meant the entire renovation of the legal power of a military ruler in Rome. Indeed, together with the restructuring of the provinces as set out in the year 27, it was to constitute no less than the legal foundations of the principate. At the same time, the special form of the renovations now made affected the structure of the legal power transferred to him in a way that was finally to separate it from the old order, determining its form as the 'imperial' legal power of the future. So it was not until the year 23 that the new structure of state, which had first begun to take shape in 27, assumed the form in which it was to remain for over 250 years.

In the summer of 23, Augustus resigned his consulate. That was the real 'republican' part of this second great constitutional settlement: the highest office, vacated by his mighty figure, would in future be restored to its function of offering rank and honour to many deserving men. Augustus emphasized the return to 'republican' ideas yet further when he had a republican of the old school chosen to replace him as consul for the rest of the year. This was Lucius Sestius, son of the famous tribune of the people who had been a friend of Cicero. Sestius junior had fought on the side of Caesar's murderers to the bitter end, had then been on the proscribed list and after he was pardoned had even continued to honour Brutus and Cassius. No one could be more republican than that. So one of the problems, how to resign the consulate, had been successfully solved. There remained the construction of a new legal power, which was to make up to some extent for what Augustus had lost in the way of legal competence and a position of supreme rank in Rome when he laid down the consulate.

Instead of it, Augustus fixed upon the official power of a tribune of the people (*tribunicia potestas*). The tribuneship of the people, ever since the days of the 'struggle between the orders', had given its holder wide-ranging power for making decisions and obstructing other officials – the tribune of the people could even veto official business proposed by the consul. The office was suitable compensation for the competence that he had lost in giving up the consulate. So far Augustus had possessed only the 'sacrosanctity' of the tribune of the people; now he received full official tribunician power. If he did not immediately take up the office of tribune of the people (*tribunus plebis*), but only the legal competence (*potestas*) inherent in it, his reason was that, as a patrician, he could not properly become tribune of the people. Now that he was again in a phase where he sought to integrate his power with the old framework of the law, he could not overrule that regulation. In addition, to hold the tribuneship of the people without interruption might have aroused the same kind of protest as his permanent occupation of the consulate.

The separation of the power of the office, that is to say of the legal competence proper to it, from the office itself, was something entirely new and, in itself, contradictory. No one had ever thought of distinguishing between an office and its powers. If it was happening now, it was out of the political necessity to clothe the ruler's legal competence in the forms of traditional law, in the process distorting that law to make it suitable for him to assume the requisite legal power. The outcome meant adjusting the tradition of public law to the ruler's requirements.

Equipped with the official power of a tribune, Augustus was not in fact a tribune – could not and did not want to be a tribune – and thus he was not an official, but nor was he simply a private person. He held the rights and competences proceeding from tribunician power, for instance the right to summon and preside over the Senate, the right to make laws in front of the assembly of the people and the right of assistance (*ius auxilii*). As holder of tribunician power he was in the public arena 'for life' without being a magistrate and thus a member of the traditional colleges of the magistracy, while his legal position was above that laid down in the other state regulations, but without being fundamentally different in its public and legal concept. It was not a special power, like that of a dictatorship or a triumvirate. In addition Augustus also took over tribunician power in the 'republican' manner, in so far as he maintained a show of resigning it at the end of every year and resuming it at the beginning of the next. It was not, incidentally, reckoned by the calendar year, but from the day when it was first assumed – which was 1 July or perhaps 1 August of the year 23 – and all the emperors after Augustus observed the holding of the office in the same way.

Meanwhile, his official assumption of tribunician power was not the end of it. It was true that the tribune could summon the Senate and propose laws at its meetings, but that right belonged first and foremost to the consuls as formally the supreme heads of the state. Consequently Augustus had to give tribunician power special privileges if its opportunities for taking the political initiative were not to be subordinate to those of the consulate. So at the same time as he assumed tribunician power he had himself granted the right always to be able to speak in the Senate when he wanted (and before anyone else) and also to summon it whenever he wished – which in this instance was not until the next year.

Now just one more thing was needed to make the *tribunicia potestas* equal to the consulate. The consul, formally the holder of the highest office, also took precedence over the proconsuls, that is to say the governors of the provinces administered by the Senate. It was true that he could not simply give the proconsuls orders, but he could do so if he personally were *in* their provinces. Now that he was not consul himself any more, Augustus also had to secure his potential supremacy over the administration of the Senate's provinces, and in another way. He therefore, through privilege, had this supremacy of his proconsular *imperium* over that of the Senate's governors (proconsuls) separately acknowledged. The fact that the proconsular *imperium* was invalid, according to the old regulations, inside the sacred city boundary of Rome was another difficulty arising from his resignation of the consulate: in Rome only the *imperium* of the magistrates of the state structure, the consuls and proconsuls, was valid. If Augustus had observed this rule, governing his provinces from Rome would have been impossible. From a purely formal point of view – and that was the only imaginable way of looking at this integration of the power of the ruler into the traditional legal order – every time he went to one of his provinces he would have had to ask the Senate for the power of command there that he had lost on entering Rome. This was an intolerable prospect, and accordingly Augustus requested, and obtained, the legal privilege of not laying down his proconsular *imperium* when he crossed the boundary of Rome and thus did not have to take it up again when he left the city.

Augustus now seemed to have achieved his aim. He had all the legal consular powers that he needed to take the political initiative without actually being consul himself, and through his tribunician power he even had opportunities that went further. In addition his legal power now looked yet more republican, particularly as, with the tribunician power, he was also surrounded by the centuries-old glory of the office-holder who was responsible for the needs and rights of the people. It was a fact that with all this, traditional public law had to a great extent been abolished. Out of individual fragments of an office, and special privileges, a new legal power had been created, especially tailor-made for Augustus. But however much had been destroyed in the process, the desire to create a formal framework binding on the potentate was obvious.

The next three years were to show that the unease prevailing in the capital after the rulings of the year 23 had not yet died down. Once again it was the question of the consulate that drove many an ambitious man to unwise behaviour and induced others, through the acts of violence that occurred during voting, to give Augustus full powers running counter to all that had logically followed the settlement of the year 27 – the consolidation of his power in the forms of traditional constitutional law. As early as 22 there were riots in Rome. They were set off by price rises, together with the effects of an epidemic that had been plaguing Italy since the previous year, as well as a devastating flooding of the Tiber that even carried away the famous wooden bridge, the oldest bridge in Rome (the Pons Sublicius). Crowds of citizens, banding together, tried to make Augustus dictator by force, or at least to transfer the permanent consulate to him. In addition, they wanted to force on him official responsibility for provisioning the city and even make him censor for life, which would have made him permanently responsible for the composition of the Senate. All this would have destroyed his political efforts to achieve an understanding with the leading men of the city, and so he refused all these applications except that of provisioning the city (*cura annonae*). He discharged even this obligation, cleverly following his former political line, not with his own staff but by transferring it to two senators of praetorian rank who were to change every year. His moderate conduct, in line with tradition, which would not let him depart from the way he had chosen even under pressure from outside and in circumstances of general emergency, won him respect. The fact that in addition he was always announcing a 'return' to the old ways gradually created corresponding expectations and finally something like an awareness that this policy would be the established horizon of his future government of the state.

In early autumn of the year 22, Augustus set off for Sicily and went on from there to the east. Since Agrippa had come back from the east only in the year 20 and then set off for the western provinces in haste after a short stay in Rome, the city was without its ruler and its supreme general for several years. However, Augustus made sure that for the next four years one of the two consuls was always a close friend of his, beginning in 22 with Lucius Arruntius, who had distinguished himself as an admiral at Actium. But the ruler's long absence led many to the entirely erroneous belief that the old state, allowing free play to all powers, had now returned, and the efforts of Augustus himself to clothe his power in the trappings of the old traditions made many feel further confirmed in this mistaken view. Naturally the consulate was the main focus of attention again, and even though Augustus had made provision for the occupant of at least one of the two posts, there was still the other. In the year 21 two members of distinguished old families were in contention for it. In addition a certain Marcus Egnatius Rufus, from a family of equestrian rank and aspiring to rise higher, seems to have misunderstood the political signals and, as aedile, showed himself willing to help the city of Rome with measures on behalf of the fire service. He organized teams of servants and hired workmen to put out conflagrations and thus brought free competition back into favour with the population of the city, just as if military rule were over and the good old days had returned. Rome was indeed often plagued by fires, so a public show of help for the fire service was a clever political move. Egnatius even, contrary to the law, succeeded in receiving the praetorship from the people immediately after his year as aedile. Augustus, seeing the danger, ordered Agrippa back to Rome, where with some difficulty he restored peace as the ruler's deputy.

At this time Agrippa, by his master's wish, married Julia, the widow of Marcellus. As the husband of Augustus' daughter, he was politically more powerful. Not only was he twenty-four years older than Julia, to enter into this marriage he had to divorce his wife Marcella, Octavia's eldest daughter, with whom he had several children. He dealt with the divorce expeditiously: we may doubt, however, whether he did so entirely willingly, and whether he was personally happy in his new role. Considering all that Augustus expected of him, Agrippa presents almost too self-effacing a picture. One might think he went along with this demand because it seemed to make up for his humiliation in having Marcellus preferred to him, since he was now, so to speak, taking over the role of Marcellus as his friend's new son-in-law. However, Marcellus had been Augustus' nephew, and if Augustus was principally concerned with children who might be born of this new marriage, leaving aside all other family concerns, his new son-in-law was not related to him. Augustus will have seen the successor he longed for not in Agrippa, but in a son who might be born to Agrippa and Julia, in fact seeing such a successor as an even more likely prospect than a son of Marcellus. Was Agrippa, like Marcellus, merely to keep the place ready for the grand-children that Augustus hoped for? In political weight Agrippa was very different from Marcellus – he was the empire's supreme general. Future events would have to show how this marriage was to be understood and how Agrippa himself saw it. Provision was made for the divorced Mar-cella: she married Jullus Antonius, the eldest of Mark Antony's surviving sons. We know nothing about any protest against this kind of 'provi-sion' by those most directly affected.

Augustus stayed away from Rome for three years. In the east, he amended and corrected the measures taken after the battle of Actium in the eastern provinces and their client kingdoms. It was the first time since the settlement of January 27 that he had been there, and his stay might be seen as the counterpart of the time he had spent in the west between the years 27 and 24. The ruler now established as *princeps* was inspecting his dominions.

There were all kinds of administrative matters to be settled on this journey, problems that had been neglected or had only just arisen. Petitions had to be answered, rewards and punishments handed out. In Sicily, Augustus conferred the rank of Roman city (*colonia*) on several towns, including Syracuse, and he took Eretria in Euboea and the island of Aegina from Athens. Kyzikos and the Phoenician cities of Tyre and Sidon paid for their inability to keep the peace at home by losing their independence; they became tributary cities. In these measures Augustus drew no distinction between the provinces under his command and those under that of the Senate. As he held proconsular power, which placed him above the proconsuls of the Senate when he was present in a province, this was correct from the purely legal viewpoint, but he must have maintained the responsibility of the Senate in the process, at least in form, as we know from his later intervention in circumstances in Cyrenaica.

From Sicily, Augustus travelled on by way of Greece to Samos, and on again from there to Syria, passing through Asia Minor. Two tasks in particular awaited him in this part of the world. The system of client princes set up after Actium had to be examined, and the relationship of the Parthians to the empire, left open at the time, must now be permanently settled. The latter question in particular could not be postponed, for the matter of revenge for the defeat of Carrhae in the year 53 was still outstanding. The dictator had not been able to exact it, and when Antony tried to do so he had failed miserably. To the Roman way of thinking, it was unimaginable that the matter could be left to rest at that. As if naturally, that is to say in agreement with public opinion, soon after the settlement of January 27 the poet Horace had felt called upon to encourage the young *princeps*, whom he addressed in this poem for the first time by his name of Caesar, to embark on a war of revenge against the Parthians. So the new lord of the world, who insisted so much on Roman tradition and the essential nature of Rome itself, had to go into action.

But first the Armenian question must be cleared up. Ever since Pompey the Great had extended the empire as far as Armenia, that country had been regarded by the Romans as a kind of glacis or defensive rampart, possession of which must be gained to secure the border with the Parthians. If that were to be done, the Armenian throne had to be occupied by a king friendly to Rome. Antony had had great difficulty with the Armenians and perhaps not entirely unreasonably held their king Artavasdes in particular either wholly or partly to blame for his failed campaign. When Augustus turned to settling the Parthian question in the year 20 the son of Artavasdes, Artaxias (Artaxes), was on the throne of Armenia. Under the protection of the Parthian king, he was engaged in a foreign policy of expansion on the eastern border (Atropatene) and western border (Armenia Minor) of his kingdom. This was where the Roman presence must first be restored, and it turned out fortunate that the Armenians themselves asked to have the brother of their present king, Tigranes, instead of Artaxias. Tigranes had been living in exile in Rome, and Augustus had brought him along, so to speak, in his baggage. Whoever or whatever was behind this request – a minority of the leading men of Armenia, or simply no more than Roman publicity at work – the matter solved itself, for Artaxias was murdered by members of his family before there could be any Roman intervention. So Tigranes was enthroned without more ado as the new king of Armenia, a ceremony performed by Augustus' stepson Tiberius, who was not yet twenty-two. Tiberius was in command of an army of intervention consisting of six legions, no doubt under experienced legates. He performed the solemn enthronement in the Roman camp.

King Phraates IV of Parthia yielded even before the Armenian question was finally settled. He agreed with Augustus to consolidate the Parthian–Roman relationship on the basis of the status quo. That meant, first, that the Parthian king accepted the settlement of the Armenian problem as Rome wanted it, undoubtedly a bitter pill for him to swallow. It meant that he was leaving Armenia to the Romans as a buttress for them, while he himself, as seen from the Mesopotamian plain, would have his kingdom constantly threatened from the mountains of the north. In addition, he renounced any expansion over the natural border formed by the Euphrates and finally, complying with a long-standing demand from the Romans, handed over all the surviving prisoners of war and the standards that the Parthians had taken from Rome at Carrhae and during Mark Antony's failed campaign. These were concessions that the king brought himself to make, not least, with the internal situation of his kingdom in mind. Like most Parthian kings, he had a rival for his throne. The rival's name was Tiridates, and the Romans held him as a kind of last trump card to be played in the political game. As the rule of Phraates was extremely despotic by the standards of the nobility of the Iranian area of the time, he was not anxious to face war against both Rome and a usurper simultaneously, particularly as the Parthian kingdom, at the size it had attained and in view of the tension constantly arising from a strong oligarchy, would not have been in any position to expand further safely. The king might also have thought, in making his decision, that at this point his country was not so badly off. It had defended itself successfully against a Roman foreign policy of expansion and at the same time had gained independence from its great neighbour. The agreement with the Romans is thus not to be seen as the humiliation of an intimidated king, as it is sometimes considered today in the light of Roman propaganda.

Augustus had the return of the prisoners and the standards celebrated as a great victory. The standards were placed in a small sanctuary of Mars on the Capitol, specially built for the purpose as their temporary residence until they could be transferred to the temple of Mars Ultor, then still under construction in the new Forum of Augustus. A great triumphal arch – a second, following the one to celebrate Actium – was erected in the Forum as a token of victory, spanning the 'Sacred Road' between the temples of the deified Caesar and Castor. Its rich ornamentation depicted, among other subjects, the return of the standards, and we know that it was crowned by a quadriga with Augustus himself driving the chariot. Augustus thus appears as lord of the Parthians and bringer of peace at the same time, and that is how Horace celebrates him in the closing lines of an epistle written in the year 20: the Parthian king bows before Augustus, kneeling, and after the famine from which Italy had suffered in the year 22, there now follows, in the year 20, the 'golden plenty' (*aurea copia*) of a good harvest. The scene of the return of the standards and prisoners, uniting the themes of dominion and peace, was to be one of the key pictorial motifs of Augustus' political concept of himself. It also appears on the breastplate of the statue of Augustus that was found in Livia's house at the Prima Porta, although here in the context of a cosmic scenario. However, in the whole empire, not just Rome and Italy, and above all in the east, the surrender of the standards was celebrated on provincial coinages and buildings as a great achievement on the part of Augustus, and was sometimes seen as a victory over the east and a revival of the great Greek war of liberation, particularly the victory of Athens over the Persians in the fifth century.

Matters looked different beside the Euphrates. No war justifying a triumphal arch had been won here, and the Parthian king was not a client of the lord of Rome. On the contrary: Augustus had refrained from exacting revenge, either for Carrhae or for the attacks on the eastern provinces between 41 and 38. The ruler of Rome had also accepted the course of the Euphrates as a frontier; his policy was undoubtedly cleverly calculated in view of the claims made in the time of the late republic, when foreign policy had been extraordinarily dynamic, and during the triumvirate period, and was guided by insight into the opportunities now open to Rome in the provinces, but it was still essentially a case of abstaining from action. However, Augustus could not present it as such against the background of the military achievements of men like Pompey and Caesar; nor could it be presented as merely a policy of peace-keeping. The outcome of his eastern mission was indeed to be the successful conclusion of peace, but his Parthian opposite number must appear the dependent partner, begging Augustus for peace, and that was how Augustus saw it himself at the end of his life, when he wrote his account of his achievements: 'I forced the Parthians to return their booty and the standards of three Roman armies to me, and to plead humbly for the friendship of the Roman people.' And he added: 'The king of the Parthians, Phraates, son of Orodes, sent all his sons and grandsons to me in Italy, not after being defeated in war but as one begging for our friendship by pledging his children.' In these remarks the reality has become a means of self-glorification: the king of the Parthians has sunk to the position of a client king pledging his dearest possession, his own family, in return for peace. In fact Phraates did not beg for peace but negotiated it, and he sent his children to Rome only ten years later – not, incidentally, as a pledge that he would keep the peace, but because he was anxious to ensure the royal dignity for the son of his young queen, Musa, and to that end wanted to get those of his older offspring who had a right to the throne out of the country.

Similarly, the solution of the Armenian problem is turned upside down in the official version. According to that account, Augustus had given the kingdom to Tigranes – or to employ the internal logic of the way he describes the event, he had made Tigranes a present of it, although he could instead have commandeered it as a province. That was simply not true, for unless he had refrained from making Armenia a province of Rome, there could have been no treaty with the king of Parthia. That had been the prerequisite for an amicable outcome. Augustus, however, deliberately made it a means of implementing his own policy without any loss of face. In his rulings of the year 20, he had firmly confirmed in principle Antony's policy of strengthening client kings while limiting the extent of the provincial area in the east. He did it by giving Armenia Minor, which was not in contention, and several towns in the west of Cilicia to Archelaos of Cappadocia, and other parts of that area to one Tarcondimotus. He left parts of the central Syrian area with Emesa (now Homs) to Iamblichus, allowed Mithradates III of Commagene to succeed to his father's inheritance, and Herod too was able to enlarge his kingdom by adding several cities and rural areas to it.

Meanwhile many in Rome were heartily wishing for the return of Augustus. As Agrippa too was kept away by unrest in Gaul and Spain, tension within the Senate had flared up again, the flames being fanned by certain ambitious individuals in the Senate, and, even if many adherents of Augustus, including some of the most uncompromising, saw what was going on in the city as a storm in a teacup in view of the fact that the centre of power had shifted from Rome itself to the army and the empire, it was up to Augustus to consolidate the political situation in the capital on as broad as possible a basis. Indeed, as Augustus himself saw clearly, that was crucial for a lasting peace at home. It could be achieved, however, only by means of such agreements as had been reached in the years 27 and 23, and that called for calm circumspection. A concerned Augustus made haste back to Rome.

Travelling by way of Athens, where Virgil joined him, he reached Brundisium in early autumn. The poet died there on 21 September at the age of nearly fifty, of a feverish illness that he had contracted while he was in Greece. A consul, with other magistrates and many senators, came from Rome to meet their ruler in Campania, a ritual more fitting for kings than for the *princeps*, and it once again emphasized the hybrid nature of the principate. On 12 October 19, Augustus entered the city again, and a few days later, in gratitude for his return, an altar was dedicated to the goddess Fortuna, who had brought him safely home to his native land after a long journey in the overseas provinces. The dedication named her Fortuna Redux. Her altar stood close to the gate through which Augustus had entered the city, the Porta Capena, to which the Appian Way leads from Campania. In addition, the Senate decreed that the day of his return should be marked by annual festivities of Augustus (the Augustalia).

Rome was in considerable turmoil that year as the result of subversion by the same Egnatius Rufus who had already made a less than glorious name for himself in the year 22. The point at issue was the tenure of the second consulate, which the Romans had wished to offer to Augustus, against his will and not at all in the spirit of the settlement of the year 23. Egnatius, however, had his eye on it, and as a result there was violent rioting. It seems that on the return of the *princeps*, Egnatius had already gone so far that he now saw nothing for it but to turn the rioting over the election of a consul into an attack on the life of Augustus, or at least that is how it was presented after the event. Obviously Egnatius was a blinkered activist with no sense of what was politically possible. Arrested with a few of his companions, he was thrown into prison, condemned to death and executed.

These events show that the magistrates were no longer in a position to keep peaceful elections going in Rome, even with the help of the Senate. The nobility, who had once been in charge of everything, no longer existed, and the minions of powerful men, which is how most of the senators are to be regarded, were usually governed by narrow-minded self-interest and concentrated solely on their own careers – hardly surprising, for they had not learned anything else from their potentates. Many of them had no code of conduct, no ethos combining their own with the common interest, and they were consequently overtaxed in the face of the necessity of respecting the present limits of their political latitude. Even before entering Rome again, Augustus had to intervene directly in the voting process and more or less decide for himself on someone to fill the office. He appointed a man called Quintus Lucretius, who had fought on Pompey's side in the civil war between Pompey and Caesar and had even been proscribed. Augustus was showing moderation and reason in continuing along his chosen path, even when he faced a chaotic set of ambitious fighting-cocks. The strength to do so can't have been derived solely from a wish to see his political ideas carried out, it must also have stemmed from a lack of respect, indeed something more like contempt, for considerable sections of this new society.

Augustus took this rioting as the occasion, and one that went hand in hand with his official position, to clear a problem still not fully solved out of his way. Acting in the spirit of the political settlements of 27 and 23, he disposed once and for all of the wish frequently expressed to him at times of emergency and unrest from various sides, although not by his closest adherents, for him to resume the consulate. At the same time he even succeeded in furthering the establishment of his legal position in the capital, without doing any injury to the idea of the restoration of the old state (*res publica restituta*).

With this end in view, he did not accept the permanent consulate, which he had resigned for the very reason that it looked unattractively close to tyrannical power, and in any case he did not need it now that he had taken over tribunician power and the legal privileges that went with it. He no longer even needed the *imperium* of a consul, which naturally did not entail tribunician power, because the privilege of not having to resign his proconsular *imperium* on entering the mile around Rome already gave him that. What he lacked, and what set him apart from the consuls, if purely to outward appearance, was the outer signs of supreme official power. A consul was preceded by twelve official servants, the lictors, carrying bundles of rods; he sat on a raised platform in the Senate on a special official chair, the *sella curulis*, a backless folding chair with ivory ornamentation. As the holder of tribunician power, however, Augustus had not a single lictor, and in the Senate, if he did not sit in the body of the house he had to content himself with the tribunes' bench, the *subsellium*. That was now rectified. Augustus received twelve lictors and the right of sitting on a *sella curulis* between the two consuls. He thus had the legal competence and outer signs of rank of a consul, without actually being consul. It could be said that enough had been done to satisfy the idea of a republic. However, it might equally well have been said that the old official hierarchy had been so undermined by such manipulations that the name of monarch was disguised only by the countless titles held by the commander of the army. So was the 'republican' framework of the new order only pretence? Were the senators, who knew very well that Augustus was permanent consul in all but name, content with a well-intentioned lie that allowed them not to acknowledge that his was a monarchy and feel that they were the elite of a free state? We shall look at that question later.

The principate was now established. None the less, the *princeps* was still working tirelessly to bring it to completion and to renovate the society on which it was based. His endeavours to improve the moral and physical consolidation of the elite were to occupy the coming year, 18 BC, but we shall look at them too later. Here I will mention only the new and second 'cleansing' of the Senate. Whereas the first, in the year 28, had been in preparation for the great settlement of January 27, the second was to achieve a final consolidation, concluding the development. Once again it was a difficult operation, arousing great displeasure in some quarters, and so the question of why Augustus experimented so persistently with the composition of the Senate is justified. Did not such a move mean interference with the independence of the Senate that had been so loudly and emphatically proclaimed as restored in the year 27? Could it not be seen as an open admission of the complete dependence of that institution on the *princeps* and did it not therefore damage the legal constitution of the principate as it had only just been created? Obviously Augustus was tackling these social questions in the same way as he had dealt with the legal structure of the state, that is to say, he thought he could regulate them by prescription. However, he was aware that such decisions must be disguised by measures signalling self-determination, and thus 'liberty'. The revision of the Senate carried out in the year 18 is a model of those tactics. Augustus was trying to maintain what was correct, but at the same time, through overemphasizing it, he did the opposite.

First he cancelled the entire list of senators, something that had never been done before. Then, for the new formation of the Senate, he picked thirty men, each of whom was to choose on oath five other men, members of his family excluded, who in his opinion were the best. One of each of these groups of five, that is to say another thirty in all, was chosen by lot to be a senator. And by these thirty – the first thirty had to retire but could be re-elected – another five each were chosen by lot. The process was to continue in this way until the Senate had the number envisaged by Augustus – initially it was 300, but after great protest the number rose to 600. This painstaking process took several days, but even before it ended fraud came to light, and finally Augustus lost patience, gave up and filled the remaining places with men whom he himself thought suitable. There were painful scenes in the Senate, and Augustus had to make some adjustments, which meant adding new names and removing others. The end result was to show exactly what he had wanted to conceal: Augustus had a free hand in the composition of the highest body in Rome.

The new 'cleansing' of the Senate was obviously to be the conclusion of a development that placed the state and society on a new foundation in the spirit of old tradition. Most people now had the uplifting sense that the time of need and danger was over. They thought they saw a new and better age ahead. And even those who had been among the enemies of Augustus now looked with confidence to the future, like that formerly despised man to whom Octavian then showed favour, and who, in an eulogy of his dead wife, said that after twenty-seven years of life spent with her: 'The circle of the earth was at peace, the state restored, and thereafter we were to see a calm and happy age.'

At the time Augustus clearly thought that a certain final point, or at least a resting point, had been reached and he had marked it with the reconstitution of the Senate. In addition he was looking for something that would also give outward expression to the new sense of life of the present time, with its hopes for the future, and would enduringly recall to all minds what had been achieved. He therefore decided on a huge festival of celebration. Like everything he did, it was a construct of mingled tradition and innovation that would serve above all to secure his rule. In it and through it, people were to look back at the past and forward to the future; the suffering but also the achievements of the dark years and the future good fortune of all Romans were to be displayed to the public at large. For this purpose Augustus looked back to the ideas of the early republic of successive ages (*saecula*). At the end of a cycle, there should be a religious festival to show that the sorrow and guilt of the past were atoned for and forgotten as a better future dawned, free of guilt and misery. Such a 'secular' festival had already been organized once, in the last phase of the First Punic War, a good 200 years earlier, when Rome, in great need, had begun to doubt ultimate success in a struggle that had been going on for fifteen years. The idea was not just to atone for any wrong that had been done, but to win back divine goodwill and ensure that the future, at the time more particularly the struggle against the Carthaginians, was under better auspices. A good hundred years later, after another completion of the secular cycle, the ritual was repeated, and another repetition was foreseen when the same length of time had again been completed. However, the civil war had prevented that when it broke out in the year 49. Now, however, Augustus planned to make up for the omission.

He intended to hold a great national festival uniting all Romans, celebrating the subject as Virgil had expressed it in his Fourth Eclogue. Great preparations were necessary to bring the old ideas of a secular new beginning into harmony with the new concepts that Augustus himself had introduced. In the old days the festival, as a sacrificial ritual of atonement, had been addressed principally to the gods of the underworld. A better future would then arise of its own accord, so to speak, from the propitiation of the gods. The sacred rites thus referred to the past but had an eye on the future.

Augustus shifted and indeed reversed the relationship of cause and effect inherent in the festival. The idea of civil war as the reason for a plea for appeasement directed to the gods was played down; attention was to be guided above all to the future. For that, however, the traditional rites and the entire ceremonial must be entirely rethought. After much work the general outlines of the festival quickly took shape on the authority of their initiator. First the Sibylline oracle necessary for the new purpose must be reshaped, indeed formed anew. In addition the whole ceremonial must be rethought and remodelled, and the requisite gods chosen to suit

323

its new purpose. The gods of the underworld and nocturnal festivities did not disappear entirely, but they took a back seat; daytime ceremonies were to come to the fore, and new gods besides Jupiter and Juno appeared in them, above all Apollo – Palatine Apollo, of course – Diana and Sol, who had played no part at all in the old rite, but who were essential to feature as the guarantors of good fortune and Roman greatness in the new age. It was no less important to fit the chronology according to which secular festivities could take place to the date that Augustus wanted, which was the year 17 BC. Scholars, among them the still very young Gaius Ateius Capito, did everything to the satisfaction of the *princeps*. Instead of the 100-year period, there would now be a *saeculum* of 110 years, as both the sacrificial ritual and the hymns specified.

The site of the festival, by old tradition, was a cult site called Tarentum on the west of the Field of Mars, near the present Ponte Vittorio Emanuele II leading to the Vatican. As president (*magister*) of the priestly college of fifteen responsible for the festivities, Augustus took over the staging of it. In that capacity he himself made the nocturnal sacrifice, which served in particular as atonement for past guilt, and then, with Agrippa, made the daytime sacrifice, while Horace wrote the words of the festival hymn (*carmen saeculare*) performed by three times nine choirs of boys and girls. The song announces the fortune of the new age, beginning with peace brought by the descendant of Anchises and Venus, and of the revival of ancient virtues that will bring mankind and nature fertility and blessing, and goes on to proclaim that Roman power (*res Romana*) and the fortunate land of Rome (*Latium felix*), that is to say imperial rule and the people of Rome, will be granted an even better century. Here the beginnings of Rome are linked as if by an arch to Augustus, and Roman history is presented according to its new master's image of it. The spirit of the time is presented as being in harmony with the morality and reasons of state of the ancient days of Rome, but conversely the ancient days (not Augustus) are seen as the source of the new attitude, and the honourable virtues are presented, as well as modesty and honesty. Personal happiness, a mind loyal to the state and the will to rule thus forge an insoluble link, as Horace and before him Virgil, presented it when the latter made the series of future Roman heroes, shown by Anchises to his son Aeneas in the underworld, close with a prophesy of the coming of Augustus. 'This is Augustus

Caesar, often promised to you, son of the deified one, who will found anew the golden age for Latium once ruled by Saturn, and extend the empire to the Garamantes and the Indies.' The festivities organized in the year 17 thus had very little in common with the old festivals of the same name. Atonement was still mentioned, but the gaze looked forward to a bright future. The festival had become the celebration of cheerful expectations of what was to come.

The building was erected: the people stood under the shelter of its roof, Romans and provincials alike, with the prospect of a future of peace and prosperity. It had taken Augustus ten years to build it. At the age of forty-six, he could feel secure in his position as *princeps* and commander of the army. There was no rival to dispute his power with him, and no foreign enemy threatened the borders of the Roman empire. The previous year the Senate had extended his two fundamental powers, the tribunician power and for his provinces the proconsular *imperium*, by another five years, and it could be expected that they would be extended again at the end of that time. The future of his house also seemed secure. His daughter Julia had borne Agrippa a son in the year 20. The child was called Gaius, after his grandfather, and in the year of the secular festival of rejoicing Julia had another son, Lucius. Not long afterwards Augustus adopted both children, who thus moved from the Vipsanian into the Julian family, and Gaius and Lucius now bore the name Julius Caesar. Undoubtedly the adoptions had taken place with the consent of Agrippa, who knew very well that his children had a political future only as Julians. His own position in the state was provided for. While in the year 23 one of the two basic powers had been transferred to him on a par with the *princeps*, if only for the east, in the year 18 the Senate also granted him tribunician power for five years, at the same time, of course, also extending the two basic powers of Augustus by five years. The position of Agrippa as successor presumptive to the *princeps* was confirmed. None the less, as the adoption of Agrippa's sons by Augustus indicated, he was intended to succeed only in an emergency. The regular hereditary succession, passing to the next generation, would fall on Gaius and Lucius Caesar, and, as both were descended from the dictator as well as Augustus, it would be undisputed.

# 8

# The Principate as Idea and Reality

'Man can want nothing more from the gods, nor the gods grant anything more to man ... than Augustus, on his return to the city, has already given to the state, the Roman people and the world.' Thus Velleius Paterculus, a man who had risen to prominence in the time of Augustus and was one of the generals to serve Tiberius when he became emperor, begins the chapter of his short *History of Rome* describing the return of Augustus from the Actian War and the restoration of the state. He had ended the civil war, says Velleius, as well as the war against the foreign enemy, and now peace reigned: 'The law was observed again, authority given to the courts and sovereignty to the Senate, and the power of the magistracy had been restored to its old form ... The state as known of old [the republic] was set up anew, enabling the fields to be cultivated again, the gods to be worshipped, the people to know security, and every man to rejoice in the secure possession of his property.' Velleius sees no break between the old state and the new one 'restored' by Augustus. In his eyes, the coming of Augustus links the old days to the new, bridging the interim period of the civil wars.

Undoubtedly only a man without any personal experience of the old days could see it like that. 'How many still lived who had known the *res publica*?' asks Tacitus of those who were alive in the year of Augustus' death (AD 14). The *res publica* that Tacitus means is the state of the era before the outbreak of the great civil war in the year 49 BC, known to us as the republic. In fact on the death of Augustus most older people had not been born until the time of the civil wars, and their juniors, like Velleius Paterculus himself, born in 20 BC, not until after the battle of Actium. In AD 14, anyone born when the civil war broke out was now sixty-three and an old man. A man's view of the structure of the state was obviously a question of his generation. Velleius might see the 'constitution' of the old state restored in the structure set up between the years 27 and 19, viewing it as identical with the state of Augustus. However, those born between 60 and 50 BC, who had personal knowledge of the great constitutional settlements in the decade after Actium, had more difficulty in their attitude to the new order. Their fathers had known the republic and had perhaps been active at that time themselves. They thus had an idea of it – even if, perhaps, only a vague idea – and noticed the distance between that state and the state as restored in the year 27.

Officially the principate was a structure legally drawn up to continue the centuries-old institutions of the Roman *res publica* or, as it was more precisely put, to 'restore' them after the turmoil of civil wars lasting for over twenty years. In fact even opponents of Augustus could not have denied that after his 'cleansing' of the Senate it was an organ capable of functioning again, that it administered half the provinces through the governors it sent out to them and that it had a say in the affairs of the city of Rome and of Italy. They would also have to admit that the consuls once again stood at the head of the state, everyone looked up to them, and on application to the magistrates the people voted on laws in their assemblies. Nor could it be overlooked that the powerful military potentate, by his own wish, was integrated into the order of the state. He was a special part of the legal constitution, but in spite of his elevated position he did not dominate its central areas, such as the consulate, the tribuneship of the people or the provinces as a whole, and so did not appear to crack the structure of the state. His legal power stood *beside* that of the holders of high office. He was not even a magistrate, but merely held an assortment of the martial powers and legal privileges of the magistracy. He had extensive official authority at his disposal, and through it he could gain access to any area of the business of state, but it did not represent legal power set above all other institutions, as the dictatorship and the triumvirate had. It was a power not superior to, but concurrent with, other, traditional legal powers.

And looking at these new circumstances purely from the legal viewpoint, even a critic could not deny their connection with the traditional state. No one would have claimed that the traditional state was actually restored, but that was not the point, even for those who could still remember it and treasured the memory. There was no doing away with the military factor in the shape of Augustus' sole command of the army now. Only a fantasist, of which there very few around at the time, or at least fewer than are to be found among modern students of the period, could think of such a thing or hope for it. The question was not whether the power of sole command could be integrated into the state, only how it was to be done. The omissions of the late republic had to be rectified now: central military power had become essential to the security and cohesion of the huge empire, and it must become a permanent part of the legal system of the state.

The act binding the military potentate to the law was addressed to the new elite. This elite, the officers and civil servants indispensable for the administration of the city and the empire, could not be induced to carry out its tasks in the long run unless its own security was guaranteed. Only in a climate of legal security, where the actions of the potentate were predictable, was lasting cooperation possible. The settlements of the years 27 to 19 were closely observed by the new elite in particular. Anxious as its members were to see a public legal framework put in place, no one could forget for a moment that in the 'constitution of the principate' the man who described himself as the 'first' (*princeps*) among those who in principle were his equals was really a monarch and he was only 'granting' Rome its constitution. It derived its validity not from a consensus of all the Romans or at least of the noble families, even if the monarch said it did, hailing that fact in official declarations. The principate rested solely on the will of the ruler to observe the constitution. No one but the *princeps* stood for its validity; he alone was its guarantor.

The 'constitution', then, depended entirely on Augustus, and his conduct reacted upon on it directly. In the forty years of his rule after the 'restoration' of the state – or it might be better to say after the beginning of his government – he displayed extraordinary stamina in setting an example to the people of Rome of the 'correct' way for the constitution to function. By conscientiously observing his own rules, he stabilized the new structure of the state, reinforced confidence in his person and gave the 'constitution' a certain existence of its own during the decades of his regime. It thus finally acquired something like a validity that could be seen as independent from the person of its creator. People forgot, or if that was hardly possible banished from their minds, the fact that the new order existed only by the goodwill of the ruler. Its precarious character was lost in time, or at least retreated from view to the extent that the ruler who first brought it into being had made himself a part of it.

The tireless efforts of Augustus to create and maintain a legal framework for the power that in reality he held was hard for many observers to understand, both in antiquity and today, and it is not easy to reconstruct his struggle to achieve acceptable forms for the legal power of the *princeps*. His fight for legal competences seems too petty, the artifice of a new set of rules made out of many fragments of the old order too strange. We are therefore inclined to ascribe too little weight to his constant efforts in that respect, because ultimately, after all, everything did depend on the ruler's goodwill. He toed the line of the 'constitution', even though he could obviously determine his own competences as he liked, and having done so could also observe or ignore them as he liked without fear of any repercussions. It seemed to be a mere façade, and the 'constitution of the principate' no more than fine words. The nub of the matter was his command of the army and the dependence on it of the citizens of the towns of Italy. By comparison, the 'constitution' might seem an illusion, and Augustus nothing but a hypocrite hiding his lust for power behind a glittering façade, putting on a show for the people of Rome.

Such an evaluation of the principate is wide of the mark, because it assumes that a society can live without the security of a predicable form of state for the long term, while still maintaining such a powerful political structure as Roman Italy and the area that it ruled. A form of government had to be sought that bound the ruler's power to Roman society, and first and foremost to the elite that was indispensable for administration. That form of government could derive only from the tradition that had made Rome all it represented. Criticism and failure to understand Augustus' structuring of the state were not to be expected from those whose sense that they were living under great threat had not for a moment left them in the twenty years of civil war. Such ideas could be entertained only by men who looked back at those years from a time of peace and security and had no memories of a world in turmoil.

Augustus knew that his power had to be based formally in the law, and he also knew that only the state as it had been in the past could provide the tools for establishing that base. He never tired of pointing out the rules of proper political conduct to the Romans, literally setting them an example and seeking to build up their confidence in those rules throughout his long reign. He hardly ever missed an opportunity to appeal to that idea and the spirit of it. It is impressively recorded for posterity in the account of his deeds on behalf of Rome that Augustus ordered to have displayed outside his mausoleum. In it, he represents himself as the man who saved the citizens from the servitude of tyranny, and who steadfastly refused all the requests made to him to assume full powers that might well destroy the framework of the *res publica*, fitting himself into the general order as a simple link in its chain, indeed subordinating himself to it. His ideas of the significance of the law for the construction of the new state are summed up in his remark that his legal power (*potestas*) had been no greater than that of any of his colleagues in office, although in social authority (*auctoritas*) he had towered above them all.

For all the many privileges vested in him, then, the ruler was a normal member of the state administration. He belonged to the sphere of the magistracy and did not consider himself above the constitution. If Augustus rejected the appellation 'lord' (*dominus*), the usual way for slaves to address their master in his time, although it was also a conventional address by free men to those who held high positions, he was not just putting on a show; his rejection of it went to the heart of the new order. He could indeed assert his will everywhere and do just as he wanted, but he still continued to remain within the framework of the *general* administration of the state. If the Senate and magistracy did not use their legal power to oppose his will, it was the *auctoritas* of Augustus that held them back, and for the same reason they deferred to him even in areas that were formally outside his jurisdiction. If he wanted to carry a point in a Senate debate, within an area for which the Senate was responsible, then he did it by a vote during the proceedings. It could be taken for granted that the Senate would do as he wanted, but that fact did not restrict free discussion. Contradiction was as hard to imagine in this system as any idea that Augustus would humbly or even flatteringly surrender of his own free will. The readiness of the Senate and magistrates to yield to him had its counterpart in the self-restraint of the *princeps* himself. Both modes of conduct were essential parts of the 'constitution'.

But in practice this self-discipline, incumbent on both parties, made government through the new order a balancing act in which either party could fall at any time. The more difficult role here was that of the *princeps*. He had to stand back when facing a recalcitrant adversary who took the new order seriously and made a legal objection, even though he had the power to intervene forcefully, and when, on the other hand, he was dealing with someone only too eager to fawn on the ruler and allow him more than the rules required, he had to remind the man gently of his independence. The critic must be answered with restraint, the flatterer reproved. His opposite numbers, the senators and magistrates, were not in an easy situation either. Every one of them needed the *princeps* if he was to get ahead in life, particularly public life. No one could rise without him. Finding the right path to tread between the dignity of a senator and the constraints of society had its problems. The principate demanded equilibrium between what the *princeps* could do and what was still permitted to a senator. Everyone understood the tipping point at which the balance was disturbed, but it was not formally defined and could therefore be seen clearly only when someone flagrantly overstepped the mark. Situations in which one party or the other did indeed overstep it were frequent, and usually the one who did that was the *princeps*, who had the opportunity to take the initiative, less frequently the senator doomed to passivity.

Realizing the idea of the principate was made harder by the fact that pressure of public business often simply would not allow the *princeps* to act in the spirit of that idea. This was not just a question of situations in which security at home or abroad was threatened – they could be dealt with by immediate action on the part of the commander of the army, with the Senate then presented with a *fait accompli*. The greatest obstacle to conduct fitting the idea of the principate was the political disparity between the true power factors of the state and the empire. All eyes and minds, not just in Augustus' own provinces but also those of the Senate, were turned not to the Senate but to the *princeps*, as the man who had the power to give and to take away, with the result that even envoys from the cities in the Senate's provinces usually turned to Augustus. It would have been more correct for him to receive only envoys and petitioners from his own provincial area, directing those who came from the other provinces to the Senate. That did not always happen, and in fact a good deal of business, not just immediately pressing problems but also those affecting the administrative organization or reorganization of provinces, did call for the decision of the *princeps*, who alone had a full view of what went on in the entire empire. As the control centre of government that the Senate was not and could not be, only he, again, could properly assess the necessity of a settlement, formulate a solution with an eye to the whole picture and implement it. The political difference favoured the *princeps*, and the presence of monarchical rule behind the 'constitution' showed more and more clearly. Critics might assume that this development had been intended from the first. Tacitus did, for one. He described Augustus as a man who at first, in the year 23, contented himself with the power of a tribune of the people but who, after the soldiers had been corrupted by gifts, the people by donations of grain, and everyone by the sweetness of peace, had taken all the business of state, the tasks proper to the Senate, the magistracy and the assembly of the people, into his own hands, thus leading the Romans into servitude (*servitium*). Although Tacitus certainly did not do justice to the first *princeps*, his view was not entirely unfounded.

The 'constitution of the principate' was the contract between the new elite and the commander of the army. It made his rule possible in form as well as fact. The constitution was the political and social context that also suited the empire after the collapse of the old system; Augustus could consider it the best possible situation while at the same time priding himself on being its originator. That did not conceal the fact that the Roman world – together with its elite – had a monarch who was even equated, for instance by Ovid, with the state (*res publica*), and no one ever tried to conceal it, at least not in the time of Augustus. The 'constitutional' monarchy thus set up was, however, not the only means that Augustus had of ruling, and not even the most striking of the methods at his disposal.

Most Romans were aware of the monarchical character of the principate, particularly because of the elevation of the person of Augustus himself, something that had been unusual in the old days. It is true that some individuals in the late republic had higher status than others, but the extent and nature of the distinction accorded to Augustus were much greater, and it was already taking firmer shape even before the establishment of the principate. For instance, his arrival in Rome after an absence of any length of time became a festive occasion for which all important men and many of the people assembled, calling out congratulations to the *princeps* and hailing his entry into the city with solemn hymns. His distinction was marked by the honour of an escort consisting of high-ranking senators, delegations of equestrians or even the entire Senate, and by the raised seat he occupied at all major occasions. Even clearer recognition of his person was shown by the declaration of not only public but also personal dates in his life, such as his birthday on 23 September, as public holidays (*feriae publicae*). In addition, by decree of the Senate and the people, the name of the sixth month (Sextilis) was changed to Augustus – just as the name of the fifth month (Quintilis) had already been changed to Julius in honour of the dictator Caesar. By decision of the Senate the sixth month, Sextilis, was chosen for the change of name because that was the month in which Augustus had first become consul and had captured Alexandria. However, that seems rather far-fetched. September, as the month of Augustus' birth and of the great victories of Naulochus and Actium, would have been far more suitable. Obviously Sextilis was chosen because it followed Julius, formerly Quintilis, the next of the 'numbered' months in the Roman calendar. Another feature of the recognition of Augustus as First Citizen, or monarch, was the habit of including his name in public prayers, in which the gods were petitioned to ensure his well-being (*salus*).

Purely worldly and human honours were accompanied by those of a religious character. Their origins went much further back than the settlement of the year 27. As the deified Caesar's son, Octavian had acquired some of the religious aura that surrounded his adoptive father during his life and after his death. He was *divi filius*, the son of the deified one, and as a Julian through his ancestor Aeneas, son of Anchises the Trojan and Venus, he was of divine descent. Since Romulus was descended from Aeneas, his family was also linked to the myth of the founding of Rome. However little religious power there might be behind the apotheosis of the dictator and the myth of the origins of Rome, they still set the person of Octavian apart from ordinary citizens, placing him above other men and surrounding him with a dignity that created distance between them and his own person. Above all, however, while observation of the myth and the apotheosis in themselves might not be especially binding on the people of Rome, that was rectified when they were institutionalized as a cult with a temple, acquiring distinct form through the cult and its pictorial representations. The dictator himself had erected a temple on the second Forum that he built, the Forum Julium on the north-eastern slope of the Capitol, dedicating it to Venus Genetrix, the cult name of the goddess in her capacity as founding mother of the Julian clan. After his murder his apotheosis manifested itself in the temple of the deified Caesar in the old Forum. Augustus was thus ever present to the Roman mind as a man of divine descent.

Octavian/Augustus was very anxious to consolidate his sacred aura. The sanctity of the tribuneship of the people, which he took over as the son of the dictator, had already served that purpose. While the tribune-ship existed mainly in the administrative area of the state, Augustus was making efforts at quite an early date to align himself with two widely venerated gods with well-established cults, Mars and Apollo. We have met Apollo already as the god to whom Octavian dedicated a part of his house. He felt an even closer bond to the same god after his victory at Actium, which was fought close to a temple of Apollo. And Mars had helped him ever since he first came to Rome to take revenge on his father's murderers. Before the battle of Philippi, Augustus had promised that if he won the victory, he would build the god a temple in his aspect as the god of vengeance (Mars Ultor), although it was not to be com-pleted until forty years later, when it became the central temple of the third large square in Rome to be called, after Augustus, the Forum Augustum.

The tendency to personalize special qualities as divine abstractions, which was rooted in traditional Roman religion, was influential in the religious elevation of the ruler. The 'sanctity' he had gained as the trib-une of the people already pointed in that direction. The significance of victory as a divine power in itself, whether as the victory of the Roman people (*Victoria populi romani*) or the victory of Augustus (*Victoria Augusti*), continued that development along the same lines. Octavian had taken it into account when he presented the statue of Victoria at the dedication of the new Senate house. The altar erected at the same time made this statue of the goddess into a cult image.

The veneration of the Genius Augusti had different connotations. The term *genius* was used by the Romans to indicate a man's power during his lifetime – but not his purely material power; it denoted, in particular, generative power. The *genius* of Augustus was linked to the worship of the Lares in a way formalized only decades after the year 27. The Lares, as household gods protecting property, were generally wor-shipped in the places where Romans lived, by the side of fields or, in the city, at crossroads (*compita*). Two Lares were worshipped in small chap-els at such road junctions. They were represented as dancing spirits, and the Genius Augusti now joined them in the form of a third deity depicted as a statuette wearing a toga. When Rome was redivided between 12 and 7 BC into fourteen districts (*regiones*) and 265 subdivisions of those districts (*vici*), the cult was entrusted to the care of a special supervisory authority, the *vici magistri*. It spread fast, and soon the cult of the *genius* of Augustus combined with the cult of the Lares was established in those towns of Italy that followed the example of the capital. Its distribution was further promoted by the fact that at all public and private banquets everyone had to pour a libation to the Genius Augusti. The cult owed its power and its binding nature as much to its broad institutionalization as it did to the protection that it offered in combination with the worship of the Lares. The cult of the *genius* of Augustus led on to the veneration of the *numen* of Augustus. By *numen* the Romans understood not the god himself but a divine power or quality, and therefore *numen Augusti* does not mean Augustus as a god but the divine power in him. We know of an altar to the *numen* of Augustus (*ara numinis Augusti*) in Rome, where the priests of the four great priestly colleges made sacrifice at certain times.

The veneration of Augustus spread everywhere that Romans lived: in Rome itself, in Italy and on into the Roman cities now proliferating all over the empire. The form of worship of the monarch was of a different kind for those who lived in the provinces and did not have citizenship rights, since in the Greek east of the empire at least they had already had a formal cult of their ruler in his lifetime for centuries. From the time of Alexander the Great onwards the Greeks had developed a system whereby important and powerful figures, especially the members of established royal houses, were closely associated with the supernatural world and the dividing line between the divine and the human appeared fluid. They now felt it was appropriate to allow great Romans to assume the role of their own kings, who had abdicated or were politically powerless, thus moving them, too, into a supernatural world. Even in the late republic, the people of towns and cities in Asia Minor had venerated various powerful members of the republican nobility. They therefore felt no scruples in raising Antony and Octavian (or Augustus) to such heights. Indeed, the cult set up for such figures became one of their ways of communicating with the man who stood above all others in the empire, and proclaiming their loyalty to him.

However, there were different forms of the cult of the ruler for the

Roman and non-Roman inhabitants of the empire, who were usually designated as 'provincials' or 'foreigners' ('peregrines') or else lumped together into the non-technical but commonly used category of 'subjects'. Immediately after the end of the war against Antony, even before he returned to Rome, Augustus had established through various decrees fundamentally different ways of relating to his person for the two groups. In the year 29, in reply to petitions from cities and urban associations (*koiná*, 'provincial parliaments'), he drew an important distinction in terms of religious veneration between his father, the deified Caesar, and himself. He allowed the Roman inhabitants of Ephesos and Nikaia (Iznik) to venerate the deified Caesar in a moderate form of worship in a temple shared with the goddess Roma. Although the dictator thus still received divine honours by virtue of his office, and his reflected glory also fell on his son, attention was focused instead on a Roman state cult through the worship of the goddess Roma. Later, however, when Pergamon and Nikomedeia (Izmit) also asked permission to venerate his person, he allowed the creation of sacred precincts for himself only to non-Romans, and then only together with the goddess Roma, and forbade them to name him as a god. This form of worship was expressly not allowed to the Roman inhabitants of those cities.

The separation of Romans from non-Romans in the veneration of the living ruler also expressed itself very clearly in the organization of worship. Whereas the cult of Roma and Caesar was organized by the assembly (convention) of the Romans who lived in a province, the cult of Roma and Augustus was organized by the non-Romans, that is to say the Hellenes, who met in the parliament (*koinón*) of the province. Anyone who had attended a *gymnásion* of the Greek style counted as a Hellene, whether or not he was of Greek descent. The parliaments had begun to take shape in the winter of 30/29, when Octavian/Augustus, coming from Egypt, stopped in the eastern provinces, and the envoys of the *koinán* of the provinces of Asia and Bithynia asked him to allow them to set up a cult for him and Roma in Pergamon and Nikomedeia. The other provinces also introduced this form of the veneration of the Roman ruler, and the settlement remained in force under the successors of Augustus. The cult was institutionalized in a similar form everywhere: a temple was built, a priest of Roma and Augustus appointed, and every four years games were held, as both a festival and evidence of the loyalty of the 'peregrines' of the province. Other honours were paid to Augustus, all of them demonstrating a link to the *princeps* that was both personal and religious. In addition, many cities drew up a new calendar beginning the year with the day of the battle of Actium or the birthday of Augustus. In the year 10/9 BC, for instance, at the suggestion of the governor, Paullus Fabius Maximus, the *koiná* of Asia decided that the Hellenes of that province would begin the new year on Augustus' birthday and at the same time they adjusted the calendar to the Julian solar year. Although that calendar was not the same for all the cities in the province, it gave many of the provincials a new, Roman and monarchical framework for the course of the year.

Places for the veneration of Augustus were set up everywhere in the empire: in city centres and in rural districts. He was regarded as a divine figure, a benefactor of mankind and ruler of the world, and his cult very quickly took on a distinct shape. Specially appointed priests made solemn sacrifices and performed the other rituals connected with the cult. In Italy and the west they were called the priests of Augustus (*Augustales*) after Augustus himself, and over the course of time they came to include the living *princeps* in the cult in many places – not Rome itself, but in many Roman towns and cities. These priests were recruited from the ranks of freedmen and were inclined to form a group of their own in the cities. But the cult became established in the central sanctuaries of the empire as well as urban residential areas. For instance, in Olympia the Metroon, north-east of the temple of Zeus and within the *témenos* (the sacred precinct), was used as a place for the veneration of Augustus. The cult statue was a colossus, two and a half times as tall as a man, and represented Augustus in the attitude of Zeus, equipped with the god's insignia of sceptre and lightning bolts.

This religious policy enabled all the inhabitants of the empire to elevate the figure of the military potentate who had risen to the status of monarch. It bound the people of the provinces to Augustus and thus to Rome, at the same time linking the ruling class of Romans to the peoples below them. Careful as he was to respect the provincials, Augustus never questioned the political and legal precedence of the Romans themselves, and on an official level he wanted to ensure that the Roman people, as masters of the world, were set apart from those whom they ruled.

But the development of the concept of the ruler as divine very quickly led to the removal of the dividing line between Romans and provincials. Pressure came from below, from the cities of the provinces and even Italy, and there was an increasing willingness to yield to it, or at least not to work actively against it. In the year 3, for instance, the Greek and Roman population of a city in Paphlagonia, and soon after that the inhabitants of all cities in that province, took an oath at the altar of Augustus (and Roma), naming Augustus himself as one of the gods by whom they swore. Here as elsewhere, the initiative came from the people of the cities, not the Roman authorities, and the act of veneration was thus carried out without actual permission. If a request for such permission had been put to Augustus himself, he would certainly have turned it down and asked for a different, more moderate form of worship. However, if the people, Greeks and Romans alike, in an excess of veneration and to express their loyalty with particular force, honoured him in his absence as ruler and bringer of peace to the world, poured libations to him or actually called him a god, then Augustus did not forbid the honour shown to him after the event but left well alone. At no time was the cult of the ruler forbidden, particularly because in the Greek east – from which the custom had increasingly spread to the west and many centres of population in Italy – religious worship had been the form in which people communicated with their legitimate ruler ever since the time of Alexander the Great, and in the new political climate, after all, the Romans themselves did not want to be excluded from the general veneration of that ruler.

Augustus was not, like the kings and princes of the Hellenistic states, officially worshipped as a god. At no time was he a god of the Roman state and nor did he want to be. If he had really tried any such thing, or made it central to his strategy of rulership, he would probably have failed, as his adoptive father had. Both Roman tradition and his own view of the importance of religion in the Roman state made it incumbent on him to proceed with caution where divinity was concerned. Precisely because he was in fact human, the sacred aura around him worked on the basis of his link to the gods and their goodwill shown to him in countless signs and omens, whether they appeared as direct manifestations of divine approval or in the form of victory.

The various elements from which the close relationship of the ruler to the gods was constructed were, as we can see, of many different kinds, and there were also different groups of people on whom the different sacred aspects were binding. It was not the unity but the very diversity of the manifestations that was the crucial determinant in the development of a sacred superstructure. But however diverse their forms might be, in the end they built up into a whole that was part of the new form of rule: in future the monarchy was also religious in character, becoming more so as time went on and the forms it took were established. It therefore based its claim to legitimacy on the idea that the monarchy was elevated because it was sacred. A Roman contemporary would hardly have put it so simply; it was at odds with the other idea of the monarchy as a principate based on public law. But on many levels the people, particularly ordinary Romans who were not concerned with the legal foundation of the potentate's rule, perhaps were not even really aware of it, saw their ruler as sacred. This development gave Augustus sacred power as well as the divine nature that had already been officially honoured. Of course, he was not going to compete with Jupiter or Apollo; on the contrary, he showed particular reverence for all the gods as superior entities, expressing his veneration in sacrifices, dedications, petitions, gifts and expressions of gratitude. However, he still appeared side by side with the old gods as a new sacred manifestation, and although he was beneath them in his religious status, everyone could see that he was a part of the public rite of worship.

The variety of forms encouraging the idea of the ruler's supernatural nature, which was not defined as a god-like power, excluded and was meant to exclude any cult of his person. For the Romans, Augustus stood apart from and even outside the worship of the gods. Leaving aside his carefully constructed proximity to some of the individual deities, the ruler's relationship to the Roman gods was the same as that of any other citizen of Rome.

Although a sacred figure himself, Augustus was concerned with the general state administration of religion as a citizen, and in particular as the holder of official power. His activities in this sphere were of various different kinds and formed another specific aspect of his relationship with the gods. He was an object of veneration and at the same time a means of access to the gods who were to be venerated. Ever since its origins, the Roman state had felt that it was closely linked to the supernatural world in many different areas. The public sphere (*publicium*) and the religious area (*sacrum*) could easily be regarded as two faces of

the same coin. The major cults, headed by that of Jupiter Optimus Maximus on the Capitol, were state cults, meaning that their observance was
entrusted to official organs, and worship was incumbent on society as a
whole. The officers of state, the magistrates, therefore also had official
religious duties: they represented the city to the gods, asked for approval
of official acts, were present during the rituals of worship and dedicated
the buildings promised to gods on military campaigns or for other reasons. As well as the sacrificial priests, for instance the *flamens* and Vestal
Virgins, who performed cult ceremonies in the narrower sense, above all
during sacrifices, there was a whole series of priesthoods organized into
colleges, which, without being attached to one particular cult, were
responsible exclusively for organizing the relationship between the state
and the world of the gods.

Among the many colleges, four were particularly prominent. At the
head of the religious hierarchy were the *pontifices*, who exerted a kind
of supervision over religious activities and were responsible for many
separate tasks; then there were the augurs, specialists in interpreting the
divine will; the College of Fifteen for sacrificial rites (*quindecemviri sacris faciundis*); and finally the College of Seven (*septemviri*, also known
as the *epulones*), who, besides preparing the meal of the gods for Jupiter,
supported the *pontifices* in many ways. While the *pontifices* and the
College of Seven looked after administrative tasks in the religious area,
including the daily observance of the cult through sacrifices and other
ceremonial acts, the augurs and the College of Fifteen were notable for
the fact that they had a direct relationship with the divine world because
they asked the gods questions and interpreted the answers from signs.
The augurs were associated with the magistrates, who employed them
as experts in the questioning of the gods (taking the auspices) before
any official act. The Fifteen were the keepers of the collection of oracular sayings of the Sibyl of Cumae, which they consulted when required
to interpret unusual signs (prodigies) and for purposes of atonement
(*procuratio*); they were sometimes questioned by the Senate about the
meaning of an omen, and asked for advice on putting matters right. If a
cult was of Etruscan or Greek origin, the priests performed religious
ceremonies by the Etruscan or Greek rite. The priesthood of *haruspices*
was also responsible for questioning the gods and interpreting divine
omens. They questioned the gods by inspecting the livers of slaughtered
sacrificial animals and interpreted divine omens including bolts of

lightning. Their tasks arose from the Etruscan religion, and the rites associated with them were so strongly marked by Etruscan ritual that only those of Etruscan origin could carry them out.

All the priests were co-opted to their colleges for life. They formed no special caste in themselves but belonged to the distinguished families of Rome. The magistrates and priests were from the same social class, and, given that the public and religious spheres of life interacted so closely, that could not be otherwise if there was to be no disruption to the political arena, for religion was present in every official action, and if, for instance, there were bad omens or some reason for atonement, it intervened directly in political decisions. Rome had no distinct priestly caste with its own political dynamic based on particular religious views; the priests were always members of the ruling class, who sought to carry out their policies through priestly offices that were occupied by themselves, members of their families, or their friends. Taking on a priestly office was another form of public influence. Only a senator could fill a priestly position in one of the great priestly colleges, although men of equestrian rank could be priests in a whole series of smaller colleges, such as that of the 'wolf-men' (Luperci), who were responsible, in particular, for ceremonies of purification.

Because the great priestly colleges could cause obstruction and delays on all imaginable levels of political decision, Augustus had to be a part of the religious administration himself. In the age of the republic priesthoods, especially in the four great colleges, were fiercely fought for by the nobility, for they conferred political influence. Augustus aimed to prevent any such thing in future. Nor did he want the priests to be able to play politics with religion. However, the priests of the various colleges were not in a very good position to do that, for as administrators of the religious domain that had regulated relations between the gods and the state as they developed over the centuries they had to concentrate on the existing state of affairs rather than trying to reorganize or actually change it.

Mastering the intricate apparatus of religious administration obliged Augustus to consolidate his mastery of the political arena first. There could be no independent political will present in that quarter. Control over the colleges could best be achieved from within, that is to say by becoming a member of them himself. So Augustus belonged to all four main colleges; he was one of the College of Pontifices, into which the dictator Caesar had already introduced him in the year 48, and since the end of the forties he had also belonged to the College of Augurs. He became one of the College of Fifteen in around the year 27, and a good decade later he finally joined the College of Epulones. In addition he was a member of several of the smaller priestly colleges.

Augustus exercised his influence on the colleges not only through taking part in their meetings and performing priestly tasks; he also guided the elections to colleges and finally, after his return from the war against Antony and Cleopatra, he received the right to appoint priests beyond the usual number. The number of priesthoods had already been extended by the dictator, and now first Augustus and then his successors expanded it until no one could say just how many priests there were. The priesthood developed into a purely honorary office, while more and more often the *princeps* made the real decisions on his own. His influence on the priestly colleges and its political significance cannot be overestimated. Through it, he worked on the entire area of religious life so industriously that the will of the colleges could hardly be perceived behind his own.

The highest priestly office of all was regarded as that of the first among the *pontifices*, the *pontifex maximus*, who had unusually wide-ranging powers to intervene in religious life. For the dictator Caesar, that office had therefore been an important aid in his political rise. After his death, Lepidus was given the post as a political reward, and after he was excluded from the triumvirate Augustus did not strip him of it. He took the post himself only after the death of Lepidus in the year 12 BC. However, although that priestly office was formally supreme, Augustus did not actually need it in order to restore and complete the entire sphere of religious life, and so taking up the office did not mark any sharp change in his religious policies.

The basic principles of Augustus' rule were multifarious and were regarded by various individuals and groups in widely different ways. The recourse of the principate to the authority of the old Roman state, the 'republic', was directed mainly at the elite, but it also struck the right note with the distinguished men of the country towns of Italy and even the soldiers, who had always seen their commanders as magistrates, regarding their sworn duty as a purely personal affair only in the extreme situation of civil war. Religious factors had a stronger effect among the people of the Roman and provincial towns. For all the legal and religious legitimacy of the rule of the *princeps*, the links depending on the direct consensus of the holder of power and individual citizens or subjects were not lost, but might express themselves as military allegiance, political friendship, the obedience of a soldier or a relationship of dependence in which give and take alternated. All of these varied very much in intensity in both civil and military life. None of this was anything new; it had been in existence for centuries. Indeed, Roman society had always existed within this network of relationships. The only innovation was the steady and ever more distinct increase of such connections after the late republic, their concentration on individuals and their militarization. The future would show how, and how intensely, personal connections would influence the rule of Augustus as it had now been set up, and as it was continuing to develop. In what relation did they stand to the other elements in his rule? Did not making the army into a clientele, geared entirely to the holder of power, neutralize the ideas of the principate? Behind the fine façade of the old order of state that was now restored did there not still stand the menacing figure of the general who owed his power entirely to his soldiers?

# 9

# The Government of the Empire

So far as most Roman citizens and all provincials were concerned, the question of who held the power of government could be answered simply by reference to Augustus. He was the all-powerful commander of the army, the patron of countless men and cities, so consequently the administration and control of all imaginable areas naturally seemed to be his business and his alone. The term 'government', in this respect, means the exercise of actual power, leaving open the question of whether or not that power was legitimate. It glosses over the construction of the state as a principate, although the inclusion of the *princeps* in a group of leaders does address the issue of legitimacy. However, the nature of the principate as the legal constitution of the restored state, deliberately introduced by Augustus in the year 27 and revised four years later, cannot simply be ignored when we come to the question of who was responsible for controlling it. If the new constitution was not to be a farce, then government must stay within the framework of the new order, that is to say the Senate and the *princeps* must exercise power in it together. Moreover, the idea of Augustus as sole ruler of Rome, Italy and the empire takes no account of whether or not the *princeps* was objectively qualified to assume the administration of the world. After all, he had neither a bureaucracy nor governmental headquarters available to him, and it is hard to establish an administration without either of those. Nor was he surrounded by a 'court' that could have provided the staff for his administration, and indeed there was not even any tradition on which to base the idea of central government. In view of the construction of his rule as a principate, and of the opportunities for central control of the empire, Augustus could not therefore simply figure as the head of an 'imperial' government. He was not the master of the Roman state, and the state and the empire themselves were far from ready for central administration.

The reasons were to be found in tradition. In the time of the old republic, there had been no 'government' in the sense of a central administration for discharging state business. In fact such a thing was out of the question, considering the political prerequisites for government in the republican period. The Roman state and its area of command were controlled by the Senate, which turned to the assembly of the people when deciding on major regulations and applied to the magistrates, particularly the consuls, the legal authority of the praetors and the provincial governors to implement those decisions that were thought right and important. In fact, however, decisions were really made not by the Senate as an institution but by the authoritative group in it, the nobility. In so far as auxiliary staff were required to carry them out, the nobles resorted principally to their own households, and above all their freedmen and slaves. They did not need special experts, since they themselves were responsible for affairs of state, relying first and foremost on personal connections.

This form of government had suited a city state and thanks to the success of the nobility had been able to persist even after the expansion of the state into a larger territory. But once the area occupied by Roman citizens covered the whole of Italy, and Rome ruled the entire Mediterranean area, a city-state type of government was bound to break down. Italy and the provinces – the provinces in particular – were not really governed, only ruled, or alternatively left more or less to their own devices. Not only were the nobles incapable of governing all the citizens and subjects of Rome with proper attention to their welfare, they were not at all interested in doing so. They had the well-being of their own protégés most at heart, and even if motivated by some sense of wider interests, they would still have been unable to govern the world effectively. The old Senate, several hundred men strong, simply could not act as the head of a large bureaucracy, and a ruling clique of families could not provide an administrative centre. Ultimately rule by the nobility could not survive because of its structural inability to administer large areas. It was replaced towards the end of the republic by some of the individual noblemen who, although opposed by others among contemporaries, had succeeded in gaining control of large parts of the area under Roman rule. They thus left the circle of the nobility, so to speak, and concentrated the management of whatever district they now controlled in their own persons, a development that finally led to the militarization of all politics and ultimately – under the dictator Caesar and the triumvirs – to the total exclusion of the old nobility from the government of the world.

It had been the military potentates of the late republic and the triumvirate who had set up the nucleus of an administration in their own commands. Their administrative centres, however, were not essentially very different from the staff of servants and employees whom the magistrates, for instance the consuls, had employed to carry out their official tasks for them under the rule of the nobility. The only difference was that the number of staff thus employed had multiplied several times over. A group of friends and officers formed an advisory committee (*concilium*) called in to make important decisions. Tasks were performed and errands run by members of this group or by persons dependent on them (clients) from whatever local area was concerned, while freedmen and slaves from the personal households of the great men did the office work, in particular dealing with correspondence. In addition, holders of office were surrounded by a troop of armed 'bodyguards', not very large, but indispensable in military campaigns.

The dictator and the triumvirs increased the numbers of the administrative staff they employed, although without giving the institution a more distinct shape, let alone a new form. It was still much as it had been in the republican period. Above all, there were no local centres of government for the various districts – neither under the dictator, who was preoccupied for easily the greater part of his time with defeating his enemies, nor under the triumvirs, who after eliminating the murderers of Caesar also had to maintain their power, and to that end spent more time in the field than in the centres of the areas they ruled, whether those centres were Rome or Alexandria. Once Octavian had defeated his rivals, there were opportunities for change. After the establishment of the principate, the autocrat who had now become Augustus could devote himself more intensively to the tasks of government, and his long journeys in the west (27–24) and the east (22–19) can be regarded as the first significant step in ushering in a proper form of imperial administration. In fact the prerequisites for effective government do seem to have existed at the time: the nobility had been replaced by a military potentate who no longer needed to trouble about winning the support of contemporaries of his own rank. He was politically independent, and for the government and administration of the land he ruled he relied on a series of assistants whom he himself had chosen and whom he could easily dismiss again should the occasion arise. Some of them might belong to the old noble families, but they were still dependent on the commander of the army. Free of the pressure to compromise and negotiate with his equals, something that had determined all politics until now – and indeed had been its real object – the man who now held power could turn to the tasks confronting him in ruling an international empire. His concerns in foreign policy were security, and at home public confidence in the rule of law and the relief of social hardship among his subjects, whether they were Romans or provincials.

However, the change from a purely or mainly personal concept of government to a more objective one was not as smooth as might perhaps have been expected, in view of the political decline of the old elite, and to a large extent its physical dissolution. The concept of the principate itself stood in the way, the idea of a compromise between traditional and oligarchic forms of government. It was true that most of the nobility had disappeared, but new families had replaced them, men who might not have the social prestige of their predecessors but had given evidence of merit and had helped Augustus to victory. Now they expected him to secure their position in society. Augustus himself had them to thank for their support, and they would continue to be indispensable in helping him with the administration of the empire and the army. As former holders of the most important offices of state, posts they had held for several years or even decades, they occupied the highest ranks of the Senate. The concept of the principate made them the new political partners of Augustus. But did that mean that he really had to take them into consideration in coming to his own decisions? Did they oblige him to take those decisions, as in the republican period, within a complex interpersonal network, thus making himself dependent on it?

The great historian Theodor Mommsen did in fact present the situation in that way in his famous work on Roman state law. According to Mommsen, the principate entailed dual rule (a diarchy) by the *princeps* and the Senate, in which the administration of the provinces as well as of Rome and Italy was divided between them as partners in power. Few knew better than Mommsen that in point of fact the *princeps* was the master, but in the eyes of Augustus himself that was so only in reality, not in concept, and concept was the key. That being the case, and if the concept was really as Mommsen represented it – with the power of the *princeps* featuring as part of the traditional magistracy – the tension between concept and reality must be regarded as tension between the ideal of partnership and the reality of sole rule. To an extent this would be a partnership between comrades: Augustus was in theory the 'first among equals'. But the settlement of 13 January 27 and its revision in the year 23 did not fulfil the conditions for a partnership between *princeps* and Senate. Those settlements meant, instead, a change from what had previously been power only in fact to power also as legally understood and therefore as the titular rule of one man. This 'concept' was not of a power-sharing partnership, but of the participation of the new elite in the administration of the empire, with reference to traditional legal forms, and it involved securing the social standing of that elite.

That makes the principate not a diarchy but a monarchy, the rule of Augustus and his heirs. None the less Augustus in particular, as the first *princeps* and founder of the principate, had to consider the Senate in all the business of government, because in line with the concept of the new order it was formally responsible for the administration of Rome and Italy, as well as a good half of the provinces. Government was therefore difficult for him. It called for a sense of whether he could safely take a decision in spheres belonging to the Senate or whether he would do better to get the Senate to take it instead, either by petitioning the Senate himself or getting some third party to do it for him. And in addition, if a delegation from the Senate's provinces approached him, should he redirect it to the Senate for the sake of propriety or deal with the matter directly himself? Should he create a new office of the city of Rome and hold it himself, or should he leave that to the Senate? In every individual case the decision depended on the particular situation and subject; but a kind of working arrangement must soon have developed in which routine matters usually remained the business of the Senate, while decisions of principle in foreign policy and all administrative innovations were made by the *princeps*, even when the occasion for making them had arisen from an area under the Senate's administration. However, in that case too the *princeps* had to discuss his decisions, formally at least, with the Senate and gain its approval. For instance, when Augustus saw a new legal code for the province of Cyrenaica, one of the Senate's provinces, as desirable because of certain incidents, he decreed it himself by edict but had the matter discussed previously in the Senate, or least by a senatorial committee, and thus prompted the senatorial decision he wanted.

Governing the world in the spirit of the principate was the art of bringing what was politically necessary into line with the wishes of the senatorial elite, or rather, since that elite was the passive side of the relationship, of taking his own political initiatives with such moderation, and adjusting them to the idea of the order of the new state so well, that even while the Senate strove for its own security and political standing it took no offence, let alone felt forced into opposition. In all this the problem lay in the existence of two views of the public position of Augustus: one was his position as the senator first in rank and holding the highest powers of office (i.e. the *princeps*), and the other was his position as the man who did in fact hold power, particularly the power of military command (making him *imperator*). Both views were real in political terms and perceived by everyone as the reality. Keeping the balance called for great political tact and an unflagging will to ensure that the *princeps* did not take second place to the monarch. However, that very thing was difficult to achieve in practice, since it presupposed self-restraint, a virtue not necessarily to be assumed in an all-powerful ruler – which Augustus was. He knew, however, that it was exactly what his creation of the principate required, implying as it did the reconciliation of the senatorial aristocracy with the monarchy, and so he never tired of demonstrating a sense of proportion in public.

Countless examples could be cited. When Augustus left or returned to Rome, for instance after his long absence in Gaul in the year 13 BC, he quite often entered or left the city by night, so that no one would feel obliged to make a show of respect or loyalty. He often declined honours to his person proposed by the Senate. If he was then put under pressure to accept, as he was after his appointment to the office of high priest (*pontifex maximus*), he might rise abruptly from his seat and leave the Senate building. At meetings he would greet the senators individually in their places and he did not need a servant to whisper their names to him (a *nomenclator*) but addressed them all as his personal and familiar acquaintances. On leaving a meeting of the Senate, he said goodbye to the senators in the same way and did not expect them to rise for him.

Actions of this kind were public evidence of Augustus' wish to take the senators seriously as partners. In view of the flattery regularly shown to him – repellent instances of gross flattery had been rife under the dictator and the triumvirs – he must have meant it genuinely, and his conduct was not just calculation. Sometimes Augustus even went so far in this demonstration of prudent reserve that it became an obvious problem, for all the senators knew that they were not so much his partners, strictly speaking, as the recipients of his goodwill. Moderation displayed against a background of factual power could be misunderstood as the gracious evidence of favours granted to them. How was anyone to be sure whether, on some state occasion, the *princeps* was acting in line with the system of the principate or as a gracious monarch? How was Augustus himself to know? Fundamentally, the only real actions of the principate were negative, defining what should not be done; and the evidence of his moderate and exemplary conduct remained in the twilight zone between graciousness and duty. That was why Augustus and his successors did not question the ambivalence of their position. The attitude of the *princeps*, taking his guidelines from the concept of the principate in carrying out affairs of state, and expressed in many ways, appears in the abstract as the proper state of mind for a citizen (*civilitas*), and to behave as a citizen was thus the maxim of the principate in action: the ruler held power in partnership with the Senate.

The appropriate relationship under the new order between the first citizen and the senators had to be maintained in their practical work. According to the basic ideas of the principate, the Senate was the central institution of the state, the centre of government of the world, and during the forty years in which he guided the state as its *princeps* Augustus spared no pains to show all Romans that the Senate remained what it had been for centuries: the heart of the Roman polity. It was the source of the fundamental powers of the *princeps* as well as of all important decisions and official acts. As he did with individual senators, Augustus made sure that the institution of the Senate itself retained the dignity of the leadership of the state, and indeed he reinforced it in that capacity.

There were a number of measures designed to equip it for its tasks as the central political body. An important one was introduced in the year 9 BC, when its procedure was revised. The occasion for this was the very lax attendance at meetings, which were scheduled in a disorganized way. Regular days for meetings were now fixed, a quorum was prescribed, and an agreement was reached on occasions when a smaller quorum would suffice for decision-making. Precise regulations were also laid down for senators to send apologies for absence, and sanctions for overstepping the rules, and finally regulations were set out for senatorial decisions that could be made by the tribunes of the people or without the requisite quorum present. Although this procedure had yet to be ratified by the assembly of the people, the Senate itself adopted it, and Augustus was very anxious for all present at a meeting to be aware of the nature of the propositions before them, express their opinions and suggest possible corrections before an application was laid before the people for ratification.

In this way the Senate was made aware of its independence, or rather of a form of procedure that suggested independence. However, if the equilibrium between form and reality arising from the nature of the political situation was to be maintained, Augustus had to restrain himself in order to preserve the appearance of senatorial independence. In fact many of the senators sometimes acted on impulse and took liberties, and while they did not really believe that such conduct restored the situation that existed under the republic, they were at least testing the freedom of the formal relationship between them and the *princeps*. For instance, a senator might venture to call out to Augustus during a speech in the Senate that he did not understand him, or would contradict what he said if given the opportunity, or if Augustus continued to speak angrily after a heated argument there might be an indignant protest to the effect that he must allow the senators to speak on affairs of state. And Augustus let such remarks pass. He was not only showing his determination to put the ideas behind the principate into practice, but also demonstrating his now well-established authority, which enabled him to accept such conduct without impairing his status in any way.

For there was no doubt that Augustus was the stronger and more active partner in this situation, albeit he did not want to detract from the standing of the Senate as the central administrative organ, let alone belittle it. The efficacy of the Senate, and its dignity as formally the highest authority of the state and the empire, were and remained part of his policies as a whole, and without that the principate itself would have been something of a farce. In his late period of government, but before the year 4 BC, Augustus tried to make the discussion of motions more efficient. In a group 600 men strong, discussion was difficult, sometimes almost impossible, in practice. He set up a committee (*consilium*) of about twenty men to do the groundwork before senatorial decisions, consisting of one of the consuls, a praetor, an aedile, a quaestor and perhaps also a tribune of the people, as well as fifteen other senators chosen by lot. The committee, which was to remain in office for six months before handing the task on to another set of members, was obviously not made up of experts, since choice was by lot, but it was intended to present a cross-section of opinion in the Senate. In the year AD 13 its constitution was revised; the number of members chosen by lot was raised from fifteen to twenty, and the consuls designate also sat on it, together with Tiberius, already chosen to succeed Augustus, his son Drusus and his adopted son Germanicus. In future Augustus was also to be allowed to add further persons as he pleased, and the time for which a committee sat was extended to a full year. The decisions of the committee should be seen as preliminary votes, despite the contrary opinion of our source for these facts, which equates them with actual decisions in the Senate. The point of the committee was to make the Senate more effective and to establish the climate of opinion, but above all it was intended to take some of the pressure of the strain of meetings in the full Senate off the now ageing Augustus. In its revised version it was also intended to introduce his successor and that successor's sons to current affairs of state and involve them more closely in the process. But although the commission sped up the transaction of state business and made it more effective, it was dropped in later times. The reason may have been principally that the Senate, which after the introduction of the committee had virtually nothing to do but approve decisions already made, thus sank to the level of a mere rubber stamp and lost its reputation as the partner of the *princeps*; in the previous few decades, in fact, with the groundwork committee separated from it, it had been little more than such a ratifying body anyway, and once the committee and its decisions took precedence, it became that in form as well as in fact.

Augustus succeeded in giving the state and the empire a proper administration again. Even critical contemporaries not only perceived but approved and even praised the fact that laws were being passed once more, the law-courts were carrying out their duties properly, and taxes from the provinces came in without scandalous sums being embezzled. Augustus had pursued his aim thoroughly, persistently, and with a fine sense of what was necessary and feasible. Rome was already getting used to the smooth transaction of public business as the norm. Nor could anyone fail to see that he called on the assistance of the Senate in every aspect of the administration that he tackled. Year by year, about one-fifth of the senators were active in one official function or another, a sign of both the political significance ascribed to them by Augustus and the heavy workload carried by individual senators. The new order of the principate was visible here not just as a concept but in practice: the new elite – the senators of the time – shared the administration of the Roman state and empire with the *princeps*. And even if it was also clear that Augustus was master of them all, when he called on the senatorial class to ratify his actions they were taking part in government in reality, not just in concept.

Some might feel that the eagerness of Augustus to involve as many senators as possible in such duties was unwelcome, and it did allow his over-didactic element to emerge very forcibly at times. The senators did not like the way in which, as his biographer Suetonius tells us, he did not call upon them in a set order for their opinions on questions arising during Senate meetings but picked men to speak as it suited him, thus ensuring that everyone paid attention. They may even have seen a restriction of their independence in such practices. To be reminded of his duties, even in the spirit of what was presented as a revival of freedom and the 'republican' tradition, might make a man of distinction feel that the principate was showing its true face. What are we to make, for instance, of the fact that Augustus agreed to stand by a friend in the law-courts only after letting the Senate know in advance – much praise was lavished on him for that – and later, after the acquittal that was only to be expected, informed the man who had brought the charges that he bore him no grudge? It was his duty to defend a friend in court, yet in view of his monarchical position such support largely superseded an impartial decision by the judges. No tactical finesse or voluble explanations in the Senate and in public could really gloss over this conflict of interests. Much as Augustus aimed for the 'political correctness' of the principate, he was bound to appear to the senators as a monarch when he personally supported a friend in court, thus forcing his acquittal. And when he then rather theatrically forgave the accuser in front of everyone, did that not also imply that, by bringing a case against a friend of Augustus, the man was guilty of an offence requiring forgiveness? This was not the exercise of justice, which was in point of fact suspended by the intervention of the *princeps*. It was even less effective to suggest that liberty reigned by dint of ostentatious restraint. Augustus therefore devised a scheme whereby, when opinions were asked in the Senate, he would give his last so as not to restrict impartial discussion. That sounded good, but senators might still make desperate efforts to say whatever they thought might please the *princeps*. Freedom and monarchy are at odds with each other, and freedom cannot be decreed or cleverly enticed into existence. Decree or no decree, one way or another the same thing always happens: the general public bows before the man who holds power. The attempts of Augustus to keep the senators collaborating with him in an independent state of mind, however, were not pointless or in vain. They might be ineffective or awkward, but they still demonstrated again and again that the principate was not an autocracy. Instead, as a monarchy, it was a case of sole rule in accordance with certain norms.

Despite all the efforts of the *princeps* to behave correctly, a certain sense of resignation was soon felt by many of the senators. It was not because of a realization that any fundamental opposition to the system was doomed to failure; its origin did not lie in any rejection of the principate, but arose from their adjustment to it. It was now clear to many who had not yet understood it that the office of senator meant first and foremost service to the state – meaning service under the rule of the *princeps* – that it entailed a great deal of work and left almost no scope for a senator to put any ideas of his own into practice. If you had acquired a certain social standing, it was therefore advisable to spend your days at leisure, devote yourself to your own interests and for the rest just enjoy life. On a larger scale, however, such tendencies were visible only after the turbulence of internal struggles was over, when it became clear that the removal of political power from the Senate had not been merely a feature of the dictatorship of Caesar and then the triumvirs, but to a certain extent applied to the principate too. While it was not a case of rule by power alone, the principate was still a monarchy. For all their appreciation of present conditions, many must have wondered what the point of it all was. Those who thought like this included members of the old noble families, who lived with the memory of the glorious past, as well as capable men of lower birth whose fathers had proved their worth and risen in the administration, and of course first and foremost many opportunists who, giving way to every kind of pressure, were looking for the best *raison de vivre*.

The consequences of this development showed in the fact that there were no candidates for quite a number of civil service posts, principally, of course, those offices that had lost most in prestige under the new regime. They included the tribuneship of the people, once the most highly regarded position after the consulate, and also an office hallowed by tradition. Augustus soon found himself obliged simply to choose candidates by lot from among former quaestors, who in the normal course of a career were the first to spring to mind for the post. Later, when candidates still failed to come forward, he decreed that all magistrates holding office should propose a man of equestrian rank owning a fortune of at least a million sesterces (as required for the rank of senator), and then the people should choose the requisite tribunes from the list of proposals. In the year 5 BC, we are told, there were no candidates for the office of aedile. The aediles, among other duties, had to organize the great games held in the city. In spite of large state subsidies, these games could be expensive for an aedile and, if his games fell short of expectations, could also make him unpopular with the citizens. Augustus had no option but to resort to emergency measures again: he ordered the candidates for office to be chosen by lot from former quaestors and tribunes of the people. In fact the unwillingness of many young men to take such responsibility went so far that, although they came from a senatorial family, they did not want even one of the lowest-ranking offices, for instance membership of the Group of Twenty-six or the Group of Twenty, as a way to gain a seat in the Senate. Sometimes Augustus had to encourage members of the group just below the senators in rank, the equestrians or knights, to apply for these offices and finally he actually had to force senatorial rank on the younger members of senatorial families, men under the age of thirty-five, so long as they had the requisite fortune and were not disabled. The fact that there were not always enough senators present at meetings meant more difficulties for the work of the Senate. That had also, it was true, been a problem in the days of the republic, and so for certain meetings a quorum had been established. Augustus fell back on that precedent. In the year 11 BC he decreed that the quorum required for all meetings, 400 senators, two-thirds of all members, could be lowered for taking certain decisions. The revision of the conduct of Senate business, mentioned earlier, also served to force senators to attend.

None the less, where the new form of administration was concerned, even critics admitted that its positive aspects predominated, especially as it was clear that Augustus did not want to set up any rival to the senatorial group in the shape, perhaps, of a social rank to which he would give preference. Later emperors did create a new branch of the administration drawn from the knights or equestrians (*equites Romani*), described today as the 'imperial administration' to distinguish it from senatorial holders of office, and Augustus must certainly have thought of doing something similar. He would have been able to draw support in the administration above all from those of equestrian rank, where no rivals to him could have arisen, as they might among senators of distinction, and whose ambition and wish to rise would have been even more useful to him. And he did draw on the equestrian class again and again, in particular for politically sensitive tasks. For instance, the governor of Egypt and the commander of the legions stationed there were knights, because Augustus had to ensure that the governor of the richest province in the empire was no threat to him. Similarly he appointed commanders of equestrian rank, usually with the title of prefect, for military areas that, until they were entirely pacified, had special administrative units similar to those of a province, such as the Rhaetian and Vindelician area, or for smaller provinces such as Judaea. He also recruited the commanders of his bodyguard from among the knights, as well as the higher financial civil servants, for whom this was particularly advantageous because the financial administration, as we shall see, was to be regarded largely as part of the personal services linked with the household of the *princeps*. In addition some new offices, with functions mainly to do with expenditure, were filled by knights. In all Augustus created over thirty high-ranking offices for men of equestrian rank, apart from those with moderate ranking. None the less, the proportion of equestrians in the higher service of the state was not on the whole conspicuously large, particularly as their functions did not conflict with those of the senators except in rare cases, for instance the high offices of state in Egypt.

For Augustus, the most difficult aspect of ruling the empire lay in appointing men to the high offices, particularly in the administration of the army and the provinces. In this area, for one thing, personal suitability had to be considered, especially such qualities as reliability, expertise and a man's ability to assert himself, but so too did a candidate's merits and social skills, so various interests had to be carefully weighed up in every individual case. Close friends on whom Augustus knew he could count had a claim to special consideration, and so did capable new men whose status as part of the younger nobility was a guarantee of their loyalty. Nor could men of the old nobility feel they had been overlooked, or the sons of the 'new men', who had grown up absorbing the lifestyle and thinking of the families of the old nobility and formed a self-contained society with them. Then there were special achievements to be honoured and personal connections to be borne in mind. In every appointment, the suitability of a particular candidate for a certain military command or province had to be taken into account, so that his abilities could be put to the best use, and it must all comply with the requirement of the *princeps* himself for security. On the one hand, loyalties that might endanger Augustus should not be allowed to form because a man was left in command over a province or an army for too long a time. On the other hand, suitable men must be chosen for whatever task was concerned. It is not surprising that the nobles of the old families were over-represented in highly regarded provinces where there were no standing armies, while the administration of most of the provinces where strong military contingents were stationed, and the more recently acquired territories, was entrusted to men of the new nobility. Augustus had the knack of choosing the men he needed. He saw society as a levelling force standing above all partisanship and jealousies. And whenever, despite that, discontent or actual hostility developed, the system of appointments as a whole was well enough balanced that no group formed a unified resistance, even though the *princeps* was entirely on his own in exercising the art of maintaining a balance between domination and partnership. Neither Agrippa nor Maecenas had a strong sense of the necessity of this balancing act. Augustus, on the other hand, was or became a master of the art and conveyed a sense of it to those around him and through his daily practice. In a process lasting decades, his finely honed personal policy ultimately came to be acknowledged as a kind of new set of regulations; to infringe them could be registered as an offence against good order.

Government by the monarch affected three different territorial areas: the part that Augustus had kept at his own disposal in the settlement of the year 27, namely the provinces allotted to him and already known as the imperial provinces; the area that had been allotted to the Senate and was known as the senatorial provinces; and finally the city of Rome and Italy, which were administered by the Senate and Augustus together, or rather administered with an eye to what Augustus himself wanted. The administration of the empire as a whole, whether controlled by Augustus or the Senate, was at first still carried out in the form that had developed during the republic. Its outstanding feature was the absence of any bureaucratic apparatus, which could not have been constructed under the republic if only because of the aristocratic practice of rule, and which also seemed unnecessary because over the previous three centuries it had been possible, in most of the Roman-occupied territories, to rely on the cities and their administrations for support. In so far as Rome had any central tasks to be performed which, like tax-gathering, could not be carried out by the towns and cities of the empire, they had been entrusted to private men or various kinds of private bodies. The intolerable drawbacks of this practice, as felt by those affected, had been accepted. They included the acquisitive selfishness of the permanently or temporarily appointed nobles, as well as the Roman tax-farmers and merchants. There was no alternative at the time, not only because of the close relationships of members of the noble ruling class but also in their many connections with the tax-farmers and merchants to whom tasks on behalf of the state had been entrusted. Even at the beginning of the principate, in spite of the gradual dissolution of the old nobility, there was still no alternative, because no other form of governmental organization was known, and in any case no one yet saw any need for one. So the Roman administration continued to depend principally on the existing organs of administration, state business was leased out to private individuals, and the governors and their staff confined themselves to controlling those to whom the state had handed the task.

Initially, for all these reasons, Augustus could carry out the administration of his own provincial area with a relatively small staff. The administration was comparatively easy to handle. He picked his governors, the propraetorial legates (*legati Augusti pro praetore*), without reference to the Senate, guided only by his personal judgement, and after the year 27 he hardly resorted at all to the old noble families but gave preference to men of lower birth who had risen through his patronage and had proved their worth. As his deputies, they could easily be controlled during their period of governorship. They could be replaced by other men as he pleased or could continue in office after the deadline of a year, and he left many of them in place for several years. One such was Gaius Poppaeus Sabinus, grandfather of the emperor Nero's wife, who was legate of Moesia from 11/12 BC until the death of Augustus, and continued to hold that office for another twenty years under Tiberius.

In Rome, the task of the central administration of the 'imperial' and 'senatorial' areas alike consisted, for one thing, in mandating provincial administration (*mandatum*) to the governors, who carried out all the business affecting their provinces. In general, apart from certain local peculiarities and innovations, it was the same for all of them. There were also many applications that governors passed on to the *princeps*, petitions from cities or from private persons to be dealt with, including requests for decisions in legal matters where the governor, in the opinion of some other party, had not made a just decision, or those for which he was not responsible. Naturally Augustus sometimes intervened himself in the interests of a province. But he was then, or at least in the majority of cases, reacting more to an application from that province than as head of an administration acting on his own initiative. The system did not allow anything else, and so initiatives generally came from below.

In two areas, however, the central administration was the really active party, and here at the same time, contrary to traditional practice, there were some innovations. These were in the administration of the troops stationed in the provinces, and the management of the private property of Augustus himself, which consisted mainly of landed estates. Augustus paid special attention to the administration of the army. He had learned his lesson at the time of the triumvirate and knew what he must reckon with if the soldiers' pay did not come up to expectations, or discontent spread in the ranks for some other reason. Here the main task and the main burden were in the appointment of officers. This was always done by the central administration, because if distinguished men of merit were ignored in favour of men of less worth, the potentially explosive aspect of such appointments might endanger the stability of Augustus' personal rule. Hardly less important, and in some cases even more so, was to ensure supplies to the army and navy, principally the former, and in the army first and foremost to the Roman legionaries. As well as the supply of weapons and material for the army's daily needs, there was the pay of serving soldiers and officers, as well as provision for the later years of those being discharged. Army pay came out of income; the pensions, however, were separate, and naturally the soldiers took a particular interest in them, for when they were discharged from military service they did not go into retirement – they were only around forty by then – but embarked on a second career and they needed security in taking it up. Augustus paid the bill ultimately by creating a special 'military treasury' (*aerarium militare*) for the soldiers, and when it was set up in the year AD 6 he paid 170 million sesterces into it. High as it was, however, this sum was not enough. So the income from a 5 per cent tax levied on large inheritances and legacies and a 1 per cent tax on valuables sold at private auction also went into the fund. In addition, it received special contributions. At the same time Augustus was industriously seeking other sources of money. He was glad to receive donations from client princes, cities or other organizational entities, but he excluded private sources of finance. In the eyes of the soldiers he had to remain the only provider of money; and no second name was to be linked with his, for the sponsor who came up with the money was the patron of the army.

Making the management of his private fortune an affair of state was an innovation on the part of Augustus, in that for the first time the highest-ranking man in the state was creating a long-term or indeed permanent form of administration tailor-made for his person. It was called the *patrimonium*, 'fortune of the father', but in spite of the clear reference in that term to the private area it was regarded from the first not as a purely private possession available for testamentary disposition. That, in particular, was because the public financial assets and incomes of Egypt, in the tradition of Hellenistic rule, were regarded as private possessions. So were the mines, at least in the provinces administered by the *princeps* himself. The *patrimonium* as an institution in public law showed for the first time, and particularly clearly, that the *princeps*, who was equipped with full power in many official positions, was only partially in charge of his private sphere of action. His person and property were of a public character; the *princeps* would never again be able to retreat into a purely private area. His house on the Palatine Hill, as he himself never tired of pointing out, was not a private refuge but belonged instead, and in a special way, to the sphere of public life. Hardly any other feature of the principate illustrates its monarchical character more clearly. Gradually, and under Augustus not yet perceptibly, the Romans began to see the private and personal property of the *princeps* (*res familiarius*), which could be left in his will, as distinct from his property as a whole.

A new type of official was created for the administration of this private fortune: the procurator (*procurator*), and holders of that office were to have a great future in the imperial period. The name in itself shows that it was in the private sphere, for the idea was that the procurator was administrator of the property of a private person; only because he was in charge of the property of the *princeps*, a post situated between the public and the private areas, did he acquire a public character. Augustus chose his procurators, as those bearing his personal commission, from citizens who were close to him or to members of his immediate family. Many were up-and-coming men from the Italian cities, such as Publius Vitellius from Luceria in Apulia, grandfather of the later emperor Vitellius. Most, however, were freedmen.

The procurators looked after their master's property in all the provinces except those directly under the control of Augustus himself. Their dependence on him – for a freedman who committed a grave offence against the man who had freed him or against his heirs could be returned to slavery – seemed to reduce any danger of the misuse of office, and their personal closeness to the man who gave them their posts made their control of the business entrusted to them easier. Such will indeed normally have been the case, but there was no lack of corrupt elements, and Augustus displayed patience sometimes bordering on complicity towards the corrupt, and towards many of his close friends. The freedman Licinus, appointed procurator of Gaul, was notorious. A Celt taken prisoner in war, he had already served the dictator, who freed him because of his business acumen. Augustus had then taken him on. Licinus, an arrogant man who craved recognition, squeezed his old countrymen the Gauls outrageously, but although their complaints finally came to public notice Augustus supported his man in spite of his obvious flaws of character, perhaps because Licinus cleverly presented himself in a good light by contributing generously to the erection of various buildings, and because Augustus intended at least a part of the property he had acquired to go back to the state in the end. The structure of the procurators' tasks depended on the province. Smaller provinces, however, and those in which Augustus had little property, were combined in a single authority, so that the *patrimonium* in his day kept barely more than twenty procurators busy at any one time. The income from the *patrimonium* was, incidentally, considerable, and provided Augustus with large sums.

In principle the same work had to be done in the provinces administered by the Senate as in those under Augustus, but the military aspect was largely absent because there were fewer troops stationed there, and most of those provinces had no troops in them at all apart from small contingents of guards for the governors. Similarly, as already pointed out, the administrative process of the 'senatorial' provinces was different in several respects from that of their 'imperial' counterparts. The reason was that the Senate, as a body several hundred men strong, could form no effective focal point, unlike the person of Augustus: the political emphasis shifted, and the great mass of administrative work from the senatorial provinces was transferred to the responsibility of the *princeps*. And there was something that weighed even more: every new norm could arise, in the provinces no less than in Italy, only from the centre of real power, a point from which the whole situation could be surveyed. If, for instance, a new legal code was set up somewhere, then it also had to be introduced wherever similar conditions and requirements existed, in the same or a related form, regardless of whether a province was under Augustus or under the Senate.

If it became particularly clear in setting up new norms that the *princeps* was a rival authority in the Senate's provinces, he would in fact prove to be the sole military authority responsible there. In Africa, for instance, a senatorial province, the legion that had to be stationed there because of the steppe and desert tribes was under the command of Augustus. Above all, however, the division of provinces between the Senate and the *princeps* established in the year 27, depending on whether provinces were pacified or 'still endangered', by no means indicated that whenever there happened to be unrest in a 'pacified' senatorial province the Senate and its provincial governor took military action. In such cases, the province might go over temporarily to the command of the *princeps*, as for instance in the year AD 6, when Augustus took over Sardinia for several years because of the pirates there, sending a prefect of equestrian rank to the island as his military commander.

Meanwhile the formal division of provincial business between the Senate and Augustus also led, in some areas, to innovations in the administration in general. Here, above all, we must bear in mind the duplication of state treasuries. The income from the Senate's provinces and the indirect taxes from Italy went into the old treasury known as the *aerarium*, called the *aerarium Saturni* because it was located in the cellar vaults of the temple of Saturn, while taxes and other dues from the Augustan provinces were to be paid into a new treasury, the *fiscus Caesaris*. There was a tendency to pay income from many good sources into this *fiscus* even if it really belonged to the Senate. The *aerarium* quite often suffered from acute financial shortages and needed the help of Augustus, and not only in the early days of the principate, when the state was still suffering from the after-effects of the unhappy triumvirate period. Four times, according to his own account, Augustus gave the Senate large sums amounting in all to 150 million sesterces. In addition he took a leading part in the administration of the treasury, though no doubt not without the consent of the Senate. So on his initiative the treasury, which had hitherto been in the hands of the quaestors, was entrusted in the year 28 to two men from the group of former praetors (praetorians) and five years later to two full praetors. All this shows that the financial administration of the Senate's provinces was also controlled by Augustus. It is not surprising to find that he alone had a good idea of the financial situation of the state, and the financial accounts of the entire empire were kept at his centre of operations. When he was severely ill in the year 23, he had given the consuls notes on the financial position at the time (*rationarium imperii*, 'the accounts of the empire'), and similarly the extensive writings he left for the Senate and his successor included a survey of all the funds then present (*breviarium totius imperii*), the property in his direct administrative area as well as that of the Senate's treasury and the credit balance in tax owing.

The transition from aristocratic to monarchical rule in practice entailed some radical changes for the citizens of Rome and Italy, and for the subjects of the provinces of the empire. Although the Senate had already been the governmental centre during the republican period, political power at the time had really been wielded by the families of the nobility, and implementing their decisions had been left to what, by comparison with the new state of affairs, was a rather small group of officials. But although the most urgent tasks had been dealt with in that way, control of the administration as a whole had not been entirely satisfactory, and

sometimes opposing interests among the nobles had led to their working against one another. An aristocracy cannot build up and manage a
bureaucracy, and so those in power, particularly the cities but also private men, had generally resorted to pre-Roman forms of organization in
order to get the necessary official business done. The reason for mismanagement under the republic did not therefore lie, as contemporaries
often claimed, in the decline of its ethos, but in the structurally limited
resources on which the administration of large areas could call. Only a
few men had developed a talent for administration and a sense of
responsibility towards those they ruled, and in so far as a Roman,
particularly a member of the leading families, mingled with other, less
highly placed Romans or provincials of non-Roman origin, showed any
interest in them and was ready to help them, his commitment was usually to those who depended on him, his clients. To have a clientele was
evidence of a nobleman's personal power and social influence, which
meant that supporting it served to maintain his own political standing.

This changed under Augustus. And as his administration covered not
only the 'imperial' provinces, but in practice and through direct intervention those of the Senate as well, the change affected more or less all
inhabitants of the empire. None the less, it was perceived only gradually, and more clearly in some areas than others. That was to do not
just with the fact that Augustus set particular store by certain branches
of the administration, but also with the way in which centralization
changed its entire structure.

It is obvious that the *princeps* took the greatest interest of all in the
administration of the army and the fleet. The necessity of controlling
them himself arose from the significance of the armed forces for the
ruler's own security. Management of the army had previously been
entirely unknown as a section of the administration; those in the army
and navy, with the exception of a few troops of guards assigned to the
magistrates, had always been discharged as soon as their military task
was performed. Soldiers were militiamen; there was no standing army.
Armies serving for any length of time did not appear until the extraordinary military commands of the late republic, and this development
continued apace during the triumvirate. The civil wars and the great
foreign campaigns undertaken by the triumvirs, to train their soldiers
and reinforce their loyalty, called for bands of men who could operate
in the long term and could not be fully discharged if their commanders

wanted to maintain power. So if we look at the relationship of Augustus to the army, the principate proves the immediate successor to the military despotism of the triumvirate. Augustus could not do without legions standing ready under arms if he did not want to risk bringing a rival on the scene. The management of the army, therefore, was both a new branch of the administration and the most important one of all. However, I shall return separately to that subject.

The administrators themselves, and those they were dealing with, could expect that with the monarchy the principles of the practice of government would change. Provincials in particular hoped that the change would go hand in hand with a general improvement to their situation, which could only be described as dismal after the endless civil wars, while their experience had also been poor under aristocratic rule. At that time the reasonably benevolent – or at least merely orderly – administration of a province seemed worth mentioning, if not very hopefully, because exploitation and oppression by the governors and their staff as well as those to whom tax-gathering was farmed out seemed to be the norm. But for that very reason even a monarch who wanted to exploit the resources of the provinces could not, it was thought, be quite as bad as the nobility or the triumvirs, and, if nothing else, at least it might be hoped that he would keep the tax-gatherers under control. Only now, in fact, had it become possible to rule and manage the provinces properly, with some consideration for the lives and security problems of their people, and only an administration that was not based solely on domination, but also took account of welfare or at least did not exclude it, could create the conditions for anything like a sense of responsibility, at the same time bringing the ethical background of provincial rule into focus. In the Roman mind, the idea of welfare for the socially weaker was linked to the ideas of patronage which provided protection and security for those who attached themselves to a patron. Cicero had already described the just and equitable activity of the Senate and magistrates in the provinces as a 'mission to protect the world' (*patrocinium orbis terrae*). In practice, however, it was not like that, and so even under the republic the people of the provinces, well knowing that the Roman authorities gave them nothing like adequate protection from exploitation, were already trying to gain individual noblemen as their patrons. Now, in the new circumstances, the *princeps* was the only man who could offer them secure protection. In future, he had 'protective rule over the world', and so the provincials sought his favour. Of course he himself also required one and all to take their guidelines from his person, not least because he was bound to see the old patronage of the nobility as a rival to the omnipotence that he claimed. With that aim in view, he even forbade senators to travel in the provinces without his express permission – the only exception being Sicily, where many of them had long had close contacts and owned extensive tracts of land – and although patronage on the part of many highly regarded senators continued, the influence of the old families or of new rising men was always countered in this way. At the same time, what was largely a monopoly of patronage required the *princeps* to show greater responsibility to his subjects. Patronage did not just demand obedience from clients, it also called on the patron to do the duties he had undertaken.

The provincials' first experiences of sole rulers had not been happy. The dictator and the triumvirs, latterly including Octavian, had ransacked the provinces out of a sheer instinct for self-preservation. Who else was going to pay for their wars with each other and against real or imagined enemies of the empire? But that had been in times of war. The *princeps* had brought peace, and he never tired of keeping that fact in the public eye. In so doing he seemed to have satisfied the most important prerequisite for the welfare of the provinces, perhaps to have ushered in their welfare already. At the same time, it was up to him to justify Roman rule to the inhabitants of the provinces. Cicero, looking at the Greeks of Asia Minor, had already regarded subservience and tribute as the price paid by the provincials for peace, a price that he thought by no means too high for the Greeks, who had fought each other endlessly and ought to have been paying tribute earlier. The Pax Romana meant not just a short interruption in an endless chain of wars, as it had at the time of Greek independence, but the lasting peace of the whole world. It seemed to mean the same as the good fortune of a Golden Age. And no one could deny that for all those who were part of the Roman empire, the 'Roman peace' of which Cicero spoke had really begun under Augustus.

So the patronage of one man over all or at least most of the inhabitants of the empire and the public assurance of peace after the end of the civil wars created the necessary conditions for a considerate administration. There were no revolutionary changes. It was more a case of keeping close control over the existing order, although new forms of administration did in fact emerge, particularly in respect of tax-gathering. Romans and provincials alike were soon aware that a sharper eye was now being kept on both the central Roman authorities and the private tax-farmers who gathered state income. The concentration of power in one man did away with a diversity of individual interests and focused the entire attention of the administration on a single point. The dependence of a holder of office, for instance a governor, on a central authority restricted his opportunities of enriching himself unsupervised. It was now difficult for him to get his hands on more money than the sum allowed since republican times as his expenses. Instead, the new group of financial trustees (the procurators) appointed by Augustus received a fixed sum from the start, more like a salary in the modern sense than compensation for the expenses that they had to incur. The business of the administrative officers, in particular the governor and his representatives, thus became clearer and easier for Romans and provincials alike to calculate, observing the legal requirements was easier, and the threshold of difficulty when anyone wanted to make a complaint through administrative channels was lower. Making administrative decisions taking into account not only Roman interests but also those of the other party concerned thus became a basic principle of Roman administration, and although that had really always been the theory, only now did it become a part of administrative reality in practice. 'In addition the voice of allies affected [i.e. the people of the provinces] shall be heard,' decreed Tiberius in the year AD 23, when he was *princeps* and a complaint was laid against a financial administrator in the province of Asia. Arbitrary acts on the part of the magistrates were a thing of the past.

But as well as the keener supervision, a more fundamental change in tax-gathering also relieved the burden on the procurators and brought more justice into the fiscal system. Particularly important was the taking of a census for each province. The census was to form the basis for the rate of taxation. Earlier, of course, the cities and the governors of the provinces, in particular those of long standing such as Sicily, had lists of landed properties and other items of value, on which the amount of tax to be levied was based. But now the entire register was revised by state officials, standardized and brought into line with the latest state of affairs, for instance where changes in financial circumstances were concerned, or in the quality of the items on which taxation was based.

Farming out taxes, which in principle still existed under Tiberius, was no longer decided in Rome by the censor but on the spot by state authorities, mainly procurators, and they also supervised the process. The census was brought up to date province by province, and repeated if necessary. For instance, Augustus held the first census in the part of Gaul conquered by Caesar, Gallia Comata, when he went there in the year 27, and his stepson Drusus, as governor, repeated the census fifteen years later.

The reform and supervision of the tax-gathering system quickly brought the provinces perceptible relief from the oppressive burden of their dues and justice in the allocation of those dues, something that had long been desired. If the political change was to be regarded as the result of a system of administration that now depended on the ruler alone, it also brought with it new institutions in other areas that proved beneficial for the inhabitants of the provinces.

Probably the most important innovation concerned the system of complaints within the legal process. It was now easier, under the rule of the *princeps*, for individual subjects or cities to make petitions or complain to the central power. As all the governors of the 'imperial' provinces held a mandate, that is to say they were not independent but were acting on behalf of Augustus, it was now simpler to lay a complaint against orders issued by the provincial authorities, or to apply for help to the central ruling authority through administrative channels. In addition, the conditions were created for a revision by the supreme authority (the mandator, i.e. Augustus) of judgements made by lower authorities. In the republic, every governor had been a magistrate himself, and his judgements and decisions had been final. At that time the only recourse had been through complaint to the Senate by sending envoys, a tedious and expensive business, or through the influence of a powerful patron if there happened to be one available. Now in principle anyone, Roman citizen or not, could object to the decision of the governor or some other holder of public office by appealing to Augustus, as the origin of all magisterial power, and the subject of a senatorial province who was dissatisfied with measures taken by its governor could pursue the same course. Augustus, as the holder of tribunician power, could veto even official actions on the part of the magistrates in the city of Rome, including judges, and thus extend the possibility of objection to the entire system of justice in the city. Since an appeal for a new investigation of the case concerned had been made to Augustus, his judgement not only superseded the verdict of 'first instance', but could also change it, that is 'reform' it.

Soon the number of appeals grew to such proportions that the *princeps* could not deal with them all himself. Consequently he had to appoint a senator of consular rank to each province as his representative, while he delegated answering appeals from those Romans living in the capital who turned to him to the praetor responsible for civil affairs among Romans (the *praetor urbanus*). It is true that the 'reformed' appeal system now possible developed only slowly into a fully fledged official channel, but the foundation stone had been laid. Incidentally, the construction of that official channel, as we see it in the period of the late imperial empire, was the model for our modern system of appeals.

The cities and tribes of the provinces could breathe again. The Greek communities of the east in particular, who still retained a very distinct awareness of their former independence or even glory, and thus found it hard to bear subjection to a humiliating system of government and any kind of injustice, thought that better times lay ahead under Augustus. He himself did his part by showing them special esteem, respecting their traditions and allowing them a sense of internal independence, indeed a certain political importance. In addition, the *princeps* proved a generous benefactor. He helped cities in misfortune, for instance Tralleis in the valley of the Meander (close to modern Aydın), when it suffered an earthquake in the year 25, and in the east and the west alike he was a patron of architecture, for instance in Corinth, where he had a temple built to his sister Octavia after her death, and in Athens, where he followed his adoptive father in laying out the new, Roman agora, while Agrippa built a great Greek theatre, the Odeion, on the site of the old agora. There were grounds for new hope: peace and the respect on the part of the ruler for the great past of the Greek cities had an uplifting effect and brought the Greeks to agree voluntarily to the new state of affairs. Not only the *princeps*, his subjects too praised the blessings of this new age and found ways of expressing it, as did the council of the city of Halicarnassus in Asia Minor. Even taking into account the council's florid style of eulogy, its praise still tells us something about the basic mood of the time: 'For the eternal and immortal world order, to the great benefit of mankind, brought Caesar Augustus as the greatest benefit, ensuring a happy existence. The father first of his homeland, divine

Rome, he thus became paternal Zeus and saviour of the whole human race, not only fulfilling but even exceeding the wishes of all in his care for them. There is peace on land and on the seas, the cities flourish under just government through inner harmony and well-being; there is a wealth of all goods, and human beings are inspired by great hope for the future, and are of equally good courage in the present.'

A governmental headquarters with such extensive tasks as envisaged by Augustus required a central point from which orders were to be issued and all lesser authorities were to take their guidelines. The house of Augustus has been seen as such a place. He moved into it as a triumvir, after living previously on the Forum Romanum. His new home on the Palatine Hill lay on a site sloping to the south or rather the south-west and falling towards the cattle market (the Forum Boarium) and the Circus Maximus. At its heart was the former house of the famous orator Quintus Hortensius. Extended by the addition of several adjoining plots of land, as time went on it grew into a complex of some size comprising, as well as the rooms and courtyards now described, in the narrower sense, as the House of Augustus, the so-called House of Livia as well as the rest of the site, where the temple dedicated to Apollo and the buildings belonging to it also stood. Even later the complex as a whole was never entirely built over, although in the end it fell into decay. In particular, the huge palace that the Emperor Domitian built at the end of the first century AD deliberately spared it. Although it went out of use, the House of Augustus, as we can tell from the remains still to be found, was preserved by the piety of his successors in the same state as when its first and only occupant lived there. At least, modern excavations have uncovered large parts of the ground-plan, although the architecture erected on it, including upper storeys, can be only fragmentarily reconstructed.

Although the two complexes now described as the Houses of Augustus and Livia are not small – the House of Augustus alone is 150 metres wide and 80 metres long – and we also have to add several rooms that have not yet been excavated or have been entirely destroyed, it is not easy to see these buildings as the centre of government for an international empire. It is also difficult to be sure whether some rooms were of a public or a private character. To the south, near the entrance to the temple of Apollo, an epistyle can be made out, with a small atrium

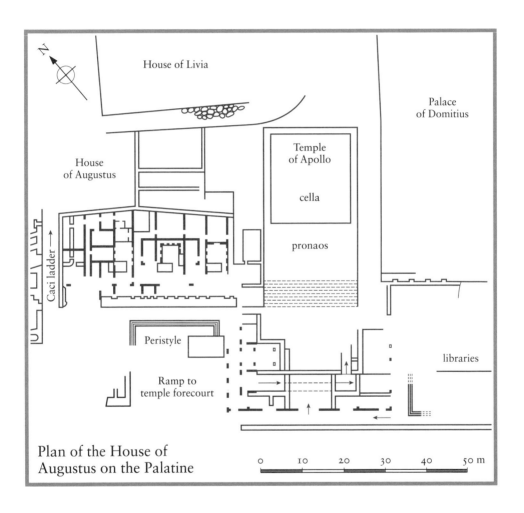

House of Livia

Palace
of Domitius

House
of Augustus

Temple
of Apollo

cella

pronaos

N

Caci ladder →

Peristyle

Ramp to
temple forecourt

libraries

Plan of the House of
Augustus on the Palatine

0    10    20    30    40    50 m

around the upper part of which the rooms were arranged. Perhaps one small room can be identified as the room, mentioned by Suetonius in his biography, to which Augustus retired when he wished to be alone. Suetonius also knew how modestly the whole building was furnished. According to his account of it, the columns of the house were made of tuff stone, and there were no long pillared halls or other architectural features made of marble, nor any magnificent mosaic floors. Augustus did not deny his rural origins, and nor did he change the lifestyle of his forefathers; indeed, he emphasized it. In summer and winter alike, we are told, he slept in the same bedroom, and his bed, the rest of the furniture and even the household utensils were apparently Spartan in their simplicity. And although we cannot, of course, apply the remarks of Suetonius to all parts of the complex of buildings, there were undoubtedly more magnificent houses even in its immediate vicinity. Augustus did not like large palaces. Perhaps he was happy to have his way of life compared to that of the owner of a small country estate.

Yet Augustus did set great store by the fact that this house, being his residence, also had something of the same political aura as surrounded its owner. It was not only the integration of the temple of Apollo into the complex that elevated the importance of the site. The building lay on the eastern side of the Steps of Cacus (*scalae Caci*) leading up from the 'Cattle Market' to the Palatine and was not far from the place regarded as the house, or hut, inhabited by Romulus on the other, western side of the Steps. Like the name of Augustus, denoting the distinction of the man who bore it, the proximity of his house to the dwelling of Romulus seemed to emphasize the link between the *princeps* and the founder of the city, and indeed the fact that it was close to the hut of Romulus was thought to have played a considerable part in the decision of Augustus to buy Hortensius' house.

In later years, Augustus deliberately encouraged the idea that his house had the character of a sacred and public building. Not only were the two doorposts garlanded with laurel by the senatorial decree issued to celebrate the settlement of January 27, but when Augustus became high priest on the death of Lepidus in 12 BC he moved the location of the priestly office, hitherto a small building in the Forum called a 'regia', to his own house, and thus made part of the place a state building. The character of the house as a mixture of private dwelling, head office and seat of the gods, all inextricably mingled, was further reinforced when by senatorial decision a statue and altar of Vesta were set up there, turning the worship of that goddess, regarded at the time mainly as a deity protecting the state of Rome, into a kind of domestic cult of Augustus himself. The old temple of Vesta in the Forum was still her central place of worship, but the goddess so important for the sacred history of the city now had a second place for her cult on the Palatine. When Augustus grew older and found the walk to the Forum difficult, the temple of Apollo or the pillared hall south-east of the library of the house were sometimes used for meetings of the Senate. In this way the temple, the centre of government and the residence of Augustus seemed to form a single unit, and there was no doubt that the Romans regarded this complex of buildings as the seat of their ruler. Incidentally, in the texts that have come down to us the first mention of the House of Augustus as the place where the ruler of Rome resided in state is by Ovid, who refers to it as *Palatia*, 'the House on the Palatine'.

We are used to speaking of the residential and administrative centre of the Palatine as the 'court' of Augustus. The term is inappropriate, and not only because of the unassuming exterior of the place. A 'court' calls for a society that understands itself as a permanent part of such a centre, living by rules that are peculiar to it and to nowhere else. The House of Augustus, on the other hand, judging by its extent and the number of people who lived there, was only the *domus* of a Roman nobleman grown to outsize dimensions. It was therefore to be judged beside the houses of the great potentates of the later republic, for instance the houses of Gnaeus Pompey and the dictator Caesar. In this sense, 'house' means primarily the place where the nobleman concerned lived, although the variety of business transacted there and the large staff required, as well as the necessity of receiving friends, partners in negotiation and petitioners, meant that rooms principally for public purposes were set apart from the purely private area. In its extent and furnishings, the House of Augustus did not even stand out from other large villas in the city. Many of the great figures of the late republic, like Pompey and Mark Antony, and also such friends of Augustus himself as Agrippa, had houses that could easily equal it. And in regard to size and splendour many men of far lower social rank lived in buildings that cast the House of Augustus into the shade. In the late republic, for instance, Marcus Aemilius Scaurus, member of a famous clan of the old nobility and successfully defended by Cicero in a trial, owned a magnificent city villa on the Palatine (he also owned the first great collection of gem-stones), and Publius Vedius Pollio, son of a freedman and a favourite of Augustus, had a luxurious palace on the Oppian Hill, one of the outrun-ners of the Esquiline, and a no less magnificent villa in Campania called Pausilypum ('Sanssouci'). And both men also owned many other houses.

There is no doubt that Livia had a separate part of the house on the Palatine to herself. Other extensive areas were the household rooms in which a large domestic staff, mainly slaves, worked. The tutors of the children and grandchildren of Augustus will certainly also have lived in the complex on the Palatine, as well as the famous philologist Marcus Verrius Flaccus, a freedman, who had to move there along with his whole school (scola). A considerable amount of space and a number of staff were required for educational purposes, particularly as Augustus also took in the children of friendly kings to be brought up with his own. He himself, as mentioned above, had his bedroom and the room to which he retired to think in private, but there will also have been an area for public business, including at least one large sitting room, although we cannot locate it for certain in the ground plan. The public rooms were more important and more closely associated with certain kinds of business in their use after Augustus had passed his fiftieth year of life and spent most of his time in Rome. After his return from his expedition in the year 13 BC to Gaul, where he stayed for several years, and apart from journeys inside Italy, especially to spas and country houses in Campania or Latium, he left Italy only twice, in the winter of 11/10 BC and in 8 BC. When he was in Rome he did not always spend the night on the Palatine, but might stay with friends or freedmen if he had public business to transact somewhere close to their houses next morning. He did not like rising early.

Of his immediate family, besides himself and Livia those who lived in the house were his daughter Julia and Livia's sons from her first mar-riage, Tiberius and Drusus, until the time came when they set up their own households. The majority of those living in the house were slaves and freedmen who served and looked after the family members by doing all the menial work about the place. The real assistants of Augus-tus, however, those who supported him in his official business, did not live in his house. They were of very different importance in influence and rank. The core of his staff of advisers was formed by his friends (*amici*), some of them bound to the *princeps* since their early youth, who had long ago risen to positions of wealth and influence. They had their own palaces, which were often luxurious. On the model of the Hellenistic rulers and many of the noblemen of the late republican period, Augustus is said to have divided his friends into three groups, distinguished from each other depending on how easily they could gain access to him (*admissio*). But although these formal categories did not at first seem to have been very strictly observed, it was clear to everyone that among those friends there was a small group very close to Augustus, who therefore had great influence. They were not just called upon for certain missions, as for instance Lucius Cornelius Balbus, whom Augustus had inherited, so to speak, from the dictator and to whom he had entrusted certain delicate missions at the beginning of his own political career; they also formed a close council (*consilium*) of advisers (*consiliarii*) who could gain access to him at any time, even if they were not engaged on a special task. On all important affairs of state, for instance in the year 4 BC, when the succession of Herod the Great had to be settled, they were called together. First among them was Agrippa. Then there was Marcus Valerius Messalla Corvinus and certainly the two other friends of Augustus' youth, Salvidienus Rufus and Cornelius Gallus, until they fell out of favour in the years 40 and 26 respectively. Another early friend of long standing was Maecenas, who was some years older than Augustus and had deputized for him as a military commander in Rome and Italy but performed no more such tasks after the end of the triumvirate. In his later years he even withdrew from political life or was virtually obliged to do so. Maecenas had no political ambition to hold great posts; he did not even become a senator, although such a career would certainly have been open to him, but remained a Roman of equestrian rank. However, his influence behind the political scenes cannot be too highly estimated. Augustus valued his silence and also his flexibility and was willing to overlook his taste for luxury and his casual conduct, although it was so different from his own lifestyle, or at least his lifestyle as he took pains to present it to the Roman elite. However, they were linked by the same interest in encouraging young poetic talents. Virgil, Horace and Propertius were among those whom Maecenas patronized. These poets sat at his table in his tower-like palace on the Esquiline and allowed him to urge them to write certain works – in the case of Virgil, for instance, Maecenas suggested his great poem on country life, the *Georgics*.

Another close friend, Gaius Sallustius Crispus, did not strive for office either, although he was of a senatorial family, but was content with equestrian rank all his life. A great-nephew of the historian of the same name, and also his adopted son, he possessed an enormous fortune, and like Maecenas had a marked taste for luxury and a lavish lifestyle, but he also had good taste and was generous. As an adviser to Augustus, he can be seen as the successor to Maecenas, who died in the year 8 BC. At a great age – for Sallustius outlived his patron by six years – he also showed Tiberius that he could serve him by committing acts of brutality, for he helped his new master to dispose of Agrippa Postumus, the last grandson of Augustus in the direct line and the most dangerous potential rival to Tiberius for the throne. With both Maecenas and Sallustius we see the great thoughtfulness that Augustus could show to his closest friends, a characteristic that, if not natural to him from the first, had probably been encouraged by the magnanimity he was forced to show during his rise to power. He also showed it to friends of more humble origin like Publius Vedius Pollio and Gaius Proculeius. The former was the son of a freedman and with the patronage of Augustus not only rose to equestrian rank but also acquired great wealth. A useful assistant to his master, he was a man without morals and could be harsh and cruel to those dependent on him; when he condemned slaves to death he had no scruples in feeding their flesh to his moray eels, a very fashionable fish at the time. Although Augustus did not approve, having no taste for such excesses himself, and on a visit to Vedius Pollio he saved a slave from being thrown to the fishes, there was no interruption of their friendly relationship. Named by Pollio as his heir, Augustus seems to have wished to distance himself from him only after his death. He had Pollio's magnificent house on the Oppian Hill demolished – according to Ovid it took up as much space as a small town – and built a large pillared hall on the site, naming it after his wife as the Porticus Liviae. It was meant as an island of rest and recuperation in a densely inhabited area, and Ovid for one took the gesture as a reaction to the wasteful luxury of the former owner of the place.

Proculeius, on the other hand, stood out from the sometimes unedifying figures around Augustus. A high-minded man, he was of equestrian rank and, like Maecenas, to whom he was related through the latter's wife Terentia, had no ambition for a political career. He had accompanied Octavian at the time of the Sicilian War, and when, in an apparently hopeless situation, he had thought of suicide Proculeius refused his request to kill him, one of the many dispositions of providence that preserved Octavian from a premature end. A number of missions of considerable importance had been entrusted to him; among others, he had conducted the negotiations with Cleopatra in her mausoleum after the suicide of Antony. Despite their friendship, it is barely credible that Augustus seriously thought of marrying him to his daughter after the death of young Marcellus. If there was anything at all in that rumour, it must at the most have been at a time when Augustus was still intending to keep Julia out of politics.

However, these friends and others too were not part of the central bureaucracy. They were advisers, carrying out certain important missions on political business. The office work meanwhile was done by slaves and freedmen. They received and sorted incoming documents, sent out their own, were scribes and messengers, provided their master with news and factual expertise, reminded him of his engagements and filed documents in the archives once they had been dealt with. At the time the various duties were not yet organized according to their functions, as they were at a later date after several generations of experience with the central administration of the empire. Strict separation of the business of administration into departments was unknown, although one assistant would be more intensively concerned with letters coming in from Italy and the provinces, while another occupied himself with researching the data for certain purposes. We know of one freedman, Julius Marathus, who wrote a history of Augustus and was probably considered suitable for writing documents and checking their facts on the grounds of his literary abilities. Another man, a scribe called Thallos, was a slave whose lower legs the *princeps* had broken as punishment for taking a bribe in return for giving away a secret from a letter. We may note here that Augustus asked Maecenas to let him have Horace, out of the circle of poets whom he knew, to help with letter-writing. Horace will certainly not have been expected to work as an ordinary scribe or researcher, but to polish up the literary style of the correspondence in his capacity as a writer.

In the same way as the bureaucratic apparatus grew out of the domestic staff of a Roman nobleman, the seal of Augustus was not a state seal of the kind known to us from the Hellenistic kingdoms, but a personal seal, and when the *princeps* used it for public business he was following the tradition of the republic, when the magistrates had also ratified documents of a public nature with their private seals. Octavian/ Augustus used several seals in succession for this purpose, first one showing a sphinx, an emblem which cannot have had very deep political significance for him, since he had inherited it from his mother. After the death of Antony, he used a seal showing Alexander the Great, a change that must have been made after his visit to Alexandria, when he had been to see the Macedonian king, but it will also have been because the measures of the triumvirate had brought the sphinx seal into disrepute. His last seal showed his own head. It had been made by the best gemstone cutter of the time, Dioscurides, and is said to have been a very good likeness of Augustus. His successor Tiberius also used it, and after him all the emperors up to Galba in the turbulent year of the Four Emperors (AD 68/69), and only through its constant use by them did it gain a public and legal character as a state seal.

The administration of Rome was a special task. In so far as Rome was a city state, its government was at first to be equated with that of the entire Roman area of rule, as it had been in fact for hundreds of years. The Roman magistrates, with the consuls at their head, had ruled the world from Rome, and settling questions relating purely to the city, such as supervision of the civic buildings, had been only a part of their duties. By the time of the late republic, however, the area of Roman citizenship no longer comprised just Rome and central Italy, but extended over the whole lower part of the Italian peninsula, and in the time of Augustus it also took in the low-lying plains of Upper Italy. The Roman city state was no longer able to cope with the administration of such a large area, let alone the huge and ever-growing territory represented by the provinces. Ever since the triumvirate, and increasingly after the establishment of the principate, large areas of the state and the empire, particularly the government of the provinces, had been largely removed from the authority of the city of Rome and transferred to the control of the *princeps*, which meant that the responsibility of the old system of government represented by the Senate and magistrates of the city of Rome was largely confined to Rome and Italy. But the administration even of Italy was no longer managed by Rome alone; it was some while since the *princeps* had become an authority rivalling the Senate, and in view of the new circumstances a time could already be envisaged when Rome was administered in the same way as every other town or large city in the empire. However, those who, under Augustus, were still far from that time still felt a fundamental change in the institutional order by comparison with the republic. First, Augustus featured along with the old administrators, the Senate and magistrates (consuls, praetors, aediles, tribunes of the people, quaestors), and second, a whole series of entirely new official positions was now created for certain tasks which, even when functions of the older magistracy were transferred to them, were notable for their new and special powers. In addition, and of particular importance for the future, the area of responsibility for all these new tasks was largely confined to the city itself. So began a development in the course of which a city ruling the world became one ruling the population of the city of Rome, so that in the end all that was left of its former grandeur was the fact that the new ruler, the *princeps*, had his official seat in Rome.

The administration of the city of Rome did not change all at once. And here, at the heart of the Roman state and in the face of the long-established institutions, where every strong intervention offended traditionalists and any change could seem to run counter to the idea of reconciliation with the political past, Augustus showed moderation and a sense of proportion. Above all, he did not work according to a plan. He had no overall plan for transforming the administration of Rome; the change arose more from the wish to eradicate individual ills. Even where the reform of existing administrative structures proved essential, he avoided alienating the Senate by taking decisions on his own but usually made sure he was asked to take on the task, and sometimes even urged to do so by the people. Although no accounts to that effect have come down to us, he must have had all reforms of the official life of the city of Rome ratified by the Senate and he would have placed the innovations officially under senatorial control. In addition, although Augustus was the official authority (*curator*) for the new concerns of the state, he always appointed officials, when they were senators, only by agreement with the Senate itself and sometimes even asked for its formal vote (*ex consensus, ex auctoritate senatus*).

None the less, the collaboration of the Senate and individual senators who held office was certainly not a real division of labour in official affairs, either in this area or others. Even when senators filled the newly created offices and the Senate took part in making the appointments, they were conceived as *curae*, that is to say official tasks performed on behalf of the *princeps* himself. The fact that senators or the Senate had a say in making such appointments shows the underlying political intention of involving the supreme group as much as possible in all affairs of state, and thus consolidating an awareness that being a senator was not just an honour but also meant joining in the administration of the city and the empire. That became particularly clear when Augustus transferred small affairs that he could well have dealt with himself to senatorial committees, such as the committee set up in the year AD 6, consisting of three consulars, to examine public items of expenditure, prune them or abolish them entirely. Augustus could easily have left such matters to the close circle of his staff, men of equestrian rank, or members of his household, including freedmen and slaves.

That the first reform of the administration of the city of Rome concerned the supply of grain for bread to the people, known as the *annona*, was certainly not just chance. The huge city had suffered severely from high prices for food and shortages of basic foodstuffs in the previous century, but remedying the situation was expensive and had increasingly become a matter of belonging to this or that party group, so the problem could not be tackled at its root under the republic. During a famine in the year 22 BC, Augustus let himself be persuaded to assume the duty of dealing with it in what was known as the Corn Office (*cura annonae*) and he quickly found a solution to the problem. However, as he did not want anyone to see this post as a substitute for the permanent office for emergency situations, Augustus did not take it on in the long term himself but first transferred it to senators of the higher ranks, who were to hold office for a year according to a special arrangement, and then, after a transitional period, finally placed it in the hands of an official of equestrian rank (*praefectus annonae*), who worked closely with him in that capacity. And the office did what it was set up to do. It ensured that sufficient grain was supplied to the Roman market, and later other foodstuffs, that the grain was distributed and that granaries on the Tiber were built and extended. It was a difficult and politically significant business calling for a firm hand. When there was famine in Rome, a not infrequent state of affairs, the people were often close to rebellion, as for instance in the year AD 6, when in spite of welfare measures – Augustus evacuated part of the population – the famine continued, and many citizens began murmuring about a potential coup, while others put up slanderous placards by night.

After the death of Agrippa in 12 BC other offices had to be created. Agrippa, who for a time had taken on the aedileship, had been in charge of the building and repair of the Roman aqueducts and had also erected many new buildings, devoting a great deal of his energy to these tasks. His extraordinary powers, which may be seen as complementary to and supportive of those of the *princeps*, were now formalized into specific areas of responsibility. For the first time in the history of Rome, a permanent office of waterworks was created, and another for road-building. Such measures of civil engineering, which under the republic had been carried out by individual magistrates – censors and consuls – as needed and as those magistrates saw fit, or sometimes on the initiative of the Senate, could now be systematically dealt with by transference to permanently appointed officials. That meant they could be planned with a view to the long term, coordinated and carried out by experts who were always available. The Roads Office (*cura viarum*) goes back to the year 20, while the Water Office (*cura aquarum*) was not created until after the death of Agrippa. For that purpose Augustus took on the experienced staff of slaves left to him in Agrippa's will, and made them state property, so that the work of building and inspection, which at least in part had been carried out on Agrippa's personal initiative, was so to speak nationalized. As the first man in charge (*curator*) of the Water Office, Augustus appointed Marcus Valerius Messalla Corvinus, who held the post for almost a quarter of a century until his death – a sign of the close link between the office and Augustus, and of its importance.

Both offices, for roads and for the water supply, were filled on the collegiate system and could be held only by senators. Here again we cannot but see the cautious hand of the thoughtful *princeps*, who saw the necessity of entrusting important and permanent tasks to equally permanent offices. He might have set them up by himself, but he did his best not to overlook the Senate in filling the posts they created. And the new office for state-owned building works in Rome (*cura operum publicorum*) arose as if of itself from the death of Agrippa, who in the end had been arranging and carrying out most such public works in Rome, both erecting new buildings and restoring those in need of repair. The great fires of the years 14 and 12 did their part in speeding up the institution of the office and showing the necessity of coordinating the renovation of public buildings by private persons, for which purpose Augustus had called on men of fortune.

The new offices meant considerable changes to the official administration of the city as a whole. In particular, they reinforced the purely local powers of the city institutions in Rome itself and its immediate surroundings. Their usefulness was therefore recognized and welcomed by the people of Rome, for now important municipal needs could be permanently met and well planned. These were measures previously carried out without any planning and only in extreme emergency. And as the *princeps* was the driving force behind all these innovations, the people naturally looked to him as the man whom they had to thank for the benefits they brought. In view of his efforts to supply the city with food and make it architecturally attractive, he now seemed the real helper and new patron of all the citizens of Rome.

Meanwhile, this activity was complemented by another, one that left a yet greater mark on the face of the city, and was to distinguish it even more clearly from what Rome had been under the republic. It concerned the provision of barracks for soldiers, who until now had been banished to the area outside its walls.

In the change of Rome from a demilitarized city to a 'garrison town', the people did not see anything like military occupation, but recognized it as a measure taken for their own security; the soldiers came to help them to combat crime in a large metropolis and to fight fires, which periodically reduced large areas of the city to rubble and ashes. As early as the year 27 or soon afterwards, perhaps in the time of unrest between the years 23 to 19, Augustus first set up a protective force of three military cohorts, called *cohortes urbanae*, 'city cohorts', dedicated to the *urbs Roma*. These men served for the same twenty-year period as legionaries, but the men's pay, to make the difference between it and that of the Praetorian Guard less obvious, was one and a half times that of the legionaries, 375 denarii. The task of the cohorts was to protect the city from criminals, and also from slaves who had run away from their masters and might form riotous mobs. Roman society, which depended on slaves to do a great deal of its menial work, had never been able to suppress a certain uneasiness about them, particularly when, as quite often happened, a crowd of slaves met a free citizen on his own. Nor was that all; criminality in general among free citizens gave rise to alarm, first because of the size of the city, second because there was no effective police force. While in former times the noble patrons had exercised a certain amount of control over their huge clienteles, many clients had later escaped supervision by their patrons because of the vast extent of the city. The number of inhabitants grew, and the tangle of streets into which malefactors could plunge at any time encouraged crime. The organs of state responsible for keeping order in the city, particularly the aediles and the 'three-man college for criminal acts' (*tresviri capitales*), were simply in no position to deal with the tasks facing them. The aediles could at most protect public places, and the 'three-man' committee could do little more than carry out, as best they could, their functions of supervising the prisons and the execution of sentences and acting as the authority to which crimes should be reported. Now and then emergency measures had to be taken. In Rome during the last decades of the republic, shaken as it was by political unrest, there had sometimes been a great deal of fear and insecurity. Then again, the larger the city grew the more dangerous its streets became – and not just at night.

For all these reasons it is obvious that the cohorts, acting as a police force, were welcomed by the great majority of the inhabitants of the city. Augustus also played his own part in preventing any discontent among the population. The number of soldiers, or police officers, was kept low, and in relation to the population of the city as a whole, which must have been well over half a million at the time, it was not high enough to represent a threat. It is true that there is still dispute about the size of the cohorts, but if we assume that a single cohort consisted of 500 soldiers, and the whole contingent was therefore 1,500 men strong, that seems as close as we can get to the facts. At first the unit had no commanding officer of its own but was directly under Augustus himself, as if it were not a new institution but a small troop attached to him personally. If he was not in Rome they were commanded by a deputy. Tiberius was the first to give them their own commander, the *praefectus urbi* (commander of the city). The *princeps* also allowed only a part of the soldiers in the cohorts to be on duty in Rome, while the others stayed in their quarters outside the city.

The regular fire brigade of Rome was also set up by Augustus. Fire-fighting was at a very low ebb during the republic, for the same reason as there was no police force: military or paramilitary groups were not allowed to be stationed within the area of a mile around the city. The security of the city had once been in the hands of the great noble patrons, who were responsible for those citizens who were their clients, even if in fact they were mainly concerned for their own houses, and perhaps those of a few clients who were particularly close to them. Officially, there were only a handful of junior officers responsible for putting out fires and no permanent organization for that purpose, so on occasion resourceful entrepreneurs or politicians, such as Marcus Egnatius Rufus in the year 22, mentioned above, had taken on the job in order to make political capital out of it. After Augustus had eliminated Egnatius, he tackled the situation himself, set up a fire-fighting team consisting of 600 slaves and in the new division of the city into districts in the year 7 BC he set up fire-fighting areas for the districts, making the aediles, as the traditional administrators of the city, responsible for them. However, this idea does not seem to have worked very well, and after a great fire in the year AD 6 the fire-fighting force was restructured into its final form. The new service was now set up as a paramilitary troop consisting of seven cohorts of 1,000 men each. They were free citizens recruited from the ranks of freedmen. These cohorts, each responsible for two of the new city districts (*regiones*), were called *vigiles*, 'watchmen'. A commander of the 'watchmen' (*praefectus vigilum*), a man of equestrian rank, led them, and they were under the direct supervision of the *princeps*.

As well as the city cohorts and the fire-fighters, Augustus set up a bodyguard. Even back in the time of the republic, senior military commanders had had personal guards, but they consisted of friends, clients or veterans, were armed with a motley assortment of weapons and had never been very extensive. Since their place was at the commander's base (*praetorium*), they were known as the 'commander's guard' (*cohors praetoria*). In the republican period, these cohorts were exclusively appointed in the field and then discharged again at the latest when the commander entered the *pomerium*; they were soldiers on active service. Naturally the great commanders of the late republic also had bodyguards, quite often recruited from foreigners. The dictator Caesar had had a Spanish bodyguard, and Octavian himself had a Spanish troop and also, until the battle lost by Varus, a troop of Germans. The real forerunners of the 'imperial' guard, however, were the bodyguards set up by the military potentates after the assassination of the dictator. They too were called *cohors praetoria*, but in manning and size the troops were very different from the older praetorian cohorts. They consisted almost exclusively of foot-soldiers of the line (legionaries) and were battle units, sometimes considerably stronger in numbers than a normal cohort, so that they could also be used in battle as an independent troop. Along with them there was a small cavalry troop, its men known as 'scouts' (*speculatores*) because they carried news and messages. The new kind of praetorian cohort was an elite troop such as we have already met in the War of Mutina, when Antony and Octavian each had such a cohort, and Octavian's had been called up in the battle of Forum Gallorum. For the potentates of the triumvirate they were still typical units, but they had no permanent quarters, because the triumvirate was not set up as a permanent organization and so had no established centre.

Augustus had not dissolved his Praetorians after the end of the triumvirate. Characteristically, in the settlement of the year 27 or soon afterwards, he got the Senate to grant them twice the pay of an ordinary soldier. This officially confirmed that the bodyguard was a military unit stationed in close proximity to the supreme commander of the army, which could mean within the mile where soldiers were not usually permitted, and at the same time marked the guard out as a special elite troop, distinct from all other units. The character of the 27 BC settlement as a declaration of monarchy could hardly have been more clearly demonstrated, for no magistrate had ever yet had a permanent bodyguard, and certainly not in Rome.

To mitigate the provocative effect, at the time Augustus gave his guard quarters within the city not at its full strength, but only one section at a time, to ensure the security of his house on the Palatine Hill. Later, in the year AD 2, probably after making changes now unknown to us in the preceding years, he reorganized the bodyguard thoroughly in respect of both its size and the terms of command. The number of cohorts was raised to nine, and their strength was then established, if not before, as 500 men to a cohort. Of these nine units, including the three city cohorts, only three were stationed in Rome itself; the others were billeted in the country towns nearby.

There was no Praetorian barracks in Rome in the time of Augustus. The famous barracks outside the Viminal Gate (the *castra praetoria*, its name still present today in the area north-east of the Stazione Termini and called Castro Pretorio) was set up by Tiberius. The guard, until then directly under Augustus, was also given two commanders in AD 2. As officials of equestrian rank they bore the title of prefects and so, as they were at the head of the military command post, each was called 'prefect of headquarters' (*praefectus praetorio*).

Here the principate was conjuring up ideas of the old republic: the man of highest rank, the supreme senator, standing above all others by virtue of his personal achievements and his extraordinary and official full powers, ruled the world in and through the Senate. The *consilium mundi*, the Council of the World in Rome, was at the centre of the empire; no magnificent palace of the *princeps* could compete with the assembly buildings of the Senate. It was possible to see the situation in that way, and some vague sense of proximity to the freedom of the old republic of the nobility might have been enough to satisfy the new society as it proudly trod in the footsteps of its predecessor. Such proximity meant a great deal, and even the no longer very numerous descendants of the ancient noble families who had survived the storms of the civil wars might not have been able to make much headway if they had wished to restore the republic of Cicero unchanged. Any of them who had not perished then now wished, if they had secured a major position in the new circumstances, 'to enjoy security in the present rather than strive dangerously for the past', as Tacitus put it. But not even the tension between these possibilities, as Tacitus set it out several generations later, was taken seriously after the establishment of the rule of Augustus. There was no sign of a new Cato, or even a Favonius. Everyone sought the major position that would guarantee influence and honour; security (*securitas*) was more in demand than freedom (*libertas*).

This desire for security, and the tendency to moral cowardice that went with it, were reactions to enormous pressure, but the compulsion engendering such attitudes was felt less and less. The advantages of the new life were as clear as their disadvantages to a man who did not adapt to them. The overwhelming power of the *princeps* sprang not from his official full powers, although in their extent and quality they were greater than any that a Roman had ever held before – we need think only of his power of command over half the provinces and the unlimited opportunities that his official role offered him. It was with some pride that Augustus announced, in his account of his own rule, that he had held no more purely legal power than any of his colleagues in the magistracy, and he glossed over the fact that he possessed not just one but many legal powers with which to face down any individual colleague isolated in his own area of office. Even greater, however, was his social power, which the Romans expressed by the term *auctoritas*. The soldiers and officers obeyed him not just, or even primarily, because he was legally their commander, but because he was their patron and guaranteed their pay during their period of service; he also materially secured their 'civilian' life after their discharge, and they therefore owed him loyalty and gratitude. The people of the city of Rome looked to him as the man who provided free food and staged exciting games; the country towns of Italy saw him as the patron to whom they could turn in need; and the provinces as the saviour who had freed them from oppression and now gave them security and justice; and they all, soldiers, citizens and provincials, were linked together by the blessings of the peace that this man had ushered in and now maintained for the long term with his army.

There was a price to be paid for the benefits – principally security and peace – bestowed by the *princeps*. It was a price of a political nature and one exacted upon the very idea of the principate. For as Augustus was the sole guarantor of these new blessings, everyone looked up to him and listened to what he said. The Senate, on the other hand, was no longer really an authority involved in decision-making; under Augustus it never had been, not even on 13 January 27 BC. The supremacy of Augustus over all other potential decision-makers was felt daily, as all and sundry made their way to him, or to someone close to him, or at the least to one of his civil servants, even when other men would have been more competent to deal with individual cases.

Everyone recognized the de facto monopoly on the power of decision-making by the *princeps*, simply in the fact that there was no discussion of political decisions, or only very seldom. The decisions had been made in the house of Augustus long before they came to the ears of the public, by which time they were mere announcements. Politics had become the business of the ruler's cabinet, and here we come up against the guesswork of historians on when, where and on what grounds some decision or other had been taken by someone or other. From now on, in the interests of shaping public business in the right way behind the closed doors of the palace offices, politics disappeared as an activity involving advice and negotiation, yet the vacuum thus publicly created was immediately filled. Instead of discussions, speeches and voting by a succession of various magistrates who used to fill public places and rooms, the figure of the man who acted as if he were merely presiding over public business but in fact was conducting it himself was ever more prominent. Augustus was in charge of most festivals, whether they were games or other performances, and he or one of his close circle dedicated the great buildings of Rome. The *princeps* was to be found not only at festivals, but everywhere that the power of the state had to be represented, and to the same extent as he filled the public arena representatives of the old magistracy of republican times retreated into the background.

In the end the most important festival in Rome, the celebration of a triumph, which had been granted so frequently in the time of the triumvirate – and was granted by Octavian himself to over thirty generals – was not held at all for persons who were not of the ruling house. The last such man to be granted a triumph was Lucius Cornelius Balbus in 19 BC for his victory over the Garamantes, a tribe in Libya. Just as his uncle had been the first consul not born a Roman, Balbus the nephew was the first triumphator marked by the same brush and at the same time the last who, as triumphator, was not a 'Caesar' or a member of the Caesarian house. After that, under Augustus, military success by proconsuls or legates was rewarded only with the right to wear the insignia of a triumph (*ornamenta triumphalia*), but not to hold a full-scale triumph. Augustus was reluctant to grant one even to his stepsons Drusus and Tiberius, who were brilliant generals: after their very successful campaigns they were rewarded only with the triumphal insignia or the minor triumph, the *ovatio*. Tiberius was first granted a triumph on 1 January 7 BC for his great success in his campaign against the German tribes, and he had to share it with Augustus. The triumph became a monopoly of the *princeps*; in the year 36 Augustus had already acquired the right to wear the laurel wreath in perpetuity, and after the settlement of the year 27 the Senate had had the doorposts of his house garlanded with laurel. Augustus was the supreme victor and triumphator; victory was one of his personal attributes. No other triumphator, therefore, might stand beside him unless a member of his own family shared the triumph.

And the good old custom of allowing a victorious commander to be hailed (acclaimed) by his men after a military success as *imperator* was hardly followed at all now, because the supreme commander might feel it was a slight to his own leadership, might perhaps even scent a would-be rival. One of the last to be distinguished by Augustus in this way was a proconsul of Africa in the year AD 3. The acclamation at the scene of a victory, usually the battlefield on which the victory had been won, was replaced by the now very tedious – because planned in advance – acclamation of the *princeps* as *imperator*, accepting the honour not only for the military successes he himself had won but also for those of all his generals. Augustus was acclaimed *imperator* in this way twenty-one times.

With all this, it was almost to be taken for granted that divine honours, which had been bestowed so profusely on the governors of eastern provinces in the republican era, were in future exclusively reserved for the *princeps*. For a while the governors of this or that province received cult or cult-like honours under Augustus. Then, in the year AD 11, he issued an edict forbidding all governors to accept any honours during their governorship and for sixty days after the end of it, giving as a reason the prevention of any kind of corruption. That will not have been the only and probably not even the main reason. No one other than Augustus was to be venerated with cult honours, particularly not in the provinces under the administration of the Senate. The last governor, as far as the sources tell us, to receive divine honours and the appointment of a priest to go with them was Lucius Munatius Plancus, the dictator's famous legate, governor of Asia between 40 and 38; the last to whom games were dedicated were Paullus Fabius Maximus, governor of Asia, probably in 9 or 10/9 BC, and Gaius Marcius Censorinus, consul in the year 8 BC and a member of one of the most distinguished families of the republic. The latter administered Asia about ten years after his consulate, but although described by the provincials as their 'saviour and benefactor' (*sotér* and *euergétes*) he received that honour only after his death.

# 10

# Rome, Italy and the Roman Empire

At the time of Augustus, Rome had long been the greatest city of the ancient world both in size and population. No other great city could compete with it, neither Athens, which was threatened with declining into a tourist attraction, nor Alexandria. The sheer size of the city brought its own difficulties, and the generous resettlement policy of Caesar and after him Augustus, both of whom tried to tempt Romans away to such far-flung places as Corinth and Carthage, now rebuilt as Roman colonies, did little to alleviate the problem. Most of the citizens of Rome were used to the comforts of city life. There were also many foreigners who had settled in Rome or lived there for long periods, and tens of thousands of slaves. The resettlement policy did nothing to reduce the number of slaves in Rome, since the majority of them toiled in the factories and palaces of the empire, and their owners had no intention of moving to the provinces. It is difficult to estimate just how large the total population of Rome was at the time, but on the basis of the number of citizens, which can be roughly assessed, from data known to us about those qualified to receive gifts of money or grain for bread-making, at 500,000 to 600,000, there must have been at least 700,000 to 800,000 people living in the city in the time of Augustus,

Rome was surrounded by the walls built in the fourth century BC of rough blocks of tuff stone and called the Servian Walls (*muri Serviani*) after the legendary King Servius Tullius. Only a few fragments of it still survive today, near the Stazione Termini and the Italian Finance Ministry. The great brick wall that now surrounds the entire city was not built until the third century AD, when it was erected by Emperor Aurelian to keep out the tribes attacking from the north who also threatened Italy at the time. The city in the strict sense lay inside the Servian Walls and was a unified, self-contained built-up area (*continentia*). In the wider sense it extended for over 2 kilometres (1.5 Roman miles) beyond the walls, and that entire area was correctly regarded as part of the city. The older city district, on the other hand, comprised only the quarters within the Servian Walls, and only they were surrounded by the *pomerium*, the sacred, legal boundary of Rome, which coincided with the walls. The *pomerium* separated an inner, 'domestic' area (*domi*), where the civil and political business of the citizens was transacted, from an outer, military area (*militiae*) under the command of the army. In the time of Augustus, however, when all Italy was at peace and inhabited by Roman citizens, that distinction was less important than the distinction between Italy and the provinces.

Under Augustus, the larger part of the inner city area apart from the large parks was either already built up or gradually having buildings erected on it, most of them of a good size. Apart from the public buildings, the houses were mainly quite simple, and some of them, particularly in the poorer quarters, were like modern slums: tiny, often dark dwellings in dirty surroundings. There were also buildings of several storeys, generally in the form of large apartment blocks (*insulae*) in such densely populated parts of the city as the Subura, and usually rented out to tenants. The building materials used were tuff stone, cast concrete (mortar mixed with stone fragments) and brick, with timber for the floors and ceilings of the multi-storey buildings. These high-rise structures had no inner courtyard to provide light, like the normal Roman house (*domus*), only windows or shafts through which some light could fall. The city gates were large, and the wide thoroughfares could accommodate two-way traffic, but most of the other streets were narrow alleys in which people lived among dirt and bad smells. There was an extensive sewage system, but its network was not evenly distributed through all quarters of the city. When Augustus boasted of finding Rome a city built of brick and leaving it a city built of marble, he was referring only to the public buildings. The Rome of gilded temple rooftops, mentioned by Propertius, ended where the dwellings of ordinary citizens began. But Augustus also put his mind to the quarters where the common people lived, looked at the existing regulations for maintaining buildings and drew up new guidelines. The latter served not only to keep the traffic moving but, most important of all, to prevent fires and accidents from the collapse of buildings. One important regulation, for instance, banned the use of bricks for buildings of more than a single storey.

Rome was the home of every Roman citizen, and it remained so even after the extension of Roman residential areas by the building of new settlements and the transfer of Roman citizenship to those who lived well outside the city. The area of citizenship soon covered all Italy including the plain of the river Po, then large parts of the provinces and finally, after the beginning of the third century AD, the entire empire. The idea that everything Roman came from the city of Rome, and every Roman belonged to it, outlived the city state itself and lasted as long as the Roman empire itself, so that Romans living outside Rome in another Italian town or in a province always had two home cities, Rome and the place where they actually came from. The idea of this dual origin – *origo* – is evidence of the strength of the idea that the community of all Romans proceeded from the city on the Tiber.

In the time of Augustus, and for hundreds of years after it, to be a Roman who lived in the city of Rome was special. Romans who lived there had featured as lords of the world; they had voted for laws and for the holders of office in the assemblies of the people; they had sat in court to hear the trials of criminal cases. The ruling families had competed for the favour of the people who lived in the city (*plebs urbana*), who not only derived material gain from that fact but also, even as the republic fell into decay, could retain a sense that they still had a hand in political power. The complaints of Cicero about the people of the city, whom he often abused roundly for following individual holders of office, particularly the tribunes of the people, and thus interfering with the political circle of the nobility, show that the people still had some influence even as the republic was in transition to monarchy. But when he cited citizens living in Italian country districts far from Rome, contrasting their traditional lifestyles close to the land with the attitudes of the more astute and go-ahead inhabitants of the metropolis, his adjurations were unlikely to have any effect, since a Roman citizen could exercise his political rights only if he were personally present in Rome. As a result, the nobility of Cicero's time had to come to terms with the common people who trod the city streets and whom they despised, but who saw a late flowering of their former importance when they exercised those rights.

The political role of the people of the city of Rome, particularly in their participation in the election of holders of office and in law-making, was further restricted in the principate of Augustus, and in the end was eliminated entirely. Directly after the year 27, however, the people still profited at first from the wish of Augustus to restore the legal order of the state and its observation of tradition. The election of the magistrates holding high office was of the first importance here, for now, in contrast to the days of the triumvirate, those who attended the assembly of the people could sometimes choose from among several candidates, and there is evidence that Augustus, following the old custom, campaigned personally in the Forum for the candidates whom he himself supported. Any individual election was, of course, subject to the publicly expressed wishes of the *princeps*, and to the recommendations (*commendationes*), not exactly legal but undoubtedly binding in fact, that Augustus also made to the assembly of the people in favour of certain candidates, especially for the consulate. He sometimes also put these recommendations in writing, making them known through a herald or a public notice. To be the candidate favoured by the *princeps* was considered a special honour and was soon elevated to a title (*candidatus Caesaris*, the candidate of Caesar), and the pride such men took in it showed very obviously how little the idea of free election was worth by comparison with the growing importance of a link with Augustus as their patron. Augustus further influenced the voting by presiding over elections himself and examining those who offered themselves as candidates. The further his influence took on the character of a normal transaction, the more restricted was the scope of voters themselves, even when there were more candidates on the list than posts to be filled, so that a vote had to be taken.

In the year AD 5 this procedure changed. In future, committees of men of both senatorial and equestrian rank decided on candidates for the posts of consuls and praetors, and their names were then presented to the assembly of the people for the final vote. As the number of candidates was thus very probably the same as the number of offices to be filled, the assembly of the people now had no opportunity at all to make decisions, and the voting process was reduced to mere acclamation of the men already chosen. As well as his normal influence on individual senators and knights, the influence of Augustus on the decisions of these committees was particularly evident in the fact that the men of equestrian rank whom he appointed to administrative bodies of ten (*decuria*) were ultimately those whom he chose as the equestrian members of the committees.

So free elections were gradually abolished without any drastic break with tradition. The old criminal jurisdiction of the assemblies of the people in the late republic had long ago given way to trial by juries picked from men of distinction, so now nothing was left to the people but the right to decide on laws put before them by the consuls, the tribunes of the people and Augustus himself as the holder of tribunician power. We do in fact know of consular and tribunician laws at this period, but it is very doubtful whether there was any serious voting on them. The decision was no longer between several options, as it had been, at least when it came to voting, up to the year AD 5, but merely between accepting or rejecting a proposed law. Fundamentally, acceptance could be taken for granted, so the assembled people had to content themselves with mere acclamation.

However, the reputation of the inhabitants of Rome was not entirely lost, despite the gradual erosion of their political rights under the monarchy. The respect they still retained arose, in particular, from the role of a Roman as theoretically a representative of the entire Roman people (*populus Romanus*), a privilege that was to last for centuries longer. To whom were the monarch, the Senate or the holders of office to turn when they wished to address the Roman people, if not to those who lived in the city of Rome? As a body, they were certainly not always the exact image of what a Roman of the old school had regarded as his people; their assemblies contained many freedmen or descendants of freedmen, who were of far lower status than free-born Romans. Furthermore, most of them were shopkeepers, craftsmen, construction workers or other kinds of tradesmen; these were the kind of people that a big city needs and were likely to be found there. The idea of the farmer leaving his plough when his superiors called on him to do his public duty was a thing of the past.

There had been some difficulty in regarding the people of Rome as potential voters and law-makers even in this time of freedom. The motley crowd more and more in evidence in the growing city had largely ceased to consist of the clienteles of the great families, and those who made it up were increasingly open to the influence of anyone who would make them the right promises and could be expected to keep those promises. This development had speeded up in the time of the triumvirate, when power was the prime consideration, and sometimes the city had been entirely beyond the control of Octavian himself because of the proscriptions, the blockades of Sextus Pompey when he was trying to starve out Rome and recurrent harsh tax-gathering methods. This state of affairs was to go with the end of the civil wars and the establishment of the principate. The military despot presented himself in a new guise, and the people of the city of Rome were a part of it.

The people of the city did have some internal organization of their own in this new age. The various districts (*vici*), with street junctions (*compita*) at their centre, played a large part in maintaining links between the city-dwellers. They had their own leaders (*vici magistri*), and through the veneration of the Lares at those junctions and the organization of local games they formed relatively well-established structures. Under the republic it had been difficult for their official supervisors, the aediles, to control the local leaders and the groups they led, and special associations (*collegia*) had also formed. These were used by political opponents of the aristocracy and, depending on the course taken by politics, might be either banned or reintroduced. Augustus had to make sure he had firmer control of the organization of the plebs. At first he rigorously cut back on the local associations by allowing only those that were of long standing and legally established, while banning all the others. And the division of Rome in the year 7 BC into fourteen regions and 265 smaller local districts (the *vici*) also helped him to control the people of the capital more efficiently. The small districts themselves, divided according to the regions, were subject to a supervisory authority chosen from among the senators. The cult of the local Lares, including, as we have seen, the veneration of Augustus, and the new division into districts were helpful, and a new era began in the relationship between the political leadership, now represented by the *princeps*, and the people of Rome.

All the inhabitants of the city came under the jurisdiction of the *vici*, slaves and foreign visitors as well as citizens, and the citizens were also divided into their old local organization by tribes. All Romans, not just every inhabitant of the city, belonged to one or other of the thirty-five tribes. Originally Rome had had four local tribes for its citizens, but in the course of time many citizens of other tribes had moved to the city without giving up membership of their old tribe somewhere in Italy. By now all thirty-five tribes had developed urban groups which also distinguished Roman citizens from the mass of foreigners and slaves by the fact that they had their own organization. Of course the four old urban tribes had by far the most members, but the others, at least on certain occasions, were also represented in large numbers because of the arrival in Rome of members of those tribes (*tribules*) coming to the city from near or far. The tribes had public tasks to perform, and indeed existed for that very purpose. In particular they were the units for voting in the assemblies of the people. The provision of grain and money, donated only to citizens, was mainly by tribes, not least because the fact that members of the tribes knew each other made cheating during the distribution process more difficult. The tribes were under administrators (*curatores*) and had subdivisions (*corpora*), not just for the more effective control of their members but also to establish personal groups of smaller units.

Besides these remnants of the political importance of the people, for instance the casting of votes now and then, and occasions on which public addresses were made to the people, Romans living in the city had certain privileges that survived into the principate from the time of their independence. The proverbial provision of 'bread and circuses' (*panem et circenses*) was typical. Not only was the staging of festive games and other performances part of a tradition going far back to the days of the republic, so was the distribution of cheap or even free grain for making bread.

However, the relationship of the *princeps* (or monarch) to the people of the city of Rome after the citizens had largely, and in the end almost entirely, lost any right to a say in public affairs is not to be seen solely in the light of the provision he made for them. There was indeed a supply problem for the largest city in the Mediterranean world, a city that was still growing, and the *princeps* was bound to see it as his business to protect the people of Rome from famine. But the population of the city could also expect him to pay it a certain if limited amount of attention in future as a political partner. The people of Rome might now be almost entirely excluded from political decision-making, and after the spread of Roman citizenship to the whole of Italy they were deprived to a great extent of their privileged position, but they were still indispensable politically. They represented the entire Roman people (*populus Romanus*).

Only the mass of the citizens, assembled as they always had been by the edict of a magistrate, could play that part, and, although their influence on political decisions decreased to the same extent as they ceased to take an active part in voting and in passing laws, when the political order became a monarchy they did have a new political role. The people of the city of Rome did not, like the Senate, rise to formal partnership with the new ruler, but they increasingly acquired the function of a sounding-board for the representation of the dignity of the *princeps* and the actions on which he decided. Octavian had already used them in this way on his first political appearance in Rome, when he sought recognition as the dictator's son. The matter at stake then had been payment of the dictator's legacy to the Romans, and the people, who could make no decision on that point themselves, had merely agreed spontaneously and informally to Octavian's proposition. When the crowd around the ruler's residence acted and reacted, whether asked to or not, in response to all that he did, that fact alone gave the people political weight, because they lived densely concentrated around the centre of government and, in bearing the dignity and name of the Roman people, they also symbolized the great past. Even in the new political circumstances, they continued to stand for the Roman people as a whole in what they accepted and what they did not. The agreement that the *princeps* wanted from them was not what it had been in the days of the republic, when they took a formal part in voting and law-making; and it had no legal basis. But it was still effective, and in becoming a ritual on those occasions when the appearance of the people was required it very soon acquired a contextual framework.

Concern for the daily lives of the people of Rome must therefore also be seen as an encounter between the ruler and those he ruled, the public expression of the patron's duty to ensure the welfare of his clients, as the people had now become, and their acknowledgement of it. In the process, and because of the greatly superior position of the *princeps*, that duty came to look like a virtue conveying the idea of generosity (*liberalitas*). In carrying it out, Augustus was acting very much in the tradition of the republic. He was the successor of the aristocracy of republican times, who had now left the political arena.

The supply of grain was of central importance in such *liberalitas* toward the plebs of Rome. There were two points at issue: one was to ensure that the market had enough grain for bread, and the other to distribute grain free to the population of the capital. The first point was especially vital at times of crisis, for instance the years 23/22 BC and AD 6, when there was famine, but also in years of normal harvest in order to prevent bottlenecks in the supply system. Augustus took over the regular distribution of free grain from the tradition of the late republic and made new regulations affecting both the numbers receiving it and the organization of the process. Restructuring the authority in charge of the distribution served to secure supplies, so now it had all been placed on a new foundation.

Most of the grain came from Egypt, which produced large surpluses that were used to supply the needs of Rome. As ruler of Egypt, Augustus could make its harvests freely available in so far as they were not needed to supply the province itself. The provinces of Africa and Sicily were also important suppliers. Giving away grain for bread entailed great expense and was also against the interests of the small farmers and grain dealers of Italy. Augustus knew that, but for social and above all political reasons he could not call a halt to the practice. However, he tried to limit obvious abuses of the system. Senators and knights, understandably, were excluded from the distribution, and so were children below the age of ten. As in the days of the republic, those receiving free grain also had to be Roman citizens; foreigners and slaves received nothing. Augustus also had all those with a right to receive grain (the *plebs frumentaria*, the 'corn people') closely checked, and in the year 2 BC he reduced their number from what had probably been over 300,000 to 200,000. Lists of them were sent to the thirty-five tribes. To decrease the expense of the administration, there were plans for the rations to be distributed only three times a year in future, for periods of four months each, but after protests from the people the system eventually reverted to monthly distributions. Ration tokens (*tesserae frumentariae*) were handed out to speed up the procedure and keep a check on it.

Besides the regular distribution of grain and the voluntary special donations in times of emergency, there were sometimes distributions of other foodstuffs, for instance oil. To the population of the capital, monetary donations (*congiaria*) were even more important. Octavian had begun his career in that very way when he paid the dictator's legacy to the people of the city, and payments continued even after he had set up the principate. Indeed, they were paid so often that in the eyes of those who received such donations they almost came to seem like a wage due to them. Augustus rejected any such idea, and for that reason he did not make donations in a regular cycle, but always sought special occasions for them, such as his victories at Actium and in Spain, the death of Agrippa or the day when his grandson first put on the toga of a grown man. In addition the sums paid, which on the three occasions between the years 29 and 12 BC had amounted to 400 sesterces per person, were reduced over the course of time. As these payments were irregular they retained the character of a voluntary gift dependent on the munificence of the *princeps*, although the expectations of the people, which could not simply be ignored, made that view of them only relative. Public expectation had to be satisfied from time to time. Considering the large number of recipients, especially before the regulations introduced in 2 BC, the entire sum paid out in this way was high. Figures that have come down to us put it at just under 600 million sesterces, an amount that could have paid the wages of the entire Rome army for several years.

While the *princeps* was active only in the background of the donations system, he was prominent and very present as the organizer of games, for the theatre and the circus were the real point of contact between him and the people. The box where the *princeps* sat, his arrival, his commands during the festivities and the moment when he left all provided a focus for the attention and acclamations of the people, relating to both the performances and to other events. The importance that Augustus ascribed to the games can be seen from the fact that he financed and organized many performances himself and even took on games for which the other magistrates could have been held responsible. He sometimes used such events for political demonstrations, for instance when he had the four children of the high king of Parthia, who had been surrendered as hostages, and their families led to him in the theatre. Similarly, the games helped him to present himself as a man close to the people and anxious to ensure their pleasure. The same aim was served, not least, by certain interludes that he himself staged at public performances, such as a show put on by a dwarf, or the appearance of exotic animals at various arbitrary places: a rhinoceros at the Saepta games in July on the Field of Mars, a snake over 22 metres long in the *comitium* of the Forum.

There were plenty of occasions for games. They were all held in connection with festivals dedicated to the gods, and a glance at the Roman calendar of such festivals is enough to show that if you did not want or need to work you could attend a major performance at least once a month, not to mention the many smaller spectacles of a more private character. Performances were held in the semicircular theatre built on the Greek pattern (for tragedies, comedies, contests), or in the Circus (for athletic competitions, gladiatorial fights, foot races, horse races), and in specially excavated basins for the staging of mock naval battles. Public places were also sometimes used for gladiatorial combat and other contests, for instance the Forum, or large halls in which ad hoc scaffolding was built to accommodate the audience. Before the time of Augustus a wooden theatre had mainly been used, but it had to be specially erected for every occasion, although sometimes it stood for a little longer if put up on such places as the Field of Mars. However, tiers of wooden seating had their dangers, since the sheer mass of spectators crowded together on them could make them collapse. The first great stone theatre in Rome, built by Pompey, was inaugurated in 55 BC and restored by Augustus in 32 and was part of a large complex in the southern area of the Field of Mars. The outlines of its semicircle are still clearly visible today in a row of buildings on the site. Caesar began building another theatre of tuff stone, brick and cast concrete on the bank opposite the island in the Tiber, but it was not finished until the time of Augustus, who named it after his nephew Marcellus, who had died young. It was completed in 17 BC but not inaugurated until four years later, and with a diameter of just under 130 metres could hold over 15,000 spectators. The third and most recent stone theatre was built by Lucius Cornelius Balbus, nephew of the famous friend of the dictator, who like his uncle had attained the rank of consul and was even granted a triumph. His theatre, inaugurated in the year 13 BC, lay between the theatres of Pompey and Marcellus, like them in the southern part of the Field of Mars. It was smaller than the other two theatres, preserving an appropriate distance from them by virtue of its size, since Balbus could not compete with their builders.

The use of these theatres as places where the *princeps* and the Roman people met presupposed that the inhabitants of the city did not attend performances as an amorphous mass. Rather, their presence could be seen as a gathering of the citizens of Rome acting as a self-sufficient society. The citizens therefore sat in the middle of the semicircle (*cavea*), senators in the front row, men of equestrian rank in the rows behind them, while non-citizens (peregrines) and the wives of Roman citizens had to be content with the worst seats in the top tiers. Augustus devoted close attention to the organization of the theatres. He wanted to ensure that the wives of citizens sat separately from their husbands and excluded them entirely from all athletic contests because he did not approve of their seeing the naked male body. Once, when he was organizing games in his capacity as *pontifex maximus*, he moved the timing of a boxing match to the morning of the second day, banning all women by edict from arriving before the fifth hour (about 10 a.m.) on that day, by which time the boxing would be over. Soldiers had to sit apart from the rest of the audience, and the *princeps* provided special seats for boys and places close to them for their tutors, also decreeing that any citizens who turned up in clothing inappropriate to their status must sit in the top rows. In line with his laws on marriage, he also allotted better seats to married men than bachelors. He had similarly decided views on the question of whether men of distinction should or should not take part in performances and contests, a point on which the regulations had previously been very lax. Even members of senatorial families, as well as those of equestrian rank, had once taken part in the games. That was now forbidden by a senatorial decision taken, no doubt, at the behest of Augustus. His ideas of discipline and decency were more marked than those of many of his contemporaries, although the idea that the conduct of crowds is more predictable if they are divided and thus easier to survey was very much in line with Roman thinking in general, and distinct from the Greek idea of large gatherings.

In all these measures Augustus showed great respect for the institution of the games, which were so popular with the people. He made great efforts to keep them running smoothly and properly and even made sure that during the games a watch was kept on the relatively empty streets, so that thieves would find it hard to practise their trade. He frequently watched the performances and contests with members of his family and his friends, quite often from his house on the Palatine, which had a good view over the valley where the Circus lay, and it is evident that he shared the pleasure taken in them by most Romans, although with Augustus it never degenerated into a passion for one kind of contest or another. He showed particular interest only in boxing, which he watched not only on official occasions but sometimes when small groups were pitting their strength against each other in the streets.

The plebeian class of the city of Rome, once representing the people as a whole and still their respected surrogate under the late republic, had found a new role, but in the process had changed its point of reference. Instead of the magistrates – for instance the consuls and the tribunes of the people – and instead of the Senate a new political factor had appeared first in the figure of Caesar and now in that of the *princeps*. And although the people went on steadily losing real political importance, and had lost it almost entirely by the end of the reign of Augustus, they remained a 'partner', in spite or perhaps even because of the loss of their legal relevance. For while the city magistrates and the Senate, besides their role in serving the *princeps*, saw themselves in traditional terms and represented that tradition to the *princeps* for the sake of their self-esteem, none of this played any part in the life of the plebs of the city. The constitutional rights of the people had been too severely curtailed in the previous few decades, and the discrepancy between the status of the people of Rome and that of the Roman citizens of Italy and the empire as a whole was too obvious for much to be made of their role now.

So the people of the city of Rome found themselves a new function. Representing all the Romans, even representing all the people of the empire, they became, as mentioned above, a kind of sounding-board for the new ruler's decisions and his presentation of himself, their monarch. The events of the last few decades had prepared them for their new part, and they assumed the role all the more easily because Augustus could be seen as the successor to those 'popular' politicians who since the Gracchi had allegedly supported decisions close to the interests of the common people. The 'father' of Augustus, the dictator Caesar, had already seen or more probably pretended to see himself as a supporter of popular policies, despite his half-hearted attitude to the people. The political tradition of the plebs of the city of Rome, however, lay more in the social than the political sphere. It concerned their welfare and entertainment, and the respect due to them. So the loss of most of their right to take part in law-making was not much mourned, and in fact had long ago been transferred to the Senate; the emphasis was on their welfare and their recognition as an informal point of reference for monarchical decisions, even though there was nothing resembling a plebiscite in the principate of Augustus. The people of Rome not only had no decisions to make – which as the term indicates is the point of a plebiscite – they were also politically insignificant by comparison with the army and the administrative class as represented by the Senate. At the time of Augustus, and under his successors, the people neither did nor caused to be done anything of political significance. They were the backdrop against which the monarch presented himself, and their importance was in that capacity. For all the impression that an audience ten thousand strong might make in the theatre, the crowd was not an independent political power but remained part of the show, an entertaining spectacle and at the same time the stage for monarchical self-presentation.

Until the beginning of the first century BC, the area to which Roman citizenship extended (the *ager Romanus*) had been confined to the west of central Italy and the land reaching north-east from there to the Apennines. Only the wish of the cities and tribes of the Italian peninsula for Roman citizenship, allied to Rome and in a league with each other, opened the way to the legal unity of Italy. It is true that the allies first had to achieve the right to the citizenship that they wanted in a fierce war (90–88 BC), but after that almost the whole of Italy was the land of the Romans. Only Upper Italy was excluded at first; remaining a military district (or province) administered by governors, although many Roman towns had already been founded there. However, once Augustus had granted Roman citizenship to the inhabitants of all of Upper Italy, including those who did not yet have it, the whole country from the peaks of the Alps to the southern tip of the peninsula (apart from the large islands) was now a legal as well as a geographical unit: the area in which the holders of Roman citizenship lived. At the same time civic awareness that Italy was the native land of the Romans formed. Thereafter Roman pride was linked not just to the cities of Rome but to all Italy (*tota Italia*), which to some extent could be seen as the vessel in which Rome had grown to greatness, casting all other lands into the shade not only through its historical achievements and divine mission, but because of its natural advantages and its climate. The praise of Italy (*laudes Italiae*) thus stood for praise of the Roman homeland, and it is celebrated by poets such as Virgil, whose *Georgics* sing the praises of the generous but moderate natural advantages of Italy, as distinct from the world of the east, which had apparently unbounded blessings in many respects, but spread terror and so seemed sinister.

In the time of Augustus the Italian peninsula was densely populated. The number of just adult Roman citizens at the time was over four million, so the entire Roman population will have been around twelve million people, and another million Romans lived in the provinces, the great majority of them in the towns and cities founded there under Roman law. The landscape of Italy contained more towns and cities than any other part of the empire. Not only did the Etruscans and the Greeks who had settled in the south of the peninsula since the eighth century contribute to the urban life of Italy, so did the Romans themselves when, as the heirs of Etruscan and Greek culture, they founded many Roman settlements (*coloniae*, 'planted towns') and encouraged urban development everywhere. Italy was now, so to speak, covered with towns and cities both old and new (*municipia* and *coloniae*). Urban areas stood close to each other, and in all there were over 400 towns, some of them quite small. Such purely rural districts as could still be found in the northern Apennines and on the southern slopes of the Alps were associated, as far as possible, with neighbouring towns and cities, without entirely giving up their traditional legal and social structures.

In the high and late imperial period, the cities and towns of Italy assimilated their various differences into a largely unified urban culture. That was not yet the case in the time of Augustus himself. Greek was spoken in large parts of central and southern Italy, and that was to continue in remote areas until the late period of the Roman empire. In addition, the dialects of Italian tribes that had survived from the old epoch of freedom were still in use, and Latin superseded them only in a very slow process. The Roman settlements founded all over Italy after the fourth century contributed to its spread, and so did the use of Latin in the army and the administration. Latin thus became the *lingua franca* in Italy (and in the entire western part of the empire), the common language used by almost everyone and finally spoken by every inhabitant of the country instead of or as well as his local dialect, although a Roman-born senator might shudder at the accent of a colleague from Upper Italy or Samnium.

Since the civil wars of Sulla's time, Italy had suffered severely and repeatedly, particularly in the vicissitudes of the fighting after 49 BC. The proscriptions and the settlement of veterans had changed the property situation all over large areas, and high taxes had paralysed economic activity for a long time. When at last peace returned, the country recovered relatively quickly, and with the breaking-up of many large estates to provide land for the veterans, partly at the expense of the cultivation of large areas by slaves, there even seemed to be some support for a free peasantry and thus a positive change in the structure of the population. In fact at the time many farms and small estates were initially created for hundreds of thousands of veterans. Many small property owners, however, soon sold their land back to large landed proprietors, and many of those who stayed had their small or medium-sized estates farmed by slaves and tenant farmers while they themselves enjoyed city life on the proceeds. In addition, large estates depending on slave labour did not entirely disappear, since otherwise growing grain and breeding livestock were hardly worthwhile; only the production of wine and oil promised good profits to the owner of a small or medium-sized tract of land. In the end, and for these reasons, the extensive settlement of soldiers in Italy did not lead to a revival of Italian agriculture. On the contrary, the large estate increasingly became the usual way to run the Italian rural economy again after the civil wars.

The decades of the reign of Augustus are notable for the relative economic prosperity of Italy. Towns and cities were adorned with fine buildings, the road network was improved and extended, and everywhere the rich and distinguished built country houses and fine villas in town, while most of the tribute and other dues from the provincials was spent in Italy when it was not needed for the armies stationed on the borders. But although there was no lack of agricultural produce, and many commodities, like oil and wine, could even be exported, while Italian craft products such as ceramic ware also enjoyed great popularity throughout the empire, the balance of trade was negative. The country itself was far from rich in metals and had to import many objects made of iron and copper, as well as luxury items from the east. There was also a shortage of timber, as well as other forest products, now in short supply because of what in many places had been the unthinking clearances of once well-wooded districts in central and southern Italy.

With increasing trade, the importance of the harbours of Italy grew. Among them, Ostia, as the harbour of Rome itself, ranked first. Many harbours profited from the fact that the seas were now at peace, and from the growing prosperity of Italy. They included Puteoli (Pozzuoli) on the northern coast of the Bay of Naples and Tarentum and Brundisium (Brindisi) in the south and south-east of the peninsula. At the same time Campania became more developed. It had always been an area of central importance to the peninsula, and its mild climate and proximity to the coast made it the favourite resort of the upper classes, who went there for rest and relaxation. Even in the time of the republic most of the nobles had villas in Campania, to which they withdrew from political business, and from the time of Augustus onwards the rulers built large palaces here. Augustus himself owned the island of Capri, as well as other landed property, and his successor Tiberius was to make Capri his permanent residence in the last years of his life.

Augustus divided the Italian peninsula into eleven large districts (*regiones*). Today it is hard to be sure what his intention was, since the regions had no leaders of their own provided with a bureaucratic apparatus, so they were not administrative units with regular tasks. Nor did they restrict the power of the cities as a superior regional administration; cities remained the lowest administrative units of Italy, while the regions obviously had only a small amount of administrative business to deal with, and that only periodically – perhaps because they provided a framework more easily surveyed for that purpose. For instance, the regions were responsible for assessing the fortune of citizens and collecting the inheritance tax set up by Augustus, and later for other public purposes.

The division into regions went hand in hand with the precise establishment of the borders of Upper Italy beyond the Po. First, however, the often refractory tribes living in and close to the Alpine area had to be subdued, an aim that the Romans pursued in many vigorous operations often conducted very harshly – in the years 35, 25, and in and after 16 – and finally achieved. The inhabitants of these 'pacified' regions, or those of them still alive, were sometimes exiled and the land given to soldiers, sometimes assigned to neighbouring towns or, as in certain parts of the western Alps, placed under native client princes dependent on Rome.

Thereafter the line of the Alpine peaks was the border with the regions of Italy to the north and west, while the river Arsia (Arsa, immediately west of present Rijeka in Croatia) formed the eastern border.

The terms used to describe the regions indicate the great tribes or groups of tribes that had given their names long ago to those parts of the country, for instance Etruria, Umbria and Samnium in central Italy, Brutii et Lucania and Apulia et Calabria in southern Italy. The four northern Italian regions were Liguria (north of Etruria) and Aemilia (the plain north of the Apennines to the Po, called after the builder of the Via Aemilia, the great road running through it, Marcus Aemilius Lepidus, consul in the year 187), as well as the two regions north of the Po and divided by the river Addua (Adda), Transpadana in the west and Venetia et Histria in the east. The name of the part of the country from which first Italy and then the entire Mediterranean had become a Roman world, Latium, was no longer used for a region. From now on old Latium was part of Campania, the reason being that the name of the Latin tribe (*nomen Latinum*) had been used to denote the 'colonies' founded by Rome in many different areas under Latin law (*coloniae Latinae*) and with the extension of Roman citizenship to those colonies in the years 90/89 had disappeared from use. Only the ancient point of origin of all that was Roman, the *urbs*, the city of Rome itself, remained outside these major divisions, retaining both Latin and Roman names.

Italy was the land of the Romans, and the Romans, meaning all male citizens of Rome, made up the Roman people (*populus Romanus*) in the political sense. In fact the Roman people could take political decisions only in Rome, which was and remained a city state, so the exercise of political rights was bound to the city. None the less, every Roman could feel that in concept he was a part of the people, wherever he lived, whether in Italy or the provinces, whether he was a soldier, a civil servant or an ordinary civilian. The progressive extension of citizenship, once confined to the city, to the whole of Italy had, however, weakened its political aspect, and even a man living in Rome or staying there from time to time no longer, as we have seen, had much of a chance to make his opinions known in the assemblies of the people now that the exercise of political power, first in fact and then also in form, had been monopolized by the *princeps* and, within certain limits, by the Senate. And now that political rights meant less and less for Roman citizens, citizenship could be extended without further detriment to areas further from the city within whose walls all citizens had once been able to gather. Even in the time of the late republic, there had been Roman cities outside Italy, for instance Narbo (Narbonne) in southern Gaul.

A new development began with the dictator Caesar and with Augustus, making Roman citizens more and more likely to be living outside Italy in the provinces. Veterans and parts of the Roman population now found new homes in the many large cities and smaller settlements all over the Mediterranean area, sometimes built entirely from scratch in rural districts, for instance Augusta Emerita (Mérida) in the west Iberian province of Lusitania, which indicated the origin of those who settled there in its name: they were *emeriti*, soldiers now retired from the army, or veterans. Some of the cities, like Corinth and Carthage, were built on the sites of ancient cities that had been destroyed. At this time several native settlements had already been elevated to the rank of Roman cities, if they had grown in size and structure to be urban in nature, and had among their inhabitants a large contingent of Roman citizens or a population assimilated to Roman life, for instance Tingis (Tangier) in western Mauretania (as early as 38 BC) and Tarraco (Taragona), capital of the northern Iberian province of Tarraconensis, in 23 BC. However, the Romanization of non-Roman cities was not a major development until several generations later. In the time of Augustus most of the inhabitants of the Roman settlements built in the provinces still came from Italy, and in many cases the settlements themselves were new foundations. Settlement in the provinces had become necessary, if only because there was no available land left in Italy itself. Hundreds of thousands therefore streamed out into the provinces, taking with them the Latin language, Roman ideas and the Roman way of life, for in the organization and outward appearance of their cities the settlers, naturally, took their guidelines from what they had been accustomed to in Italy, with the result that the face of the Mediterranean world was more and more Roman. Under Caesar, and, since only in a very few cases was he able to see his foundation of cities through to the end, more particularly under Augustus, this development was not gradual but sweeping. It altered whole tracts of land, and seemed to make the borders between Italy and the provinces easier to cross, thus also endangering the special political position of the land of the Romans. At an earlier date, it is true, Roman citizens had settled in the provinces for a length of time or permanently, joining in their own associations there (*conventus civium Romanorum*) to maintain their standard of living and secure their privileged position. But only now were whole cities with Roman rights, some of them large, built on provincial soil. For those who looked back to the past, this was the beginning of a development at the end of which travelling to a province no longer meant moving from the ruling land to a subject one, a district characteristically under the direct administration of Rome or the Roman army, but from one Roman country to another. However, the complete or partial move to equal status of the former land of the rulers with those of the subjects was barely perceptible to the contemporaries of Augustus. To them, Italy was still pre-eminent, as it traditionally had been, and no one, not even the inhabitants of the provinces, doubted that Italy, the land of the Romans, ruled the provinces.

The political difference was retained in the minds of Romans and provincials alike and found concrete expression in the fact that the citizens of Italy did not have to pay direct taxes. A Roman was free of tax (*immunis*), a provincial must pay tribute (*stipendiarius, vectigalis*). With the exception of the 5 per cent inheritance tax imposed by Augustus, indirect taxes were therefore levied, for instance the sales tax on goods acquired at auction or through purchase agreements, and duty as well as a tax on the manumission of slaves. The property and capital taxes paid by provincials, in contrast, were a sign of subservience. Here we see the deliberately sharp distinction between Italy and the provinces which led, not least, to the fact that the soil of Italy, being tax-free, acquired a special legal quality. Augustus bestowed this Italian land law (*ius Italicum*, Italian law) on certain Roman cities outside Italy as a privilege. As a result, the colonists of these cities owned provincial land as if it were Italian land, and thus paid no land tax. Conversely, the existence of areas of non-Italian land under 'Italian law' gave the impression that provincial land was legally less valuable. Given this situation, in fact many lawyers of the imperial period developed the concept that the Roman people were overlords on provincial soil. And while this was a rather vague legal concept, devised for political rather than practical legal ends, it tells us that the Augustan period still took a political distinction between Italy and the provinces as a principle, one that might on occasion have legal implications. It was Augustus himself who wanted to preserve this distinction. To him, borrowing as he did from all the political and moral ideas of Roman tradition, the difference between a ruling and a subject society – and similarly between an area where the rulers lived and another where their subjects resided – was part of the constitution.

A man wishing to leave Rome for one of the provinces in the western Mediterranean area could rely on a good, dense road network running both along the coasts and into the interior, and linking all the countries under Roman rule with each other and with Rome. The journey to the provinces of Gaul and Iberia took the traveller first to the coastal road, the old Via Aurelia, north to beyond Genoa and then along its continuation, the Via Julia Augusta, to the Rhône delta, on along the Via Domitia, and thus to the Pyrenees and beyond them to Spain. Even more new roads were built in the west than the east, sometimes along older routes, particularly but not solely on the initiative of Agrippa. They had opened up the part of Gaul conquered by Caesar (Gallia Comata) and linked it to the southern Gallic province of Narbonensis. Once the Alpine areas had been conquered, road-building also made them accessible and linked them to the old Roman areas to the east and south. The roads were very well constructed, with milestones giving information about distances and posting stations where horses could be changed and travellers could rest, and they were maintained in good order. In general, and not just for short distances, the roads promised safety and opportunities to stop and rest at any time. You could cover as much as a hundred kilometres a day in a travelling carriage. The armies in particular preferred the road for long journeys, and they marched so efficiently that they could cover long distances in a relatively short time. A sea route took you to your destination more quickly, but many travellers disliked sea travel, because unfavourable winds – the art of cruising before the wind was not yet known – calms and storms often made it hard to calculate a voyage in advance, and there was little travelling by sea in the winter months. If the winds were very good, a merchant ship of medium size needed no more than ten days or even only a week to sail from Ostia to Gades (Cádiz) on the Atlantic. The voyage from Ostia to Carthago Nova (Cartagena) took about four days, and the voyage to Carthage in North Africa about the same. In some circumstances warships went faster. Good roads and harbours, as well as the certainty that the peace of Augustus had eliminated danger from war at home or abroad as well as the risk of encountering pirates and highway robbers, brought Italy and the west closer together and reinforced the relationship that had now existed for centuries.

When the Romans celebrated the Secular Games in the year 17 BC, the countries of the western Mediterranean had been part of the Roman sphere of power for over 200 years. In conflicts that often lasted for many years, Roman armies had laid waste large parts of North Africa and Spain, eradicating whole communities and bringing severe hardship on most of the survivors, particularly in Spain, for almost 100 years. After the Celtic, Iberian and Celtic-Iberian tribal communities of the west had been physically decimated, as conquered peoples they could no longer summon up the strength to maintain their independence and traditional ways of life in a changed world, and many also lacked the intellectual and cultural background that might have enabled them to do so. The independent cities of the coasts of southern Gaul, Spain and Mediterranean Africa, founded centuries before by Phoenician traders and Greek settlers, survived this dismal time better. But there were not very many of them, and the largest, Carthage (today Tunis), had been razed to the ground by the Romans in the year 146 BC. Many smaller towns were able to maintain something of their old glory, for instance Massilia (Marseille), although because they sided with the republicans they had been robbed by the dictator Caesar of large parts of their out-lying possessions.

Caesar had added to the areas already ruled by Rome all the Celtic land from the province of Narbonensis to the Atlantic and the Rhine. The Romans had based the conquest of the western land masses, and finally their subjugation as provinces, on anxiety for their own military security. While that could constitute an acceptable reason for the conquest of large tracts of land in the struggle against the great power of Carthage, the Celtic lands conquered by Caesar were a different case. His conquests were made not to defend the empire against an enemy, but so that he could have a large army available to him stationed on provincial soil outside Rome, giving him a secure base for winning the position of power in the empire that he wanted. The unrest in the province of Narbonensis before his campaign, which he cited as his reason for invading free Celtic territories, was a threadbare pretext that hardly anyone believed.

The peoples of the west had paid for their existence as states with subservience to Rome. They were often largely eradicated, any survivors being made into subjects who paid tribute to the Romans and in return were allowed to live in quasi-communities, whether as a tribe or as a city. In the early Augustan period these territories might be considered 'pacified' (*pacatus*), as the Roman put it, meaning totally subjugated. At least subjugation brought peace, although with many more advantages to the power of Rome than to its subjects. After conflicts that sometimes lasted for hundreds of years, they generally lived in conditions of great hardship. In many places, the peace was like the peace of a graveyard. That was certainly true of large areas of the parts of North Africa made into provinces by Rome (Libya and Tunisia), where life did not really begin again until Caesar refounded Carthage. Matters were not much better even in large parts of the Iberian peninsula, where two centuries of freedom fighting ended in the year 19 with the defeat by Agrippa of an uprising by the north-west Iberian Cantabrians, most of whom were eradicated. Southern Gaul (Narbonensis) had long been considered a pacified province. Only in parts of West Africa (Mauretania, comprising what is now the east of Algeria and Morocco) was there still occasional unrest, mainly involving the Gaetulians, Berber tribes living on the outskirts of the desert. However, Augustus left the job of quelling them to the local client princes, supported by Roman troops from the African and south Iberian provinces.

With the exception of Mauretania, which except for part of the eastern area (Numidia) had been governed since the year 25 by King Juba II, who had been educated in Rome, the entire west had now been divided into military districts (the provinces). The foundation of the two oldest provinces, Sicily and Sardinia with Corsica, went back to the third century BC. Augustus merged the two provinces on the African coast into one, calling it Africa Nova, and conversely after the complete pacification of the Iberian peninsula made the two provinces of which it had consisted into three, Tarraconensis in the north-east, Baetica in the south and Lusitania in the west. The Gallic land mass had been divided into four provinces since the twenties: besides the old province of Gallia Narbonensis in the south, the three provinces lying in the Celtic country conquered by Caesar, Belgica in the north, Aquitania in the south-west and Lugdunensis in the east. In all, the western empire thus contained ten provinces, but we should also count Illyricum, comprising the Adriatic coast up to the Macedonian border, as well as the Dalmatian and

Pannonian inland areas conquered by Octavian, for although they were geographically a part of the Balkan peninsula, there as in the west Latin was the everyday *lingua franca*. To the east of a line reaching from the city of Scodra to the western border of Cyrenaica, Greek predominated.

All eleven provinces could be regarded as, on the whole, 'pacified'. However, certain potential flashpoints had decided whether a province was allocated to the administration of the Senate or of the *princeps* in the year 27, and still did. The Senate had control of the African province, which had long been spared unrest, of equally peaceful Baetica and of the large islands. The two remaining provinces of the Iberian peninsula, where individual tribes still rose against Roman rule until the year 18, along with all the provinces of Gaul, were under the control of the *princeps*. The pacified part of Illyricum went to the Senate. At first the real source of unrest in the west was still the Celtic country conquered by Caesar (Gallia Comata), and that must have been why Narbonensis, although pacified long before, at first went to the *princeps* as the area through which troops marched to the north of Gaul, and to reach his two Iberian provinces. But after a few years, by which time it could genuinely be considered peaceful, Augustus handed it over to the authority of the Senate. The unrest in Gaul died down only gradually, after energetic measures on the part of Rome. In the year 43 Lucius Munatius Plancus, as governor of the Celtic country conquered by Caesar, was still involved in struggles with the Rhaetians, and he reached Lake Constance. In the year 38 Agrippa had to take the field against the Aquitanians. He secured the Rhine border by crossing the river and settling those Ubians who had already moved to the left bank of the river on a site near what would later be Cologne. Between 30 and 28, in the years before the great constitutional settlement of 27, there were reports of several uprisings at the same time in various parts of Gaul: one of the tasks that fell to Gaius Carrinas, as governor, was to fight the Belgic tribe of the Morini on the shores of the English Channel. His legate Marcus Nonius Gallus had to fight the rebellious Treveri and their German allies, and Marcus Valerius Messalla Corvinus, as governor of Aquitania, had to put down another Aquitanian rising. Quelling rebellions was an arduous business, and both Messalla and Carrinas were granted triumphs for their victories. But although the constant presence of several legions in the Gallic provinces was necessary, the disproportionate military strength there was not solely because of these last flickerings of resistance to the Roman occupation, and the intransigence of individual German tribes on the right bank of the Rhine who now had to learn to accept the river as a frontier, although they had so often crossed it in the past to go raiding or looking for more land. Obviously Augustus soon formed the plan of continuing his father's Gallic campaign by undertaking a large-scale expedition over the Rhine and the Alps, and the fighting force gathered in Gaul was destined for that purpose.

Only gradually did the tormented and humiliated people of the west begin to sense the coming of a new era and realize that, after the cruel wars of conquest, the extermination policies of many Roman commanders and the civil wars that had their aftermath even in the western countries, their new ruler offered prospects not just of the peace of everlasting subservience but of active welfare, a certain prosperity and even a degree of freedom never allowed them before. The prerequisite, naturally, was that they should adapt to the new conditions, that is to say keep their eyes turned to Rome and refrain from pursuing any independent policy. However, the blessings brought by the Roman Peace (Pax Romana) and the concern for their welfare of the *princeps*, as their patron, were not felt to the same degree everywhere. It all depended on how old and durable relations with Rome were, and on the peaceful demeanour of the subjected, the many vicissitudes of the wars of conquest and the cultural proximity of those concerned to Rome and their willingness to foster it. Sicily, on which Phoenician and above all urban Greek culture had left their mark, found the situation easiest, in spite of all the hardships of the late republican period. The going was harder for many tribal societies of the Iberian peninsula.

If the provincials had come to terms with Roman rule, their ability to adapt to Rome pointed the way to a better future. The standards to which they had to adjust were the urban way of life and recognition of a class of notable leading personages in it who guided the fate of the city. Adapting to an aristocratic and urbanized system was the way forward. The urbanization process could lean for support on the Phoenician and Greek settlements along the coasts established centuries earlier, and on the typically Celtic fortified settlements (*oppida*) in their administrative districts, which were to be found everywhere in the Gallic and Iberian provinces. Long before the time of Augustus, a number of cities in the west had been set up by Roman magistrates as *coloniae* organized on the Roman pattern; they included, for instance, such cities as Pollentia on Mallorca (123 BC). Many residential centres had also gradually formed into Roman towns when individual veterans, traders and their families decided voluntarily on a life in the provinces, and naturally chose the urban form of settlement. In that way Italica in the south of Baetica, not far from Hispalis (Seville), gradually gained the status of a Roman city (*municipium*).

But although there were cities or early forms of cities everywhere in the west to serve the Romans as points of departure and bases for the urban and cultural Roman penetration of the surrounding country, urbanization of the western possessions was most durably encouraged and continued by the colonization policy of the dictator Caesar and after him Augustus – and above all, for decades, by the necessity of settling many thousands of veterans and other urban Romans on their own land. In many places, the dictator had already laid the foundations of a city, and Augustus built on those foundations. However, he himself also founded many Roman towns (*coloniae*) or, if they had previously been non-Roman cities, introduced innovations. They might then, as well as many foreign ('peregrine') cities, acquire the status of a *municipium*, while others were granted Latin rights, which distinguished the holders of urban office as magistrates with Roman citizenship, a preliminary stage to granting them full Roman legal status.

The extent of urbanization is most clearly obvious on the Iberian peninsula, and particularly in Baetica, where there were several dozen such Latin towns in the Augustan period, as well as a number of *coloniae* and *municipia*, and in Tarraconensis, where the military colony of Caesaraugusta (Zaragoza) developed into a flourishing city. Lusitania was a little way behind the other two provinces, but it had its capital Emerita (Mérida), mentioned above, also a veterans' colony. Narbonensis already had many cities and now saw further foundations such as Forum Julii (Fréjus). The dictator himself, and after him Lucius Munatius Plancus as governor, founded few cities in the recently conquered Celtic country, but exceptions were Equestris (Nyon) and Augusta Raurica (Basel-Augst). Far more new towns under Roman law were founded in the province of Africa, where several formerly 'peregrine' settlements also rose to the status of Roman *municipia*. Even Mauretania, administered by King Juba after the year 25, contained a series of military colonies, especially in the phase between 33 and 25, when the country was under direct Roman administration, such as Saldae (Bougie), and quite a number of native settlements were promoted to the status of cities under Roman law (*municipia*). The island of Sicily, which had long been largely urbanized, needed no new foundations. Urban life there had, however, suffered severely during the slave rebellions and in the civil wars, and parts of the countryside had been devastated, particularly along the south coast. Now there was a new spirit of activity abroad, thanks to the veterans who reinforced the existing communities and/or the rise of towns to the status of Roman colonies or cities under Latin law. In Illyricum, which was close to Augustus' heart after his campaign there, and was certainly popular with a number of veterans because of its proximity to Italy, several new *coloniae* and *municipia* were also founded. Salonae (today Solin near Split) and Narona (Vid), for instance, were Julian foundations.

But Augustus was not concerned solely for the Roman cities. In the countries of the west, ravaged for decades by wars and rebellions, there were many places where the old native (peregrine) settlements stood in particular need of his support. In Gaul, Spain and the Illyrian area there were reconstructions to be carried out, and in fact in the time of Augustus many new settlements were founded to accommodate exiles and the homeless. In Gaul, for instance, the old mountain settlement of Bibracte took new form as Augustodunum (Autun) lower down the mountains, and Lutetia Parisiorum (Paris), destroyed in the great Celtic revolt of the year 52, was rebuilt, while the 'town of the Ubians' (*oppidum Ubiorum*), later Cologne, was founded on the right bank of the Rhine. In Lusitania, Bracara Augusta (Braga in northern Portugal) was founded. The new foundation or the encouragement of peregrine communities occurred in many places along the great roads that were now extended or built from scratch, and the stations along those roads did not just offer supplies for the immediate needs of travellers, but grew to become urban centres with their own local administration. This was how the early form of what would later be the large Roman city of Augusta Treverorum (Trier) came into being. Situated in terrain where there does not even seem to have been a fortified Celtic settlement (*oppidum*) earlier, the city must have grown from the requirements created by the bridge built there across the Moselle. The purpose of the bridge was to be part of the long-distance road leading from Lyon to the Rhine valley – although without any complex of buildings to guard the bridge, with a station for changing horses and other travel services and accommodation for what must already have been a tribal assembly of the Treveri here, it could hardly have been called a town at all in Augustan times, let alone a Roman city. Here as in many other places, the measures of the Roman administration served non-Roman communities and the general infrastructure of the province. Concern for the welfare of the 'peregrine' settlements and the extension of the traffic network were in fact no less important for opening up the country than the building of new towns under Roman law.

With the thousands, indeed hundreds of thousands, of Roman settlers, the Latin language spread in the countries of the west. By now it was not spoken only in Roman settlements, it also acquired greater importance as a *lingua franca*, although it could not entirely displace the old languages in general use, Phoenician and Greek. In the Augustan period Greek was also in use in the west, even outside Sicily, where of course it was still the dominant language. In Africa and parts of southern Spain the Berbers, Iberians and Celts also spoke Phoenician, and although it was in decline it lingered on for several centuries.

The west was quick to adopt the Roman way of life without any deliberate attempt by the Roman authorities to impose it. The difference between Roman and local power, and the shattering of the pre-Roman world, guaranteed relatively swift adjustment. Narbonensis and the two Spanish provinces facing the Mediterranean led the way. Hardly any trace of the pre-Greek and pre-Phoenician inhabitants of the Iberian peninsula, the Iberians and Celtic-Iberians, was left; their pre-Indo-Germanic substrate of language was still spoken only in a few mountainous areas. The Celtic language and way of life was able to assert itself for longer in the Celtic country conquered by Caesar.

In terms of the land mass alone, the balance was about equal between the east and west of the empire. There were eleven western provinces in the year 17 BC, as against ten eastern provinces. But the number and extent of client states in the east was far greater. The usual way from Italy to the east was by sea, whether you took the shortest way there, from Brundisium to Apollonia on the other side of the Ionian Sea, and then continued along the great army road, the Via Egnatia, going by way of Thessalonika to the straits, or whether you took the direct sea route for longer journeys, setting off for the great harbours of Ephesos in the province of Asia, Seleukeia (Seleucia) in northern Syria or Alexandria in Egypt. The land route from Italy to the east led by road along the Dalmatian coast to the point where the route joined the Via Egnatia. This route was mainly used by travellers going from the north-east of Italy or from Dalmatia to Greece.

The ten eastern provinces represented an old cultural heritage; some of them, such as Egypt and large parts of Syria, still bearing the mark of the great civilizations of the ancient east. They had all, however, even those with an original tradition of their own, long formed the core area of Greek culture. As far back as anyone could remember, the city had been at the centre of social and political life in these countries, a development fostered by many new foundations created by the Hellenistic rulers, both great and small, who divided up the huge empire of Alexander after its founder's death. When the Romans had taken over from them as the new rulers, the new provinces set up on their soil often reflected the extent of the former areas of rule, with Macedonia corresponding to the former Antigonid kingdom, Asia to the kingdom of Pergamom and Egypt to the Ptolemaic kingdom. The many languages of the pre-Greek world still survived; they were spoken by many people, but the *lingua franca* had been Greek for centuries.

Of these provinces, seven were under the control of the Senate. They were Macedonia, Achaea, which was a separate province from Macedonia after the year 27 – the old Greek motherland, with the Aegean islands – and in addition the western part of Asia Minor (Asia), the coast of the Black Sea (Bithynia et Pontus), the farther Anatolian area of Galatia, declared a province after the death in 25 BC of its last king, Amyntas, and Cyrenaica, merged with Crete to form a province in the year 27 (Creta et Cyrene) as well as the island of Cyprus, which, previously probably united with Cilicia, was given to the Senate in the year 22. Augustus controlled only three provinces in the east: Syria, Egypt and Cilicia. Of these three, the first two were important areas in both economic and military terms, while Cilicia, still a large territory in the time of Cicero, had now shrunk to the great plain around Tarsos, and lost a good deal of its importance. The many principalities within the provinces or on their borders were controlled either by the governors of the provinces next to them or around them or directly from Rome. Among the most important of them were the kingdoms of Cappadocia under Archelaos and of Armenia under Tigranes in the east of Anatolia, as well as the kingdom of Judaea, which on the death of Herod in the year 4 BC was divided between his three sons, and the Thracian kingdom east of the province of Macedonia and north of the straits (roughly speaking the east of Bulgaria today). Only two of the smaller principalities need be mentioned: Commagene in the north of Syria, between the rivers Pyramos (Ceyhan) and Euphrates, which was still ruled by a branch of the Seleucid house, and the small kingdom of Pontus in the north-east of Galatia (Pontus Polemoniacus).

The east did not need to have any new cities founded. Only in special cases was a city built, for instance near battlefield to celebrate a military victory. When Pompey won his victory over Mithradates Eupator in the year 66 BC, he built a city called Nicopolis ('victory city') in Asia Minor, and Octavian did the same in the year 30 after his victory at Actium. His Nicopolis, on the northern peninsula of Actium, was populated by merging many communities in that area and quickly grew to be one of the most densely inhabited cities in Greece. Although many veterans had been settled there, it was considered not a Roman but a Greek city and was endowed with special privileges on its foundation. Augustus further fostered its status among the Greeks by giving it one-sixth of the votes in the council of the reorganized Protective League (Amphictyony) of the Delphic oracle.

But while Nicopolis remained a unique case, owing its foundation to special circumstances, the dictator and after him Augustus saw themselves frequently obliged to turn to the eastern as well as the western provinces to settle many veterans and citizens from Rome and other Italian cities. However, the forms of that settlement differed in principle from the shape it took in the west. First, it is striking that in the east no city with a Greek population was transformed into a Roman city, that is to say, using Roman terminology, became a *municipium*, and, in contrast to the west, no town or city was under Latin law. Instead we find great numbers of Roman colonies (*coloniae*), that is to say new urban foundations under Roman law. The basic principle can easily be explained: in the absence of an all-embracing bureaucracy reshaping the empire everywhere, Romans had to regard the city as the basic unit of their administrative rule and thus had to work to build up urban centres where they found none in existence. They did not have to think about urbanization in the east, with its many existing cities, because no settlements there had to be built up to the form, or early form, of a city with the help of Roman municipal ordinances and a Roman or Romanized population. The settlement of veterans and other Roman citizens could therefore take place only where there was land to spare, meaning above all on the sites of towns that had been destroyed, confiscated or depopulated by war. Roman veterans and civilians, sometimes with some of the original Greek inhabitants, were settled in such places, and in this way the newly rebuilt cities were given the Roman organizational form of *coloniae*. Although it was impossible to naturalize the Latin language in the east, Latin did spread specifically Roman ways of life and thought and thus contributed to a balance between east and west within the Roman empire. Of the many cities built at the time as Roman colonies, we may mention Sinope (Sinop) on the Black Sea coast, already founded by Caesar, Dyrrhachium (Durazzo), Patrae (Patras), Alexandria Troas (near old Troy) and Berytus (Beirut).

The west of the empire profited most by the land settlement policy of the Augustan period. But there still remained a great difference between east and west on several levels. The eastern countries were well ahead of those in the west in economic development of almost all kinds, particularly in all areas of handicrafts. In addition they had a considerably greater wealth of agrarian products and minerals. They exported manufactured products as well as raw materials, and the balance of trade on the whole was to their advantage; only Narbonensis and of course Italy could compete in the west. Similarly, income from taxation was considerably higher in the eastern than the western provinces.

In addition, there was also a considerable cultural difference between east and west. The ancient Orient and Greece had left their mark on the east, where there was a written culture millennia old and a well-developed literary tradition which the west, initially without a written culture of its own, could share only in certain cities founded by the Phoenicians and Greeks. Furthermore, the eyes of the Romans had been turned eastwards for centuries. The Romans had been influenced in successive waves by the Greeks, Greek religion and literature, Greek domesticity and Greek forms of architecture, first by contact with the Etruscans, who, themselves influenced by the Greeks, brought the urban life and Greek lifestyles to the Latins and then directly by the Greek colonies in southern Italy and Sicily. Later, direct contact with the Greek motherland brought the Greek cultural heritage, and under military Roman occupation of the east these links and influences were further reinforced and multiplied. The nobility of the republic, and not they alone, had already felt Greek influence in the second century, and in the time of Cicero Greek was the second language of almost every man of distinction. The Greek spirit was part of the Roman world, and Latin became able to encompass Greek ideas. Many prepared the way for this development, particularly the Roman poets and – in philosophy and rhetoric – Cicero. So Rome and Italy in the time of Augustus had long been culturally a Greek province: the political decline of the Greeks went hand in hand with a Hellenization of the Roman world.

# 11

# The New Leadership Class

The upper class in Rome and the Italian cities had suffered severe set-backs since the outbreak of the civil war. Although some of the noble families still had a certain amount of influence in public life during the later years of the Augustan period, between the entry of Caesar into Italy across the Rubicon and the time of the death of Augustus there had been a complete reshuffle of the leadership class, in both its social composition and its fundamental intellectual and political ideas. Roman society did still bear the mark left on it by the aristocracy, but the nobles of the year 49 BC and those of the year AD 14 were worlds apart. Many old families who had survived, like the Calpurnii Bibuli and the Licinii Luculli, paid for it with a loss in social prestige, since they could no longer boast of any consular appointments; others retained their former status, but were submerged in a sea of new names filling the lists (*fasti*) not only of the lower ranks of magistrates but also the highest of all, the consulate. Between the years 39 and 26, for instance, although many consular names still had a fine old traditional ring about them, there were already twice as many consuls from families whose members had never before held that post, nor even a praetorship. Beside families such as the Cornelii Lentuli, Domitii Ahenobarbi, Valerii Messallae and Licinii Crassi the names of men 'of no family' now featured. There were many able men among them who had proved their worth in the army or the administration, including Gaius Calvisius Sabinus, Lucius Arruntius, Titus Statilius Taurus, Marcus Cocceius Nerva, Gaius Sosius and Marcus Vinicius, and not a few of these new men were the founding fathers of families famous in the imperial period, giving rise to a new nobility. Other and no less gifted army commanders, however, such as Lucius Tarius Rufus, who rose from a very obscure family to the consulate, were unable to pass on their new social rank. Special political circumstances meant that the lists of consuls in these years show a mingling of famous and unknown names, with members of the old families sometimes more strongly represented, as in the years soon after the founding of the principate, particularly between 19 and 6 BC, but sometimes new men featured prominently over a long period, most of them former army officers, as in the last decade of the life of Augustus. A number of these families, like the Statilii, Cocceii and Vinicii, managed to maintain their newly won social status in the long term, or at least for several generations, and could hold their own with the families who had the old tradition behind them.

A large number of the new senators came from parts of Italy that had not previously provided them. While before the civil war the great majority had been from the west of central Italy and the Sabine country, areas already settled by Romans long before the wide extension of citizenship in the years 90–88, senators now came from all parts of Italy, including the north. The Emperor Claudius later justified his policy of opening up the Senate even further, so that Romans from the Gallic provinces conquered by Caesar could now be candidates for a senatorial seat, by saying that Augustus (and Tiberius) had brought men of fortune and loyal to the state, the flower of the cities of Italy, into the Senate. Now and then senators also came from provincial cities, for instance from Gallia Narbonensis (Provence), where many Romans lived, but only a few of them were not Romans born. Those few included the Cornelii Balbi from Gades in southern Spain and Quintus Pompeius Macer from Mytilene on Lesbos, the grandson of Pompey's supporter Theophanes. Pompeius Macer was the only senator in the Augustan period who we can be certain was of Greek origin. There were no Sicilian senators at all.

In the time of Augustus, the senators formed an *ordo*, a class or order, that is to say a unified and self-contained group working in the same sphere, with the same view of life and the same ethical convictions. Although even in republican times the members of the Senate had been regarded as a firmly established order (*ordo senatorius*), there had not been any sharp dividing line between them and the next highest-ranking group, the knights or equestrian order, for since the minimum fortune (*census*) that senators and equestrians must possess was the same at the time, set for both at 400,000 sesterces, the adult son of a senator, if he was not yet in the Senate himself, was of equestrian rank. Augustus made the senators into an exclusive, clearly defined group by including the sons of senators when they reached the age of sixteen and were allowed to wear the toga reserved for grown men (*toga virilis*). In addition he required all senators to have a minimum fortune of a million sesterces, thereby distinguishing them from the equestrians, whose *census* was set at the same level as before. Entry to the Senate was thus no longer connected only with holding an office, but also with membership of a family of senatorial rank.

In the republican period, the Senate had been replenished by means of elections to the magistracy. A man elected to office entered the Senate after his term and once in the Senate he was assigned a rank depending on the office he had held, the highest being the consulars (the former consuls), then the praetorians (the former praetors), and so on. The influence of a senator both in the Senate and in social life depended mainly on this ranking order, which was based on a man's achievements for the state. Under Augustus that order was maintained with only one difference, but a crucial one: in future the Senate no longer drew new members from free election by the people, but from a mechanism in which the assembly of the people, or the committees of senators and equestrians later set up to decide on the candidates in advance, constituted only a formal framework for the election, and the crucial factor was the directly or indirectly expressed wish of the *princeps*. As senators held the highest offices in the army and the administration in general, Augustus had to pay close attention to the replenishment of the Senate. On the other hand, he must not appear to be overriding the wishes of a group of men who were indispensable to him, as successors to the aristocratic society of the republic, and indeed he expressly did not want to appear in that light because of the idea behind the principate, so he had to disguise his actual influence on the make-up of the Senate as far as possible, to cover up the fact that the power of disposal was his.

First, however, Augustus carried out several 'purges' of the Senate. These were rather drastic measures, for here he was indeed dictating the mechanism for replenishing the Senate. The earliest and very thorough 'reading of the Senate' (*lectio senatus*) of this kind, carried out in 28, had reduced the then overblown Senate by several hundred to 600 men and had certainly been seen by most as the opening move in the restoration of the state. The 'purge' of the year 18 entailed another thorough scrutiny of the Senate. It might be seen as the conclusion of the long process of devising a new state structure, and its main aim was to make the Senate an organ capable of functioning efficiently by establishing a maximum number of 300 members. But the attempt to limit membership so rigorously failed, and neither the last scrutiny of the Senate carried out by Augustus himself in the year 11 BC nor those that he did not conduct personally but were carried out by officials specially appointed for the purpose, naturally under his supervision, could do anything to change that.

It was the process of replenishing the Senate from the holders of magistrates' posts, not the great purges, that decided in the long term whether it was an administrative organ capable of functioning, and doing so in the spirit that Augustus wanted. During the triumvirate period, he had had almost unlimited opportunities to influence elections, since the senators of that time had been an amorphous mass brutally intimidated by the military potentates. Often he had not even found it necessary to have formal decisions taken in the assembly of the people on the men for whom posts in the magistracy were intended, but simply had them appointed without any formality. There was a fundamental change after the principate had been set up, for the idea of a return to 'normal' circumstances made it impossible to admit that the *princeps* was going to select the holders of administrative power himself, while the people, or the committees of senators and equestrians that suggested candidates for office, were not to curb his will. So what was in fact the deciding influence of the *princeps* had to be disguised by a veneer of elections. The will of Augustus was maintained by a variety of different methods: he might make a formal, binding recommendation, or he might make his personal interest known in some other way, for instance by appearing in the Forum with the candidate he favoured.

Everyone knew that Augustus managed the elections and appointed the magistrates, and there was no public criticism. Ultimately it did not matter much how far the people were still involved in the election process; what counted for more was the amount of personal support that the *princeps* gave to an individual. A special degree of interest on his part was an honour to the candidate and raised his social reputation. To be the candidate of Augustus guaranteed a man's further rise up the hierarchy of office. The importance of whatever office he held was not, therefore, the only factor determining his rank; his proximity to the *princeps* weighed just as heavily. If a candidate favoured by Augustus did not own the minimum *census* for a senator, the *princeps* might even support him by supplying the sum of money necessary to make it up. He did that for the grandson of the famous orator of Cicero's time, Marcus Hortensius Hortalus, and for Gnaeus Cornelius Lentulus Augur, later consul for the year 14 BC. Acceptance of a senator among the patricians was a particular honour. Following the example of his adoptive father, Augustus had had himself granted the right to appoint patricians quite early, in a law of the year 30. The fact that age-old tradition said a man was a patrician only by virtue of his origin, meaning membership of one of the old noble families, did not make the honour any less desirable. It might also illustrate the widening gulf between the present and the society in which the patriciate had once been part of an immutable tradition, but none the less, in its new form, it was part of a ranking order which distinguished between members of the new society in many ways – and made it easier for the *princeps* to control.

The Romans were a society divided by social status, even within the various groups. Senators, for instance, had clear and generally acknowledged gradations. A number of signs of rank helped the ignorant and outsiders to recognize the differences. Senators, who had to wear the toga of their forefathers on all official occasions, were distinguished from other citizens by a purple stripe (*clavus*) on their undergarment, the *tunica*, which was visible beneath the toga from throat to waistline. Further signs of senatorial rank were a gold ring and red shoes; in addition, patricians were distinguished by an ivory clasp on their shoes at the ankle. Equestrians, who originally were not strictly distinguished from senators, also wore the purple stripe and the gold ring, but once a distinction had been made between men of senatorial and equestrian rank, the stripe on the senators' undergarments was broader (*latus clavus*) than the stripe worn by the equestrians (*angustus clavus*).

Social esteem was naturally linked primarily with the number and importance of the offices a man had held, and these were expressed in the Senate in a ranking order that made them clear to everyone. But the origin of senatorial dignity also played a part. If a man from a non-senatorial family had become a senator through the support of the *princeps*, it depended on what degree of that support he had enjoyed in his candidature for office. To have been the candidate of the *princeps* raised a man above other senators who were really of the same rank. If a man came from a distinguished family, then quite apart from the support of the *princeps*, which was given to many, the age of that family mattered. Men like Cornelius Lentulus and Valerius Messalla, whose families had figured in major events of the republican period and had provided several consuls, ranked higher than others, however great the more recent achievements of those others. Their ancestors spoke for them. Now in particular, when the number of those with distinguished family trees was decreasing, the glory of their great names gained in significance, and even if the Augustan age was also well disposed towards new men, the honouring of tradition in the same period did its part to show that the old names had not entirely lost their resonance. Even under the republic, members of distinguished families had taken care that in cases of adoption the memory of the family of the birth father, if it was of any significance, was not lost in a man's new adoptive name; the cognomen of the birth father was simply attached to the name given in adoption. As descent through the maternal line could not be deduced from the traditional nomenclature, which took account only of the paternal line, in the last decades of the reign of Augustus it even sometimes happened that a man added to his name either the gens name (*nomen gentile*) or the cognomen of a distinguished relation on his mother's side. Such names sometimes grew to monstrous length. The second cognomen of the consul of the year AD 5, Gnaeus Cornelius Cinna Magnus, referred to his maternal grandfather, the famous Pompey the Great, and Cinna did yet more when, contrary to a centuries-old custom of naming family descent by mentioning the first names of a man's father and paternal grandfather, he gave not the latter but that of his other grandfather, i.e. Pompey (*Luci filius Magni Pompei nepos*, 'son of Lucius, grandson of Pompey the Great').

Acceptance into the Senate took place, if not through exceptional selection, for instance in a reduction of senatorial numbers, then through the holding of an office. Under Augustus, as in the republican era, the senators made up a functional elite. A young man usually began his career (*cursus honorum*) between the ages of eighteen and twenty-eight, by holding one of the lower posts in a group of offices known as the 'Group of Twenty-six' (vigintisexvirate) and later, when several of those offices were abolished in the lifetime of Augustus, as the 'Office of Twenty' (vigintivirate). They included the three-man college for the judicial system, whose members, among their other duties, supervised the carrying-out of death sentences and were the authority to which criminal activities were reported, and the office of the masters of the mint, who supervised the striking of gold, silver and copper coins on the directions of the Senate and magistrates. After that the adept became an officer, generally a military tribune, an appointment usually entailing two years of military service with a legion, and on his return would be a candidate for the quaestorship, although that was a post that he could not fill before completing his twenty-fifth year of life. As a quaestor, he was in charge of certain funds in Rome or the senatorial provinces, or he could be a personal assistant to Augustus (*quaestor principis*). Only after holding the post of quaestor did he enter the Senate, where he could sit with the other quaestorians, the lowest-ranking senators. The aediles and the tribunes of the people, posts held as alternatives to each other, stood on the next rung of the ladder of office, and then came the office of praetor, which no one could hold until the age of thirty at the earliest. As a praetor, a senator took on tasks of civil or criminal jurisdiction, or after the reform of the treasury in the year 22 one of the two new financial positions. While there had been twenty places available for quaestors, the pyramid of office narrowed towards the top. Since 22 there had been only ten praetors, and the next rung, the consulate, an office that could not be held before a man was forty-three, had an even narrower base, although in several years, particularly late in the reign of Augustus, when the two 'consuls by ordinance' (*consules ordinarii*) who gave their names to the year retired, two more consuls were appointed, but seldom more. The consulate was the top rung of the ladder of office and, together with the praetorship, the point of departure for major activities outside Rome, perhaps as governor of a province or commander of a legion (*legatus legionis*). The most distinguished offices were reserved for former consuls, and in particular only consulars were considered as governors of important senatorial provinces such as Asia, or the provinces of Augustus where more than one legion was stationed.

The holder of senatorial rank was not entirely free to determine the course of his life. Although it was open to him to retire and devote himself to art and literature, or enjoy his wealth at his leisure, family and tradition, ambition and Roman pride usually caused him to follow in his forefathers' footsteps. He was entangled in the expectations of his class, and that included ideas of a suitable career. Once he was in the

Senate the very order of rank in itself made him look up to the highest ranks on the ladder. The inscriptions of the time that have come down to us, and that soon increased enormously in number, especially those recording honours and on tombstones, give us an idea of the importance that a man's career had for him.

Senatorial society was a self-contained group. Its thinking embraced not just the political sphere but all areas of life, including intellectual interests. First and foremost, the senator was a landowner, although there were considerable variations in the extent and nature of the property he owned. Many senators possessed large landed estates, usually in Italy, but some owned land in provinces like Sicily and Gallia Narbonensis. Setting a senator's minimum fortune at a million sesterces does not tell us much, since that was not a very large sum for a man of senatorial rank; if he held the post of governor of one of the more important provinces, the same amount would be his annual salary. Extensive land ownership was a prerequisite for senatorial rank, but there were also many Romans, members of the equestrian order or the upper classes in the city, who owned large estates without being senators, so other factors were equally important in fostering a certain awareness of rank. They included a ban on a senator's engaging in trade either openly or surreptitiously – indeed he was legally forbidden to do so. The notion that a man of distinction had to be a countryman reflected the old ideal of the Roman peasant soldier, and the tradesman or craftsman was always to some extent at odds with it through the whole course of Roman history. However, a large landowner was a countryman only in so far as he sometimes withdrew to the country, more for rest and relaxation than to supervise the management of his estates; he was not a real farmer. The centre of his existence was his town house, and its palatial dimensions banished any idea of a life of rural toil. So far as his awareness of his rank went, then, the ban on engaging in trade was primarily to distinguish him from that line of business, not to define him as a countryman. The sense of a coherent group was thus reinforced by an ethos arising from the senator's special tasks: his activity in the administration and the defence of the empire. The education of senators' sons, which rested entirely on private initiative, was determined solely by his future avocations, so it included legal and rhetorical training to help him develop the linguistic agility that he would need in dealing with the common people, the soldiers, those who were subjects of Rome and administrative committees. It was also essential for him to see active service in the army as early as possible.

The ideas instilled into a young senator were geared to the performance of his duties to the state, as now represented by the *princeps*: the maintenance and promotion of the stature of Rome and the ideological foundations of Roman rule. Every senator's son could cite examples of dutiful service and heroic courage in every conceivable situation from the annals of Roman history. Not only the members of the old senatorial families but above all the 'new men' eagerly subscribed to the regulation of the entire senatorial order. The lower their own origin, the more they complied with it, for only within the group could you rise further. The eyes of all were turned upwards to the ladder of office, and that meant looking to the *princeps*, who alone could help an adept up that ladder.

The *princeps* himself was more anxious than anyone to help the senators in their efforts to prove worthy of their great empire and the deeds of their forefathers. As monarch and military potentate, he was also the main obstacle to the free operation of the Senate – or, more accurately, to its sense of being able to make decisions in relative freedom. The man who was in fact their ruler, and whose massacres of distinguished men in darker times they still remembered very well, inspired considerable physical fear in them, and that fear was not unjustified. If Augustus did not want to risk the whole idea of the principate – which was that the senators took part in the government of the empire – then he had to counter their sense of insecurity and uneasiness. So he refrained from accusing individual senators of criminal offences, citing the Senate itself as an authority if necessary, and even proposed a law reserving to it the criminal prosecution of those of senatorial rank. Although this did not reduce his influence on debates, in the field of criminal jurisdiction it helped the Senate to become a law-court of peers, which was in line with the thinking of the *princeps* and the idea of the principate.

To support the senators in political life, Augustus therefore had to keep presenting himself to the Roman public at large as one who promoted both the political position of the senators and the Senate itself as an institution. Where necessary he would readily and energetically lend his aid to a knowledgeable and well-disposed senator. But that support was quite often coercive and would brook no contradiction. This perceptible pressure, which might often meet resistance, was reinforced to a high degree by many of the new ideas and regulations affecting the lives of individuals. For Augustus did not just show support for the performance of duties to the state and for old-established standards of conduct, he was anxious to renovate or actually reform society as a whole, with particular reference to the senators, and that reform was to extend to their morality. He regarded this aim as the restoration of an older society: tradition, meaning the morality of the ancestors of the Romans (*mos maiorum*), was the criterion. Naturally, the implication was that the customs of the past were better than those of the present. In his idea of the value of tradition – or what he presented as tradition – as a standard for his own time, Augustus could feel at one with both his contemporaries and with past generations. The adoption by the leadership class of a way of life similar in essentials to that of their forebears had long been the concern of Roman statesmen, ever since the inexhaustible opportunities offered by rule over large parts of the Mediterranean world had helped men of distinction to acquire not just fame but sometimes a large fortune, something that in itself entailed considerable distortion of the traditional, tried and trusted forms of both political and private life. There had been repeated attempts to correct this deviation by returning to the old ways, since it seemed that only what had brought Rome to its leading position could secure its future greatness. A huge variety of laws to limit extravagance (*leges sumptuariae*, sumptuary laws) had affected almost every imaginable aspect of life, for instance new decrees on clothing, expenditure on banquets, the nature and extent of the dishes served at them and the giving of presents, and as these laws were not very successful, for the obvious reason that the conduct they criticized was now normal, a succession of variations was introduced to reiterate and tighten them up.

Augustus himself was active here, and while his own laws on such matters, like their predecessors, affected all citizens, in the nature of things it was mainly the senators and after them, at the most, the equestrians who really bore the burden of the innovations. They were, of course, specifically directed at that group. Although all laws of this kind regulated the expenses of the leadership class, thus restricting its freedom, those affected accepted them and recognized their necessity, at least in principle. However, they did not let the infringement of their liberty stop them acting as they liked. They still had many other legal means of demonstrating social status and they also persisted with their proscibed conduct, perhaps toning it down to some extent, while society at large turned a blind eye. There could not be spies and informers lurking everywhere, ready to denounce them, and everyone knew that an authority unused to handling complaints was not anticipating such denunciations. If a senator spent more than the maximum 100 sesterces stipulated by Augustus in giving a dinner on an ordinary day and invited more than the regulation number of guests, it was unlikely that charges would be brought against him.

There was one area, however, that had not previously attracted the attention of the law, and here Augustus went beyond the traditional framework for the regulation of society. He wanted to introduce a new concept of marriage and the conduct of married life. It seemed to Augustus that married couples no longer fulfilled the purpose of marriage, which to his mind was having children and bringing them up, and he thought that marriage as he now found it lacked the social significance of earlier times. Like many of his contemporaries, Augustus believed that the political downfall of the republic was principally due to a decline in morality among the upper classes, and that included a decline in the concept of marriage. Two things, he felt, had to be done to stop it: the will to contract a marriage must be revived, along with an awareness that having children was its prime purpose. Both, in his view, could be achieved only by legal decree.

Augustus' view of marriage is purely functional, but the idea that the welfare of the state depended on marriage as an intact institution, and above all on a wealth of children, was not entirely new. For over a hundred years politicians, historians and writers had denounced the moral conduct of the Romans, particularly the upper classes. They did not simply point out this deplorable social conduct, they manufactured a crisis out of it. There had long been criticism of the modern concept of marriage. Even before the great settlement establishing the principate, Horace had bewailed the decline of marriage in a famous ode, presenting it as the main cause of the downfall of the state. This was the point taken up by Augustus: he could call for support on the words and measures of famous men whose names were known to every child in Rome and whose authority no one disputed. One of them was Publius Cornelius Scipio

Aemilianus, the destroyer of Carthage, who had even suggested rewarding the fathers of many children. In his sweeping legislation on marriage, Augustus could have cited him, or Cicero, who had also included precepts on marriage in his catalogue of the conduct befitting an ideal Roman state. But he had a wide choice among public figures who had pronounced on correct marital conduct and he cited the equally well-known Quintus Caecilius Metellus Macedonicus, who as censor in the year 131 had encouraged marriage, giving the procreation of offspring as his reason. This precisely echoed the ideas of Augustus himself.

Correct marital conduct in line with the ethos of the state was therefore laid down by law. Augustus was clever enough to reject the idea suggested to him of an office for enforcing morality and the law (*cura morum et legum*), which would have been too like the interference of dictatorial or censorial full powers in private life. But how would anyone have thought of that suggestion if his intention of reforming marriage had not been known? Perhaps, in view of his laws on morality, he himself had at first wanted to be in charge of enforcing them but then sensed discontent among the senators and decided against it. At any rate, he contented himself with bringing the laws he proposed before the assembly of the people, on the grounds of the full tribunician powers that he held, and in his own account of his reign he skilfully presented his conduct later as an honourable refusal to take an office which, since it contravened the norms established by the founding fathers of Rome, he could not have accepted. Of course, the subject of his decrees was unaffected by any change in their form.

In the year 18 Augustus proposed the new law on marriage ('Julian Law on the Order of Marriage', *lex Iulia de maritandis ordinibus*). A generation later, in the year AD 9, it was extended and corrected by a law on marriage (the *lex Papia Poppaea nuptialis*) proposed by the consuls of the year, Marcus Papius Mutilus and Quintus Pappaeus Secundus. The first law has not come down to us intact and since it was superseded is less well known than the second, which makes it hard to distinguish between the two.

The jurisdiction applied to all Romans in equal measure, although not to foreigners. As the penalties to be exacted show, it was directed chiefly at senators. At the heart of the new laws were compulsion to marry and the injunction to have children. The monstrous nature of this intrusion into private life was not mitigated but, if anything, emphasized by the detailed legal provisions. Every Roman of marriageable age, men between twenty-five and sixty, women between twenty and fifty, had to be married. If one of a married couple died, or the marriage ended in divorce, the man had to marry again within 100 days, while the law generously allowed the woman a period initially of a year, then of two years after the death of her husband, although after divorce the period of grace was at first only six and then eighteen months. In addition several legal provisions, some of them centuries old, that might be obstacles to marriage were set aside. A father's refusal to give his daughter in marriage and pay her dowry was circumvented by making it the duty of a magistrate to appoint a guardian for the daughter, thus depriving paternal power (*patria potestas*) of force in this respect. The quota of children was precisely set as at least three, while a freedman had the number raised to four. If a marriage was childless, it should be dissolved after a certain time so that the parties could enter into another marriage. Senators and their female relations, although not other Romans, were forbidden to marry freed slaves and actors, in order to keep senatorial families free of persons of ill repute and low origin. All Romans were forbidden to marry prostitutes, pimps or convicted adulteresses.

At first, however, refusing to marry had no direct legal consequences, and a marriage contracted or continued in defiance of one of these bans remained legally valid. That was inevitable, if only because in the absence of comprehensive measures to monitor marriages there would have been great legal uncertainty. Augustus therefore tried to ensure that the legal regulations were observed by methods of punishment and reward (because of the unpopularity of the new laws, he could not rely on those who transgressed them incurring any social stigma). Anyone of marriageable age who was not married could not attend the games, although that measure was softened later. A senator who had fewer children than the law specified must expect considerable disadvantages on his way up the ladder of public office. Conversely, a senator blessed with sufficient children received privileges. A consul who had the requisite number of children took precedence over his colleague who did not, and the senatorial father of a large family could choose his own province and apply for offices as many years before the legal age for them as he had children. There were also disadvantages to rights of inheritance. A person who, against the regulations, remained single could not accept any legacy except from his or her closest relations; while half of any legacy was withheld from those who were married but had only one child. These regulations did not restrict the liberty of legators in any way; you could go on leaving property as you wished. Only the legatees were affected, since the regulations might make them unable to accept a legacy. There were also gradations, depending on the number of children you had, and the ability to leave property within the marriage relationship was also restricted.

A man had no relief from the rigour of these laws until he was sixty, a woman until she was fifty or had borne three children, although the only children who counted legally were those who had been born alive and had not died before a certain age. Up to that point everyone had to try to fulfil the legal requirements, but many tried to evade this plethora of laws in some way. That was easy enough for the common people of Rome and probably most of the equestrian order as well, since there was no supervising authority to note non-observation or transgression of the legal specifications. There were indeed informers who could be prevailed upon to report offences, sometimes for money, and in the absence of a public prosecution system to step in officially in the case of such offences these informers were in fact an important aid to the implementation of the laws. Resort was often made to them to enforce the law, including the laws on marriage. But only the easily surveyed senatorial order could really be watched, and it was to this group that marital jurisdiction was geared.

However, it was still possible simply not to comply with the law by remaining single or refusing to marry again after the death of a wife or husband. You had to expect the legal sanctions, but you could remain independent. Many widows must have chosen this way, which enabled them to remain faithful to their dead husbands. Against Augustus' express command Antonia, the younger daughter of Mark Antony and Octavia, did not marry again after the death of her husband Drusus, Livia's son, although when he died she was only twenty-seven years old. Such an attitude to marriage, considered particularly praiseworthy in the past, now detracted from your reputation and even became officially undesirable because of the legal policy intended to produce a large number of children.

The new regulations entailed many instances of injustice, which the legislators ignored. The blessing of children, for example, could be denied a couple for reasons for which neither marriage partner was responsible, as was very well known even at that time. In addition, no one could overlook the fact that many leading figures did not comply with the legal requirements – first and foremost Augustus himself. He had only one daughter and, at the time when the first law on marriage was passed, two adopted sons, who for legal purposes did not count. Strictly speaking, he should have divorced Livia in order to comply with the law and have many children. As he was the ruler, it was conceded, willingly or unwillingly, that his was a special role, but since as *princeps* he placed himself on a par with the other senators, he did not like to see it in that way and, pedantic as he was, at some point he had himself granted a dispensation for some unimportant reason. Whether that also applied to the quota of children we do not know. But could similar liberties be allowed to Maecenas, who had no children at all? And what about the two consuls of the year AD 9, Papius and Poppaeus, who had proposed the second law on marriage? They were both bachelors, and in effect their own law was declaring them inadequate members of society. Others would have been available for the consulship in the year 9; there were enough tribunes of the people who did meet the legal requirements. Perhaps such candidates for office would have objected to having their names associated with the unpopular law, and it is possible that the situation of the two unfortunate bachelors was the very reason why they could not oppose the wish of the *princeps*.

Despite all the complaints of the senators, and all the inconsistencies and injustices of the laws, Augustus stood firmly by them. Feelings sometimes ran high in the Senate during discussions of the subject, and now and then, when Augustus appeared in public, there were even protests. Many are said to have pointed out his own far from irreproachable life, which to a great extent ran contrary to his legislative intentions. It was no use. Apart from a few alleviations, and a period of grace of at first three and then another two years before the legal requirements came into force in individual cases, Augustus made no concessions, and he also took many opportunities to demonstrate what he thought proper in marriage. When the equestrians protested, he led the children of his granddaughter Agrippina and his great-nephew Germanicus, who had married when he was twenty and had not failed to carry out his conjugal duties with enthusiasm, into the theatre, sat the children on his lap and their father's and through gestures gave the people present to understand that the burden was a light one, and these model parents had set an example that should be followed. Another public spectacle that he staged in the year 3 BC was rather embarrassing. For this purpose, he had an old man from Faesulae (Fiesole) in the north of Etruria and his many descendants brought to Rome and made them walk in an official procession to a sacrifice to Jupiter on the Capitol. The old man arrived with 8 children, 27 grandchildren, 18 great-grandchildren and 8 great-great-grandchildren. It had taken Augustus some time to find this paragon of fertility. The old man was one of the ordinary people, although a free-born Roman; no suitable example was available among the senators.

We should not assume that the laws were so very successful. Instead of the enthusiasm for the joys of married life that he had hoped to instil into men of distinction, there was widespread hypocrisy; mock marriages were concluded, and men of marriageable age became betrothed to small children, giving the future bridegroom a period of grace. These arrangements could be dissolved again, and betrothals to other children concluded, putting off the day of marriage for ever. The attempt to bar such practices by stating that an engagement to a girl under ten did not free a man from the disadvantages of unmarried status is evidence of the impotence of the legislator rather than his power. Discrepancies between the norm and compliance with it in fact finally made concessions necessary, at least for individuals. The wish for a dispensation from the rigour of the law, expressed by many senators, led to the creation of a legal privilege allowing its holder all the rights of a person who really did have three children. The 'Three Children Law' (*ius trium liberorum*) fundamentally represents capitulation to the difficulty of enforcing the law on marriage.

Augustus crowned his investigation of the marriage beds of high society by making adultery a criminal offence. In the old days, adultery had been subject to the husband's domestic jurisdiction; he could reject his adulterous wife or kill the adulterer caught in the act with her. In effect, it was self-help. But that was not always the case. In the public area, damages might be required, but only in particularly drastic cases. In the late republic, prosecution for adultery was rather lax. An immoral way of life was only occasionally publicly rebuked by the censors, who would investigate and remove really flagrant offenders from the Senate. That was to change now.

In a law introduced by Augustus himself 'on the prevention of adultery' (*lex Iulia de adulteriis coercendis*), probably in the year 18, adultery (*adulterium*) as well as extra-marital sexual intercourse between a man and a woman and sexual relations between free men (*stuprum*) became criminal offences. So did procuring. The law on adultery addressed the wife, since she was responsible for the descent of her children, and affected the husband only if he committed adultery with someone else's wife; there was no penalty for unfaithfulness to his own spouse. The right to prosecute for adultery was open to any Roman, but the husband and those who had authority over the wife took precedence in bringing charges. On conviction, a male adulterer was fined half his fortune, while the woman in the case forfeited half her dowry and one-third of her fortune. In special cases exile to some remote place (*relegatio in insulam*) seems already to have been envisaged as a penalty. A special court to try the crime of adultery (*quaestio de adulteriis*) was set up, with a praetor presiding over it.

Augustus' legislation on marriage had many consequences, and not only for his contemporaries. With some alterations, it remained in force until the third century AD, and certain features of it until the end of the Roman state. Indeed, the treatment of adultery as a criminal offence even survived classical antiquity. Few other aspects of legislation in either antiquity or modernity attracted as much comment. The classification of adultery as a public matter traced a deep dividing line in the history of the interplay of public and private life; the private sphere was made more vulnerable to state intervention. It became a crime, liable to legal prosecution, and also affected personal ideas of marriage, for it made social and ethical conduct in the most private area of human life the subject of legislation and thus of public discussion. Under the respectable cloak of law-abiding concern, the door was wide open to gossip about marriage in the homes of distinguished Romans, and the subject was even openly debated in the Senate. In the year 13 BC, for instance, a man called Cornelius Sisenna had to hear aspersions being cast on his wife's way of life. We do not know what gave rise to this incident, but one can only hope the matter had not been raised as a special point in the order of business of the day. In the debate Sisenna, clearly not a man at a loss for words, defended himself by saying that, after all, he had married his wife on the advice of Augustus and with his knowledge. The senator thus had no scruples about presenting

Augustus himself as a guilty party, which set off one of the *princeps'* not infrequent fits of rage, although for the sake of remaining on good terms with the Senate he curbed it outside the door of the Senate house. The question here was not the general one of what went on in the marital bed, it was the discussion of a concrete case, and the Senate was used as a place to wash dirty linen in public. Augustus obviously saw nothing offensive in that.

The remarkable aspect of this state intervention in what had previously been a private sphere of life is not only the fact in itself but also its special legislative treatment. What appears surprising, indeed repellent, is the clever casuistry of the laws, which paid pedantic attention to individual areas of behaviour and decided whether they should be forbidden or compulsory, subject to reward or to punishment. The application of a casuistical approach, conventional in all other areas of criminal legislation, is alienating when it is applied to social behaviour. The legislator has obviously studied the most intimate sphere of private life closely, covering almost every conceivable aspect of human behaviour and its treatment by the authorities. Nothing seems to have been forgotten, even the possibility that a cuckolded husband might *not* report and prosecute his wife's conduct. Since he tolerates her adultery, it is clearly what he wanted, so his passive attitude is to be prosecuted as if he were a pimp. When, at the end of his life, Augustus boasts of reviving the morals of the founding fathers of Rome by his legislation when they were threatening to fall into oblivion, that is true of many but not all his legal measures. In some, including his legislation on marriage, he was introducing a *new* law, although his reference to traditional norms, or those handed down as such, conceals the fact.

In retrospect, Augustus seems to reveal another side of his political will in his legislation on marriage. In a very general sense, it coincides with his discernible wish at this time to create a new administrative aristocracy indispensable to the state. However, it is not the political aspect that strikes the impartial observer and no doubt struck those affected, but the way in which he wanted to impose his own aims, making the production of many offspring incumbent on society. The means he used, the individual regulations, created not only new and previously unheard-of laws but also a changed awareness of the importance of the relationship between the public and private spheres, and thus at the same time of social and ethical behaviour. In a way Augustus seems to stand apart even from classical antiquity as a legislator here. For although the desire for children born in wedlock, felt by not just married couples and their families but the state authorities as well, certainly has its place in the thinking of the ancient world, his thoroughgoing regimentation is a qualitative leap that we might expect to find in a totalitarian regime. The idea of reward by the state for trying to produce descendants is like a bridge from the ancient to the modern period, for whether the prize is privilege in a man's official career or the award of a Mothers' Cross, the wish for children is separated in both cases from the private area and regarded as important state business. Another institution going back to Augustan times links them with the modern period: the introduction of registers of births, listing the success of the efforts made by married couples while also certifying that their offspring were born in legal wedlock.

A final evaluation of the political intention of the Augustan laws on marriage as the creation of a 'healthy' society, meaning a morally pure society producing many children, will probable evoke little sympathy. Examined closely, the legislation of Augustus may well elude understanding and even create perplexity. But predictable as it was to anyone of sober judgement, the uselessness of such efforts is not the main issue. Those who would point to Augustus' own lax attitude to marriage or indeed his lack of children in order to deny his right to bring in any such legislation do not do him justice either. It may be ideal for a legislator's personal conduct to comply with the law he introduces, but that does not affect assessment of its political intention. The question of whether the desired end related appropriately to the means employed is more difficult. Augustus inevitably fell out with a number of senators and alienated many of them. Above all, however, he featured here not as the *princeps* who regarded the senators as aides and partners, but as a ruler and judge, abandoning the role of restrained guide and teacher for that of a disciplinarian acting with remarkable lack of feeling, indeed with contempt, for others and no consideration for the relationship between husband and wife, a legislator who saw marriage as nothing but an institution for producing offspring. That he could do it at all shows how secure his position now was. But the fact that the great majority of senators accepted this legislation, and a number of them, including some writers, even praised it, was certainly not only because of the now undisputed authority of Augustus, but also because its theme, at least in the attempt, followed tradition, and visible behind it was a moral concept that every senator could and perhaps even must share. So the legislation itself may well not have seemed very strange to the contemporaries of Augustus, and they may not even have considered the possibility that it might fail in its aims, since most of them – like Augustus himself – did not think about that aspect at all. What seems strange, however, not just to us today but to those contemporaries of Augustus who were familiar with casuistry, is the precise classification of social behaviour for the purpose of its control by authority. Even a contemporary of Augustus must have seen that his legislation replaced the family, or the father as head of the family, by the will of the state, in this case the ruler. By agreeing to his laws, society gave up a part of its freedom; those who submitted to it now felt at home in a monarchy. We hear of no resistance to it on the grounds of principle.

Augustus' marriage legislation brings up the question of opposition to the new spirit and the man who stood for it. Was there any opposition at all to Augustus? Here we must first define what we mean by 'opposition'. Is it resistance on principle, aiming for elimination of the ruling political system, or is it rejection from within the system of individual persons or aspects of it? The latter comes closer to today's use of the term for conditions in the imperial Roman period, but modern accounts often do not use it in that sense.

Opposition to the ruling system at this time would have been like returning to the political conditions of the republic. The proponents of such views would not have recognized the measures taken by Augustus and leading to the establishment of the principate as a political compromise and would have wished to eliminate the monarchy standing in full view behind the new order, even in the formal sense. Illusory as such ideas might be, and had been even in the lifetime of Brutus and Cassius, they could have been in the minds not only of many representatives of the old nobility, but also of men from the new aristocracy who – in line with the wishes of Augustus – had adopted the old nobles' awareness of their own status. However, there was no political resistance to the monarchy; it cannot be said of a single one of those who conspired against the life of Augustus, not even Varro Murena, that he clearly adopted that political aim. During two decades of civil war most members of the old nobility had gone, and with them any idea of the possibility of restoring the old order.

All the same, the memory of the republic as a better form of state, based on liberty – aristocratic liberty – had not entirely disappeared from the minds of many senators, especially as the principate, in turning to a new aristocracy, seemed to have taken the old political order as its model. Although Augustus excluded a return to the republic as a political concept grounded in reality, the basically positive image that even semi-official opinion claimed to have of the republic was dangerous to him, and there were potential grounds for opposition in the fact that an aristocrat, as senator or magistrate, might take upon himself what the principate claimed to be its political guideline, that is to say might try to put into practice the purely formal theory that as a senator he could take some initiative of his own, or try to make an independent career for himself. But any behaviour of that kind would have represented a grave misunderstanding and even, in view of the visible balance of power, an intentionally false assessment of the opportunities offered by the new order. For liberty, if such a term is to be used at all for the principate, was merely *granted* by the holder of power and was thus fundamentally different from liberty in itself. Political liberty as an independent force was abrogated by the establishment of the military monarchy, and all political action was subject to consideration by the one man who really held the power to grant that liberty. The principate had changed nothing there. So if the 'republic' now and then provided a backdrop to the principate, it was not with any idea of its actual restoration. If someone took the idea at face value and said so, it could be seen as non-political enthusiasm, but could also be taken as an attack on the powerful ruler, in which the resentment of many members of the old nobility became intermingled with honest veneration of a past political world that was barely understood now, personal hostility to Augustus or simply a show of political actionism.

More significant and real than this kind of opposition, behind which there was hardly any genuine political will, was resistance to Augustus in person, with the aim of removing him and replacing him by someone else. This opposition operated within the system, was linked to the hope of an extension of the political ideas represented by the principate and, given the political balance of power as created by the civil war, was ultimately the only opposition that Augustus really had to fear. A rival is the nightmare of every military potentate and one that Augustus still had to fear in spite of the constitution of the principate. After the death of Antony there was no serious competition in sight, but all the same Augustus took great pains to nip any potential plots in the bud. A coup could hope for success only through the army officers and soldiers, and so he worked hard to ensure their loyalty by promoting their careers, providing for them generously and giving lavish presents. He could handle soldiers with remarkable skill and he could keep officers far enough away from each other that no serious body of resistance, so far as we know, was able to form anywhere.

Those conspiracies of which we do know – or rather, since they had no discernible plans or aims, those bands of disaffected men – did not therefore come from the armies, but from individual aristocrats who, so far as their resistance could boast of any tangible political intent or genuine plan, sought support in Rome and not from the legions in the provinces. The attempted coup by Terentius Varro Murena in the year 23 might have been based on the fact that Murena felt he had been driven into a corner and was trying to find a way out of a sticky situation. In the intrigues of 31 of young Lepidus, son of the triumvir, we are more likely seeing a mild after-shock of triumviral rivalries, and his attempts to put them into practice were simply amateurish. If this was a case of the son trying to continue his father's feud and pick up where his power had left off in the past, then the largely obscure machinations in AD 2 of Jullus Antonius, second son of Mark Antony and Fulvia, and married to the elder of the two Marcellas, Octavia's daughters, call for a different interpretation. Jullus Antonius was accused of adultery with Julia, Augustus' daughter, and seems to have been killed (or driven to his death) because of the suspicion that he saw this adulterous relationship as a means to rise higher in the succession to Augustus. If those suspicions are in any degree correct, then this attempt to oust the *princeps* from his dominating position came not from outside but from the house of Augustus himself. Jullus Antonius, relying on his marriage to Marcella, his relationship with Augustus' daughter and not least his descent from the triumvir Antony, formerly Augustus' rival, might have calculated that he had a good chance. Augustus constantly feared assassination. He sometimes wore armour under his toga in the Senate, and when in the year 18 he carried out a rigorous 'purge' of unworthy persons from the Senate he allowed the senators to enter the Senate house only one by one, having their clothing searched in advance in case they were carrying hidden daggers.

Augustus had to live with the idea of a violent coup aimed at removing him from power. Nothing had changed there since he first embarked on a political career, although he was now better protected, and the majority of his enemies had made their peace with him. In his eyes the clemency of the ruler, which his father Julius Caesar had made a central virtue (*clementia Caesaris*), was to be regarded only to a limited extent as an instrument to protect himself from attack. After all, it had not done his father much good. He had to be on his guard, and a shirt of mail under his toga and treating his opponents severely were safer measures than following the eloquent recommendations of philosophers to show clemency. Augustus certainly has not gone down in history as a merciful monarch. Pardons were rare during his reign. When he did once exercise clemency and pardoned a prominent man who was planning to assassinate him – Gnaeus Cornelius Cinna, a grandson of the famous populist who had been consul four times, and on the maternal side a grandson of Pompey the Great – one contemporary historian was moved to devote a special literary work to this occasion, with Livia appearing as the figure who persuades Caesar to show mercy. However, the facts about the 'conspiracy' of Cinna are not clear, and there is good reason to think that the case has not been accurately reported to us. In any event, any willingness to remove Augustus by force clearly decreased after the establishment of the principate. The conspiracy of Cinna in the year AD 4, according to one classical historian, was the last against the *princeps*.

The historical reflections of historians and other writers deserve special study in the context of resistance to Augustus. Apart from secret pamphlets, which were not so much historical records as libels against the *princeps* (*libelli famosi*), there is no literature rejecting the principate or expressing fundamental criticism of it. The new order, brought in and now maintained by force, could not be open-minded enough to tolerate anything of that nature. All the same, historical writing in the time of Augustus and the following centuries was not undiluted eulogy. Within the limits set by the monarchy, it could express a dissenting or even critical opinion on this or that event or even the principate itself. Virgil, who in his *Aeneid* depicts the Augustan age as the point to which Roman history tended and its zenith, wove politically independent and sometimes clearly critical remarks into important passages, even those referring to Augustus. In the great speech of Anchises to his son Aeneas in the underworld, he inserted a relatively wide-ranging passage which takes the civil war between Caesar, the father of Augustus, and Pompey as an occasion to urge the Romans to live in harmony. Virgil and his contemporaries could equally well have been thinking of the more recent events since the year 44 BC, in which proscriptions were only one of the crises. And in his account of the making of a shield for Aeneas by the god Vulcan, Cato Uticensis, the implacable champion of the republic, is depicted as one of the great men of Rome whose deeds have found their reward in the world beyond the grave. Virgil, like most Romans of his time, knew that after the misery of the great civil war he was of the same mind as Augustus, but that did not make him suppress the memory of the discord for which Augustus bore his share of blame, or lose his power of independent judgement of the republic trodden underfoot by that same Augustus. If the poets did not want to express direct criticism of a definite event of their time, for instance the civil war, then like Horace they opted to transfer it to the realm of myth.

The real problem of historical writing, however, increasingly lay in gathering information, as historians were writing further and further from the time when opinion could be freely formed. True, the Senate archives were open to everyone, but the real centre of power, the *princeps'* house, did not open its doors to all seekers after the truth, only to those who were ready to accept and pass on the official interpretation of political actions. It was possible, however, for a historian in the Augustan age to combine praise of the republic with recognition of the new order in the form of Augustus himself. Linking the principate not just to the old order, but to the way of life and moral conduct of the forefathers of Rome, as well as connecting the ethos of the state to the history of the old society, could disguise the contradictions present. The most important historian of the time, Livy (Titus Livius, 59 BC–AD 17), united both positions. He was regarded as a man who venerated the old republic and at the same time was a friend of Augustus, who even in jest called him a 'Pompeian' (*Pompeianus*), meaning an adherent of the republic.

\*

The most distinguished group of Romans after the senators were the men of equestrian rank (*equites Romani*), whom modern German- and English-language historical researchers also call 'knights', a term suggestive of the Middle Ages. A clearly defined group (*ordo equester*) with fixed functions in the time of the republic, their cohesion was gradually eroded. The equestrian order occupied some of the seats on the jury of the criminal courts of Rome (*quaestiones*), and the management of most of the taxes, duties and state commissions (*publica*) had also been in their hands, so they were called *publicani*. In the time of Cicero, business of this kind dominated all their other activities so much that the knights were mainly seen as 'publicans'. However, formally speaking, all who had the minimum fortune set by the census still belonged to the equestrian order. The self-contained nature of the group was lost first in the blood-letting of the Sullan proscriptions, later by a lack of audits of personal fortune. After the census of the year 70, the next was not until the year 28, so for a generation or more no men with the requisite fortune could be classified as knights. This was all the more disturbing when, after the war between the allies in 90–88, the number of citizens, and thus of those who could claim equestrian rank, increased dramatically. The group was falling apart, or at least no one could still work out who really belonged to it. In addition, after the extension of citizenship to the whole of Italy, and since Caesar and Augustus also extended it to the Roman cities founded all over the empire, many men with the fortune necessary to be an equestrian no longer perceived Rome as the natural centre for eventual public duties.

As the senators were no longer able, if only because of their numbers, to deal with the duties of the empire, which were increasing all the time, Augustus had to resort to a larger circle of men capable of assuming state functions. Here, if they were prepared to take them on, he could call on prosperous citizens who, although they did not belong to senatorial families, qualified through the 'equestrian' *census*, the amount of fortune necessary for a man to be engaged in public life. Not every prosperous man will initially have been inclined to give up his pleasant, independent life for a state career entailing subordination as well as some insecurity. Ovid (Publius Ovidius Naso), for instance, who belonged to a comfortably situated family from Sulmo (Sulmona) in the central Apennines, could not commit himself to public service.

It is clear that the *census* alone was not a sufficient qualification for a future equestrian active in public life. Loyalty, initiative and competence were called for. Augustus reconstituted the equestrian order. Referring back to republican usage, the equestrian was called in future – with an eye to his potential state functions – a 'knight with a state horse' (*equites Romani equo publico*), and the group as a whole was relatively large compared with the senators, who numbered 600. In contrast to the equestrians of Cicero's time, the group was remarkably cohesive, for anyone who wanted to belong to it first had to approach Augustus: it was he who formed, added to and when necessary 'purged' the equestrian order, and so the group was created through nomination by the *princeps*. Membership of it was not, as with senators, hereditary. As an established order (*ordo*) it formed the reservoir for the official functions intended for it. As well as the 'knights with a state horse', some of those who had only the minimum fortune for an equestrian seem to have been described as 'knights on the grounds of the census' (*equites a censu*), but they had no kind of organization and were of no importance for public work. However, Augustus showed that in his time the idea of equestrian rank as denoting a certain fortune was never entirely lost by stating that those who themselves qualified, or whose fathers had qualified, only through the equestrian *census* could sit in the seats at the theatre reserved for knights.

This measure further confirmed the corporate character of the equestrians, sometimes expressed in resolutions, and also denoted by signs of rank such as the narrow purple stripe on the *tunica*. Since the idea persisted that men of equestrian rank were 'horsemen' (*equites*), as the Latin word tells us, as a social body they also expressed their unity in military terms by division into six squadrons (*turmae*). They appeared in that way to the public at large on 15 July, the day of the annual parade, when all equestrians with 'horses of state' filed past Augustus. This was known as the *transvectio equitum*, 'parade of the equestrians'. On this occasion the physical prowess of the men and the state of their horses were checked. One historian, a contemporary of Augustus, tells us that 5,000 knights sometimes took part in the parade. Since at the time all equestrians aged thirty-five and over were allowed to stay away from the parade without any loss of status, and many must have been unable to attend because they were on service outside Rome or lived far from the city, the actual number of the equestrians 'with a state horse' will have been considerably higher, possibly up to around 10,000 men.

Another contemporary of Augustus, the geographer Strabo, notes that in both Patavium (Padua) in northern Italy, and Gades (Cádiz) in the south of Spain, 300 men owned the minimum equestrian fortune required by the census, but he adds that no other city in Italy (barring Rome) had such a high number. The men mentioned by Strabo were not necessarily 'knights with a state horse', only those who had passed the financial test of the census, but even so the figures give some idea of the huge reservoir of prosperous men from whom following generations of equestrians could be drawn.

The equestrians also had a youth group (*iuventus*) founded by Augustus. This group was not confined to the city of Rome, but had branches in the Roman cities of Italy and the provinces. Augustus placed at its head his two adopted sons Gaius and Lucius, his grandsons from the marriage of Agrippa to his daughter Julia. As the 'first among young men' (*principes iuventutis*), this position conveyed the idea that they were the leaders of distinguished Roman youth. Augustus promoted what amounted to a cult of equestrian youth, particularly in connection with the two young Caesars. Fundamentally, however, this was simply the backdrop for the concept of Gaius and Lucius as the successors to Augustus, and the parade of young equestrians and the games they organized were a deliberate act of monarchical self-presentation which was distinctly at odds with the idea of the principate.

The complex tasks of the administration, which were becoming ever more diverse, called for more and more reliable and capable officials below the level of the senior magistrates of Rome and the governors and generals. The equestrians were an obvious choice here, and in making use of them Augustus looked back to the public functions they had already exercised in the time of the late republic. Of primary importance here was their activity as sworn jury members in the courts trying criminal cases (*quaestiones*); the gathering of state finances was of secondary importance, for although that was undertaken by men who satisfied the equestrian property qualification in the Augustan age, it was essentially a private matter and not the central task of a group that distinguished itself by its public character. The various law-courts were divided according to the kinds of cases they tried; there were ten permanent courts for crimes such as murder, forgery and adultery, each under a praetor. Special courts could also be set up under a presiding judge specifically chosen for the purpose. The sworn jurors were chosen from among the senators and the equestrians and were divided into three departments (*decuriae*) of 1,000 men each. Augustus, whose legislation revised the entire system of jurisdiction, set up another, fourth *decuria* for lesser legal disputes, and the pool from which these jurors could be drawn need have only half the equestrian property qualification. In major trials, the number of 2,500 sworn equestrians was considerably higher than that of senators, and perhaps juridical activity was opened up in this way to take some of the burden off the latter. The committees for deciding on candidates for the consulate and praetorship and presenting them to the assembly of the people also drew on members of the equestrian *decuriae*. Unlike the public functions previously performed by equestrians, this was an innovation, and shows the growing importance that Augustus attached to them for the administration of the state. There were equestrian voters as well as equestrian sworn jurors.

Another and extremely important role for the future development of the administration of the empire was undertaken by equestrians on military service. The middle-ranking officers' corps serving under a legion commander or an even higher military man, mainly men commanding cohorts and cavalry formations, had already often been men of equestrian origin in republican times. As there was no standing army at that time, no general rules about the qualification and career of these officers existed. Instead, the magistrate to whom a military mission was entrusted had always chosen his own officers, and as a rule they were recruited from the circles of his friends or men recommended to him who had served in earlier wars and proved their worth. The introduction of a standing army brought change here. For now there was a permanent need not only for senior military officers (the commander of a legion, the commander of a corps of several legions), but also for a considerably larger number of officers below that level but above that of the centurions, who may be regarded as equivalent to captains and as a rule were men of humbler origin.

The middle-ranking officers, that is to say those commanding the units within a legion and contingents from allied forces, were also a distinct social group to which not everyone could belong, only a man of relative distinction. Recruiting them from among the equestrians was an obvious course of action, and, as Augustus was supreme commander of the army, thanks to his monopoly on appointments he had the opportunity of appointing these indispensable officers from what had become a firmly established group of functionaries only when the standing army came into being, choosing men personally known to him or suggested by those whom he trusted. Through his unrestricted power of choice, he could form them into a corps devoted to him and trained under his supervision, in fact his willing tool. In addition, he could promote a man who was not yet an equestrian through his army service.

Under Augustus, we already see the first instances of professional groups being forged within the officers' corps of the middle ranks of service. Later they came to be called the 'three equestrian military offices' (*tres militiae equestres*), which in stages led to the administrative positions intended for equestrians in the service of the state. Through equestrian military service, Augustus could also enable ambitious and capable men from the upper classes of the Roman cities of Italy and the provinces to rise in his service, and even perhaps in this way help them to reach the highest of the offices open to equestrians at some date or, once promoted to quaestor, to enter the Senate. Even in the time of the triumvirate, when the chances of rising in the world had been almost unlimited, centurions could enter the equestrian ranks after holding the post of *primipilus*, chief centurion, the highest open to them at centurion rank. Augustus had made this post a regular army rank from which further promotion was possible, and although that did not mean there was any clearly defined career ahead yet for such men, and much was still in flux, still the rank of *primipilus* shows us two things: first, the equestrian order was open to new groups, and second, such promotion was linked to army service, during which the candidate could be observed for years and his suitability for further service to the state assessed.

However, it was only under the successors of Augustus that an equestrian career was to develop into the foundation stone of an effective imperial administration. Under Augustus, the administration he supervised was still characteristically searching for forms that would suffice for the practical needs of the new state order, and for political aims that had also changed. Below the high offices reserved for senators, as mentioned above, the group of procurators, active principally in finance, was the first to be established. Although men qualified by the equestrian *census* do appear among the procurators, this group was not determined by its separate group character but by its proximity to Augustus, to whose 'household' in the widest sense the procurators belonged. At the same time, however, equestrians featured among them in growing numbers and importance. They were, it should be emphasized again, not intended by Augustus as a counterweight to the senatorial members of the administration, who as senators remained at the heart of its bureaucracy. But certain official positions were closer to the person of the *princeps* than others, and it was obvious for him to fill them with men who knew him particularly well, or of whose abilities he could make almost unlimited use. The richest province of all, Egypt, which could not be entrusted to any independent magistrate because of the financial temptations it offered and which Augustus, as successor to the Ptolemies, had to regard as a personal base for his rule, therefore went to a governor of equestrian rank with the title of prefect, and it was no coincidence that the first prefect of Egypt was a close friend of Augustus, Gaius Cornelius Gallus. As the province was governed by an equestrian, the commanders of the legions stationed there could not be of senatorial rank either, but must also be equestrians. Similarly, military formations in Rome such as the fire-fighting service organized by the army were led by equestrians if they already had commanders of their own under Augustus. These men also held the title of prefect (*praefectus*), a rank that for a long time had been usual for a highly placed officer, but one who was responsible to the senatorial magistrate. Besides the governors of Egypt and the commanders of the guard in Rome, it was also held by the admirals of the fleets in Misenum and Ravenna (*praefectus classis*, 'prefect of the fleet'), who were also directly responsible to Augustus. Smaller provinces or administrative districts which had only just been subdued by the army, or had been taken over by a client prince, also had prefects appointed by Augustus. Judaea, within the province of Syria, was a prefecture from AD 6 onwards, and so were many areas inhabited by the recently defeated Alpine tribes, such as the districts where the Ligurian tribes of the maritime Alps lived.

The gratitude of the Romans for a world at peace and the prospect of a relatively secure future knew no bounds. Today, the eulogies of the time sound servile, sometimes positively embarrassing, but although they increasingly came to be couched in a style of formal homage, at first they were the expression of genuine feeling in which relief after all the misery that had been suffered mingled with hope for a better future. Unlimited appreciation was expressed to Augustus, in particular, by hundreds of Roman towns and cities in Italy and indeed all over the Roman world. On the local urban level, political life was often livelier there than in Rome, where ordinary people were largely excluded from the political process. Outside it, however, holders of local office were still chosen by the people after elections, even though they were sometimes turbulent. In all the cities a well-to-do upper class set the tone. Citizens chose the holders of urban office from that class, and after their term of office they entered the local senate, here known as the *curia*. The group of curials (*decuriones*) formed the leadership in every town, the municipal nobility, and as such had a clear group awareness of itself (*ordo decurionum*). Augustus felt particularly close to this urban class; he never disowned his origin in the equestrian families of Italian country towns and sometimes, on public recommendation (*commendatio publica*) – which will have come above all from the council of decurions – he also promoted members of it, even if they were not known to him personally, to equestrian rank through their military service.

Augustus was more reserved in his attitude to freedmen as a group. In contrast to the Greek cities, where a freed slave was classified with the foreigners resident there, the slave manumitted formally by a Roman, that is to say by the civil law (*ius civile*), became a Roman citizen. Freedmen owed that not to any special generosity on the part of the Romans but to the peculiarities of Roman family law, whereby freed slaves counted as children of the household, and consequently there was also a reverse side: the freedman as a rule had to see the father of the family as his patron, to whom he owed not only material duties but a legal duty of respect. The man who freed a slave therefore retained considerable rights over the slave he had manumitted, and if a freedman did not carry out his duties he could be returned to the condition of slavery. Only a man who was free-born (*ingenuus*) and not born into slavery was free of the most pressing duties. In principle, Augustus shared the general prejudices of Roman society against freedmen; it was made clear in the fact that he forbade senators to marry freed slaves. However, he placed no other restrictions on the marriage choices of freedmen, and in the context of his marriage legislation even freed them in part from their duties to their patrons if they could fulfil certain conditions stated in the law.

While the wish for a Roman society rich in children sometimes kept prejudice against freed slaves in the background, in two laws of the years 2 BC and AD 4 Augustus drastically curtailed testamentary manumissions, through which several hundred slaves at a time had sometimes been freed. He decreed that only a fraction of a man's slaves might be freed on his death and in addition set the maximum number to be freed (100 if a man owned 500 or more slaves), and the minimum ages of those freed (twenty) and of the owner freeing them (thirty). The figures show that the problem existed only because of the huge numbers of slaves kept by a considerable number of Roman families. In view of the careers in trade and industry preferred by freedmen, and the protection they might expect from the owner who freed them, the population of large parts of all Rome and of other large Roman cities felt a not unjustified fear that these people could usurp their livelihoods. So Augustus also hesitated to distinguish freedmen with higher offices and social privileges unless they were from his own household. The gift of the gold equestrian ring to the doctor Antonius Musa, who cured Augustus of a severe illness in the year 23 BC, should be seen as a special and isolated case, and, while in addition the commanders of the fleets of Ravenna and Misenum were freedmen, that was because the crews of the fleet anyway were to a great extent recruited from freedmen themselves.

# 12

# Self-presentation of the Monarchy: the Romans' Understanding of Their Time

Augustus begins his account of his own achievements, which after his death was inscribed on two bronze pillars in front of his mausoleum and on the walls of many temples, with the following words: 'At the age of nineteen, on my personal initiative and at my own expense, I recruited an army with which I led the state to liberty after its oppression by the tyrannical rule (*dominatio*) of a political group (*factio*). In the consulate of Gaius Pansa and Aulus Hirtius I was therefore accepted, by decrees awarding me honours, into the Senate, where I was given a place among the former consuls, and military command was transferred to me. It [the Senate] entrusted to me, as propraetor, the task of working with the consuls to ensure that the state suffered no harm. After both consuls had fallen in war, the people made me consul that same year, and chose me as a triumvir for the restoration of the state.'

The events of the years 44–43, to which he refers here, look back at the early political career of Augustus and his rise to the consulate and the triumvirate. Fifty-five years separate those events from the version Augustus gave of them in his account written in April AD 13, sixteen months before his death, when he wanted to make sure that posterity would see them as he presented them. It is easy to prove today that his account is inaccurate. But how many of those who themselves had lived through the years 44–43 were going to give the lie to the *princeps*? Few of them were still alive in AD 13, for like Augustus himself they would now be in the middle of their eighth decade of life.

Most of the incidents of 44–43 mentioned by Augustus in fact bear only a very superficial relation to what really happened at the time, and with the best will in the world not even that can be said of many of them, which must be regarded as false or at least presented in a very distorted way. First and foremost, the motives claimed by Augustus for his actions are so far from the facts that we can only say he embellished or misrepresented the truth. Augustus simply turned the real events upside down, and his interpretation of them was no less outrageous for being officially announced from on high. The effrontery with which Augustus rewrote the history of the time is likely to shock anyone looking back at it now. The 'faction' from whose rule he allegedly liberated the state was that of Antony, the rightful consul and after that the legally appointed governor of Cisalpine Gaul. And to what kind of liberty did Augustus claim to have led the state? He was able to perform that heroic deed only as an ally of Cicero and other like-minded men, to whom liberty really meant something. But are we to suppose that he then defended the old order shoulder to shoulder with Cicero? Furthermore, the raising at his own expense of an army with which he claims to have saved the state – meaning the republic – amounted to high treason. Did Augustus really think it had been forgotten that no private person was permitted to raise and equip an army? That was the business of the Senate. The acceptance of Caesar's young adopted son, a political nonentity at the time, into the highest ranks of senators was another break with the legal system of the republic and one that had never occurred before. So was legalizing the military command that Augustus had usurped, of which he goes on to speak. Both the appointment of Octavian as a senator and the transfer to him of a military command had been the work of Cicero, who believed that in the hour of need the young man and the army he had recruited could be pitted against Antony. Imposing the state of emergency declared by the Senate, to which Augustus next refers, may perhaps pass muster as a legalized form of resistance to Antony, but he would have done better to draw a veil of silence over what follows. Describing both the consulate that he had acquired by brute force with his march on Rome and the tyranny of the triumvirate that was then set up in glowing terms, as meritorious acts, was bound to appear to anyone who knew what had really happened an outrageous lie.

But hardly anyone could now remember the events described by Augustus. Even the few who could have set the record straight refrained from doing so, and not just out of fear of the all-powerful *princeps*. Political reality had changed; the events of over fifty years before now appeared only in the light of that new reality and had no other significance. No one was interested in taking a close look at the early years of

Augustus. Some day historians might ascertain the truth about the past, or what was taken for the past, but who was interested? As far as historical awareness went back, all Romans knew about a long period of two decades of the utmost danger and unspeakable misery, in which Augustus had played a prominent and not always glorious part. But that was long ago now, and the Romans knew that it was also Augustus who had freed them from the horrors of those times, maintaining the security and welfare of Rome in a peace that had lasted for over forty years. The present was superimposed on the past and made it difficult to remember what life had once really been like.

In all that he told the Romans about his political past, Augustus was counting on their present state of mind being very different from what it had been in the past. However, he did not content himself with appealing to that new awareness; he himself reinforced it in what seemed to him the right spirit, indeed shaped it and turned it in a particular direction. In so doing – and this is important for our understanding of that time – he could rely on the willing acceptance of his ideas by Roman society. Those ideas had not simply been imposed on the people from above, but were linked to concepts that already existed. Augustus had not always been able to expect such ready acceptance by the Romans. Coming on to the political stage as the son of Caesar, at first he was welcome only to those to whom the figure of the dictator really meant something, in practice Caesar's soldiers and closest clients, and even among those Octavian's authority was not undisputed; he had strong rivals to contend with. A little later, indeed, a majority had seen him only as a terrorist and a tyrant who murdered the people of Italy and seized their land. His path to his reputation as a man generally respected and even praised had been long and thorny. His campaigns as a triumvir against the corsair Sextus Pompey and in Illyria had been staging posts along that way, the culmination of which was his victory at Actium, showing him not just victorious against the alleged threat of control from the east, but also as the bringer of peace. But he did not let his military successes and his efforts to consolidate peace at home speak for themselves; in his own account he provided them with a commentary, which revised the facts through interpretation, careful selection and an editing-out of the unfavourable aspects and made them the carriers of his message. The most important part of this message related to the political values dearest to the Romans: peace and liberty. Augustus laid particular emphasis on the former, for all the inhabitants of the empire, Romans and provincials alike, had wanted peace more than anything after the misery of the past.

And peace appeared to have been restored with the victory at Actium. However, it was not peace itself, the mere absence of war, but its symbolic abstraction that Augustus wanted to leave its mark on the minds of the Roman people: the fact that they now lived in a peaceful world, and that this world was indissolubly linked to his person. The peace that the Romans had brought to all their subject peoples, and that they now themselves enjoyed after the end of the civil wars, derived from Augustus (the Pax Augusta). It was identical with the peace of the Roman empire (the Pax Romana).

The symbolic proclamation of peace in the empire took place in January of the year 29, immediately after the end of the war against Antony and Cleopatra and even before Octavian returned from the east, through the closing of the temple of Janus. In his account of his achievements Augustus prides himself on the fact that this procedure was repeated twice more during his reign: 'During my principate, the temple of Janus Quirinus, which our forefathers had decreed should be closed only when, after a victory, peace prevailed throughout the empire of the Roman people on land and at sea, was closed three times by order of the Senate, while before my birth, the records tell us, it had been closed only twice since the founding of the city.' The other occasions for the closing of the temple – the second was after the end of the Spanish campaign of the year 25, and we do not know the occasion for the third time – and the question of whether there was really no warlike conflict going on in the empire at this time carry less weight than the repetition of the act itself, which after that first occasion in the year 29 continued to present the *princeps* as not only the bringer of peace but also the man who preserved it. Pax, the personified goddess of peace, became an established symbol of his reign from now on, allowing no tension to arise between reality and the idea of peace, even when conflicts broke out again after the year 16. For peace still remained unbroken in Italy and the provinces, and the extensive military operations on the borders served to secure peace at home. The Roman army is not pictured as a belligerent Fury, but as the means of bringing and maintaining peace. In a poem written just before Augustus' return from Gaul in the year 13, Horace praised the peace of the world and the sense of security felt by the Roman people, despite many

Ara Pacis Augustae, dedicated on 30 January 9 BC.
Southern frieze: Augustus with priests and lictors; behind, Augustus leading members of his family.

dangers threatening them on the borders. The army was not at odds with the idea of peace but appeared as its prerequisite.

Peace stood for both the welfare of the state and concord between its citizens, and both now seemed to have been finally won. Peace (Pax), concord (Concordia) and the welfare of the state (Salus Publica) were all interdependent, and Augustus had given the Romans all three by defeating their enemies, ending the civil war and setting up the principate. That was how he meant his actions to be seen, and so in fact they were. When, in the year 12 BC, the Senate was once again collecting money for statues to Augustus, he declined the honour, but allowed the erection instead of statues of Salus Publica, Concordia and Pax personified as goddesses. He himself was included in this divine trinity, for the three goddesses were only another aspect of his person, and so Concordia, after the restoration and consecration of her temple by Tiberius at the beginning of the year AD 10, was called Concordia Augusta.

Augustus ensured that the idea of peace received visible expression in a cult devoted to the goddess Pax. Her cult venerated peace and was also related to the *princeps* and his entire house. When he returned in triumph from three years away in Gaul and Spain, the Senate vowed to erect an altar to 'Augustan Peace' (*ara Pacis Augustae*), which Augustus himself mentions in his account of his achievements. It was built on the Field of Mars over a period of several years and solemnly consecrated on 30 January 9, Livia's birthday.

From left to right: Livia, Tiberius, Antonia Minor, Drusus I.

Slabs from the altar were already being discovered in the Renaissance, although no one recognized their provenance. Once they had been identified, proper excavations were carried out under very difficult conditions in 1903, and again in 1937–8, bringing to light large parts of the altar and about a third of its decorative reliefs. The structure consisted of the altar table and a precinct wall entirely surrounding it, with access to the altar itself through two entrances. It stood in the middle of the Field of Mars, on the Flaminian Road (now Via del Corso), a few hundred metres from the present exhibition area and close to the mausoleum of Augustus. Even in its reconstructed form, which reveals regrettable gaps in our knowledge, it is easily the most impressive architectural monument of Augustan Rome, striking for the quality of its figurative and ornamental reliefs, while the political statement they make is unique of its kind.

At the centre of the pictorial decoration are the friezes on the outer wall surrounding the altar precinct. They show the procession on the solemn occasion in the year 13 when the Senate vowed to build it. Augustus walks at the head of the procession with his lictors, followed by priests (*flamines*), then Agrippa and all the prominent members of the family of the *princeps*, accompanied by their wives and children. Augustus, who was not yet *pontifex maximus*, appears not as a priest but as *princeps*, and his function is therefore not in the technical act of making the vow, which is shown, but in his presence as the bringer of peace to the Gallic and Spanish provinces. The vow was made by the Senate, together with the priests whose part it was to perform the sacred rites, but as the bringer of peace Augustus is its point of reference. The reliefs

459

on the broader sides of the wall, by the large entrances to the altar precinct and fitted at the same height as the procession, trace Roman history far back into the past. One slab shows Aeneas as a priest after his arrival at what was to be Rome, sacrificing to the goddess Juno the sow which, it had been prophesied to him, would appear and show him the site of the future city (this episode is known as the prodigy of the sow). Another slab shows the twins Romulus and Remus, with their father Mars and their foster-father the shepherd Faustulus, being suckled by the she-wolf in the cave on the Palatine Hill (the Lupercal) where Rome was later to rise. Two more reliefs show the elements of earth, water and air with the goddess Roma, setting the earthly scene in a divine context. The elements and Augustus' ancestors thus join him and his house in presenting a unified image of history under divine protection. By relating the entire past history of the Latins and the Romans to his person, he appears as the sum of all their achievements, more particularly as the bringer of peace and good fortune. The references to the divine world conferring benefits and fortune extend to the twining vegetative motifs and their animal inhabitants, some of the creatures shown symbolizing deities. Their significance would have been well known to viewers of that time.

The clear reference of the altar to Augustus as the bringer of peace also explains the significance of another structure, erected not far from the altar in the year 9. It is a sundial (*horologium solarium*) consisting of an obelisk surmounted by a bronze globe – the obelisk was the first to be brought to Rome from Egypt and stands today in front of the parliament building in the Piazza Montecitorio. It relates to the altar in the way that the equinoctial line of the dial would pass right through its centre, thus pointing to Augustus, who was born at the autumn equinox on 23 September. The sundial was perhaps also meant to refer to the nearby mausoleum of Augustus, which had been standing completed by the Tiber for two decades at this time, since the orientation of the obelisk, which is not precise and in fact is a good 18 degrees out, seems to point to the mausoleum.

The idea of peace did not stop there; it was linked to the expectation of a better time. What Virgil had yearned for in his Fourth Eclogue, and like other poets of his time later never tired of praising as a wish that had been fulfilled, was what Augustus himself very obviously believed. His efforts to convey his own view of the future to the Roman people culminated in the Secular Games of the year 17, formally proclaiming the dawn of the new age and sanctioned by the gods. He himself had been born under the sign of Capricorn the goat, the sign of the rising sun, and by the old uncorrected, pre-Julian calendar possibly on 17 December, but 23 September was his officially sanctioned birthday, bringing him under the sign of Libra, the scales, designating the equal length of day and night. Perhaps that day became his birthday after the dictator's reform of the calendar in the year 46 BC and the resulting adjustment of dates. In view of the general confusion of the calendar at the time of his birth – in the year 63 it was several months out of joint – many kinds of reckoning were possible, and it is difficult for us to get a clear picture today. At any rate, despite celebrating his official birthday on 23 September Augustus kept the goat as his birth sign. It denoted a time marked by winter sowing and thus the beginning of new growth, and he therefore took it as an omen that the special constellation of the stars at the hour of his birth or perhaps his conception pointed to the future. We find the theme on coins and other items in general use, and also on the famous Gemma Augusta, where the gem-cutter showed it above the head of Augustus: with him the new time had come, and its confirmation was visible to everyone in his star sign.

The idea of peace was part of a specifically Roman view of the way history linked the present with the past, indeed the very distant past. We speak today of Roman 'national consciousness' or 'national pride'. This modern concept does not correspond entirely to conditions in the ancient world. It would be more accurate to say that the Romans saw themselves as a political community, and not exactly what the modern term 'nation' would suggest. They were a people without any 'national' partners. In their sense of belonging together, the Romans formed an isolated community, acknowledging no other nations as their equals. They had not reached this political self-awareness by confronting other nations, but by doing away with the very idea that such nations existed at all. That sounds paradoxical, but the Roman sense of cohesion arose from the dissolution of all other political structures in the Mediterranean world.

As a political community the Romans were a product of their isolation. That did not, however, apply to their intellectual and moral lives, which were more like the result of intensive confrontation with the Greek intellect and sense of form. The cultural influence of the Greeks

461

on the Romans is as old as Roman history itself. It begins with the Etruscans and continues in waves lasting into the time of Augustus, and it is marked by very different approaches to the heritage of the Greek mind. Periods when Greek ideas were readily adopted alternated with times of arrogant resistance, a reaction with a perceptible touch of the inferiority complex about it. On the whole, however, relations with Greece were fruitful, and it is the great achievement of the Romans to have taken the intellectual foundations laid by the Greeks and built on them an intellectual life and a literature of their own, not simply in imitation but with independent ideas and forms, in particular a specifically Roman morality and view of the world which was ultimately able to hold its own even with Greek culture. At the time of Augustus this process was mainly complete, but the Romans were still trying to reach new heights – again in competition with the Greeks.

Over the centuries the political isolation of the Romans and their understanding of themselves, as created and reinforced by Greek ideas, resulted in a cast of mind giving moral support to the political unity of Rome and its dominion over all the peoples of the Mediterranean world. It embraced all areas of life and outlasted all crises. Its two mainstays were reverence for the gods and the head of the family (*pietas*) and justice to fellow men and conquered enemies (*iustitia*). In line with these ideas, the Romans did not fight against the gods; respect was owed even to the gods of an enemy city, and if that city was defeated its gods were duly offered a new residence in Rome itself. War was always waged in response to attack and was therefore a just war (*bellum iustum*). Other ethical concepts developed from these two mainstays of Roman thinking, particularly unconditional obedience to the master of the house and the magistrates (*disciplina*) and the observance of obligations towards fellow citizens and the community (*fides*). The historical consciousness of the Romans emphasized the idea of their ethical superiority over other peoples, and the certainty of having received divine aid throughout their history. So the city on the Tiber became mistress first of the cities of the Latins, then of all Italy, finally of the world, and with the help of Greek mythology the Romans constructed a history of its origins going back into the ancient times populated by gods and heroes. It linked the ancestors of the Romans to the Trojan War, with which the Greeks also began their own history, and thus incorporated the gods into their history as guarantors of the grandeur of Rome.

The image that the Romans had of their history in the time of Augustus, however, was not defined solely by its fame and glory; it also had dark aspects. They concerned the last hundred years, when despite the state's outward stability it had been plagued at home by terrible unrest in which thousands of people lost their lives, sometimes brutally slaughtered for no fault of their own. The climax had been reached in the ill-starred triumvirate period. Since Rome had owed her rise to a fundamental ethical attitude, a decline in the old customs was held responsible for her fall. In the generations before Augustus avarice and sensual indulgence, egotism and a thirst for power in which personal interests took precedence over those of the community had led to conflict and economic misery. Against a background of growing insecurity as they faced the future, leading men in the republic, together with writers and historians, presented the Romans with a picture of the life of their forebears as a model of conduct that would bring back the good old days. The thinking of their ancestors was held up to them in thousands of examples and codified, so to speak, as the right way to behave (*mos maiorum*). Writers of the calibre of Sallust and Livy preached a return to the old values, and, as they as historians saw it, that meant turning to the tradition of Rome in the past. 'What chiefly makes the study of history wholesome and profitable,' says Livy in the preface to his great history, 'is this, that you behold the lessons of every kind of experience set forth as on a conspicuous monument. From these you may choose for yourself and for your own state what to imitate, from these mark for avoidance what is shameful in the conception and shameful in the result.'

Augustus did not need to construct this image of history himself. It was there before him: the leading men of the ruling families had created it and constantly reworked it, particularly those of them who criticized and admonished, who harped on about political decline and tried to halt it by turning back to tradition, or what they understood to be tradition. They were all particularly anxious to emphasize the greatness of Rome and their own part in it and they used the history of the Romans to that end, as well as to demonstrate and justify their own political influence. The death masks of all a man's important forebears were taken to his funeral as evidence of the great past, and Romans were also familiar with their history from the many statues and countless inscriptions honouring great men, especially funerary inscriptions, and from images on historical reliefs and coins. The fact that Augustus' own family, the Octavians, had no great name in the history of Rome did not matter, for he came on to the political stage as Gaius Julius Caesar. The Julians and above all the person of the dictator vouched for him. Many of his sayings and symbolic actions show how important he felt it to associate himself with the history of the Julian clan. In his first years in power he had had to exploit his adoptive father's name to secure the support of the soldiers, and it also represented his link with the history of Rome. Venus was one of the ancestors of the Julians, like Romulus, the founder of the city, and it seems that initially he wanted to give himself the name of Romulus. From Venus to Aeneas, her son by Anchises the Trojan, Julian history spanned the arc to Romulus as the descendant of Aeneas and then, as Rome rose to a position of international power, to the dictator Julius Caesar and so to himself.

But Augustus was not solely concerned to place his Julian family in the tradition of the nobility; he now set about demoting other noble families which had once been rivals for power and influence in Roman society but had now largely left the public arena, and taking their place himself. He let slip no opportunity of demonstrating his links with old Rome. Without actually forcing the families of the old nobility entirely into the background, his pre-eminent position and wholesale use of all available means to raise the historical profile of the Julian clan served to make the Romans aware of their importance in historical events, especially of the early period. Augustus was always to be seen as the point at which Julian history was culminating, and the dictator Caesar, although Augustus could not have managed without him early in his political career, gradually retreated into the background. It is tempting to say that in the end he almost lapsed into oblivion. In his account of his achievements, Augustus no longer calls on the name of Caesar or the title of *divi filius*, both of which had been so useful to him earlier as the basis of his right to rule. He mentions the temple of his deified 'father' only in enumerating the buildings he erected, and as the place where plunder taken in war was received, and he even expressly distances himself from the dictatorship. Proudly he says that, although the Senate and people had asked him to assume it himself, he refused. He wanted dictatorship to recede into the background behind the idea of the principate, and by this time Augustus had long been able to stand on his own feet.

This view of the Roman past as a precursor to Augustus is

particularly clear in the writers of the Augustan period. In the sixth and eighth books of his great Roman heroic epic, the *Aeneid*, written in the twenties, after the year 27, Virgil expresses it with the utmost clarity. The hero, Aeneas, learns what the future of his people holds from his father, Anchises, in the underworld. In the great speech in which Anchises tells his son about the future figures who will define the Roman empire, Virgil lays stress on the link between ancient Rome and Augustus: the entire first part of the speech is devoted to the early period up to the time of Romulus, and after mentioning the omens at the foundation of the city and the honorific name of Augustus, he goes on to write a hymn of praise to the *princeps*. He sets Romulus and Augustus side by side, so that the latter is presented as the man who brought to perfection all that divine fate had planned in the early days of Rome. After the untiring efforts of the Romans to achieve and maintain a position of political power, and after the misery of the civil wars, he stands for the dawn of a better time, expressed in the image of a 'Golden Age'. 'This man,' Anchises tells his son, 'is he of whom I have so often spoken to you: Augustus Caesar, of divine descent, who will found a new Golden Age in the fields of Latium, where once Saturn reigned.' Through the mythological agency of Hercules and Dionysus, two wanderers through the world, Augustus is also presented as the epitome of the high international standing that the Romans had won over the course of centuries. A peaceful world, united by Augustus, promises welfare and happiness – that is the message of these lines. Only then does Virgil – or Anchises – turn to the rest of the history of Rome, mentioning other Roman rulers, followed by Lucius Junius Brutus as the liberator of the Romans from the rule of the last tyrannical king, and finally a few heroes from the fourth to the second centuries, but he devotes only a few words to them. The connection between Romulus and Augustus and the contrast between modest political beginnings and complete mastery of the world determine the tone of the whole composition.

In the second and longer passage, devoted to the future history of Rome, Virgil describes the shield made for Aeneas by the god Vulcan at the request of Venus. Virgil begins this excursus not with ancient history, but with the image of the she-wolf suckling the twins Romulus and Remus, and thus with the prehistory of the founding of the city, and then he covers the time of the kings and the emergent republic's struggle for freedom against Porsenna and the Celts who besieged Rome. After that the narrative leaps forward to continue with two figures from the late republic, Catiline and Cato, whom Virgil, however, mentions only in passing, before describing the battle of Actium at length. However, the battle itself – its course is directed by the gods of war and spirits of revenge, with the rejoicing figure of Discord (Discordia), while Cleopatra leads the enemy in the person of the Egyptian goddess Isis – is not really the ultimate destination of Virgil's line of thought, only the medium through which the reader reaches the next great scene, the triumph of Octavian over the enemies of Rome, when at last the rule of Rome over the world is secured. In an impressive image, the victorious Octavian looks down from the threshold of the temple of Apollo on the Palatine to see nations bringing gifts from all over the earth, the peoples of the Sahara in the south, of the east as far as Scythia, of the Euphrates, the Rhine and the Araxes in Armenia. Again, Virgil sets Augustus in a line of historical thought linking the early days of Rome with his victory over his rivals and his dominion over what is now the whole world. This image unites the Roman empire with the world, Augustus appears as the 'guardian of the Roman empire' (*custos imperii Romani*) and 'he who presides over the whole circle of the earth' (*totius orbis terrarum praeses*), as a decree of the Senate of Pisa of the year AD 4 puts it. He stands for Roman rule of the world, and the pictorial symbolism conveys the same message. He is shown as Jupiter ruling the world on both the famous gen of Augustus in Vienna and one of the silver goblets from the Boscoreale villa near Pompeii: on the front of the goblet Augustus, sitting on his chair of office and surrounded by a throng of lictors and soldiers, receives the surrender of a party of barbarians. Whatever actual event this refers to, the scene serves mainly as background to the other side of the goblet, where Augustus, again seated on a kind of throne (not the chair of office this time), takes the orb of the world in his right hand and, attended by Roma, Mars and other divinities, and Venus as the ancestress of his clan, receives victory in the form of a statuette. Here he is shown as a divine personage among gods, who are transferring dominion over the world to him and who guarantee its permanence.

Augustus was not dictating to his poet in the presentation of the *princeps* as the culminating point of Roman history in the two central passages from the *Aeneid* cited above, although naturally they were not written without any idea of what he would like. The main feature of Virgil's account is that it captures the general mood of the time. The

Romans liked to raise their image of history to idealized heights and, under the spell of the restoration of peace at home and the declared political intention of reviving tradition, were happy to see both symbolized in Augustus, and where the references attached to that historical image are incompatible with the prominent position of Augustus or even at odds with it, Virgil traces those too in the literary sphere. Typical are constant reminders of the liberty of the republic and references to the civil war, a subject that Virgil addressed not only in his early work, the *Eclogues* and the *Georgics*, but also later, in lines written when peace had been secured. In the catalogue of heroes in Book 6 of the *Aeneid*, for instance, he suddenly interrupts his listing of the great figures of Rome, which is only loosely connected to the context, by a nine-line reference to the civil war between Caesar and Pompey, closing it by condemning bloodshed among Roman citizens. While Virgil presents the father of Augustus here as one of the parties in the civil war, and thus an active element in discord, in the description of the shield in Book 8, 'pale Discord' appears at the battle of Actium, and here Octavian himself is represented as a party to civil war. Even the peace restored by Augustus cannot quite banish the memory of that terrible experience, especially not in a man who, like Virgil, had himself seen the outbreak of war between Caesar and Pompey. In addition, the description of the shield sets up a memorial honouring Cato Uticensis, representing the aristocratic rule of the declining republic and an implacable enemy of the dictator, as the man who 'speaks justice in a remote area to the pious, and thus to the better part of Roman society' and at the same time allows scope to mourn the liberty of a great Roman society that was lost with him. There is also direct mention of the liberty of the old republic in both passages: in the underworld scene Lucius Junius Brutus, the first consul of the republic, is introduced as the champion of 'noble liberty' (*pulchra libertas*). In the description of the shield the Romans also fight (in view of the threatened return of the last tyrannical king) for the maintenance of liberty, with Augustus seen as the main guarantor of its preservation.

The image of history propagated by Augustus is illustrated with particular clarity by his most important architectural work, the Forum of Augustus. With its central building, the temple of Mars Ultor, it is the most historically significant complex of the time. No other building gave better and more concrete expression to the ideas of the *princeps* about the past of Rome and its role in the new state. The message of its structure and its statues is not that of an ordinary contemporary or a poet, but of the ruler himself, and the extremely direct and massive manner in which it is conveyed makes it clear that here Augustus did not simply see himself as a part of Roman history but was staking a claim to the whole of that history for himself.

The term 'forum' describes the large area or square in the centre of every city that served for political purposes, the assemblies of the people, legal transactions, public performances of every kind and also for trading. In Rome, the old Forum (Forum Romanum) had been used for that purpose for centuries. The dictator had added a second forum on its north-west side, the Forum Julium. The forum constructed by Augustus was therefore the third large central square. The new squares provided for a growing need in Rome for space for public and private business but above all they demonstrated the magnificence and glory of the men who built them, which made them items of monarchical architecture.

The old market place, which had been at the hub of Roman political life for over half a millennium, was not untouched by the new developments. It changed under Augustus, and indeed over the course of the years its structure and function were altered so much that it gradually lost its old republican look and assumed a monarchical and Julian appearance. The colourful medley of private and public business transactions in a square surrounded by public buildings, and linked on all sides by streets and smaller alleyways to other markets and living quarters, now became an enclosed and therefore more restricted area. It served more for public than private purposes, and expressed the character of the ruling house through its many connections with the Julian family. The temple of the deified Caesar, dedicated in the year 29 and closing the Forum at its south-east end, introduced the changes of the time, along with the Parthian arch on the south-east side and the new Senate house completed by Augustus, the Curia Julia. At the same time as the temple of the Divine Julius was erected, Augustus also built another speaker's rostrum, so that the square now had two rostrums, one at each end. Later, in AD 6, the temple of Castor and Pollux to the west of the temple of Caesar and after it the temple of Concordia at the north-west end of the square were completely renovated, and finally the two basilicas were entirely rebuilt along both long sides of the Forum.

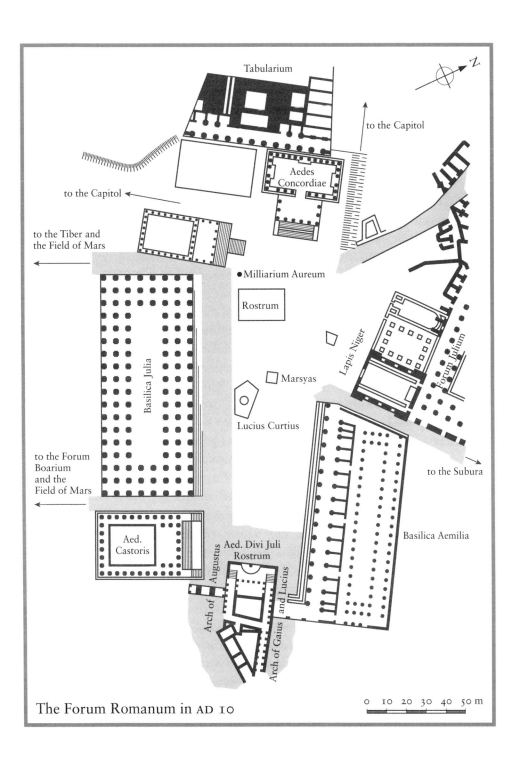

The Forum Romanum in AD 10

The old Basilica Sempronia on the western side was replaced by a larger building, named after the Julian family (Basilica Julia), and a fire in the year 14 BC was the occasion for the restoration of the Basilica Aemilia opposite it, also built in the early second century BC. Augustus contributed to the cost of its restoration, which was incumbent upon the Aemilian family. The old central market place of Rome thus became a complex in which almost every building and monument spoke of the new ruling house. Symptomatic of the ruthless expulsion of the old republican spirit was the disappearance of the circular space north of the Forum known as the Comitium, which had been the centre of all political life for centuries. It was where the Senate, the people and the magistrates had conducted business, and many of its time-hallowed monuments to the Roman past had been firmly anchored in the minds of the Romans, such as the old speakers' rostrum, the assembly room of the senators (*senaculum*) and a whole series of statues.

The second forum, the Julian Forum, provided a new central public place which, unlike the old Forum, led the eye to a temple. Caesar had begun building it in the fifties, but the forum and temple were not completed until 46 BC, and Augustus had more work done on them after that. The temple was the temple of Venus Genetrix, dedicated to Venus as the ancestress of Caesar, and thus had a very pronounced political aspect in relation to the dictator's own divinity.

The forum built by Augustus also led the eye to a temple, the temple of Mars the Avenger (Mars Ultor). He had vowed to build it in the year 42, before the battle at Philippi against the assassins of his adoptive father, but it was not completed until forty years later in 2 BC. The layout was to have been more extensive, but as the owners of the site obstinately refused to sell a larger area Augustus had to content himself with the space available. The temple and the pillared arcades were remarkably extravagant in appearance; the material used was white Carrara marble, and the rich ornamentation, with its reliefs and caryatids symbolically supporting the upper storeys of the pillared arcades, was notable for its high quality. The completed complex must have made a lasting impression on all who saw it at the time, although what remains today gives us little idea of its original magnificence. The dimensions of this forum were only a little larger than those of the Julian Forum, but the temple itself was more spacious than the temple of Venus in the Julian Forum, so that it dominated the entire forum. Two

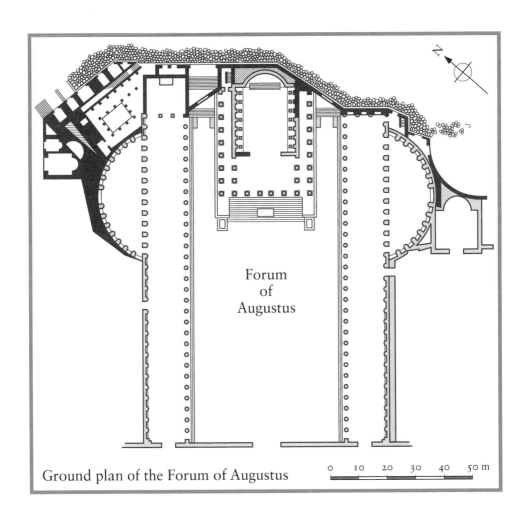

Forum
of
Augustus

Ground plan of the Forum of Augustus

0    10    20    30    40    50 m

long pillared arcades (*porticus*) bordered the square on its long sides, each of them with a large exedra.

A particularly notable feature of the Forum Augustum was its statues, which did not just provide decoration but as an ensemble were intended to convey a political statement to the observer. A triumphal chariot drawn by four horses (a quadriga) with the statue of Augustus occupied the centre of the square, and the names of the peoples he had defeated were listed on its pediment. The chariot, like the equestrian statue of the dictator in the Julian Forum, stood on the same axis as the temple and had been donated to Augustus by a decree of the Senate. The central position of the triumphal chariot showed that Augustus was the point of reference of the entire layout. From the quadriga, the eye of an observer fell first on the statuary group in the tympanum of the temple. It showed, among other figures, Mars, Venus and Fortuna, along with Romulus, the latter perhaps as having performed the solemn rite of the *augurium augustum* when he asked the gods their opinion on the founding of the city. The nine-metre plinth for the cult statues inside the temple accommodated not only Mars Ultor and Venus but also a third statue, possibly of the dictator. The pillared arcades flanking the temple continued the pictorial sequence. The great heroes of the mythical and historical past of Rome stood, as triumphators, in the niches of their exedras. A plinth inscription with the name and the highest position as magistrate that each had occupied provided brief information on the statues, and another, longer inscription mentioned the offices occupied by the person honoured and celebrated his achievements (a eulogy, *elogium*). Augustus himself wrote many of these eulogies, for instance that of Scipio Africanus, and perhaps all of them. Only fragments of the statues and inscriptions have been preserved, but many can be reconstructed from similar complexes in Italian cities, for instance Arretium (Arezzo), Pompeii and Emerita (Mérida) in Spain. The exedras must have been occupied by the two main figures: Aeneas fleeing from Troy with his son Ascanius, carrying his father Anchises on his shoulders, along with the household gods (*penates*) of the city that he had rescued, and at the centre of the northern exedra and opposite him would have been Romulus, with the 'magnificent armour' (*spolia opima*) taken from an enemy leader over his shoulders.

This statuary programme traces the descent of Augustus from his divine ancestors Mars and Venus to Aeneas and Romulus, founder of the family's rule in Latium and of Rome itself, and on from them to the heroes of Roman history. They are not displayed for their own sake but to illustrate the line of tradition linking them, leading from the early history of Rome to its final culmination in the reign of Augustus. With their arrangement in a long series pointing to that one man, the great figures of Roman history lose their own individual character and become indissolubly linked with the historical position they occupied. Marius can stand beside his arch-enemy Sulla and members of the aristocracy who were at daggers drawn with him. The picture as a whole was intended to confirm – or if the observer had not yet taken the point, to demonstrate once and for all – that the whole history of Rome led to this one man and culminated in him. We can also tell that from the words of Augustus himself in an edict relating directly to the statuary group in his forum. 'My intention was to be judged myself, as long as I live, and the *principes* of the time following me also to be judged, by the citizens who took those men as their example.'

Augustus also emphasized the central political significance of his forum by reserving the temple and its forecourt for a whole series of state ceremonies. Among other things, it was decreed that every magistrate who received a command abroad would set out for his province from here, and it was the place where the Senate would receive foreign legations and decide on the granting of triumphs. In addition, a triumphator was to conclude his triumphal procession here and dedicate his laurel wreath to Mars, and finally the standards already returned by the Parthians and other former enemies were to be kept in this forum, along with all standards that might be returned to Rome in future. The solemn ceremony of assuming the toga of manhood (*toga virilis*), in which Roman boys were received into the ranks of adult citizens fit for military service, also had to be held in this temple. The temple precincts thus became a centre of Roman foreign policy. Financed, as Augustus wished, out of the plunder taken in war, the complex bore witness to the fame of the Roman past and the greatness of the present reign in the statues on display and the public business transacted in it and in front of its steps. Past and future were combined in what every stone of the buildings represented.

The image of history that we are shown by Augustus and that we encounter in the figures of the Augustan age calls for critical reflection.

A modern observer will probably begin by assuming that, given the circumstances, history was being manipulated in order to legitimate contemporary policy. That idea cannot be entirely dismissed, but the suspicion is accurate only to a very limited degree. First, we have to bear in mind the fact that none of the literary records of the Romans, from the very earliest, telling us about their attitude to the state itself and to the Roman position of international power contains, at least in principle, any fundamental ideas other than those that we encounter under Augustus and that he presented to the world of his time as worthy of imitation.

However, we have to make two major and closely connected reservations here. For one thing, the emphasis that the historical presentation, both written and in pictorial images, clearly lays on the early history of Rome is new. Display of the achievements of noble families in public, a guiding principle of the Roman idea of history for centuries at funerals and triumphs, on reliefs and the coinage, and to which they had always looked up, now retreats further and further into the background with the political decline of those families and their increasing loss of importance. The achievements of the men of the great days of Rome, the fourth to the second centuries, are reduced to instances of exemplary behaviour, collected for purposes of instruction and edification. Their place is taken not by the family tradition of the *princeps*, but by his links to the myth of the ancient and early period, to which Augustus relates his position of supremacy and special authority. Equally momentous for the change in the historical ideas of the Romans is the way the entire course of history is presented as leading to Augustus himself. The changes in historical thinking thus spring not so much from the content of statements as from the fact that they all lead to Augustus, and the way in which he selects, emphasizes, publicizes or plays down historical events.

The monarch absorbs history, and in so far as he does that, the past assumes a colour all its own. It gains greater weight through its close connection with the ruler, who speaks for everyone and everything. We see this with particular clarity when Augustus himself, or a poet of his time, speaks of the aims of government. Probably the most famous lines of Virgil, known to everyone with even the most fleeting knowledge of classical antiquity, are the closing lines of the speech of Anchises in the underworld. They deal with the different skills and talents of the Greeks and the Romans. The Greeks, says Virgil, are brilliant sculptors in stone and metal, and know more about oratory, the sciences and astronomy, but a Roman should remember that he understands how to rule nations with the military power of command, how to impose the good behaviour required in times of peace on them, how to spare the conquered but defeat the haughty in war. This comment takes it for granted that Roman rule over the peoples of the Mediterranean world is justified, and its justification serves above all the idea of peace. Of course, the Romans were aware that they had ruled the world in the past, but the positive change of direction to the idea of Roman world rule justified by world peace is new. Cicero was the first to express it; here it becomes part of an official view of the world. And it means more than the boastfulness that we might infer from the remarks in Augustus' account of his achievements when he says that delegations came to him from all over the world, from the Indians and the nations on both sides of the river Tanais (Don), from the peoples of the southern Caucasus and the Medes. The idea of world peace implies a turning to those who have been conquered: they are no longer merely subjects, exploited for purposes of material greed, but also the recipients of the benefits given to them as they are also given to Roman citizens. In this understanding of the right way to rule, there is a perceptible focus of attention on the empire, a change that the aristocratic rulers could not have introduced for sociological reasons, and so the foundations were laid for the abolition in the empire of the old opposition between the Romans who ruled and the provincials over whom they ruled. The empire could become an empire consisting entirely of Romans.

A different political aim is evident in the monopoly of history by the monarchs, and it had retrospective influence on the historical image, distorting and deforming it. Even if the basic concept of the virtues to which Rome owed its stature remained the same as the older ideas, historical thinking was no longer moulded by the idea that a Roman (whether a politician or a poet) had of himself as a free and independent agent, in the light of history and the traditional records. Rather, it increasingly concentrated on the one man who claimed a monopoly on the past. Many traditional sources of independent historical ideas became muted or died away entirely under pressure from the semi-official formation of opinion. For instance, both in the late republic and under Augustus (after the years 19 and 18) the masters of the mint, often young noblemen or adherents of certain noble clans, had illustrated the feats of their distinguished ancestors on the reverse side of silver coins (denarii). Such coinages disappeared between 5 and 2 BC, making way for the monarchical image.

Linked to this development, the elevation of recent historical events and those involved in them was bound to lead to an even more idealized view of the past than in the republican period. The course of history was frozen in timeless images, intensified as abstractions, and human behaviour was reduced to stereotypes. The early days of Rome and the distant events of the great age when the Romans set out to become masters of Italy – events that had taken place before the middle of the third century and predated any independent Roman literature – became formulaic, and their contours blurred. The great men of Rome are all the same: towering figures, brave, god-fearing, just and considerate, virtuous. They are completely frozen rigid, as we can tell from the fact that not one of those virtues can be removed without the whole heroic figure itself collapsing. Imagine Aeneas committing some impious action, or growing tired of his companions! The great figures of history have become colourless, tedious prigs. The attempt to make all these heroes, whether they belong to mythology or the early history of Rome, available in order to legitimize the present made them the plaything of current necessities. Now just vague sketches, subjected only to present needs, they lost any kind of individuality and could be interchanged at will. They sometimes seem to be figures from another world. The observer feels the discrepancy between historical reality and the artificial rigidity of this image of history, senses the tension inherent in it and finally understands it as an ideal that does not seek to describe and account for the past, but to give it a certain relevance to the observer living in the present. However, the puppet figures of the past seem to be out of reach, and this image of history unresponsive to any claims made on it. The observer sees the didactic intention, sees what is wanted, indeed demanded, and on the strength of the fact that it cannot be attained he moves away from the image of history presented to him or feels increasingly indifferent to it.

Romans encountered the new political world in literary accounts of past and present events, in inscriptions, public declarations and symbolic acts, as well as the images that adorned public buildings and squares and were to be found in private houses. It was also on display in the many new buildings and their ornamental furnishings, in the renovation or rather rebuilding of the old Forum, in the two new fora, the Julian Forum and the Augustan Forum, in the large-scale extension of the Field of Mars with its temples, baths, pillared arcades and many public buildings, some of them intended for the recreation of the people of the city. Augustus' boast of leaving Rome a city of marble when he had found it a city of brick says as much about the number as about the quality of his buildings, and they were indeed remarkable in both their design and their furnishing by comparison with the old days. The new buildings were not distinct from the older ones by virtue of size; there were no vast and showy structures. Many of them were even on a rather modest scale; the dimensions of the Ara Pacis did not reflect the real importance it had for Augustus himself and the architects and sculptors who later took their guidelines from it. The new architecture was particularly notable for its form, its strikingly well-executed ornamentation and the materials employed. Not everything could command the same attention, and there was also a distinction between the religious and the political in the execution of architectural works. The large number of small shrines devoted to cults that Augustus wanted to revive were restored in the old style. However, some larger new shrines or shrines restored by Augustus and other public buildings stood out because of the use of Carrara marble, annexes, remarkable new forms of ornamentation and imposing façades. These buildings seldom had wooden ceilings or terracotta ornamentation of the kind usual in temples of an earlier period. Although a Roman temple still differed from a Greek one in standing on a raised podium, and thus retained its Italian nature, it had acquired an architectural style of its own that was indissolubly linked to the Augustan period in both the building and its figurative ornamentation, which favoured the classical and, for religious purposes, even the archaic style. For all its brilliance of ornamentation, the execution of the design was remarkably plain and clearly related to classical Greek architecture in a way that indicates a deliberate choice. The ornamentation and its vegetation motifs show that it belongs to the Augustan period, suggesting a playful wealth of movement symbolizing fertility and at the same time a strict sense of order. It thus seems to illustrate both the good fortune and the dignity of the time, banishing any remaining oppressive weight and allowing viewers to forget the past, whatever an individual's opinion of it might be. The new forms, colours and motifs are not confined to public buildings; we also find them in private houses, even purely political motifs such as ships' prows and signs of victory (*tropaeum*, trophies), which call to mind the victory at Actium.

In view of the indisputable structural intentions of these buildings, consisting as they do of different elements, as well as the high quality of their design, we may speak of Augustan classicism. But that does not mean a break with tradition: continuity was still in evidence everywhere, as it was in the political world. Recourse to classical and archaic forms is often not a direct reversion to an earlier time, but rather picks up Hellenistic themes, which in their own turn took their guidelines from an earlier style. Augustan classicism, if we may so call it, is not all of a piece; it experiments, even in the late Augustan period, which, as in the case of political development, appears to be a time of standstill.

The very obvious efforts of Augustus to guide the Romans' ideas of their history and their political present does not mean that we should suspect a political motive behind every work of art and every building of the time. Even the Ara Pacis does not try to make a political statement with every ornament; Augustus is not sitting on every tendril of the decoration. Above all, by focusing on the public and religious buildings we fail to take account of the large amount of private architecture and everyday objects, of pictures and domestic decoration, and the private religious trends of the time remain to a great extent neglected. We should not forget that the older cults revived by Augustus did not really appeal to the people any more, that most of them, once restored, did not last long, and even the official state cult had little religious power of its own left. It had long ago been replaced. The old and usually abstract nature gods had little left to say to the people. They had been replaced by gods from the eastern mystery cults, which promised their devotees a closer relationship with the divinity they worshipped and created a sense of security in the small communities where the faithful assembled, something that the depoliticized cities of Italy and the provinces with their semi-official cults could no longer provide. The Egyptian goddess Isis had long ago made herself at home in Italy. Her worshippers were not exactly persecuted by the Roman authorities, but from the time of the late republic the cult had been kept as far as possible from the inner area of the city of Rome. In the long run attempts to suppress semi-official foreign cults were doomed to fail. In the first century of the monarchy the mystery cults made deep inroads into the Roman empire;

and by the second century AD there was no city in the empire where they did not have many small communities.

Yet for all the general political alignment with the *princeps*, there was no climate of intellectual oppression. For the very reason that the semi-official view of state and society in the past and the present did not conflict with traditional thinking, and the propagation of such ideas, no one felt any excessive pressure. The restrictions on free speech related only to the person of the *princeps* and his house. Here, however, it was wise to show restraint, and those who did not were punished. If the *princeps* had not reacted sternly to attacks on his person, the door would have been left wide open to his rivals for power. In such cases, the usual grounds of complaint were injury to or disparagement of the dignity of office (*maiestas laesa*), and in such circumstances charges could be brought on behalf not only of Augustus but also of members of his family. Cassius Severus, a gifted orator and writer, had to go into exile in Crete in the year AD 6 or soon afterwards, by decree of the Senate, because of such charges, and his writings were destroyed. But although Severus made no secret of his dislike of the present regime, and heaped invective on it, Augustus took him to court only after showing patience for a long time. Similarly, one Titus Labienus (unlikely to have been a relation of the famous general of Caesar's Gallic campaigns), who proved to be a rabid agitator against the course the state was taking and the man steering that course, was allowed to continue his ranting for a long time until at last, a few years before the death of Augustus, the Senate put him on trial, and his books were burned – the first book-burning in world history, incidentally. The charge in such cases was always of slandering the *princeps*, not of showing any definite political opinions, for instance openly confessing allegiance to the old republic. A man like Labienus could act for a long time unpunished as a supporter of Pompey, and thus of the republic, speaking enthusiastically of the old liberties, and Augustus himself almost affectionately called Livy, the great historian and his friend, a 'Pompeian'. Marcus Antistius Labeo, the most outstanding lawyer of his time and the son of one of Caesar's assassins who took his own life at Philippi, confirmed his love of the old republic and its liberty more sharply, indeed in uncompromising terms, and thereby deliberately distanced himself from Gaius Ateius Capito, the other great lawyer of the period, who was known to be an unconditional supporter of Augustus. Augustus would have given Labeo, who had been only praetor, the consulate if he had wanted it. But Labeo proudly declined the honour, another reason probably being that his rival Capito had held the office before him. However, despite his refractory conduct, he suffered no harm. One could even praise the men most hated by the *princeps*, Brutus and Cassius, and eulogize Cassius as 'the last Roman', as the historian Aulus Cremutius Cordus ventured to do, without being prosecuted for it in the lifetime of Augustus. Their portraits could be put up with impunity on private premises for anyone to see.

The ideas of the time did not entirely coincide with the semi-official view of the world, but did agree with it to a considerable extent. Augustus needed no propaganda in the modern sense to spread his political ideas, nor did he indulge in brain-washing to drive out old concepts and replace them with others or politicize the Roman world entirely in the way he wanted. But by strongly emphasizing current trends and aligning them with his person, while covering up other tendencies, he ultimately brought about a standardization of the world of political ideas which inevitably, by dint of its massive nature, introduced a general code of political ethics and behaviour, the point of which was gradually lost because the conduct encouraged was so generalized, interchangeable and unattainable.

Just as the aristocrat and the ordinary Roman did not have a process of re-education imposed from above, the writers did not act as mere organs to carry out the ruler's will, certainly not as 'court poets', even when they allowed themselves to be urged to write a work, and not infrequently struck up a hymn of praise to the *princeps* and members of his family of their own accord. More probably they shared a general mind-set that, after the miseries of the past, thought it saw the dawn of a new age and felt in harmony with the great Roman tradition. They considered the acts and wishes of the *princeps* an appropriate sounding-board for their own ideas about the world, not a demand for a hymn of praise. Virgil, as we have seen, could also form his own independent political opinion and did not conceal his ideas of the republican past. No poet had to sing the praise of the new policies. Tibullus did not, Propertius did so only late and in moderation. Even the banning or burning of books, something that shocks us today, did not entail the severity of ideological condemnation. Ovid's works were banned only from public libraries, and naturally the book-burnings affected only those works that were publicly available. They were more in the nature of punishment accompanying a legal condemnation, or the abrogation of friendship (which could also isolate the author), than a ban on reading. For instance, in the late Augustan period it was not forbidden to read the works of Brutus or Antony, and Augustus did not even ban Brutus' *Cato*, a widely distributed small book of republican leanings, but, following his father's example, he himself wrote a work in rebuttal of it. We also have to realize that many poets, historians and scholars came from Upper Italy, an area that had attained its own political identity only through the dictator and Augustus. Livy came from Patavium near modern Venice, Virgil from Mantua, and although that city had long been a *colonia* of Roman citizens, it took part in great events only once it was unified with Italy. The inhabitants of what had once been the back yard of Rome represented, even more forcefully than citizens of the old days, the Roman tradition in which the citizens' morale and pride in the achievements of Rome, their courage and loyalty to those who wielded power, had merged them into a unit. It was a development even more marked than that of the former Italian federations, which themselves had been granted citizenship rights since 90–88. Part of one of these federations was Sulmo in the Apennines, the birthplace of Ovid.

In one area Augustus' wish to leave his own mark on his reign and his time was expressed with particular clarity and permanence: in the art of portraiture, more specifically the portrayal of his person. Everyone probably knows what Augustus looked like and is aware what an influence his portrayal exerted in many ways on the portraits of Roman rulers after him. Portraits of Augustus can be classified as belonging to three or four main types, all of them obviously deriving from an original image that he wanted and allowed to be seen. It is instantly identifiable, and not just because of the way he wore his hair. The first portrait will have been commissioned by Octavian not long after his first arrival in Rome, perhaps as early as the year 43, and certain features such as his noticeably hooked nose, his long throat and prominent Adam's apple are emphasized more strongly than in later likenesses. It was followed after a few years by a portrait differing from the first in many respects, but the type more usual after the early twenties BC, and copied until the death of Augustus, is the one really familiar to us. It is the portrait of a fairly young man, in a form owing much to classical Greek art, and appears fundamentally ageless. The indications of individual features that can be seen in the earlier types are missing or very much toned down. Particularly characteristic is the way his locks of hair are arranged on the right-hand side of his head. In the course of this distribution, the various versions of his portrait through Italy and the empire influenced each other in a number of ways without cancelling out the basic types. The type widely found after the early twenties, that is to say from around the time when the principate was set up, is clearly intended to convey a message. The man it shows is portrayed as an ideal ruler, and its very immutability signals that fact. The ruler and his reign are linked in the portrait in a way that speaks of the high-minded convictions of his reign and their durability.

# 13

# The Army of Augustus

In republican times the army had been raised from the ranks of Roman citizens. The soldiers were militiamen who regarded doing their military service as their duty to the people. Anyone fit to join the army was bound to serve, and a man was fit if he had a minimum fortune allowing him to equip himself with his own armour and weapons, as long as he had no severe physical or mental disabilities. There was no training period, because men had practised sword-fighting and spear-throwing in their native towns and villages since their youth and they refined these skills during service. Soldiers were raised only for the purpose of war, to avert an attack or to gain land and plunder, and the citizens recruited to that end were discharged once the military operations were over. In wartime soldiers were usually in the field only between harvest and sowing; they served for a longer period only in exceptional cases, for instance during the Second Punic War (218–201) and the Spanish campaigns of the second century. In line with the instructions of the Senate, they were raised for whatever military campaign was impending by officials responsible for the purpose, using a system that took account of a man's earlier periods of service. As a rule the recruits had to assemble on the Field of Mars outside the city wall of Rome, where officers appointed by a magistrate drew them up into units. Military service was arduous; very few reasons could exempt a man from serving, and those few reasons had to be confirmed by witnesses.

Although the army had changed a great deal in the last hundred years of the republic, its fundamental principles remained the same. It consisted of infantry with only a small cavalry contingent, and on the whole the horsemen played little part in conflict as a strike-force. The legion was the basic unit. Ever since the reforms of the great general Marius at the end of the second century, a legion had consisted of ten cohorts (*cohortes*), each of 600 men, the cohorts in turn being subdivided into three maniples each of two centuries. However, a legion was not always up to its full fighting strength of 6,000 men. The legionaries were armed with an assortment of weapons such as the short sword (*gladius*) for hand-to-hand fighting, and the spear (*pilum*), which as a rule was thrown just before the two fronts engaged in battle. The cohort was the tactical battle unit, while the legion was only the overall administrative unit, but the men's *esprit de corps* bound them first to the legion and only second to their cohorts. When the legions were raised they were numbered, and since they would be disbanded again at the end of a military operation no durable traditions formed.

The power of command was safeguarded by rigorous punishments for any miscreant, including the death penalty, and entire units that refused to obey orders suffered decimation, the execution of every tenth man. The Roman army depended on acceptance of the principle of obedience to command, and indeed the Romans regarded any breach of it as a crime worthy of death.

The leadership of the army was the business of the magistrates, who by virtue of their office had the *imperium*, the military power of command: the consuls and praetors, and any proconsuls and propraetors acting for them. Under these officials six military tribunes (*tribuni militum*) had originally commanded a legion in republican times, but in the last century leadership had passed to a legion commander (*legatus legionis*), and although military tribunes were still appointed, on the whole they assumed only administrative functions. With very few exceptions, the legate of the legion was appointed from among the senators, while the tribunes also belonged to the upper social classes and were generally men of senatorial or equestrian rank. In command below the level of the legates were the tribunes and prefects of the cohorts, while the subdivisions of the cohorts were commanded by centurions. To our modern way of thinking the centurions were officers; they formed the backbone of the army, and most of them had risen from the ranks of common soldiers.

The main difference of military organization before Caesar and Augustus lay in recruiting methods. After the end of the third century, war was almost exclusively waged outside Italy. The distances that had to be travelled made it a longer affair, and when it entailed bitter conflict over several years, as it often did, it called for the presence of Roman troops stationed abroad. The job could no longer be done by an army of militiamen, for the soldiers, who were from the peasant farmer class, could not cultivate their land when they were away for such long periods, and what loot they brought home was not enough to provide for their families. The peasant farmers of Italy soon fell on hard times, and quite a number of them were impoverished by the neglect of their land. Discontent, long pent up, was discharged in the riots of the time of the Gracchi.

When, after several decades of relative calm at the end of the second century, large hordes of German warriors invaded Illyricum and Gaul, and the Romans suffered devastating defeats costing the lives of more than 50,000 soldiers, there were alarming bottlenecks in the recruiting of replacements. Marius, mentioned above, therefore changed the qualifications for joining the army to open it to men who could not afford to equip themselves, as well as those raised in the usual way. For that purpose, the minimum amount of property a man owned had to be set at a lower level, and in the course of time, after the minimum figure had dropped lower and lower, penniless men, usually impoverished farmers and farmers' sons with no prospects, joined the army in their thousands. They were provided with armour and weapons by the state, and the Roman armoury became a permanent institution.

Some of the legions who, under Marius, had defeated the Germans had been in the field for several years. When the danger was over, it was taken for granted that all the soldiers would be demobilized. The soldiers themselves wanted to disperse, but only those who had land of their own knew where to go with their share of the loot. Most of the volunteers, however, had no homes, so the commander of the army had to act as patron of his soldiers and ensure that all the landless men among them were given a plot of land to farm. Roman ideas of patronage obliged their commander to help them. In civilian life the patron, a man of distinguished family, succoured his clients in an emergency, for instance supporting them in the law-courts, and now, in the field, the general was patron of all those soldiers who were citizens and had been entrusted to his care. The generals did their duty and demanded land from the Senate to provide for their soldiers, or if the Senate could not agree turned to the assembly of the people. But in the time of Marius, and again later under the triumvirs, it was not easy to acquire land in

Italy, which was where the soldiers were naturally most anxious to set-tle. Marius finally failed because he could not solve this problem.

It did not go away, however. The major military tasks of Rome, repel-ling enemy incursions into the empire and averting the danger of pirates, called for large and sometimes long-serving armies, and for the commanders who offered to perform these military tasks the quickest and surest way to raise a strong army was by recruiting volunteers. In addition many politicians, hoping to gain more influence in the state by undertaking even greater military responsibilities, began to construct military problems that did not really exist, or inflated minor sources of danger into a real threat for their own ends. That was the case with Caesar's Gallic War and the campaign of Crassus against the Parthians. These great military commands shook the traditional political struc-tures to the point where the republic fell, and the last military potentate, Augustus, built the monarchy on its ruins.

For the army and for the state as a whole, this development was linked to far-reaching changes. It was not just that after every major military operation the state was cast into great perturbation by the problem of settling the veterans, while the victorious general pestered the Senate with political demands that could not be met. The structure of the army itself changed, and, more significantly, the relationship of the soldiers to the state was completely reversed. The change first made itself felt when the question of providing for the soldiers, not just after they were demobilized but during their service, became more and more pressing. Their pay, which originally had been intended as compensa-tion to cover their expenses and provide for their families while they were away on service, was raised and gradually became a proper wage. Finally, Caesar doubled the men's pay to 225 denarii a year. Much more money now had to be raised for an army than before, and an equally serious consideration was that only reliable supplies made it possible for a man to stay in the army for a long time; that again encouraged the development of the army into a body of volunteers. A soldier without land or a family might even regard life in the army as a career.

Other changes were less obvious. Long service with a unit created strong psychological bonds between soldiers who lived and fought together for years, and as their emotions were linked to the immediate community of the legion and cohort to which they belonged, differences in the status of individual units arose in what had once been a homogeneous army. Ambition and rivalries developed among the soldiers, for the military life, even if it was not actually seen as a career, took up a considerable part of their lives or at least their youth. A sense of having more experience than other soldiers and being better at the job was expressed in strong attachment to a man's own unit or even veneration of it. The long history of the traditions of certain units began. A legion with long service behind it had higher status than one only recently raised, or a legion made up entirely of recruits, and success in battle also gave one legion a higher reputation than another. Caesar's Tenth Legion was the first unit in the Roman army to have important traditions; its men felt superior to all other soldiers, and even the general had to consider these feelings of theirs. To show more favour to one legion and less to another in the allocation of rewards had more than purely material significance; it affected a soldier's emotions. The longer a legion had been in service, the greater was the difference in status between it and more recently formed units. At the time of the triumvirs there was such a clear difference in quality between a legion of veterans and one of recruits that an army without long-serving soldiers was thought to have little fighting force, and sometimes a single legion of veterans determined the outcome of a battle.

The long period of service also changed the entire internal organization of a legion. That was evident, for instance, in the growing importance of military ranks on all levels, beginning at the top. As a rule, a legion raised just for a short time in war had previously had no leadership of its own; it was led by military tribunes under the supreme commander. Over a long period it came to need its own commander, and he had to be a man dependent on the supreme commander if the chain of command were to be maintained. Pompey and Caesar had already introduced this institution; some of their legion commanders, the legates (*legati legionis*), were capable military men but of course were pledged to total obedience to their general. In the old days there had been no marked differences of rank between the officers below the leadership of the legion, particularly the centurions. When it became clear that one or several centurions filled the leading positions within a cohort, only the fact that the legion would soon be demobilized prevented the formation of an established hierarchy and a normal structure of promotion. That was different now. The long duration of time for which a legion stayed together brought with it ideas of a hierarchy of officers and a military career even below the level of general. The phenomenon was most clearly visible among the officers who led the subdivisions of the cohorts under the legion commander, that is to say the centurions.

In line with the subdivision of the cohort into three maniples, each made up of two centuries, every cohort had six centurions, their status being determined by the position of the century within the cohort. The leader of the first century of the first maniple was the highest-ranking centurion in a cohort, the centurion of the second century of the third (and last) maniple was the lowest-ranking. The first centurions were described as of the 'first order' (*primi ordines*). Ranking order in the well-developed legions of the imperial period was continued between the cohorts of a legion, and as a result, in an even further extended hierarchy, the centurions of a higher cohort had more status than those of the lower cohorts. The first centurion of the first cohort, known as the *primipilus* (*primus pilus*), ranked highest of all the centurions of a legion. The hierarchy of centurions is the best illustration of the absolute nature of the chain of command and is readily comprehensible by every man in a modern army. Its development was gradual, but once again its origins lie in the Augustan period.

The military unit as it was set up over a long, even an unlimited period created definite ideas of the characteristics of individual groups within the hierarchy, and in the minds of those concerned they became distinct types. The legion legate was one such type, so was the centurion, and within the ranks of centurions again so was the first centurion of every cohort and the common soldier (*miles gregarius*), although among those there were many distinctions: one man might be a technician, another a bridge-builder. And rivalry, for instance between centurions, which hardly had time to develop in short periods of army service, could now unfold, and so could the dislike of one group for another, for instance the dislike of the common soldiers for their immediate superior officers, the centurions. Such resentment was expressed with particular force after the death of Augustus among the legions stationed in Pannonia. A military apparatus slowly came into being and was already fully fledged at the end of the reign of Augustus. In form and spirit, it already bore all the trademark features of a standing army.

When Augustus set up the principate at the end of the civil war, thus leading the Romans back to 'normal' circumstances, the state of emergency was not over for the army. It is true that the bulk of the soldiers were discharged, but in spite of the peace that had now been won a considerable number of legions remained under arms. The state had not gone back to the republic, it had become a monarchy, and a monarchy that, even if it made itself out a civil institution and pledged itself to tradition, depended on the swords of the soldiers. The *princeps* needed legions not only to protect the still endangered border provinces, but also to deter any potential rivals who might entertain ideas of usurping his power. For the return of peace revealed what the long war had hidden until this point: the presence of armed force on a permanent footing. The existence of a standing army gave Augustus new problems, and they were to dog the monarchy until its end.

The first and most important problem was how to finance the army. Equipping it with weapons and war matériel, as well as supplying its other needs, called for large sums of money, and besides the pay of men on active service there were also special bounties to be paid. These had originally been granted on special occasions, such as the first time Gaius Caesar, grandson and adopted son of Augustus, took part in a successful campaign (with Tiberius against the Sugambri tribesmen of the Lower Rhine), but soon they came to be regarded as regular payments. In addition, the soldiers had to be provided for when they had finished their service. Augustus had finally set up a special military fund (*aerarium militare*) for this purpose and paid large sums into it himself.

The greatest drain on the fund was the regular pay of soldiers. At a salary of 225 denarii (900 sesterces) a year, and assuming a number of twenty-five standing legions, the money to be provided for that purpose alone amounted to 33,750,000 denarii (135 million sesterces). In fact the sum was very much higher, because provision also had to be made for the troops stationed in Rome and the auxiliaries recruited from non-Roman tribes (although they received less), as well as the naval crews of the fleet. Many soldiers received higher pay, and that meant extra expense. The salaries of the bodyguard in Rome amounted at first to nearly twice and then more than three times normal pay, 750 denarii; the officers received many times basic pay, and several ranks among the common soldiers also received a higher wage, as a rule one and a half times basic pay. The difference between the salary of an officer and the basic pay of a common soldier is particularly striking. A centurion was paid fifteen times as much as a common soldier; the centurions of the first order got twice the amount of an ordinary centurion, and the first centurion of the first cohort, the *primipilus*, received double that sum again.

Even without the considerable sums needed to provide for discharged soldiers, the sum of annual payments as a whole to the army must have been well above 60 million denarii (240 million sesterces) and may have been as high as 80 million denarii. The size of the sum can be best illustrated by its ratio to state income as a whole at that time, although we do not know exactly the amount that came in to the state coffers, and it can be only imperfectly reconstructed from the many separate items of information that have come down to us. However, if we remember that income from the Gallic provinces conquered by Caesar amounted to ten million denarii, and from the much richer eastern provinces reorganized by Pompey (Bithynia, Cilicia and Syria) it was 135 million denarii, and we further regard these figures as gross income from which a not inconsiderable amount must be subtracted for the expenses of provincial administration, we have some idea of the drain of military expenses on the budget of the state as a whole. Could Augustus have managed with fewer soldiers? That will be considered when we come to look at the functions of the army and the navy.

Under the militia system there were no set times of service, and the question of providing for demobilized men emerged only when those without property of their own were recruited. The standing army under Augustus, however, could not dispense with regulations affecting the duration of service and provision for the veterans' old age. Although it was clear than an army was needed in the monarchy even in peacetime, ideas of established regulations in the standing army developed only gradually, and seem to have been adopted mainly because of pressure from the soldiers themselves. It was, in fact, essential for them to know for certain when their army service would come to an end, and it was just as important for new recruits to the army to know the same facts.

The idea of a military life as a career did not immediately occur to every soldier. But once it did, vital questions faced him. How long would his physical constitution make him fit for army service? What would he do after demobilization when he was old, or approaching old age? What would he live on? Where was he to go when he had been torn away from his former environment for many years, sometimes almost two decades? How long would he need to start a family and find a new career? There must have been lively discussions of these questions in military camps, and opinions will sometimes have been expressed with the anger and bitterness that Tacitus puts into the mouths of the mutinous legions of Pannonia in the year AD 14. Certainly there were many veterans who had found a home in the army because it provided for them and they felt secure. Higher ranks in particular, like the well-paid centurions, must have been happy to serve for longer than was required of them. But most of the men, in particular older men who were better able to assess the decrease in their physical powers, and those who in the long term could not endure the brutal drill and the arrogant behaviour of many centurions, will have wanted to know for certain what would happen to them when they left the army.

Periods of service and provision for the men were not precisely established until 13 BC, but for a decade and a half before that date they must have fluctuated in accordance with the draft resolutions laid before the Senate in that year. According to these proposals, praetorian guards were to serve for twelve years, legionaries for sixteen years. Then in AD 6, in the context of the great military operations in Germania and Pannonia, the length of service for a praetorian guard was extended to sixteen years and for a legionary to twenty years. In principle an even longer period of service was possible. If necessary, former soldiers could be recalled to the standards, in the same way as Augustus himself, when he was just setting out on his political career and needed support against Antony, mobilized troops of veterans who had already left the army. Of these former soldiers, known as 'men called upon' (evocati), those who had been in the higher ranks were the most likely to be recalled.

Initially, Augustus had provided for his veterans by giving them a plot of land, the usual practice since the time of the reformer Marius. These plots were of generous dimensions, and the higher-ranking men often received so much land that they sometimes leased it out, moved to the city and lived there on their rents. Augustus continued this practice until the year 13 BC. After that, however, the veterans received money when they left the army, a legionary being paid thirteen times his previous annual salary, a praetorian eleven times his salary (3,000 and 5,000 denarii respectively).

At the end of the reign of Augustus, there were twenty-five legions in his army, that is to say, if they were all at full strength, 150,000 legionaries. In the course of the great demobilization in the years after 30 BC there were initially twenty-eight legions left under arms, and finally, after three legions were lost in the battle of the Teutoburger Wald in the year AD 9, the number stabilized at twenty-five.

Besides being numbered, the legions were known by honorific epithets and under these names became traditional institutions. Two hundred years after Augustus, in the time of Cassius Dio, nineteen of the legions of the Augustan period still existed. The legions of Augustus were numbered up to the figure twenty-two. Many of the numbers among the first ten were given twice; in the case of some of them that was probably because units with old traditions in the armies of Lepidus and Antony had been taken on by Octavian and they were allowed to keep their old numbers. There was no confusion because the legions, as mentioned above, had honorific epithets (with a few exceptions, such as the three lost legions of Varus). The epithet Augusta was a particular honour, and it was disgraceful for a legion to be deprived of its epithet for cowardice or indiscipline, as happened by order of Agrippa in the war against the Cantabrians of north-west Spain in the year 19. Other legions adopted the names of the provinces in which they had successfully campaigned, for instance some (from the dictator's time) adopting the epithet Gallica, others Cyrenaica (probably units taken over from Lepidus) or Macedonica. Others again bore the name of a god with whom the legion had associations, for instance the Legio XV Apollinaris, or received an epithet on the grounds of conspicuous courage, such as the 'Victorious Sixth' (Legio VI Victrix) or the 'Merciless Twenty-first' (Legio XXI Rapax). In addition all legions had their own emblems. They were carried both on the standard of the legion, which was crowned with an eagle (*aquila*), and on the standards of the subsidiary units, and often related to the dictator or to Augustus, for instance the Ibex, the sign of the Zodiac for the birth date of Augustus, or the Bull, the sign of the Zodiac ruled by Venus and thus the sign of Caesar and the entire Julian house. Other emblems referred to great deeds, for instance the Legio X Fretensis (from *fretum*, strait, 'the legion that distinguished itself in the Sicilian straits'), which also bore the additional emblem of a trireme in reference to the legion's campaign against Sextus Pompey. Others were the Legio XI Actiacus, signifying that it had distinguished itself at Actium, and the Legio V Alaudae, the 'Crested Larks', which also displayed the symbol of an elephant in reference to the dictator's African campaign, in which it had taken part.

*

As well as the regular Roman troops, there were the foreign auxiliaries and the fleets. Foreign troops had always played an important part in the Roman army. Under the late republic, they consisted at first of local contingents commanded by men of the allied group concerned, often by its prince. Such units continued to exist under Augustus, but as in the republic they were discharged again after the campaign was over. Another category of foreign auxiliary troops acquired considerably greater importance once there was a standing army; it was made up of soldiers of foreign origin who served for many years, as a rule longer than the Roman legionaries, and sometimes for as long as twenty-five years. They were known as *auxilia* and were under Roman commanders holding the rank of prefect. As infantry they were divided into cohorts, as cavalry into squadrons (*alae*), of 500 and 1,000 men respectively, and obeyed the commander of the legion to which they were assigned. The squadrons were regarded as elite troops. There were also occasional mounted cohorts (*cohortes equitatae*), but they were more like infantry on horseback than a troop of cavalry.

The soldiers of these foreign troops were initially recruited mainly by tribes. But when long service and the transfer of their units meant that they gradually lost contact with their native area, men of other tribes were recruited as substitutes. In the end Romanization removed distinctions between the auxiliaries and the Roman legions, but that process was far from complete in the Augustan period. Auxiliary troops were not always recruited on a voluntary basis; there were instances of forced recruitment, in some circumstances with the deliberate aim of weakening a particular tribe. The Rhaetians (and Vindelicians) who lived in what is now south Germany, and who had been overcome in the year 15 BC, lost a considerable number of men able to bear arms in this way, and so did the Breuci of the Save-Drau area after the Pannonian revolt of AD 6–9.

Within the armed forces, warships had played a considerable part in the years of civil war, and in the final phase even a decisive one, but most of their crews had been demobilized after the battle of Actium. The fleet was distinct from the other military forces in two ways. First, the Mediterranean had become a Roman inland sea, and after the end of the civil wars a war fleet was required only to keep the seas safe from pirates and to provide a courier service. As a result, there were no major operational functions for the deep-sea fleet, if such a term may be applied to vessels that were seriously at risk in heavy seas and suitable only for brief missions. Second, the crews of the ships were usually recruited from non-Roman peoples, and more rarely from the poorer people of Italy, as well as from Roman freedmen and even slaves. The last, however, were freed when they entered the service. The captains themselves were very often freedmen, and thus were Roman citizens, but the overwhelming majority came from the Greek-speaking east. The commanders of the fleets had the title of prefect (*praefectus classis*), the rank of an equestrian, and like the governors of the provinces were answerable directly to Augustus. In Italy after 27 BC there were two prefectures of the fleet, independent of each other.

The deep-sea vessels were powered by oars, since they had to be rowed fast for manoeuvrability in battle or to get under way quickly, and so they had strong crews of 180 to 200 men. For longer voyages warships known to us in modern terminology as 'galleys' also used sails, which were stowed away in the hold or left on land during battle. While large quinquiremes had been typical of the final years of civil war, with five rowers manning each oar, the smaller, lighter triremes with three men to each oar predominated in the imperial fleet, having proved their worth over the centuries.

Once there was peace throughout the empire after the battle of Actium, the fleet was concentrated in at first three and later two naval ports. One was Forum Julii (Fréjus) in Gallia Narbonensis, to which Antony's ships taken at Actium were also taken. In Italy itself many good harbours, for instance Naples and Puteoli, were unsuitable for warships because of the unusually large amount of merchant shipping that used them; others were ruled out as naval ports for military purposes because of the poor state of their harbour basins, for instance Ostia, which was silted up with mud from the Tiber. The Julian Harbour constructed at Puteoli in the war against Sextus Pompey had quickly filled with sand, and so a new harbour for warships was built rather further south on the Bay of Naples at Cape Misenum. It came to be the main bastion of the Roman fleet as the closest naval base to Rome itself. As well as Misenum on the Tyrrhenian Sea, Ravenna on the Adriatic, which had already been used during the civil war years, served as the second naval port for warships. The harbour at Ravenna was joined to the southern branch of the Po by a canal (the *fossa Augusta*), and its sheltered position made it an excellent anchorage for ships.

Besides the main fleet, there were smaller flotillas. Under Augustus there may have been one in Alexandria, but they were certainly to be found in the Augustan period on the great rivers: the Rhine and, after the expansion of Rome into the Balkan area, the Central and Lower Danube.

The most important military problem arose from the change in recruiting methods, and it mainly concerned finding the next generation of legionaries. While soldiers in the time of the militia army had been raised by age and the areas where they lived, they had in principle been volunteers. But although the armies of the late republic and the civil war period had still consisted largely of volunteers, most of them were discharged after a campaign. The army left under arms after the end of the civil war, however, was an army of professional soldiers for whom regular replacements would have to be found. The legions alone demanded 7,000 to 8,000 new men a year, and that made it necessary to have a new structure for the recruiting system.

As the principle that legionaries (and bodyguards in Rome) had to be Romans was maintained, and the central recruiting office in Rome could not find enough men for an army now widely dispersed over the empire, every man had to see about getting accepted as a recruit for himself. The bulk of new recruits in the time of Augustus still came from Italy, often from Upper Italy, but men from the hinterland of wherever a legion was stationed now also applied. In the west, they came from Roman cities, for instance those of Baetica and Narbonensis; there were also cities under Roman law in the east, but new recruits here also came, among other places, from Galatia, Egypt and other provinces with a Greek-speaking population. The latter were Romans without a link to a specific Roman city, most of them probably the sons of freedmen, and the fact that none the less they were accepted as recruits is evidence of the shortage of applicants. If the need for new troops was particularly urgent, even in the time of Augustus many capable men had been accepted from the wider catchment area of a legion and on entry into the army had to be given citizenship rights. This was the beginning of a development in which the hinterland of the place where a legion was stationed ultimately became, to a great extent, its recruiting area.

None the less, there were bottlenecks in the recruiting process. Whereas the Romans of a previous generation had regarded military service as their duty to the state, and so accepted it without demur even if the burden was a very heavy one, it was a very different matter to choose the military life as a career. The pay of a common soldier was not particularly high, especially as there were deductions for weapons, food and clothing, and the provision for demobilized men could not be called generous, at least after the change from an allocation of land to money payment for veterans. In addition, the number of Romans capable of bearing arms, which in the year 28 amounted to a good four million men, was rather too small to supply an army of at least 160,000 soldiers with the necessary annual replacements by finding some 9,000 to 10,000 new recruits. So it is not surprising that when there was a sudden need for new men, for instance after the loss of three legions under Varus in the year AD 9, Augustus resorted to raising them by force along the lines of the old militia system. Nor is it surprising that he met with dogged resistance.

Finding new officers was at least as important, and the existence of an established officers' corps as well as the standing army was fraught with consequences for the general political and social development of the Roman empire. These officers had to be recruited and trained for an army career. Such a career was necessary to give the officers a social prospect that, together with the pledge of loyalty made when a man swore his oath on the standard, became one of his most important links to the *princeps*. The *princeps* himself had to pay close attention to the origins of his generals. The settlement of the year 27 had established that they were to be drawn from the senatorial class, but that in itself forced Augustus to proceed very cautiously in case he had any possible rivals. To avert the danger of a possible coup, he carefully sent his generals to troops that were now widely dispersed, and subtle differences in the promotion of individuals were intended to keep them from forming too much solidarity as a group. The candidate for command of a legion, or for the governorship of a province where two legions were stationed, could at first be kept under close observation in a career leading him from a middle-order officer's rank, where separate cohorts or cavalry divisions were to be commanded, to a quaestorship and then a praetorship. Just as, earlier, the ambition of candidates for the magistracy had been channelled and controlled by its firmly established hierarchy of office, the military officer now had to envisage his career in accordance with the regulations not of an aristocratic society, but solely of Augustus. The *princeps* thus not only promoted his candidate but also disciplined him to ensure his devoted and obedient conduct.

A key position for further rise in the army soon turned out to be service in the middle ranks of the officers' corps. Holding command of the cohorts and auxiliaries could lead on to employment in many fields, among others various prefecture posts. The middle-ranking officers' corps was reserved for equestrians, but in the future a loyal and capable officer who was not an equestrian could be raised to that rank for his achievements and could even rise higher and become a senator. The historian Velleius Paterculus and his family provide a good example of the career of a tried and trusted officer. After his grandfather and father, as prominent members of their local municipality, had served as officers of the middle rank first in the armies of the late republic and then under Augustus, the historian himself, born around 20 BC, began his own army career. He was first a military tribune, i.e. a member of the middle-ranking officers' corps, and then, after several campaigns in which he held several higher ranks, became a quaestor and so entered the senatorial class and rose yet further, along with his brother, to become a praetor. Although he had already been designated for that office by Augustus, he did not take it up until the year AD 15, under the principate of his patron and commander of many years Tiberius, to whom he was devoted. In spite of his senatorial offices, he remained an army man.

Within the officers' corps, the centurion occupied a central position as leader of the lowest unit, the century. Centurions had proved their worth in the various campaigns of the republican period, but for lack of a career system offering better prospects in future they had been denied further promotion. A capable soldier could himself rise from the ranks to become a centurion, but no higher. That changed in the armies of the civil war, although no regular system of promotion could develop at that time, and the changes became established and went on developing in the Augustan period. Long service, and the large, well-differentiated nature of the army, opened up the way to higher ranks for a centurion who had proved himself in action and in leading his men and in some circumstances also brought a rise in his social status. If the centurion had already risen within a legion and finally achieved the highest rank of this group of officers, the *primipilus*, he could now rise further through the middle ranks of officers, that is, by way of the post of commander of a cohort of legionaries and of the cohorts and cavalry formations of allied auxiliaries and finally could even reach equestrian rank, although that would not have been a regular career path for a *primipilus* under Augustus. It seems, however, that Augustus himself formed the *primipilares*, as those who had finished their service with the rank of *primipilus* were known, into a division known as a *numerus*, from which he might if necessary choose a man for further employment.

The security of the reign of Augustus was built on his soldiers' unconditional loyalty to the *princeps*. As a young man at the time of the civil wars, Augustus had spent a long time fighting for that loyalty in competition with the dictator's experienced generals and he paid a high material and personal price. He had had to invest huge sums of money and in spite of his proven generosity not infrequently had to put up with arrogance and insubordination. All that had now changed fundamentally. He had eliminated any competition, and the Roman world had returned to relatively normal conditions. But as the army remained the basis of political power, relations between the *princeps* and the soldiers were still a sensitive area. The camaraderie of those early days was gone now. Augustus was the undisputed master of the state and the empire, his personal charisma was on a par with that of the dictator Caesar, and he was revered as their patron by all the soldiers. The difference was also expressed in the way the *princeps* spoke to the soldiers. In the early days he had sought their favour by addressing them as 'comrades' (*commilitones*), a term replaced after the end of the civil wars in personal addresses and official decrees by 'soldiers' (*milites*), and he told his stepsons Tiberius and Drusus to stick to that term. He based his decision not just on the requirements of the military hierarchy and the now peaceful times, but above all on the fact that the new form of address was a more appropriate way of distancing his dignity (*maiestas*) and that of his house from the soldiers.

Their loyalty at first depended simply on the fact that Augustus was the rightful and legally appointed supreme commander of all the troops. His *imperium*, the military power of command, had initially been granted for ten years, and after the expiry of that period was twice extended by the Senate for another five years and three times for another ten years. The loyalty of the troops was also ensured by the religious bond created by the oath to the standard (*sacramentum*) made by every soldier to his *imperator* on entering army service and annually repeated.

Over and beyond the formal relationships, a soldier felt bound to the *princeps* on a personal level, and that was the source of his real loyalty to the house of Augustus. The social relationship was doubly evident. First, the dangers that he and his men had survived during campaigning together and the final success of military victory created a bond between the army and the *princeps*; a bond of the same kind had always been at the heart of the relationship of patronage between a soldier and his general. Second, it was particularly well established and durable because it appealed to the feelings of the soldiers themselves. Even though Augustus himself did not very often go into the field with his army, all the soldiers knew that their generals were only mandated by the supreme commander, and Augustus was still the man to whom they really related. As he could not be present everywhere in the now widely scattered army, his image was present instead. The troops bore a portrait of him (*imago*) on their standards, particularly the eagle of the legion, wherever they went. Where an established camp had been in existence for a long time, in the late Augustan period they were probably already also putting up a statue of the *princeps* in the *praetorium*, which was the centre of the camp and at the same time the place for the religious cult of the monarch.

Augustus was also responsible, as patron of his soldiers, for their material needs while they were on active service, and for providing for them after their honourable discharge, meaning the gift of a plot of land or, later, monetary payment. Once a soldier had been settled somewhere, then no matter who dealt with the concrete details of the transaction, the *princeps* was still regarded as the real founder of his new home. As a result the towns where veterans spent the evening of their days generally bore his name or that of his father and were Julian or Augustan towns.

It was on these social relationships with the soldiers that the security of the person of the *princeps* and his rule depended. Augustus could never for a moment forget that the army had brought him to power and was the foundation of that power's continued existence. That applied to the time of the principate just as it had during the civil war. The new institutions set up by public and religious legislation might sometimes make people forget how they depended on each other but could not do away with that relationship. It took a long time for the principate of Augustus to be consolidated and become an institution legitimated by custom (*mos*), for the new order to become sufficient unto itself. It took time for the idea of the charisma of the entire family of the *princeps* (*domus Augusta*) as a dynasty to take shape in the minds of the people, turning the unique nature of the principate of Augustus into a durable monarchy.

It is characteristic of a standing army that its units are stationed at specific places and, if the military situation does not call for a campaign, have permanent accommodation there. Of course it had been the same in republican times for the small military contingents at the disposal of the provincial governors to protect their district from thieving hordes on its borders, and to ensure their own safety and that of their staff. But while those had been small units, and do not signify a change from the militia system to a professional army, the army stationed between 54 and 49 in the two Spanish provinces, administered by Pompey from Rome through legates, can be regarded as a standing army. The eight and later seven legions stationed in Spain had little to do there and remained inactive for five years until the outbreak of the civil war. There can be no doubt that Pompey had raised his Spanish army of that time because of his rivalry with Caesar, and it would disappear along with the situation that had created it. In fact the extraordinary powers of command of the late republic always entailed temporary concentrations of forces designed to fight the real or imagined enemies of Rome, and that in turn meant that, after doing their job, these huge armies were discharged.

The civil wars that broke out in the year 49 had at first concealed the problem of finding a military base for a long-serving army. For the legions did not stay in one place; on the contrary, they waged war at enormous expense, and at the end of a given episode of belligerence the soldiers were supposed to be discharged, wanted to be discharged and usually were. Such demobilization, with its painful consequences for the people of Rome, looked like a revival of the old system whereby militiamen returned to civil life. The change in the situation became clear only when peace returned, welcomed by all, in the year 30, and, even if it may not have been immediately obvious to the ordinary citizen, the problem faced the *princeps* and the leadership class at the time of the settlement of the year 27, which touched upon the allocation of army units to the various provinces.

At the time the provinces in which most legions were stationed had been assigned to the control of the *princeps*, on the grounds that they were still in danger and therefore needed the power of command of a supreme commander, as well as a stronger military presence. In retrospect, that may have aroused a suspicion in the minds of many critics that this had been merely a device to hide the true political situation: the existence of a military monarchy. However, while there were indeed provinces with great potential for conflict (Tarraconensis, Lusitania) and borders considered to be at risk (the Rhine, Illyria, the Euphrates), there was still no appropriate term for their situation in the new regime, so the permanent presence of troops there was defined in conventional terms.

To speak of the 'military base' where a long-term army was stationed, at least in the early Augustan period, is therefore wrong. At first it was not a matter of sending certain units to established military bases; the bases, conversely, arose in response to military necessities. It can be quite confusing to trace the various changes of base for the legions between 27 BC and AD 14. Units were always being moved back and forth, and not only after the annihilation of the three legions under Varus, which merely led to additional transfers of men. The great majority of the legions and other military units were stationed in northern and western Spain (four to five legions), in the eastern region of Gaul on the Rhine (five to eight legions, depending on the current situation), on the Macedonian and Illyrian border and then, after the new order of rule in this area, on the Central and Lower Danube (eight to nine), as well as in Syria (three to four). Africa (one legion), Egypt (with three and later two legions) and the Rhaetian area were far less strongly guarded in the normal way.

Institutionalizing supreme command of the army in the person of the *princeps* had been a necessity for the new regime; it was introduced with the settlement of the year 27 and was never questioned again.

However, knowing what to do with such a vast army, ready to go into action, was another matter. The army handbooks said nothing about it; they could not, and nor were there any previous examples of such a situation to act as points of reference. For in the past an army had always been raised by the leadership of Rome to go into attack or be ready for defence. Earlier, a standing army had been unknown in principle; the Hellenistic monarchies with their armies of mercenaries were a different case. So there was nothing to be done with the Roman army but what had always been done with an army: move it from place to place. That was advisable, if only because of concern about what soldiers not in action and left to their own devices might think up. In a camp of idle soldiers, discontent seemed to be pre-programmed, and the triumvirate period offered many examples of recalcitrance and insubordination. Both the commanders who had experienced them at the time and those who heard about them later looked back with horror. What was an idle soldier going to do but work out, as he had since the days of the dictator, how he could be better off and what his future prospects were?

The supreme commander wondered what to do with his enormous army, and it was an urgent matter because one question had to be answered immediately: where was the army to stay anyway? Where was it to be stationed? There was the camp (*castra*), which as a typically Roman institution offered the army shelter in the event, for instance, of a siege, and had to be regarded as one of the arcana of Roman rule of the world. But it had always been the camp of an army on the move, defending itself against actual attack or going on the offensive itself. It was therefore set up somewhere new when the army marched on. On major campaigns in distant parts, the camp had sometimes also served as winter quarters (*castra hiberna*), and then it had a longer life; Caesar's winter quarters in Gaul provide much evidence here. But even the camps in use for a long period were not standing camps erected to last permanently, and once the campaign had moved on or the operation was over they were raised, as they had been in the foothills of Actium. Caesar kept his legions together after he had subdued all the Celtic tribes west of the Rhine, but that was for political reasons and did not mean that he was setting up garrisons for the soldiers. Nor did the military policy of the triumvirs provide permanent garrisons for their legions. Indeed, the triumvirs had been intent on keeping them involved in action to ensure that their men were in good fighting fettle. After the victory of Augustus and the coming of peace to the empire, an abrupt break with the policy up to this point was not to be expected.

In fact we do not know of any military camps for the existing legions of several years' duration in the Augustan period. As in the time of the dictator, there were of course camps that were in use for some time, particularly as winter quarters, but even when a unit intended to return to its old camp after a campaign, it did not leave the camp itself intact when it marched away. Remains of six different camps have been found in Castra Vetera (Xanten) and in Novaesium (Neuss); there are even traces from the time of Augustus and Tiberius of seven superimposed camps. Excavations show that in the oldest of these camps the men still used tents; only later were wooden huts erected, and it seems that these later camps did serve as a regular base, at least for long operations, so that when the soldiers marched out they did not demolish everything but left some of the huts standing. However, as they could not be certain of returning to their point of departure in autumn, there was no reason to worry about the maintenance of what they had left behind. These standing army camps were still a long way short of being considered to be established military bases. The 'barracks' changed according to the aim of an operation.

We cannot overlook the fact that, after the year 16 BC, the policy of expansion to the north and in the Balkans had its origin in keeping legions available for action when at present they lacked any way of occupying themselves. Of their very nature, the legions wanted to be active. If the frontiers of the empire were not in immediate danger, the mere presence of a large military potential could be made to look like a far-sighted security policy, linking possible danger points and new discoveries about the situation abroad into a plan for forward defence. It was not at all difficult to present it to the public as a strategy for preserving peace, in view of the responsive reaction of Roman society to matters of security and reputation, and centralized manipulation of opinion was well versed in planting ideas in people's minds.

# 14

# Military Expansion after 16 BC

When Augustus celebrated the Secular Games, there was no unrest giving cause for concern either on the frontiers or in the provinces. The huge empire seemed to be free of any threat from rebellious provincials or aggressive inhabitants of the bordering regions. The Romans could have leaned back, reassured, to enjoy the peace so often lauded and celebrated. They did the opposite. In the next year, 16 BC, they embarked upon large-scale offensives on their northern borders, operating from several bases. These offensives, of dimensions previously unknown, bore comparison with the dictator Caesar's Gallic War. If foreign policy at the beginning of the principate had been confined to consolidating the existing areas of Rome's dominion, for instance on the Iberian peninsula, or had expressly relinquished the policy of expansion hitherto pursued, perhaps on the Parthian border, the signal for a reversal of those previous targets now seemed to have been given. We shall look in vain for any distinct reason for this change of direction. Nothing fundamental had changed on the borders; there were no major military problems, either old or new, calling for action, and in so far as there was still anything to be regulated – the Romans had suffered a not inconsiderable setback in Gaul, to which we shall be returning later – it was not so grave that eradicating the problem would have justified the expense incurred.

There has been much speculation by historians on the motives for the period of military expansion that now set in, lasting up to the death of Augustus, and in the course of time many hypotheses that cast only superficial light on the question have become so entrenched that a critic must refute them before presenting other ideas. There is a wide range of opinions, not to mention certain rather outlandish views that have staked their claim for consideration. In view of the extent of the expansion, how anyone can speak of a defensive foreign policy remains a puzzle, and we may leave the proponents of that thesis to solve it. At the most we can try to explain the origin of this concept. Its intellectual author will then be found in Theodor Mommsen, who – with more reason – proposed, as an explanation of the time of the great expansion of the third and second centuries BC, the thesis of a fundamentally defensive foreign policy, although its effect was expansion because of the endeavours of the Romans to achieve security ('defensive imperialism').

Sometimes an opposite opinion is expressed: that Augustus was a conqueror who wanted to extend the borders of the Roman world beyond the river Elbe. In view of the obvious wish for expansion shown by the *princeps*, historians not otherwise inclined to indulge in fantasy when interpreting our sources sometimes abandon their usual distaste for extreme positions and, influenced by many quotations from the time when Rome ruled the world, allow their gaze to extend not only to the whole of northern Europe but as far as India, even to the China Sea. They justify their imaginative ideas, or those that they impute to Augustus, by pointing out that Roman knowledge of geography was incomplete. The people of Rome did, however, have an idea of the distance between Syria and India (at that time including present-day Pakistan), gleaned from the conquests of Alexander the Great, a subject familiar to every educated person in classical antiquity. They knew about the difficulties of such an expedition and the large population of that area (their knowledge was not, as is sometimes claimed, confined to nomads) and they also knew that the end of the world to the east, as seen from the Land of the Five Rivers, the Punjab, was still so far away that even Alexander, with his boundless ambition, had to turn back at the prospect. But did it make sense for a Roman to regard dominion over the world as ruling the entire geographical world, especially to the north and the east, where large areas still had to be measured and for that purpose must first be explored? Trying to present Augustus as a new Alexander, a political fantasist acting without thought for the traditional society of his time, is to abandon the discipline of history and enter the realm of the adventure novel. Quite apart from the fact that the Roman empire, in the minds of those who lived there, was already a world empire, the idea that Augustus, like Alexander the Great before him, contemplated the conquest of the whole geographical area of the earth, or a large part of it, is a disconcerting one. By this time the Romans had long since come of age as conquerors and had no intention of rushing headlong into an enterprise with a wholly uncertain outcome. They were not adventurers like Alexander, who, with his ambition to conquer first the huge Persian empire and then the rest of the world, had taken leave not only of the traditional policies of the Greeks but also of all sense of the possibilities of political action. Alexander had stepped out of his time with his boundless ambitions, and accordingly no classical or modern idealization of him based solely on his success can absolve him of the insanity of the notion.

The idea of Augustus as conqueror equates the ideological elevation of Roman rule to world dominion, as it was widely discussed and praised in the literature of the time, with the aims of a practical military policy. The idea of ruling the world, however, itself arose from the achievements of the past and did not mean setting out now on world conquest. When Virgil makes the father of the gods, Jupiter, say to Venus, the mother of Aeneas: 'I set no limits to them [the future Romans] in space and time. I gave them an unlimited empire,' he was referring to the state of affairs already existing in the early years of Augustus, not anticipating further conquests. As a reason for the expansion that began in the year 16, the idea of a threat to Rome from its northern borders is more widespread today. Even if, according to modern investigations, that was not the case, and tribal pressure in the Germanic, Alpine and Illyrian regions in general is to be seen more as a reaction to the Roman urge for conquest in previous decades, we cannot exclude the possibility that the Romans did feel there was a security problem in the years 16/15, especially as the northern border had been greatly extended by military operations in the recent past. However, the general public of Rome must certainly have known that there was no serious threat to Italy from the north, and any areas of threat that still had to be dealt with – the frontier as drawn by Octavian in the Illyrian–Pannonian area was the real problem here – could have been pacified at far less expense.

The most widely held thesis is that the Roman leadership was looking for a suitable line of defence to replace the one that, since the time of Caesar, had been marked by the Rhine with one further to the east, and had its eye on a 'river border' formed by the Elbe and the Danube. Even if the more thoughtful supporters of this thesis concede that such an aim could have been envisaged only once operations were in progress, not before they began, it remains a thesis constructed *ex eventu* and it cannot be proved valid even for the late period of the Augustan conquests. According to our sources, Augustus had not yet reached the whole of the Middle Danube area, and there is nothing to suggest that he had nurtured a wish early on to make a continuous frontier line of the rivers. A commonly held variant of the 'river border' theory as his aim is that the idea was to shorten the line of the border or round off the frontiers of the empire. The argument is that, with the Elbe–Danube line, the angle formed by the lower reaches of the Rhine and the Danube could be avoided, and there would be a shorter line to be defended. Hardly a word is ever said about the fact that such theses arise solely from the study of modern atlases. Anyone setting out to accommodate them would have to support them by the investigations of Roman concepts of the intended geographical area of occupation in the year 16, what idea they had of its geopolitical significance and what in the opinion of the theorists the Romans, who thought about such matters mainly in practical terms, might expect to encounter before achieving this imaginary aim.

The grounds for a foreign policy of expansion must derive from the operations undertaken, and that means going to our sources to discover what the Romans' ideas of the geography of the frontier areas and the hinterland really were. Then, after sober study of all the factors involved, we shall see whether a result can be deduced. However, the main consideration in assessing Roman military and foreign policy in the years after 26 is whether we can discern a purposeful plan in its operations from the start. Or did they instead derive from the success or failure of what was going on at home and abroad and alter themselves accordingly – that is to say, were the decisions taken influenced by newly acquired knowledge of the geographical nature and ethnic characteristics of hitherto unknown areas? In any case, we must take care not simply to assume that these ventures were based on a deliberate plan.

But even if no advance planning can be deduced from the outcome of Roman military operations abroad, we can discern two circumstances on which the idea of expansion to the north-east or east would have depended to a high degree. One has already been mentioned, and I need only refer to it briefly here. The military apparatus for expansion was ready to hand. It had not been created for that purpose, but its mere existence was bound to influence all decisions on foreign policy and would have had a dynamic effect, because the presence of a standing army with nothing to do meant potential danger in the minds of Augustus and his generals. The other circumstance is the example of Caesar, which we can assume was a factor in the consideration of all military ventures in the north, for not only was Augustus Caesar's son, his future campaigns set out from the areas – Gaul and Illyria – that had been conquered by the dictator or on which he had his eye for future expansion. The knowledge of both the dictator and his adopted son must have been similar where their familiarity or unfamiliarity with the areas they meant to occupy and their inhabitants were concerned. Before the beginning of his campaign, Caesar knew very little more about Gaul, which he went on to occupy, than Augustus knew later about the Germanic and north Pannonian areas. But we may also take it that they had plenty of reliable information, for there was an intricate network of trade routes, and not just along the rivers and coastlines. They were not setting off at random into the unknown.

However, it is very difficult to make out how much weight Caesar's example carried, because the motivation for his Gallic War was entirely different from any that Augustus might have. Caesar had started the war in order to strengthen his political position at home. At the beginning of his own campaigns on the Rhine, Augustus had for years held the position that Caesar had set out to create for himself; now he was looking for a field of action for his legions. Gaul, the area conquered by Caesar, could hardly provide the inspiration for further conquests, since it was a geopolitically self-contained area, although the dictator had not found it in that condition: before his campaigns in Gaul neither the Rhine nor the English Channel had been regarded as frontiers by the people living there. He created those frontiers, and left Gaul to Augustus as a regional unit. Did Augustus perhaps, in contemplating occupation of the area east of the Rhine, have in mind the aim of creating a similarly self-contained Germania? We may set out from the fact that Augustus and his generals as yet had little definite spatial idea of the imperial borders to the north and north-east in Germania and Pannonia. They could make their plans and decisions only on the basis of the nature of the border regions themselves, the threats they had come to represent to Rome in recent decades and the known geographical conditions that an invader would face. The first operations of the campaigns that now began show that initially Augustus and his commanders had to assess the geography of the region into which they were advancing in an exploratory, almost tentative spirit, and we should therefore start by surmising that no decisions about future borders were made, or at least not at the beginning of the venture.

We can therefore find few real reasons for Augustus to plan a major policy of conquest, and the events of the year in which the great expansion began themselves suggest that there was no such plan, but that he embarked on military operations to counter a limited danger. If those operations took on large dimensions in view of the military potential available, thereby creating the conditions for further military ventures, that was not necessarily the consequence envisaged at the beginning of Augustus' campaigns.

In the year 16 there was so much unrest in frontier areas to the north that a responsible leadership was bound to feel called to take action. There were attacks and uprisings at a number of points on the borders, even in many parts of the provincial regions themselves. More and more bad news kept arriving. Adjoining provinces were in danger in three frontier zones at the same time. In the north of Macedonia several tribes were putting pressure on the border, among them the Scordisci on the Lower Save and the Upper Morava; there was trouble from the tribes of the central and eastern Alpine areas, among them the Pannonians and the Norici, the latter inhabiting the Alps east of the river Inn; and in the region of the Central and Lower Rhine a number of German tribes were now crossing the river between Lake Ijssel, the Lippe and the Lahn, including the Sugambri, the Usipetri and the Tencteri.

Above all, movements in the north and north-east of Italy gave cause for concern. They involved tribes such as the Camunians and the Vennians, from the southern Alps near present-day Lake Garda. Publius Silius Nerva, an able commander, dealt with them relatively quickly. Silius had proved his worth as a legate of Augustus in the Cantabrian War and now, as proconsul of Illyricum, he subdued first the Alpine tribes of northern Italy and then the Norici of the eastern Alps. He belonged to a family not previously distinguished, and we hear of him for the first time when he became consul in the year 20. He was typical of the military man who had risen in the world, staking his own and his family's claim to join the nobility.

The situation on the Rhine was more difficult. The tribes mentioned above had crossed the river early in the summer, defeated a troop of Roman cavalry and then even challenged the governor of the part of Gaul conquered by Caesar, Marcus Lollius. Lollius was a good friend of Augustus, whose companion he seems to have been from his early youth. On hearing that the German tribes had crossed the river, he set out against them with at least a legion, but although he expected to meet the enemy he was obviously insufficiently prepared and was defeated with considerable casualties, even losing an eagle, the legionary standard. Lollius immediately rearmed for another engagement, but the German forces avoided it by retreating back across the Rhine. Although this setback, which went into the annals as the defeat of Lollius (*clades Lolliana*), had no further consequences, it was a great shock. In that same summer Augustus made haste to Gaul, although there does not seem to have been any acute danger by the time he arrived. He took with him his stepson Tiberius, who was then twenty-five years old, and had just taken on the Rome judicial praetorship. Although the 'city praetor' (*praetor urbanus*) was not supposed to leave Rome during his term of office, Augustus overrode that convention and simply transferred the business of the praetorship to Drusus, younger brother of Tiberius – a striking break with the law on the part of the *princeps*, who was usually rather meticulous in observing the old ways. It showed clearly that public law applied to Augustus and his family only in certain circumstances.

Although all was quiet on the Rhine border when Augustus arrived, he went to the Rhine himself, initially leaving Tiberius in charge of the administration of the Gallic provinces. It was obvious that Rome could not take the defeat of Lollius lying down; the German tribes must be punished, if only for crossing to the left bank of the Rhine. At the moment, however, there was an even more pressing problem. The tribesmen might have withdrawn, but once again there was a threat to Italy, and now also to Gaul, from Alpine tribes living in the central and western Alps. Some kind of action was called for, and the presence of Augustus with the legions on the Rhine, so that he was directly confronted with the military situation, seems to have led to the decision to demonstrate the military might of Rome with a particular show of force to the tribes of the frontier between eastern Gaul and northern Italy. That is also indicated by the setting-up of a mint in Lugdunum in the year 15; its unusually high production of gold, silver and bronze coins must have been intended to finance the military operations.

The first thing to do, in view of the menacing activity of the Alpine tribes, was to intimidate them, and that meant restoring the centuries-old function of the Alps as a barrier to all that lay north of them. The initial position differed from that of earlier ventures only in that the necessary military potential was already present. Indeed, this was an essential factor, allowing the Roman leadership to deal with the security problem more effectively than had been possible in the past. The next priority was the permanent prevention of attacks mounted from the Alpine area on eastern Gaul, to which the raiding Rhaetians were storming in from the north-west of the Alps, and also of similar attacks on Italy from those quarters. Roman forces set out from these two areas – Italy and central Gaul, which had been the main aim of the Alpine tribes – advancing towards the central Alps, to be precise the area between the Swiss Jura and the high Alps, and went on into the northern foothills of the range. Augustus gave the leadership of the two army groups to his stepsons Tiberius and Drusus, who of course had the support of experienced officers, advising them to prove themselves quick learners on this campaign and emerge from it as independent generals.

Here Augustus was promoting members of his own family in an entirely new style of military leadership, and his decision clearly shows that he had not the slightest reservations about Livia's sons. With the appointment of his two stepsons, the younger generation of his family now stood side by side with him and Agrippa. In fact the generals as a body were being rejuvenated. Not only was Augustus himself now approaching fifty, so were the generals of the time of his struggle for sole leadership, if indeed they were still alive. He did indeed have at his disposal able younger men who had already proved their worth, and they were also men from whom, as their origins were not in the old nobility, he need fear no political ambition. We shall soon be meeting some of them. But the appointment of younger members of the house of Augustus sent a clear signal. Even though peace had now reigned for over a decade in the empire, not only Augustus himself but his whole family, the *domus Augustus*, represented here by the younger generation, were to preserve direct contact with the army, particularly the troops on active service, thus both maintaining their personal proximity to the source of their power and reinforcing it to consolidate the permanent establishment of the ruling house and secure its position for the future.

Operations began in the following year, 15 BC. Drusus, now using his family cognomen and known as Nero Claudius Drusus, advanced from the south and went on to the place where the southern Alpine tribes had defeated Silius the previous year. The main army probably made its way through the valley of the Etsch and Eisack rivers and over the Brenner pass into present-day Tyrol. Ahead of it were the Rhaetians, who had settled there, particularly in the valleys of the central Alps (the South Tyrol to the North Tyrol, in the present canton of Graubünden). The term Rhaetian covers a group of small tribes who had lived in the Alpine valleys for centuries, mingling repeatedly with new arrivals in the area, and the core of original inhabitants still belonged to a group predating the Indo-Germanic immigrants. Drusus succeeded in weakening them so much in many skirmishes that they could be considered subdued after only a few months. He had the support of Tiberius, who was pressing on from the west to Lake Constance over the Swiss Jura.

Tiberius had to deal not just with the Rhaetians but also with other tribes, including the Celtic Vindelicians – also made up of several small tribal groups – whose main centre of settlement was on the high plains of present-day Upper Swabia and Bavaria. He built a small fleet on an island in Lake Constance, probably Mainau, defeated his adversaries with this fleet in a battle on the lake and then moved on north-east to the sources of the Danube. He also inflicted a heavy defeat on the Rhaetians in a land battle. By the end of the campaign the brothers had taken a large number of fortified camps and settlements. It is extremely unlikely that the important Celtic settlement (*oppidum*) of Manching, south of the Danube valley in the present Ingolstadt region, and probably an outpost of the Vindelicians, was destroyed, although that assumption has been made again and again by previous historians; it was probably conquered several decades earlier.

In only a year all the peoples of the central and western Alps and their foothills had been so completely subjugated by the Roman army that we hear no more of uprisings by the indigenous inhabitants of the area. However, some of the Rhaetians in particular, whom their contemporaries considered the fiercest of all the Alpine tribes, had resisted tenaciously. It was said that the Rhaetians and Vindelicians killed all enemy men and boys who fell into their hands, and did not even spare the unborn child in its mother's womb if their soothsayer predicted the birth of a boy. In a hopeless situation Rhaetian women, so the legend goes, would dash their children to death on the ground and fling them at the Romans. Although ideas of barbarism in general may have contributed to such stories, the indomitable will of these people to resist remains at their heart. The Romans were in no way inferior to the Rhaetians in their violence and indeed cruelty. Those men among the enemy still able to defend themselves were rounded up and forcibly pressed into Roman service as auxiliary troops, while the entire area was organized as a province in the form of a special district under the military jurisdiction of a prefect. As well as the Rhaetian and Vindelician area in the central Alps and the present-day north of Switzerland, Upper Swabia and the area known to the Romans as the Vallis Poenina, meaning 'river valley' (the river in question is the Upper Rhône), now the Pennine Alps in the Valais, also became a part of the new military zone (Raeti, Vindelici et Vallis Poenina). To secure it, the Roman military leadership stationed two legions with their auxiliary troops here for the long term, but only one camp for the legionaries is known to us from this early time, at Dangstetten on the northern bank of the Upper Rhine. The Nineteenth Legion, among others, was billeted here from time to time.

Later, in the year 7/6, the defeat of the Alpine tribes was marked by the erection of a large victory monument in honour of Augustus, the *tropaeum Alpium*, at the foot of the western Alps near Turbia, now La Turbie, north of present-day Monaco. It lists all the Alpine peoples defeated under his supreme command, forty-six of them in all. In Rome the poet Horace dedicated two odes to the victors, one referring more specifically to Drusus (4, 4), the other to Tiberius (4,14).

It also seems to have been in 15 BC, the year of the capture and occupation of the Rhaetian and Vindelician area – rather than a few years later or even in the Claudian period – that the whole of the kingdom of Noricum bordering that region to its east, and extending from the rivers Inn and Danube and Illyricum to what is now the border of eastern Slovenia, was occupied and placed under Roman administration, although in the Augustan period it was not a full province. It may have been under a prefect, but it is not impossible that a member of the former royal house of the Norici was allowed to remain in place as a client prince, at least for a while. An eastern area consisting of Poetovio (Ptuj, Pettau) and Carnuntum was separated from Noricum and added to Illyricum.

To the north, the area was bordered by the Danube, which also formed the frontier of the empire here.

If the Pax Romana had brought peace to the Alps, the situation was not so good in the Pannonian–Dalmatian region, known to the Romans at this time by the inclusive name of Illyricum. The Danube extended to several parts of it, for instance present-day Lower Austria and in the area where the central course of the river reached Moesia, but it did not form a continuous border, and most important of all it was not yet a military frontier secured by fortified camps. Consequently, the Roman-occupied area not only suffered recurrent uprisings by local tribes or parts of tribes, but was also open to invasion by Dacians and other groups from the Danube area beyond it. In the years 14 and 13, Scordisci tribesmen who had settled on both sides of the central Danube around what is now Belgrade invaded Pannonia and reached Sirmium. A major mopping-up operation seemed necessary. It was entrusted to Agrippa, who went to Illyricum, but his death put an end to the operations. Augustus then sent Tiberius, now twenty-nine years old, to Pannonia. He managed to restore peace in the years 12 and 11 but, although the province seemed to be pacified, he had to return to Illyricum next year after an invasion of Dacians across the frozen Danube, and he was still there in the year 9, operating mainly in the Dalmatian part of the province.

In the years 14 and 13 there was relative peace on the Rhine border and in the Alps. The Romans were not involved in any major military campaign, and the only unrest was in Pannonia. In the year 13, Tiberius became consul for the first time, with Publius Quinctilius Varus, and in the summer Augustus himself left Gaul, where he had been since the year 16. He left Drusus behind as administrator of the Gallic provinces, and Drusus immediately ordered a second census of the Gauls to be taken. There was nothing to suggest that in 12 BC, the following year, the great occupation of the area on the right bank of the Rhine was to begin, in what were later known as the German campaigns. It is not certain that such far-reaching plans had yet been made. The Romans had first to adjust to a fundamentally changed geopolitical idea of the north. In so far as policy, particularly military and security policy, focused on the north and east at all, it had hitherto concentrated entirely on the Alps and the line of the Rhine already secured by Caesar. There is not

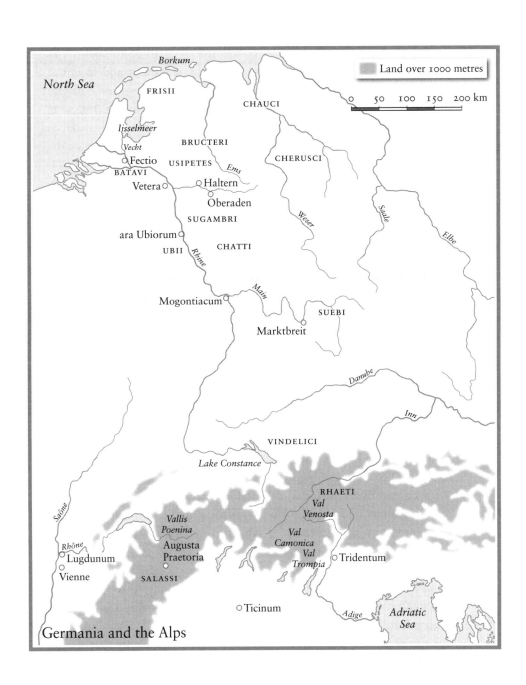

North Sea

Borkum

FRISII

CHAUCI

Ijsselmeer

Vecht

BRUCTERI

Fectio

USIPETES

CHERUSCI

Ems

BATAVI

Vetera

Haltern

Oberaden

SUGAMBRI

Weser

Saale

Elbe

ara Ubiorum

CHATTI

UBII

Rhine

Main

Mogontiacum

SUEBI

Marktbreit

Danube

Inn

VINDELICI

Lake Constance

RHAETI

Val
Venosta

Vallis
Poenina

Val
Camonica

Saône

Val
Trompia

Tridentum

Rhône

Augusta
Praetoria

Lugdunum

Vienne

SALASSI

Ticinum

Adige

Adriatic
Sea

Germania and the Alps

Land over 1000 metres

50    100    150    200 km

the slightest evidence that the Roman leadership had looked across the mountains and the river, setting its sights on the hinterland of the right bank of the Rhine. Why should it? A plan to curtail the corners and angles of the frontier line is very unlikely; the new situation was the result not of an extensive plan of conquest, but of an unforeseen series of rebellions. The swift conquest of the Alpine valleys and foothills, which must certainly have surprised the Romans themselves, had created a new frontier, and a new view of the problems to which it gave rise. Nor can the return of Augustus from Gaul to Rome be regarded as a fanfare signalling a major assault on the tribes of the right bank of the Rhine. At first all that was at stake was vengeance for the defeat of Lollius, along with the advisability of keeping the German tribes from further incursions over the river. There were plenty of troops stationed in the area, so punitive operations could be carried out thoroughly with a view to establishing a permanent deterrent. Operations were therefore to go far into the region on the right bank of the Rhine, but because of defective knowledge of its precise geography they must also entail gleaning more reliable information about the terrain and the tribes living there.

Accordingly, the venture upon which Drusus now embarked gives the initial impression of an expedition to explore and reconnoitre the land on the right bank of the Rhine, rather than to conquer it. A prerequisite for the subsequent operations, which lasted for several years, was of course the transfer of troops stationed in the interior of Gaul to the Rhine; archaeology has established that the earliest traces of the camp at Xanten (Vetera) and probably the camp at Mainz (Moguntiacum) date from this time. Drusus had five to six legions and troops of auxiliaries available. Before beginning his campaign he summoned the sixty Gallic tribal communities (*civitates*) to Lugdunum (Lyon), founded as a small military colony by Munatius Plancus in the year 43. It had been the site of an important Roman mint for some time now. Drusus set up an altar to Roma and Augustus here, and it soon became the organizational and religious centre of the part of Gaul conquered by Caesar, Gallia Comata, which either now or a little later was to be divided into three provinces. The altar was dedicated on 1 August of the year 12, and Gaius Julius Vercondaridubnus, a Haeduan who held Roman citizenship, was appointed the first priest of the cult. Gaul now had a centre that would be indispensable for further operations to the east.

Drusus began his German campaign in the year 12 with an expedition to explore and pacify the northern section of the border. He had obviously been waiting for an occasion for it, and that occasion was provided by another foray of the Sugambri across the Lower Rhine. Once they had been repulsed, Drusus immediately crossed the Rhine at a more northerly point and then advanced south along the right bank of the river into the land of the Usipetri and Sugambri on the rivers Ruhr and Lippe, laying it waste. He then, mainly using the Rhine itself as a traffic route, went back beyond his point of departure to a place from which he could go by the shortest route to Lake Ijssel, probably the site of the later camp of Fectio, now Vechten. To get further north he had a trench built for his ships (the *fossa Drusi*) from the arm of the Rhine to Lake Ijssel and then turned towards the North Sea. Here he occupied an island, probably in the vicinity of the island of Borkum, and went on into the river Ems, where he successfully fought the Bructeri, who had settled on the upper course of the river. The Frisii and Chauci who lived on the coast do not seem to have offered much resistance; the former even rescued him from an emergency which faced him because he was unaware that tides here were much stronger than in the Mediterranean, and his ships were suddenly beached. The march back obviously presented no problems. The outcome of the campaign was not only precise knowledge of the situation on the northern border: Drusus had also gained allies in the Frisii, and the country through which he had passed could therefore be regarded as an area of Roman influence.

That winter Drusus returned to Rome and took up the office of city prefect to which he had been appointed for the following year, but he immediately left the city, ignoring the business connected with the office that might have kept him there, and was back on the Rhine so soon that he was able to begin his second campaign in spring of the year 12. He crossed the river again, as he had done the year before, to fight the Usipetri and Sugambri, and his task was eased by the fact that the latter were at war with their neighbours to the south, the Chatti, because the Chatti had refused to join their army the year before. Advancing from the north and crossing the river Lippe over a bridge, he met with little resistance from the local tribes, including Tencteri and Chatti tribesmen, so he marched on east as far as the Weser. Finally forced to turn back because provisions were running low, as he passed through a ravine-like valley on the return march he fell into an ambush which, in retrospect, seems to foreshadow the disaster that was to befall Varus. But the military discipline of his men and the prudence of their leadership averted any worse outcome. Exploiting the disorder of the enemy ranks, Drusus succeeded in fighting his way out of the trap, and he crossed back over the Lippe and reached the Rhine. He had a fortified camp set up on the Lippe about 40 kilometres from the Rhine (presumably Haltern, which may be the camp of Aliso mentioned by writers of antiquity), and another camp was built that year or the next in the land of the Chatti, a clear sign that he intended to come back and was even apparently envisaging eventual occupation of the territory.

In the autumn of the year 11 Drusus returned to Rome. He was awarded the lesser triumph (*ovatio*), but Augustus withheld the title of *imperator*, although his soldiers had already hailed Drusus by it. On this point Augustus was grudging even to his stepsons, despite the military success they were achieving in the field, because the official bestowal of the title could be interpreted as designating his successor to rule the principate of Rome. Augustus claimed a monopoly of all acclamations as *imperator* for himself, and so he now received his thirteenth such triumph. However, when his sister Octavia died that same autumn, his stepson Drusus had the honour of delivering her funeral oration.

In the winter of that year Augustus was in Lugdunum. Tiberius also went there, but another Dacian invasion soon summoned him back to Illyricum, which he had been administering as legate since the year 12. In Lugdunum Augustus, Tiberius and Drusus must have discussed, with particular attention, the outcome of the campaigns in Germania and the policy that they should adopt towards the Germans. As Drusus began another campaign against the Germans living on the right bank of the Rhine the next year – his third – it seems likely that the policy of exploring and securing the border, which undoubtedly had the consent of the *princeps*, was now taking the shape of a policy also approved by Augustus for the occupation of large regions to the east of the river. If we remember that the area envisaged in these plans lay between the river Main and the coast of the North Sea, it is clear that such a decision had nothing to do with any idea of 'curtailing' the borderline along the Elbe. Drusus had not yet set eyes on the Elbe, and no link existed between the lands he had subdued and the foothills of the Alps.

Drusus returned to the Rhine in spring, with the title of proconsul, to begin his third campaign. This time he was marching against the Chatti, who had settled north of the lower Main and east of the Sugumbri and Tencteri. He crossed the river and made his way over the Taunus range and the Wetterau area, going far into the country of the Chatti. However, he encountered some resistance and finally withdrew back over the Rhine again without achieving any decisive success.

After his return to Rome, Drusus began his first consulate on 1 January 9. Back in Gaul, he set out across the Rhine on his fourth German campaign and first attacked the Chatti again, then the Suebi who lived to the east of them and finally the Cherusci of the Weser district. He crossed the river and reached a place not far from where the Elbe is joined by its tributary the Saale. He could not cross the river here and press on; instead he set up a monument to victory (*tropaeum*) and then turned back, although it was not yet winter. While still quite close to the farthest point of his campaign, in a region west of the Saale, he fell from his horse, broke his ankle and died from the consequences of the accident a month later, aged only twenty-nine. The summer camp where he died was known thereafter as 'the wicked place' (*scelerata*). Tiberius, who had made haste to Germania on hearing news of the accident, found him still alive. The speed with which he made for his brother's sickbed makes one suspect that once the commander of the army was out of action, Augustus feared for the whole campaign.

It is said that a woman of titanic proportions had appeared to Drusus on the Elbe, denouncing him for his insatiable urge to make new conquests and foretelling his imminent death. There was talk of other omens predicting it. There is evidence that the contemporaries of Drusus were very much aware of his importance and saw, at least in retrospect, that his death marked a turning point in Roman foreign policy.

The death of Drusus was a heavy loss in many respects. After the death of Agrippa in the year 12, he had been by far Rome's best military commander. Despite his youth, he acted independently in the field, planned operations carefully, was imaginative and steadfast when faced with difficult situations and, above all, was a dynamic, thrusting, forward-looking general. Unlike his brother Tiberius, who although also an able general was considered hesitant, Drusus could carry his men along with him. The energetic policy in Germania of the years 12 to 9, even if Augustus planned it as an operational line of forward defence, undoubtedly owed its wide-ranging dynamism to Drusus, who could inspire enthusiasm in his soldiers and was popular with the people of Rome. The idea that he planned to restore the old republic and had thus aroused the suspicion of Augustus is a fantasy of classical historians, anticipating the hatred of the aristocracy for his brother, who was to become emperor, and is entirely unrealistic. Drusus seems, in fact, to have been a man whose perhaps not very complex nature allowed him to mingle with men of his own rank with relatively little conflict, and he was also surrounded by the aura of a man close to the people (*civilitas*); he had, in fact, the qualities suitable to a man representing the principate.

From all that we know, Augustus was very close to his stepson, and his grief was genuine. Drusus had married Antonia, the younger daughter of the marriage of Mark Antony to Octavia, and he was thus not only the stepson of Augustus but also a member of the Julian family. His children were the great-nephews and great-niece of Augustus. There were two sons of his marriage to Antonia: Germanicus, outstanding as a general in the early reign of Tiberius, and Claudius, who was to become emperor, as well as a daughter, Livia Julia, known as Livilla.

The funeral of Drusus befitted his rank and the high esteem in which the Romans held him. Soldiers carried his body to the Rhine, distinguished citizens of Roman cities took it on from there to Italy. Augustus met the funeral procession in Ticinum (Pavia) and accompanied it to Rome. He himself and Tiberius delivered funeral orations on the dead man, of which only a fragment has come down to us, but we also have a speech of comfort for his mother Livia by an unknown author; stylistically it had its flaws. The remains of Drusus were cremated on the Field of Mars, and the ashes interred in the Mausoleum of Augustus beside the Tiber. Among the honours paid to him was an arch on the Appian Way and a cenotaph at Mainz, and it was also decided that he and his descendants should be granted the honorific Germanicus. Augustus himself composed the eulogy inscribed on his tomb and wrote a biography of him.

As expected, Tiberius succeeded Drusus in command of the army of the Rhine. Augustus himself went to Gaul in the following year, 8, a clear sign not only of his concern for the army but also of his intention of holding on to what Drusus had achieved. Tiberius took energetic measures and with the support of Augustus himself was not squeamish in his choice of methods. Envoys of German tribes asking to conclude a treaty with Rome were sent away empty-handed; perhaps Augustus did not want to grant them the international legal sovereignty that would go with a treaty. When envoys of the recalcitrant Sugumbri finally also arrived, he had them unceremoniously detained. To take pressure off the Central Rhine, he finally forced 40,000 of the Sugumbri and Suebi, particularly large and pugnacious tribes, to move to the left bank of the Rhine.

Tiberius remained supreme commander on the Rhine until the year 6 BC. Although the Romans had not entirely occupied the area between the Rhine and the Elbe, and most important of all they had no civil infrastructure there and thus no members of the aristocracy who in certain circumstances could be induced to carry out administrative tasks, its extent was now known, the army had been there, and it was ready for an administration to be set up. To the historian Velleius Paterculus, later a legate of Tiberius, Drusus features in retrospect as 'conqueror of the greater part of Germania', and he adds, with reference to the operations of the years 8 and 7 BC, continued by his brother Tiberius and certainly anticipating the latter's glorious campaign of 5 BC, that he, Tiberius, 'administered Germania as victor over every part of it, and could pass through it to his army without coming to any harm'. Germania was at his feet, to such an extent 'that he had almost brought it to the form of a province owing tribute'. A new Roman province was taking shape.

If after his return to Rome, probably in the year 8, Augustus solemnly extended the bounds of the *pomerium*, the sacred city limit of Rome, an act allowed only to one who had extended the borders of the Roman empire itself, it must have been with reference to Germania, which had thus officially become a part of the empire. It looked as if Drusus had left his brother only the task of consolidating an already subjugated area now willingly waiting to acquire full provincial status. Matters did not turn out like that, not least because Tiberius, exasperated by the policy Augustus was pursuing over the succession, suddenly retired into private life. He relinquished his command and went into voluntary exile on Rhodes. At that point the theatre of war in Germania lost a capable general who was extremely familiar with the nature of the terrain.

Tiberius remained aloof from all public activity for ten years, and in the end was even expressly barred from it. Not until AD 2 was he permitted to return to Rome, where he moved into the former house of Maecenas on the Esquiline which the Julian family had inherited. In AD 4, after the death of Gaius Caesar, whom Augustus had intended to succeed him, Tiberius once again took on supreme command of the army on the Rhine. In the meantime, and in the years until the army suffered its great catastrophe, it had been under the command in the north of a whole series of generals, among them some outstanding military experts. The first to take over from Tiberius was also a relation of Augustus, Lucius Domitius Ahenobarbus. He was the son of the famous supporter of Antony who had been consul in the year 32 and thus belonged to one of the most distinguished noble clans of the late republic. When Antony and Octavian were reconciled in Tarentum he was still under age and became betrothed to Antonia, the elder of the two daughters of Antony and Octavia, a child only two years old at the time. The marriage did not take place for another seven years. Their union produced three children, two daughters and a son, the father of the later Emperor Nero. After pursuing the customary career, Domitius had been consul in the year 16, had gained experience as governor of Africa and Illyricum and had shown himself a capable general in those provinces. He was regarded as arrogant and supercilious, but was a man with a zest for life, a characteristic that he shared with Gaius Sentius Saturninus, another legate of the army of invasion in Germania at this period and also of distinguished descent; his family tradition went far back into the republican period. Sentius' family had defended the republic, but Gaius had been pardoned by Octavian and in the end, only a few years younger than Augustus himself, he became one of his most reliable companions. We know nothing about his activities before his consulate in the year 19. After holding that office, he went as governor to Africa and Syria; in Syria he came into sharp conflict with Herod the Great over the latter's execution of his sons by Mariamne.

Publius Quinctilius Varus, also related to Augustus, could boast of even more distinguished descent as one of an old patrician family. His father had been on the republican side at the battle of Philippi and had taken his own life when the republican forces were defeated. The younger Varus married Claudia Pulchra, a granddaughter of Octavia and thus a great-niece of Augustus, probably when he was still quite young. We know little about him before his consulate in the year 13 BC. He was several years younger than Sentius and like him had been governor first of Africa, then of Syria, where he proved his worth in putting down the riots that broke out in Palestine after the death of Herod. It is very likely that he, rather than Publius Sulpicius Quirinius as the evangelist Luke claims, was governor of the province at the time when Jesus was born.

The fourth and last of the governors or legates in Germania to be mentioned here is Marcus Vinicius. His family, originating in Campania, is known to us only from the time of the late republic. His uncle, Lucius Vinicius, was tribune of the people in the year 51 and an adherent of Caesar and became consul in the year 33, but we know almost nothing about him. All we know of the career of his nephew Marcus Vinicius before his consulate in the year 19 is a few dates, and similarly little is known of his period as army commander in Illyria in the year 11, through which he rose to the ranks of the most prominent generals. He is one of those military men whose origins were not spectacular, but who distinguished themselves in the service of the *princeps* by their loyalty, ability and expertise in administrative and military leadership and enjoyed a steady – or as their rivals of more aristocratic descent saw it, a meteoric – rise in the world.

As commander of the army of the Rhine, Domitius brought new life into what one is inclined to call, at this point, the administration of Germania. He brought a new outlook to his new post, a fact deserving mention here. Before taking command in Germania, he had been appointed by Augustus to the governorship of Illyricum, where the second-strongest contingent of the army was stationed – it was even sometimes of equal strength to the army in Germania, because of the rebellions that kept breaking out in the Illyrian area. The main focus of military activities at the time was on the north-west border of his province, in the region of the Danube, and here he also had to deal with the Hermunduri, who for reasons unknown to us were moving south from their homes in the region of the rivers Elbe and Saale. He seems to have diverted them to the former homeland of the Marcomanni, who themselves, probably to avoid being surrounded by Romans, had emigrated to the Bohemian Basin vacated by the Celtic Boii tribe. Domitius thereupon advanced to the Elbe, probably reaching the upper part of its course in Bohemia, and even crossed the river and dedicated an altar to Augustus on its banks. He negotiated treaties with the German tribes who had settled here but probably avoided a clash with King Marbod (Maroboduus) of the Marcomanni, who was consolidating his rule in

Bohemia at this time. We do not know the details of Domitius' operations, but they were unusually bold and successful. He had gone much further into German regions than any other Roman commander. The failure of Velleius Paterculus to mention him at all in his account of the German wars of the period casts a light on the bias of his history, which was meant primarily for the eyes of Tiberius, whom he venerated, and he simply left out anyone whose deeds outshone those of his idol. Of course only the death of Drusus, whom Domitius replaced as the dynamic element in the German campaigns, had opened up the way for his achievements, and he was also free to make his own arrangements because, while Tiberius was not far from the Rhine at this time, he left the operational part of the campaign to Domitius. There is much to suggest that the two men did not have opposing views of the campaign in Germania, but on the contrary discussed their military operations and the aims they were pursuing together, so that Germania, or the part of envisaged as a province, was to be 'pacified' and secured on two sides.

After Domitius had taken over supreme command of the army of the Rhine from Tiberius, he was active in the years 4 BC to AD 1 in a Germania that he obviously already saw as a Roman domain. We have evidence of that in his efforts to improve the traffic network in countryside where the movements of the army were often severely impeded by forests and marshes. He laid out corduroy roads ('long bridges', *pontes longi*) in the marshy area between the Rhine and the Ems and could then move relatively freely in the area between the Rhine, the Elbe and the Main. However, his policy with tribesmen, the usual method adopted by Roman occupiers of playing off one group of Germans against another and securing the Roman presence by resettling them, brought him into conflict with several tribes at the end of his governorship, particularly the Cherusci. In AD 1, Germania was in a state of turmoil.

Marcus Vinicius now succeeded Domitius as commander of the army of the Rhine. He had already proved his worth in Pannonia, putting down the rebellions that kept breaking out there after 16 BC. When the Dacians crossed the frozen Danube into Pannonia in the winter of 10/9 BC, he had halted them with the second-strongest army in the empire and threw them back across the river. In Germania he was mainly occupied with fighting the rebellious German tribes. We do not know many of the details, or indeed much about his command there in general, but he campaigned successfully until he was recalled, and was therefore honoured with the award of the triumphal insignia.

His successor in AD 4 seems to have been Gaius Sentius Saturninus. At least, we find him as legate of the army of the Rhine under the supreme command of Tiberius in that year. After returning from his self-imposed exile, Tiberius not only had been adopted by Augustus and designated his successor by the award of tribunician power but also at the same time had received supreme command of the army of the Rhine again. On his arrival in Gaul, which had to wait until high summer of the year 4 because the adoption could not take place until the end of June, he received a warm welcome from the officers and men. The historian Velleius Paterculus, who at the time held the rank of a cavalry colonel (*praefectus equitum*), was one of his retinue. Tiberius went right through Gaul to the mouth of the Rhine, where, advancing from the north just as Drusus had done, he began his march into Germania. It cannot be called a campaign because much of the country was already occupied. Once again his object, as well as dealing with the small tribe of the Canninefati on the Batavian peninsula formed by the two great arms of the Rhine (the Waal and the Lek), was to engage first the Bructeri and then the Cherusci, who offered little opposition. After reaching the Weser, by which time the season was already well advanced, Tiberius took the army into winter quarters in one of the fortified camps on the Lippe. This was the first time a large Roman army had spent the winter in Germania. Velleius Paterculus writes exultantly of the successful conclusion of this venture: 'Our armies had traversed the whole of Germania.'

In the year 5, back from Rome again after the winter break, Tiberius and the army first marched north, probably through the valley of the Weser, into the region where the Chauci lived on the coast between the Elbe and the Ems, and then along the Elbe. Here he fought a battle against the Langobardi, who thereupon vacated the left bank of the Elbe. Going on up the Elbe, he encountered first the region inhabited by the Semnoni on the central Elbe and then the Hermunduri, pitched camp beside the river and received envoys from the German tribes there. At this same place he met the fleet, which had been on a major reconnoitring expedition. It had first sailed along the coast of Jutland, had ensured that the Cimbri and Charudi who lived on the Jutland peninsula were on friendly terms with Rome, and at the farthest point of its voyage reached Skagens Horn (*Cimbrorum promontorium*). On returning to the mouth of the Elbe, the fleet then went on, using the river as its route, to reach Tiberius at his camp. The combined venture by land and sea, a great achievement of military strategy, showed that Tiberius was a capable organizer. He was hailed as *imperator*, of course together with Augustus, and his deputy Saturninus was distinguished with the award of the triumphal insignia. The German venture seemed to have been successfully concluded. The scene of Tiberius receiving the German envoys on the banks of the Elbe may be regarded as the symbolic conclusion of a policy to incorporate Germania into the Roman empire that had begun sixteen years earlier.

By way of an interim report, we should try to establish more clearly the aims of Roman policy in Germania in the years from 12 BC to AD 5, so that we can draw conclusions about the following years against the background of what had been achieved. On the conclusion of Tiberius' great venture in the year 5 Velleius Paterculus, who had taken part in the campaign, sums it up with the words: 'Nothing was left to be conquered in Germania apart from the tribe of the Marcomanni.' It sounds as if he is drawing a line at the end of a final conquest. There is much to suggest that the campaign was not seen in that light from the first; rather, it began as a large-scale exploration of the region on the right bank of the Rhine to ease the strain on the border formed by the river. This idea is supported by the fact that in the year 12 the German venture began with a comprehensive exploration of Germania from the north, where there was no threat to the Romans and Drusus encountered no resistance, not a move that can easily be understood as purely a plan of conquest. The exploration of the unknown east, the weakening of the German tribes from the right bank of the Rhine who were threatening to cross the river and the occupation of important points from which to observe them and if necessary engage in 'forward defence' could well have formed the operational aims of the venture in the year 12, and were no small task in themselves.

The success of Drusus, and the urge to conquest that it then probably aroused, changed the aims of Rome. Most of all it seems to have been the events in the Illyrian and Norican border area, and the uncertainty of the military situation, which was already clear in the year 16, that influenced further strategic planning in Germania. The line of fortified camps along the Lippe initially founded by Drusus, including Oberaden (left unoccupied after Drusus' death) and Haltern, set up rather later, speaks for itself. These were not temporary camps pitched in the course of a march, but established bases never left ungarrisoned. They served as stations for departing and returning expeditions, and as supply points where provisions, equipment and other war matériel were not only stored but in part manufactured. The Lippe with its camps traces the line of the army road secured by fortified posts that led into Germania. However, there must have been another army route further south, starting at Mainz, from which Drusus had set out on his last campaign. It presumably did not lead north-east through the Wetterau area, but rather directly east into the region of the Central Main, that is to say in part through the region of the much-feared Hercynian forest (*Hercynia silva*), a term denoting all the forested mountains north of the Danube. This assumption is confirmed by the archaeological evidence showing that as well as the large camp of Rödgen/Bad Nauheim in the Wetterau, which must date from the time of Drusus, there was soon another large permanent fortified camp at Marktbreit on the southern end of the great loop described by the river Main. This was certainly a legionary camp, and can be dated to between the campaign of Domitius in the year 8 BC and the battle of Varus in AD 9. As a permanent base it may have been just one in a long line of fortified camps linking Mainz with this area, although no trace of the others has been found to this day. The theory of this conjectural southern line of fortified camps, which we can make out only at Marktbreit, is supported by the natural assumption that Roman strategy in Germania was conceived as setting out from Gaul and the Illyrian area, rather than the foothills of the Alps, and that consequently the aim was to secure the northern border area against the particularly warlike Pannonian and German tribes, rather than to 'curtail' the border.

For the year AD 5 we may assume that operations, in so far as they affected Germania and judging by their geographical extent, were considered concluded by the expedition of Tiberius that year. The Rhine, the Elbe and Saale and the Main marked out an area that at this time was intended to be a new administrative sphere of Roman rule, that is to say a province. At the same time, it is the area that now featured as Germania in the Roman mind. Its borders could not be clearly enough discerned to the east, as later Roman and above all modern opinion sees it, for Augustus to look for large rivers to form the frontiers of his expansion. If only for that reason, the Elbe cannot be as important as has been supposed, because an Elbe border at the mouth of the Saale would have found its natural continuation in that river. Above all, however, the Romans would soon have discovered that the Elbe/Saale region (and northern Bohemia) was much more densely inhabited than the areas further west, and defining a border without taking account of that fact would hardly have led to swift consolidation of the area. From the evidence of our sources, the Roman leadership none the less thought military security operations were largely concluded, and so they began dividing up the area, establishing meeting places as the early stages of an administration, intervening in tribal problems and in particular distinguishing individual noblemen with Roman citizenship and thus winning them over to the Roman cause, even already gathering taxes and exercising jurisdiction. Everything was in the early stages, and Germania – like, for instance, Noricum and the Rhaetian-Vindelician area – still formed a military district; it could not, of course, be regarded as finally pacified, but the outlines of a future province were already clearly visible.

After the great German venture of Tiberius in the year AD 5, only one opponent still seemed to stand in the way of peace in the Roman sense, meaning subjection to Rome: the Marcomanni under their king, Marbod. Velleius Paterculus had said exactly the same, of course implying that this ought to be the next target for the Romans. And in fact, under the supreme command of Tiberius, the invasion of Marbod's kingdom began in AD 6. Twelve legions in all with their auxiliary troops, half of the entire Roman military potential, were summoned to Germania. The plan was for two army groups to advance into Marbod's territory, Saturninus with the army of the Rhine to the east, and Tiberius from Carnuntum on the Danube (between modern Bad Deutsch-Altenburg and Petronell in Lower Austria), where he had gone into winter quarters, advancing west and north. Each of them had roughly six legions and auxiliary troops. They were making for the 'land of the Boii' (*Boihaemum*), as Velleius Paterculus spells it, which we may feel can safely be identified with the Bohemian Basin. The two halves of the army were to meet at a place previously decided on, evidence not only of Roman knowledge of the area, but also of the precision with which they thought they could calculate their marching speed. Previously there had been offensives of a similar size only in the civil wars, and we have to look a hundred years ahead to the Dacian wars of the Emperor Trajan to find anything comparable in the future. Velleius Paterculus, serving in Pannonia at the time, cites the reason for the war as the strength of Marbod, who could apparently raise 70,000 infantry soldiers and 4,000 cavalrymen, and therefore represented a danger not only to Germania, which Velleius rightly regards as an established Roman zone of influence at this time, but also to Noricum and Pannonia, even to Italy. He calculates that the distance between the kingdom of Marbod and the line of the Alpine crests was only 200 Roman miles (300 kilometres). This calculation indicates the change in geographical ideas since the year 16 BC. Back then, the Alps formed a barrier against any enemy in the north and north-east, as they had for centuries; now an enemy 300 kilometres to the north-east was a danger that it was the army's duty to avert. Was this sufficient reason for the gigantic offensive?

Marbod had been to Rome as a young man, and after military training returned to his people familiar with Roman thinking – Velleius calls him a barbarian on the grounds of his origin rather than his intellect. Having risen to the highest position of power in his tribe, presumably by exploiting the insecurity of the Marcomanni in their retreat to Bohemia, he was now pursuing from their new area of settlement a policy of expansion principally at the expense of the German tribes of the Elbe (the Semnoni, Langobardi and Lugii). The Romans very soon saw that his policy was a danger to this area of Germania, where they had only recently gained control, and as the pressure on the tribes of the Elbe could be relieved only by an attack on Marbod himself, the target of their campaign must be the Bohemian region in which the Marcomanni had settled. Nothing but such a long-term aim justified the huge military effort involved. A successful outcome would be the inclusion of the Bohemian Basin in the Roman empire, whether as a province or under a client king. The urge to expand was extending to borders ever new, developing its own dynamic, and by now the Romans were obviously not entirely in control of it.

The campaign began in the spring of AD 6. There can be no doubt that Augustus had agreed to it, for without his consent half the army would not have set out. But even the usually rather circumspect Tiberius seems to have supported the offensive, thus stepping into his great brother's shoes. He did not have to wonder if they fitted him.

Tiberius set out in spring. We do not know the precise route taken by the two armies. Tiberius could either march along the Danube, first west and then north-west, joining Saturninus in more familiar territory, or set out north from Carnuntum for the Bohemian Basin. If he went straight to Bohemia, their meeting place would have been far from the terrain which to some extent they already knew. It is more likely that they joined forces in or near one of the fortified camps of the southern part of Germania, but here we know only of Marktbreit on the great southern loop of the river Main, and that was also in the direction that Saturninus was taking on his way east ('through the land of the Chatti and the dense Hyrcanian forest'). Since they must have guessed that they would be not far from the enemy here, somewhere further to the south-east of modern Marktbreit seems more likely. However, they never did join forces. When Tiberius was only five days' march away from the enemy, and as many days again from his meeting with Saturninus' army group, he received news of a rebellion of the Pannonians at the base camp that he had only just left, and it was of alarming dimensions. The cautious Tiberius thereupon broke off the mammoth campaign at once, and both army groups returned to the bases from which they had set out. However, Tiberius did not omit to conclude a treaty of friendship with Marbod, thus covering his back for his difficult task in Pannonia. Marbod was probably glad to have escaped a dangerous situation so suddenly and now he was able to continue pursuing his plans on the north and north-west border of his sphere of influence unimpeded.

Since Octavian's campaign in the years 35 to 33, the Pannonian-Dalmatian area had been frequently shaken by rebellions both small and sometimes quite large. As we have seen, several troublespots had to be dealt with in the years after 16 BC. But when Tiberius set out on his campaign against the Marcomanni, peace had reigned for a number of years, so the Roman leadership thought it safe to take the army to a neighbouring region. However, it seems that the preparations for the campaign, in particular the raising of auxiliary troops for the Roman army, actually kindled the flame of rebellion or perhaps more likely fanned embers of resentment that were still glowing. The almost total withdrawal of the legions from Pannonia finally tipped the scales. Even the governor, Marcus Valerius Messalla Messallinus, son of Corvinus, was away in Tiberius' retinue. How secure the Romans must have felt to leave the province virtually unguarded!

The unrest very quickly took hold of large parts of Pannonia and Dalmatia, in particular the entire region of the rivers Save and Drau and the hinterland of the Dalmatian coast. The Breuci on the upper course of the Save and Drau, under their leader Bato, as well as the Desidiati in present-day Bosnia around Sarajevo with their leaders, Pinnes and another Bato, were at the heart of the rebellion. Only the coast and north Pannonia were to some extent spared. Velleius, who as legate was on Tiberius' staff during the war, estimated the strength of the rebels at 200,000 men. Even if that seems excessive, the enemy at least outnumbered the Romans, and the recent decades of Roman rule had also familiarized them with the Roman use of arms. They could also travel on the roads that the legions habitually took, and then withdraw into impassable country if they felt they were at a disadvantage. The rebellion seems to have drawn the small tribes, whose cohesion had already been greatly weakened, more strongly together again. According to Roman sources, the rebels spoke confidently of attacking Macedonia and Italy, although that could have been just anxiety on the part of Romans who imputed such ideas to the rebels.

Augustus further increased the general hysteria by declaring in the Senate that the enemy could be at the gates of Rome in ten days' time. He must certainly have known better, but with this claim he could make the Romans more willing to accept the impositions he thought necessary: new taxes, and above all the raising of more troops for military service from the ranks of slaves who first had to be freed. Including among the infantry freedmen who had so recently been slaves was a measure to be adopted only in the utmost need, and restrictions were imposed to the effect that they should form units separate from the other soldiers and be used only to guard the Roman cities of the Illyrian border area. Among those who brought Tiberius the substitute troops from Italy was not only the historian Velleius Paterculus, but also Germanicus, son of Drusus and adopted son of Tiberius. Germanicus, who was only twenty-one at the time, took the office of quaestor in the year 7 and now gained his first military laurels under the command of his adoptive father.

The aim of the rebels, as it turned out, was less ambitious than supposed. First they murdered all the Romans they could lay hands on, merchants or veterans who were, or were to be, landowners in their area; then they stormed the Roman fortresses, in particular Sirmium on the Save (present-day Sremska Mitrovica), at the time the farthest advanced military bastion, and the coast city of Salonae (today Solin near Split). In the first year of the rebellion, the Romans had to begin by organizing their resistance. The governor, Messallinus, boldly made his way to Dalmatia, and the commander of the neighbouring Moesian military district, Aulus Caecina Severus, made haste there with his Thracian auxiliaries to protect eastern Pannonia and Sirmium, but soon had to turn back to repel an invasion of Dacians in his own province. The war was fought on widely dispersed fronts, sometimes here and sometimes there, and the enemy was elusive.

The following year, AD 7, brought no relief and was if anything even more difficult, although not only Caecina but also the governor of Asia, Marcus Plautius Silvanus, came to the aid of the campaign with a number of units of all kinds hastily raised in the eastern provinces. With their five legions in all, and the ten led by Tiberius, along with an equally strong contingent of auxiliaries, of which Tiberius alone led seventy cohorts of infantry and ten squadrons of cavalry, besides the 10,000 veterans recalled to service and many volunteers, there were just under 150,000 men in the Pannonian area (not counting the Thracian auxiliaries)! But Caecina and Plautius found themselves in great difficulty in all but impassable country, and only just escaped the fate that the legions led by Varus were to suffer two years later: on this occasion it was not the leadership but the courage of the soldiers that saved the day.

Tiberius avoided concentrating his troops in one place and prudently divided them between the different battlefields, trying above all not to allow their supply links to their base camps to be broken. He was cautious, reviving his reputation as a general who knew what he was about and was not going to endanger his men unnecessarily. He also concerned himself with the physical and psychological well-being of his soldiers, trying to give them new courage when they felt dejected or despondent. His personal commitment and human proximity did much

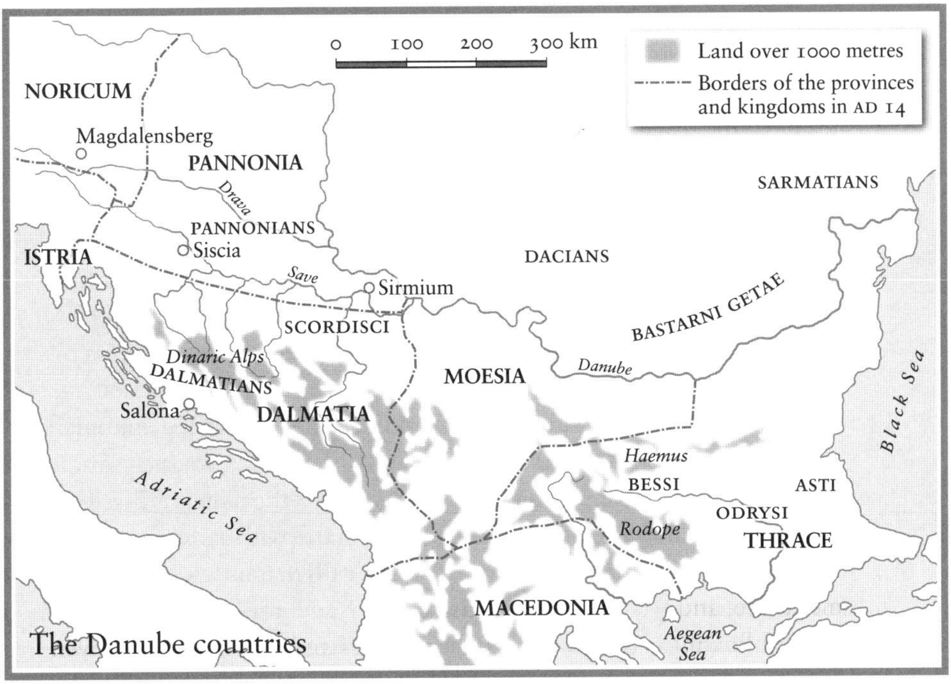
0 100 200 300 km
Land over 1000 metres
Borders of the provinces and kingdoms in AD 14
NORICUM
Magdalensberg
PANNONIA
Drava
PANNONIANS
Siscia
ISTRIA
Save
Sirmium
SCORDISCI
DACIANS
SARMATIANS
BASTARNI GETAE
Dinaric Alps
DALMATIANS
Salona
DALMATIA
MOESIA
Danube
Black Sea
Adriatic Sea
Haemus
BESSI
ASTI
ODRYSI
Rodope
THRACE
MACEDONIA
Aegean Sea
The Danube countries

to ensure that the army withstood this apparently never-ending war, which allowed hardly any conflicts on a battlefield, only laborious searching for an enemy who was then difficult to fight, since the rebels used guerrilla tactics. His hesitant way of waging war, averse as he was to making quick decisions, made the men miss his brother's brilliant forward-looking strategy, but was appropriate to this warfare of imponderable risks on many fronts.

Only the next year brought a change for the better. Added to the general exhaustion of the rebels were bottlenecks in their supplies, since no more provisions could be gleaned from the devastated countryside. First to surrender were the Breuci, with their leader Bato. At this point, obviously considering that the rebellion was as good as quelled, Tiberius left Pannonia, handing supreme command to his legate Marcus Aemilius Lepidus before returning to Rome. However, the war was not over yet. In the eastern, Dalmatian part of the rebel area a new danger arose in the shape of the other Bato, Bato of the Desidiati, who now rallied the rebels to him. Once again Tiberius had to return to Pannonia. His army, divided into three columns, combed the countryside thoroughly for the last of the rebels. The body of troops led by Tiberius himself, accompanied by Germanicus, who was still there, finally managed to hunt down Bato, defeat him and take him prisoner. Since Bato had once allowed Tiberius to escape a very dangerous situation, his life and the lives of his family were spared, and not much fuss was made about the other insurgents. Many of the younger men had to pay for their resistance by enslavement. For the rest, Tiberius used measures of forced recruitment to weaken the power of the tribesmen, as before with the Rhaetians. These measures affected mainly the Breuci.

As a result of new geographical knowledge, and the experience of security policy acquired during the war, the unusually large Pannonian-Dalmatian area, extending from the Central Danube to the Adriatic coast, which had formed a single province under the name of Illyricum, was now divided into two. The northern part, with its centre in the Save-Drau area, received the name of Upper Illyricum (later Pannonia); the southern part, with the coastal region and present-day southern Croatia, as well as Bosnia-Herzegovina and Montenegro, became Lower Illyricum (later Dalmatia). Extension of the road network in Illyricum now began. The main roads, running south-east along the rivers Save and Drau into the southern Balkans, were later among the great traffic routes of the empire. Equally important in the Augustan period, however, was the road leading north, from Aquileia over the lowest point of the eastern Alps, the Birnbaumer Wald pass into the Julian Alps (520 m), to Emona (now Laibach), founded by Tiberius, and on to Carnuntum by way of the Augustan military camp at Poetovio (Ptuj, Pettau). Beyond the Roman empire it continued north to the Baltic and was known as the Amber Road.

The triumph of the Romans was complete, but only a long war with many casualties, calling on all the forces of the empire, had made that triumph possible. Tiberius and Augustus were acclaimed by the title of *imperator*, and the former was even allowed his own triumph. But only a few days after the decrees honouring them for putting down the last rebellion in Pannonia had been passed, news arrived in Rome of the annihilation of Varus and his three legions. The result was another rebellion as bitter as the unrest in Pannonia; all the trouble, it seemed, was beginning again. When Tiberius arrived in Rome he refrained from celebrating his triumph for the time being and merely entered Rome

Gemma Augusta, sardonyx, 18 × 23 cm, probably AD 10/12.

Upper picture: Augustus in the attitude of Jupiter, sitting on a bench with Roma, the augur's staff in his right hand as a sign of his link with the gods, a lance in his left hand as a sign of dominium. Below him, the eagle of Jupiter, above him his star sign Capricorn. The personified goddess of the world, Oecumene, holds a citizen's crown (*corona civica*) above his head honouring him for saving the citizens. On the left, Tiberius (identified by his sign of the Zodiac, Scorpio) on a soldier's shield in the lower section) alighting from the triumphal chariot driven by Victoria to approach Augustus. An imperial prince, very probably Germanicus, stands between him and Roma. Below right, Italia or the earth goddess Tellus, above her a divine figure often interpreted as Oceanus or Chronos.

Lower picture: Roman soldiers and prisoners of war erecting a sign of victory (*tropaeum*). The figures to the right probably personify allied troops.

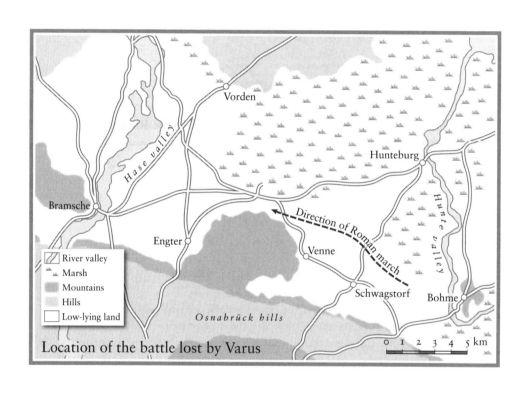

Vorden

Hunteburg

*Hase valley*

Bramsche

*Hunte valley*

Engter

Direction of Roman march

Venne

Schwagstorf

Bohme

*Osnabrück hills*

0  1  2  3  4  5 km

Location of the battle lost by Varus

with the laurel wreath of an *imperator* to receive solemn greetings from the state and people. He was shown particular honour as he sat with the consuls and Augustus. The famous Gem of Augustus in Vienna probably shows this triumphal return of Tiberius: marked as commander by his star sign of Scorpio, he descends from the triumphal chariot to approach Augustus, who, depicted as Jupiter by his attitude and symbols, receives him sitting on a bench with Roma. The warrior standing beside the triumphal chariot is probably Germanicus, who supported his adoptive father Tiberius so successfully in the war. The deities surrounding Augustus and Tiberius – Victoria and Italia, as well as Oekumene (the inhabited earth) and Oceanus – symbolize victory and the idea of world dominion, which is emphasized by the erection of the sign of victory (the *trophaeum*) and the captive barbarians in the lower part of the picture.

During the suppression of the Pannonian rebellion, all had been quiet in Germania. Sentius Saturninus had brought his army of the Rhine back in good order in the year 6. He seems to have known how to control the district entrusted to him with a mixture of diplomatic skill and the display of strength, while increasing Roman influence over Germania. It is possible that it was he who set up the altar of the Ubii (*ara Ubiorum*), the nucleus of what would one day be the city of Cologne. Just as the altar of Augustus at Lyon was intended to be the centre of the Celtic tribes and cities, the intention of this east-facing altar may have been to assemble the German tribes around it.

Germania was still only a military district and in addition it had not yet been fully explored, nor had detailed information been recorded, but it did seem to be merely waiting to be transferred to the administrative system of a province. Sentius, who was already over sixty years old, returned to Rome as one of the most esteemed members of the senatorial aristocracy. Much decorated himself, he was able to spend his old age in the knowledge that he had also ensured an established place in the upper ranks of the aristocracy for his family. His two sons Gaius and Gnaeus had been consuls in one and the same year (AD 4), a unique event at that time – one *consul ordinarius*, i.e. appointed at the beginning of the year, the other *consul suffectus*, suffect consul, appointed part of the way through the year. It was more likely early in the year 7 than at the end of the previous year that Saturninus was replaced as legate of the army of the Rhine and Germania by Publius Quinctilius Varus.

Varus was a skilful administrative official, but had acquired a certain amount of military experience in Syria in putting down unrest among the Jews. Although that fact, seen against the background of the catastrophe for which he was to be partly responsible, was unlikely to impress a professional military man like Velleius Paterculus, his appointment to commander of the army of the Rhine and governor of the Germanic military district does suggest that Augustus thought the qualities of an administrative expert were called for here. When our sources speak of Varus beginning to act in the manner of a provincial governor, administering the law, levying taxes and issuing edicts, that will have been an accurate account of the salient points of his activity, even if, in retrospect, it was held against him, sometimes viciously, as reprehensible. Velleius, for instance, comments that he behaved in the middle of Germania not like an army commander but like a Roman praetor legislating in the Forum in Rome. The main task facing Varus was undoubtedly to keep the peace in the German military district during the years of unrest in Pannonia, and his campaigns, or they might be called military displays, in the years 7 and 9 served that purpose. So did the time he spent in the summer camps, which he saw as administrative centres for his district.

In the year 9 Varus and his army pitched their summer camp on the river Weser. His retinue included Arminius, a man of distinguished origin among the Cherusci tribe. He had been brought up in Rome, had made his mark in the army while doing his military service, had become a Roman citizen and, although only in his mid-twenties, had even achieved equestrian rank. When Tiberius was commander of the army of the Rhine and Germania, he led the Cheruscian auxiliary contingent as military tribune.

Early in autumn, Varus and his army set out for their winter quarters on the Rhine. Before he began his march, he had been warned by Segestes, another eminent member of the Cherusci who had also received Roman citizenship, of a plot against him by German princes, but he clearly ascribed little importance to this warning. Roman armies had made the journey from the Weser to the Rhine by way of the fortified camps on the Lippe several times already; the terrain was not unknown. However, in the country of the Bructeri the three Roman legions advancing with a large baggage train and in loose formation – they were the Seventeenth, Eighteenth and Nineteenth Legions, with six cohorts of auxiliary troops and three cavalry squadrons – suddenly encountered strong German forces. These forces were led by Arminius, who had withdrawn from the Roman camp. He had chosen for the attack wooded, marshy land that had been prepared ahead of the coming battle in various ways, for instance by constructing obstacles. The Romans had to contend not only with this unexpected attack on difficult terrain but also with poor weather. Rain and storms presented the Roman soldiers with problems, making the going extremely difficult on the softened ground, and in addition they could not get a clear view of the various directions from which they were being attacked.

After the first assault Varus ordered his legions to erect a proper camp of the kind normal on the march. But the Germanic tribesmen, encouraged by their first success, prevented them from marching on in good order, so they soon became strung out along the ravines and narrow passes that had to be traversed. Even after the baggage train, in which there are said to have been women and children, was finally abandoned to its fate for the sake of the restoration of military discipline, the units, rapidly growing weaker, could no longer maintain any kind of marching order on the near-impassable terrain and were unable to hold their own for long as the tribesmen attacked again and again. The soldiers passed through rather more open country again for a small part of their way, but then the forest and the marshes closed in on them once more.

The ordeal of the legions and their auxiliary troops lasted for four days. The men managed to erect another camp, if only a provisional one, but after that the last of those still on their feet were cut down. Varus and his officers took their own lives, and many of the soldiers with them. Others flung themselves into the thick of the battle, intending to die. One of Varus' legates, Numonius Vala, tried to get away with those members of the squadrons still capable of fighting and reach the nearest fortified camp, but very few of them succeeded. Only a minority managed to flee from the battle; many were taken prisoner. The German tribesmen sacrificed the tribunes (colonels) and highest-ranking centurions (captains) to their local gods and shared out the others between themselves as slaves, or as loot for which they could demand ransom. There were many tales of heroism and desperation. Two of the legions' standards, the 'eagles', were taken and handed over to the Marsi and the Bructeri, though the standard-bearer of the third seems to have got his standard far enough away to elude immediate capture. This eagle, the standard of the Nineteenth Legion, was found five years later by the soldiers of Germanicus when they visited the battlefield; the other two eagles were also recovered on later campaigns in Germania. It was the greatest defeat of a Roman army since the disaster of Carrhae.

The first consequence of the battle was that the Romans abandoned those of their fortified camps in Germania that had not already been captured by the rebels. Only Aliso on the Lippe, where a few survivors of Varus' army had managed to take refuge after a long march, was still left to Rome, although after the withdrawal of the Germans the men of its garrison left the fort of their own accord and made their way to the Rhine. Here, they were received by Varus' legate Lucius Nonius Asprenas, commanding the two remaining legions of the army of the Rhine, stationed in Mainz. When news of the disaster had come he had kept a cool head, maintained discipline among the terrified soldiers, and by marching to the northern camp of Vetera (Xanten), to which Varus had meant to go, kept the Celtic tribes of Gaul from rebelling and the Germans from crossing the Rhine.

Until a few years ago the details given in our sources were not clear enough for the site of the battlefield to be determined. For a long time it was described as 'the battle in the Teutoburg forest' because Tacitus, who gives the most concrete details about the site of the battle, locates it 'in the Teutoburg forest' (*Teutoburgiensis saltus*); the place, he says, lay not far from the more distant part of the land of the Bructeri, in the country between Ems and the Lippe. However, it is not clear which of the many mountain ranges of moderate height in this region we are to understand by that. The range that was given the name of the Teutoburg Forest in the seventeenth century (and not before; its older name is Osning) was rather arbitrarily identified with the site mentioned by Tacitus. In the course of time many other suggestions have been proposed, including some that diverge entirely from the data provided by Tacitus, which do at least allow the scene of the battle to be roughly located.

A hundred years ago Theodor Mommsen suspected, on the grounds of extensive finds of coins, that the battlefield was in the Barenaue district east of Bramsche in the country near Osnabrück, but he was not believed. After further finds of coins more recently, and then successful investigation and excavation (since 1987), an extensive battlefield was discovered there. Its situation and size, as well as the finds already made, show that, with probability verging on certainty, it can be identified with the site of the catastrophe that overtook Varus. The identification is backed up by the huge number of finds made on the battlefield, in particular Roman coins, amounting by 1996 to 360 denarii and just under 500 bronze coins, as well as military objects including 600 bronze items of good size, and recent finds of collections of bones buried over a period of one to ten years (confirming what Tacitus tells us about the visit of Germanicus and his army to the battlefield in the year 15 and the subsequent interment of the fallen). Ramparts have also been excavated, obviously set up as a short-term means of barricading the valley, and the finds are copious here. Above all, however, the fact that none of the coins found on the battlefield was minted after the year AD 9 will hardly admit of any other interpretation. At least, we know of no other great battle of that time that would account for this complex of finds.

The burial place lies in a valley between a foothill of the Wiehen-gebirge range, Mount Kalkriese, which is from 60 to 120 metres high, and the Grosses Moor (Great Marsh). The marsh here extends so far into the hills that only two narrow reinforced tracks over sandy soil make it passable today, one directly up the slope and the other some 150 metres further north on the borders of the marsh (known as the old army road). An army coming from the mid-Weser, wishing to avoid this moderately high range of hills, and thus making for their northern edge by way of the present Münsterland region, to reach the forts on the Lippe and go on to the Lower Rhine, would have to pass through this valley.

Once news of the battle had reached Rome, the first question asked was how such a thing could have happened. The place had been known for almost a generation, the Romans were familiar with the locality, and operations in terrain that could be easily surveyed were no great problem for a battle-hardened army. Many of the survivors, including some ransomed prisoners, gave the Roman leadership very good information about the course of the battle, echoed by our sources and to a very high degree confirmed by the Kalkriese excavations. Varus was blamed for heedlessly ignoring the warnings of Segestes that a plot was brewing, but he cannot be said to have been particularly remiss. There was a great deal of wrangling among the German princes; the Roman commanders were certainly well accustomed to that, and few could have regarded Arminius, a man who had received special honour from the Romans, as a potential rebel. As for the military side of the catastrophe, we do indeed have to consider Varus culpably careless on the march back to the Rhine. He must have felt he was already in a reasonably well-secured province, or at least that no particular precautions were necessary. That is the only way to explain the clear indication in the sources that the army was advancing in too loose a formation, or at least not in the good military order required for the march, and that the narrow pass on Mount Kalkriese had not been reconnoitred well enough.

While this failure on the Roman side is clear, there remains the reason for the German revolt. Attempts have been made to present Arminius as the man who freed Germania from Rome, with reference to Tacitus, who expressly calls him 'the undoubted liberator of Germania'. However, Tacitus wrote this – like Cassius Dio, who is also cited on this point – at a time when the aim of making Germania a province had long been abandoned, and the German tribes, on the basis of a critical survey of contemporary political and moral conditions, could be presented as a positive counterpart to Roman society. It was a long time since the conquest of Germania and thus its 'liberation' had been a political reality. The late interpretations which see the battle of the German forces against Varus as a joint revolt by several tribes against foreign rule by Rome and which chiefly derive from national or even nationalistic modern interpretations of the battle spring from a wish to consider the German rebellion as a spontaneous uprising of the people against the Roman occupying power.

Taking our knowledge of the mentality, politics and society of the German tribes of the time as our starting point, however, there is little room for ideas of a broad popular uprising against Roman rule. The picture of an aristocratic upper class guiding decisions in its own interests, and itself rife with rivalry, fits what we know better than a movement of 'the people'. There is something to be said for seeing the basic motive for the 'rising' in the tensions in the lives of many German aristocrats, including Arminius, divided between two entirely different worlds, one Roman, one German. Perceiving it as merely a rebellion incited by Arminius, leader of an auxiliary contingent of Cherusci warriors, is a thesis in which the actual motive for his defection – whether tension between German chiefs, personal differences between them and the Roman military leadership or opposition to certain Roman administrative measures – remains entirely in the dark. Perhaps the unrest was also set off, like the Pannonian rebellion a few years earlier, by indignation at the introduction of taxes and the specific way in which they were levied, and our sources do suggest that. However we assess it, we should remember that Arminius was not acting on his own, for not only Cherusci but also Bructeri and Marsi took part in the attack, and the evidence is the standards found in their territories. After their victory over the Roman troops all that the German tribesmen tried to do was to impress the mighty Marbod, who had ambitious plans for expanding his area of influence, by sending him the head of Varus to deter him from taking action against their tribes. It was certainly not an invitation to him to join the 'uprising'.

The catastrophe horrified Rome; many probably thought of the invasion of the empire by the Cimbri and the Teutones a hundred years earlier, and saw the German tribes already marching on the city. Augustus was deeply distressed by the loss of one-eighth of his legions. It was said that, on hearing the terrible news, he knocked his head against a door, crying out, 'Quinctilius Varus, give me my legions back!' and that he tore his garments and would not have his hair and beard trimmed for months as a sign of mourning. To nip any unrest in the bud, he had Rome secured by the army, dismissed his German bodyguard and extended the period of service of all Roman governors to avoid further turmoil and ensure continuity. He also tried to create a replacement for the lost legions by raising more troops and recruiting volunteers. Since the Romans, no longer used to the militia system, did not flock to join the army, he punished a certain number of those who refused to join by imposing large fines on them and cancelling their civil rights and even had some executed. Above all, however, the army of the Rhine was not only restored to its old strength, it was further consolidated. It very soon had eight legions. This naturally meant that the strength of the army in other parts of the empire was reduced; legions were transferred to the Rhine from the Spanish and Illyrian provinces, which could on the whole be considered pacified. None of the new legions formed now or later were given the number of any of those annihilated in Germania: the Seventeenth, Eighteenth and Nineteenth Legions. Those numbers were felt to have ominous significance.

\*

Tiberius was appointed to supreme command of the troops on the Rhine. He went there in the year 10 and made it his first task to discipline the troops, who had been demoralized by their crushing defeat. He did this in two ways: first by demonstrating that he felt particularly close to the soldiers and officers, and second by showing patriarchal severity towards any lax or insubordinate conduct, sometimes dealing rigorously with offenders, even in the case of a legionary legate, a man holding the rank of general. With his army now reinforced, and its morale restored, he crossed the Rhine in the year 11, but operated in enemy territory with a caution even greater than his typical circumspection. He not only had to regain the terrain that had been lost, he must also restore the faith of the troops in themselves and their leaders. There was no major battle: Tiberius was content to lay waste enemy territory, extend the army roads and lay out fortifications in many places, for instance between the camp at Xanten and the Lippe. In the year 12 he also carried out naval manoeuvres, where the Chauci on the coast, as it happened, had remained loyal to the Romans, and he even chalked up some military successes. He had to break off any further actions for the time being because of a rebellion in Vienna (modern Vienne), a city in Gallia Narbonensis.

In the year 11 Germanicus, Tiberius' adopted son, took part in the campaign in Germania. After his brilliant success in Pannonia, also achieved under the supreme command of his adoptive father, this campaign in a second great theatre of war which, like Pannonia, was also an area in crisis, meant more than just further training in military leadership. It could not be concealed from either soldiers or civilians that Augustus saw Germanicus, who through his mother was directly related to the Julians, as the successor he ultimately wanted. Tiberius, successful general that he was and officially the heir designate of Augustus, cannot have found this easy to bear, particularly as he had a son of his own blood, Drusus (II), only a little younger than Germanicus. It was bound to look as if Germanicus were being preferred to him. In the year 12, when Tiberius was also campaigning in Germania, Germanicus, not yet twenty-seven years old, held the consulate, while his cousin (and brother by adoption) Drusus was only quaestor. Augustus, who was beginning to feel his strength fail, was obviously preparing for the succession. His arrangements for the following year show that equally clearly. Germanicus was now appointed governor of the three parts of Gaul, and as successor to Tiberius in supreme command of the army of the Rhine he went there, as Velleius writes, 'to deal with the remains of the war'. He stayed there through the year 14, and among other things held a census. Tiberius was to go to Illyricum to consolidate the peace there. He was not able to leave until summer, but as soon as he had set off, news of Augustus' serious illness recalled him to Campania.

There is nothing to suggest that the activities of the Romans on the Rhine and in Germania after the battle lost by Varus were merely a rearguard action designed to weaken the German tribes and prevent them from crossing the river. The policy of occupation was still being pursued even if, after the Varus catastrophe, in a very circumspect and initially low-key way. In his account of his deeds, written just under four years after Varus' battle, Augustus regards Germania as a Roman province: 'I extended the borders of all those Roman provinces to which people who were not under our sway were neighbours. I pacified the Gallic and Spanish provinces, as well as Germania, with the Ocean from Gades (Cádiz) to the mouth of the Elbe.' At the end of his life, Augustus regarded the land between the Elbe, the Rhine, the North Sea and the Main as the Roman province of Germania.

The main centre of gravity in foreign policy in the mid-Augustan and late Augustan period was the German and Illyrian area. Because Illyricum was so important, particularly after the great rebellion between AD 6 and 9, special attention was also paid to the district extending to the Lower Danube north of the province of Macedonia. Incursions by the tribes living here, or by Dacians crossing the river to raid the countryside, not only disturbed the peace near Macedonia, but also impaired the security of Illyricum. Since the campaigns of Crassus, the Roman military leadership had treated the area between Macedonia and the Lower Danube as a Roman sphere of interest, but obviously not with a view to annexing it, rather to ensuring its loyalty to Rome through client princes. Only if there was resistance to Roman supremacy, or invasion by tribes from the other side of the Danube, for instance the Sarmates of Scythia or the Thracian Getae, who lived on both banks of the Lower Danube, did the military troops stationed in Macedonia go into action. Many tribes, like the Scordisci, could also be repelled from

Illyricum. The armies of Macedonia and Illyricum worked very closely together during the Augustan period, and military aid sometimes also came from the provinces further to the east.

The most extensive military campaign here, after Crassus, was that of Lucius Calpurnius Piso (*pontifex*). Initially active in the east, he had the mission of opposing the Thracian Bessi, who were putting pressure both on the Thracian princes allied to Rome and on the province itself. He fought them very successfully between 13 and 11 BC. Another major operation in this area was the war waged nearly twenty years later by the consular Sextus Aelius Catus against the Getae on the Lower Danube, 50,000 of whom he forced to settle on the nearer bank of the river in order to take pressure off the Danube. While the area between the Lower Danube and Macedonia, later to include the province of Moesia, was not made a full province by Augustus, a special military district was set up here even before the Pannonian and Dalmatian rebellion, the legions stationed in Macedonia being moved further north for that purpose. The district was bordered to the east and north by the Black Sea and the Lower Danube, and to the west by a line west of the Magus (Morava). Thrace itself was exempted from the military district.

The second potential flashpoint in Roman foreign policy was the border with the Parthian empire. In 20 BC the Euphrates had been agreed as a border, and the Armenian question was solved by deciding that their region should not be made a province but instead have a ruler installed or at least recognized by Rome. On the whole the agreement held good, although there was still some danger because of the convoluted Armenian and Parthian palace intrigues. When Tigranes, made king by Rome in the year 20 BC, died, the Armenians could not agree on a successor, and several rulers followed one after another. Gaius Caesar, whom Augustus sent to the east with special full powers in the year 1 BC, was unable to sort out anything final.

Whether the agreements of the year 20 BC really represented a permanent solution would be discovered after the death of Phraates IV of Parthia, with whom the settlement had been made. After he was murdered in the year 2 BC, everything pointed to a new understanding in the spirit of the old one. In AD 1 Gaius Caesar, in discussion with the successor in the Parthian royal line, young Phraates V, known as Phraatakes, did confirm the earlier agreements – despite the warlike remarks of Ovid in his *Ars Amatoria*, which had just appeared. Ovid already saw young Gaius as the avenger of Carrhae and conqueror of the east and may have been expressing the hopes of many distinguished armchair strategists at home. To demonstrate that the meeting was between equals in rank, it took place on an island in the Euphrates, and both Gaius and Phraates came with a military retinue of considerable size. There could not, or course, be any question of independence from Rome for the Parthian empire, but the king had very good reasons for showing that he wanted peace and would comply with the old agreements. His elder brothers, the sons of his father's earlier marriage, also had a legitimate claim to the throne but were still in Rome, where their father had sent them in order to ensure the succession of his younger son, and the existence of this Roman bargaining counter left the king in a difficult predicament. Consequently a condition of the renewed agreement was that his brothers should stay in Rome.

But the royal carousel of Parthia kept turning. Not only was Phraates V assassinated a few years later, so was his successor, and after the Parthians had asked Augustus to send them one of the sons of Phraates IV living in Rome, Vonones arrived. His countrymen so disliked the Graeco-Roman manners acquired by the prince during his education in Rome, which he did not abandon now he was king of Parthia, that he was soon exiled. Artabanos III then ascended the throne and was still ruling at the time of the death of Augustus. Vonones, now in flight, managed to seize the throne of Armenia. This was the state of affairs at the beginning of the reign of Tiberius.

The region could not have been described as pacified in the year AD 14. There was unrest because the Armenians were busily involved in the question of the occupation of their throne and so did not always do as Rome wished. There was also the fact that in view of the problem of the Armenian succession the Parthians were doing their utmost to exploit every opportunity to install a king in Armenia whom they liked. On the whole, however, the agreement of the year 20, even in a critical situation, was still the point where the political conduct of those involved converged. In view of the instability of the Armenian throne and the Parthian situation, not much more could be expected, and for that reason, despite the general confusion, the Romans did not take the chance of behaving aggressively, so that there was still an impression that this border was in a desirably peaceful state. Augustus remained on the defensive here, and in principle this restraint applied to Roman policy in the area for another hundred years.

For centuries, the borders with the tribes of the north on the Rhine and the Danube, as well as those with the Parthians on the Euphrates, remained the line of defence, guarded with watchful suspicion, against what went on just beyond the frontier. In retrospect those frontiers seemed like a firm line for which Augustus had striven from the first. We have seen that in fact that was not the case; at least, at the time of his death all was still in flux in Germania, and the Danube did not form an established unbroken border. The other borders of the empire – the Black Sea, the Arabian desert, the Sahara and the Ocean – seemed to present no problems, and yet three areas required special attention.

First there was the north coast of the Black Sea, where the Romans showed an interest in the so-called Bosphorean empire, the centre of which was the Greek cities on both sides of the Cimmerian Bosphorus (the straits at modern Kertsch). The region had long been part of the Hellenic cultural area. In the late republic Mithradates, ruler of the kingdom of Pontos on the coast of the Black Sea in Asia Minor, had seized it, and in 14 BC King Ptolemon of Pontos, installed there by Antony and confirmed in his position by Augustus, united his region with that of the Cimmerian Bosphorus. When Agrippa travelled to the east after the Secular Games of the year 17, equipped with full powers as a colleague of Augustus, he supported the ambitions of Ptolemon and in 14 BC, on hearing news of hostility to Rome in the Crimea, even went at once to the north coast of the Black Sea. However, when Agrippa arrived in Sinope (Sinop), the situation in the Crimea had stabilized again, and he no longer needed to intervene. Even after political affairs there had changed, when Ptolemon died in 8 BC, his successors recognized Roman supremacy in so far as they sought confirmation from Rome of their right to the throne. The region could therefore continue to be regarded as within the Roman sphere of interest. Incorporation of this region in the Crimea and on the Cimmerian Bosphorus among the client principalities of Rome, however, did not entail any dynamic move into the south of Russia. The Bosphorean empire turned its eyes towards the Black Sea and as a part of the Greek world was more of an appendage of Asia Minor; with only a loose link to Rome. None the less, Roman activity in that region meant that the Black Sea, its coast now

Roman as far as the mouth of the Danube, was declared a Roman inland sea.

It was different on the land border of several thousand kilometres in Africa, to the south of the three provinces of Egypt, Cyrenaica (Cyrene) and Africa Proconsularis (today roughly equivalent to Tunisia and eastern Algeria), as well as the kingdom of Mauretania (western Algeria and Morocco), a client kingdom of Rome under Juba. Here, especially on the southern border of Egypt, beyond the First Cataract or rapids of the Nile, the frontier had been unstable for thousands of years. The Ethiopians kept making incursions into the Nile valley from the south. They were Nubians from the north of present Sudan – the land of Kush of ancient Egypt. Roman operations in the south of the province may be regarded as campaigns in the tradition of the Egyptian pharaohs, defensive battles rather than expeditions of conquest to gain access to the Nubian gold-mines.

The first prefect of Egypt, Gaius Cornelius Gallus, had taken the field against the Ethiopians in the years 30 and 29, operating from the southern province of Thebais. Similarly, when his successor as prefect, Aelius Gallus, set out in the year 25 on his Arabian expedition, he is said to have received orders from Augustus to keep an eye on Ethiopia on the other side of the Red Sea. Nothing came of that because the Arabian expedition failed. Only a little later the successor of Aelius Gallus, Gaius Petronius, mounted an expedition over the southern border of Egypt into Ethiopian territory. The occasion for it was an attack on the most southerly garrison of Egypt in Syene, which had three cohorts to secure it. Not only the garrison itself but also Elephantine on the opposite bank and the Nile island of Philae had been overrun. Perhaps the incursion was connected with the extensive military exposure of Egypt during the Arabian campaign of Aelius Gallus the year before. At any rate, Petronius' expedition was not an independent campaign of conquest; its aim was to secure the southern border. After Petronius had repelled the attack on Syene, he went on into Nubian territory in 24–22 and even reached Napata, the ancient outlying city of the Ethiopians, situated a little way above the Fourth Cataract, destroyed the city and came back with a large amount of plunder. After another campaign he sent the envoys of the Ethiopians who had come to him to Augustus, who was on Samos at the time, and Augustus did not miss his chance to mention, in his account of his deeds, that under his rule the Romans had reached

Ethiopia. That did not mean that Ethiopia had been conquered; the operation had only pushed the border a little further south to what was known as 'twelve-mile land' (Dodekashoinos).

On the southern border of the other two African provinces, and in the south of Mauretania, the Romans had to contend with the nomadic tribes of the steppes and the deserts, particularly the Garamantes and Gaetuli. Their hostility was probably due not least to the settlement of Romans who took over their fertile grazing areas. South of Cyrenaica and Africa Proconsularis there was repeated fighting to hold back the Garamantes, as we can tell from the award of several triumphs to the governors in office there between 34 and 28 BC. In the years 21/20 Lucius Cornelius Balbus was very successful against them, and in AD 5/6 so was Cossus Cornelius Lentulus against the Gaetuli, both as governors of Africa Proconsularis at the time. Balbus had even advanced to Garama, an outlying city of the Garamantes far in the south. However, that did not mean that the tribes were conquered; fighting continued after the death of Augustus. He dealt with the threat represented by the desert tribes by stationing a legion in the south-west of the African province, the *legio tertia Augusta*, at Ammaedara (today Haidra in the west of central Tunisia).

The third region to be mentioned in connection with Roman expansion was in the north. Ever since Octavian's command of the west of the empire as a triumvir, there had been repeated talk among Roman writers, particularly Horace, of an expedition to Britannia. Such a venture would of course have been in the tradition of Caesar, who had landed there twice, more to discover the lie of the land and the difference between British and Gallic Celts than with any idea of conquest. Horace was already seeing the Britons as enemies to be defeated in the year 39, and when Augustus set off north after the great settlement of the year 27, the *princeps* seems in fact to have thought at first of a crossing to Britannia. It cannot have been more than a wish to emulate the dictator. In his account of his own deeds, Augustus mentions only two British princes who had fled to him, and if other princes from the island brought gifts to Capitoline Jupiter in Rome, it was no more than a sign of mutual goodwill between all concerned. At this time, and during the reign of Augustus, the Romans never seriously set their sights on Britannia. The Ocean was the border, here and elsewhere.

*

At no time, whether before or after Augustus, were the borders of the Roman empire extended so far as during his reign. The Alpine area with its foothills to the Danube, the region that today is Austria (Noricum), the entire Dalmatian hinterland to the Drau and again on to the Danube, as well as the region between the Lower Danube and Macedonia and the north-west of Spain, all these regions were turned into provinces or else – as on the Lower Danube – were governed by client princes dependent on Rome. From the Iberian peninsula to the Crimea, from the coast of the North Sea to the Sahara, all obeyed the orders of Rome. The great achievements of Augustus were not ignored even a hundred years after his death. Augustus, so Tacitus writes, had enclosed the empire within the bounds of the Ocean and rivers lying very far away; legions, provinces and fleets had linked them all. To anyone looking in retrospect there seemed to be a plan behind it all, with frontiers drawn principally in the interests of security. This was bound to seem all the more plausible because the empire as a whole consolidated itself within the boundaries as they existed in the year AD 14, and Augustus therefore seemed to have established them in advance as lines that could be particularly well defended.

The beginnings of this expansion do not, as we have seen, point that way. At the start we find action not freely chosen but pre-decided in order to secure the empire, namely the final 'pacification' of the entire Iberian peninsula, the protection of Italy and Gaul by the occupation of the Alpine region and the securing of rule over any rivals, resulting in the first conquests in the hinterland of Dalmatia. And it was not the dictates of security that led to continuation of the military policy of expansion after these initial aims were achieved, it went on because the means to carry it out were available and thus the chance to put such a policy into practice. The state was now ruled by a monarch who had come to power and was kept in power by soldiers. The standing army was the engine of expansion.

It is obvious that the policy of achieving security through 'forward defence' very soon became an independent entity. Once you were on the other side of the Alps, there were new conclusions to be drawn from it. The Rhine could and must now be watched from a different viewpoint, from the south-east, and measures of military policy adjusted accordingly. In the south-east, the Romans had reached the Save during Octavian's campaign of 35 to 33 BC, and had advanced beyond that river. Octavian had not aimed to pursue any policy of security or expansion by his campaign at the time; he had been concerned with reinforcing the link between him and the army and strengthening his position against his rival Antony. With his campaigns against the Alpine tribes and the Germans on the right bank of the Rhine between the years 16 and 9, the borderlines reached in Dalmatia and Pannonia acquired very different significance. A policy no longer motivated by home affairs but aiming for expansion had to look for regions that it might overcome, and in addition the positions achieved in the year 33 proved untenable, given the geographical and ethnic problems of that region. If there was no further advance, then territory would have to be given up, but that – leaving aside the loss of prestige entailed – would have been pointless because, with the occupation of the foothills of the Alps and Noricum, a link to the south, Macedonia and the eastern provinces by way of Dalmatia/Pannonia had become essential.

In fact before the Alpine campaign, the Roman leadership will already have felt called upon to improve the land route from Italy to Macedonia, so there is some justification for modern historians who see the conquest of the entire Illyrian area, beginning with Octavian's venture into Dalmatia, in this light. The coastal road from Aquileia to Macedonia was difficult going, indeed near impassable, so the usual way from Italy to the east had been by the sea route across the Adriatic and the Ionian. But there were much more suitable conditions for a long-distance road in the interior of the Balkan peninsula. However, we should not reconstruct the aim of a conquest of the whole of Illyricum *ex eventu*, from the fact that the great army road later ran from Aquileia by way of Emona (Laibach), Siscia, Sirmium, Naissus (Niš) and Philippopolis (Plovdiv) to Byzantium (Istanbul). With the borders of the empire in the year 35 in mind, it seems absurd to suppose that Rome would have set out to conquer territories hitherto entirely unknown for the sake of building a road to the Bosphorus rather than extending the coastal road. In retrospect, however, the acquisition of these regions proved important and useful, and seen in this light Germania looked like a desirable extension of Roman influence, not just because of the Rhine border, which was under repeated pressure from the German tribes, but also as seen from Noricum and Pannonia. Perhaps, looking back at that time later, one would have had to say that the acquisition of the Dalmatian and Pannonian region was not absolutely necessary, but it was worth striving for. The eastern policy pursued by Augustus shows that ideas of security rather than imperialism were uppermost in his mind. Once easily defensible positions on the Euphrates and the highlands of Armenia had been reached, he left matters as they were. If he had wanted to do more, and cross that line – which as it happened Pompey had reached back in the sixties – in order to gain more land, he would have been venturing into the heartland provinces of Persia and would then have faced the necessity of overthrowing the entire Persian empire. Augustus was not Alexander; he followed Roman tradition and out of consideration for the security of his own regime he could not abandon the positions he had reached.

In the later years of Augustus, it was clear that the military expansion had been a severe drain on the powers of Rome. The extraordinary opportunities apparently offered by a standing army, not raised for a particular purpose but always present, made it difficult to see the point of limiting military activities. The tried and tested Roman army, a vast body of men, faced nothing even remotely comparable beyond the borders of the empire. Caesar had shown how easy it was to advance into large territories and occupy them – apart, that is, from the Parthian empire. The rebellions in the Pannonian and Dalmatian area and in Germania slowed down this dynamic advance. Not only did recruitment become more difficult; the specific conditions of the years 44 to 35 were not likely to recur. The expense of the army also became a serious problem, for it had to be met by taxation and could no longer be provided by funds seized from the property of proscribed men and cities, or plunder of the kind taken from Alexandria after the battle of Actium. War would no longer feed the army; the inhabitants of the empire had to provide for it. In addition, the question of a smooth succession to the principate that arose in the last years of Augustus was also affected by the army. The *princeps* had to consider the appointment of generals and the number of legions and provinces to be transferred to them very carefully before making any decisions. The army and the rule of the empire were locked in an indissoluble relationship.

According to Tacitus, Augustus added to the sheaf of notes in his own hand that he left to be given to his successor Tiberius on his death a piece of advice: to stay within the bounds of his *imperium* in future and refrain from further expansion. We may leave aside the additional remark made by Tacitus that it was not certain whether he wrote this out of concern for the empire or malice (directed against Tiberius), since that derives from Tacitus' own claim to be able to reveal the truth about Augustus and the principate, which we shall not be studying here. There has been controversy among historians on whether in giving this advice Augustus was thinking of the frontier of the empire on the Euphrates, or on the Rhine and the Elbe. Since he considered Germania a part of the empire in his last years, it must have been the border with the Parthians that he had in mind, and we also know that Roman society was at least subliminally considering a Parthian war even after the year 20 BC. But perhaps what he wrote says more: it is evidence of a certain resignation, in contrast to a dynamic foreign policy. Military setbacks, the difficulty of financing and supplying the army, and the recurrent and virulent problem of rivalry between successful generals made Augustus not faint-hearted, but certainly more modest in his aims.

There was no further thought of rounding off border areas to the north on a large scale. The sudden loss of three legions in the year 9, and the difficulty of finding replacements for them, raised the question of whether the number of legions was sufficient to secure the empire. Compared with conditions today, the Roman part of the army was not unusually large, consisting of less than 1.5 per cent of Roman citizens. But the burden of taxation on the population did not match modern standards; it was much less. The financial problem therefore tempered plans for any enlargement of the army, and so did the fear of a rival who, with the support of part of the army, might take power. Augustus was fortunate to have had such a loyal man beside him as Agrippa, as well as capable generals within his own family on whom he could rely. Twenty-five legions, together with the guard of the city of Rome and the soldiers of the fleet, as well as auxiliary contingents of roughly the same strength, seemed enough to secure the borders against invasions and put down any rebellions in provinces not yet fully pacified. But further expansion, imponderable and risky as it would be, was impossible with the arsenal in its present state, as Augustus must soon have realized. Pannonia and Germania had muted the vigour of the army. The empire remained as it was, with the inclusion of Germania between the Rhine and the Elbe.

Augustus therefore left behind him an international empire well secured by the army. Nothing like it has been seen to this day. It provided not only the conditions for maintaining order at home, that is to say for the survival of the monarchy as a principate in the following centuries, but also for development from an empire based on rule over defeated subjects to an empire made up entirely of Romans, and thus the conditions for the creation of our Western world. However, let us look once more not at that future prospect, but at the ideas of contemporaries. Augustus saw the empire as dominion over the world, and himself as ruler of that world, and so did the people who lived in it at the time. The Romans accepted and praised their world empire as a political achievement, without the slightest doubt that their dominion was justified, and as in the future the provincials too were cared for by the empire they were all the more likely to agree. Rule over other nations was never seen in classical antiquity as a phenomenon requiring thought; the concept is always seen in a positive light, whether we think of the Persians, the Carthaginians or the Athenians. The Romans were no exception, and why should they be, when they were obviously more capable than any other people?

So everyone, first and foremost the Roman writers, hailed the domination of the world by Rome. We have already discussed Virgil, but it is easy to list many others who rejoiced. Horace often did so, and after the great victories of Tiberius and Drusus against the tribes of the Alps and their foothills in 15 BC he wrote another celebration of victory. Hardly a line is devoted to the idea of revenge as the occasion for war, or any other theme to justify it; a surge of pride in the victories of Rome hides all the misery of the defeated, their loss of freedom as well as devastation and death; the real victor, Augustus, is seen surrounded by the glory of world dominion that blanks out all those moving outside the borders, including them in the victory even if they were defeated peoples who happened to live in the empire now, for instance the Cantabrians and Indians, the Medes, Persians, Scythians, Sarmates or Britons, among whom not a single Roman cohort was stationed. Rome was everywhere you looked, and the same justification for its supremacy was always given: the Roman law and Roman peace. How could the Vindelicians be ignorant of Roman law? Once defeated they knew about it. The Pannonians, says Velleius, had become over-bold after the benefits of a long peace, and so rebelled against the rule of Rome. They showed themselves unworthy of the blessings of Rome and did not value the Pax Romana as they should. But it was possible to help these stupid

barbarians. They had to be taught what they did not know for themselves, the virtues of peace and the law, that is to say civilized Roman
behaviour. Bato of the Desidiati showed his understanding of Roman
ways when, after he had been taken prisoner, he replied to Tiberius, on
being asked why he had defected from Rome and waged war for so long
against the Romans: 'It is your own fault. For you sent wolves to guard
your flocks, not dogs and laws.' Once again the Roman empire was in
good order, for Bato had assumed unthinkingly that Roman rule lay in
the governors and orders sent from Rome – the 'dogs and laws' – while
all he was complaining of was poor treatment of the defeated by the
Romans. Here before Tiberius stood a subject complaining of the blessings that Roman rule brought the peoples. Bato was to have the Pax
Romana. World domination is a fine thing when you are on the side of
those who dominate. Perhaps not Bato himself, but his descendants had
a chance to be on the right side, always assuming, of course, that they
adopted Roman law and the Pax Romana as their own.

# 15

# The Struggle for the Succession
# and the Last Years

When Rome celebrated the Secular Festival in the year 17 BC, the monarchy seemed to have been consolidated in the form of a principate, the empire was in good order, and its frontiers secured. Augustus could look at his work with satisfaction and pride. We can detect his sense that he could now rely on the stability of his regime, trusting in the consent to it of the citizens of Rome and the inhabitants of the provinces, in many events of the time, including the magnificent organization of the Secular Games, intended to feature as the high point of his government so far and sum up its achievements.

In 16 BC Augustus embarked on his policy of expansion to the north, and he himself set off for Gaul in the summer of that year. He stayed in the western provinces for three years. Agrippa had gone to the eastern provinces a year earlier, and he was not to return to Rome until the year 13, only a few months before Augustus himself. In the year 18 Augustus had arranged the granting to Agrippa of one of the two fundamental powers of the *princeps*, official tribunician power (*tribunicia potestas*), conferring on him the rights necessary for political activity in the administrative centre of Rome, and before he set off for the east the Senate also renewed, for the same length of time, his tenure of the other power, proconsular power (*imperium proconsulare*), relating to provincial administration and military leadership. He thus held the two fundamental powers of the *princeps* in parallel with Augustus, whose proconsular power the Senate had also extended for the same period in the year 18, and although many official and honorary rights held by Augustus were not also given to Agrippa, he could be regarded as the former's colleague in the principate. He was clearly second to Augustus in rank, but equal in respect of their fundamental powers. The division of tasks between them is undoubtedly to be understood as a division of labour between the two outstanding men of the empire, although Augustus carried much more weight as *princeps* and the man responsible for active military policy in the west.

As the husband of Augustus' only daughter, Julia, Agrippa belonged to his close family circle. He was not only friend and aide, but also the father of the male descendants of the Julian family so much desired by Augustus. By the time Agrippa went to the east, Julia had already borne him two sons: Gaius, three years old when his father left, and Lucius, who was not born until the summer of 17. Augustus adopted them, making them his sons as well as his grandsons. The adoption made it clear to the Roman public that Augustus had not designated Agrippa his successor, and if he himself were to die when the boys were still under age, Agrippa was merely to deputize for them.

At this time Augustus was in the prime of life. He had only just passed his mid-forties, so his obvious concern about the succession may seem excessive. But in fact some indication of his intentions had long been expected, not only by his immediate circle but also by hundreds of thousands of people who depended on him. A monarchy now ten years old had followed the struggle for power, when such considerations were far from anyone's mind, and for fear of a new outbreak of civil war the Romans might well be anxious to have some idea of the succession to Augustus. Without a decision on that point, would not several candidates feel called upon to claim the inheritance and finally seek to settle the matter by force of arms? When the principate was founded in the year 27, the youth of the *princeps* had kept the problem of how this new order of things could continue after his death in the background. Now, however, a new generation had grown up: young people who, like Julia, already had children of their own.

There was a particular difficulty inherent in the succession to the principate. Formally, it was not a monarchy but an office set up by the Senate, and Augustus was not a dynast but the holder of a number of powers legally granted to him. While the soldiers, like most of the citizens, also saw him as their patron whose word was law and whose authority (*auctoritas*) stood for legal power, that was so only in practice, not in the legal formalities, and of all the Romans his closest and most powerful aides from the senatorial aristocracy saw that most clearly. For the principate was a compromise between them and the holder of military power, who

derived his strength and his claim to legality from the constitutional law
of the republic and thus from a legal constitution. Without the cloak of
legality worn by the man who in fact wielded power, Rome would have
been back with the military dictatorship of the triumvirate period. However, the *princeps* could not leave his official position to anyone else; it
could be passed on only through his fundamental tribunician and proconsular powers, and those were in the gift of the Senate. Since Agrippa
now shared them, he appeared as the successor-designate who, if Augustus were suddenly to die, would also receive the other rights and honours
not yet granted to him, and which he would need in order to take the
place of Augustus fully. But if Augustus survived Agrippa, some day Julia's
sons, whose adoption by Augustus had marked them out as his heirs,
would have to be granted those powers by the Senate.

The question of the succession to Augustus was prominent in the
second half of his reign. Earlier, perhaps until the late twenties, threats to
the principate had always come from individuals or groups of distinguished men wishing to set Augustus aside and hand power to a candidate
of their own or to a different political order, the aristocratic order of the
old republic. Now, after the consolidation of the position of Augustus as
ruler and with the enlargement of his family, the potential danger from
members of his own close circle became more obvious. Not that there
were already would-be murderers in his house; the authority of Augustus
remained uncontested until his death. Only then was the power struggle
among members of the Julio-Claudian family to leave a bloody trail
behind it. At the moment the sole question was which of the potential
candidates was to be preferred as his successor, and which was not. However, decisions, assumptions and speculations on the subject in themselves
created great tension, sometimes poisoning the political climate.

Augustus had no son of his own. Those male members of the family
who were descended from him did so through the women of his family, principally his daughter Julia and his sister Octavia. His close family,
however, was not confined to Agrippa and Julia with their two sons,
and Octavia with her four daughters. There was also Livia, his wife, and
her two sons by her first marriage, Tiberius and Drusus. Both men were
not only closely related to Augustus but had grown up to be capable
generals. That did nothing to simplify the problem of the succession,
and the question of how Augustus felt about them arose. While both
Drusus and Tiberius stood very high in his esteem, that did not

necessarily mean that he intended to prefer them to his grandsons as successors. On the contrary, his adoption of Julia's sons in their infancy showed every Roman which way the wind was blowing. Discord in the house of Augustus now seemed inevitable.

Other potential successors from the Julian family, besides Julia's children, might possibly come from the ranks of Octavia's offspring. Octavia had four daughters from her two marriages, (Claudia) Marcella the Elder and (Claudia Marcella) the Younger from her marriage to Gaius Claudius Marcellus, and the two Antonias from her marriage to Mark Antony. Her only son had died in the year 23. Her daughters had all married distinguished and influential men, and in the year 17/16 some of them already had children, the great-nephews and great-nieces of Augustus. The elder Marcella had been married first to Agrippa in about 28, her younger sister to a nephew of the triumvir Aemilius Lepidus and then to one Valerius Messalla, both of them members of old patrician families who had held the office of consul. The husband of the elder Antonia was Lucius Domitius Ahenobarbus, the outstanding commander of the war in Germania. Many of the men who had married into the Julian family had presumably been hand-picked because of their close friendship with the *princeps*.

The practice of marrying female family members to distinguished men and friends of Augustus continued in the next generation with his great-nieces. Claudia Pulchra, daughter of the younger Marcella by her second marriage, to Valerius Messalla, married Publius Quinctilius Varus, the luckless military commander in Germania. Whether Augustus was seeking contact with old families here – and in the process burnishing the unspectacular origins of the Octavians – or strengthening his links with friends, the marriages of his stepsons Tiberius and Drusus to women of the Julian family served to connect Livia's children, and thus the Claudian branch of their extended family, more closely with the Julians. After the death of Agrippa, Tiberius was forced to marry his widow Julia – divorcing his first wife Vipsania in order to do so – and Drusus married the younger Antonia. Of their children, in turn, Drusus (II), the son of Tiberius, married his cousin Claudia Livilla, the daughter of Drusus (I), who had previously been married to Gaius Caesar, and Germanicus, son of Drusus, married Vipsania Agrippina, Agrippa's daughter by his marriage to Julia.

The marriage policy pursued by Augustus sought, first, to integrate

Agrippa, and with him his not very distinguished Vipsanian family, into the Julian house, and second, to consolidate the internal structure of the Julio-Claudian extended family by introducing into it representatives of the old nobility. The many and various links between the different branches of the Julio-Claudian family are quite hard to survey in themselves. It is particularly difficult to get a clear view because of the lack of direct descendants in the male line: relationship with Augustus was exclusively through the women related to him by blood, particularly his daughter and sister, and anyone looking around for a potential successor had to bear several candidates in mind. The scarcity of male descendants even bestowed an aura of brilliance on women whose relationship to Augustus was quite tenuous. Thus the children of his half-sister, the elder Octavia, counted among his immediate family, and so did her son Sextus Apuleius, whom Augustus promoted to the consulate in the year 29. Similarly the descendants of Atia, mother of Augustus, by her second marriage to Lucius Marcius Philippus, and the offspring of her sisters of the same name, could also claim a place among those of 'almost equal birth'. In the generation of Atia's grandchildren, for instance, a Marcia married the distinguished Paullus Fabius Maximus, consul in 11 BC, who was related to the patrician Fabian and Aemilian families and was a friend of Augustus. The considerable number of women who could pride themselves on their close relationship to the *princeps*, and the long life of Augustus while more and more such relationships resulted from marriages in the younger generations, makes it difficult to get a clear view of all the circumstances, particularly any given person's precise degree of proximity to Augustus. A modern observer, even one familiar with the period, is obliged to consult the family's complicated genealogical tree quite frequently. Here we do not have the order of precedence among later generations typical of established dynasties, made incumbent on them either by force of custom or by legal statute.

As Augustus had made clear, descent as direct as possible from the Julian side of his family was a very important consideration in the choice of the man to be granted constitutional rights as potential successor to the *princeps*. None the less, previous achievements for the state were also desirable where the army, the Senate and Roman society were concerned. If the designated successor could not boast of those, he must at least have held high office and must therefore be a grown man whom everyone could recognize as capable and willing to hold such office. Although the question of the succession was vague and provisional in many ways, it was soon as clear as day to the Romans that in adopting the children of his daughter Julia and showing them public favour, Augustus had announced to the general public, at least for the immediate future, that the direct female line leading from him through his daughter had been chosen for the succession. Julia's sons were to take precedence over the sons of Livia or the descendants of his sister Octavia.

In the year 13 Augustus returned to Rome after three years of administration in Gaul, to be greeted jubilantly by Horace in an ode, the last he ever wrote, hailing Augustus as a scion of the house of Aeneas and identifying him with an age distinguished by peace and the majesty of Roman dominion. While Augustus travelled the west, Agrippa had been travelling the east, and in his four-year absence – he had set off soon after the Secular Games – had settled many problems that were still pending. By this time the two basic powers of the principate (the proconsular imperium and tribunician power) granted to or already held by Agrippa on his departure had run out, so they were now renewed for another five-year term, and his power of military command, like that of Augustus, was made supreme over any potential rivals. Then, at the turn of the year 13/12, he had to make haste to Pannonia when news arrived of uprisings there.

At the turn of the year Marcus Aemilianus Lepidus died. Once Augustus' colleague in the triumvirate, he had lived under house arrest for nearly quarter of a century, a man ostracized and almost forgotten. At the time of his fall in the year 36 Augustus had not stripped him of the dignity of *pontifex*, although the priestly office was a not inconsiderable power factor in view of the pontifical duty of supervising all the most important priests. The patience of Augustus was rewarded, since now that the post, which for ninety years had been subject to the vote of the people, had become vacant in the normal course of events, he himself could be a candidate for it, that is to say have himself elected and stage a great spectacle demonstrating the political freedom of the people and the wide support he himself could expect in the election. It became a popular festival; the crowds streaming into the city were, in the words of Augustus himself, greater than ever before, and so the act of election became a rally of support for the new ruler, an act in which freedom consisted of electing the *princeps* to the post of *pontifex*, thus showing public approval of Augustus and his principate. The election was held on 6 March, and after that he added this new dignity to his titles, just as all the emperors did after him until the year 382, when Emperor Gratian, under pressure from Ambrosius, bishop of Milan, relinquished the title. His successors all followed his example.

In his account of his own deeds, which was meant for public consumption, Augustus did not mention the name of Lepidus, whom he had hated, but he indulged in another dig at the dead man without naming him by claiming, although he knew better, that the previous holder of the office (i.e. Lepidus) had seized the pontificate in a period of civil unrest. This was a rather crude distortion of the fact that Antony had let him have it as a reward for good behaviour after the dictator's assassination. At the time, in addition, Augustus contrived to present it as creditable and kindly on his part not to have simply stripped Lepidus of that dignity, although it should have come to him, Augustus, because his 'father', the dictator, had held it. The people had asked him to take it, he said, but he had declined. No one asked for the truth, and no one could have expressed any doubts. The past was used in the service of the present. The pontificate was now to be the inherited property of the holder of power, and it was to be hoped that Lepidus appreciated being allowed to call himself *pontifex* for so long.

When Agrippa arrived in Pannonia the unrest, contrary to expectations, had died down again, so he soon returned to Italy. He went straight to Campania, where he died suddenly in the second half of March 12 BC. He had probably fallen ill in Pannonia. On hearing the news that he was seriously ill, Augustus made haste to Campania at once, but he was not in time to see Agrippa alive. The body was taken to Rome and cremated in a solemn ceremony. Augustus delivered the eulogy on the dead man, a few fragments of which have come down to us on a papyrus. He made use of his dead friend as imperiously and ruthlessly as he had when he was alive. Although Agrippa had built a tomb for himself, Augustus had his ashes placed in his own mausoleum; as Julia's husband and the father of her sons, whom Augustus expected to succeed him, Agrippa now belonged to the Julian family even in death. That is the only way to explain the fact that he was the only man outside the Julian family whose name two cities bore, in a custom reserved only for dynasts; they were Phanagoria on the Cimmerian Bosporus (today Sennaya on the Taman peninsula), its name being changed to Agrippias, and Anthedon on the coastline of Herod's kingdom, west of Gaza, now renamed Agrippeion. In his will Agrippa made Augustus his principal legatee, although he would have had hereditary rights in respect of Agrippa's children anyway, as his adoptive sons and his grandchildren. He inherited by far the larger part of Agrippa's landed property, including Chersonese (today Gallipoli) in Thrace. Agrippa gave his gardens on the Field of Mars to the people, saying that the baths situated there should be free to all, and devoting the yield of several plots of land to that purpose. On the occasion of his funeral Augustus gave every citizen in Rome 100 denarii.

Agrippa had been the son-in-law of the *princeps*, and at the end he was formally of equal rank with him in the sharing of power and thus the mightiest man in Rome after the *princeps* himself. The two had been bound by their youthful friendship, which had taken them both to Rome and elsewhere in the dictator's lifetime, but their relationship was consolidated and proved its true worth in the difficult days after the Ides of March. Agrippa had been at the side of Augustus at every stage of his rise to become sole ruler of Rome and had proved himself an outstanding general and brilliant organizer who could turn to some very unconventional methods in his practice of military leadership and administration. He was dynamic and industrious, tireless in action and able to turn his hand to almost anything. That would have been impossible if he had not been rigorous with both himself and others, although many of his contemporaries criticized him for that rigour. They saw him as a peasant who had been unable to deny his origin even when he reached the highest positions, and whereas it could be said with goodwill of Augustus that he was a man of 'rural simplicity' (*rusticitas*), the same term applied to Agrippa did not convey approbation. It was a word used in aristocratic society to denigrate jumped-up men of equestrian rank without openly insulting them. To aristocrats, Agrippa was a classic example of the parvenu, typical of those who had profited by the civil war. He had risen from nowhere to stand side by side with Augustus at the head of the empire and he had indeed been a nobody at the beginning of his career. Not even at the height of his power or after his death is there any mention of his place of birth, which may have been somewhere in Dalmatia. No one had ever heard the name of his family or even the name of his father. The 'newness' (*novitas*) and indeed wholly unknown nature (*ignobilitas*) of the family was a subject of general discussion; to most senators he was simply not a part of established society, or society as it was now reshaping itself. Quite a number of the distinguished men of Rome showed what they thought of the dead man's humble origins by staying away from his funeral.

Those origins, however, were not the only or even the main reason for his unpopularity. Similar origins were tolerated better in other men. Distinguished Romans found the uncompromising stand he took in the recognition of Augustus and his actions difficult to fathom and unforgivable. He was his master's most loyal servant and showed what seemed like impervious stamina in the performance of his duty. Certain people wanted to make him suffer for what they could not, or would not, blame on his master, and the fact that Agrippa took so little notice of their disfavour infuriated them. He obviously shrugged off the poor figure he cut when, at the wish of Augustus, he divorced his wife Marcella to marry Augustus' daughter Julia, although he was twenty-four years her senior and could have been her dead husband's father. Nor did he protest when Augustus adopted his two sons of his new marriage in their infancy, making him appear merely the man who had sired children for his master. He seemed to ignore malice and mockery, or at least he did not give his enemies the satisfaction of showing open resentment. It was enough for him to be more powerful than anyone else after Augustus. His preference for remaining aloof from the world of distinguished men around him may also have been the reason why even well-meaning commentators described him as unapproachable, sometimes grim. His disdain for those of noble origin went so far that he gave up sending reports of his activities to the Senate, which Augustus still regarded as the centre of the state. Feeling that as general and administrator he was responsible to the *princeps*, later his partner, he wished to report back only to the authority to whom he owed a duty, thus showing the senators (and the Senate as an institution) what he thought of them.

His friendship with Augustus withstood all dangers and any differences of opinion between then. Perhaps Agrippa's awareness that his own origin could not be reconciled with any ambition for the imperial purple contributed to his much-cited and praised loyalty: what looked like modesty sprang from his knowledge that there was a barrier he could not cross. Roman society was dominated by the aristocracy, so he made up for the stigma of his origin by giving more and more evidence of obedience to the rules of the regime. He was – together with Augustus – the greatest general and admiral of the period after Caesar but he did not accept any of the three triumphs he was offered. Such trumpery was for the socially eminent; he could look down on them all and at the same time teach them, with some arrogance, that triumphs were only for the master and not his servants. For however distinguished the rank of his colleagues was, and however much they might pride themselves on their noble names, he showed them that they too served a master. Clever calculation could be seen as moderation. He also shared many of the bad habits of the 'new men', although these were also those of men of the old nobility but were more easily overlooked in them. As a general he was inflexible towards his soldiers and he could be cruel to the defeated who failed to understand the meaning of the Pax Romana, that sign of the times. Nor did he despise wealth. He must have been one of the richest property owners of his time, perhaps the richest of all after Augustus.

Agrippa also outshone many of his contemporaries in his under-standing of literature and science, and was notable for his remarkably original mind. He made a famous speech saying that important paint-ings and sculptures should be made accessible to the public, which, as Pliny the Elder comments, would be better than driving such works of art 'into exile in private villas'; it was probably the first time public sup-port was given to the idea of museums. Of course, nothing came of it. He was more successful with his work on the use of water from the public conduits, written apparently when he was aedile in the year 33, and its principles remained valid. However, the geographical work in which he systematically described the world of classical antiquity was his most creative. Until now geography had been a Greek domain: in spite of their growing empire, the Romans had hardly studied the land they ruled at all scientifically. Agrippa's interest in geography had been aroused by the campaigns that took him west, north and east to the borders of the ancient world, and by his intensive work on road-building. It seems that he wanted to have a map of the world compiled from the data in his book. However, it was not until long after his death that the map was completed according to his plans, at the wish of Augustus, and it adorned the walls of the pillared hall which Agrippa's sister Vipsania Polla had had built on the Field of Mars (the *porticus Vipsania*). He also had his own ideas about matters of style, which for a member of the upper classes at the time were not simply a question of fashion or whim but could show how a man saw the world as a whole. He was a critic of Virgil, who did not lack for those who envied him or carped at him anyway. Agrippa called him the inventor of a new kind of bad taste (*cacozelia*) foisted on them by Maecenas, by which he did not mean a poor or bombastic form of expression but the use of words from everyday language.

It is particularly curious that historians of the Augustan period have presented Agrippa as the champion of 'democracy', meaning equality between aristocrats and thus the order of the old Roman republic. How Agrippa could be regarded a symbol of democratic or even aristocratic equality is hard to understand, and we are likely to be alienated by an account from classical antiquity of Agrippa as a 'democrat', and even more alienated by a modern historian who takes the term at face value. This remarkable transformation of Agrippa can be traced back to the historian Cassius Dio, who devoted almost half a book to this question, clothing it in the form of a conversation between Agrippa, Maecenas and Augustus. Cassius Dio, over 200 years after their time, was staging a discussion on the best or better kind of state, and in searching for a pendant to the monarchy found Agrippa, whom he managed to present as a 'democrat' beside the 'monarchist' Maecenas. Chiefly interesting is the way in which he could choose Agrippa, that keen watchdog of the holder of power, and a man who despised aristocratic arrogance, for the role of a speaker for the republican constitution. This misconception can have been due only to very external characteristics and achievements, his personal modesty and frugality as well as his buildings and the terms of his will, which showed concern for the people of the city of Rome and goodwill towards them.

Augustus was growing lonelier. The next year saw the death of his sister, the blameless Octavia, whom he loved dearly. She had stood by her husband, Mark Antony, bridging the two fronts, and after his death had given his children and hers a secure home, devoting her life to her own family and keeping clear of politics. At the end she lived very quietly. She was given a magnificent public funeral, although such things were not normally accorded to women. Those who did not already know could tell from this that they were living in a monarchy now. She lay in state in the temple of the Divine Julius, and both Augustus himself and her son-in-law Drusus delivered funeral orations, one from the rostrum

567

in front of the temple, the other from the speaker's rostrum opposite it. Two years later Drusus died after his riding accident, the next year, 8 BC, saw the death of Maecenas, who had been ill for a long time, and in the same year the death of his protégé Horace. The ranks of the early companions and aides of Augustus, on whom he had been able to rely in his times of greatest need, were thinning out. He often lamented the loss of Agrippa and Maecenas, whose advice he had been able to ask. Who was still left of his great companions in arms in the days of his early struggles? Of the men of unknown origin who had at first rallied to Caesar's young son in such numbers, many were now dead or had retreated into the shadows of history. Of those still alive, the first and foremost was Messalla Corvinus, who, probably only a little older than Augustus, had already come over to him in the days when he was known as Octavian, before the war against Sextus Pompey, and since then had been his loyal friend, general and expert administrator. He was to be Augustus' companion for almost another quarter of a century, until he died a little while before him at a great age. There was also Lucius Munatius Plancus, an experienced party politician, who had also ensured his political survival by coming over to Octavian at just the right moment, but Plancus, who craved recognition, whom many despised and whose ostentatious mausoleum in Gaeta, ancient Caieta, was obviously not in proportion with his political importance and reputation, was certainly not among the close circle around Augustus. Most of the men who now surrounded him were younger than he was. Although he was only fifty years old when Agrippa died, it became clear to him then that he now belonged to the older generation and so he left Italy only once more, in the year 8 BC, when he and Tiberius went to Gaul.

The death of Agrippa had major consequences for the succession to the principate. It was initially assured by the two Caesars, the sons of Agrippa and adopted sons of Augustus, the elder now eight years old, the younger five. After the death of Agrippa a third son was born, and was called after his father, with the cognomen Postumus usual for all children born after their father's death. As Augustus was not formally a monarch, only the holder of official legal powers, the children could not succeed him in any emergency that now arose. Only when they were adult and of an age to hold office was it possible to introduce them to the public at large as his presumptive successors. Agrippa had died much too early for the function intended for him, so Augustus needed to find 'another Agrippa' in case he died suddenly. Since he wanted and indeed must look for such a man in his own house, as things stood only Tiberius, the elder of the two sons of Livia by her marriage to Claudius Nero, and after him his younger brother Drusus, conqueror of the Germanic tribes, were in the running.

Augustus did indeed mark Tiberius out as a potential successor. He not only gave him the military and political rank that Agrippa would have held, he also expected him to take on the same family position in the succession policy. First, Tiberius had to marry the now widowed Julia and to that end divorce his wife Vipsania, Agrippa's daughter by his first marriage, Caecilia, daughter of Atticus. The importance of Agrippa's family in the succession policy being pursued by Augustus can be deduced from his insistence on Tiberius' divorcing his wife: only the children of Agrippa by his marriage to Julia counted now. The fact that Vipsania, who had already borne Tiberius a son, was pregnant again at the time troubled Augustus no more than he himself had been troubled by Livia's pregnancy when he intervened in her marriage to Claudius Nero.

At first all went according to plan. Tiberius obediently rejected his wife Vipsania, although theirs had been an unusually harmonious union, and was betrothed to Julia. The marriage – that much decency was at least observed – was not to take place until the end of Julia's year of mourning. Tiberius thus seemed to be the perfect substitute for the role that Augustus had intended for Agrippa. But there was a major difference between them. Tiberius was related to Augustus only through his mother, and he also, above all, belonged to the younger generation who might be considered for the succession. That meant that, unlike Agrippa, he was a genuine rival to the two young Caesars, a situation that was very soon to lead to bitter conflict.

The damage done to Augustus' family policy on the death of Agrippa, however, at first seemed to have been mended, and Tiberius now also took over the political function that Agrippa had exercised. He had already shown his talents as a military leader in the Alpine war and he now became Augustus' legate in Pannonia. A revolt had broken out there when news came of the death of Agrippa, and Tiberius now had a chance to consolidate his military reputation over a period of several years (12–9). He succeeded in doing so and was distinguished on the grounds of several successes by the award of the triumphal insignia and

the 'minor triumph' or *ovatio*. A full triumph, however, was still withheld. When his brother Drusus died in the year 9, he succeeded him as
supreme commander of the army of the Rhine. Further honours soon
raised his position above that of all other men in the empire. He had
been hailed as *imperator* in the years 9 (in Pannonia) and 8 (in Germania), and after his first success as commander in the war in Germania
was finally allowed to celebrate a full triumph on 1 January 7 BC. He
had already been consul in the year 13; now, also in the year 7, he
became consul for the second time. Finally, when the Senate granted
him tribunician power in the year 6 BC, and Augustus was thinking of
sending him, again in succession to Agrippa, to Armenia to disentangle
the intrigues surrounding the throne of that country, he could be considered in every respect the counterpart of Agrippa both in family policy
and in his official rights.

Had Augustus given up his wish for Gaius and Lucius Caesar, his
grandsons and adopted sons, to be his political heirs? By no means. It
seemed as if he could not wait to show them off as his preferred successors, despite the official position of Tiberius, whom he himself had
promoted to it, and his stepson's great military achievements. In the
years following the death of Agrippa, the boys were an established part
of public life and were, so to speak, handed round at occasions when a
large crowd had gathered. They were popular and won the hearts of the
people of the city. By comparison with them the taciturn, grim-looking
Tiberius was sure to be cast into the shade if he was present at all. In the
year 6 the people even urged Augustus to make Gaius consul; the boy
was then fourteen years old. One does not know whether to blame this
idea on the devaluation of the consulate or the sycophancy whereby
unbounded honours were bestowed. As was to be expected, Augustus
rejected the proposition, but probably without seeing it as an unreasonable request, for he gave the adolescent a major substitute; he ensured
his election to *pontifex*, a hardly less outrageous affront to tradition. He
seemed to be obsessed by his grandsons, and by the wish for a man
related to him by blood to succeed him. When Gaius Caesar took part
in military exercises for the first time at the age of twelve, his troop
received a monetary gift from Augustus as if they had won a victory,
and no sooner was he qualified to wear the toga of a man at the age of
fourteen that he was given the right to attend Senate meetings and sit
among the senators at the theatre and at public banquets. People could

have thought they were living not at a time when the principate was still in its early stages, but under an absolute monarchy that no longer took its leader's official character seriously, and on the death of the monarch could see a legitimate heir to the throne even in a child not yet of age. However, the time of 'child emperors' had not yet come. Augustus was well ahead of his time in his fanatical endeavours to ensure that his own blood would still be ruling after his death.

Obviously Augustus did not stop to think much about the effect on Tiberius of all these honours granted to the young Caesars. His was not the foolish stupidity of a besotted grandfather but the position adopted by the ruler to his succession, which was of vital importance to the whole empire. Supposing that Augustus had suddenly died, would not the Caesars, so clearly designated his presumptive political heirs, have represented a heavy burden on a *princeps* Tiberius? And was there not also a danger that the clear will of Augustus to see the two Caesars as the heirs he really wanted might set off a civil war if mighty generals sided with them over the inheritance? Even those who could understand the wish of Augustus to present his own grandsons as his successors would surely see that problem; it was latent in the interim solution represented by two army generals of proven ability. Agrippa and Tiberius, unlike the young Caesars, were marked out for their leading position in the state by their legal and official positions and their own achievements. Probably Agrippa had not ultimately wanted that position; however, Tiberius, before his voluntary exile, did not show that it was unwelcome, and as a candidate of the younger generation he could not simply be pushed aside.

There was another misjudgement in the succession policy. Julia was unsuitable for her intended role, and she now rebelled against the pressure that had been put on her all her life to subordinate her own wishes to politics. Augustus had brought her and Tiberius together like two chess pieces, and at first they both seemed to comply fully with the new marriage laws that made the procreation of children the aim of the union without regard for such emotions as love. Julia had a son in 10 BC, but his life was to be short. The animosity between the married couple, previously under control, now weighed on them more heavily. Tiberius could not forget his beloved Vipsania, and Julia's pride and domineering nature became more pronounced. Augustus might see her first and foremost as a procreating machine, but as the only daughter of the *princeps*, the centre of his family policy, and more particularly as the mother of the two young Caesars, she ranked second only to Livia among the ladies of the empire. She may have seen herself as taking precedence even over Livia, who was not a Julian, and she will not have forgotten that Augustus rejected her mother Scribonia immediately after her birth in order to marry Livia, or that she had been cast out together with her mother at the time. The rivalry for the succession between her own children, the Caesars, and Tiberius may have further reinforced her dislike of Livia. And the brutality of Augustus in first rejecting her mother and then forcing her, Julia, into marriage successively with Agrippa and Tiberius can hardly have fostered the warm relationship common between father and daughter.

The question of the succession tore the family apart, and not only the men but also the women helped to deepen the rift. Livia and Julia played their part in the game, and the force of natural bonds between parent and child or married couples were not simply cancelled out by the way that Tiberius and Julia had been paired off with each other. Political family interest alone was no guarantee that their relationship would last, and the marriage of Julia to Tiberius, the Agrippa substitute, failed.

In the year 6 BC, entirely unexpectedly, Tiberius suddenly abandoned his political career and withdrew from public life. It is not easy to say what made him give it all up, or rather what finally prompted his retirement. To his contemporaries, his decision was like a thunderbolt coming out of a clear sky. In the years 8 and 7 Tiberius had been successful in Germania; he had celebrated his great triumph on 1 January 7 and had begun his second consulate on the same day. In the following year, the Senate even extended his tribunician power for five years, and thus, like Agrippa before him, he stood beside Augustus. What more did Tiberius want? He could climb no higher. And then he asked Augustus for leave of absence (*commeatus*) on the grounds that he had had enough of honours and needed peace and quiet. No one believed that excuse, and rumours were rife. The claim that he himself made later, saying that he did not want to stand in the way of the young Caesars, could be explained by his fear of assassination in the isolation of his self-imposed exile. In fact, however, it is more likely that Tiberius felt that the publicly expressed wishes of Augustus for more progeny to succeed him constituted a constant humiliation, and he would not endure it any longer. He was in a dilemma, trapped between loyalty and (useless) resistance to the preference given to the young Caesars, and since he could not cope with such a dead-end situation he avoided it by retiring from public life. All attempts to dissuade him failed. It was in vain for Livia to plead with him, or for Augustus to lament in the Senate his own situation as a man abandoned. At first Tiberius' request to leave was not granted, whereupon he refused food. After four days he was allowed to go. He went to Rhodes, leaving Julia behind, and lived there quietly as a simple countryman. He was not stripped of his tribunician power, but he made no use at all of any of his official rights.

It was on Rhodes that Tiberius heard, a few years later, of the scandal in which Julia was involved. Among the messages he received was the information that Augustus had sent her a letter of divorce in his name. Nothing makes the way in which the patriarch disposed of members of his family more ruthlessly clear. Tiberius will not have mourned for the end of his marriage, but the circumstances of the divorce were another humiliation for him. He had the decency to ask for some alleviation of her punishment and to let her keep all her presents from him. Meanwhile, he was beginning to feel less secure, particularly after the five years of his tribunician power ran out. Everyone seemed to have deserted him. Most people had cut him dead directly after his retreat into private life, and he was accompanied to Rhodes by a single senator, one Lucilius Longus, whom Tiberius held in high regard all his life. Quite a number of people even referred to him as 'the exile', and now despised him for it. He was considered politically finished, and, as things stood, so he was. In Nemausus (Nîmes) his statues had already been overthrown, and when Gaius Caesar went to the east, with extraordinary full powers, one of his table companions is even said to have offered, over-zealously, to bring him 'the exile's' head. Tiberius felt afraid and withdrew even more, hardly even receiving officials who, sailing past Rhodes, wanted to visit him. He kept quiet, and the humiliations he had suffered, as well as his insecurity in the face of an uncertain future, gradually made him want to return to the capital city, where, under the protection of Augustus, at least he need not fear for his life and might hope for an improvement in his personal and political situation.

Political relationships in Rome, especially those concerned with family policy, changed fundamentally while Tiberius was away. The two Caesars were now young men, and when Tiberius came asking for reconciliation Augustus let him feel the force of his anger for not doing as he was told. Augustus had no Agrippa and no Tiberius now to keep the throne warm for his heirs, but he was showing everyone that he could do without them. He could hardly wait to see his grandsons grown up and ready to follow in his footsteps. In 5 BC, when Gaius solemnly put on the toga of a grown man and was thus accepted into the circle of adults, Augustus, after a gap of seventeen years, had himself appointed to the consulate again so that, armed with what in form was the highest office, he could accompany his grandson on his first official appearance in the Forum, thus introducing him to the Senate and people of Rome as his political heir. Obediently taking the hint, the Senate thereupon designated Gaius consul for the year AD 1 and authorized him to attend meetings of the Senate from now on. The equestrian order also made him leader of the (equestrian) young people (*princeps iuventutis*) and presented him with a silver shield and spear. Augustus had 60 denarii each paid to those citizens of the city of Rome who already received grain in celebration of the day. Three years later the ceremony was repeated for his younger grandson, Lucius, and once again Augustus was not going to let anyone else be the consul who accompanied his grandson to the Forum. This was his thirteenth and last consulate, and he did not hold it for the full term of office, nor had he done so three years before. At this time the mint in Lugdunum (Lyon) began producing coins in a series of denarii and gold pieces with the two Caesars portrayed on the reverse as 'leaders of youth', with the attributes of shield and spear given to them. Coins of this kind continued to be minted until AD 4, so many of them that no more silver coins were minted until the year 13. These coins were obviously put into circulation to introduce the Caesars publicly as the presumptive heirs of Augustus, more particularly to present them to the army, since most of the coins were used as army pay. Provincial cities did not lag behind in honouring the young men: the temple dedicated to Gaius and Lucius Caesar in the year AD 1 in Nemausus (the Maison Carrée, Nîmes) is impressive evidence of that to this day.

The year 2 BC, which had begun so brilliantly with the introduction of Lucius into public life, brought a special honour for Augustus. At the beginning of February he was hailed by his companion of many years, Marcus Valerius Messalla Corvinus, with the agreement of the Senate and the people, as 'Father of his Country' (*pater patriae*). For a long time, Augustus had declined that title, but now he accepted it in a moving scene in the Senate. That form of address meant more than just an honour for Augustus, now an old man. As 'father' of the Romans, he was the equal of Romulus and had thus risen, so to speak, to be the second founder of the city. Since a father was at the same time lord over all the members of his household, wife and children, freedmen and slaves alike, the title also implied his patronage of all Romans, an arrangement demanding care for the household from the father, obedience to him of all in his power. It marked out Augustus as a caring father figure, over and beyond his legal authority. While as *princeps* he guided the Senate, all Romans, senators, men of the equestrian order and ordinary citizens obeyed him because of his authority as their 'father'. The term was another Roman word for the sole ruler, and we can see its value and political importance in the fact that Augustus – like all the emperors after him – added it to his official titles.

Another high point in this year, which was full of solemn festivities, was the dedication on 12 May of the temple of Mars Ultor in the new Forum of Augustus. The occasion was accompanied by contests in the Circus and was celebrated a few months later with further events. Their splendour and ingenuity bear witness to the importance of the temple in Augustus' eyes. He had 260 lions hunted to death in the Circus Maximus to the south-west of the Palatine, 36 crocodiles were hunted in the Flaminian Circus on the Field of Mars – the Circus had to be filled with water for the purpose – and there were gladiatorial contests in the Saepta Julia. The climax of the entire show was the depiction of the naval battle of Salamis between the Athenians and the Persians, for which a huge basin was dug and fed by the waters of the Tiber. Nothing remains today of the building known as the Naumachia ('naval battle') in the present Trastevere district of the city. It was over half a kilometre long and about 350 metres wide.

However, then a discordant note rudely disturbed this apparent harmony. Julia, the only daughter of Augustus and wife of Tiberius, himself now living in exile, was publicly accused and found guilty of adultery with several men, including some of very distinguished birth. Her co-accused included such names as Claudius Pulcher, Cornelius Scipio, Quinctius Crispinus and Sempronius Gracchus, all of very distinguished families, although their names were of more importance than their political positions. But then the scandal acquired a politically explosive

*Julia's adultery)* (handwritten margin note)

note with the naming of Jullus Antonius, the younger son of Mark Antony, as one of Julia's sexual partners. Antonius, who had been too young to accompany his father to the east and had thus been spared by the judgement of Augustus in the year 30, was brought up with loving care by his stepmother Octavia, and with the support of Augustus himself even became consul after her death. The love affairs of Julia and in particular her relationship with Antonius had been the subject of gossip for a long time, and many variations on the theme went the rounds both before and after the official version of the liaison was made known. In view of the fact that this state of affairs had been more or less common property for some time, we can hardly speak of the 'discovery' of these incidents, but apparently Augustus himself knew nothing about them. The rumours current in Rome, and the way the scandal was exploited as a political tool, have probably obscured the true background of the affair for all time. But the reactions of Augustus are remarkable, and give a possible clue to our assessment of it. He accused his daughter in the Senate, and thus very publicly, of adultery, and involved the Senate itself in the criminal investigations without actually making it formally her judge. He did at any rate show enough restraint, perhaps even shame, to have the main prosecution charges read out by one of his quaestors. Julia's offence was officially regarded as injuring the dignity of the *princeps* (*lèse majesté*), and the delinquent was banished, by a household court in which the *pater familias* had power over those under his rule, to the small island of Pandateria. Her mother Scribonia went with her. Many of the others involved, both men and women, were killed or sent into exile. Antonius was either executed or forced to commit suicide, we do not know for certain which.

Not only is the public involvement of Augustus strange, the motives for the behaviour of Julia and Antonius as the suspects and Augustus as their prosecutor are blurred in what evidence has come down to us. Was all this a conspiracy, led by Antonius in the attempt to oust Augustus, as a number of historians, perhaps the majority, assume today? We can dismiss that idea. Antonius, a man without an army or followers, would not have had the faintest prospect of success, and it is unrealistic to suppose that he himself did not know it. And supposing he really was so blind, would Julia, the mother of the young Caesars whom Augustus wanted to succeed him, have helped to stage such a coup? It is extremely improbable. The affair must have been solely a case of adultery. We can imagine that Julia, the natural centre of Roman society, had a certain lust for life, if only to make up for the psychological abuse to which her father untiringly subjected her.

The motive of Augustus himself for the 'public condemnation' of his daughter was probably far more normal than is usually supposed. Having arranged his daughter's marriages as part of a policy for his own blood to succeed him, he found her in the arms of the one surviving son of his former arch-rival and reacted with uncontrolled fury. Instead of settling the affair discreetly, he made it very public by reading out his accusations or having them read out in the Senate. What gossips had dared only to whisper privately now became a subject for public discussion. His daughter had wounded his honour and disrupted his family policy; as he saw it, she was the only culprit, not the weakling Jullus Antonius, and for that he brought her to court in public. He had seen her only as an instrument of his policies, and when the instrument stopped functioning as he wanted he destroyed it with a brutality that revealed more about his true nature than many of his utterances had ever been able to do. It says much about his harshness that he did not even consider the feelings of Julia's two sons, his beloved and pampered grandsons. And his thirst for revenge did not seem to be quenched even by her punishment. Julia was guarded closely on her little island north-west of Ischia, and could not receive any male visitor without express permission. Augustus would listen to no pleas for pardon, and only after five years did he allow her to move to Rhegion (Reggio di Calabria) on the mainland and to rather more comfortable accommodation. Pleas from the people of the city of Rome to bring Julia back from exile fell on deaf ears, and even years after the scandal were met by the theatrical response that water and fire would mingle sooner than he would lower himself to do that.

Not even the failure of his daughter's marriage taught Augustus a lesson. Once that vessel of his hopes was broken, he started to construct the next. The following year, before his beloved grandson Gaius Caesar, already publicly presented as his successor, set out on his great mission to the east, he swiftly married the nineteen-year-old to Livia Julia, known as Livilla, daughter of the elder Drusus by his marriage to Octavia's daughter Antonia (Minor) and thus the granddaughter of Livia and great-niece of Augustus. While the succession in the Julian line was

now assured, this marriage, like the marriage of Tiberius to Julia, renewed a link between the Julian and Claudian branches of the extended family that might be interpreted as a gesture of reconciliation, and as the bride was of the same generation as Gaius, at least they were well matched in age. Neither complained of being paired off like this, and how could they? The patriarch was obviously enamoured of his idea and thought that with his exaggerated notions of Gaius figuring on his travels as a new Pompey or even a new Alexander, he had added extra lustre to the arrangement. Gaius set off for the east before the birthday of Augustus on 23 September. For this mission, which Augustus undoubtedly saw as following his own and Agrippa's journeys to the east, he was granted the fundamental military power of the *princeps*, the proconsular *imperium*, giving him precedence over all the governors of the eastern provinces. That gave him a share in the power of the *princeps*, whose designated successor he now was in due form. A brief inscription after his death explicitly describes him in those terms.

Gaius went first to the Danube to introduce himself to the armies stationed there, and then to Samos and on to the eastern provinces to settle Armenian-Parthian affairs, which were in turmoil yet again. He was greeted solemnly and respectfully wherever he went. Presumably with the praises of Augustus ringing in their ears, the people of Athens, who did not like to be outdone by anyone else in flattery, addressed him as 'the new god of war' (Ares). Considering his age, the cult of his person was bound to seem excessive. It made the young man seem to embody the durability of the principate.

The authority of Tiberius steadily decreased the longer he was away from Rome. In the year 1 BC, his tribunician power ran out, and now he held no office at all. The meteoric rise of Gaius Caesar made it clear to him that he had lost all his political status. He feared for his safety, became anxious and tried to show the public how harmless he was by emphasizing his retired way of life. His fears, as it turned out, were not entirely unfounded, for it was suspected that through certain centurions who were devoted to him he had tried to find out about the present situation in Rome with an eye to a political change. It was undoubtedly a malicious insinuation, but Augustus let him know about the rumour, thus openly expressing his own distrust. Thereupon Tiberius of his own accord asked him for a guard in a remarkable gesture of self-humiliation. He might well feel like a prisoner, and indeed he did not cut a good figure. When Gaius Caesar stopped off in Samos on his mission to the east, Tiberius thought that he ought to pay a courtesy call on the young man, and met with a very frosty reception. Gaius and his retinue, including Marcus Lollius, that arch-enemy of Tiberius, whom Augustus had given his grandson (and adopted son) to go with him as an adviser, let him see how little he meant to them; such deliberate humiliation made Tiberius feel like a troublesome petitioner. Finally Livia managed to get him a position as a legate, so that at least he represented something, and at last, in the summer of AD 2, he was allowed to return to Rome with the express permission of Gaius. While that in itself was a humiliation, there was another and greater one in the strict condition that he was to keep out of all state business in Rome. The former triumphator slunk quietly back to the city and took up residence in the former house of Maecenas on the Esquiline.

On 2 August, just before the return of Tiberius to Rome, Lucius Caesar had died on the way to Spain at the age of only eighteen. His sudden death – he had left Massilia in good health, but swiftly died of a disease that obviously struck him down only when he was on board his ship – gave rise to rumours that he had been poisoned, and among the names of those suspected, on the principle of *cui bono*, was the name of Livia. Augustus mourned his grandson deeply, and the whole of the population of Rome grieved with him for the young man whom they had loved. Even Tiberius ranged himself with the mourners by writing an elegy for him. He can hardly have been expected to grovel in such a way, which made it embarrassing.

Only a year and a half later Gaius Caesar too was dead. He had been wounded while laying siege to a fortified Armenian city; he had thoughtlessly agreed to a discussion with its enemy commander and was attacked from the rear. Although his wound did not seem to be dangerous at first, his condition deteriorated so much that he fell prey to melancholy, resigned his official authority and expressed a wish to withdraw from political life. Augustus persuaded him to return to Italy only with difficulty. Gaius sailed for home on a merchant vessel rather than a warship, which casts light on his condition, but he got no further than the Lycian harbour of Limyra, where he died in February AD 4. His ashes were taken to Italy and placed, like his brother's, in the Mausoleum of Augustus. Honour upon honour followed the news of his death. Statues were erected to the two brothers, days of remembrance were fixed, sacrifices announced, triumphal arches built, and there were plans for a pillared hall, the *porticus Iulia*, to be built along both sides of the temple of the deified Caesar. The lamentations for their deaths were mingled again and again with awareness of the importance of the loss that Rome had suffered. The grief of Augustus was boundless and genuine. A letter to Gaius that has come down to us by chance reveals something of their close relationship, and Augustus' account of his own deeds begins with the words, 'Since cruel Fate has torn my sons Gaius and Lucius from me . . .' He goes on to leave instructions for his successor Tiberius – another humiliation whereby, even in death, at the solemn moment when his will was opened in the Senate in September AD 14 and his heir took over the principate, Augustus publicly presented Tiberius (or perhaps we should say stigmatized him) as the successor he had not wanted and did not love. In his grief at the death of his grandsons, Augustus lost the moderation of which he was usually a past master.

The early death of the two Caesars left the question of the succession wide open once again. In the interests of the principate, a man had to be found who belonged to the family of Augustus, and to whom the army would also respond. There was potential danger in the present situation: if Augustus died suddenly the outcome could have been chaotic, and Augustus was now sixty-six years old. He had no option but to designate Tiberius for the role of successor, or rather ask him to resume it. With his fortunes in the ascendant again, Tiberius could require guarantees that his stepfather's intentions were genuine. Granting him one of the fundamental powers of the *princeps* was no longer enough. Tiberius had to become a Julian so that he could take up his inheritance as the son of Augustus. The outcome of the negotiations was a compromise to which Tiberius seems to have agreed only after some hesitation. Augustus decided to adopt him on condition that in return Tiberius adopted Germanicus, the son of Drusus and the younger Antonia, and thus the grandson of Augustus' sister Octavia. The adoptions took place on 26 June AD 4. Tiberius adopted Germanicus, Augustus adopted Tiberius, and at the same time he also adopted Agrippa Postumus, the youngest son of Agrippa and his own youngest grandson.

With his adoption by Augustus, Tiberius became formally the appointed successor to the principate, in line with both the concept of that institution and the dynastic ideas that had already taken deep root in the army and the people. But even in this extreme situation, when Tiberius represented the only option still open to Augustus, we can see the strength and persistence of his desire for the succession to go to his immediate family circle in the fact that he also made Germanicus and Agrippa Postumus members of the Julian family, thus imposing them on Tiberius as *his* successors, although Tiberius himself had a grown son (Drusus II). It was obvious by implication that he still entertained ideas of the succession of his own blood, and in addition, when he adopted Tiberius and Agrippa Postumus on the same day, he commented in front of an assembly of the people that he was adopting the former for the sake of the state. He certainly did not intend the remark to be disparaging, and it was undoubtedly passed on later, for instance by Velleius, with approval, but in the context of the entire process such a comment, made only on the adoption of Tiberius, could be taken to mean that his situation forced him into the adoption: Augustus was abandoning his old Julio-Octavian policy of succession and choosing the able and successful general Tiberius for reasons of state, or so it could appear. Considering the situation of his family policy and the adoption of two Julians on the same day – Agrippa Postumus by himself, Germanicus by Tiberius – contemporaries could even suppose that the whole process, together with the admission by Augustus that his adoption of Tiberius was for the sake of the state, was an emergency solution, deprecating the idea of succession by the Claudian part of his family, or at least making it clear that it was his second choice, and his first would have been for a Julian solution. It was not surprising that the apparently mystifying adoptions immediately set off rumours, some of them daringly speculative. Further rumours were rife immediately after the death of Agrippa Postumus and the succession of Tiberius to the principate. Tacitus, among other remarks, circulated the story that Augustus had contemplated making Germanicus his successor, but Livia had vetoed the idea.

The Senate now granted Tiberius tribunician power again, on this occasion, it appears, not just for five but for ten years. Tiberius took his time over accepting, first privately and then in the Senate. That was not simply the expression of a hesitant character, as is commonly assumed; it can also be seen as a means of bringing pressure to bear to ensure that this time his nomination as successor to Augustus was meant seriously and was final. Tiberius now became supreme commander in Gaul and

Germania again, and he immediately resumed his successful military career. He was warmly welcomed by the soldiers, and the brilliant success that he achieved first in Germania and then in Pannonia, sometimes under extremely difficult conditions, was evidence of his great military talent and his tenacity in pursuing a plan once he had made it. Augustus also publicly showed that Tiberius, who was forty-five years old on 16 November AD 4, was now officially the successor to the principate by transferring to him tasks that were really his own to perform. When Parthian envoys approached him in the year AD 5, he referred them to Tiberius, who was then in Germania.

It will have been at around this time that the equestrian order presented Tiberius' own son Drusus (II) with a silver shield, denoting that he was 'youth leader' (*princeps iuventutis*). The example of the two Caesars shows that the bearer of that title was to be regarded as a kind of crown prince, so this seems to have been a gesture of reconciliation, indicating that Drusus, who was entirely Claudian, was at least not excluded from the succession. Naturally Germanicus also received the same title. The ambiguity of the policy of succession still remained. Would Tiberius some day, once he was *princeps*, feel bound to follow the guidelines laid down by Augustus?

The years after the adoption of Tiberius were filled with battles in Germania and Pannonia. But at this time the inhabitants of Rome and its surroundings had troubles of their own that made news from the north retreat into the background. In the year 5, the city suffered a flood and an earthquake, and even worse, supplies of food for a metropolis the size of Rome proved inadequate. The people went hungry, and famine recurred in the following years; it seemed to be an uninterrupted affliction. In the year 6 it was so bad that Augustus had part of the population, in particular slaves, gladiators and most of the foreigners, turned out of the city and resettled, some of them 150 kilometres away. To placate the people of Rome, those entitled to receive grain were given double rations, but even that was hardly enough to keep the angry inhabitants of the capital quiet. There were rumours of impending political coups, defamatory writings denouncing the administration went the rounds, and the fact that the authorities offered rewards for helpful information about their anonymous authors was not likely to stabilize the situation. In addition a great fire devastated large parts of the city in the same year. We hear reports of famine in Rome and Italy until the year 9. It seems that the difficulty of ensuring supplies was directly connected with the tense military position in the north. The hard-fought Pannonian War went on and on, keeping large parts of the Roman army engaged, and forcing the government to give supplies to the troops precedence over providing for Italy and in particular the capital city. In the year 9, when all this misfortune was at its worst, no sooner had the Pannonian rebellion been crushed than the Romans were shattered to hear news of the terrible defeat of Varus and the death of 20,000 of his soldiers.

In the year AD 7, the family of Augustus suffered a new scandal. Augustus banished Agrippa Postumus, Agrippa's youngest son, whom he had only recently adopted at the same time as Tiberius. The young man was sent first to Sorrento, then to the tiny island of Planasia, 12 kilometres south-west of Elba. The exact details, in particular the reason for his exile, remain vague. The monarchical character of the principate is only too obvious in the way that Augustus dealt with this and all the other affairs of the ruling house: the true background to his decisions usually remained hidden behind the closed doors of the palace, and although official reasons were given they were often felt to be threadbare and were not believed. Instead, there were rumours and suppositions, and some malicious insinuations.

According to the official version Agrippa, who was eighteen at the time and obviously a difficult character who had a troubled relationship with Augustus and Livia, had been at odds with them to such an extent that finally his grandfather – and for nearly three years also his adoptive father – felt he was beyond his control. The obvious conclusion to be drawn is that the background of this family conflict was argument about the private and above all political future of Agrippa. After Augustus' drastic change of course in his succession policy, Agrippa obviously misjudged his own position in the ruling house and could not adapt to the new circumstances. He must have felt like a deposed prince, as indeed he was, and it ruined him. It was therefore advisable simply to say that the young man who could not or would not adapt to the intricacies of politics was mentally disturbed. He seems to have been a victim of the change in the succession policy after the death of the two Caesars. As their younger brother, he may have hoped, in view of the policy pursued by Augustus before their deaths and the adoptions of the year 4, when he and Tiberius became adopted sons of the *princeps*, that he himself would have a stronger position, perhaps equal to the position enjoyed by the two Caesars. When we are told that he called Livia, slightingly, a 'stepmother' and spoke of being deprived of his inheritance, that may express some of his disappointment over his lost political future. But there was no way past Tiberius now. Augustus was sixty-nine years old and could not begin the game of the Julian succession from the beginning all over again. Why had he adopted Agrippa Postumus in the first place, setting him beside Tiberius and thus raising his political expectations?

In the following year, AD 8, there was another scandal, one that affected the ruling house as badly as the scandal of the previous year. This time the central figure was Julia (Minor), the sister of Agrippa Postumus and granddaughter of Augustus. The fall of her mother Julia in the year AD 2 seemed now, nine years later, to be repeated in her own fate. She was accused of adultery and banished to the island of Trimerus off the Apuleian coast, where she lived for twenty years, supplied with the necessities of life by Livia to the end. She died in the year 28. This incident too remains largely obscured by the veil of semi-official utterances and well-meaning or deliberately distorted attempts to explain it. The younger Julia was married to Lucius Aemilius Paullus, a member of one of the most distinguished patrician clans. He was accused of conspiracy, probably in connection with the events of the year 8, and executed. His connection with Julia's offence cannot be made out even in rough outline. The accusation of immorality was probably just a pretext, for we hear only of one lover mentioned in connection with Julia, Decimus Iunius Silanus, and Augustus punished him only by withdrawing his friendship, which Silanus took as a command to remove himself voluntarily from Rome. Julia does not seem to have done anything so very bad. Today it is not really possible to get even an approximate grasp of the facts of this case, whether real or alleged.

The lack of guilty parties in this scandal can lead one to suppose that adultery was not the primary transgression, but to think of a genuine conspiracy seems entirely outlandish. Lucius Aemilius Paullus was an insignificant figure who had achieved no status in the army or the administration, and distinguished birth alone no longer counted for much. It seems more likely that the condemnation of Julia was closely connected with the banishment of Agrippa the previous year. Julia, like Agrippa, may have been at odds with her grandfather, perhaps even actively expressed her opposition to his about-face in the succession policy. Tiberius as *princeps* would mean the end of any political future for both her and Agrippa; the new political line taken by Augustus was for them a fall from the heights as the most likely representatives of a Julian succession. They were no longer flattered like royal children but were a political nuisance and after the death of Augustus must even have felt that they were in danger.

The question of the succession destroyed the Julian part of the family, and it was the patriarch himself who, with all the energy he had previously devoted to promoting the interests of the young Julians and pampering them, now consigned them to obscurity and indeed to ruin.  His anger with the insubordination of his daughter and his grandchildren never died down as long as he lived. In particular, he could not forgive the two Julias for their independence, which ran counter to his own moral ideas, probably because they made him look ridiculous as the champion of the new morality in marriage. He even stated in his will that his daughter and granddaughter were not to be interred in his mausoleum, and he had no intention of ever recalling them from exile, indeed he hardly troubled to ensure that they had the means of sustaining life. Nor did Tiberius relieve their sad fate; although he meticulously followed the instructions of Augustus after his death, he could have made a personal exception here. After the death of her father Augustus, Tiberius' former wife Julia had to endure even harsher conditions; she wasted away in Rhegium, hungry and exhausted, until in the year 14 death finally released her from a wretched existence. Augustus even forbade his granddaughter Julia, who had a baby after she was exiled, to bring it up as her own, and her beautiful palace was razed to the ground. The loving father and grandfather had become a furious brute. He used to call the two Julias and young Agrippa his three boils, his cancerous sores. However, his conduct towards his daughter and granddaughter, who are now thought to have been merely weak and too fond of pleasure, was and still is defended by most modern scholars. Then as now, the two of them had little chance when the finger of the guardian of morality pointed their way.

Whether Agrippa Postumus and his sister Julia set off these family tragedies, or whether they were drawn into an existing conspiracy, there can be hardly any doubt that political motivation played a crucial part and led to their harsh punishment. Augustus' succession policy had failed, and he now had neither suitable candidates from the Julian part of his family to continue it nor time to wait for a new generation. So he had to disappoint the justified expectations of those still left of his grandchildren's generation, and he did more by simply crushing the brother and sister who at the worst had merely been immature or perhaps incompetent. Another indication of the political character of the scandals is the fact that people spoke of attempts to free the two exiles; there was even a suggestion that after they had been 'liberated' they were to be presented to the armies. Of course, the leaders of this plot were described by those anxious to oblige Augustus as criminal, senile, physically defective and semi-barbarian fiends, and as a result we know very little today about how much truth there was in the affair.

The fate of Ovid was also linked with the banishment of Julia, another matter that eludes explanation today. In the year 8, when he was on Elba, Augustus brusquely exiled the poet by personal decree to Tomis (Constanza in Romania) on the furthest border of the empire. Through his third wife Ovid was in close contact with Atia, an aunt of Augustus, and her daughter Marcia, but we have no idea whether this connection also meant that he was personally close to Augustus' granddaughter. His part in the allegedly immoral conduct of Julia is pure speculation. He had not been condemned in the proper way by a judge, only by the despotic word of Augustus, and he obviously dared not mention the reason for his exile, or perhaps did not even know it, since whether he had committed a criminal offence or not was irrelevant. Speaking of his exile, Ovid blames himself only for his stupidity and naivety, not for any wrongdoing. Several times he calls his personal inadequacy a mistake (*error*), and he also mentions a 'disgraceful poem' (*turpe carmen*) as a second 'deed' for which he has been denounced as a writer who encouraged adultery. He also confesses to causing Augustus pain by his behaviour. By this disgraceful poem we are probably to understand his 'Art of Love' (*ars amatoria*), published just under ten years earlier. In fact the sentence of exile passed on him by the *princeps* might well have been the result of it. An 'art of love' as a didactic poem was bound to arouse the ageing man's displeasure, in spite of all the amours in which he himself indulged even in old age. It contravened his matrimonial legislation, which was to reach new peaks the next year

(AD 9), and was obviously already being discussed the previous year. In addition Augustus obviously did not like the genre at all, particularly because historical characters were cheerfully satirized without inhibition by Ovid in the 'Art of Love', as well as his other works, and even the Julian ancestors did not escape. He introduces Romulus, for instance, at the time of the rape of the Sabine women, as the ancestor of all later lovers. Augustus did not care for such jokes, and not only did he fail to find them funny, he might even have felt that he himself was being mocked. The timing of the exile suggests that the scandal over Julia let loose the fury of Augustus at the whole light-hearted genre and the cheerful freedom of the Ovidian style. It is possible that, as a member of Julia's wide circle of acquaintances, Ovid had aroused the ire of the *princeps* in some way, perhaps through an occasional poem rich in allusion. We cannot tell today; at the most we can discount the idea that Ovid had an intimate relationship with Julia.

Augustus' anger with the poet did not die down. In spite of many petitions, he never reversed his decree, and nor did Tiberius after his predecessor's death. After nearly ten years in exile, only a few years after the death of Augustus, Ovid died at the age of sixty. He had defiantly continued to devote himself to writing poetry, 'to which alone', as he wrote, 'Caesar has no right', and Augustus had not touched his right to publish either.

When his granddaughter was forced to leave Rome, Augustus had already begun his eighth and last decade of life; he celebrated his seventieth birthday on 23 September AD 8. His close family had shrunk to a very few now that he had sent his daughter and two grandchildren into exile. He had won back Tiberius, but that taciturn, surly man, who to Augustus represented a living memory of the loss of his beloved Caesars and who shared with him the recollection of their long dispute and the injuries they had inflicted on each other, was certainly not likely to make his old age and isolation easier to bear. He still had two people, above all, with whom his relations were warmer: his wife Livia and Germanicus.

Since his adoption by Augustus, Germanicus had been a member of the Julian family and was now called Germanicus Julius. Aside from his adoption a blood relationship linked him with Augustus, for his mother Antonia (Minor) was a daughter of Octavia, sister of Augustus, so

Germanicus was his great-nephew. He gave Augustus great joy in two ways: he ensured that there were more children in the family and he proved an able general. His children also belonged to both parental sides of the Julian family, for through their father they were great-grandchildren of Octavia, and through their mother Agrippina, a daughter of Julia, they were great-grandchildren of Augustus. Germanicus officially introduced himself to the Roman public in the year 6, when he and Tiberius organized games held in honour of his dead father Drusus. The Senate granted him, as it had granted the two Caesars, permission to hold all the offices of state five years before the legal age. He was also appointed an augur, and in the year 7, at the age of only twenty-one, became quaestor. He was in Pannonia between the years 7 and 9 and distinguished himself both there and later in Germania as a military leader under the command of his adoptive father Tiberius.

Germanicus was a man after Augustus' own heart, but their closeness inevitably clouded his relationship with Tiberius, since Germanicus was, so to speak, the last remnant of a policy of Julian succession. Claudius, the younger brother of Germanicus, was sickly, malformed and also appeared to be mentally backward. Those who knew him considered him good for nothing much except the study of history, in which he showed a remarkable interest. Augustus and Livia avoided him, and so did his sister; even his mother Antonia kept her distance from him and described him as 'a monster of a man whom Nature began to form and then left unfinished'. She considered him a fool, and Augustus and Livia, as several passages from their correspondence show, were united in regarding him as unfit to appear in public. Careful thought went into the question of how he could best, meaning least conspicuously, be presented to a wider public if absolutely necessary without making the family ridiculous. He had to attend the games mentioned above, held in honour of his father – he was fifteen years old at the time – but he wore a hooded cloak and kept the hood over his head. No one could have imagined, at the time, that he would one day become *princeps* and in that role would prove to be the most capable of all from the house of Augustus who succeeded to that position.

Livia was extremely close to her husband all her life. The fact that the marriage was childless seems not to have troubled their relationship very much. There is no doubt that Livia's ability to adapt to Augustus contributed to what was obviously a model marriage, particularly the way she organized everyday matters just as he liked them. Praise of Livia's maternal attitude to her own children and the others entrusted to her care, and of the plain simplicity of her way of life – she was averse to all luxury – may reflect her own nature, but it will also have been shaped by Augustus. She had the same capacity for getting her way and the same rigorous approach in dealing with everyday life as he had in politics. She kept her household firmly under control and disliked any kind of change in it. All her life, for instance, she drank only one kind of wine, a rare variety made from grapes grown only in north-east Italy, because she thought it good for her health and every day she ate a certain salad plant (*inula*, elecampane) for the sake of her digestion. In their marriage of over fifty years, Augustus and Livia seem to have grown more and more like each other through mutual respect. We know of no serious dispute, and Livia's upright moral character will have contributed much to the harmony of their union. She would not allow herself the lapses that she overlooked in her husband.

Livia was not only a support to Augustus at home, she was also his political confidante. He regularly asked her advice and made notes of important points before a conversation with her as he would for other important discussions. She accompanied him on several journeys, some of them quite long. The Greek east saw her as the wife of the ruler and paid her the same divine honours as were paid to Augustus. While this Greek attitude was based on a tradition centuries old, the western provinces followed eastern habits only with a certain delay. Livia always kept a cool head, even in critical moments, and showed none of the sometimes heated reactions of Augustus. She appears to have been ruled entirely by reason. Her great-grandson, the later Emperor Gaius (Caligula) called her, sarcastically, an Odysseus in skirts.

For all her personal charisma, and in spite of the many opportunities of exerting influence available to Livia, she was clever enough to stay in the background, never directly interfering in politics. In so far as she did want to exert influence, she did it through the person of Augustus and when she broached any political subjects herself she confined them to matters affecting women. But of course she could not prevent herself from being regarded as not just part but also a formal part of the monarchy, and she probably wanted that. At a very early date, in the year 35, both she and Octavia were granted the 'sanctity' (*sacrosanctitas*) of a tribune of the people, which Augustus had also had conferred on himself as successor to the dictator Caesar. In its new form this sanctity, detached from the office of tribune, was to symbolize the inviolability and religious consecration of the monarch and, as its bestowal on Livia and Octavia shows, of his house as well. And just as cities were called after Caesar and Augustus, at least two smaller cities, Livius in Palestine and Liviopolis on the Black Sea, took Livia's name. She was closely connected with many senatorial families and with a number of foreign dynasts; she was a good friend of Herod's notorious sister Salome. She also seems – like Octavia – to have been granted at an early date the right to dispose of her own property; her fortune grew all the time, through legacies and gifts, and was managed by her own staff of freedmen and slaves. The Villa ad Gallinas near Prima Porta, north-east of Rome, where the famous statue of Augustus stood, was only one of her many properties.

Livia has not usually had a good press in modern literature, where her virtues are presented in contrast to her alleged thirst for power and her desire to promote the interests of her own sons at almost any price, and a number of authors are inclined to suspect her of the political murder of Augustus' grandsons Lucius and Gaius Caesar and Agrippa Postumus. These views derive from historians of antiquity, particularly Tacitus, who saw Livia as responsible in many respects for the tensions between the Julian and Claudian branches of the family. Many scholars speak of the existence of a political trend or even 'party' connected with Livia. There is no question of any such thing. Clearly and after all understandably as she wished to further the careers of her own sons, Augustus was not to be swayed by her in matters of importance, least of all in his succession policy, which – against the interests of the Claudian part of his family, and thus counter to any alleged potential intentions of Livia – he pursued to its ultimate conclusion. Livia herself was well aware of the limits within which she could operate and observed them with care; the Livia who kept an eye on all political tendencies from within the palace and engaged in intrigue is an invention of the historians.

Although Livia was venerated in the provinces, her role outside the house in Rome remained restricted. She often appeared in public with Augustus, but public response to her was muted. She frequently features in reliefs or small pictorial works, but the poets hardly mention her – Horace never does. She was formally raised in the estimation of the Roman public only on the death of Augustus. In his will, he gave her the title of Augusta and took her into the Julian family; in other words, he was adopting her. As for the adoption, it remained to be seen whether Livia, in view of the fact that the future of the principate belonged to the Claudians and not the Julians, set much store by it. In death, Augustus was taking her into his own family, a sign both of his tenacity and of his resentment of the fact that the family was ultimately displaced. The title of Augusta meant more, for it went hand in hand with a rise in her rank and meant that she now stood side by side – not in the legal and formal sense, but in the political and social hierarchy – with the *princeps*, although his name was now Tiberius. Augustus probably did not ask her advice about this elevation in rank. Any reaction of Tiberius to it is one thing, what the bestowal of the title on a woman said about the new Augustan order is another. While 'Augustus' was the title of the head of the principate, initially given just as a special honour to the officially appointed first among equals, 'Livia Augusta', or after the adoption 'Julia Augusta', showed that the principate had become a monarchy, since the wife of the holder of the highest office in the principate had no official place in the conception of that constitutional form.

Augustus remained healthy and able to work until the end of his seventh decade of life. Although his health had been poor in his youth, after his severe illness in 23 BC, the year of crisis, we hear very little of any serious impairment to his physical condition. In a letter written to his grandson Gaius Caesar on 23 September AD 2, his sixty-fourth birthday, he says in good humour that he has now cheerfully and in good health completed his sixty-third year of life, which was regarded as particularly dangerous for the male climacteric. He does not seem to have suffered from any major health problems in his old age. However, once he had passed his mid-fifties he gave up going on long-distance journeys to the provinces and confined himself to travelling in Latium and Campania. Of course, he was not spared some of the ailments of old age. He suffered from bladder-stones and frequent itching of the skin, and at an advanced age from weak vision in his left eye. At night he would wake too early and be unable to get to sleep again. But he did what he could to preserve his physical health. He habitually ate moderately; he liked plain country fare, hand-pressed cheese, sardines and fresh figs, and drank wine sparingly, preferring Rhaetian wine. His sensitive stomach, which would rebel after too much of it, helped him to drink in moderation. In winter he dressed very warmly, wrapping himself in four tunics as well as a thick toga, and having his legs wrapped; in summer, as he did not tolerate the sun well, he wore a broad-brimmed hat (*petasus*). To prevent illness he was careful, as a biographer remarks, not to take a bath too often. In his old age he often went riding or walking and would hop the last part of the way when walking back to keep himself fit. As far as we can tell his psychological condition remained stable even in old age. He always regained control of himself quickly after an outburst of rage, and if such a thing happened in the Senate he would sometimes leave the meeting and come back once he was composed again. Only a ruler could do such a thing, but for whatever business was under discussion – and for the preservation of the idea of the principate – cooling off outside the Senate was certainly better than discharging his anger when it was in full session. When he had been under great psychological stress in his youth, for instance during and after the battle of Philippi, he had suffered severe disorders of the stomach and bowels, but we hear little of them later.

In his last years he was clearly slowing down, but without losing track of the business of state or giving it up entirely. The senatorial committee already formed by the year 4 BC and reconstituted in AD 13 to prepare for decisions in the Senate was a help to him here. It met in his house, sparing him the walk to the Senate house and the tedious hours spent at meetings. He did much business lying down now, and if he felt weak or tired he would more and more frequently get someone else to speak on his behalf at public meetings, whether a personal quaestor or a family member such as Germanicus, who sometimes read out speeches for him in the Senate during his consulate in AD 12. In the same year he also found a pretext for asking the senators to refrain from delivering a daily greeting (*salutatio*) outside his house, and to excuse him for staying away from public banquets in future.

If we leave aside his conduct to his grandchildren Agrippa and Julia, Augustus in old age appears more human than before, or at least better-disposed and certainly less stern. We seem to get a glimpse behind the official façade. Perhaps old age makes the mask brittle, allowing us to see some of his very personal preferences and passions, as well as the pressure of the political burden that he had to bear. Or perhaps the picture of a more human and accessible Augustus is deceptive, for in his early years the pulsating political life of the time overshadows the private area, and an observer could see only incidentally or by chance characteristics that emerged more strongly in the aged Augustus. His unrelenting attitude to members of his own family who had been unwilling to subordinate their lives entirely to his wishes should warn us against the idea of a man grown milder in his old age.

Among his close friends at this time was Paullus Fabius Maximus, descended from two old patrician families and related to Augustus through his wife Marcia. However, Fabius was considerably younger than Augustus. Among the company of old gentlemen who played dice together there were also two consulars not much younger than Augustus himself, Publius Silius Nerva and Marcus Vinicius, the old soldier who had won so many laurels on the northern border of the empire. Both came from families of equestrian rank and could now claim nobility for themselves and their families. In their origins and the way their own achievements had enabled them to rise in the world, they were very close to Augustus. The game of dice, of which Augustus had been passionately fond from his youth, was played with four-sided dice (*talus*). They played for high stakes; in a letter to Tiberius, Augustus confesses once to having lost 20,000 sesterces, a sum equivalent to twenty years' pay for a legionary, allegedly because of his easy-going or negligent manner of play. He also played with balls, both large and small, and knew other games involving movement and skill. As fellow players of these games he liked to recruit little slave boys, who had to be well formed because of his distaste for dwarfish or deformed people; he bought them like toys for himself from the farthest corners of the empire.

Augustus cast no more doubt on the succession of Tiberius, but he made sure that he had marked out Germanicus as the successor next in line. Naturally enough, without losing sight of Augustus himself, the people of Rome now paid more attention to his presumed successor and gradually began taking their guidelines from him, some willingly, many more hesitantly, several with severe forebodings. At least in his last years, Augustus did not oppose but rather encouraged this development. His premonition of his imminent death was also evident in personal decisions, where he now obviously gave Tiberius a free hand. Although we cannot say that an established circle distinct from other persons in the leadership group formed around Tiberius, some of his close friends and assistants now gained important positions. They included members of old noble families such as Lucius Calpurnius Piso (*pontifex*, consul in 15 BC), who had won the highest regard and was prefect of the city uninterruptedly from the year 13 to his death in the year 32, and men from families of the new nobility who had not previously achieved consular rank but now did, such as Lucius Apronius (consul in AD 8).

On 23 October of the year 12, Tiberius was finally able to celebrate his triumph over the Pannonians, delayed because of the Varus disaster. The entire population of the city of Rome took part. They were fed at a thousand tables, and every man was given 300 sesterces as a gift to celebrate the triumph. The high point of the festivities was a demonstrative gesture of reconciliation, for before Tiberius climbed to the Capitol to dedicate his laurel wreath to Capitoline Jupiter, he descended from his triumphal chariot and knelt before Augustus.

In his last year of life, only weeks before his death, Augustus was still working on his account of his deeds, his only written work of any length to have come down to us, but much of it had been composed well over a decade earlier. There is nothing else exactly like this account; as a work of monarchical autobiography it does not aim to be simply a eulogy of or reflection on himself, but takes his relationship with the Roman people as its point of departure and derives its content from that relationship. It is one of the most original works to be found in the political literature of the Romans. Its succinct clarity is evidence of the style that Augustus preferred, and we encounter it not only in this account, intended as official documentation, but also in his letters to Livia, to his grandson Gaius Caesar and to Tiberius. From these few letters, which have come down to us either complete or as fragments, and from a few direct answers by Augustus to spoken questions, we know that he liked a plain style close to everyday language. He was certainly not a man to emulate the ornate periods of Cicero, and his deep dislike for mannered oratory or writing is clear to us from several remarks in which he expressed his distaste for affected, ponderous language and for archaism. He mocked Maecenas in particular, calling his sentences 'perfumed ringlets' and parodying them. He is a striking example of the type of Roman aristocrat who took it for granted that he would not only be closely acquainted with literature but would also strive to develop his own style in speaking and writing. Part of that was a training in rhetoric, essential for a man in public life in Rome if he was to appear before the people, the Senate and the army. Augustus had had that training and never ceased developing his own stylistic abilities. They became a well-tuned instrument helping him to write and speak successfully. He liked to deliver speeches extempore, revising them later for the record so as not to leave anything out, but saving the time it would have taken to learn them by heart. He had one remarkable weakness: although of course he read Greek without any difficulty, his mastery of the spoken language was inadequate, so for addressing Greeks he worked on certain texts in Latin and then had them translated.

He was a productive author, writing mainly small works including pamphlets or answers to other men's writings. His memoirs did not get very far, breaking off at the Cantabrian War in the year 25 BC, after thirteen books. His attempts to write poetry were not very well thought of, and he himself regarded them with scepticism. He tried his hand at a tragedy, *Ajax*, but then abandoned his Ajax 'to the fungus', as he put it, alluding to one version of the suicide of the Greek hero, and destroyed what he had written.

In the first half of the year AD 13, when his fundamental military power, the proconsular *imperium*, ran out, Augustus had it extended. Tiberius, whose civil equivalent, tribunician power, had been renewed the previous year, now received the military power again by consular law, and this time it was equal to that of Augustus. Another clear sign that Augustus was gradually retiring from politics is the fact that, also in the year 13, he designated Tiberius' son Drusus for the consulate in the year 15, but even now he was not letting go of the reins entirely. In the year 13 he even fought a hard battle with the Senate for the inheritance tax that had been introduced a few years earlier. Its proceeds went into the military treasury, which made it particularly dear to his heart. Although the tax was moderate, and was paid mainly from the legacies of the closest blood relations of the deceased, the senators did not like it. In the end Augustus was able to carry his point only by threatening that, if the Senate persisted in rejecting the tax, he would introduce a land tax in Italy, which had so far been free of it. It seems unlikely that, as tradition claims, he visited the exiled Agrippa on his island in the last year of his life, and the story linked with it that thereupon Livia, fearing that the succession of Tiberius would be endangered, poisoned her husband is entirely incredible.

Many omens announced the imminent death of Augustus, and whether they were actually seen, were interpreted as omens after the event or were simply invented, it makes no difference to what people believed. Among the many signs and wonders a total eclipse of the sun was reported, and in addition a flash of lightning that struck the statue of Augustus on the Capitol and melted the first letter of his name Caesar. As the letter C also stands for the number 100, and the remains of the name, AESAR, mean 'god' in the Etruscan language, the augurs explained that this omen meant Augustus would die in a hundred days' time and be received among the gods.

Tiberius was to take over command in Illyricum again in the summer of the year 14, to consolidate the peace so laboriously achieved there, and Augustus decided that in spite of his age he would go with him as far as Beneventum (Benevento) in the south of central Italy. He seems to have felt not only able to undertake the long journey, but also healthy enough to manage the business of state during the absence of Tiberius. It was his last journey, and he was not to see Rome again. Because it was usual for writers of classical antiquity to pay particular attention to the last days of great men, particularly the hour of their death, we are relatively well informed about this journey and the subsequent death of Augustus.

Augustus and Tiberius travelled south at their leisure. In the small Latin harbour of Astura, they boarded a ship that took them to Capri. The island was the personal property of Augustus; he was particularly fond of it and called it 'the city of idlers' (*apragopolis*). On the way there he had contracted a gastric disorder that weakened him. None the less, he remained cheerful, gave his companions presents and paid his respects to the Greeks of Campania. He stayed on Capri for four days, watched the games held for the ephebes and gave those around him Roman togas and the broad throw worn by Greeks (the *pallium*) on condition that the Romans among them wore the *pallium* and spoke Greek, while the Greeks were to wear the toga and speak Latin. However, his health did not improve. In spite of his poor state of health, he went on to Naples to watch athletic contests and continued to Beneventum with Tiberius. There they parted. On the journey back, however, the condition of Augustus deteriorated so much that his party had to stop in Nola. As his end was in sight, Tiberius was summoned back at once. He is said to have found him still alive and to have held a long conversation with him. According to another account Livia, who was also present, kept the death of the *princeps* secret for reasons of security until the arrival of Tiberius, who had allegedly reached his province already. The discrepancy between the two versions characteristically derives from the roles assigned by ancient historians to Livia and Tiberius immediately before the death of Augustus. As Velleius Paterculus, the contemporary and close acquaintance of Tiberius, expressly says that he was in time to see the dying Augustus, and we cannot assume that in this case he was lying or had any motive for lying, familiar as he was with personal relationships between the leadership class in Rome, preference must go to his version of events.

On his deathbed, Augustus is said to have been calm and composed. He thought about his appearance, and after a glance in the mirror had his hair combed, and his chin, which was already out of his control, bound in place. He asked the friends standing around him whether he had reached the end of the comedy (*mimus*) of life, adding in Greek the request for applause, a standard concluding phrase from an Attic comedy now lost, 'If it was well played clap your hands, and accompany us on our way with cries of applause.' Then he said his goodbyes, asked after the welfare of the sick daughter of the younger Drusus, son of Tiberius, and died in Livia's arms with the words 'Livia, remember our marriage, and farewell.' It was 19 August AD 14, a month before his seventy-sixth birthday. He died in the same house and the same room where his father, Gaius Octavius, had died seventy-two years earlier.

The lines from the end of the comedy have been interpreted in various ways, but it is unthinkable that the dying man looked back at his life without reflecting on the political role that he had filled as the first man in Rome and ruler of the world. Augustus had in mind his part on the political stage, and as the herald and mentor of a new form of state, the principate, he had been an actor to a very high degree. He may have had before his eyes the labour of the forty-year struggle to consolidate that state and win over the new aristocracy to it, and also of the struggle with himself against the temptation that omnipotence brings with it. Despite all setbacks and defeats, he will have hoped for approval, and it was not withheld, at least by those looking back at the history of his reign later. For many contemporaries and those who immediately followed that time, the achievements of Augustus soon paled beside the needs of the present, the envy of less able men and the superior attitude of those who judged the past in the light of the problems of their own time.

The body of Augustus was brought to the city by night because of the heat of the season. It was carried by councillors of the surrounding cities, from whom men of the equestrian order took it over just outside Rome and bore it into the city, to lie in state in front of his house on the Palatine. Honours for the dead man from the Senate came thick and fast, including the description of the entire period of his life as the 'Augustan age' (*Augustum saeculum*). Perhaps the instructions left by Augustus himself for his funeral muted this excessive enthusiasm slightly.

Before the funeral, his will was opened. Augustus had written this last version of it on 3 April of the previous year, partly in his own hand, partly taken down from his dictation by two freedmen. It had been deposited with the Vestal Virgins and was now brought from them and read aloud in the Senate, like the public document that it was. In it, Augustus made Tiberius and Livia his main heirs, Tiberius with seven-twelfths of his property, Livia with four-twelfths, while the remaining one-twelfth was divided between Drusus the son of Tiberius, and Germanicus with his three children, as secondary heirs. He also left several legacies to be paid by his heirs. Most of the sum from those legacies went to the Roman people and the soldiers. The people received in all 40 million sesterces, and the members of the thirty-five tribes, probably only those who lived in the city, received 100,000 sesterces per tribe. Of the soldiers, the men of the Praetorian Guard (the bodyguard) received 1,000 sesterces, the members of the cohorts of the city of Rome 500 and the legionaries 300 sesterces each. In addition, he decreed that Livia was to be taken into the Julian family and receive the title Augusta. He considered his daughter Julia, still living in exile, worthy only of a few presents, he did not reprieve her and he stipulated that when she died her ashes were not to be placed in his mausoleum. Finally Augustus decreed that the sons of all those who had made him their heir at a time when their offspring were not yet of age should have the whole property left by their fathers, interest included, repaid to them when they did come of age. This was the practice that he had followed in his lifetime.

Apart from the will, Augustus left four written scrolls to be opened on his death. One contained instructions for his funeral, the second was his account of his own deeds, the third was a list of all the most important affairs of the empire (*breviarium totius imperii*), a survey of all the groups of the armies and the monies in the state coffers at the time, with a list of the names of freedmen and slaves who could account for them. The fourth and last scroll was for Tiberius personally. It contained instructions, advice and injunctions for him. Among them was the advice to limit the numbers of freedmen and not to extend the empire beyond its existing frontiers. Coming from a man who had expanded the empire like no other Roman before him, and even in the year of his death still aimed to make the area between the Rhine and the Elbe a Roman province, this was bound to seem strange. Did he think that the powers of the *imperium* would not allow further conquests? Or did he not trust the cautious and already ageing Tiberius? Although he bore that last point in mind, Tiberius was to follow his advice only so far as it suited his own policies.

On the day of the funeral, the body was first taken in solemn procession from the house on the Palatine to the Forum Romanum. A considerable and particularly impressive part of the procession consisted of the apparently never-ending series of likenesses (*imagines*) of famous ancestors of Augustus, including Romulus, and allegorical representations of all the peoples he had defeated, along with large tablets describing his deeds. In the Forum, Tiberius and his son Drusus delivered eulogies on him, the first from the rostrum outside the temple of the deified Caesar, the other from the rostrum opposite. Then senators took the body on their shoulders and carried it to the Field of Mars, where it was cremated. One senator, the former praetor Numerius Atticus, swore later on oath that he had seen the figure of Augustus ascend to the heavens from the burning pyre, for which Livia gave him generous monetary recompense. It meant that the dead man had been received into the ranks of the deified (*divi*). Later it was said that an eagle carried the soul of Augustus aloft, and it seems that an eagle had already been set free on the day of the funeral. Men of the equestrian order, clad only in unbelted *tunicae*, gathered up the remains and waited beside the pyre for a while, together with Livia. The ashes found their last resting place in the mausoleum that had been ready to take them for over forty years.

On 17 September the Senate decreed, in due form, that Augustus had been raised to the company of the gods (*consecratio*). The cult of the Divus Augustus received, as priests, the Sodales Augustales, drawn from the highest-ranking senators and members of the ruling house. When it was set up, this committee of twenty-one men included, as well as Tiberius and his son Drusus, the two sons of the elder Drusus, Germanicus and Claudius. A special priest (*flamen*) was appointed for the ceremonies of the cult, and a temple erected. It lay in the valley between the Palatine and the Capitol behind the Basilica Julia; its precise site was long the subject of controversy. It was not ready for consecration until the time of the second successor of Augustus, Gaius (Caligula). And Caligula's successor, Claudius, also erected a statue of Livia in it.

As the new master of the principate, Tiberius took over smoothly. He already held the fundamental powers of the *princeps*, and if at first he had everything carried out by the consuls, he certainly did not pretend to be undecided about whether to assume the business of government, as Tacitus suggests; it was in the nature of things that he should do so. As he was not consul himself at this time, it was taken for granted that the consuls in office should act as representatives of the Roman state in the hiatus between the death of the old *princeps* and the accession to office of the new one. On the other hand, Tiberius himself called the Senate meeting to discuss the funeral of Augustus and the opening of his will, on the grounds of his tribunician power, and, what was yet more important, even before that meeting he gave the password of the day to the Praetorian Guard as the new *imperator*. There were soldiers everywhere at the funeral. At the same meeting on 17 September when the deification of Augustus was formally proclaimed, Tiberius himself received the title of Augustus, and thus he had formally succeeded Augustus as *princeps*.

Among the first events of the new principate was the death in exile on the island of Planasia of Agrippa Postumus, the last grandson of Augustus, who had adopted him in the year 4. Several leading members of the Julio-Claudian house have been and still are suspected of having ordered his death: Augustus himself, said to have given the order before his own death; Tiberius and even Livia; and finally Sallustius Crispus, believed to have carried out the order. It is possible that the young man died a natural death, but very improbable in view of the fact that it coincided with the succession to the principate by Tiberius. Agrippa was no danger to Tiberius as a rival at this point, but with Germanicus he was all that remained of the Julian policy of succession that, in spite of his adoption of Tiberius, Augustus had continued to pursue by adopting Agrippa at the same time. It was in the interests of Tiberius to dispose of him, and he was probably a victim of reasons of state, with Sallustius only acting as an executioner with either vague or clear instructions.

In principle, Augustus had prepared well for the transition in the principate. But it was none of his doing, for he had not wanted Tiberius to succeed him, that a man now took over who had excellent military and administrative experience and in addition knew all the problems of the principate, particularly the proper form of conduct towards the high senatorial aristocracy. Nor was it owing to Augustus that the new *princeps* observed his instructions with great care. The previous few decades had worn Tiberius down, and his long period of passivity left him, now fifty-three, disinclined to make a new start. In his reign of over twenty years he kept the army and the administration firmly under control and thus ensured the lasting existence of the principate after the dangerous gulf of the first transition of power. If his principate was notable for strong tensions among the senators, sometimes threatening to degenerate into bloodshed, that was less because of any deviation from the line that Augustus had taken than because he lacked the strong hand that was the essential corrective for the 'freedom' of the Senate, and that Augustus had known how to apply. Tiberius, a patrician born, may have felt closer to the senators than Augustus as the descendant of country gentlemen. But authority founded on noble origins did not count for as much now as it had in the republic. The great men in the Senate sometimes had to be shown what mattered in this new state.

# 16

# Epilogue

Various tales of the childhood and youth of Augustus were current in classical antiquity. One widespread legend about his birth was told in a religious work by Asclepiades of Mendes in Egypt. According to this legend Atia, the mother of Augustus, had visited a temple of Apollo, and while she was sleeping in her litter there a snake embraced her and then immediately left her. On waking, she felt as if her husband had been lying with her and cleansed herself. As a sign of what had happened, a mark shaped like a snake appeared on her body, and after that she did not like to go to the public baths. Augustus was born nine months later and was regarded as the son of Apollo. Just as he had been born a god, he vanished like a god on his death, to be venerated as divine by all the inhabitants of the empire. And in the same way as he appears like a being outside human existence at the beginning and end of his life, that life itself seems to have been lived entirely on stage, in a performance showing what Augustus wished to present, but not who and what he really was. We perceive him as a conglomeration of ideas which, refracted thousands of times over by the literary and archaeological records, tell us what we ought to know about him and his achievements. All his statements and sayings that have come down to us, even in his personal letters, seem to serve that end. Although we may think we discern something of the 'real' Augustus from early letters (for instance to Cicero written before his rise to power), from his outbursts of anger and from the facts provided by contemporary informants who were interested in the man's personality, physiognomy or education and tried to see behind the façade, even so we usually suspect that the picture has been retouched. And in any case, most of what we are told about him dwells on the 'façade'.

However, the interest of biographers in the physical appearance of famous men does give us a relatively clear idea of what Augustus looked like. We are told that his height was about 1.70 metres, and although that was not short by the standards of the time, he wore thick-soled shoes in order to look taller. His figure was rather sturdy, but otherwise regular, except that his left leg was not as strong as his right leg, and he sometimes dragged it. His facial expression, on the whole calm and composed, contrasted with the intense brilliance of his blue-grey eyes, of which he was particularly proud. His eyebrows grew close together, his nose was slightly hooked, his teeth small with gaps between them, and not particularly white. His hair was dark blond, and he did not usually grow his beard. We are even told that he had a number of birthmarks on his skin, and several calluses. But the citizens of Rome did not see him as literature describes him to us. His statues, and his portraits on reliefs and coins, show the stereotypical likeness of a ruler, and were approved by himself. The more he aged, the less they reflected his real appearance. In his portraits he seems to be looking past the observer with a sublime expression.

Nor can we get much idea of Augustus from his personal habits, his family life and his intellectual interests. The little we do gather from what we are told is not enough to provide a fully rounded picture of his character and mind. What emerges far more clearly from our sources is his political will, together with his actions and what we can reconstruct, on that basis, of his motivation. They tell us something about his political ambitions and real achievements, but still they are not enough for a character study. However, taking into account the vague nature of the evidence that has come down to us, and therefore keeping a suitable distance from both the eulogies and the strictly political statements, we can perhaps say something about the personality of Augustus along the lines of what follows. If it does not seem very positive that may be because his political life is the part of him we know best, contemporary records concentrated on it, and a veil conceals his private life where it was not also political. In addition, the records of the time quite early turned to uncritical polemics which, mingling with paeans of praise, add up to an image that it is difficult to interpret clearly.

He was no model of all the virtues, but then how could anyone be that if he wanted to make his way in the world during the decades of the civil war? He was especially bloodthirsty in pursuit of his enemies, but knew how to cover up his cruelty as the demands of his time required. He appeared to be mild-natured but rather calculating, and he always kept an eye on public opinion. He never tired of emphasizing his much-vaunted love of his adoptive father Caesar, although it served him mainly as a pretext for disposing of his enemies, and his piety towards the gods, in so far as it was not intended to demonstrate his loyalty to the old Roman tradition, was in his own interests. His sense of justice, which also won him much praise, was nothing but a tool used for political ends and to reward his supporters. Long and close friendships bound him to many men as long as they were useful to him, but mere suspicion was often enough for him to break with them abruptly or even drive them to their death. He seemed to have no softer feelings or sense of humour – or if he did have a certain amount of humour, as certain passages in his letters may suggest, he kept it well concealed. His emotions were worn for show, and there he performed his role so poorly that anyone could see through it – which cannot have troubled him, for a theatrical display of emotion was all he needed to achieve whatever political aim he had in view. His life was full of public appearances to demonstrate or to conceal his political intentions, and countless times he proved himself a master of the art of presenting his commands as exactly what those who received them wanted themselves. His official actions showed a great gift for managing people, even or most of all en masse, as well as his ability to understand the way they thought and their current concerns. Even a rather critical senator could feel flattered and edified by such a performance, at least while he was part of a large audience; if he thought about it later he might demur, but it was necessary only for him to agree in the first place. The virtues of Augustus as they were proclaimed all over the empire, not just in Rome, and in the temples and public buildings of the people, were intended to show that he was the acknowledged holder of all power in ancient Rome. They were not meant for those who knew better, but for the millions of Romans and provincials who saw him, or were intended to see him, as the incarnation of the benevolent ruler.

The objection to such an idea of Augustus is obvious. Politicians are not models of virtue; they can be expected to be in basic agreement with the values of their society, but not to give evidence of any special moral fervour. The very nature of the profession seems to exclude politicians from being judged by the standards of steadfast morality. And if we think of the period in which Augustus had to make his mark, the mere idea seems absurd. He could not have survived the period when he was fighting for political recognition without being hard, even brutal. Consequently he had to go along with the proscriptions. If he did not actually wade in blood, that is to his credit – but the point is debatable.

After the end of the civil war he liked to feature as an example of the merciful ruler. As early as the year 27, when he received the shield listing his virtues, the Senate testified to his clemency (*clementia*). Undoubtedly this was more of a semi-official declaration than a reference to actual instances of magnanimous conduct in the past. Augustus possessed 'clemency' first as an inheritance from the dictator, who had tried to spare his own class after the outbreak of the civil war. At the end of it Augustus could have followed in his footsteps, but he did so only hesitantly. The virtue of clemency is a quality of rulers, not of a free society, for it cancels out the law in force – apart from the granting of pardons to enemies taken prisoner in the civil war, a situation which, like the war itself, was outside the legal order. Clemency, the principle of which was to be seen not as a form of rule but as an attribute of the monarch Augustus, was less easily adjusted to the idea of the principate. No biographer would claim any special instances of clemency for him, but there is no doubt that after the end of autocratic rule, that is to say after the year 27, he did try to create a legal order in society. Augustus did much to reorganize the system of procedural and criminal law, and he also made great efforts in legal practice, whether as judge or witness, to set up good jurisdiction. The virtue of justice (*iustitia*), with which he is also credited on the shield, therefore seems more apt. He showed in many ways that in a harsh or even ruthless legal situation he could see the human side of a case, even where it concerned slaves, the least important members of society. It cannot be said that the legal policies of his time already set out to make the laws affecting slaves more humane, but he did show that he disliked seeing them killed for no reason, for instance by the cruel slave-owner Vedius Pollio. And his efforts to reform the houses in which slaves lived in miserable conditions – those who worked on the land in particular – might be thought to show his humane side, although the main aim was probably not so much to improve their working conditions in general as to restore those free persons who had been arbitrarily forced into slavery to their original status.

No biography of Augustus that casts light on his political aims and intentions can be written solely on the basis of what we know, directly or indirectly, about his person, his intellectual interests, his moral attitudes and his human relationships. Quite apart from the shortage of records on those subjects, anything capable of being considered a statement about them has been distorted many times in transmission, or reduced to a formula, or ossified into a moral example. A biography of Augustus is possible mainly because we are well informed about the events that played a part in his life, and those which he largely determined and ultimately strongly influenced. We also have reliable information about his work, its gradual development and the ideas behind it. We can gain access to Augustus only through a presentation of the complex of events comprising the decades of change from republic to imperial empire that, at the same time, trace the stages of his own political career. Only in this context can we interpret what is said about his person, and indeed his own statements. For assessing the man and his work, then, the few personal statements of his that we have and the occasional contributions of third parties are less important and informative than what he said officially about the principles governing his conduct, that is to say his ideas of ethical values. They point to the political aims and concepts behind his actions.

Where the importance of religion for his policies is concerned – we may recollect his revival of the ancient Roman cults, and the sacred superstructure bestowed on his own dignity as ruler – it would be intriguing to know what Augustus thought about the supernatural world. Although as a member of the upper class he naturally took an interest in philosophical questions, we can say that he certainly did not guide his own hopes and fears by means of philosophy. Its precepts seem merely to have given him an opportunity to utter banal truisms, or at best sensible maxims. The gods at first served him as a means to a political end; there can be no doubt of that either, but we may assume that he believed in the deities closest to his heart and their divine powers, and that his political success reinforced this belief. However, it is hard to hear any note of genuine piety in his semi-official pronouncements. We are on safe ground only with what we know about his attitude to a form of faith outside the religion of the Roman state: he was not drawn in any way at all to the mystery cults, a form of religion with major implications for the future and already widespread in his own time. In the mysteries, humans experienced the divine as a personal encounter. He himself remained an adherent of the old Roman religion, in which ancient Roman traditions combined with Etruscan and Greek piety. For Augustus, its aura of religious power, however close worshippers might feel to a deity and however much the numinous was made part of a mythical event, never lost its original impersonal character, which largely excludes the idea of any purely individual relationship, and this kind of religion was merged indissolubly with the state of which it was a constituent part.

Augustus did, as we can see more clearly, share the widespread religious or pseudo-religious behaviour that is described as superstition. If he put on his shoes the wrong way round in the morning, and found that he had his left shoe on his right foot, he saw it as a bad omen, and conversely he believed that when a heavy dew had fallen there was a good prospect of coming back from a journey safe and well. He also thought the nones (*Nonae*), the name for the ninth (*nonus*) day before the Ides and thus the fifth or seventh day of a month, was an unlucky time, and so was the nundine (*nundina*, containing within it the word *novem*, nine), the word for a Roman market day, perhaps because both words contain the idea of the word *non*, the Latin for 'no'. His fear of thunderstorms seems positively absurd. Although he was supposed to be a favourite of Jupiter the Thunderer, when a storm approached he would hide in a deep, solidly built cellar, and when he travelled he always took with him the skin of a monk seal, which was supposed to act as protection against lightning bolts.

Where his personal religious feelings were concerned, Augustus was the same as his contemporaries of the upper class in Rome; he had no special interests in this field, and shared the opinions and prejudices of other citizens with the same fervour or lack of it. Only in one point did he differ from all of them, casting everything tried and achieved in the sphere of religion before him into the shade, and that was his exploitation of human religious feeling for political ends.

Even at a fleeting glance, his rise apparently from nowhere to rule a world empire seems a truly astonishing feature of his career. It points to what is probably Augustus' outstanding talent, his ability to get what he wanted. No politician can make headway without that ability, and in his youth as Octavian he had it to a remarkable degree. He came to

Rome at the age of eighteen, with nothing behind him but a certain amount of encouragement on the part of the murdered dictator, and the clause in Caesar's will naming him as his son. He had no supporters outside the dictator's hangers-on and had to stake his claim in the midst of a large pack of members of the old nobility, Caesarian generals and greedy soldiers, none of them well disposed to him. The distinguished men whom he suddenly joined could regard him, with some justification, as an upstart backwoodsman – for that was how the small-town background from which he came could be described. However, he embarked on his game and played it for the stake of power. Few thought he had a chance. But he cleverly (or with cold calculation) associated himself with different partners, playing off one against another as the necessity arose. First he took the people of Rome as his political allies, then the veterans who had fought under his 'father', after that those who sympathized with Caesar's assassins and even one of those assassins himself; finally he fought with Antony against all the others, and in the end against Antony himself. He had become a master of the uses of political rancour at an early age, and it was a great help to him when he became part of the political power structure in only a few months. His lonely struggle, in a society that was consuming itself with hatred, envy and ambition, and in which every man struck out ruthlessly around him, explains his harsh and enigmatic conduct in the first two decades of his political career. He had to search all the time for the way leading upward, had to beware of those lying in wait to ambush him, deal with setbacks, and keep his supporters happy once he was enjoying success. Genuine friendships stood little chance in that pitiless struggle. His only truly close friends at the time were Agrippa and Maecenas, and the former in particular was such a loyal and talented aide that his friendship must be considered essential to Augustus' ultimate success. The struggle for political influence, and very often for mere survival, could not, however, be won solely by dint of ruthlessness, cruelty, bribery and the betrayal of others who happened to be his allies at any given time. For success Octavian, and then Augustus, needed an understanding of human nature and the ability to carry conviction; he needed flexibility and mastery of the art of illusion, and ultimately none of that could have worked without his gift for rhetoric. He could deliver a speech impromptu and make engaging conversation in a company of friends or soldiers; he undoubtedly had personal charisma. On occasion he also showed courage, admittedly not on the battlefield, where he was able to prove bold enough only so far as it was essential for him to show himself brave in front of the soldiers, but in the Senate or an army camp he held his own, even in a menacing situation. He would not have got far if he had not been so steadfast, and it showed not only in his will to stake his own claims, but also in the way he achieved his political ideal of the principate. Once he had seen what it was right for him to do, he would fight for it doggedly.

It is difficult to explain where Augustus found the strength to assert himself against hostility both overt and covert for almost sixty years. He certainly did not owe his success to the circumstances alone, however much we assume them to have been in his favour. Without a shadow of doubt, we have to look to his person for the cause of his resolute mind, his ruthless rigour as well as his gift for leadership and ability to adapt to political and, above all, personal situations. Heated as he could be on occasion, he compensated for his outbursts of temper by his capacity for self-control – with a few but remarkable exceptions affecting close members of his family and his circle of friends. On important occasions he could bide his time, and he used that ability to cover up many of his weaker points, for instance in military expertise. It is said that he justified the caution and hesitation he sometimes employed with such maxims as 'Hasten slowly' or the line from Euripides: 'A cautious general is better than one too daring.'

Augustus must surely have derived considerable strength from his rural origins. Although he made much of the nobility conferred on him by adoption, he did not deny those origins. Their main merit was that they distanced him from the aristocratic elite with its cliques, jealousies and intrigues. He could not have succeeded in creating a new leadership elite without that sense of distance and its accompanying lack of prejudice against new men who were rising in the world. He deliberately isolated himself to a certain extent by disdaining to conceal his rural background and continuing to follow a plain way of life. He could open up, but his isolation still made itself felt, creating the conditions for his long term in office as ruler. He cultivated and even deliberately emphasized it. We have evidence of that in his almost archaic lifestyle in his house on the Palatine and in his stern, patriarchal education of his grandchildren, partly in person – for instance, by teaching them reading and writing and other elementary branches of knowledge, instilling ideas of good behaviour into them, even making his daughter and granddaughters learn to spin wool as well as other household skills.

His realization that he must depend on himself called for constant watchfulness and a capacity for untiring work, for until the structure of the state was politically consolidated Augustus could not let its affairs out of his own hands even for a short period. Because the question of the succession remained in the balance for a long time and was finally decided only ten years before his death, he could not let himself indulge in leisure even in his old age. He might speak of his longing for peace and quiet in a letter to the Senate, and he might genuinely mean it, but the senators he was addressing could see it only as a hollow phrase. In fact he could not for a moment think of retiring from public life. The great reformer Sulla, who abdicated his dictatorship when he retired in the year 79, could do so because he left behind him a society that had existed much as it then was for centuries. Augustus had to construct his state on new foundations, even creating a new leadership class, so his was the sole responsibility for maintaining his work and supervising those charged with carrying it out. He knew that he was indispensable and he had the strength to follow the path on which he had embarked to the very end.

We must not forget that, without the long life granted to him, Augustus could not have completed his political work. If he had died in the twenties the civil war would probably, indeed almost certainly, have begun again, and there would have been no principate. He lived to be very old, although he had faced many great dangers. He was saved from them more than once by the goddess Fortuna, who looked kindly on him. Even his contemporaries saw that he was her favourite, and in fact he owed his survival to a considerable number of coincidences. They included not only assassination attempts, which he escaped by pure luck, but also unpredictable situations and sudden changes in the course of events that brought him entirely unexpected success, for instance in the spring of 43 BC, when the death of both consuls meant that leadership of the Senate's entire army fell into his hands, or in the spring of 40, when he was surrounded by armies, but the sudden death of an enemy general changed what had been a very difficult situation for him into a very favourable one. In addition, he profited to a great extent by Antony's all but inexplicable easy-going attitude to him.

*

The outstanding achievement of Augustus is his rescue of the state and the empire from a major crisis that seemed to offer almost no prospects. The Roman state was in danger of total collapse; the ruling class in society was breaking up entirely and threatened to carry everything down into the abyss with it. It had controlled the fate of Rome for 500 years, and there was no substitute ready to hand. The attempt to replace it with naked military dictatorship had failed on the Ides of March. The assassination of the dictator had also shown that the state could be saved only by an aristocratic society able and willing to take over its administration; it could not survive without that leadership class, let alone in opposition to it. If not quite everything had already fallen apart in the civil wars – for a new elite could not, after all, simply emerge from nowhere – that was solely because every hint of political independence in the structures of those Mediterranean states over which the Romans had established their ascendancy had been snuffed out during centuries of conflict. The powerlessness of its subjects was a prerequisite for the salvation of the Roman state from apparently inexorable decline.

Augustus kept the state of Rome and Roman rule alive and truly earned the citizens' crown that since time immemorial had been given to a Roman soldier who saved a comrade from mortal danger, even if the first time it was awarded to him, during the proscriptions, does not seem quite the right moment. The year 27 would have been better.

The work of Augustus was not confined to creating a new organizational framework, absorbing and reinvigorating the old constitution that no longer matched present developments in the state and society, thus becoming useless. That was what Sulla had done when he reformed the state after the civil war in the late eighties, and Diocletian was to do the same 300 years later. Augustus, on the other hand, had first to reconstitute the society on which the state had depended, something that Sulla had not thought necessary and Diocletian did not need to do. What Augustus had to achieve was far more difficult. Constructing a new leadership class, without which the state and the empire could not have functioned, could not be done overnight, and it seems almost incredible that he achieved that aim in what, considering the vast extent of the task, was a relatively short time. With great patience and personal commitment he brought together representatives of families both old and new and at the same time made sure that the never-ending work of forming a new aristocracy remained in his hands.

Without firm ideological and moral foundations for society, his task would have been impossible, and constructing them must have been the most difficult and also the most daring aspect of his work on the new state. He not only gave the senators and knights – and the notable men of the cities – the concept of a Greater Rome, which could be taken for granted anyway, above all he 'restored' the idea of the old state, that is to say he made them feel that it had never ceased to exist and that they, in partnership with him and under his guidance, were in charge of it. However, there was a latent danger in the 'restoration' of the old state and the traditions that went with it: it lay not in the fact that a member of the upper class (the senatorial aristocracy) might see it as a return to old, 'republican' conditions (that is a view reserved for modern observers), but that he might assume there was greater political scope for individuals under the new monarchical regime than was actually the case. The incessant efforts that Augustus made to involve the senators in public life and get them to express their opinions freely should not be understood as encouraging them to strike out on independent initiatives. His aim, instead, was to consolidate the state and his regime by means of a system of regulations adapted to the new circumstances, and the formation of an elite able to undertake the tasks of its administration under the monarch and guided by him. To achieve this aim, the monarch's constant contact with individuals who were to join or remain in the leadership group was necessary. Augustus constantly had to enlist the aid of others, accept disappointments and put up with being slandered as the tyrant he certainly was not. It was a labour of Sisyphus that he had to perform, starting from the beginning over and over again. That called for a steadfast mind and a strong will, and if his persistence sometimes seemed didactic there was no help for that. He always had to keep his balance between the monarch and the teacher of behaviour conducive to the new 'liberty', he had to hide the extent of his actual power and even do the best he could to conceal the legal opportunities open to him. For while they might allow him to put anything he liked into practice, he deliberately did not construct them as a concentrated legal force for his own use; they were a motley collection of the partial rights and privileges of the magistracy from which he could pick and choose as necessary. There was no single term to describe the sum of his legal powers as a whole; they functioned without one. According to the old law Augustus was not even a magistrate (*magistratus*), and he himself did not bear the title of proconsul in the empire. In fact his dominant position did not correspond to any title at all. On occasion Augustus himself spoke of his *statio*, meaning position or post, a term conveying something of its military sense and presenting him as a man who was always 'on guard' for the Romans and the provincials alike. The term for his constitutional position was explicitly political: he was the *princeps*, that is to say the First Citizen, but he was also – in fact but not in title – the monarch; both were the political reality. As he had been a military potentate in the past, and his supreme command of the army remained the foundation of his rule, visible to all, he had to pay particular attention to his function as First Citizen. In spite of many lapses, he showed remarkable patience in doing so and acted the part in many scenes performed before the high society of Rome.

Well over 100 years ago, Theodor Mommsen interpreted the principate as a constitution that, despite its monarchical structure, stood within the framework of the constitutional order of the 'republic'. He consequently counted the *princeps* as one of the magistrates of the republic, thus giving his concentration of legal powers, however diffuse and contrary to republican legal thinking it was, the quality of official authority, supported by the collegiate body of office-holders of equal rank among themselves. This thesis has been, and still is, firmly rejected by many who think they know better, as if Mommsen, the foremost historian of the ancient world, and not only in his own time, did not know that the principate meant monarchy, as if his ideas of the legal order, expressing as they did the logical concepts of the legal system of his time, had led him into making the mistake of equating the *princeps* with the other holders of office, who were entirely dependent on him. But in fact with the construction he put on the principate Mommsen was trying to clarify its connection with the republic, which consisted of the survival of an administrative aristocracy and the existence of a general framework of order, in which the public life of the principate ran its course. In doing so, he restored to the principate its significance as a constitutional order, which was the way Augustus wished it to be seen and his contemporaries understood it, although little notice was taken of that in Mommsen's day. The change in public law – relating now to the *princeps* and no longer to an aristocratic elite – is a different story. But Mommsen's view allows us to see the principate, if not as a continuation of the state of the past, which had been ruled by the administrative elite, at least as an intellectual reference back to it. The continuity was complemented by many non-legal elements, above all the ideological values of the past, which were also understood to be still in force. At least as long as the senatorial aristocracy in its new form as created by Augustus lasted, and the *princeps* regarded himself as its partner, something of the republic lived on in the principate.

We cannot overlook the fact that the state built by Augustus, the 'constitution of the principate' that had to symbolize the continued existence of the old state in new political and social circumstances, was an artificial product. The confusion of modern interpreters, some of whom hail the principate as the resurrection of the republic, while others dismiss it as a deceptive façade, can be taken as an expression of the ambivalence of the artificially built structure, which was not coincidental, unintended and inadvertent but was a constituent part of the work. The principate was artificial in the sense that it was not a skilful modification of existing circumstances in pursuit of a political line. Instead, Augustus created something entirely new, a structure planned in advance and incorporating features of the old state that looked useful; his principle was always to look for practical ways of realizing his ideas. The principate of Augustus appears, so to speak, top-heavy.

Not only the state regulations but also the political ideas required to support the new structure of the state began as intellectual products that in part, like the idea of the Rome of old and its virtues and merits, were attached to what existed. Other elements, however, like the religious superstructure beneath which the First Citizen became the monarch, represented a new form of religious rule consisting of many elements, and revealing the master's guiding hand in its complexity and equilibrium. The will of Augustus to create and shape something new was particularly visible in his social policy, which, because it related to human life and thought, showed the ideas behind it sharply outlined. For while Augustus was also drawing on ideas that can be traced far back into republican times, the fundamental concept of his legislation on marriage and its practical execution are in the spirit of a will to shape it unconditionally; it is the product of a preconceived order ignoring social realities.

The succession policy was also inappropriate to the existing political situation. It would really have been best to present as successor a grown man of an age to hold office and distinguished by public achievement.

Instead, Augustus made blood relationship with him the qualification, thus setting aside the established rule that adoption gave every citizen who was adopted equal rank with the adopter's natural children. In pursuit of his aim, he took those members of his family whom he thought particularly suitable for the succession and moved them like chessmen by means of marriages, divorces, adoptions and, when these moves went wrong, as they were bound to do, by banishment until the family itself was as good as destroyed. His policy for the succession was a total failure, but it is further evidence of his belief that he must force his preconceived wishes through even in this delicate area, with no regard for the personal feelings of his family.

Augustus may be credited with more than the consolidation of the Roman state and Roman society. His governmental policy was almost equally important. The huge and ever-growing empire, with its many provinces, had almost suffocated the aristocratic governing system of the old order by the end. It was no longer suitable for administration by a number of different men and had sunk to being merely the object of exploitation by individual members of the nobility and a way for them to gain power. The new, monarchical system of government contained the prerequisite for a proper administration, meaning above all a considerate one, and Augustus energetically set about giving the inhabitants of the provinces, both those dependent on Rome and those that were formally allies, not only the hope but also the certainty that the new figure at the head of the Roman state was their patron and thought of their welfare. Not only did he bring peace to the empire as a whole, he also introduced honest and upright dealing and built up an administration that concerned itself with the needs of the people. Countless measures for the good of the inhabitants of the cities, and never-failing attention to good administration encouraging the welfare of provincials, led to a previously hardly imaginable positive attitude on their part to Rome and the Romans. The new ruler stood for the dawn of a just and peaceful age. No one doubted his divine quality, but his earthly nature as it affected ordinary people was certainly more important to the dwellers in the provinces. Augustus ruled the circle of the earth (*orbis terrarum*) and the establishment of his rule guaranteed the good fortune of all who lived under it. He appeared to them like a father figure bringing peace and prosperity to everyone, Romans and provincials alike. They revered him because, as the people of Baetica in the south of

Spain put it on dedicating a gilded statue to him, 'through his good deeds and lasting care the province is now at peace'. When the monarch turned to the provinces he gave his subjects there the status of acknowledged members of society. And if Augustus also made sure that Romans took precedence over provincials, he created the conditions whereby the latter could gradually become full Roman citizens and the empire of Rome become an empire of the Romans.

There is nothing really comparable with the special form of Augustan state-building in the history of the world. It was set up solely to serve the ruler's dealings with the leadership class and their mutual cooperation, and hardly anything like it can be found elsewhere. The mere idea of creating a new society appears unique and even absurd, and the particular form of the principate cannot be illustrated by any kind of comparison. Nothing but the political work of Augustus as a whole, comprising the revival of the Roman state and empire from almost hopeless decline and the stabilization of the new order, invites us to try looking for one. Augustus ensured that the state and empire would stand firm for the next two and a half centuries. In the whole of ancient history there are only two other men whose achievements appear comparable, and neither was an architect, but rather the destroyer of what he found.

Alexander was the more brutal destroyer. He annihilated an empire out of his sheer urge for conquest, thereby bringing down the existing political structures of the Greek world. The few attempts he made to reorganize those he had robbed into states where native and Greek systems mingled were certainly not the aim of his endeavours, as his own contemporaries knew when they saw him, directly after he had overthrown the Persian empire, preparing to annihilate other domains. When Caesar returned to Rome in the year 49, he too came to destroy the old state. Although a number of his measures indicate a wish to change it, and the grand style of some of them in their initial stages inspires some modern interpreters with such enthusiasm that they occasionally even think Caesar one of the greatest statesmen of all time, we cannot see even the framework of a new order shaped by him, let alone a society that could have maintained it. He too remains, first and foremost, a conqueror and a destroyer.

And yet Augustus is not considered by either ancient or modern historians to be the equal of these two, or other outstanding men in classical antiquity. No one ever thought of calling him 'the Great', like Alexander or Pompey. He is not a figure to inspire liking, either then or now. Obviously, qualities of intellect and character are associated with the term 'the Great', and people thought they saw them in other men rather than Augustus, or perhaps simply ascribed them to such men. He was not 'noble' or 'high-minded', or any of the other things that are supposed to make a man great; he was considered, indeed, cruel, underhand and hypocritical. Nor was he a talented man of letters whose books were read by children before they regarded him as a politician. On the contrary, he was responsible for the killing of Cicero, the most eloquent orator and outstanding philosopher of the day, or at least allowed Antony to put him on the list of those to be killed. Nor was he of the distinguished descent that might have made others regard his failings with indulgence. He not only seemed to lack the qualities of greatness, he ran counter to them in his didacticism and pedantry, in the appearance of being a plain and affable man that he wore for show, in the modest nature of his literary interests and abilities. Indeed, he seems to be boringly average, and for that very reason the cruel deeds of his youth were not forgotten as they were overlooked in a man like Antony. Augustus was not and is not considered exceptional, and to be an Everyman figure is unpardonable in one who aspires to greatness.

His political achievements also seem to lack what we value in 'great men'. He was not a charismatic general who could sweep his men away with him or a brilliant tactician and strategist; in fact he was so far from it that we are sometimes inclined to regard him as a man controlled by his generals or even as a coward, and then as now we find ourselves reading the tales of his failed attempts to play the part of military commander with a certain glee. His apparently average nature makes him a target for malice. Was he hanging back like a coward at Philippi when he was out of sight for so long or was he suffering from diarrhoea? We do not entertain such speculations about Alexander; even when he murdered his friend Cleitos we do not wonder whether it was the work of a furious tyrant or perhaps an alcoholic, we try to understand. And few wish to expose Caesar sitting in judgement over his enemies in his private house as a tyrant setting himself above the law. It is easier to accuse Cicero, as a lawyer, of discreditable political ideas and indecision. Augustus did expand the empire, adding large tracts of land to it, an achievement that can be ranked with the conquests of Caesar and Pompey, but he did not win the battles himself; other men won them for him: first Antony, then Agrippa, Salvidienus Rufus, Drusus and Tiberius, to name only a few of his generals. A critical observer may add that while his 'servants' were in the field, Augustus was behind the lines or sitting in Rome counting up the acclamations as *imperator* that others had won for him. There are reports of a correctly dressed lecturer in a German university lecture hall, when the death of Alexander was about to be announced, shedding a tear of emotion as the last soulful word died away in his throat. No one has ever been known to show grief or even melancholy over the account of the death of Augustus.

His political achievement, then, arouses no elevated feelings, nor did it in his own day. Most of the senators who, whether from old or previously obscure families, formed the new senatorial aristocracy did not thank him for the security of their social position, for as they saw it they had lost something. That something was political liberty, and even if they had never really had it but did indeed owe their rank in society to Augustus, they looked back to the past sadly and let men of letters, including some who called themselves historians, whisper that because of that loss they should regard the monarch with suspicion. In fact the tedious business of leading the aristocracy to adjust to the new political facts, to which Augustus devoted himself for almost fifty years, was not likely to inspire political enthusiasm even in those who had benefited by it. It was not only the members of the old families who found it difficult to adapt to the circumstances. They all had to subordinate themselves, work hard for the sake of their social standing and could not think of idleness; they always had before them this man who so often reproved them either singly or en masse, perhaps lecturing them from a scroll or from notes made while he was reading at home, quoting examples of proper conduct from the good old days or sending them off to consult with civil servants. Indeed, he was always delivering lectures, either in the Senate or in edicts to the people of Rome. Public life had become a school in which the teacher – there was only one – dinned the rules to be observed in public work into gentlemen who were not as eminent as before, and he could lose his temper if everything was not done by the book. When he let fly, they were very ready to whisper privately that he was a tyrant and a hypocrite and to listen to the writers who 'unmasked' the idea of the principate as mere pretence, declaring that the principate itself was a disguise for tyranny. The politician as pedagogue is not calculated to be an appealing figure. Even modern historians prefer to write about violent events, so Alexander and Caesar are dear to their hearts.

Augustus was the architect of the Roman empire. With him begins the line of *imperators* whom we call the Caesars (a word that of course survives into modern German as 'Kaiser'), although initially their title was 'Augustus' or '*princeps*'. But for him Rome would have ended up as a military dictatorship – or the military dictatorship that had already existed since the year 49 would have continued. However, an empire the size of Rome's could not be maintained in the long term by such a form of government. It is idle speculation to wonder how the empire would have developed without Augustus. The consensus between an administrative aristocracy and the monarch, secured in the principate, did at least place the Roman state and empire on firm foundations that lasted, in the form he had given them, for over 200 years, and that were also a prerequisite for the continued existence of the empire in following centuries. The monarchy and the senatorial aristocracy were the two pillars on which government rested. As the consensus between them was not achieved simply by a set of rules working automatically but was reached, or rather kept having to be restored, in continuous interplay, the system broke down now and then, usually on the side of the monarchy. A monarch born into the purple, often an immature young man, might not always see why, in view of his great powers, he should regard a good relationship with the senatorial class as necessary to his regime. But these occasional failures, which were rare and could quickly be corrected, were not typical of the principate itself; its outstanding characteristic was its long duration, and consequently a long period of peace at home, which to a later observer used to wars and unrest may seem almost like the peace of the graveyard. Augustus the architect had little in common with Alexander the destroyer and he was understandably surprised – or has been reported by others to have been surprised – that Alexander, wondering what to do with the rest of his life after so many victories, did not think it would be a greater achievement to preserve the empire he had won than to conquer it in the first place.

The historian Cassius Dio, writing 200 years later, a man who himself held high office, correctly signalled the importance of the consensus between the monarchy and the aristocracy in his assessment of Augustus – or better, anyway, than Tacitus 100 years before him, whose verdict on Augustus and his immediate successors had not emerged from the orbit of those senatorial circles where they still indulged in sentimental regrets for their freedom, and who was not, therefore, in a situation to judge the principate properly. Dio, on the other hand, clearly presents the principate as the ideal constitution for a state – that is to say, out of those basic forms of state that could be imagined in his time: 'Not alone for these reasons did the Romans [grieving for the death of Augustus] greatly miss him, but also because by combining monarchy with democracy he preserved their freedom for them and at the same time established order and security, so that they were free alike from the licence of a democracy and from the insolence of a tyranny, living at once in a liberty of moderation and in a monarchy without terrors; they were subjects of royalty, yet not slaves, and citizens of a democracy, yet without discord.'

# *Notes*

CHAPTER I

## Main Sources

Civil war and Caesar's rule (49–15.3.44 BC): App. b.c. 2,134–469; Cass. Dio 41–3; Cic. Att. 7,10–13,58, also many letters from the collection to his friends (*ad familiares*) (all letters quoted as numbered in the editions of the Bibliotheca Oxoniensis, those from the collection of Brutus' letters also from the more recent edition by W. S. Watt); Nicol. Damascen. 1–106; Suet. Div. Jul. 31–44; Plutarch: Caes. 32–61; Pomp. 60–80; Cic. 37–42; Brut. 7–18.

Conspiracy and Ides of March: Nicol. Damascen. 17,48–50; 19–27; 58–106; App. b.c. 2,470–508; Cass. Dio 44,12–22; Suet. Div. Jul. 80–82; Plut. Caes. 62–7.

## Explanatory Notes

p. 1 *Caesar's remarks*: Suet. Div. Jul. 86,2: 'non tam sua quam rei publicae interesse, ut salvus esset; se iam pridem potentiae gloriaeque abunde adeptum; rem publicam, si quid sibi eveniret, neque quietam fore et aliquanto deteriore condicione civilia bella subituram'.

p. 2 *The Ides of March*: The words of Brutus after the assassination: Cic. Phil. 2,28. Assistance rendered by Calvisius and Marcius: Nicol. Damascen. 26,96. They were both rewarded when Antony and Octavian, after their reconciliation in Brundisium in the year 39 BC, appointed them to the consulate.

p. 4 *The name of Marcus Brutus*: As the son of his birth parents his name was Marcus Junius Brutus. After his adoption by one Quintus Servilius Caepio, probably a brother of his mother Servilia, in the year 59 (Brutus was twenty-six years old at the time) he should have been known, according to Roman usage, as Quintus (or Marcus) Servilius Caepio Junianus (in such cases the *nomen gentile*, the gens name of the birth father, was added in its adjectival

621

form with the ending -*anus* as a second cognomen to that of the adoptive father). Officially, however, he was known as Quintus Caepio Brutus. The suppression of the *nomen gentile* was less conspicuous because, among the large number of bearers of that name, including freedmen, it often went unmentioned at this time, so that a bearer of the name was usually addressed if not by his forename, *praenomen*, by the more clearly distinctive cognomen. If the *nomen gentile* was meant to allude to the birth father, Brutus dealt with the matter by using the cognomen 'Brutus', instead of the adoptive form of the cognomen 'Junianus'. That was, of course, because the *cognomen* 'Brutus' referred more clearly than 'Junianus' would have done to his famous ancestor, Lucius Junius Brutus, one of the first two consuls of the republic.

p. 6 *Antony on Cicero*: Cic. Phil. 2,30: Cicero as a man who had known about the conspiracy (*conscius*); fam. 12,2,1: Cicero as instigator (*auctor*) of the assassination.

p. 7 *The Tyrannicides group in Athens*: The original sculptural group showing Harmodios and Aristogeiton was by Antenor and was stolen by the Persians as the spoils of war after their occupation of Athens in the year 480. After the overthrow of the Persian empire by Alexander the group was returned to the Athenians, probably by one of the first Seleucid rulers. In 477/6, Kritios and Nesiotes created a new group of which we have only copies; see Antony E. Raubitschek, *Dedications from the Athenian Akropolis*, 1949, 481ff., 513ff.; Werner Fuchs, *Die Skulptur der Griechen*, 1969, 337ff.

pp. 9–10 *The decreasing numbers of the nobility*: The most important group for political decision-making consisted of the former consuls (consulars), who were the first to be asked their opinion in the Senate. In September 44, when Cicero began organizing the resistance of the 'republicans' to Antony, whom he described as a new tyrant, the senators included the following twelve consulars, who – except for Isauricus – had held the office before the outbreak of the civil war, and thus in a time of free voting (see Cic. fam. 12.2ff., letter of 25.9.44): L. Aurelius Cotta (cons. 65, seldom attended the Senate), L. Julius Caesar (cons. 64, unwell at this time), M. Tullius Cicero (cons. 63), C. Antonius (cons. 63), L. Calpurnius Piso Caesoninus (cons. 58), L. Marcius Philippus (cons. 56), M. Valerius Messalla Rufus (cons. 53), Cn. Domitius Calvinus (cons. 53), Ser. Sulpicius Rufus (cons. 51, out of Rome at the time), L. Aemilius Paullus (cons. 50), C. Claudius Marcellus (cons. 50), and P. Servilius Isauricus (cons. 48, but had begun his career before 48). Several of them were supporters of Antony. Among the consulars there were also a number of supporters of Caesar, all of them except Lepidus *homines novi*: Q. Fufius Calenus (cons. 47), P. Vatinius (cons. 47), M. Aemilius Lepidus (cons. 46), C. Trebonius (cons. 45), C. Caninius Rebilus (the one-day consul of 45); and to them should be added the future consuls of the year 43, C. Vibius Pansa and A. Hirtius. The consuls of the year 44, Mark Antony and P. Cornelius Dolabella, had risen to prominence through Caesar but belonged to old noble families. Not all the consulars were available for discussions in the Senate; apart from brief absences from Rome, illness or disinclination to attend, many were active outside Italy as governors or army commanders. For instance, Vatinius was in Illyricum in 44, and Lepidus and Trebonius went to their provinces in the same year, as did the consuls Antony and Dolabella. See also, on the weakness of the group of consulars, Syme, *Revolution*, 164ff.

p. 13 *Caesar on his dignitas*: Caes. bell. civ. 1,9,2: 'sibi [sc. Caesaris] semper primum fuisse dignitatem vitaque potiorem' ('to him, Caesar, *dignitas* always meant more than life'; see 1,7,1, 8,3, 32,4.

p. 15 *Cicero on the consulate of Rebilus*: Plut. Caes. 58.2ff.; see Cic. fam. 7,30,1.

pp. 15–17 *The Senate under Caesar*: See Jehne, *Caesar*, 80ff., 392ff. Senators descended from formerly non-Roman families, for instance of Spanish descent, remained few and far between, while among the centurions who formed the backbone of every army there were some members of respected families from Italian country towns; they were not all brutal, uncouth men of humble origin, slave-drivers of the recruits. Most new senators still came from families of equestrian rank, who were just below senators in the hierarchy or belonged to the upper class of the country towns of Italy. However, fewer of them now came from the towns of the old Roman citizenship area in Latium, Campania and central Italy. The majority were prominent men from towns and cities that had been included in that area only since the civil war of 90–88 BC, known as the Social War, or not until the time of Caesar. Upper Italy, which he had administered as its governor for ten years, and from which he recruited men for a number of his legions, was undoubtedly over-represented among the new senators. Caesar also made another move towards the dissolution of senatorial rule by taking it upon himself to appoint new patricians. Members of the oldest aristocratic families had always been termed patricians, and after the middle of the fourth century they, with a few plebeian families, formed the new aristocracy, the nobility. It was a man's origin that made him a patrician; he could not be promoted to that rank, as Caesar, himself from a patrician family, of course knew. And if he, who as a patrician could feel no resentment of the patrician part of the nobility, introduced that innovation, it makes the political aims he was pursuing by such means all the clearer. Cicero on the Senate under Caesar: Macrob. Sat. 2,3,11.

p. 17 *The assembly of the people under Caesar*: See Jehne, *Caesar*, 110ff., 416ff.

p. 20 *Caesar on the republic*: Suet. Div. Jul. 77: 'nihil esse rem publicum, appellationem modo sine corpore ac specie'.

pp. 20–23 *The honours given to Caesar*: See Jehne, *Caesar*, 191ff. Roman religion in the time of Caesar presented a complex picture. In the account given in the text, I have dwelt on one feature – but certainly the dominating one – of early Roman religion, because over a long period that feature made it very difficult for the Romans to elevate a human being to divinity. The Greeks themselves had not taken the deification of mortals for granted. The first Greek to whom divine honours were intentionally paid was Lysander, the Spartan commander of the end of the fifth century BC; see Christian Habicht, *Gottmenschentum und griechische Städte*, 1956, 3ff. For Roman religion see Muth, introduction to Habicht; idem, 'Religio'; Carl Joachim Classen, 'Gottmenschentum in der römischen Republik', *Gymnasium* 70, 1963, 312–38.

pp. 24–6 *The question of the formal outlines of Caesar's rule*: Cicero on the rule of Caesar: Cic. Phil. 1,3: 'dictaturam, quae iam vim regiae potestatis obsed-erat, funditus ex re publica sustulit' (sc. Mark Antony). Modern scholars have discussed at length the form taken by Caesar's rule: see the survey in Jochen Bleicken, *Geschichte der römischen Republik*, 1988³, 210ff. Here I will men-tion only the position taken by Jehne (*Caesar*, 15ff., 186ff.). According to his line of argument, Caesar also gave his actual (military) power legal form through the dictatorship and logically extended it by adding special rights, honours, etc. The dictatorship for life, he argues, could add nothing to Caesar's existing, extensive and comprehensive area of jurisdiction and consequently – here one must agree – 'has to be interpreted as a sign of the permanent reshaping [of the actual power of Caesar] to make it an autocratic regime' (p. 38). Theodor Mommsen, in a note directing readers to Cic. div. 2,110, rightly dismissed the traditional idea that at the Senate meeting of 15 March 44 (when he could not be king in Rome) Caesar wanted to be given the title *rex* for the non-Roman area of the empire. This belongs in the realm of slander. The question of the deification of Caesar has also been controversial. Those who support the idea that Caesar aimed to become a king in the Hellenistic tradition must presuppose that this was his deliberate policy. Helga Gesche (*Die Vergottung Caesars*, 1968; cf. idem, *Caesar*, 162ff.) has suggested a new methodological approach distinguishing between a deifica-tion policy to be seen merely as a rise in rank and one placing the deified person on a par with the gods. Using this model, she tries to show that Cae-sar aimed only for the former in his lifetime but wanted the latter after his death (cf. finally Jehne, *Caesar*, 217ff.). A survey of research on these prob-lems will be found in Gesche, *Caesar*, 142ff. (up to 1973), and *Jehne*, Caesar, 191ff.

p. 26 *Caesar's will*: Nicol. Damascen. 13,30, 17,48 (testamentary adoption and inheritance of three-quarters of his property); Suet. Div. Jul. 83 (the phrasing of the adoption of Augustus: 'in ima cera Gaium Octavium etiam in familiam nomenque adoptavit'; see Liv. per. 116); App. b.c. 2,596ff.; Cass. Dio 44,35,2ff. The two co-heirs of Octavian, Quintus Pedius and Lucius Pinarius, are mentioned only in Suet. Div. Jul. 83,2 as nephews of Caesar: 'tres instituit heredes sororum nepotes, Gaium Octavium ex dodrante, et Lucium Pinarium et Quintum Pedium ex quadrante reliquo'. The use of the genitive plural of *soror*, the naming of the last two together and the fact that they are treated equally all show that they were descendants of another sister of Caesar, about whom we know nothing, from two different marriages. They could have been nephews or – like Gaius Octavius – great-nephews of Caesar. We know little about Octavian's two co-heirs. However, Quintus Pedius must have been considerably older than Gaius Octavius, for he had been Caesar's legate in the Gallic War in the year 57. Assuming an age difference of about twenty years, he could have belonged to the generation of Octavian's father, and thus may have been his uncle. But if the two co-heirs were Caesar's great-nephews, we have to presume that there was another generation between them and the second Julian sister. Since Pedius and Pinarius are named together in the will and received identical legacies, it is at least probable that they were *both* either nephews or great-nephews of Caesar. On this problem, see Friedrich Münzer, 'Aus dem Verwandtenkreise Caesars und Octavians', *Hermes* 71, 1936, 222–30. Antony on 'the boy' Octavian: Cic. Phil. 13,24ff. (20.3.43): 'et te, o puer, qui omnia ... nomini debes id agere' (from Antony's letter to the consuls Hirtius and Pansa quoted by Cicero). On the subsidiary heirs: Cass. Dio 44,35,2; Suet. Div. Jul. 83,2; App. b.c. 2,597.

p. 26–32 *The testamentary adoption of Octavian*: For the career of Octavius before the Ides of March, see in particular Vell. Pat. 2,59. The funeral oration of Octavius for his grandmother Julia: Suet. Aug. 8,1; Quintil. Inst. 12,6,1. The appointment of Octavius as Master of the Horse is also disputed, but see Helga Gesche, 'Hat Caesar den Octavian *sic* zum Magister equitum designiert? Ein Beitrag zur Beurteilung der Adoption Octavians durch Caesar', *Historia* 22, 1973, 468–78. Cicero last mentions him as 'Octavius' in mid-May 44, and from 10 June calls him 'Octavianus': see Att. 15,2,3; 12,2; 16,9,1; 11,6. Plancus expressly says that Cicero recognized the testamentary adoption *filii loco* in a letter to him (fam. 10,24,5). For the imputation to Octavius of vicious practices leading to the making of the will: Suet. Aug. 68. Acceptance of the will before the praetor Gaius Antonius: App. b.c. 3,49. Curiate law on the adoption of Octavian: App. b.c. 3,389. On the testamentary adoption of Lucius Licinius Crassus (Scipio or Cornelianus), whose birth father was Publius Cornelius Scipio Nasica, praetor in 93, see Cic. Brut. 212; on the adoption of Atticus by his uncle Quintus Caecilius in the year 58, when he was around fifty-one, see Corn. Nep. Att. 5,2: 'Caecilius ... moriens testamento adoptavit eum heredemque fecit ex dodrante' ('The dying Caecilius ... adopted him in his will and made him heir to three-quarters of his property'). Not a testamentary adoption, but an instance of the adoption of an adult was that of the son of Publius Cornelius Lentulus Spinther, consul in the year 57, by a member of the Manlian family (Cass. Dio 39,17,1ff.), and in his will one Marcus Gallius adopted the four-year-old Tiberius Claudius Nero, later to be emperor (Suet. Tib. 6,3). On the question of the potential posthumous son, see Schmitthenner (see below) 25ff. The appointment of guardians: Suet. Div. Jul. 83,2. The fact that Caesar still believed in, and probably hoped for, the birth of a son of his own has come down to us from a note found only in Cassius Dio, to the effect that he had himself given his name of Imperator (as a first name) and the dignity of *pontifex maximus* as hereditary titles (name of emperor: 43,44,3; 52,41,4, 40,2; *pontifex maximus*: 44,5,3). However, the veracity of Dio's account is not beyond all doubt, as we can tell from the context of the note. He may simply have assumed, from the bearing of those titles by all emperors up to his own time, that it was Caesar who had made them hereditary. On the testamentary adoptions of the late republic, see the list in Walter Schmitthenner, *Oktavian und das Testament Caesars. Eine Untersuchung zu den politischen Anfängen des Augustus*, 1952, 1973[3], 44ff., and Gerd Alfs, 'Adoptionen in der Zeit der römischen Republik bis auf die des Caesar Octavianus', Cologne, typewritten dissertation, 1950, 83ff. Alfs presupposes arrogation for all who were adopted *sui iuris*. However, arrogation had not been an instrument of regular legal adoption, but was used in the late republic only for public documentation of a change of gens, usually for political reasons. Scholars are divided in their assessment of the adoption of Gaius Octavius. Schmitthenner, in his highly regarded study of the subject (see above), supported the opinion that no testamentary adoption in the late republic could be proved, and that the adoption of Octavius was merely a case of his taking the name. On the whole, other scholars have not followed him, but recently Christiane Kunst, 'Adoption und Testamentsadoption in der Späten Republik', *Klio* 78, 1996, 87–104, has agreed with him at least in principle; on testamentary adoption in the late republic, as well as the works mentioned above, see M. H. Prévost, *Les Adoptions politiques à Rome sous la république et le principat*, Paris, 1949; idem, 'L'Adoption d'Octave', *Rev. Intern. des Droits de l'Antiquité* 5, 1950, 361–81; Alfs (see above) and Rudolf Düll, *Ztschr. Sav. Stiftg.* Roman. Abt. 93, 1976, 3ff. Our sources do not appear to distinguish between the transfer of a name (*nomen inferre*) and adoption (see, for instance, Cic. off. 3,74). In respect of testamentary adoption, and in particular the adoption of adults, in spite of a lack of general legal regulation the practice of equating the legal consequences of a testamentary adoption with the adoption of a child seems to have become established so far as the transfer of property, a name and the family *sacra* are concerned. Of course the practice of adoption under the principate, including the adoptions carried out by Augustus himself, proves nothing about the adoption of adults in the late republican period, since the adoption of Octavius in itself influenced the further development of the law on adoption. The radical views of Herbert Rosendorfer, 'Die angebliche Adoption des Augustus durch Cäsar', *Abhandlg. d. Akad. d. Wiss. u. Liter. Mainz*, geistes- u. sozialwiss. Kl., 1990, 1, who thinks the adoption clause in the will is to be considered a forgery, take into account only a part of our sources, and his rather polemical line of argument does not carry conviction. For the present state of research see Gesche, *Caesar*, 175–9, and Kienast, *Augustus*, 4ff.

## CHAPTER 2
# Main Sources

The family and youth of Gaius Octavius/Octavianus: Nicol. Damascen. 1–15, 1–36; Suet. Aug. 1–8; Cass. Dio 45,1–2.

15 March–Aug. 44 BC: App. b.c. 2,509–3,122; Cass. Dio 44,21–45,10; Nicol. Damascen. 16–31, 37–139; Cic. Att. 14,1–16,7, and letters from the collection to his friends (*ad familiares*).

# Explanatory Notes

pp. 35–6 *The time Octavius spent in Campania mid-April 44 BC*: Cic. Att. 14,12,2 ('nobiscum hic perhonorifice et peramice Octavius, quem quidem sui Caesarem salutabant; Philippus non, itaque ne nos quidem, quem nego posse esse bonum civem; ita multi circumstant, qui quidem nostris mortem minitantur' – 'Octavius showed me great friendship and honour here. His men addressed him as Caesar; Philippus did not and so nor did I. I do not think that he can be a citizen true to the constitution; there are too many around him who threaten our friends with death'; 22.4.44) and 14,10,3 ('mecum in Cumano, illum hereditatem aditurum' – 'He was with me at my villa in Cumae; he means to accept the legacy'; 19.4.44). On the first political moves by Octavian, see Andreas Alföldi, *Octavians Aufstieg zur Macht*, 1976; Heinz Bellen, 'Cicero und der Aufstieg Octavians', *Gymnasium* 92, 1985, 161–89; and finally Gotter, *Diktator*, 56ff. On the chronological problems of those months, Erich Becht, *Regeste über die Zeit von Cäsars Ermordung bis zum Umschwung in der Politik des Antonius (15. März bis 1. Juni anno 44 v. Chr.)*, 1911 (not '*bis 1. Juni anno 43 v. Chr.*', as erroneously given in the title of the book).

pp. 37–8 *The origins of Octavian's family*: Vell. Pat. 2,59 and Suet. Aug. 1–7. Suetonius (2,1–2) contains the genealogy of the Octavians obviously constructed as evidence of their origins in the old nobility. It suggests that at a very early period they split into a branch of the family with a future in the nobility and another with a future in the equestrian class. Significantly, Velleius (2,59,1), a fervent admirer of the Julio-Claudian house, remarks that little can be said about the descent of Octavian. Suet. Aug. 2,3 quotes what Augustus himself said about his origins, and also (2,3 and 4,2) on the denigration of his ancestors. On the youth of Octavian, see Gardthausen, *Augustus* I, 45ff. Cicero on the origin of Octavian: Cicero defended Octavian against the disparagement of him by Antony and his adherents particularly extensively and impressively in the Third Philippic (3,15–17), a speech that he delivered in the Senate on 20 December 44. The accusation of *ignobilitas* ('obscurity', 'low birth') formed the core of the attacks on Octavian.

p. 39 *Piso ensuring that Caesar's will was read*: Suet. Div. Jul. 83,1; App. b.c. 2,566ff.

pp. 41–5 *Antony*: Syme, *Revolution*, 103ff. and *passim*, gives a sober assessment of Mark Antony at this time. He does not see him only through the lens of our sources, which are critical of Antony in many respects, nor does he interpret his conduct from the viewpoint of modern attempts at retrospective justification of his actions, but seeks to do him justice in the context of the political possibilities of decision-making that were open to him after the Ides of March. In particular, he does not see him as the 'wild man' he is represented to be at this time by a number of authors of antiquity, especially, of course, his arch-enemy Cicero. On Antony's speech at the funeral of Caesar, see Wilhelm Kierdorf, *Laudatio Funebris. Interpretationen und Untersuchungen zur Entwicklung der römischen Leichenrede*, 1980, 150ff. Cicero on the laws passed by Antony: 'tabulae figuntur, immunitates dantur, pecuniae maximae discribuntur, exsules reducuntur, sensatus consulta falsa referuntur' (fam. 12,1,1; 3.5.44, to Cassius).

pp. 44–5 *Dolabella's claim to Syria*: This does not seem to have been disputed at any time after the Ides of March, not even by Cicero, who on 17 April 44 (Att. 14,9,3) assumes that Dolabella's governorship of Syria is to be taken for granted. On the settlement laws enacted by the consuls Mark Antony and Dolabella, see W. Sternkopf, 'Lex Antonia agraria', *Hermes* 47, 1912, 146–51. In line with Ludwig Lange and others, he distinguishes between two of Antony's settlement laws but rightly regards them both as laws passed by the consuls Mark Antony and Dolabella (*leges Antonia Cornelia*; the tribune of the people Lucius Antonius, Antony's brother, had no hand in the second). The first can be dated to April and the second to June 44.

p. 47 *Quotations from the letters of Cicero*: On Antony as 'heir to the throne' (*regni heredem*): Att. 14,21,3 (11.5.44); on the persistence of the tyranny: Att. 14,14,2 (28.4.44); on fears that the new tyrant would set a bloodbath going: Att. 14,13,2 (26.4.44); on the pointlessness of the action on the Ides of March: Att. 14,12,1 (22.4.44); on the childish planning of the assassination: Att. 14,21,3 ('acta enim illa res animo virili, consilio puerili', 11.5.44); and on the tree not fully uprooted: Att. 15,4,2 ('excisa enim est arbor, non evulsa', 24.5.44).

p. 52 *The correspondence between Cicero and Matius*: Cic. fam.11,27 and 28. Cicero's central and unconcealed accusation is in 27,8: 'te ... non fugit, si Caesar rex fuerit – quod mihi quidem videtur – in utramque partem de tuo officio disputari posse, vel in eam, qua ego soleo uti, laudandam esse fidem et humanitatem tuam, qui amicum etiam mortuum diligas, vel in eam, qua non nulli utuntur, libertatem patriae vitae amici anteponendam' ('it cannot escape your notice that, if Caesar was king – which in my opinion he was – one can speak of your office in two ways, namely first in what I consider is the usual way, praising your loyalty and humanity even towards your dead friend, and second saying, as many do, that the liberty of one's fatherland is to be set above the life of a friend'). See also Alfred Heuss, 'Cicero und Matius: Zur Psychologie der revolutionären Situation in Rom', *Historia* 5, 1956, 53–73, and idem, 'Matius als Zeuge von Caesars staatsmännischer Größe', *Historia* 11, 1962, 118–22 (= idem, *Ges. Schriften*, II, 1995, 1192–212 and 1213–17).

pp. 52–3 *Portents seen on Octavian's entry into Rome*: A halo around the sun: Vell. Pat. 2,59,6 ('solis orbis . . . velut coronam tanti mox viti capiti imponens' – 'a circle round the sun . . . as if setting a wreath on the head of a man soon to be of importance'); Suet. Aug. 95 ('circulus ad speciem caelestis arcus orbem solis ambiit' – 'a circle in the nature of a rainbow lay around the sun'; ibid. also for the omen of the lightning).

p. 53 *Acceptance of the will before Praetor Gaius Antonius*: App. b.c. 3,49.

p. 54 *Antony and Lepidus*: On the appointment of Lepidus as *pontifex maximus* and the betrothal of the son of Lepidus to a daughter of Antony: Cass. Dio 44,53,6ff. On the date of the appointment, see Becht, op. cit.

pp. 56–8 *On Octavian and those around him*: Syme (*Revolution*) branded the young Octavian an adventurer and a revolutionary ('adventurer', 134; 'the cause of Caesar's heir was purely revolutionary in origin', 130), just as he considered the entire period between the years 60 BC and AD 14 in the light of a 'revolution'. His account relates entirely to the persons involved and is also almost exclusively confined to the elite. It is in the remodelling of this class that he thinks he sees the revolutionary procedure in the stricter sense. His concept of revolution, which he does not examine any further, thus remains indistinct, a vague outline. For all the recognition of his purely literary achievement, Syme has had a number of critics; see, for instance, the review of his book by Arnaldo Momigliano, *Journ. Rom. Stud.* 30, 1940, 75–80, and the contributors to a questionnaire circulated among classical scholars that also set out from Syme's book: *La rivoluzione romana. Inchiesta tra gli antichisti*, 1982 (see in particular the contributions by Alfred Heuss, 1ff.; Karl Christ, 11ff.; Francesco De Martino, 20ff.; and Carlo Lanza, 34ff.). See also the illuminating study of the character and work of Syme by Karl Christ, 'Ronald Syme', in idem, *Neue Profile der Alten Geschichte*, 1990, 188–247 (202ff. for criticism of Syme's use of the concept of revolution). On Syme, see also Alfred Heuss, 'Der Untergang der römischen Republik und das Problem der Revolution', *Histor. Zeitschr.* 182, 1956, 1–28 (= idem, *Ges. Schriften*, II, 1995, 1164–91); also Hartmut Galsterer, 'A Man, a Book, and a Method: Sir Ronald Syme's *Roman Revolution* after Fifty Years', in Raaflaub/Toher, 1–20 (especially on the prosopographic method), and Zvi Yavetz, 'The Personality of Augustus: Reflections on Syme's *Roman Revolution*', in Raaflaub/Toher, 21–41 (criticism of the lack of colour in Syme's account of his character).

p. 63 *Octavian's payment of Caesar's legacy to the Roman people*: It has been said that because the legacy was legally intended for certain persons (in juridical usage, *personae certae*), Octavian need not have paid it. That is to overlook the fact that acceptance of the will also implied the inclusion of *incertae personae*, and above all to forget that the payment was political in nature, where the amount of the sum and the recipients were concerned. Accepting a will with such a content was a political action.

p. 64 *The exchange of provinces*: This is also dated by modern historians to the end of July or beginning of August. However, as there is no doubt that the five-year period of command was granted to Antony at the beginning of June (Cic. Att. 15,11,4), and it is hard to see why the granting of that command should have been separated from the exchange of provinces, the June date deserves to have preference. In favour of it is also the fact that at exactly that time the Caesarians were all united; see Botermann, *Soldaten*, 22 note 4; Ehrenwirth, *Untersuchungen*, 6ff.; and Gotter, *Diktator*, 53ff., 270ff.

pp. 65–6 *The games for the dictator and the comet (sidus Iulium) at the games in honour of Venus*: Games: Cic. Att. 15,2,3 (preparations beginning in May); Cic. fam. 11,28,6 (the assistance of Matius); Nicol. Damascen. 28,108; Cass. Dio 45,6,4–7,2; Suet. Aug. 10,1. On the comet: Plin. nat. hist. 2,93ff. (after Augustus' own account in his memories of his life); Suet. Div. Jul. 88; Ovid metamorph. 15,749, 840 and 850; Cass. Dio, op. cit.; see Weinstock, *Divus Julius*, 378ff., and J. Ramsey/A. Lewis Licht, *The Comet of 44 BC and Caesar's Funeral Games*, 1997 (with an unsuccessful attempt to prove the historicity of the comet).

pp. 66–7 *The reconciliation of Antony and Octavian on the Capitol*: Nicol. Damascen. 28,115–19; App. b.c. 3,111–13; see Botermann, *Soldaten*, 27ff. On the dating, also see Botermann, *Soldaten*, 26ff., as well as Ehrenwirth, *Untersuchungen*, 62ff.

pp. 68–70 *On the situation of the assassins of Caesar in Italy*: Cicero on the assassins of Caesar and Antony in June 44: Att. 15,20,2. The crisis meeting in Antium on 8 June: Cic. Att. 15,11 and 12; see also 10. Finally, on Servilia and the role of women in the late republic see Maria H. Dettenhofer, 'Zur politischen Rolle der Aristokratinnen zwischen Republik und Prinzipat', *Latomus* 51, 1992, 775–95. The last edict issued by the praetors, of 4 August: Cic. fam. 11,3,4, whence the quotation comes: 'nos in hac sententia sumus, ut te cupiamus in libera re p. magnum atque honestum esse, vocemus te ad nullas inimicitias, sed tamen pluris nostram libertatem quam tuam amicitiam aestimemus'.

## CHAPTER 3
# Main Sources

September 44–April 43 BC: App. b.c. 3,123–298; Cass. Dio 45,11–46,38; Cic. Att. 15,13, 16,8–16, and many letters from the collection to his friends (*ad familiares*); idem, ad Brut.; idem, Phil.; Suet. Aug. 9–11; Plut. Cic. 42–5; idem, Anton. 14–17; idem, Brut. 18–23.

# Explanatory Notes

p. 72 *Cicero on his journey as flight from Antony*: Att. 15,20,2 (20.6.44).

p. 73 *On Cicero's Philippics*: The fourteen speeches that Cicero made before the Senate between 2.9.44 and 21.4.43 attacking Antony (for the second, see below, p. 78) form a single unit. They are modelled on the speeches made by Demosthenes attacking Philip II, king of Macedonia and father of Alexander the Great, known as the 'Philippic speeches' (*orationes Philippicae*). Four of the attacks on Philip mounted by Demosthenes had already been collected in classical antiquity under the title of 'Philippic speeches'. In them, Demosthenes defended the claim of Athens to its northern Aegean possessions and its status as a great power. Cicero had already described his speeches against Antony as *Philippicae* (sc. *Orationes*) in his letters (ad Brut. 4,2 = 2,4,2 and 3,4 = 2,3,4), thus claiming to be the equal of Demosthenes. In antiquity, Demosthenes and Cicero were already often linked together as the greatest orators of the Greek and Latin language area; Plutarch of Chaeronea also drew a parallel between them at the beginning of the second century AD in his account of the lives of Greek and Roman men.

Below, a summary of the speeches:

First Philippic: delivered before the Senate on 2.9.44. Criticizes Antony's discharge of his office, particularly with respect to his legislation, for which he claimed the support of Caesar's archives. Caustic as this attack is, Cicero is not entirely severing his links with Antony yet.

Second Philippic: Cicero's response to the speech made by Antony in the Senate on 19.9.44. Cicero did not deliver this speech publicly, and it was published only after his death. This very long text gives an account of Antony's policies in a polemic showing that we may now take the break with Antony for granted.

Third Philippic: delivered in the Senate on 20.12.44. Cicero expresses his support for the 'republican front' that he was promoting (Decimus Brutus, Octavian, and the consuls designate for the coming year, 43). He claims that the actions of Brutus, Octavian and the soldiers who had deserted Antony, although not within the law, had been carried out in the interests of the state, commends them, and describes their conduct as good. Cicero calls for all governors to remain in their posts until a different senatorial decision has been made and appeals to the future consuls to take action in support of the men he commends. He puts forward his propositions as a motion to be passed.

Fourth Philippic: on the same day, Cicero presents the decisions of the Senate to an assembly of the people (*contio*) and calls Antony an enemy of the state.

Fifth Philippic: delivered in the Senate on 1.1.43. Cicero speaks in opposition to the motion by Quintus Fufius Calenus to send a delegation to Antony, requiring him to cease military operations and withdraw from the province of Cisalpine Gaul. He proposes that motions honouring Decimus Brutus, Lepidus, Octavian and his troops be passed, among other motions suggesting the appointment of Octavian to propraetor, granting him senatorial dignity of the rank of a praetorian and allowing him to hold office before he has reached the legal age. Some of Cicero's motions are outdone in extravagance by additional motions from other senators, for instance that Octavian be granted consular rank. The Senate approves these motions next day. Cicero's attempt in the first part of the speech to get the Senate to call a state of emergency and declare war on Antony as an enemy of the state, however, fails.

Sixth Philippic: delivered before an assembly of the people (*contio*) on 4.1.43. Cicero opposes the senatorial decision to send an embassy to Antony.

Seventh Philippic: delivered in the Senate in mid-January. Cicero doubts that there was any point in sending the delegation that has now gone to Antony and once again demands war against him.

Eighth Philippic: delivered in the Senate on 3.2.43. Antony's negative answer to the envoys is discussed in the Senate after their return. Cicero turns against the previous day's senatorial decision, which, while noting the existence of 'uproar' (*tumultus*) in view of Antony's attitude, none the less, despite the obvious de facto state of conflict, avoided calling it war (*bellum*). He also opposes the attempt of Quintus Fufius Calenus to persuade the Senate to send a second delegation to Antony and suggests instead that all Antony's soldiers be called upon to report to the consuls, Decimus Brutus or Octavian by 15 March, and that if anyone goes to join Antony after the announcement of this senatorial decision, that man be regarded as an enemy of the state. The motion is passed.

Ninth Philippic: delivered in the Senate in early February 43. Cicero defends the motion to erect a statue honouring Servius Sulpicius Rufus, who died on the envoys' journey to see Antony and thus in the service of the state.

Tenth Philippic: delivered in the Senate in mid-February. On hearing the message sent by Marcus Brutus to the Senate saying that he has raised an army in the east, has occupied Illyricum, Macedonia and Greece, and his power is at the disposal of the republic, Cicero moves that Brutus be given command over the army and the provinces that he has occupied. The Senate agrees to this proposal.

Eleventh Philippic: delivered at the end of February 43 in the Senate. On receiving news of the assassination of Gaius Trebonius, governor of Asia, by the proconsul Publius Cornelius Dolabella on his way to his province of Syria, the Senate discusses measures to be taken against Dolabella. Contrary to other suggestions in this debate, Cicero recommends entrusting the conduct of the conflict with Dolabella to Cassius, who in the meantime has taken Syria, and giving him a supreme military command (*imperium maius*) for that purpose. This motion is not passed, and instead Pansa's proposition to entrust conduct of the war to the officiating consuls is adopted.

Twelfth Philippic: delivered in the Senate a few days after the Eleventh Philippic. It addresses the decision already made by the Senate to send another embassy to Antony. Cicero opposes this decision, giving reasons why, although he has been appointed one of the envoys, he cannot take part in the venture.

Thirteenth Philippic: delivered in the Senate on 20.3.43. A letter from Marcus Aemilius Lepidus, governor of Gallia Narbonensis and Citerior Spain, advising the Senate to make its peace with Antony, is read out. Cicero opposes this appeal for peace. In a second main section of his speech, he criticizes a letter to the consuls from Antony in which – in reply to the intention of sending another embassy to him – he justifies his policies and presents himself as leader of the Caesarians. Antony's letter, a significant document on which Cicero comments word by word, can be reconstructed in its entirety from this speech. Cicero's remarks do not go beyond pure polemics.

Fourteenth Philippic: delivered in the Senate on 21.4.43. Cicero comments critically on the propositions put forward in the Senate on the arrival of news of the victory won by Hirtius at the first battle of Forum Gallorum (a festival of thanksgiving to last several days, and the wearing of the toga as the garment of peace), pointing out that Decimus Brutus has not yet been liberated, nor is the war yet over. However, he finally recommends a thanksgiving festival to last fifty days, rewards for the victorious troops and honouring the fallen. His motion is passed.

p. 73 *Lentulus Sura*: Antony's stepfather. Julia, the mother of the three Antonian brothers, had married Sura as her second husband. In the year 63 he had sought to gain readmittance, through the praetorship, to the Senate, from which the censors of the year 70 had expelled him for his lax way of life. Mark Antony's claim that Cicero had handed over the body of the executed Sura only at the pleading of his own wife, to whom Julia had turned, is untrue (see Plut. Anton. 2,1; Cic. Phil. 2,17), but it is evidence of the hostility (*inimicitia*) existing between them ever since 63.

p. 74 *Brutus on Cicero's hatred of Antony*: Cic. ad Brut. 25 (= 1.17),1 (Brutus to Atticus, probably June 43): 'sed quaedam mihi videtur – quid dicam? – imperite vir [sc. Cicero] omnium prudentissimus an ambitiose fecisse, qui valentissimum Antonium suscipere pro re publica non dubitarit inimicium' ('But this man who in general is so extremely clever seems to me – how shall I put it? – to have done many things with little expertise, or out of ambition, for instance in making Antony, that very powerful man, his enemy in the interests of the state, without forethought').

p. 75 *Cicero to Cassius*: Fam. 15,15,1 (August 47): 'neque quisquam hanc nostram sententiam vere umquam reprendit praeter eos, qui arbitrantur melius esse deleri omnino rem p. quam imminutam et debilitatam manere; ego autem ex interitu eius nullam spem scilicet mihi proponebam, ex reliquiis magnam' ('and no one has ever thought badly of this view of ours, apart from those who think it would be better for the state to fall into ruin entirely than to continue in existence in a diminished and weakened condition. I, however, reflected that its downfall would naturally leave no hope, while if something remained there was still much hope left'). Cicero to Brutus: ad Brut. 23 (= 1,15),10: 'nullum enim bellum civile fuit in nostra re publica omnium, quae memoria mea fuerunt, in quo bello non, utracumque pars vicisset, tamen aliqua forma esset futura rei publicae: hoc bello victores quam rem publicam simus habituri, non facile adfirmarim, victis certe nulla umquam erit'. The fact that Cicero had foreseen the consequences of civil war and so had supported peace, in opposition to 'brave and clever men such as the Domitii and the Lentuli' ('fortes illi viri et sapientes, Domitii et Lentuli'), also emerges from a letter written in the year 45 to a like-minded friend, Toranius: fam. 6,21,1: 'solosque nos vidisse, quantum esset in eo bello mali, in quo spe pacis exclusa ipsa victoria futura esset acerbissuma, quae aut interitum adlatura esset, si victus esses, aut, si vicisses, servitutem' ('we alone have seen what misfortune would come of such a war, in which – if any hope of peace is excluded – even victory would be very bitter; in the case of a defeat it would bring downfall, in the case of victory it would bring servitude'). On the identification of this Toranius, who bears no forename in Cicero's correspondence (fam. 6,20 and 21), as the tutor of Caesar's great-nephew, see Friedrich Münzer, RE VI A, 1937, 1725ff.

p. 75 *The relationships by marriage of Isauricus*: The second husband of Servilia, the mother of Marcus Junius Brutus, was Decimus Junius Silanus, consul in the year 62. The couple had three daughters, who married Publius Servilius Isauricus (consul in 48), Marcus Aemilius Lepidus (consul in 46 and later one of the triumvirs) and Gaius Cassius Longinus (praetor in 44, the assassin of Caesar). Marcus Junius Brutus, son of Servilia's first marriage to the elder Marcus Junius Brutus, was thus half-brother to these three women.

pp. 75–6 *The consulars*: See Gotter, *Diktator*, 155ff.

p. 76 *Marcus Brutus on social climbing as Cicero's weak point*: Cic. ad Brut. 25 (= 1,17),4, Brutus to Atticus, probably June 43: 'haec [sc. exile and poverty] mihi videntur Ciceroni ultima esse in malis et, dum habeat, a quibus impetret, quae velit, et a quibus colatur ac laudetur, servitutem, honorificam modo, non aspernatur' ('this seems to Cicero the worst of all evils, and if he can find someone from whom he can get what he wants, and by whom he is revered and praised, he will not spurn servitude if only it has an honourable context for him').

p. 77 *Cicero on the concept of the* partes *as employed by Antony*: Cic. Phil. 13,38ff., esp. 39: 'istas tu partes potius quam a populo Romano defectionem vocas?' ('Would you sooner call this' – that is to say war on the fatherland, on Mutina, on the consuls – '*partes* than secession from the Roman people?').

pp. 79–81 *Octavian's activities at this time*: His attempt to gain election as tribune of the people: Suet. Aug. 10,2; Cass. Dio 45,6,3. The account in App. b.c. 3,120ff., claiming that Octavian was urged by the people to seek election, which the Senate sought to oppose out of fear that Octavian might be bent on avenging his adoptive father's death, and only then did Antony intervene, obviously assumes situations arising in the election campaign that could have been envisaged only later; see Ehrenwirth, *Untersuchungen*, 82. The recruitment of soldiers in Campania: Cic. Att. 16,8 (2/3.11.44) and 9 (4.11.44); see Botermann, *Soldaten*, 36ff. Octavian's alleged attempt to have Antony assassinated: among others, Cic. fam. 12,23,2 (to Quintus Cornificius, 10.10.44); Suet. Aug. 10,3. For Octavian's attempts to win Cicero's support, see esp. Cic. Att. 16,8,1 ('vide nomen, vide aetatem' – 'think of his name, think of his age'; also on the approach of Antony); 16,9 (4.11.44) ('non confido aetati, ignoro, quo animo' – 'I do not trust his age, nor do I know his attitude'); 16,14,1 (12.11.44) ('valde tibi adsentior, si multum possit Octavianus, multo firmius acta tyranni comprobatum iri quam in Telluris, atque id contra Brutum fore, sin autem vincitur, vides intolerabilem Antonium, ut, quem velis, nescias' – 'I entirely share your opinion that, if Octavian wins the upper hand, the acts of the tyrant will be even more clearly approved than in the Senate meeting that took place in the temple of Tellus, and that this will go against Brutus. If, however, he is defeated, we shall have an intolerable Antony, so that one does not know what to wish for').

pp. 81–4 *Octavian's march on Rome*: See esp. App. b.c. 3,164–74; Cass. Dio 45,12,3–6. Octavian before the assembly of the people in Rome: Cic. Att. 16,15,3 (early December 44): 'at quae contio! nam est missa mihi. iurat "ita sibi parentis honores consequi liceat", et simul dextram intendit ad statuam' ('but what an assembly that was! I was told about it. He swears to attain his father's honours if that be granted to him, and stretches out his right hand, pointing to the statue'). Antony's tirade against Octavian: Cic. Phil. 3,15ff. On the defection of Antony's two legions of veterans to Octavian, see Botermann, *Soldaten*, 45ff.

p. 84 *The sums promised by Octavian to the soldiers*: App. b.c. 3,197.

p. 85 *Cicero's negotiations with Oppius*: Cic. Att. 16,15,3: 'sed, ut scribis, certissimum video esse discrimen Cascae nostri tribunatum, de quo quidem ipso dixi Oppio, cum me hortaretur, ut adulescentem totamque causam manumque veteranorum complecterer, me nullo modo facere posse, ni mihi exploratum esset eum non modo non inimicum tyrannoctonis, verum etiam amicum fore. cum ille deceret ita futurum . . .' ('but like you, I too see that the dividing line on which opinions differ is certainly the election of our Casca. I discussed this with Oppius when he urged me to accept the young man and all his veterans. I replied that I could not by any means do that without being sure that he would treat the assassins of the tyrant not only without hostility but in a friendly manner. And when Oppius agreed . . .').

p. 86 *Sextus Pompeius Magnus Pius*: The significance for the political calculations in the late summer and autumn of the year 44 of Sextus Pompeius Magnus Pius, second son of Pompey the Great, remains an open question. He commanded large parts of south-east Spain, and in 44 he had been able to consolidate his position. Among his fighting forces there were both Roman and non-Roman infantry, but in spite of many successes on land against the governors sent to Spain by Caesar (Gaius Asinius Pollio) and after his assassination by the Senate (Marcus Aemilius Lepidus), it was his fleet that carried most military weight. On behalf of Antony, Lepidus had tried to get Sextus Pompey on the side of the Caesarians, or at least keep him neutral. The major factor involved in these negotiations was the return to Sextus of his father's property and payment of compensation. Although by virtue of his descent Sextus Pompey was a 'Pompeian' and thus should in theory have been a supporter of the republic and, so to speak, a natural member of Cicero's coalition, the negotiations with Lepidus and Augustus show that he felt he was a military potentate standing beside other such men. His 'republican' attitude had been largely dissipated, if it had ever been real at all. Cicero's comment on the uncertainty of his political course is significant, Att. 14,4,1: 'ipse Sextus, quo evadat' ('and what Sextus is striving for I do not know', 10.4.44). Lepidus finally succeeded in coming to an agreement giving Pompey the freedom to return to Rome (which cost little and of course did Pompey no good) and thus reinstating him as a citizen; in addition he was to be paid a high sum in compensation for the loss of his father's property. However, the precise date of this agreement is not certain, and that makes it difficult to place it in the context of the political decisions in the second half of the year 44 as a whole. Recent research generally assumes a date in August or September 44. The agreement must have been concluded in November at the latest, since the Senate confirmed it in its resolution honouring Lepidus of 28 November 44 (Cic. Phil. 3,20ff.; see also 5,41; 13,8ff.). We can at least say, then, that the agreement between Sextus Pompey on one side and Lepidus and Antony on the other emphasized Octavian's isolation and thus made it even more desirable for him to have the backing of the Senate and the new consuls. See Ehrenwirth, *Untersuchungen*, 92, and Gotter, *Diktator*, 72ff.

pp. 86–7 *Cicero on Octavian*: Phil. 5,43: 'quis tum nobis, quis populo Romano obtulit hunc divinum adulescentem deus? qui, cum omnia ad perniciem nostram pestifero illi civi paterent, subito praeter spem omnium exortus prius confecit exercitum, quem furori M. Antoni opponeret, quam quisquam hoc eum cogitare suspicaretur . . .', 49: 'eius autem filii longissime diversa ratio est;

qui cum omnibus carus est, tum optimo cuique carissimus. in hoc spes libertatis posita est, ab hoc accepta iam salus, huic summi honores et exquiruntur
et parati sunt'. 'Saviour of the state' (*conservator rei publicae*): Phil. 3,14;
'Father of the Fatherland' (*patriae parens*): Phil. 13,25.

p. 90 *The possessions of the senators looted by Antony's soldiers*: Cic. Phil. 8,9.

p. 90 *Octavian's first auspicium*: That is to say his first use of the right to request
the gods to approve the military command (*imperium*) that he had undertaken. This has also come down to us in writing (inscription of the city of
Narbo in the year AD 11, on the erection of an altar dedicated to the name of
Augustus in the forum of the city): Dessau ILS no. 112: *VII* 'idus Ianuarius,
qua die primum imperium orbis terrarum auspicatus est' ('on 7 January, the
day when he first turned to the gods to ask approval of his military power
over the world').

pp. 91–2 *Cicero on the actions of Brutus and Cassius in the east*: Phil. 11,27: 'nam
et Brutus et Cassius multis iam in rebus ipse sibi senatus fuit', 28: 'C. Cassius …
nonne eo ex Italia consilio profectus est, ut prohiberet Syria Dolabellam? qua
lege, quo iure? eo, quod Iuppiter ipse sanxit, ut omnia, quae rei publicae salu-
taria essent, legitima et iusta haberentur. est enim lex nihil aliud nisi recta et a
numine deorum tracta ratio imperans honesta, prohibens contraria. huic igitur
legi paruit Cassius, cum est in Syriam profectus, alienam provinciam, si homines legibus scriptis uterentur, his vero oppressis suam lega naturae'. The thesis
of Klaus Martin Girardet, 'Die Rechtsstellung der Caesarattentäter Brutus and
Cassius in den Jahren 44–42 v. Chr.', *Chiron* 23, 1993, 207–32, to the effect
that Cicero's phrasing proceeds from, and was the result of, an emergency law
in force, has been rightly refuted by Gotter, *Diktator*, 282ff. The republican
emergency law, if indeed it was a law at all, does not affect the validity of normal laws. Cassius writes to Cicero on 7.3.43 about the taking over of the
Syrian and Egyptian armies (Cic. fam. 12,11,1); on 5.5.43 Cicero still knows
nothing for certain about him (Cic. ad Brut. 13 (= 1,5),2; Cicero to Marcus
Brutus). On the events of this time in the east, see also Gotter, *Diktator*, 195ff.

pp. 95–6 *Servius Sulpicius Galba on the battle at Forum Gallorum*: Cic. fam.
10,30 (Galba to Cicero, 16.4.43); on the low value of recently recruited
legions, see also the letter from Plancus to Cicero of 28.7.43 (fam. 10,24,3ff.).

p. 97 *Anecdotes of the battle at Forum Gallorum*: Suet. Aug. 10.4–11; cf. Tac.
ann. 1,10,2.

p. 98 *Cicero aims to become dictator*: Cic. Phil. 14,14ff.

p. 98 *Cicero on those who envied him*: Cic. Phil. 14,13–21; on the lack of
consulars ibid., 14,17.

pp. 98–9 *Cicero on Octavian*: Cic. fam. 11,20,1 (Decimus Brutus to Cicero,
24.5.43); see Vell. Pat. 2,62,6.

p. 99 *Cicero as victor over Antony*: Cic. Phil. 14,20: 'memoria tenent me ante
diem XIII Kalendas Ianuarias principem revocandae libertatis fuisse, me ex
Kalendis Ianuariis ad hanc horam invigilasse rei publicae, mean domum

measque aures dies noctesque omnium praeceptis monitisque patuisse, meis litteris, meis nuntiis, meis cohortationibus omnes, qui ubique essent, ad patriae praesidium excitatos, meis sententiis a Kalendis Ianuariis numquam legatos ad Antonium, semper illum hostem, semper hoc bellum'. Cicero in the intoxication of victory: Cic. ad Brut. 9 (= 1,3),2; Cicero to Marcus Brutus, 21.4.43.

# CHAPTER 4
## Main Sources

April 43–November 42 BC: App. b.c. 3,299–4,581. Cass. Dio 46,39–47,49; Suet. Aug. 12–13, 26–7; Plut. Cic. 46–9; idem, Anton. 17–22; idem, Brut. 24–53.

## Explanatory Notes

p. 102 *Cicero to Brutus on the ovatio granted to Octavian*: Cic. ad Brut. 23 (= 1,15),9 (Cicero to Marcus Brutus, July 43).

p. 103 *On the senatorial envoys sent to Octavian's legions*: Vell. Pat. 2,62,4ff.; App. b.c. 3,354ff.; Cass. Dio 46,40,4–41,2.

pp. 103–4 *Lepidus and Sextus Pompey after the victory of the Senate*: The 'windy' (*ventosissimum*) Lepidus: Cic. fam. 11,9,1 (Decimus Brutus to Cicero, 29.4.43). At about the same time Cicero writes to Marcus Brutus about the 'weakness and inconstancy' of Lepidus, and his 'hostile attitude to the state' (Cic. ad Brut. 2 (= 2,2),1: 'levitatem et inconstantiam animumque semper inimicum rei publicae', 11.4.43). On the delegation sent to Sextus Pompey: Cic. Phil. 13,13; Pompey, he says, is 'paratissimo animo', his mind full of 'great readiness', whatever that may mean in the case of a pirate.

pp. 104–5 *Octavian's wish for the consulate*: He had already expressed it in May: Cic. ad Brut. 12 (= 1,4a),3 (Brutus to Cicero, 15.5.43), with a heartfelt groan, so to speak, at the end of the letter: 'quod utinam inspectare possis timorem de illo [sc. Octavian] meum!' ('so that you can form some idea of my fears of that man').

p. 105 *Octavian's meeting with Decimus Brutus*: Cic. fam. 11,13,1 (Decimus Brutus to Cicero, 10.5.43), 11,10,4 (idem to Cicero, 5.5.43).

p. 105 *The fighting force of Decimus Brutus' legions*: Cic. fam. 11,10,5 (Decimus Brutus to Cicero, 5.5.43), 11,13,2 (idem to Cicero, 10.5.43; Brutus calls his troops *copiolas*, 'little troops'); App. b.c. 3,332.

p. 105–6 *Antony's joining Lepidus*: Cic. fam. 10,23,2ff. (Plancus to Cicero, 6.6.43); App. b.c. 3,342–8; Plut. Anton. 18,1–6; Cass. Dio 46,51,1–4.

p. 106 *Plancus attempting to make peace*: Cic. fam. 10, 6 (Cicero to Plancus, 20.3.43); Plancus as an adherent of the Senate: Cic. fam. 10,8 (Plancus to the

Senate and people of Rome, 23.3.43); see also Cic. fam. 10,14 (Cicero to Plancus, 5.5.43) and Cic. ad Brut. 2 (= 2,2),2 (Cicero to Marcus Brutus, 11.4.43).

p. 106 *The mood of Decimus Brutus*: Cic. fam. 11,26 (Decimus Brutus to Cicero, 3.6.43; the last of his letters to have come down to us).

p. 106 *Plancus to Cicero*: Cic. fam. 10,24,3–7 (28.7.43), here, 24,4, on Octavian: 'cum interim aversum illum ab hac cogitatione ad alia consilia video se contulisse' ('I see that he has abandoned that idea and turned to other plans'), and §6: 'quod vivit Antonius hodie, quod Lepidus una est, quod exercitus habent non contemnendos, quod sperant, quod audent, omne Caesari acceptum referre possunt' ('the fact that Antony is still alive, that Lepidus has joined him, that they have an army not to be despised, that they hope they can venture anything, all this can be chalked up as Caesar's doing'); cf. 10,23,2ff. Plancus' link with Antony can be seen in the letter from the latter to the Senate that Cicero quotes on 20 March 43 in the Senate itself: Cic. Phil. 13,43ff.: 'nec Lepidi societatem violare . . . nec Plancum prodere, participem consiliorum' ('neither to break the link with Lepidus . . . nor to betray Plancus, my partner in my plans'). Naturally Cicero vigorously disputes that this attitude is correct.

p. 107 *The soldiers against Antony*: Cic. fam. 11,13,3ff. (Decimus Brutus to Cicero, 10.5.43).

p. 108 *Octavian's suggestion of sharing the consulate with Cicero*: Plut. Cic. 45.4–6 (later, Augustus confirmed this fact in his own memoir); App. b.c. 3,337–40; Cass. Dio 46,42,2. Isauricus described as a 'firebrand' ('homo furiosus'): Cic. ad Brut. 2 (= 2,2),3.

pp. 108–9 *On recommendations for appointment to public positions, etc.*: On the proposition to make Bibulus one of the college of augurs: Cic. ad Brut. 15 (= 1,7; letter of recommendation from Marcus Brutus to Cicero, May/June 43). On the appointment of Lucius Aelius Lamia: Cic. fam. 11,16 and 17 (letters of recommendation from Cicero to Decimus Brutus of the summer of 43). On the request for backing for Appius Claudius: Cic. fam. 11,22 (letter of recommendation from Cicero to Decimus Brutus of 6.7.43).

pp. 109–10 *The march on Rome*: The words of the spokesman for the centurions: 'hic faciet, si vos non feceritis' (Suet. Aug. 26,1; see Cass. Dio 46,43,4). Octavian's remark to Cicero: App. b.c. 3,382).

p. 110 *Octavian's augury*: Suet. Aug. 95; App. b.c. 3,388; Jul. Obs. 69; Cass. Dio 46,46,2. Romulus' augury: Liv. 1,7,1. The official questioning of the gods, asking whether they looked favourably on some forthcoming enterprise – going to war, giving battle, calling an assembly of the people, etc. – was carried out by the magistrate with the aid of members of a special priesthood, the augurs, usually by means of observing the flight of birds or examining chickens, hence its name of 'looking at birds' (Lat. *auspicium*, from *aves aspicere*, 'to observe birds'), or *augurium* (the word describes the activity of the augurs).

p. 111 *The Pedian Law*: The law condemning the assassins of Caesar to death (*lex Pedia*): the outlaw status of the killers was expressed in a ban on anyone's giving the condemned men water and fire, i.e. nourishment and shelter ('aquae et ignis interdictio'). The charges against Cassius and Brutus: Plut. Brut. 27,4. The judge who said that Marcus Brutus was innocent: Cas. Dio 46,49,5.

pp. 112–13 *Cicero's letters to Marcus Brutus*: For the first suspicion: Cic. ad Brut. 18 (= 1,10; *c*. June 43). The passage quoted is from this letter: 'sed Caesarem meis consiliis adhuc gubernatum, praeclara ipsum indole admirabilique constantia, improbissimis litteris quidam fallacibusque interpretibus ac nuntiis impulerunt in spem certissimam consulatus ... qui si steterit fide mihique paruerit, satis videmur habituri praesidii; sin autem impiorum consilia plus valuerint quam nostra aut imbecillitas aetatis non potuerit gravitatem rerum sustinere, spes omnis est in te'. The justification: Cic. ad Brut. 23 (= 1,15). His doubts of Octavian: Cic. ad Brut. 26 (= 1,18),3ff. (27 July 43). The passage from this letter quoted: 'maximo autem, cum haec scribebam, adficiebar dolore, quod, cum me pro adulescentulo ac paene puero res publica accepisset vadem, vix videbar, quod promiseram, praestare posse, est autem gravior et difficilior animi et sententiae, maximis praesertim in rebus, pro altero quam pecuniae obligatio: haec enim solvi potest et est rei familiaris iactura tolerabilis; rei publicae quod spoponderis, quem admodum solvas, si is dependi facile patitur, pro quo spoponderis?' Cicero's description of Octavian as 'light-minded': he uses the Latin term *temeritas* (ad Brut. 26,4 = 1,18.4). As early as in the letter written to Brutus on 14.7,43, Cicero fears that Octavian could leave the province of Upper Italy for the rest of Italy with warlike intent: Cic. ad Brut. 22 (= 1,14),2: 'exercitus autem Caeseris, qui erat optimus, non modo nihil prodest, sed etiam cogit exercitum tuum flagitari; qui si Italia attigerit, erit civis nemo, quem quidem civem appellari fas sit, qui se non in tua castra conferat' ('Caesar's army, however, which was excellent, is no more use now, but actually obliges you to summon your own army; if his has set foot in Italy there is no citizen worthy of the name who will not join your camp'). The failure of Brutus to understand Cicero's deep dislike of Antony: Cic. ad Brut. 25 (= 1,17),1ff. (Marcus Brutus to Atticus, summer 43). The rejection by Brutus of Cicero's attempt to persuade Octavian to behave well (the Latin term used is expressed by *salus*) to the assassins of Caesar in the east: Cic. ad Brut. 24 (= 1,16; Marcus Brutus to Cicero, probably early July 43). Evidence that Cicero saw all three Antonian brothers as equally bad and thought it desirable to eliminate them all: Cic. ad Brut. 8,2; 9,3; 11,2 (= 1,2a,2; 1,3,3; 1,4,2; the last letter is Marcus Brutus to Cicero of 7.5.43). Cicero had written to Brutus recommending him to have Gaius Antonius, whom he was holding prisoner, put to death, since the cause (*causa*) of all three Antonians (*tres*

*Antonii*) was the same, and as enemies of the state they were no longer Roman citizens. Brutus declined on legal and moral grounds; 5 (= 2,5),1 and 5; see also 20 (= 1,12),1ff. For the authenticity of the last two letters of Brutus (ad Brut. 24 and 25), also disputed by D. R. Shackleton Bailey, see finally Gotter, *Diktator*, 286ff. Gotter considers the arguments against their authenticity so far inadequate, but thinks the discussion is not yet closed.

pp. 115–16 *The conference of Bononia*: Main sources: App. b.c. 4,2–13, 26–7; Cass. Dio 46,55, 47,1–2, 15,2–20. The search for hidden weapons: Cass. Dio 46,55,2.

pp. 116–117 *The founding and nature of the triumvirate*: Cf. Bleicken, *Prinzipat*, 11ff.

p. 117 *Ventidius Bassus*: In the section devoted to Ventidius Bassus by Gellius (15,4) some verses lampooning him have been preserved; these were graffiti scribbled on the walls of Roman alleys, where many inhabitants could still remember the humble past career of Ventidius Bassus: 'concurrite omnes augures, haruspices! [the latter were priests responsible for interpreting bad omens] / portentum inusitatum conflatum est recens: / nam mulas qui fricabat, consul factus est' ('Come here, all you augurs and *haruspices*; a rare, puffed-up monster has just appeared: for he who once dealt in mules has become consul').

p. 118 *Clodia*: Clodia, whom Octavian married at the wish of the army and Antony, was the daughter of Fulvia from her marriage to Publius Clodius Pulcher, the notorious tribune of the people of the year 58, and an adversary of Cicero. Fulvia's marriage to Mark Antony made Clodia his stepdaughter. At the time of the marriage Clodia, according to Suet. Aug. 62,1, was *vixdum nubilis*, meaning, in view of what was considered marriageable age for girls at this time, under twelve years old. Two years later, when Octavian separated from her, he swore on oath that he had not consummated the marriage, for which her youth will have been the reason. Although Clodia was certainly born at a time when her father had already moved into the plebeian class and no longer gave his *nomen gentile* as Claudius but had changed it to Clodius, she is also called Claudia in recent writing on the subject, with reference to Suet. Aug. 62,1, where she is mentioned as Claudia (Plutarch calls her Clodia), and to CIL VI 1282, where her brother is called Claudius on a vase. In an official exchange of letters between Cicero and Mark Antony in April 44, Antony calls him Claudius, but Cicero uses the name Clodius (Att. 14,13a,3 and 13b,4). As neither of them would knowingly have used an incorrect name, we may assume that one was free to call the children of Clodius either Claudius/Claudia or Clodius/Clodia, depending whether the first options were used with reference to the patrician Claudian family or to their father's birth name. As I see it, however, there is no doubt that in a formally correct sense, if not a strictly legal one, the name of their father's *nomen gentile* at the time of their birth was the one to be borne by his children, and consquently Octavian's wife was called Clodia.

pp. 119–23 *The proscriptions*: App. b.c. 4,16–26, 28–224; Plut. Cic. 46–9; idem, Anton. 19–20; Cass. Dio 46,47,3–15,1; Suet. Aug. 27,1–2; Vell. Pat. 2,66–7. In addition see R. S. Conway, 'The Proscription of 43 BC', *Harvard Lectures on the Vergilian Age*, 1928, and Hermann Bengtson, 'Zu den Proskriptionen der Triumvirn', *Sitz.ber. d. Bayer. Akad. d. Wiss.*, philos.-histor. Kl., 1972, 3. The triumvirs' edict of proscription recorded in App. b.c. 4,31–4 is not to be considered authentic, and not just because of the bold naming of Octavian as Octavius Caesar. Death of the consul Pedius: App. b.c. 4,24ff. The brother of Lucius Munatius Plancus was originally called Gaius Munatius Plancus; after his adoption by one Lucius Plautus he called himself Lucius Plautius (or Plotius) Plancus. For the identification of Toranius, see note p. 634 above. On Varro: according to Cicero, Phil. 2,104, when Antony first confiscated his villa in Casinum, he changed the name of the study from a *studiorum deversorium*, 'place of studies', into a *libidinum deversorium*, 'place of lust'. At the time of his proscription Varro was seventy-three years old; after escaping death he lived on until the year 27 BC. A list of the names of those proscribed who are known to us can be found in F. Hinard, *Les Proscriptions de la Rome républicaine*, 1985, 264ff.; on other matters this book should be used only with reservations, on account of the anachronistic idealization of proscription that it represents. The funeral oration for his wife, delivered by the once proscribed husband whom she hid and saved, part of which has come down to us in writing, gives a particularly graphic account of the distress and confusion caused by proscription; the wife saved her husband, against the will of Lepidus, by obtaining a pardon for him from Octavian. Identification of the dead woman with Turia, wife of Quintus Lucretius Vespillo, later to be consul (19 BC), with which Theodor Mommsen agreed, is uncertain; see Wilhelm Kierdorf, *Laudatio Funebris. Interpretationen und Untersuchungen zur Entwicklung der römischen Leichenrede*, 1980, 33ff., and Dieter Flach, *Die sogenannte Laudatio Turiae. Einleitung, Text, Übersetzung and Kommentar*, 1991, esp. II 2a–21 of the text.

pp. 123–5 *The flight and death of Cicero*: See above all Plut. Cic. 46–9; App. b.c. 4,73–82, and Seneca suas. 6,17 (from Livy). Attempts to clear Octavian of the murder of Cicero: among others: Cass. Dio 47,7,2–5 (Cassius Dio presented Antony as the truly cruel and pitiless persecutor: 47,8); Plut. Cic, 46,2ff., 49,5 (the story of the grandson of Augustus found reading a Ciceronian text); App. b.c 4,220 (on the patronage of Cicero's son); Suet. Aug. 27 (exonerating Octavian from co-responsibility for the proscription but showing the particular cruelty of his part in the murders). For Cicero's mental state in the last months of his life see Gelzer, *Cicero*, 407ff. Mommsen's verdict: *Römische Geschichte*, vol. 3, 1909[10], 619: 'Showing no insight, opinions or useful intentions as a statesman, he figured successively as a democrat, an aristocrat and a tool of the monarchs, and was never more than a short-sighted egotist. Where he seemed to be taking action the questions concerned were regularly waved aside . . . He was forceful in opposing spurious attacks, crushing walls of cardboard with much sound and fury; he never decided any serious matter, for either good or ill, and he allowed the execution of the Catilinian conspirators rather than actually bringing it about himself. In the context of literature it has already been emphasized [by Mommsen himself] that he was the creator of modern Latin prose; his importance rests on his style, and it is only as a stylist that he shows secure self-confidence. As a writer, however, he stands as low as he does as a statesman.' This crushing verdict on Cicero arises not least from the fact that we know him better than almost any other man of classical antiquity – perhaps with the exception of St Augustine of Hippo – and we can follow his thoughts and emotions, including those he wanted to conceal, into the ramifications of his syntax. If we were as well informed about Caesar, perhaps much would appear in a more relative light, and Mommsen would at least have had something to hold against 'his' Caesar. There is a later, well-balanced assessment in Stockton, *Cicero*, 297ff. Mommsen on Cato: 3,459, and other mentions; Cicero on the idealist Cato: Cic. Att. 2,1,8.

p. 126 *The citizen's crown*: Cass. Dio 47,13,3. The full name of the crown was *corona civica ob cives servatos* ('citizen's crown awarded for the saving of citizens').

p. 128 *Virgil and Cremona*: Ecl. 9,27ff.: 'Vare, tuum nomen, superet modo Mantua nobis, / Mantua vae miserae nimium vicina Cremonae.' On the history of the time as reflected in Virgil's *Eclogues*, see note on p. 645 below.

pp. 136–43 *The battle of Philippi*: see Bengtson, *Marcus Antonius*, 135ff., and the maps in Kromayer/Veith, *Schlachten-Atlas*, 115ff., with leaf 23,6. Octavian's three days in the marshes: Plin. nat. hist. 7,148. Octavian saved by his doctor's dream: Plut. Brut. 41,6ff.; Suet. Aug. 91,1; Cass. Dio 47,41,3. Claims of Brutus' soldiers to have killed Octavian: Plut. Brut. 42,3. Brutus' fear that his soldiers might change sides: App. b.c. 4,521. Octavian's mutilation of the body of Brutus: Suet. Aug. 13,1; see also Cass. Dio 47,49,2. For the list of *nobiles* who died at Philippi, and the losses suffered in the battle, see Brunt, *Manpower*, 485ff. On the date of the battle, see App. b.c. 4,513, and for precise dating, on the basis of a recently found fragment of the Praeneste calendar, see Orazio Marucchi, 'Un nuovo frammento del Calendario prenestino di Verrio Flacco', *Notizie degli Scavi di Antichità* 18, 1921, 277–83.

p. 143 *Cassius Dio on Philippi as the dividing line between democracy and monarchy*: 47,39; see also 47,42,3. The watchword given by Brutus: Cass. Dio 47,43,1.

pp. 145–6 *Brutus*: The last remark of Brutus before his suicide is a quotation from a speech by Heracles in an unknown tragedy: Cass. Dio 47,49,2: 'O ill-starred Virtue, you were only a word; I tried to achieve you, but as it turned out you served the cause of Chance' (= A. Nauck, *Tragicorum Graecorum Fragmenta*, 1889², no. 374 = B. Snell, *Tragicorum Graecorum Fragmenta*, vol. 1 1971, 88 F 3). Plutarch wrote a biography of Brutus. He has come down to us most fully, however, in the corpus of Cicero's letters, and within them in the correspondence between Cicero and Brutus, in particular the two letters of Brutus nos. 24 and 25 (= 1,16 and 1,17). In the second letter, which may have been written in June 43 to Cicero's friend Titus Pomponius Atticus, he complains of Cicero's encouragement of Octavian; in the first, written by Brutus to Cicero himself at the beginning of July 43, he waxes indignant over Cicero's recommendation to Octavian to show restraint in approaching the assassins of Caesar. It contains fine passages on the price to be paid for the republic, and the duty of fighting for it. In the second letter (Brut. 25,6) Brutus addressed the dangers threatening the republic in concrete terms: 'ego certe quin cum ipsa re bellum geram, hoc est cum regno et imperiis extraordinariis et dominatione et potentia, quae supra leges se esse velit' ('I for my part will certainly wage war in this matter, that is to say against monarchy, against extraordinary military powers, against despotism, and the power that would place itself above the laws'). On the political career of Marcus Brutus, see also Gotter, *Diktator*, 207–32, with a look back at the opinions of earlier scholars.

p. 146 *The coins*: Denarius with the head of Marcus Brutus and the inscription BRUT(us) IMP(erator) on the obverse; on the reverse, the freedman's cap, the *pileus*, between two daggers and the lettering EID(ibus) MAR(tiis),43 42 BC: BMCRR II, p. 480, no. 68; Sydenham no. 1301; Crawford no. 508/3. Denarius with the portrait of Lucius Junius Brutus, 54 BC: BMCRR I, p. 479, no. 3861; Sydenham no. 906; Crawford no. 433/1. Head of Marcus Brutus with that of Lucius Brutus, consul 509, 43/42 BC: BMCRR II, p. 477, no. 57; Sydenham no. 1295; Crawford no. 506/1, aureus. The oldest coin with the portrait of a living Roman is the gold coin of Titus Quinctius Flamininus, consul in 198 BC (Head², 235); however, it belongs to the Hellenistic area and has nothing to do with Roman traditions of minting.

## CHAPTER 5
## Main Sources

December 42–36 BC: Vell. Pat. 2,74–81; Suet. Aug. 14–26; App. b.c. 5,1–602; Cass. Dio 48,1–49,18; Plut. Anton. 23–35; Flor. epit. 2,18.

## Explanatory Notes

pp. 153–4 *The numbers of legions and the soldiers to be demobilized*: See Walter Schmitthenner, 'The Armies of the Triumviral Period: A Study of the Origins of the Roman Imperial Legions', dissertation, Oxford 1958 (typewritten), and, with a partially critical assessment of Schmitthenner's theses, Brunt, *Manpower*, 473ff., esp. 488ff., as well as Hahn, 'Legionsorganisation', 201ff. The number of soldiers due to be demobilized has often been exaggerated; here I am largely following the sober analysis of Brunt., 488ff., 326ff. On the settlement see also Keppie, *Colonisation*, 58ff. and *passim*. The veterans' settlements have left traces on Virgil's *Eclogues* and *Georgics* (2,198). Virgil himself was among those affected, driven from his property near Mantua, which was close to Cremona, one of the places marked out for the confiscation of land. The Ninth and First Eclogues clearly refer to the expropriations of the year 41. In the Ninth Eclogue, in chronological order the first of these poems to be written, we hear of the complaints of the shepherd Moeris on being expelled from his land. The First Eclogue is a dialogue between Meliboeus, expelled when land was divided up for redistribution, and Tityrus, who is miraculously able to keep his own land through the assurances of the 'godlike youth' (sc. Octavian) in Rome. Virgil may even have been expelled from his estate twice; it is possible that Gaius Asinius Pollio had already restored it to him once, but certain that Publius Alfenus Varus, one of Octavian's generals and probably identical with the famous jurist of the same name (see Wolfgang Kunkel, *Herkunft und soziale Stellung der römischen Juristen*, 1952, 20) reinstated him in his possession of it. On these Eclogues see Friedrich Leo, 'Vergils erste und neunte Ecloge', *Hermes* 38, 1903, 1–18; Carl Becker, 'Virgils Eklogenbuch', *Hermes* 83, 1955, 314–49; and Karl Büchner, 'P. Vergilius Maro', RE VIII A, 1955, 1045–52. A small poem of 103 lines entitled *Dirae* ('Curses') has also come down to us under the name of Virgil, taking as its subject the owners' farewell to an estate in Sicily, and the curses that they utter on that occasion. There are many reasons why this poem may not in fact be by Virgil, but it assumes a knowledge of his *Eclogues* and fits the situation of the expropriations of land. Horace also lost his estate in Venusia (Venosa) through the redistribution of land at this time, as well as property from his father's estate in Asisium (Assisi).

pp. 156–7 *Lucius Antonius*: The friendly tone that he adopted towards ideas of the republic (see also the speech put into his mouth by Appian, b.c. 5,159–66, and in addition J.-M. Roddaz, 'Lucius Antonius', *Historia* 37, 1988, 317–46, who considers that his republican attitude was of real significance) seems to have been emphasized by Asinius Pollio, through whom it reached the account of Appian in particular. Pollio may have ascribed more political weight to this attitude than it had in historical reality. Syme, *Revolution*, 216, writing on Lucius Antonius' tirades on liberty, thinks that 'at Perusia he [sc. Octavian] stamped out the liberties of Rome and Italy in blood and desolation, and stood forth as the revolutionary leader, unveiled and implacable'. But Octavian was not a revolutionary, and nor were there any liberties to be stamped out at the time. On the political stance of Pollio, and on the dependence of

Appian's account on his historical work, see Bertram Haller, *C. Asinius Pollio als Politiker und zeitkritischer Historiker*, 1967, and Hose, *Erneuerung*, 259ff. There is much to suggest that Appian did in fact depend on Pollio, but it cannot be proved beyond doubt because only a very few fragments of Pollio's work survive. The citizens of Nursia and liberty: Cass. Dio 48,13,6. The story is claimed by Suet. Aug. 12 for the War of Mutina, in which the Nursians also opposed Octavian. But the declaration of liberty in the course of that war makes less sense.

pp. 158–61 *The increased political scope for action of the soldiers*: On this subject, in general, App. b.c. 5,60–71, esp. 60–67 on the rebellious soldiers in the theatre and on the Field of Mars. On the negotiations in Teanum: App. b.c. 5, 77–82, and in Gabii: App. b.c. 5,90–94; Cass. Dio 48,12,1–3. *Senatus caligatus*: Cass. Dio 48,12,3 (in Greek, recast).

p. 162 *The number of combatants in the Perusian War*: See Brunt, *Manpower*, 493ff., and in particular P. Wallmann, 'Untersuchungen zu militärischen Problemen de Perusinischen Krieges', *Talanta* 6, 1974, 58–91.

pp. 162–3 *Lucius Antonius against the triumvirate*: App. b.c. 5,118–20; see also his speech attacking Octavian, App. b.c. 5,179–81, and above p. 157.

pp. 165–7 *The siege of Perusia*: There is a map of the siege in Kromayer/Veith, *Schlachten-Atlas*, leaf 24,6. On the war, see Emilio Gabba, 'The Perusine War and Triumviral Italy', *Harv. Stud. in Class. Philol.* 75, 1971, 139 60. On the Perusian slingshots (*glandes Perusinae*): CIL. XI 6721, esp. 4,5,13 ('L. Antoni calve, peristi C. Caesarus victoria', 'bald-headed Lucius Antonius, Caesar's victory leaves you a defeated man!') and 14 ('L. Antoni calve, Fulvia, culum pandite!'). Octavian's lampoon is in Martial 11,20,3–8; see the commentary by Uwe Walter, *M. Valerius Martialis: Epigramme*, 1996, 249ff. On the belligerent scenes staged by Fulvia: Flor. epit. 2,16,2; Vell. Pat. 2,74,3; Cass. Dio 48,10,4.

p. 166 *Asinius Pollio*: His letter of 16.3.43 to Cicero (fam. 10,31) is valuable evidence of the inner conflict of a general of this time, a man who had no ambition for political power and looked at the future with a regretful backward glance at the republic, yet wanted to do the right thing in the interest of the state. Pollio reveals his character in a wonderfully phrased remark, 'natura autem mea et studia trahunt me ad pacis et libertatis cupiditatem', 'my nature and my interests lead me to wish for peace and freedom', and emphasizes his veneration (*pietas*) of and loyalty (*fides*) to the dictator. He retained those qualities in carrying out his administrative tasks, and without any sycophancy to the leadership (*dominatio*). Pollio on Octavian: Macrob. Sat. 2,4,21: 'Temporibus triumviralibus Pollio, cum Fescenninos [Fescennine verses were coarse songs of the kind sung in ancient Italy at weddings] in eum Augustus scripsisset, ait: at ego taceo, non est enime facile in eum scribere qui potest proscribere' ('when, in the time of the triumvirate, Augustus composed Fescennine verses against him, Pollio said: I for my part will remain silent, for it is not easy to criticize a man who holds the power of proscription'). On the relationship of Pollio to Antony and Octavian, see A. B. Bosworth, 'Asinius Pollio and Augustus', *Historia* 21, 1972, 441–73. Octavian's execution of Roman senators and equestrians, as reported by Suetonius (Aug. 15), Appian (5,201) and Cassius Dio (48,14,3ff.) – according to Suetonius and Cassius Dio 300 were killed – is considered historical fact by a number of classicists, for instance Kienast, *Augustus*, 39 and note 169, as well as other literature. The reported remark by Octavian, 'moriendum esse' (Suet. Aug. 15), does not contain in the Latin, as it does when translated, any personal reference, which would be *tibi moriendum esse*, it merely conveys the general necessity of death. The uniformity of the saying (and the speaker's indifference) are expressed in the very impersonality of the way it is expressed, but cannot be suitably phrased in a literal translation such as 'One must die', or 'There must be dying.'

pp. 167–8 *Fulvia*: Friedrich Münzer, RE VII, 1910, 284, described Fulvia, in a few cogent words, as the first Roman wife of a dynast. No one has written a monograph on her, and the material that has come down from that period is not sufficient for one, but see Richard A. Bauman, *Women and Politics in Ancient Rome*, 1992, 83–9. The quotation from Plutarch: Plut. Anton. 10,5. Syme, *Revolution*, 214ff., rightly rejects the idea that Cleopatra represents a motive for Fulvia's anti-Octavian commitment (see App. b.c. 5,75; Plut. Anton. 30,4). It is pure speculation that on Antony's visit to Egypt in the winter of 41/40 he had already 'forgotten all else in the arms of Cleopatra', as Paul Groebe put it in a distinctly inadequate article in RE I, 1894, 2605. There is no evidence of any close relationship between them until the year 37. Hans Volkmann, *Kleopatra: Politik und Propaganda*, 1953, 92ff., describes their meeting in Tarsos and their relationship over the next few years soberly, if in the rather aloof style of his time. There have been unsuccessful efforts to identify various portrait busts that have come down to us as Fulvia. Frequent attempts to link the woman's head on a Roman coin (see below) with her must also be rejected, particularly as such an identification would have had far-reaching political consequences; a woman's head on a coin, on the Hellenistic model, can only represent a queen or a dynast. Are we to suppose that Mark Antony really regarded Fulvia as a ruler, or at least tolerated such an idea without protest? The coin with the alleged portrait of Fulvia is a half-denarius from a series of coins that Mark Antony had minted in the Transalpine or Cisalpine area (Sydenham no. 1160 = Crawford no. 489/5); the woman's head on the obverse represents a figure of Victoria, and from the numismatic viewpoint again cannot be identified with Fulvia.

p. 168 *The lament of Propertius*: 1,22; see 1,21, and on the subject Hans-Joachim Glücklich, 'Zeitkritik bei Properz', *Altspr. Unterr.* 20/4, 1977, 45ff., and Siegmar Döpp, 'Properzens Elegie I,22. Eine unvollständige Sphragis?', in *Festschrift für Franz Egermann*, 1985, 105–17.

p. 169 *The African provinces*: It is not clear from our sources whether it was only now that Octavian allowed Lepidus to claim his African provincial area. The extremely confused circumstances in both African provinces would have made it almost impossible for him to take them over earlier. In any case, Titus Sextius, who had the area in his power at this point, handed over his four legions to Lepidus, who then, along with those granted to him by Octavian, had ten legions available to him. In the years up to 36, he raised another six, so that in the end he had sixteen legions at his disposal. On Lepidus during his time as governor of Africa, see Weigel, *Lepidus*, 81ff. It is a matter of controversy whether the two African provinces, the old one (Africa Vetus) and the province set up by Caesar (the former kingdom of Numidia) were already united at this time, but Duncan Fishwick and Brent D. Shaw, 'The Formation of Africa Proconsularis', *Hermes* 105, 1977, 369–80, produce good arguments to suggest that the unification of the two provinces as Africa Proconsularis is connected with Lepidus' taking over the governorship of Africa and can thus be dated to 40/39.

p. 170 *Mucia and Scribonia*: Mucia was the daughter of Quintus Mucius Scaevola, the consul of the year 95, *pontifex maximus* and a famous jurist, and was the third wife of Pompey the Great, by whom she had three children, Gnaeus, Sextus and Pompeia. This Pompeia was married in her turn to a son of the dictator Sulla, and then to Lucius Cornelius Cinna (son of the most important member of this branch of the Cornelian family, who was consul in 87–84), whose sister Caesar married at the age of sixteen; his only daughter, Julia, was her child. The family relationships of Pompeia thus extended to large parts of the nobility. Scribonia, the daughter of one Lucius Scribonius Libo and sister of the later consul of the same name who held the post in 34 BC, was married first to Gnaeus Cornelius Lentulus Marcellinus, consul in the year 56 BC and second to one Cornelius Scipio. By her first two marriages she had several children who rose to high office.

pp. 172–3 *The treaty of Brundisium*: App. b.c. 5,251–76, esp. 272ff.; Cass. Dio 48,28,3–30,1; Plut. Anton. 30–31.

pp. 173–4 *The criminal offence of Salvidienus*: See Richard A. Bauman, *The Crimen Maiestatis in the Roman Republic and Augustan Principate*, 1970, 177ff.

pp. 174–6 *Conditions in Rome and the riots there after the return of Antony and Octavian to the city*: App. 5,280–90; Cass. Dio 48,31; only Cass. Dio 48,31,5 mentions the overturning of the statues of the two triumvirs. The appointment of sixty-seven praetors: Cass. Dio 48,43,2.

pp. 176–7 *The meeting at Cape Misenum*: App. b.c. 5,290–313; Cass. Dio 48,36–8 (he describes the setting staged for the meeting slightly differently, with the triumvirs on land and Pompey on an artificial mound erected in the sea); Plut. Anton. 32. App. b.c. 5,303 (cf. 298) names Puteoli, the old Dikaiarcheia (now Pozzuoli), as the scene of the meeting, but this statement cannot be reconciled with others to the effect that the meeting was at Cape

Misenum and Baiae. The Peloponnese, received by Sextus Pompey, was part of the province of Achaea, which contained ancient Greece and was bordered to the north by the province of Macedonia. In the republican period, Achaea generally had no governor of its own, and its administration was by the governor of Macedonia. App. 5,326 speaks of the Peloponnese as the area allotted to Pompey; Cass. Dio 48,36,5 speaks of Achaea, but Antony would certainly not have ceded the whole of Greece, possibly including the Aegean Sea, to Pompey. According to App. b.c. 5,299, Pompey hoped to replace Lepidus in the triumvirate. In no circumstances, however, would the group of powerful men in existence up to that point have been overturned, although one can imagine that they might have thought of taking him into the triumvirate as a fourth member; cf. also App. b.c. 5,328.

pp. 178–9 *Virgil's Fourth Eclogue*: See, in particular, out of the vast amount of research on the subject, Hildebrecht Hommel, 'Vergils "messianisches" Gedicht', *Theologia viatorum. Jahrbuch der kirchl. Hochschule Berlin* 2, 1950, 182–212 (= idem, in *Wege zu Vergil*, Wege der Forschung 19, 1966, 368–415, with an appendix 415–25; also further literature there); Andrew Wallace-Hadrill, 'The Golden Age and Sin in Augustan Ideology', *Past and Present* 95, 1982, 19–36; Karl Büchner, 'P. Vergilius Maro', RE VIII A, 1955, 1195–213; Kienast, *Augustus*, 239ff.; and Walther Kraus, 'Vergils vierte Ekloge: Ein kritisches Hypomnema', ANRW II 31,1, 1980, 604–45. Gerhard Binder offers an individual attempt at interpretation, 'Lied der Parzen zur Geburt Octavians', *Gymnasium* 90, 1983, 102–22, suggesting that the announcement of the birth of a child of Virgil himself in the past, more specifically in the year 63, is to be seen as a projection relating to Octavian. In Georg. 2,532–40, Virgil looks back to a golden age of Saturn in the early days of Rome, to which a godless race put an end, but without hoping for better times yet to come. Scholarly discussion of the Fourth Eclogue concentrates chiefly on whether Virgil is referring, with the birth of the boy, to a real child born at the time or whether he sees him only as an ideal figure symbolizing longing, and also on the origin of the concept of a Golden Age, that is to say on the prophetic content of the poem. On the first question, the point is: who was the divine boy? Many candidates have been considered, for instance Octavian's child by Scribonia, but that child was not born until the year 39 and was a girl, or even a child who might be expected to be born of the marriage between Octavia and Antony, although it was not concluded until the autumn of 40, and that child too was a girl (see Werner Dahlheim, 'Augustus', in M. Clauss, ed., *Die römische Kaiser*, 1997, 32). I find it difficult to imagine that Virgil refers specifically to a boy in his poem without knowing the gender of the child in advance. In addition, if we are to think of a real child, Virgil can only have meant the son of the man to whom the poem was dedicated and who did have a son born to him at the time, since otherwise the dedication would have been farcical or even insulting (the fact that the child concerned, Gaius

Asinius Gallus, claimed later that he himself was meant is of little importance for purposes of identification). But even if the child can only be the son of Pollio, and Virgil did indeed mean that boy, it is significant in the poem only as the vessel in which longings for a better time gather. To speak, as so often, of a prophecy on Virgil's part would mean that the poet already has his eye on the future history of Italy after the year 30/29. However, the poem is closely linked with the time when it was written; the object of longing is unreal, and the Golden Age only another way of saying that the future is unknown. Lines 31–6, which speak of slight traces of 'the former wrong' and have given rise to great critical confusion, certainly do not represent a break in the poet's thinking, but set out to reconcile the new and peaceful time after the boy's birth with reality and convey no idea of the sudden advent of a divinity. The effect the poem had on its contemporaries also lies in the very fact that it does not represent some empty Utopia or even a prophecy, but links longing for a better time with knowledge of reality, projecting that into the future.

pp. 179–81 *Livia*: See Lotte Ollendorf, 'Livia', RE XIII, 1926, 900–924, and Walter Hatto Gross's treatise *Iulia Augusta*, Göttinger Akad. d. Wiss., 1962 (with portraits of her). On the love-life of Octavian/Augustus: Suet. Aug. 69–71,1. Octavian in his memoir *Res Gestae* on Scribonia: Suet. Aug. 62,2. The 'three-month' child: Cass. Dio 48,44,5. Premature birth of Livia's baby: Suet. Aug. 63,1.

p. 181 *Horace and the civil war*: Epodes 7 and 16 almost certainly date from the time after the treaties of Brundisium and Misenum, and before the new outbreak of the war against Sextus Pompey in the year 38. The verbal echoes of Virgil's Fourth Eclogue in lines 33 and 49 of Epode 16 have set off a long controversy and one that cannot be settled about priority; see Lefèvre, *Horaz*, 61ff. The quotation is epode 7,1–4: 'quo, quo scelesti ruitis aut cur dexteris / aptantur enses conditi? / parumne campis atque Neptuno super / fusum est Latini sanguinis?' (trans. Lefèvre, op. cit., 63).

p. 184 *The layout of the Julian Harbour and the building of the fleet*: Cass. Dio 48,49–50,1–3, 51,5; Vell. Pat. 2,79,1–2; Suet. Aug. 16,1. In his account of the Gulf of Puteoli, Strabo 5,4,5ff. described the geographical setting of the harbour in the Augustan period. On the harbour, see R. F. Paget, 'The Ancient Ports of Cumae', *Journ. Rom. Stud.* 58, 1968, 162ff. (with maps and photographs); Viereck, *Flotte*, 263. As the channel in Lake Lucrinus was always silting up, the war harbour was soon abandoned, and the harbour of Misenum took over from it as the central harbour for warships on the west coast of Italy.

p. 185 *Antony and Cleopatra in Tarsos*: See esp. Plut. Anton. 25–9.

p. 186 *Quintus Labienus*: He had coins minted with the inscription PARTHICUS IMP(erator) (BMCRR II, p. 500, no. 131ff.). Here, *Parthicus* denotes not the name of a victor, as for instance in *Asiaticus* and *Germanicus*, but associations with the Parthians, i.e. 'Commander of the Parthians'.

pp. 187–8 *The 'new Dionysos' of the time*: See A. D. Nock, 'Notes on Ruler-cult II', *Journ. Hellen. Stud.* 48, 1928, 30–38. Entry into Ephesos as Dionysos: Plut. Anton. 24,4; into Tarsos: Athenaios deipnosoph. 4,147ff./148ab. The marriage of Antony to Athena: Cass. Dio 48,39,2; Seneca suas.1,6. Antony named in a decree of the city of Athens of the year 38 as 'the god Neos Dionysos': IG II² 1043 Z. 22ff.

pp. 189–90 *The treaty of Tarentum*: App. b.c. 5,389–99; Cass. Dio 48,54; Plut. Anton. 36. Horace's *Iter Brundisinum* (Sat. 1,5), describing the poet's journey from Rome to Brundisium in the company of Maecenas, Lucius Cocceius Nerva and Gaius Fonteius Capito (a supporter of Antony), as well as the poets Virgil, Plotius and Varius, refers to this meeting of the triumvirs, not to the meeting of the year 40, as was once assumed. Horace cannot have known Maecenas yet in 40. On the part played by Lepidus in the triumvirs' second term of office (37–33), see E. Badian, 'M. Lepidus and the Second Triumvirate', *Arctos* 25, 1991, 5–16, emphasizing the now changed position of Lepidus.

pp. 191–7 *The second phase of the Sicilian War*: On Octavian's considering suicide after his defeat at Tauromenium: Plin. nat. hist. 7,148; on Octavian's defeat and personal danger, see also App. b.c. 5,464–7; Cass. Dio 49,5,3–5. On the battle of Naulochus: App. b.c. 5,489–503; Cass. Dio 49,9ff. On the 'gripper' grappling iron (*harpax*): App. b.c. 5,491; a drawing with an account of the way it worked can be found in Viereck, *Flotte*, 95ff. The date of the battle has come down to us from a large fragment of a calendar of feast days, from Amiternum in the Sabine country. The award of the banner and crown to Agrippa: Suet. Aug. 25,3; Vell. Pat. 2,81,3; Cass. Dio 49,14,3.

pp. 197–9 *The capitulation of Lepidus*: App. b.c. 5,506–24; Cass. Dio 49,11,2–12,4. The humiliation of Lepidus: Cass. Dio 54,15,4–8. On the economic situation of Sicily at this time, see Shelley C. Stone III, 'Sextus Pompey, Octavian and Sicily', *Americ. Journ. Archaeol.* 87, 1983, 11–22.

pp. 199–200 *The demobilization of the soldiers*: On the numbers of legions and men after the end of the Sicilian War see Brunt, *Manpower*, 499ff. On the demobilization and the indignation of the soldiers see App. b.c. 5,528–36; Cass. Dio 49,13,1–14,2. On Octavian's edict from the time of his second triumvirate: C. G. Bruns/O. Gradenwitz, *Fontes iuris Romani antiqui*, 1909⁷, no. 69, with the correct conjecture in note 7: 'triumvir rei publicae constituendae iter' (instead of the meaningless 'consul ter').

pp. 200–202 *The end of Sextus Pompey*: The account of Hannibal's deeds in the temple of Juno Lacinia: Liv. 28,46,16. Sextus Pompey giving refuge to proscribed men: App. b.c. 5,597. This passage also contains mention of his passivity as a commander, which was seen as the result of a sickness or blindness sent by the gods.

## CHAPTER 6
## Main Sources

Vell. Pat. 2,82–8; Suet. Aug. 17–18; Plut. Anton. 33–87; Cass. Dio 49,19–51,19.

## Explanatory Notes

pp. 204–5 *The scene outside the gates of Rome in the year 36*: Cass. Dio 49,15,3; App. b.c. 5,539.

p. 206 *The freedmen*: The freedmen were demoted to the condition of slavery after the Sicilian War and either returned to their former masters or executed: Aug. RG 25,1; for the numbers see also Oros. 6,18,33, and App. b.c. 5,544ff. When Horace, in his criticism of a rich freedman in Epode 4, emphasizes the rigid boundary between freedmen and slaves (1–4), and equally critically describes the war against Sextus Pompey as a struggle of the proud fleet (free Romans) against robbers and slaves ('contra latrones atque servilem manum') (17–20; these lines place the date of the epode as 37/36), he is reflecting the climate of opinion throughout Italy, and Octavian was taking it into account in his cruelty towards Pompey's freed soldiers.

pp. 207–11 *The temple of Apollo on the Palatine*: Vell. Pat. 2,81,3; Suet. Aug. 29,3; Cass. Dio 49,15,5. On the transfer of the Sibylline books to the plinth of the cult statue for safe keeping soon after the dedication of the temple, see Virg. Aen. 6,69ff., where the promise made by Aeneas of a temple for Apollo and Diana and games in honour of Apollo looks ahead to the Palatine temple and the Secular Games. The divine triad of the temple to Apollo on the Palatine appears on a relief (Museo Correale, Sorrento; illustration in Zanker, *Augustus*, no. 186) together with the Sibyl, who has sunk at the feet of Apollo and is pointing her right hand at the oracular collection stored in the plinth of his statue. On the Palatine temple of Apollo, see Paul Zanker, 'Der Apollontempel auf dem Palatin: Ausstattung und politische Sinnbezüge nach der Schlacht von Actium', *Città e architettura nella Roma imperiale*, Analecta Rom. Instituti Danici, Suppl. 10, 1983, 21–40, referring to the Hellenistic model; B. Kellum, 'Sculptural Programs and Propaganda in Augustan Rome: The Temple of Apollo on the Palatine', in Winkes, *Augustus*, 169–76 (also with special reference to the Danaids); Gurval, *Actium*, 87ff.; and Eckard Lefèvre, *Das Bild-Programm des Apollo-Tempels auf dem Palatin*, 1989. On the temple of Apollo Sosianus, see François Hinard, 'C. Sosius et le temple d'Apollon', *Kentron* 8, 1992, 57–72. On Apollo and Dionysos in the background of the quarrels of the two potentates over the minting of coins at the time, and the envoys they sent, see Dietrich Mannsperger, 'Apollon gegen

Dionysos: Numismatische Beiträge zu Octavians Rolle als Vindex Libertatis',
*Gymnasium* 80, 1973, 381–404. On the tendency of noble families to trace
their descent back to the mythological past and link it with deities, see T. P.
Wiseman, 'Legendary Genealogies in Late-Republican Rome', *Greece &
Rome* 21, 1974, 153–64. On the sanctity of the tribune of the people: Cass.
Dio 49,15,6 speaks of the transfer of sanctity and the right that went with it
of sitting on the tribunes' bench (*subsellium*) in the Senate. On discussion of
this transfer, particularly in ancient tradition, see Bleicken, *Prinzipat*, 74ff., on
the transfer of sanctity to the dictator Caesar see Jehne, *Caesar*, 96ff.

pp. 212–15 *Antony's Parthian campaign*: Plut. Anton. 37–52; Cass. Dio 49,24–
31. On relations between Rome and Parthia in general over the preceding
decades, see Karl-Heinz Ziegler, *Die Beziehungen zwischen Rom und dem
Partherreich: Ein Beitrag zur Geschichte des Völkerrechts*, 1964, 36ff.; and on
Antony's Parthian policy, see A. S. Schreiber, 'Antony and Parthia', *Rivista
Storica dell'Antichità* 9, 1979, 105–24. On Antony's campaign in particular,
see Gardthausen, *Augustus*, I, 290ff.; Johannes Kromayer, 'Der Partherzug des
Antonius', *Hermes* 31, 1896, 70–104; and Kromayer/Veith, *Schlachten-Atlas*,
121ff. with leaf 24,7. Plutarch's description of the campaign is very probably
based on an account of it by Quintus Dellius, one of Antony's legates, who
took part in the campaign himself (see Plut. Anton. 59,6). Dellius, who was
extremely hostile to Cleopatra, went over to Octavian before Actium. His
contemporaries saw him as one of those opportunists who changed sides several times, an idea graphically illustrated by Marcus Valerius Messalla
Corvinus in using the term 'horse-jumper', i.e. a cavalryman who shows his
horsemanship by repeatedly jumping on and off a galloping horse. Dellius
changed his allegiance from Dolabella to Cassius, the assassin of Caesar, then
again to Antony, and ended up – just at the right time – supporting Octavian;
he was a turncoat of the time of the civil war: 'desultor bellorum civilium'
(Seneca suas. 1,7; see Vell. Pat. 2,84,2). The location of Phraaspa, capital of
the Atropatene district, cannot be precisely established. The 'tortoise' on the
retreat from Media: Cass. Dio 49,29,2–30.

pp. 217–21 *Octavian's Illyrian war*: Cass. Dio 49,35–7; App. Illyriké 52–83. On
Illyricum, Philipp-Stephan G. Freber, *Der hellenistische Osten und das Illyricum unter Caesar*, 1993, esp. 158ff., assuming that the dictator had a restricted
aim in his conflict, to secure the old border; On the Dalmatian and Illyrian
area at the time of the dictator, see Freber, *Der hellenistische Osten* (op. cit.
157ff.); on the situation in the war itself, Georg Veith, 'Die Feldzüge des C.
Iulius Caesar Octavianus in Illyrien in den Jahren 35–33 v. Chr.', in *Schriften
der Balkankommission*, Antiquarische Abt. VII, 1914 (with good maps); also
Kromayer/Veith, *Schlachten-Atlas*, 117ff., leaf 24,1–3, and ibid. on the siege
of Siscia, leaf 24,4; on the siege of Promona, leaf 24,5. The storming of Metulum: App. Illyriké 54–61. When Octavian arrived there Siscia was very
probably one of two towns that merged together later; the other part was

called Segestiké. In Appian, the inhabitants of Siscia are therefore called Segestians. There has been a certain amount of controversial discussion of the aims and territorial outcome of the campaigns between 35 and 33, but opinions are almost unanimous on what was actually achieved; see Kromayer/ Veith (op. cit.); Syme, *Revolution*, 240; and Walter Schmitthenner, 'Octavians militärische Unternehmungen in den Jahren 35–33 v. Chr.', *Historia* 7, 1958, 189–236. Cassius Dio on the Pannonians: 49,36, 2–5. In 49,36,1 he also expressly admits that there was no good reason for this war. On the name of the Pannonians: according to Cass. Dio 49,36,5, they were called after the Graeco-Latin word for a cloth rag (Latin *pannus*), because they made their garments of separate piece of cloth sewn together. But this can at the most be the name that others gave them, not what they called themselves; see Andreas Mócsy, RE Suppl. IX, 1962, 519ff.

pp. 218–19 *Octavian's second journey to Sicily*: The alleged danger threatening from the north, and the discontented veterans: Cass. Dio 49,34,1–5.

pp. 221–2 *Octavia*: Octavia's separation from her husband did not mean that Cleopatra became the triumvir Antony's official wife. Joint portraits of Antony and Cleopatra are found on coins only after 32, and until 35 we still find coins with the joint portrait of Antony and Octavia; see BMCRR II, 520ff. (Antony and Octavia, 36/35 BC); 525 (Antony and Cleopatra, 32/31 BC).

pp. 222–6 *Antony's reorganization of the east*: In view of a certain amount of imprecision in the ancient sources, modern scholars have disputed whether Antony formally married Cleopatra; see, according to Viktor Gardthausen, in particular Álvoro d'Ors, 'Cleopatra ¿"uxor" de Marco Antonio?', *Anuario de Historia del Derecho Español* 49, 1979, 639ff. The new regulation of the client system in the years 37ff.: Cass. Dio 49,32,3, 33,2. The first transfer of territory to Cleopatra in the year 37: Plut. Anton. 36; Cass. Dio 49,32,4. On Polemon and the Pontus area see Eckart Olshausen, *Pontos und Rom (63 v. Chr.–64 n. Chr.)* and Richard D. Sullivan, 'Dynasts in Pontus', ANRW II 7,2, 1980, 909ff. and 913ff. The reorganizations of the year 34: Cass. Dio 49,41,3 describes the allocation of territory to the children of Antony and Cleopatra (Alexandros, Cleopatra and Philadelphos) as promises, while they are called actual transfers by Plutarch in the parallel passage (Anton. 54,7; the daughter, Cleopatra, is not mentioned here). Cleopatra with Antony on Roman denarii: BMCRR, East 182: obverse, head of Antony with inscription 'ANTONI / ARMENIA DEVICTA', reverse, bust of Cleopatra with inscription 'Cleopatrae reginae regum filiorum REGUM', i.e. '[Coin] of Cleopatra, queen of kings and her sons who are also kings'. Syme, *Revolution*, 271ff., vigorously defends Antony's reorganization of the east on the grounds that its division into provinces by Pompey had come too early, and therefore decentralization had become necessary. If kings now replaced Roman proconsuls and tax collectors, he thinks, that meant 'order, content and economy – they supplied levies, gifts and tribute to the rulers of Rome' (272). A favourable

NOTES

opinion of eastern princes certainly arose chiefly from knowledge of the poor state of previous Roman provincial administration. In defending Antony's reorganization Syme is carried away so far as to say that 'to the population of the eastern lands the direct rule of Rome was distasteful and oppressive, to the Roman State a cause of disintegration by reason of the military ambition of the proconsuls and the extortions of the knights. The empire, and especially the empire in the East, had been the ruin of the Republic' (272). We may doubt whether the Romans would have achieved the political results seen by Syme as desirable by setting up kings instead of governors. There was certainly mismanagement in many of the provinces, but in the time of the republic and its oligarchy, as Syme himself acknowledges, not of the monarchy. All the same, Syme also thinks that 'his [sc. Antony's] dual role as Roman proconsul and Hellenistic dynast [as the husband of the queen of Egypt] was ambiguous, disquieting and vulnerable' (273). On Antony's reorganization of the east with particular reference to the part played in it by client kings, see Hans Buchheim, 'Die Orientpolitik des Triumvirn M. Antonius', *Abhandlg. d. Heidelberger Akad. d. Wiss.*, philos.-histor. Kl., Jahrg. 1960, 3. Abhandl., esp. 49ff. Thomas Schrapel, *Das Reich der Kleopatra: Quellenkritische Untersuchungen zu den 'Landschenkungen' Mark Antons*, 1996, has recently taken a look at the historical accounts of the land transfers, particularly those of Plutarch and Cassius Dio, as well as the minting of coins and the inscriptions on them in the areas under discussion, and has come to conclusions about the extent and precise date of these transfers that differ in part from previously held ideas. Although I think that his evaluations of the material, often very meagre, are speculative, and older interpretations are at least equally well worth considering (especially in what they say of Crete and Cyprus), future research will have to take account of not just the literary evidence but the contemporary accounts put forward here, and their evaluation.

p. 228 *The rivalry between Octavian and Antony*: Cornelius Nepos, Att. 20,5: 'inter quos [sc. Octavian and Antony] maximarum rerum non solum aemulatio, sed obtrectatio tanta intercedebat, quantam fuit incidere necesse inter Caesarem atque Antonium, cum se uterque principem non solum urbis Romae, sed orbis terrarum esse cuperet.

pp. 230–32 *The mutual recriminations*: Suet. Aug. 63,2.68; Plut. Anton. 55; Cass. Dio 50,1,2–2,1 and 50,24–30 (Octavian's speech to his soldiers before the battle of Actium); Seneca ad Luc. 83,25; cf. Kenneth Scott, 'The Political Propaganda of 44–30 B.C.', *Memoirs of the Americ. Acad. in Rome* 11, 1933, 7–49; John Robert Johnson, 'Augustan Propaganda', UCLA, Ph.D. thesis, 1976 (microfilm), esp. 78ff.; and Holger Sonnabend, *Fremdenbild und Politik: Vorstellungen der Römer von Ägypten und dem Partherreich in der späten Republik und frühen Kaiserzeit*, 1986, 49ff. Antony's defence of his intoxication ('de sua ebrietate'): Plin. nat. hist. 14,148; see the explanation offered by Gabriele Marasco, which is worth discussing, in his 'Marco Antonio "Nuovo

655

Dioniso" e il *De sua ebrietate*', *Latomus* 51, 1992, 538–48, suggesting that
Antony accounts for his pleasure in drinking (perhaps as a justification?) by
the close relationship he claimed with Dionysos, Heracles and Alexander.
There was embittered dispute on whether the dictator was to be regarded as
Caesarion's father. Antony cited Caesar's own recognition of the child as his,
according to statements by his friends, an argument that Octavian denied in
writing; cf. Suet. Div. Jul. 52,2.

pp. 232–5 *Events at the beginning of the year 32 in Rome*: Cass. Dio 50,2,2–7.
On the position of Octavian and Antony with regard to constitutional law in
the year 32, see Bleicken, *Prinzipat*, 65ff., citing other literature.

pp. 236–8 *Octavia and Cleopatra in 32/31, and the declaration of war*: The
divorce of Octavia: Liv. per. 132; Plut. Anton. 57,4 (Octavia told to move out
of Antony's house in Rome); Cass. Dio 50,3,2. The opening of the will and the
rumours arising from it: Plut. Anton. 58,4–11; Cass. Dio 50,3,3–4,2, 5,1–4;
Suet. Aug. 17,1; see also, on Cleopatra, Prop. 3,11,29–72, esp. 30ff., 45ff.; on
Plancus see also Vell. Pat. 2,83. The alleged oath sworn by Cleopatra: Cass.
Dio 50,5,4. Horace on Cleopatra: c. 1,37,6ff. (30 BC). The declaration of war:
Plut. Anton. 60,1; Cass. Dio 50,4,3–6,1. The number of senators and consu-
lars accompanying Octavian to the war: Aug. RG 25.

p. 238 *The oath sworn by Italy and all the west to Octavian*: Aug. RG 25:
'iuravit in mea verba tota Italia sponte sua et me belli, quo vici ad Actium,
ducem depoposcit, iuraverunt in eadem verba provinciae Galliae, Hispaniae,
Africa, Sicilia, Sardinia' ('All Italy voluntarily swore allegiance to me and took
me as leader in the war that I won at Actium. The provinces of Gaul, Spain,
Africa, Sicily and Sardinia all took the same oath'). The enumeration of provinces omits Illyricum. Suet. Aug. 17,2 gives the wording of the oath as
'coniurare pro partibus suis' ('to swear by his cause'). The oath may be
regarded as an oath taken by soldiers to their commander required by Roman
citizens and all other inhabitants of the west; see for this sense Peter Herrmann, *Der römische Kaisereid*, 1968, 78ff. Octavian with all Italy, the Senate,
the people and the gods against the queen: Virg. Aen. 8,678ff. (the description
of the shield).

pp. 239–51 *Preliminary skirmishing and the battle of Actium*: Plut. Anton.
61–68,5; Cass. Dio 50,11–35; Vell. Pat. 2,85; Virg. Aen. 8,671–713 (description of the shield). On the numbers of troops present at Actium see Brunt,
*Manpower*, 498ff. and 502ff. After the battle the army lost track of Antony,
and thereupon marched away and finally surrendered: Cass. Dio 51,1,4; Plut.
Anton. 67,7ff., 68.4ff.; Antony's orders to the army issued from Tainaron:
Plut. Anton. 67,7ff. On the catapults and ballistas see Viereck, *Flotte*, 101ff.
Today we distinguish between arrow-firing artillery operated by hand or
mechanical devices and slingshot-firing artillery; the description of the former
as catapults and the latter as ballistas is modern; the ancient terms are not
standardized; see Viereck, *Flotte*, 101. Both types of artillery could also

operate as fire-throwers, but we know of only the Octavian fleet using them to throw fire at Actium. Antony abandoning his army: Vell. Pat. 2,85,3. The information given by Octavian/Augustus on the number of ships captured: Plut. Anton. 68,2. On the course of the battle of Actium, and in particular the interpretation of Antony's manoeuvre as a breakthrough, see Johannes Kromayer, 'Der Feldzug von Actium und der sogenannte Verrath der Cleopatra', *Hermes* 34, 1899, 1–54, and John M. Carter, *The Battle of Actium*, 1970, German translation *Die Schlacht bei Actium*, 1972, 235ff. Carter sees the reason for a decision to break through with the fleet as the poor chances the weakened army would have had in a retreat on land. The attempt, which goes back to W. W. Tarn, to give an entirely different interpretation to the course of the battle, on the evidence of Horace, Epode 9,19ff. (claiming that a large number of Antony's ships had suddenly gone back to harbour without giving battle, leaving Antony no option but flight, see Murray/Petsas, 131ff., cited in the following note), is based on a misinterpretation of this passage in Horace and need not be considered. Gardthausen, *Augustus* I, 383, is among a number of scholars who hold that Cleopatra betrayed Antony.

p. 251 *The monument commemorating the victory at Actium*: Remains of it have been excavated, see William M. Murray/Photios M. Petsas, 'Octavian's Campsite Memorial for the Actian War', *Transactions Americ. Philos. Soc.* 79,4, 1989, 1–172 (on 9ff. there, the testimonials to the victory), and on the dating of the monument see Thomas Schäfer, 'Zur Datierung des Siegesdenkmals von Aktium', *Mitt. des Deutsch. Archäol. Inst. Athen* 108, 1993, 239–48. On the inscription, see J. M. Carter, 'A New Fragment of Octavian's Inscription at Nicopolis', *Zeitschr. für Papyrologie u. Epigr.* 24, 1977, 227–30.

pp. 252–5 *The end in Alexandria*: Plut. Anton. 69–86; Cass. Dio 51,10–16; Vell. Pat. 2,87,1ff.; Suet. Aug. 17,3–5. The renaming of Antony's club of boon companions: Plut. Anton. 71,4. Death of Cleopatra and conjectures on the manner of it: Plut. Anton. 85ff. Tribute paid to Cleopatra by Horace: c. 1,37,21–32; see also Vell. Pat. 2,87,1: 'sana expers [sc. Cleopatra] muliebris metus' ('without any womanly fear'). The death of Canidius more terrible than he deserved: Vell. Pat. 2,87,3. It is also Velleius (2,87,2) who praises the clemency (*clementia*) shown by Octavian after the end of the campaign. On Cleopatra, see Edwyn Bevan, *The House of Ptolemy: A History of Egypt under the Ptolemaic Dynasty*, 1927, reprint. 1968, 359–84; Felix Stähelin, 'Cleopatra', in RE XI, 1921, 750–81; and Heinz Heinen, 'Cäsar und Kaisarion', *Historia* 18, 1969, 181–203.

p. 255 *Octavian's reaction to news of Antony's suicide*: Plut. Anton. 78,2ff. The *damnatio memoriae*: Plut. Anton. 86,9; idem, Cic. 49,6; Cass. Dio 51,19,3; see Dessau ILS no. 943 and Tac. ann. 3,18,1.

pp. 255–6 *On property prices and the rate of interest*: Cass. Dio 51,21,5.

p. 256 *On the reorganization of Egypt and the client principalities in Asia Minor under Antony and Octavian*: See Eleanor G. Huzar, 'Augustus, Heir of the

Ptolemies', in ANRW II 10,1, 1988, 343–82, and David Magie, *Roman Rule in Asia Minor to the End of the Third Century After Christ*, 1950, 427ff. and 442ff.

pp. 256–7 *Octavian at Alexander's tomb, his contempt for the tombs of the Ptolemies*: Suet. Aug. 18,1; Cass. Dio 51,16,5.

pp. 257–8 *The modern verdict on Antony and Octavian*: Ronald Syme in particular sees Antony as an aristocrat and a politician of stature, contrasting him with Octavian the adventurer, terrorist and despot. This thesis is based largely on a comparison of the people with whom they mingled and whom they used to help them, and Syme's account of Octavian's character in particular is influenced by circumstances at the time when he was writing his book (1937/8); see Géza Alföldy, 'Sir Ronald Syme, "Die römische Revolution" und die deutsche Althistorie', *Sitz.ber. d. Heidelberger Akad. d. Wiss.*, philos.-histor. Kl., Jahrg. 1983, 1, esp. 19ff. Among other objections to Syme's theory, it must be said that the adherents of Antony differed only very slightly from those of Octavian, and that those members of distinguished families who remained loyal to Antony in his last years certainly did not represent a 'republic' any longer. On the adherents of Octavian and Antony before Actium, see Syme, *Revolution*, 234ff. (Octavian) and 266ff. (Antony), as well as Anna Elisabeth Glauning, 'Die Anhängerschaft des Antonius und der Octavian', dissertation, Leipzig, 1936.

## CHAPTER 7
## Main Sources

Vell. Pat. 2,89–93; Strab. 17,3,25; Suet. Aug. 27,5–28, 2, 47; Cass. Dio 51,21–7, 52,42–54,10.

## Explanatory Notes

pp. 260–61 *The ideological emphasis given to Actium*: Horace Epode 9 (a celebration of victory written directly after the battle, at which Horace was present; he presents Antony as in thrall to Cleopatra); c. 1,37 (ode of victory on the battle of Actium); Virg. Aen. 8,675–713 (in 698ff. Actian Apollo, with other Roman gods, fights the Egyptian gods and the deities of other barbarous peoples, called *monstra*); Prop. 3,11 (31ff.: Cleopatra asks for Rome as her price for marrying Antony; the Senate is to be subject to her) and 4,6 (27ff.: Apollo as one who brings aid in battle); see on the same subject Andrew Wallace-Hadrill, *Augustan Rome*, 1993, 1ff., and in particular Gurval, *Actium*, including 47ff. on the minting of coins after Actium. The subject of Actium on monuments: Tonio Hölscher, 'Denkmäler der Schlacht von Actium.

Propaganda und Resonanz', *Klio* 67, 1985, 81–102, and on coins in particular: Simon, *Selbstdarstellung*, 89ff. – *libertatis populi romani vindex*: tetradrachm (cistoforos on a Rhodian base), minted 28/27 BC in the province of Asia, perhaps Ephesos or Apameia/Bithynia (BMCRE 691); see Wickert, 'Princeps', 2081, and Karl-Wilhelm Welwei, 'Augustus als *vindex libertatis*. Freiheitsideologie und Propaganda im frühen Prinzipat', *Altspr. Unterricht* 16/3, 1973, 29–41.

p. 262 *Closing of the Arch of Janus*: Aug. RG 13. On the god Janus see Latte, *Religionsgeschichte*, 132ff. On the architecture and location of the arch see Lugli, *Roma*, 82ff.; Richardson, *Rome*, 205ff. On the longing for peace felt at this time, see among others Hor. c. 1,2 (circa 27 BC) and Virg. Georg. 1,498ff.; idem, Aen. 1,285ff.; on the tension between the idea of peace and readiness for war, E. S. Gruen, 'Augustus and the Ideology of War and Peace', in Winkes, *Augustus*, 51–72.

pp. 262, 264 *The buildings mentioned in the text*: Triumphal arches dedicated to Octavian: the Actian arch in the Forum, of the year 29 BC, may have stood to the south of the temple of the Divine Julius, but its location is a matter of controversy. According to most interpreters it comprised a set of three arches, according to others (Nash) only one (in more recent excavations an arch with a single opening, the predecessor of the triple arch, has been discovered here), and was demolished when the Parthian arch was built on the same site. The arch with the single opening has also been linked to the naval victory of Naulochus. The dedicatory inscription on the Actian arch has come down to us from a sixteenth-century copy (Dessau ILS no. 81). The lists of consuls and triumphators (*fasti*) were carved on the walls of the two side arches (probably of the Parthian arch). Fragments of these lists have been rediscovered (and are known as the *Fasti Capitolini* because they are kept in the museum on the Capitol today). Only a few remains of both arches themselves still exist today, and most of those are not visible. On this discussion see Nash, *Rome*, I, 92ff., Coarelli, *Foro Romano*, 258ff., Steinby, *Roma*, I, 80–85, and Nedergaard, op. cit. On the temple of the Divine Julius, see Nash, *Rome*, I, 512ff.; on the Curia Julia and the statue of Victoria, see Alfonso Bartoli, *Curia senatus. Lo scavo e il restauro*, 1963 (a scholarly appraisal of what remains of the Diocletian *curia*), and Tonio Hölscher, *Victoria Romana*, 1967, 6ff.

p. 262 *The reading of the Georgics in Atella*: vit. Donati 92ff.

p. 263 *The triumph of Octavian*: Cass. Dio 51,21,5–9; Suet. Aug. 22.

pp. 264–5 *The purchase of land where soldiers could settle in the year 30 BC*: Aug. RG 16, see §15 for the triumphal gift and §3 for the fact that of the *c.* 500,000 soldiers in all who had sworn an oath to him during his reign he settled over 300,000 in the provinces or demobilized them in their native land. On the settlement of soldiers after Actium, see also Keppie, *Colonisation*, 73ff. and *passim*, and Walter Schmitthenner, 'Politik und Armee in der späten römischen Republik', *Histor. Zeitschr.* 190, 1960, 16f. (in 30 BC some 230,000 soldiers, *c.* 80,000 of them demobilized). On the equal treatment of all soldiers in settling them, including those who had followed Lepidus and Antony, see Hygin. gromat. de limit., p. 177 L. On the number of soldiers still on active service after Actium there is some controversy. So far as I can see, the thesis of Theodor Mommsen, who in his commentary on the *Res Gestae* of Augustus' thought (pp. 68ff.) that there were only eighteen legions still active, is almost unanimously rejected.

p. 267 *Voting in Italy*: Augustus allowed the citizens of twenty-eight *coloniae* founded in Italy to vote in writing in their home towns for candidates for the higher offices of state in Rome, and then seal them and send them to Rome on the day of the election (Suet. Aug. 46). This right was certainly intended as a special privilege for these colonies, marking them out from the other Italian towns.

pp. 272–7 *Crassus and the spolia opima*: For Octavian's motives in promoting Crassus, see Edmund Groag, RE XIII, 1926, s.v. 271. The campaign of Crassus: Cass. Dio 51,23,2–27; see Groag, op. cit., 272–85. Propertius 4,10 wrote an elegy on the three cases when the *spolia opima* was taken. On the *spolia opima* and Octavian's efforts to prevent the granting of this honour to Crassus, see Liv. 4,19,5, 20,2–11, and on these passages Hermann Dessau, 'Livius und Augustus', *Hermes* 41, 1906, 142–51, and idem, *Geschichte der römischen Kaiserzeit* I, 1924, 57ff. Dessau sees Crassus as a dependent magistrate (represented in his *Geschichte der römischen Kaiserzeit* as the opposite of an independent magistrate) whom Octavian could refuse the dedication of the *spolia opima* on the grounds of the evidence he had found that an independent command was necessary for him to be able to dedicate the prize, but he thinks that the evidence itself and its interpretation are untrustworthy because of the political intention behind them. On the other hand J. W. Rich, 'Augustus and the *Spolia Opima*', *Chiron* 26, 1996, 85–127, has no doubt that Crassus held an independent command, but does not see that as part of the problem in the year 28. According to him, although he was an independent magistrate, Crassus gave way voluntarily and without discussion to pressure from Octavian. There is also disagreement on the subject of when Augustus presented the inscription in the temple of Jupiter Feretrius to the public. As he himself began restoring the temple before the year 32 (Corn. Nepos Att. 20,3), he could have had it ready directly after the battle with the Bastarnae, to reveal it only at some later date. Scholars do not agree on how far Crassus was an independent magistrate. The description of him by the Athenians as *imperator* and proconsul (Dessau ILS no. 8810) is also dismissed as flattery. E. Badian, '"Crisis Theories" and the Beginning of the Principate', in Gerhard Wirth (ed.), *Romanitas – Christianitas*, Festschrift for Johannes Straub on his seventieth birthday, 1982, 24ff., firmly rejected any influence of the Crassus episode on the act of state of 27 on chronological grounds (the return of Crassus at the end of 28, the triumph on 4.7.27). However, as it has been established that there was indeed discussion of the dedication question at the time, that would be hard to understand if it did not take place directly after the battle with the Bastarnae, i.e. after the summer of 29, but only at the time of the triumph. The achievements of Crassus should not be seen as the cause of the new order ushered in during January 27, the provisions of which Octavian had certainly been discussing with his friends well in advance, but as the factor setting off its swift introduction.

pp. 281–2 *The 'reading of the Senate' (lectio senatus)*: See Mommsen, *Staatsrecht*, II, 418ff.; on the *princeps senatus* see ibid., III, 969ff., with the revisions by Christian Meier, 'Die Ersten unter den ersten des Senats', in D. Nörr/D. Simon (eds.), *Gedächtnisschrift für Wolfgang Kunkel*, 1984, 185–204. On the *lectio senatus* of this year: Cass. Dio 52,42,1–4; on the appointment of patricians: Aug. RG 8; Cass. Dio 52,42,5. Octavian as *princeps senatus* in the year 28: Aug. RG 7 (here Augustus speaks of having been *princeps senatus* for forty years when he wrote this, which would mean that he composed the *Res Gestae* in about the year AD 12); Cass. Dio 53,1,3. The phrases *me principe* and *ante me principem*: Aug. RG 13, 32 and 30; see Tac. ann. 1,1,1: '[sc. Augustus] ... cuncta discordiis civilibus fessa nomine principis sub imperium accepit' ('Augustus brought the state, laid low in the civil wars, into his power under the name of *princeps*'). Horace c. 1,2,50 calls Octavian/Augustus *pater atque princeps*, but because of its gloomy basic mood this ode probably dates to before the settlement of the year 27.

p. 283 *The census figures*: Aug. RG 8. For discussion of the total figure, which exceeds that given for the year 70/69 more than four times over, see Jochen Bleicken, 'Cicero und die Ritter', *Abhandlg. d. Göttinger Akad. d. Wiss.*, phil.-histor. Kl., III, 213, 1995, 95 note 174. Brunt, *Manpower*, 113ff., thinks that wives and adult children were also included in the census figure for the year 28 and consequently assumes a considerably lower number of citizens; for the opposite view see T. P. Wiseman, 'The Census in the First Century B.C.', in: *Journ. Rom. Stud.* 59, 1969, 59–75, esp. 72ff. The census figures for the year 8 BC were 4,233,000; the figures for the year AD 14 were 4,937,000 (Aug. RG 8).

pp. 283–4 *The restoration of the temples in the year 28*: Aug. RG 20; the banning of Egyptian cults: Cass. Dio 53,2,4. On Augustus' religious policy of restoration, see J. H. W. G. Liebeschuetz, *Continuity and Change in Roman Religion*, 1979, 55–100; Wolfgang Speyer, 'Das Verhältnis des Augustus zur Religion', in ANRW II 16,3, 1986, 1777–805, and Galinsky, *Augustan Culture*, 288ff.

pp. 284–5 *The change in the management of the state by the consuls*: Cass. Dio 53,1,1; on the prelude to it, which is not easily understood, see Bleicken, *Prinzipat*, 39ff. On Octavian's distancing himself from the time of the triumvirate: Cass. Dio 52,2,5, and Bleicken, op. cit., 83.

pp. 285–6 *The settlement of 13–16 January 27*: Vell. Pat. 2,893ff.; Cass. Dio 53,2,7–13,8; Strab. 17,3,25; Suet. Aug. 47, on his explanation see W. K. Lacey,

'Octavian in the Senate, January 27 BC', *Journ. Rom. Stud.* 64, 1974, 182ff. (a later version in: idem, *Augustus*, 77–99), and Bleicken, *Prinzipat*, 85ff. On the concept of the *res publica restituta* or *reddita*, see *Laudatio Turiae* II 25; Fasti Praenestini for 13 January; Ov. fast. 1,589; see also Aug. RG 34 and 1. In Vell. Pat. 2,89,3ff., Velleius hails the settlement of 13 January as a deed restoring the laws and the courts of law, the Senate and the magistrates, and returning them to their old form ('restituta vis ... ad pristinum redactum modum'), and his praise leads into the comment: 'prisca illa et antiqua rei publicae forma revocata' ('thus was the venerable form of state brought back into force').

pp. 286–8 *The partition of the provinces*: In the year 11 BC Octavian/Augustus acquired control of Illyricum from the Senate (Cass. Dio 54,34,4), so that after that year the Senate governed twelve provinces (with Galatia; the kingdom of the client King Amyntas was superseded by a new senatorial province combining its central Anatolian highlands with districts bordering them to the south), while Octavian had nine provinces. Numidia, set up as a province by Caesar, had probably been united with Africa earlier; see p. 648 above. Until the year 11, the Senate administered only the pacified southern part of Illyricum (Strab. 17,3,25); the northern part, which Octavian had conquered, is not likely to have had the status of a province at this time and will have been under his command as a purely military area. See on the partition of the provinces Fergus Millar, 'The Emperor, the Senate and the Provinces', *Journ. Rom. Stud.* 56, 1966, 156–66. The dating of the new provincial structure in Spain and Gaul has not been precisely established; Augustus may have introduced it only when he was in that area in the years 16–13. On the senatorial governors: two provinces, Asia and Africa, were reserved for consulars. For participation in the choice of governors by the lottery method, a term of five years after consuls and praetors had held office was usual before they took office as governors; we do not know the details of exactly how the lots were drawn; see Mommsen, *Staatsrecht*, II, 249ff., and for a suggestion based on the practice of the allocation of provinces see Werner Eck, 'Beförderungskriterien innerhalb der senatorischen Laufbahn', in ANRW II 1, 1974, 204ff. According to Strab. 17,3,25, Augustus had had the right to make war and peace since 27 BC; according to Kathleen M. T. Atkinson, 'Constitutional and Legal Aspects of the Trials of Marcus Primus and Varro Murena', *Historia* 9, 1960, 442.443ff., he acquired it only through the *lex Iulia maiestatis* of 8 BC.

pp. 288–90, 292–5 *The character of the structure of state in the settlement of January 27*: The literature on this subject is extensive. Earlier opinions have been described by Lothar Wickert in his long RE article 'Princeps' (RE XXII, 1954, 2068ff.), and he supplemented them in ANRW II 1, 1974, 25ff. and 71ff. I will mention here only two introductory sketches: Wolfgang Kunkel, 'Über das Wesen des augusteischen Prinzipats', *Gymnasium* 68, 1961, 353–70 (= W. Schmitthenner (ed.), *Augustus*, Wege d. Forschg. 128, 1969, 311–35), and Walter Eder, 'Augustus and the Power of Tradition: The Augustan

Principate as Binding Link between Republic and Empire', in Raaflaub/Toher, 71–122. Most of what has been written discusses the means of rule, looking at the instruments on which the rule of Augustus rested, whether formal (such as the form of the *imperium* used) or social (such as social dependencies, for instance clienteles, or concepts serving the purpose of such dependencies, for instance *auctoritas*). Oddly enough, now and then we come upon opinions in which the rule of Augustus is seen as a simple continuation of the organization of the state before the year 49 (and thus of the republican period) or at least that state is considered to be the model or example for the form of state that began in the year 27 (for this view see above all Helmut Castritius, *Der römische Prinzipat als Republik*, 1982; for the opposing view see among others Fergus Millar, 'Triumvirate and Principate', *Journ. Rom. Stud.* 63, 1973, 50–67, esp. 63ff.). If we see the republic as the pattern for the principate, the question arises of extending the formal changes, and indeed of entirely different forms on which the principate was built, so far that they can be forced into the republican context, as in principle is done by Walter Eder, op. cit. (for criticism of this view see Manfred G. Schmidt, in *Gnomon* 66, 1994, 241ff.). Others have gone to the opposite extreme, above all Syme, who understands the new structure of the state as 'a painless and superficial transformation' of Octavian's despotic rule, and credits the senators with knowledge of the true purpose of the use by Augustus of republican forms and phraseology, and with an undertstanding of 'the full irony in the ostensible contrast between Dictator and Princeps' (*Revolution*, 313, 340, 351), while Dieter Flach calls the efforts of Augustus to present the *res publica restituta* as a 'pseudo-republican game' (in *Historia* 22, 1973, 562ff.). Both interpretations miss the point of the political possibilities and prerequisites of the settlement of 27 January. The principate, which did not conform to any clear concepts of constitutional law and therefore is often susceptible to ambiguous interpretation, caused Syme, *Revolution*, 323, to despair of defining it: 'The Principate baffles definition,' he wrote, and 'the constitution is a façade', 340, but this denigration of the nature of the principate is a consequence of his preconceived concept of the socially revolutionary character of the radical changes.

pp. 290–92 *The honorific Augustus and the further honours*: Aug. RG 34; Fasti Praenestini of 16 January; *Feriale Cumanum*; Ov. fast. 1,587ff., 609ff.; Suet. Aug. 7,2; Cass. Dio 53,16,7ff.; on the part played by the *pontifices* in bestowing it: Lydus de mens. 4,III. Sulla had seen himself as the new founder of Rome. In Sall. Hist. I fr. 55,5 Maur. he is disparagingly referred to as 'scaevus iste Romulus'. On the connection of the title Augustus with Romulus as *primus augur* and with the first *augurium* as legitimation of the rule of Augustus, see Kenneth Scott, 'The Identification of Augustus with Romulus–Quirinus', *Transact. Americ. Philol. Assoc.* 56, 1925, 82–105, and Taylor, *Divinity*, 158ff. On the *corona civica*: Aug. RG 34; Fasti Praenestini of 13 January; see

Andreas Alföldi, *Der Vater des Vaterlandes im römischen Denken*, 1971, 40ff. On the crown of oak leaves and the laurels on the posts of his house: Aug. RG 34; Fasti Praenestini of 13 January; Cass. Dio 53,16,4; see Andreas Alföldi, 'Die zwei Lorbeerbäume des Augustus', *Antiquitas* 3, 1973 (with many illustrations from coins and reliefs). On the shield in his honour: Aug. RG 34; see Ramage, *Res Gestae* 73ff. A marble replica of the shield was found in Arles, ancient Arelate; it is now in the Musée de l'Arles Antique there. A priest of Augustus dedicated another depiction of the shield with its inscription in Potentia in the Picentine area (Dessau ILS no. 82). On the official representation of the rules made in January on coins, see Konrad Kraft, 'Zur Münzprägung des Augustus', *Sitz.ber. der Wiss. Ges. an der Johann Wolfgang Goethe-Universität, Frankfurt am Main*, vol. 7, 1968, no. 5 (= idem, *Ges. Aufsätze zur antiken Geldgeschichte und Numismatik*, I, 1978, 291–337), and Hans-Joachim Gehrke, 'Münzen im Rahmen kaiserlicher Selbstdarstellung. Die Konstituierung des Prinzipats durch Augustus', *Altspr. Unterricht* 22/4, 1979, 67–86.

pp. 295–8 *The general political and military situation in the years 27–25*: See in particular the informative essay by Walter Schmitthenner, 'Augustus' spanischer Feldzug und der Kampf um den Prinzipat', *Historia* 11, 1962, 29–85 (= idem (ed.), *Augustus*, Wege d. Forschung 128, 1969, 404–85); also see here 70ff., on the planned expedition to Britain. On north-west Spain in the Augustan period see also F. Diego Santos, 'Die Integration Nord- und Nordwestspaniens als römische Provinz in der Reichspolitik des Augustus. Von der konsularischen zur hispanischen Ära', in ANRW II, 3, 1975, 523–71. Augustus in danger of death from a bolt of lightning, and his new illness: Suet. Aug. 29,3 and 81,1. The planned expedition to Britain: Horace c. 1,35,29ff., 3.5.2ff. (26 BC); Cass. Dio 53,22,5, 25,2. The poet: Horace c. 3,14 (on the return of Augustus in the spring of 24). I cannot agree with the interpretation of this ode by Dietmar Kienast, 'Horaz und die erste Krise des Prinzipats (Die Ode "Herculis ritu")', *Chiron* 1, 1971, 239–51, who sees a Horace full of gloom and political resignation in this poem; the year of the battle of Philippi, mentioned in the closing lines, is intended to call the youth of Horace himself to mind, not the freedom of the republic. Augustus' request to Virgil, and his failure to comply with it: Verg. vit. Donat. 31ff., and Macrob. Sat. 1,24,10ff. The expedition of Aelius Gallus to Arabia Felix: Strab. 16,4,22–4 (Strabo was a friend of Gallus); Aug. RG 26; Horace c. 1,29; Cass. Dio 53,29,3–8; see Hermann von Wissmann, 'Die Geschichte des Sabäerreichs und der Feldzug des Aelius Gallus', in ANRW IX 1, 1976, 308–544, esp. 313ff. and 396ff., and Steven E. Sidebotham, 'Aelius Gallus and Arabia', *Latomus* 45, 1986, 590–602.

pp. 298–9 *The marriage of Marcellus, and the privileged status granted to him and Tiberius*: Suet. Aug. 63,1; Vell. Pat. 2,93,2; Cass. Dio 53,27,5, 28,3–4; Horace c. 1,12,45ff. (25 BC; the Marcellus concerned must be assumed to be Augustus' nephew because of the following line about 'the Julian star'). On Virgil's epilogue on Marcellus (Aen. 6.860–86), see, finally, Reinhold F. Glei,

'The Show Must Go On: The Death of Marcellus and the Future of the Augustan Principate', in H.-P. Stahl (ed.), *Vergil's Aeneid: Augustan Epic and Political Context*, 1998, 119–34.

pp. 299–300 *The building and appearance of the tomb of Augustus*: In the Augustan age this was already named after the tomb of the Carian prince Mausolus in Halicarnassus (modern Bodrum): Strab. 5,3,8; Suet. Aug. 100,4. On its modern reconstruction, the date of its completion and its interpretation, see Henner von Hesberg, 'Mausoleum Augusti (Monument und Grablegungen)', in Steinby, *Roma*, III, 234–9, and on the history of the monument up to the present day see Maria Aurora von Hase Salto, '"L'augusteo". Das Augustusmausoleum im Wandel der Geschichte', *Antike Welt* 28, 1997, 297–308. I consider it far-fetched to claim, as Konrad Kraft does in his 'Der Sinn des Mausoleums des Augustus', *Historia* 16, 1967, 189–206, that Octavian/Augustus built his mausoleum as a counterpart to the tomb of Antony in Alexandria; Antony had fallen victim to the *damnatio memoriae* and cannot therefore be regarded as a criterion for Augustus' actions.

p. 300 *Gallus*: On his over-ready tongue: Ovid trist. 2,445f.: 'non fuit opprobrio celebrasse Lycorida Gallo / sed linguam nimio non tenuisse mero' ('Gallus was not reproached with praising Lycoris, but with not holding his tongue when it was loosened by too much undiluted wine'). According to Serv. ad ecl. 10,1, Virgil designed the second half of the fourth book of his *Georgics* as a eulogy of Gallus but had to cut it again after his friend's catastrophic end; see Karl Büchner, in RE VIII A, 1958, 1311 and 1315ff. Today it is widely thought that this theory is improbable, and that Servius either misunderstood his sources or inflated praise of only a few lines into a full-scale eulogy; see a full discussion in J. Hermes, *C. Cornelius Gallus und Vergil*, 1980. On the origins of Gallus (*ex infima fortuna*) and the criticisms of him, as well as the grief of Augustus: Suet. Aug. 66,1ff.; Cass. Dio 53,23,5–7.

p. 301 *Messalla Corvinus as praefectus urbi*: Hieronymus chron. on the year 26 ('anti-constitutional': 'incivilis potesta'); Tacitus ann. 6,11,3 says that Messalla resigned from his office 'as if he did not know how to manage it'.

pp. 301–4 *The buildings*: The temple of Jupiter Tonans: Cass. Dio 54,4,2–4; Plin. nat. hist. 36,50, 34,78ff.: see P. Gros, in Steinby, *Roma*, III, 159ff.; on the *diribitorium*, Cass. Dio 55,8,3ff. On the amphitheatre of Statilius Taurus, see Richardson, *Rome*, 6, and on the Saepta Julia see Lily Ross Taylor, *Roman Voting Assemblies from the Hannibalic War to the Dictatorship of Caesar*, 1966, 44ff. The pantheon of Agrippa designed as a place for the worship of Augustus: Cass. Dio 53,27,2–4; the purpose of the pantheon built by Agrippa: Cass. Dio 53,27,1–4. On Agrippa's building work in general, see Frederick W. Shipley, *Agrippa's Building Activities in Rome*, 1933 (on the Saepta and the *diribitorium* 37ff., on the Pantheon 55ff.). On the building of the Pantheon, see also W. L. MacDonald, *The Pantheon: Design, Meaning and Progeny*, 1976. Edoardo Tortorici, 'L'attività edilizia di Agrippa a Roma', in *Il bimillenario di Agrippa* (Dipartimento di Archeologia, Genoa), 1990, 28ff., has tried to prove, through examination of the older excavations, that Agrippa himself intended it to be a round building. On the *miliarum aureum*, see Nash, *Rome*, II, 64ff. On the road-building: Aug. RG 20; Dessau ILS no. 84 (the Via Flaminia; the arch).

pp. 304–5 *The trial of Primus and the 'conspiracy' of Varro Murena*: Cass. Dio 54,3,2ff. gives the date of the trial of Primus as the year 22, but this dating is disputed by the majority of scholars; see Friedrich Münzer, in RE V A, 1934, 709. Richard A. Bauman, *The Crimen Maiestatis in the Roman Republic and Augustan Principate*, 1967, 183ff., supports the date as recorded by Dio, and so does Kathleen M. T. Atkinson, 'Constitutional and Legal Aspects of the Trials of Marcus Primus and Varro Murena', *Historia* 9, 1960, 440–73 (according to her the conspirator was not the consul of the year 23 but his cousin, and Terentia, the wife of Maecenas, was this man's sister). Lawrence J. Daly, 'Augustus and the Murder of Varro Murena (*cos.* 23 B.C.): His implication and Its Implications', *Klio* 66, 1984, 157–69, thinks that Augustus was involved in the elimination of Murena because of his open opposition to him.

pp. 305–6 *Agrippa's displeasure on finding Marcellus preferred to him*: Vell. Pat. 2,93,2; Suet. Aug. 66,3; Cass. Dio 53,31,1–32,1 (also see 31,1 for the intention of the reading of the will). Syme, *Revolution*, 340ff. and 368, has seen in the tension of this time a split within the Caesarian party, in which Augustus, caught between Maecenas as defender of the monarchical viewpoint and Agrippa opposing the adoption of Marcellus, came down on the side of the latter despite being personally inclined to entertain monarchical ideas. We do not know just where Maecenas stood on this point, but the political confessions of faith of Maecenas and Agrippa that Dio ascribes to them, in a verbal duel in front of Augustus in the year 28/27 BC, certainly influenced this theory of Syme's; in it Maecenas stood for the monarchy and Agrippa for 'democracy'; Syme, *Revolution*, 343: 'The fiction [of the verbal duel] is transparent – but not altogether absurd.'

p. 306 *The sickness of Augustus and his cure by Antonius Musa*: Suet. Aug. 28,1, 59,1 81,1; Cass. Dio 53,30,1–3.

pp. 306–7 *The death and funeral of Marcellus*: Cass. Dio 53,30,4–6; Prop. 3,18. The lines on Marcellus: Virg. Aen. 6,855–86; on the loyalty and modesty of Agrippa, see Cass. Dio 53,23,4, 27,4, 31,5. The nature of the command given to Agrippa in the year 23 and renewed in the year 18 is disputed. The main point at issue is whether it is to be regarded as a co-regency or as an independent *imperium* derived from that of Augustus. This discussion received new nourishment from a papyrus fragment published in 1970 and from the eulogy given at Agrippa's funeral by Augustus. The command must have been an independent one, but not equal with Augustus' own command. However, debate on the subject cannot yet be considered closed; see the latest (at the time of writing) contribution to it, by Walter Ameling, 'Augustus und Agrippa. Bemerkungen zu PKöln VI 249', *Chiron* 24, 1994, 1–28. On Piso: Tac. ann. 2,43,2.

pp. 308–9 *The suggestion of appointing three consuls*: Suet. Aug. 37,1; resignation of Augustus from the consulate: Cass. Dio 53,32,3.

pp. 308–12 *The new administrative dispositions of the year 23*: The main source is Cass. Dio 53,32,3–6. On the interpretation of the process, see the literature below for pp. 320–21. On the assumption of tribunician power by the dictator Caesar, see Jehne, *Caesar*, 96ff.

p. 312 *The riots and offers made to Augustus in the year 22*: Aug. RG 5; Suet. Aug. 52; Cass. Dio 54,1–2.

pp. 313–14 *The marriage of Agrippa*: Agrippa's second wife, Marcella, was very probably the elder daughter of Octavia by her first marriage, to Gaius Claudius Marcellus (Cass. Dio 54,6,5). If so, then behind his marriage to Julia lies the wish of Augustus for a descendant in the *direct* line, instead of only through Octavia, and it was thus a particularly flagrant display of his dynastic intentions.

pp. 314–18 *Augustus and the Parthian question*: Augustus on the return of the prisoners and standards: Aug. RG 29: 'Parthos trium exercitum Romanorum spolia et signa [sc. the standards taken at Carrhae in the year 53 and from an officer of Antony's in the year 40, and those lost by Antony himself in the year 36] reddere mihi supplicesque amicitiam populi Romani petere coegi'; 32: 'ad me rex Parthorum Phrates, Orodis filius, filios suos nepotesque omnes misit in Italiam non bello superatus, sed amicitiam nostram per liberorum suorum pignora petens.' In the same vein, Strab. 6,4,2. Augustus refrains from making Armenia a province: Aug. RG 27: 'Armeniam maiorem interfecto rege eius Artaxe cum possem facere provinciam, malui maiorum nostrorum exemplo regnum id Tigrani, regis Artavasdis filio, nepoti autem Tigranis regis, per Ti. Neronem tradere'; see Cass. Dio 54,8,1–3, 9,4ff. On the Parthian policy pursued by Augustus after his victory over Antony, see Dieter Timpe, 'Zur augusteischen Partherpolitik zwischen 30 und 20 v. Chr.', *Würzb. Jahrb. für d. Altertumswiss.*, n.s. 1, 1975 (Festschrift for Ernst Siegmann), 155–69 (holding that in 30 BC Octavian was not already following his later policies as Augustus), Michael Wissemann, *Die Parther in der augusteischen Dichtung*, 1982, and Holger Sonnabend, *Fremdenbild und Politik: Vorstellungen der Römer von Ägypten und dem Partherreich in der späten Republik und frühen Kaiserzeit*, 1986, 157ff., esp. 197ff. On the minting of coins on the occasion of the settlement with the Parthians: Simon, *Selbstdarstellung*, 123ff. On the Parthian arch, see Coarelli, *Foro Romano*, 285ff., and Elisabeth Nedergaard, 'La collocazione originaria dei *Fasti Capitolini* e gli archi di Augusto nel Foro Romano', *Bullettino della Commissione Archeologica Comunale di Roma* 96, 1994/95, 33–70 (the Parthian arch was to the south of the temple of Caesar, the Actian arch in another part of the Forum). On the pictorial presentation of the Parthian victory, especially the Prima Porta statue of

Augustus, see, out of the extensive literature, Zanker, *Augustus*, 188ff., and Erika Simon, 'Altes und Neues zur Statue des Augustus von Primaporta', in Binder, *Saeculum Augustum*, III, 204–33 (with further literature), as well as Walter Hatto Gross, 'Zur Augustusstatue von Prima Porta', *Nachr. d. Göttinger Akad. d. Wiss.*, phil.-histor. Kl., Jahrb. 1959, no. 8. Gross sees the statue as depicting Augustus deified and thus places it in the early Tiberian period. On the buildings in the east, particularly Athens, pictorially celebrating the handing over of the standards, see Thomas Schäfer, *Spolia et signa. Parthererfolg und augusteische Baupolitik in Ost und West* (in press at the time of writing). Horace on the Parthian settlement and its like with peace: c. 4,15,6ff. and epist. 1,12,27–9; Propertius on the same subject: 3,4 (introductory poem for those going to war). Augustus and the client princes in the east: Cass. Dio 54,9,2ff.

p. 319 *The return of Augustus in the year 19 and the riots in Rome*: See Cass. Dio 54,10,1–4; on the offices then transferred to him idem, 54,10,5–7; and see also Bleicken, *Prinzipat*, 100ff. Altar to Fortuna Redux: Cass. Dio 54,10,3. The day and month of its dedication, 15 December (19 BC), is known to us from a large fragment of the late Augustan calendar of feasts from Cumae (*Feriale Cumanum*) that has been preserved and also contains other important dates in Augustan history. See for a coin of this time, showing the altar of Fortuna Redux on the reverse: BMCRE 4: FOR(tuna) RE(dux); CAESARI AUGUSTO EX S.C.

pp. 320–21 *The alteration and extension of the fundamental legal powers of Augustus in the years 23 and 19*: The basis of any discussion of this subject is De Martino, *Costituzione Romana*, 1, 168–211. I will also mention Ernst Meyer, *Römischer Staat und Staatsgedanke*, 1948, 1975[4], 357–62; Jean Béranger, *Recherches sur l'aspect idéologique du principat*, 1953, 106ff.; Wolfgang Kunkel, 'Über das Wesen des augusteischen Prinzipats', *Gymnasium* 68, 1961, 353ff. (= W. Schmitthenner (ed.), *Augustus*, Wege d. Forschg., 128, 1969, 321ff.); Kienast, *Augustus*, 86–92; and Bleicken, *Prinzipat*, 93–105. Data from other sources that disagree with these, some of them hard to understand and contradictory in themselves, above all Cassius Dio (54,10,5) on the conferring of the permanent consulate on Augustus, have brought modern scholars to come to conclusions that are also difficult to comprehend. Dio's note has led quite a number to assume that, if the consulate itself was not conferred on him for life, then at least the consular *imperium* is to be seen in that light (these scholars include Meyer, op. cit., 359ff., and Kienast, op. cit., 95). But Mommsen, *Staatsrecht*, II, 872 note 2 (on permission to make use of the consular insignia) had already established the facts of the matter. Once the privilege of not being obliged to resign the proconsular *imperium* on crossing the *pomerium* had been granted, an *imperium consulare* was superfluous, for the *imperium proconsulare* actually *is* a consular *imperium*, known as an *imperium pro consule* only because it was exercised in the provinces.

pp. 321–2 *The second 'cleansing' of the Senate*: Cass. Dio 54,13–14.

p. 322 *Praise of the good fortune of the time*: This tribute is from a eulogy of the man's dead wife: *Laudatio Turiae* II 25: 'pacato orbe terrarum, restituta republica quieta deinde nobis et felicia tempora contigerunt' (in Dieter Flach, *Die sogenannte Laudatio Turiae. Einleitung, Text, Übersetzung und Kommentar*, 1991).

pp. 322–5 *The secular festival*: See Latte, *Religionsgeschichte*, 298ff.; Jean Gagé, *Recherches sur les jeux séculaires*, 1934; Helmut Rahn, 'Zum carmen saeculare des Horaz', *Gymnasium* 77, 1970, 467–9; Hans Kloft, 'Die Säcularspiele des Augustus und die Tradition der Herrscherfeste in der Antike. Soziale und kommunikative Aspekte', in G. Binder/K.Ehrlich (eds.), *Kommunikation in politischen und kultischen Gemeinschaften*, 1996, 51–74; Hubert Cancik, 'Carmen und sacrificium. Das Saecularlied des Horaz in den Saecularakten des Jahres 17 v. Chr.', in R. Faber/B. Seidensticker (eds.), *Worte, Bilder, Töne. Studien zur Antike und Antikerezeption*, 1996, 99–113; Duncan Barker, ' "The Golden Age is Proclaimed"? The *Carmen Saeculare* and the Renascence of the Golden Race', *Class. Quart.* 46, 1996, 434–46; and (on the Etruscan origin of the festival) John F. Hall, 'The *Saeculum Novum* of Augustus and Its Etruscan Antecedents', in ANRW II 16,3, 1986, 2564–89. On the minting of coins celebrating the games, see Simon, *Selbstdarstellung*, 84ff. The records of the games of the year 17 are known to us not only from the account of the early Byzantine writer Zosimus (2,5–7; 2,6 on the Sibylline oracle), but also from extensive fragments of an inscription found on the Field of Mars, and originally part of a marble pillar (Dessau ILS no. 5050). The place where these fragments were found lies on what is thought to be the cult site of Tarentum. Virgil: Aen. 6,792ff. (the Garamantes were Berbers living in the south of Libya); Aen. 1,286–95 – these lines are spoken by Jupiter, revealing to Venus the destiny whereby a new, peaceful age will be ushered in during the time of Caesar (= Octavian/Augustus, not the dictator, as has sometimes been assumed; see the commentary of R. G. Austin on this passage). The emphasis here is on peace as well as the idea of Roman rule, and these lines may have been written even before the settlement of the year 27.

## CHAPTER 8

## Explanatory Notes

p. 326 *The quotations from Velleius and Tacitus*: Vell. Pat. 2,89,2: 'nihil deinde optare a dis homines, nihil dii hominibus praestare possunt . . . [3] restituta vis legibus, iudiciis auctoritas, senatui maiestas, imperium magistratuum ad pristinum redactum modum . . . [4] prisca illa et antiqua rei publicae forma revocata rediit cultus agris, sacris honos, securitas hominibus, certa cuique rerum suarum possessio.' Tac. ann. 1,3,7: 'iuniores post Actiacam victoriam,

etiam senes plerique inter bella civium nati: quotus quisque reliquus, qui rem
publicam vidisset?'

pp. 330–32 *Augustus on his own legal power*: Aug. RG 34: 'post id tempus [27
BC] auctoritate omnibus praestiti, potestatis autem nihilo amplius habui
quam ceteri, qui midi quoque in magistratu conlegae fuerunt' ('after this time
I was above all others in authority, but I had no more official power than the
others who were my colleagues in their magistratures'). Augustus rejects the
appellation 'lord' (*dominus*): Cass. Dio 55,12,2. A good example of the practice of the administration of the senatorial provinces in the Augustan period
is given in the prescriptions of Augustus for the senatorial province of Cyrene
from the years 7 to 4, which have been preserved in writing, and set out regulations for the provincial courts in four edicts and a senatorial decision. The
Cyreneans, obviously bypassing the governor of the province, had turned to
Augustus instead of to the Senate. Thereupon Augustus took the initiative and
made decisions for the senatorial province, but without losing sight of the
Senate, which, as he told the Cyreneans, was responsible for the matter
(1,12ff.) and whose decision he claimed to be conveying to them. The senatorial decision itself was made not on the initiative of the consuls, but on
application from the *princeps* in consultation with a *consilium* (5,86ff.); see
Johannes Stroux/ Leopold Wenger, 'Die Augustus-Inschrift auf dem Markt-
platz von Kyrene', *Abhandlg. d. Bayer. Akad. d. Wiss.*, philos.-histor. Kl., vol.
34, 2nd treatise, 1928, esp. 61ff.

p. 332 *The references to Tacitus, Suetonius and Ovid*: Tac. ann. 1,2,1. Suet. Aug.
28.2: 'ita mihi salvam ac sospitem rem p. sistere in sua sede liceat atque eius
rei fructum percipere, quem peto, ut optimi status auctor dicar' ('may it be
granted to me to maintain the state secure and intact, and in return I would
wish as my reward to be called the originator of the best constitution'). Ovid
trist. 4,4,15 ('res est publica Caesar').

pp. 332–3 *The elevation of the person of Augustus*: On the official calendar of
feasts in the Augustan period, see Taylor, *Divinity*, 142ff.; Peter Herz, 'Kai-
serfeste der Prinzipatszeit. III 1 Augustus und seine Zeit', in ANRW II 16,2,
1978, 1147ff.; and on the political significance of dates for Augustus: Jörg
Rüpke, *Kalender und Öffentlichkeit. Die Geschichte der Repräsentation und
religiösen Qualifikation von Zeit in Rom*, 1995, 396ff. Entry into Rome with
solemn singing etc.: Suet. Aug. 57,2. On the renaming of Sextilis after Augustus: the decision of the Senate and the people: Macrob. Sat. 1,12,35; cf. Suet.
Aug. 31,2. The official Roman year still began with 1 March in the first half
of the second century BC, so that the later months Julius and Augustus were
the fifth and sixth months respectively, previously known as Quintilis (from
*quinque*, 'five') and Sextilis (from *sex*, 'six'). Naturally only those months
whose names had no religious connotations, but were purely numerical, could
be considered for alteration. The month Quintilis, which became Julius, was
the first month in the calendar to be named after a number, but it was also the

month in which the dictator was born (13.7). The fact that the real reason for the choice of Sextilis lay not in the events cited in the senatorial decision, but in its being the next numerical month after July and thus the sixth (by the old reckoning of the beginning of the year) or the eighth (after the introduction of 1 January as the beginning of the year), is proved by the planned later changes: the intention was to rename Septembris and Octobris for Tiberius and Livia (Suet. Ti. 26,2). Although Cassius Dio 55,6,7 says that the people first wanted September, the month in which Augustus was born, to take his name, that cannot be true; Augustus would hardly have refused to go ahead with the idea, particularly as wishes of that kind were usually his own doing; the passage may be a late attempt at explaining the choice of the month Sextilis for the honour, which at first sight is not easy to understand.

pp. 334–5 *The Genius Augusti*: See Latte, *Religionsgeschichte*, 103ff., and Heidi Hänlein-Schäfer, 'Die Ikonographie des *Genius Augusti* im Kompital- und Hauskult der frühen Kaiserzeit', in Alastair Small (ed.), *Subject and Ruler: The Cult of the Ruling Power in Classical Antiquity*, 1996, 73–98. The word *genius* derives from *gigno* (arch. *geno*), 'to engender'. The female power was Juno. On libations poured for the Genius Augusti: Cass. Dio 51,19,7. On the organization of the compital associations see Kienast, *Augustus*, 164ff., and Jochen Bleicken, in RE VIII A, 1958, 2480–83. On the *ara numinis Augusti* in Rome, see the Fasti Praenestini for 17 January, and on that subject Walter Pötscher, '*Numen* und *numen Augusti*', in ANRW II 16,1, 1978, 355–92, esp. 387ff.

pp. 335–8 *The worship of Augustus in the provinces*: The petitions by cities of Asia Minor to practise the cult of Augustus: Cass. Dio 51,20,6–8; cf. Suet. Aug. 52: 'templa … in nulla tamen provincia nisi communi suo Romaeque nomine recepit' ('He allowed temples to himself to be erected in the provinces only if he was venerated in them jointly with the goddess Roma'). On the provincial cult of rulers in the time of Augustus see Taylor, *Divinity*, 181ff.; Jürgen Deininger, *Die Provinziallandtage der römischen Kaiserzeit*, 1965, 16ff., 66ff., 84ff.; and G. W. Bowersock, *Augustus and the Greek World*, 1965, 112ff. On the Augustales: Marquardt, *Verwaltung*, I, 197ff.; Mommsen, *Staatsrecht*, III, 452ff.; and Robert Duthoy, 'Les Augustales', in ANRW II 16,2, 1978, 1254–309 (with an extensive bibliography). On the establishment of a new calendar in Asia: *Oriens Graecus* no. 458 = Robert K. Sherk, *Roman Documents from the Greek East*, 1969, no. 65; see also Deininger, op. cit., 54. On the cult of Augustus in individual cities, see for Olympia Hans-Volkmar Herrmann, *Olympia*, 1972, 182, and for Miletus and the province of Asia Peter Herrmann, 'Milet unter Augustus. C. Iulius Epikrates und die Anfänge des Kaiserkults', *Istanb. Mitt.* 44, 1994, 203–36. On the oath of loyalty taken by the Paphlagonians, see Peter Herrmann, *Der römische Kaisereid*, 1968, 96ff., and on the general development of the cult of rulers in the time of Augustus see Christian Habicht, 'Die augusteische Zeit und das erste Jahrhundert nach Christi Geburt', in *Le Culte des souverains dans l'Empire Romain*, Entretiens sur l'antiquité classique 19, 1973, 39–88; Robert Étienne, *Le Culte impérial dans la péninsule ibérique d'Auguste à Dioclétien*, 1958, 353ff.; and Kienast, *Augustus*, 202ff.

pp. 339–42 *Augustus and the colleges of priests*: On the right of Augustus to multiply the number of priests: Cass. Dio 51,20,3. On the position of Augustus within the priesthoods: Cass. Dio 53,17,8. On the colleges of priests see Marquardt, *Verwaltung*, 235–481; G. J. Szemler, *The Priests of the Roman Republic: A Study of Interactions between Priesthoods and Magistracies*, 1972; Jean Gagé, 'Die Priesterämter des Augustus', in Binder, *Saeculum Augustum*, II, 52–87 (German trans. of the original French contribution of 1931); and Wolfgang Speyer, 'Das Verhältnis des Augustus zur Religion', in ANRW II, 16,3, 1986, 1777–805. Gagé ascribes disproportionate importance to Augustus' role as an augur, claiming that it is identical in content with the name of Augustus (cf. the abbreviation of both to AUG) and served to symbolize Augustus as the new Romulus and inaugurator of the new Rome. The depiction of Augustus with the curved staff (*lituus*) on the Gemma Augustea does indeed show him as a priest and perhaps as the successor or Romulus in that office, but not as the inaugurator of a new age, and similarly the gem itself gives no indication of being capable of Gagé's interpretation.


CHAPTER 9

Explanatory Notes


pp. 344–9 *The imperial administration*: A great deal of new literature has recently been written on that subject, but much more is known about conditions in the mid- and late principate than in its early phase under Augustus, because later on there was an increasing amount of written material. We have to assume that the late republican beginnings of the administration were initially further developed only hesitantly, and only very gradually were new forms also created. Of literature providing more information, I will mention Hirschfeld, *Verwaltungsbeamte*, 1ff., 410ff. and *passim*; Szramkiewicz, *Gouveneurs*; H.-G. Pflaum, 'Les Procurateurs équestres sous le Haut-Empire romain', 1950; idem, 'Procurateur', in RE XXIII, 1957, 1240ff. (for a summary); Werner Eck, 'Augustus' administrative Reformen: Pragmatismus oder systematischen Planen?', *Acta Classica* 29, 1986, 105–20 (among other points, emphasizing the gradual rate of change in the forms of administration, occurring only when it became necessary); idem, 'Die Ausformung der ritterlichen Administration als Antisenatspolitik?', in A. Giovannini/D. v. Berchem (eds.), *Opposition et résistances à l'Empire d'Auguste à Trajan*, Entretiens 33, 1987, 249–89; idem, 'Die staatliche Administration des Römischen Reiches in der hohen Kaiserzeit – ihre strukturellen Komponenten', in R. Klein (ed.), *100 Jahre Neues Gymnasium Nürnberg*, 1989, 204–24 (the last three essays, by

Eck, also in idem, *Verwaltung*, 83–102, 29–54 and 1–28), and idem, 'La riforma dei gruppi dirigenti. L'ordine senatorio e l'ordine equestre', in A. Momigliano/A. Schiavone, *Storia di Roma*, II, 2, 1991, 73–118.

p. 349 *The conduct of Augustus as princeps*: Cass. Dio 54,25,3–4, 27,2 and 56,41,5; Suet. Aug. 53,3 (his behaviour in the Senate).

pp. 350–51 *The Senate*: Reform of the year 9 BC: Cass. Dio 55,3–4,1; Suet. Aug. 35,3. Laxity of the senators: Suet. Aug. 54; the passage referred to: 'licere oportere senatoribus de re p(ublica) loqui'.

pp. 351–2 *The senatorial committee*: Cass. Dio 53,21,4–6 and 56,28,2ff.; as well as Suet. Aug. 35,3. See John Crook, *Consilium principis*, 1955, 8ff., and Bleicken, *Senatsgericht*, 81ff.

p. 353 *Augustus' way of picking senators to answer at random*: Suet. Aug. 35,4. On the defence of a friend by Augustus: Cass. Dio 55,4,3. Augustus the last to give his opinion in the Senate: Cass. Dio 55,34,1.

p. 355 *On the lack of candidates for the less important offices*: Cass. Dio 54,26,3–9, 30,2 (on the years 13 and 12 BC); 55,24,9 (on the year AD 5). On the senatorial quorum and fines for non-attendance at meetings: Cass. Dio 54,18,3, 35,1 (on the years 178 and 11 BC). On the revised conduct of Senate business, see above, pp. 350ff; see also Talbert, *Senate*, 136ff.

pp. 356–7 *Appointments to high office for the provinces and the army*: See Szramkiewicz, *Gouveneurs*, II, 196ff., who, citing Syme, *Revolution*, *passim*, comes to useful conclusions, despite a number of gaps in his account. On the ratio of senatorial to equestrian offices in the early imperial period see Eck, 'Augustus' administrative Reformen' (as note above).

pp. 359–63 *The aerarium militare, the management of the private fortune of the princeps and the aerarium Saturni and fiscus Caesaris*: On the *aerarium militare*: Aug. RG 17; Suet. Aug. 49,2; Cass. Dio 55,25. On sums paid into the treasury by Augustus: Aug. RG 17, see also appendix 1; on the levying of an inheritance tax, see Lutz Neesen, *Untersuchungen zu den direkten Staatsabgaben der römischen Kaiserzeit (27 v. Chr.–284 n. Chr.)*, 1980, 136ff. On the *aerarium militare* and *aerarium Saturni* see Mireille Corbier, *L'Aerarium Saturni et l'aerarium militare: Administration et prosopographie sénatoriale*, 1974, and on the *aerarium Saturni* and *fiscus* see A. H. M. Jones, 'The Aerarium and the Fiscus', in idem, *Studies in Roman Government and Law*, 1960, 99–114 (= *Journ. Rom. Stud.* 40, 1950, 22ff.), and on the financial system in the early imperial period, especially on the *fiscus Caesaris*, see finally Michael Alpers, *Das nachrepublikanische Finanzsystem: Fiscus und Fisci in der frühen Kaiserzeit*, 1995 (also the review of this work by Matthäus Heil, *Histor. Zeitschr*, 263, 1996, 449ff.). On the landed property owned by Augustus, see Israel Shatzman, *Senatorial Wealth and Roman Politics*, 1975, 363ff.; on the mines, see Hirschfeld, *Verwaltungsbeamte*, 145ff. On the corrupt procurator Licinus: Cass. Dio 54,21,2–8; see Arthur Stein, in RE XIII, 1926, 501ff. Sardinia taken over by Augustus for several years: Cass. Dio 55,28,1. His notes on the financial situation in the year 23: Suet. Aug. 28,1; the writings left on his death in AD 14: Suet. Aug. 101,4.

pp. 365–7 *The princeps and the provinces*: Cicero on the administration of the provinces: off. 2,27: 'itaque illud patrocinium orbis terrae verius quam imperium poterat nominari' ('therefore it could be called protective rule over the world rather than forcible command of it'). The ban on senators travelling to the provinces (other than Sicily): Cass. Dio 52,42,6 (contrary to what Cassius Dio says here, they could not travel in Gallia Narbonensis without special permission until the time of Claudius). Cicero on tribute as the price of peace: Cic. ad Quint. fr. 1,1,33ff. (to his brother Quintus, governor of Asia, *c.* the end of 60 BC). The principle of giving a hearing to allies: Tac. ann. 4,15,2: 'audirent socios'.

pp. 367–8 *The provincial census*: See Marquardt, *Verwaltung*, II, 211ff., and Georg Ürögdi, in RE Suppl. XI, 1968, 1184–208, esp. 1201ff. The provincial census is to be clearly separated from the census of the empire. The latter was a headcount of all Roman citizens periodically undertaken – three times by Augustus, in 28 and 8 BC and in AD 14. The census of the empire in general mentioned in the gospel of St Luke (2,1–3) as being undertaken by the governor of Syria, Publius Sulpicius Quirinius, affected the provinces, and cannot therefore have been an imperial census, quite apart from the chronological problems (it can be shown that Quirinius held a provincial census in AD 6/7, whether as governor or not is uncertain; on that and his apparent double term as governor of Syria, see Edmund Groag, in RE IV A, 1931, 829ff.). The census described by Luke was a provincial census. On the attempt to find a solution or explanation to this problem, see Horst Braunert, 'Der römische Provinzialzensus und der Schätzungsbericht des Lukas-Evangeliums', *Historia* 6, 1957, 192–214, and on the tax declaration of a Jewish woman recently found in a papyrus and dating from the year 127, which may lead to new conclusions not only on the provincial census but also on the history of the birth of Jesus, see Klaus Rosen, 'Jesu Geburtsdatum, der Census des Quirinius und eine jüdische Steuererklärung aus dem Jahr 127 nC.', *Jahrb. f. Antike u. Christentum* 38, 1995, 5–15. On the beginning of the appeal system under Augustus, see M. Kaser/K. Hackl, *Das römische Zivilprozessrecht*, 1996[2], 501ff. On the delegation of appeals by Augustus: Suet. Aug. 33,3 and on this passage Bleicken, op. cit., with the criticism of Wolfgang Kunkel, *Zeitschr. Sav. Stiftg. Rom. Abt.* 81, 1964, 374ff. (= idem, *Kleine Schr.*, 338ff.).

pp. 369–70 *Relations between Augustus and the Greek cities*: See esp. Christian Böhme, *Princeps und Polis: Untersuchungen zur Herrschaftsform des Augustus über bedeutende Orte in Griechenland*, 1995. On the building policy of Augustus in the provinces, see Kienast, *Augustus*, 343ff. The decree of Halicarnassus: *The Collection of Anc. Greek Inscr. in the British Museum*, IV,1, 1893, no. 894 Z 2ff.

pp. 370–74 *The house of Augustus on the Palatine*: See Coarelli, *Rom*, 142ff., idem in Steinby, *Roma*, II, 40–45; Gianfilippo Carettoni, *Das Haus des Augustus auf dem Palatin*, 1983 (almost exclusively on its decoration; see on this subject W. Ehrhardt, *Gnomon* 60, 1988, 640ff.); Patterson, 'Rome', 204ff.; Mireille Corbier, 'De la maison d'Hortensius à la *curia* sur le Palatin', *Mélanges de l'École franç. de Rome* 104, 1992, 871–916 (emphasizing the evidence for identifying the 'Latin' library of the precincts of the temple of Apollo with the Senate house); and Timothy Peter Wiseman, '*Conspicui Postes Tectaque Digna Deo*: The Public Image of Aristocratic and Imperial Houses in the Late Republic and Early Empire', in Ch. Pietri (ed.), *L'Urbs: Espace urbain et histoire*, 1987, 393–413. On the hut of Romulus, see André Balland, 'La Casa Romuli au Palatin et au Capitole', *Rev. Étud. Lat.* 62, 1984, 57–80. On the Hellenistic royal palaces see W. Hoepfner/G. Brands (eds.), *Basileia: Die Paläste der hellenistischen Könige*, 1996, and in this volume Wolfram Hoepfner, 'Zum Typus der Basileia und der königlichen Andrones', 1–13. On the late republican houses of the nobility see also Rolf Rilinger, '*Domus* und *res publica*: Die politisch-soziale Bedeutung des aristokratischen "Hauses" in der späten römischen Republik', in A. Winterling (ed.), *Zwischen 'Haus' und 'Staat': Antike Höfe im Vergleich*, 1997, 73–90, and in the same collected volume, on the court at the time of the principate, see Aloys Winterling, 'Hof ohne "Staat": Die *aula Caesaris* im 1. und 2. Jahrhundert n. Chr.', 91–112. Sources for the house: Suet. Aug. 72–3; Ovid metamorph. 1,168–76 (the heavenly house of Jupiter is described with references to the house of Augustus: *Palatia caeli*; on the significance of *palatia* as a royal residence see Konrat Ziegler, in RE XVIII 3, 1949, 10ff.). Virg. Aen. 7,153, 170f., undoubtedly alluding to the house of Augustus on the Palatine, described the house of King Latinus: 'augusta moenia regis' or 'tectum augustum, ingens, centum sublime columnis / urbe fuit summa, Laurentis regia Pici' (this is the only passage in the *Aeneid* where Virgil uses the adjective *augustus*). The making of part of his house into state premises for the purpose of an office for the *pontifex maximus*: Cass. Dio 54,27,3. Marcus Verrius Flaccus, the author of a lexicon of difficult terms known to us in part in later revision, as the tutor of the grandsons of Augustus: Suet. gramm. 17; the children of other men brought up in the house of Augustus: Suet. Aug. 48.

pp. 375–7 *The friends of Augustus*: Agrippa: Rudolf Hanslik, 'M. Vipsanius Agrippa', in RE IX A, 1961, 1226–75, and Jean-Michel Roddaz, *Marcus Agrippa*, 1984. Maecenas: Alfred Kappelmacher, in RE XIV, 1928, 207–29; his influence on Virgil's *Georgics*: Virg. Georg. 3,41ff.: 'tua, Maecenas, haud mollia iussa / te sine nil altum mens incohat' ('It was your stern orders, Maecenas. Without you, the mind will tackle no high subject'). Sallustius Crispus: Tac. ann. 1,6,3 and 3,30,2ff. as well as Horace, c. 2,2 (Horace criticizes Sallust's love of riches and luxury). On Maecenas and his casual manner, see esp. Vell. Pat. 2,88,2: 'C. Maecenas equestri, sed splendido genere natur, vir, ubi res vigiliam exigeret, sane exsomnis, providens atque agendi sciens, simul vero aliquid ex negotio remitti posset, otio ac mollitiis paene ultra feminam fluens' ('Maecenas, a man of the equestrian class but of brilliant descent who, when some task required tireless activity, could be watchful, far-sighted and capable in carrying it out, yet also, when he could free himself of political business, gave himself up to leisure and casual indolence to an extent outdoing even that of women'). Vedius Pollio: Cass. Dio 54,23,1–6; Plin. nat. hist. 9,77. Ovid on the house of Vedius: fast. 6,641–4. On Pollio see Ronald Syme, 'Who was Vedius Pollio?', *Journ. Rom. Stud.* 51, 1961, 23–30 (= Syme, *Papers*, II, 518–29). Proculeius: his refusing to kill Octavian, Plin. nat. hist. 7,148; the plan of a marriage to Julia: Tac. ann. 4,40,6. The circle of advisers for settling the succession of Herod: Flav. Jos. antiqu. 17,229; idem, bell. Iud. 2,25. The faithless Thallos: Suet. Aug. 67,2; see also the whole of chapter 67 on the freedmen and slaves of Augustus, as well as Suet. Aug. 101,1 on the two freedmen Polybius and Hilarion, who wrote down a part of his will. Horace requested as a secretary: Suet. vit. Hor.: 'ante ipse sufficiebam scribendis epistolis amicorum, nunc occupatissimus et infirmus Horatium nostrum a te cupio abducere, veniet ergo ab ista parasitica mensa ad hanc regiam, et nos in epistolis scribendis iuvabit' ('Once I was able to write my own letters to my friends; now that I am very busy, and have become weak, I would like to steal our friend Horace from you. So let him leave the table of your parasites, come to the grand table here and help me to write my letters').

p. 378 *The seals*: Suet. Aug. 50; Plin. nat. hist. 37,10; Cass. Dio 51,3,5–7; see Hans Ulrich Instinsky, *Die Siegel des Kaisers Augustus*, 1962.

pp. 379–82 *The reorganization of offices in the city of Rome under Augustus*: See Mommsen, *Staatsrecht*, II 2, 1032–73. On the individual offices: Eck, *Italien*, 25ff. (*cura viarum*). On the water supply, Gunther Garbrecht, 'Wasserversorgung in römischer Zeit', in Frontinus-Gesellschaft (ed.), *Wasserversorgung im antiken Rom. Sextus Julius Frontinus, Curator Aquarum*, 1982, 9–43 (32ff. on the water supply of Rome, the city's water requirements and water distribution), and Werner Eck, 'Organisation und Administration der Wasserversorgung Roms', in Frontinus-Gesellschaft (ed.), ibid., 63–77 (= idem, *Verwaltung*, 161–78). On the public building works in Rome: Anne Kolb, *Die kaiserliche Bauverwaltung in der Stadt Rom: Geschichte und Aufbau der* cura operum publicorum *unter dem Prinzipat*, 1993. On the famine of the year AD 6: Cass. Dio 56,26,1–3, 27,1.

pp. 382–4 *The military formations in Rome*: City cohorts: Helmut Freis, 'Die cohortes urbanae', *Epigraphische Studien* 2, 1967, and idem, 'Urbanae cohortes', in RE Suppl. X, 1965, 1125–40. On the late republican 'police', see Wilfried Nippel, *Aufruhr und 'Polizei' in der römischen Republik*, 1988; on the responsibility of the aediles and the *tresviri capitales* for keeping public order, see Mommsen, *Staatsrecht*, II, 499ff., 594ff. The fire-fighting force (*vigiles*): P. K. Baillie Reynolds, *The Vigiles of Imperial Rome*, 1926, 17ff., and J. S. Rainbird, 'The Fire Stations of Imperial Rome', *Papers of the Brit. School at Rome* 54, 1986, 147–69; on Egnatius Rufus see above, pp. 313, 319; on the reorganization of the fire-fighting force in the year AD 6: Cass. Dio 55,26,4.

pp. 384–6 *The bodyguard*: The foreign bodyguards of the dictator and Octavian: Suet. Div. Iul. 86,1, and Aug. 49,1. On Octavian's praetorian cohort in the

War of Mutina, see p. 95 above. On the question of how far the little cavalry troop of *speculatores* formed an independent body, see Manfred Clauss, 'Untersuchungen zu den principales des römischen Heeres von Augustus bis Diokletian: Cornicularii, speculatores, frumentarii', dissertation, Bochum, 1973, 46ff. On the doubling of pay for the praetorians: Cass. Dio 53,11,5; on their quarters inside and outside Rome: Suet. Aug. 49,1. See Marcel Durry, *Les Cohortes prétoriennes*, 1938, idem (in summary) in RE XXII, 1954, 1607–34, s.v. praetoriae cohortes, and Alfredo Passerini, *Le coorti pretorie*, 1969.

p. 386 *Quotation from Tacitus*: Ann. 1,2,1: 'opibus et honoribus extollerentur ac novis ex rebus aucti tuta et praesentia quam vetera e periculosa mallent'.

pp. 387–9 *The monopoly of high honours by the princeps*: Drusus received the *ornamenta triumphalia* and the *ovatio* after his campaign in Germania in 12/11 BC (Suet. Claud. 1,3; Cass. Dio 54,33,5); Tiberius was promised a triumph by the Senate after his Pannonian campaign of 12 BC, but Augustus restricted it to the *ornamenta triumphalia* (Cass. Dio 54,31,4). Tiberius was not granted a full triumph until the year 7 BC, for his success in fighting the German tribesmen (Cass. Dio 55,6,5, 8,2; see Suet. Tib. 9,2), and later, in October AD 12, for victory over the Pannonians and Dalmatians (Cass. Dio 56,17,1). The award of the right to wear the laurel wreath in perpetuity: Cass. Dio 49,15,1; on the garlanding of the doorposts of his house with laurel, see p. 291 above. On the acclamations of Augustus, see Leonhard Schumacher, 'Die imperatorischen Akklamationen der Triumvirn und die auspicia des Augustus', *Historia* 34, 1985, 191–222. The number of triumphs and awards of the *ornamenta triumphalia* (over thirty): Suet. Aug. 38,1. The proconsul of Africa acclaimed as *imperator*, Lucius Passienus Rufus: Dessau ILS no. 120; he also received the *ornamenta triumphalia* (Vell. Pat. 2,116,2), which was usually linked to the acclamation as long as the *princeps* granted or accepted it. Only under Tiberius was the honour entirely discontinued. The last to receive the acclamation as *imperator*, in AD 22, was the proconsul Quintus Junius Blaesus, the uncle of Sejanus, for his military success against the rebel Numidian Tacfarinas (Tac. ann. 3,74,4). On the monopolizing of the triumph by Augustus, see Frances V. Hickson, 'Augustus *Triumphator*: Manipulation of the Triumphal Theme in the Political Program of Augustus', *Latomus* 50, 1991, 124–38. The edict of Augustus against the acceptance of honours by governors: Cass. Dio 56,25,6; on this subject see G. W. Bowersock, 'Augustus und der Kaiserkult im Osten', in Antonie Wlosok (ed.), *Römischer Kaiserkult*, Wege d. Forschg. 372, 1978, 389–402 (from the English original: *Augustus and the Greek World*, 1965, 112ff.). The games for Fabius Maximus: Ph. Le Bas/W. H. Waddington, *Inscriptions grecques et latines recueillies en Asie Mineure* 3, 1870, no. 1730b; for Censorinus: A. Boeckh, *Corpus Inscr. Graecarum*, no. 2698b. On the provincial games, temples and altars dedicated to Augustus: Suet. Aug. 59.

CHAPTER 10

Explanatory Notes

p. 390 *Population numbers in Rome*: The number given in the text for the inhabitants of Rome tends towards the lower figures given in modern attempts to calculate it. On the number of Romans living in the city, see Franz Georg Maier, 'Römische Bevölkerungsgeschichte und Inschriftenstatistik', *Historia* 2, 1953/4, 318–51. Maier is sceptical about all methods of calculation and consequently about their results, with the estimates varying from a good half million to well over a million inhabitants of Rome. See also G. Hermansen, 'The Population of Imperial Rome: The Regionaries', *Historia* 27, 1978, 129–68, attempting to calculate the number of apartment blocks (*insulae*); Brunt, *Manpower*, 376ff.; and Kolb, *Rom*, 448ff., citing other literature.

pp. 390–92 *Building methods and the traffic in the city*: See Kolb, *Rom*, 400ff. On the city walls, see M. Andreussi in Steinby, *Roma*, III, 319–24. Augustus on the city in his time: Suet. Aug. 28,3: 'urbem neque pro maiestate imperii ornatam et inundationibus incendiisque obnoxiam excoluit adeo, ut iure sit gloriatus marmoream se relinquere, quam latericiam accepisset' ('he so beautified the city of Rome, which was not yet adorned in a manner fitting for the majesty of the empire, and was plagued by floods and fires, that he could rightly boast of having left behind him a city of marble when he had taken over a city of bricks'); Cass. Dio 56,30,3. *Aurea templa*: Prop. 4,1,5; cf. Ovid fast. 1,209ff., esp. 223f. Augustus' building regulations: Strab. 5,3,7; Suet. Aug. 89,2; cf. Vitruv. 2,8,17. On the building regulations for Rome, see Kolb, *Rom*, 288ff., 445ff.

pp. 392–5 *The elections*: Suet. Aug. 40,2, 56,1; Cass. Dio 53,21,6; and see also (giving the text of fragments of an inscription on the election committees, found in the 1940s and 1982 and summarizing a *lex Valeria Cornelia* of the year AD 19) James H. Oliver/Robert E. A. Palmer, 'Text of the Tabula Hebana', *Americ. Journ. Philol.*, 1954, 225–49, and J. González, 'Tabula Siarensis, Fortunales Siarenses et municipia civium Romanorum', in *Zeitschr. für Papyrologie und Epig.* 55, 1984, 55–100. On the election procedure see Regula Frei-Stolba, *Untersuchungen zu den Wahlen in der römischen Kaiserzeit*, 1967, 87ff. (120ff. on the committees), and Dieter Flach, '*Destinatio* und *nominatio* im frühen Prinzipat', *Chiron* 6, 1976, 193–203 (Flach concentrates mainly on the post-Augustan period). Egon Flaig, *Den Kaiser herausfordern. Die Usurpation im römischen Reich*, 1992, 59–67, sees the *plebs urbana* of the empire as at least a latent political power whose 'politicization' on certain subjects, particularly those affecting the imperial family, he estimates so highly that he claims it must count as an independent political force, although ranking lower than the Senate and the army.

pp. 395–6 *Forms of organization of the plebs*: On the associations see Kienast, *Augustus*, 164ff., and Jochen Bleicken, 'vici magister' in RE VIII A, 1958, 2480–83. The associations banned by Augustus: Suet. Aug. 32,1. On the compital (local district) games and the cult of the Lares, see above, pp. 334–5. On the organization of the tribes see Mommsen, *Staatsrecht*, III, 161ff.

pp. 397–9 *The distribution of grain and money*: Aug. RG 15; Suet. Aug. 40,2, 41,2; on the organization of the supplies see p. 380 above. Augustus' reservations about the distribution of free grain: Suet. Aug. 42,3. The number of recipients: Cas. Dio 55,10,1; on the organizing of the distributions: Suet. Aug. 40,2. On the monetary donations, see the list in Kloft, 386 (see below). On the supply system of Rome see Denis van Berchem, *Les Distributions de blé et d'argent à la plèbe romaine sous l'Empire*, 1939, repr. 1975, esp. 27ff., 32ff.; Geoffrey Rickman, *The Corn Supply of Ancient Rome*, 1980, esp. 55ff.; Hans Kloft, 'Freigebigkeit und Finanzen, der soziale und finanzielle Aspect der augusteischen Liberalitas', in Binder, *Saeculum Augustum*, I, 361–88; and especially on questions of organization Catherine Virlouvet, *Tessera frumentaria: Les Procédures de distribution du blé public à la fin de la République et au début de l'Empire*, 1995.

pp. 399–402 *The games*: Suet. Aug. 43–5, in this passage 43,3ff. on the appearance of a dwarf, Parthian hostages, a rhinoceros and a snake. The magnificence of the games given by Augustus and the large number of them that he himself organized: Aug. RG 22ff.; Suet. Aug. 43,1; regulations on the seating of the crowd in the theatre and on discipline: Suet. Aug. 44. On theatrical and circus performances see Traugott Bollinger, *Theatralis licentia: Die Publikumsdemonstrationen an den öffentlichen Spielen im Rom der früheren Kaiserzeit und ihre Bedeutung im politischen Leben*, 1969 (1ff. on the measures taken for attendance at the games and conduct during performances, 50ff. on the manifestations of the will of the ruler and the public in the time of Augustus). See also Jürgen Deininger, 'Brot und Spiele. Tacitus und die Entpolitisierung der *plebs urbana*', *Gymnasium* 86, 1979, 278–303 (with a survey of the subject in the entire early principate), and on the theatre buildings in the towns of Italy see Giorgio Bejor, 'L'edificio teatrale nell'urbanizzazione Augustea', *Athenaeum* 57, 1979, 126–38.

pp. 402–3 *The role of the people of the city of Rome under Augustus*: The tribunician power assumed by Augustus, and his succession to the leadership of a popular party as claimed by some scholars, as well as the continuing importance of the plebs in the political life of Rome under Augustus himself and his successors, are sometimes interpreted in modern research as evidence of a 'plebiscitary' element in the Roman empire. Proponents of this thesis often refer to Theodor Mommsen, who sees the principate as being founded on the sovereignty of the people (see for instance *Staatsrecht*, II, 749ff.), but in this interpetation of the principate that concept is not constitutive, but has only a function holding true of the entire system of Roman constitutional law. A good and more recent account, although it is still influenced by Mommsen on this point, is by Rolf Gilbert, *Die Beziehungen zwischen Princeps und stadtrömischer Plebs im frühen Principat*, 1976; there is also a well-balanced small study of the relationship of the *princeps* (Octavian/Augustus) to the plebs of the city of Rome by Z. Yavetz, 'The Tribunician Power in Shaping the Image of the Principate', in idem, *Plebs und Princeps*, 1969, 83–102.

pp. 403–7 *Italy in general*: See T. W. Potter, *Das römische Italien*, 1992 (English original edition 1987), which considers the cities and traffic systems of Italy, its economy and its religion; also M. H. Crawford, 'Italy and Rome from Sulla to Augustus', in CAH² X, 414–33. On the economic situation of Italy in the late republic and early imperial period, see the information provided by Rostovtzeff, *Gesellschaft*, I, 1ff., 34ff., still essential despite later investigations, and the survey in Siegfried J. De Laet, *Aspects de la vie sociale et économique sous Auguste et Tibère*, 1944, 42ff. On Upper Italy in particular, see G. E. F. Chilver, *Cisalpine Gaul: Social and Economic History from 49 BC to the Death of Trajan*, 1941, and Sigrid Mratschek, 'Est enim ille flos Italiae. Literatur und Gesellschaft in der Transpadana', *Athenaeum* 62, 1984, 154–89. Virgil's praise of Italy: Georg. 21,36–76. On the figure given for the Roman population of Italy, sometimes a subject of heated debate, see finally Elio Lo Cascio, 'La dinamica della popolazione in Italia da Augusto al III secolo', in *L'Italie d'Auguste à Dioclétien*, 1994, 91–125. On the division of Italy into regions, see Theodor Mommsen, 'Die italienischen Regionen', in idem, *Ges. Schriften*, V, 268–85, and Rudi Thomsen, *The Italic Regions from Augustus to the Lombard Invasion*, 1947.

pp. 408–10 *The foundation of cities by Caesar and Augustus*: See Friedrich Vittinghoff, 'Römische Kolonisation und Bürgerrechtspolitik unter Caesar und Augustus', *Abhandlg. d. Akad. d. Wiss. u. Liter. Mainz*, geistes- u. sozialwiss. Kl., Jahrg. 1951, 14; A. N. Sherwin-White, *The Roman Citizenship*, 1973², 225ff., and Kienast, *Augustus*, 386ff. On Italian land law (*ius Italicum*) see Jochen Bleicken, '*In provinciali solo dominium populi Romani est vel Caesaris*. Zur Kolonisationspolitik der ausgehenden Republik und frühen Kaiserzeit', *Chiron* 4, 1974, 359–414.

pp. 410–11 *The roads and trade routes*: See Gerhard Radke, 'Viae publicae Romanae', in RE Suppl. III, 1973, 1417–686; Thomas Pekáry, *Untersuchungen zu den römischen Reichsstrassen*, 1968; Raymond Chevallier, *Les Voies romaines*, 1972; M. P. Charlesworth, *Trade-routes and commerce of the Roman Empire*, 1961; and Heinz E. Herzig, *Probleme des römischen Strassenwesens: Untersuchungen zu Geschichte und Recht*, in ANRW II 1, 1974, 593–648.

pp. 411–21 *The provinces*: See Theodor Mommsen, *Römische Geschichte*, V: *Die Provinzen von Caesar bis Diocletian*, 1909⁶, Rostovtzeff, *Gesellschaft*, De Laet (as above), and above all Friedrich Vittinghoff (ed.), *Europäische*

*Wirtschafts- und Sozialgeschichte in der römischen Kaiserzeit* (= *Handbuch der europäischen Wirtschafts- und Sozialgeschichte* I), 1990, see here a survey of Italy and the provinces, 375ff.

pp. 411–17 *The west in particular*: Kienast, *Augustus*, 386ff. Individually: Sicily, Sardinia, Corsica: R. J. A. Wilson, in CAH² X, 434ff. Spain: Hartmut Galsterer, *Untersuchungen zum römischen Städtewesen auf der Iberischen Halbinsel*, 1971, esp. 17ff.; A. T. Fear, *Rome and Baetica: Urbanization in Southern Spain, c. 50 BC–AD 150*, 1996, esp. 63ff., 105ff.; and Géza Alföldy, 'Spain', in CAH² X, 449ff. On Gaul, where tribal societies were very slow to develop a 'Gallo-Roman *civitas*' leading to the cities of late antiquity: Hartmut Wolff, 'Kriterien für lateinische und römische Städte in Gallien und Germanien und die "Verfassung" der gallischen Stammesgemeinden', *Bonner Jahrb.* 176, 1976, 45–121; Ch. Goudineau/A. Rebourg (eds.), *Les Villes augustéennes de Gaule*, 1991; and C. Goudineau, 'Gaul', in CAH² X, 464ff. On Trier in the Augustan period see Heinz Heinen, *Trier und das Trevererland in römischer Zeit*, 1985, 41–53. The assumption of an early form of Trier in the nature of a town around the year 17 BC, proposed as grounds for the city's 2,000th anniversary celebrations, is not much more likely than almost any other late date during the reign of Augustus. Illyricum, Noricum, Macedonia and Moesia: J. J. Wilkes, 'The Danubian and Balkan Provinces', in CAH² X, 545ff. Africa: Leo Teutsch, *Das Städtewesen in Nordafrika in der Zeit von C. Gracchus bis zum Tode des Kaisers Augustus*, 1962, esp. 52ff.; Jean-Marie Lassère, *Ubique populus: Peuplement et mouvements de population dans l'Afrique romaine de la chute de Carthage à la fin de la dynastie des Sévères (146 a.C.–235 p.C.)*, 1977, esp. 143ff.; Nicola K. Mackie, 'Augustan Colonies in Mauretania', *Historia* 32, 1983, 332–58; Michèle Coltelloni-Trannoy, *Le Royaume de Maurétanie sous Juba II et Ptolémée*, 1997; also C. R. Whittaker, 'Roman Africa: Augustus to Vespasian', in CAH² X, 586ff. On concern for the welfare and reconstruction of peregrine communities: Kienast, *Augustus*, 402ff. On the road network, see the literature cited on p. 680 above, and Kienast, *Augustus*, 412ff.

pp. 417–20 *The cities in the east (without the Greek motherland)*: See A. H. M. Jones, *The Cities of the Eastern Roman Provinces*, 1937, 1971², and Kienast, *Augustus*, 370ff.; also Joyce Reynolds and J. A. Lloyd (Cyrene), Barbara M. Levick (Greece, Crete, Cyprus, Asia Minor), Alan K. Bowman (Egypt), David Kennedy (Syria) and Martin Goodman (Judaea), in CAH² X, 619ff. On the colonization policies of Caesar and Augustus in the east, see Vittinghoff, op. cit., 1305ff., 1351ff. and *passim*. On Nicopolis in particular, a recent work is Daniel Strauch, *Römische Politik und griechische Tradition: Die Umgestaltung Nordwest-Griechenlands unter römischer Herrschaft*, 1996, 156ff., in this passage also on Patras. On the Roman colonies in the east, see also G. W. Bowersock, *Augustus and the Greek World*, 1965, esp. 62ff., and Barbara Levick, *Roman Colonies in Southern Asia Minor*, 1967.

## CHAPTER 11

# Explanatory Notes

pp. 422–7 *The senators in general*: Senatorial rank (*ordo senatorius*) is discussed in the standard works for the entire period of the principate, i.e. until the time of the Severan dynasty; these works do look at its beginnings under Augustus, but those aspects are subordinated to the entire picture. See above all Mommsen, *Staatsrecht*, III, 458ff. (here including the republican period); Alföldy, *Sozialgeschichte*, 101ff.; Kienast, *Augustus*, 126ff.; Werner Eck, 'Die Umgestaltung der politischen Führungsschicht – Senatorenstand und Ritterstand', in idem, *Verwaltung*, 103–58; Claude Nicolet, 'Augustus, Government, and the Propertied Classes', in Millar/Segal, *Augustus*, 89–128. See also the instructive little survey by Richard J. A. Talbert, 'Augustus and the Senate', *Greece & Rome* 31, 1984, 55–63, and Peter A. Brunt, 'The Role of the Senate in the Augustan Regime', *Class. Quat.* 34, 1984, 423–44 (for the involvement of the Senate in administration). On the Senate as an institution (meetings, order of business, area of responsibility, etc.) see Mommsen, *Staatsrecht*, III, 835ff., and Talbert, *Senate*; on the composition of the Senate see Siegfried J. de Laet, *De Samenstelling van den Romeinschen Senaat gedurende de eerste eeuw van het principaat*, 1941, esp. 19ff., and on the decline of the old noble families see in particular Syme, *Revolution*, 490ff. and *passim*; Helmut Halfmann, *Die Senatoren aus dem östlichen Teil des Imperium Romanum bis zum Ende des 2. Jh. n. Chr.*, 1979, and Wiseman, *New Men*, 184ff. and *passim*. Halfmann, op. cit., 71–100, mentions only a single senator from the time of Augustus who can be shown to be of eastern origin, and two from the time of his successor Tiberius.

pp. 422–3 *The individual senators*: Claudius on the origin of the senators: Dessau ILS no. 212, II Z. 3ff.: 'Sane novo more et divus Augustus avonculus meus et patruus Ti. Caesar omnem florem ubique coloniarum ac municipiorum, bonotum scilicet virorum et locupletium, in hac curia [sc. the Senate in Rome] esse voluit' ('my uncle on my mother's side, the divine Augustus, and my uncle on my father's side, Tiberius Caesar, wanted, in what was certainly a new way, those men who were true to the state and prosperous, the flower of all the Roman cities, to sit in that meeting place'). Although Italy is not named as the country of origin of these senators, the reference can be assumed to be self-evident. The sons of senators as members of the *ordo senatorius*: Suet. Aug. 38,2; raising of the minimum fortune for senators to a million sesterces: Cass. Dio 54,26,3ff., 17,3. Dio's information on the *census* is to be preferred to that of Suet. Aug. 41,1, stating that the senatorial *census* had been raised to 1,200,000 sesterces. On elections by the people, see pp. 392–3. On the three surveys of the Senate by Augustus himself, see Aug. RG 8 and pp. 281ff. and

321ff. above. On the support given to impoverished senators: Suet. Aug. 41,1; Cass. Dio 54,17,3; Tac. ann. 2,37,1. On the new patricians, see Hans-Henning Pistor, *Prinzeps und Patriziat in der Zeit von Augustus bis Commodus*, 1965, 11ff. The idea that in creating a new patriciate Augustus sought 'to replace the old aristocracy by a new patrician nobility' (Kienast, *Augustus*, 128, with reference to de Laet) is certainly not to be accepted, for in so doing he would have made the aristocracy that he had weakened (and to some extent destroyed) into a new 'closed society'. He had to aim to distinguish between the leading senators, not encourage a sense of solidarity among them. On the signs of rank see Mommsen, *Staatsrecht*, III, 887ff.; Hans Rupprecht Goette, '*Mulleus – embas – calceus*. Ikonographische Studien zu römischem Schuhwerk', *Jahrb. Deutsch. Archäol. Inst.* 103, 1988, 401–64; and Frank Kolb, 'Zur Statussymbolik im antiken Rom', *Chiron* 7, 1977, 239–59.

p. 427 *Names given on adoption*: The consul for the year 52, Pompey's father-in-law Quintus Caecilius Metellus Pius Scipio, changed by adoption from the Cornelii Scipiones family to the Caecilii Metelli Pii family, but did not then as usual add the gens name of his birth family in the adjectival-*anus* form (Cornelianus), but the cognomen of that family, Scipio, indicating the most distinguished branch of the Cornelian gens.

p. 430 *The senatorial court as a law-court of peers*: See Jochen Bleicken, *Senatsgericht und Kaisergericht: Eine Studie zur Entwicklung des Prozessrechtes im frühen Prinzipat*, 1962, 17ff., and (casting doubt on the existence of a senatorial court as early as the Augustan period) Wolfgang Kunkel, 'Über die Entstehung des Senatsgerichts', *Sitz.ber. d. Bayer. Akad. d. Wiss.*, phil.-histor. Kl., 1969, 1 (= idem, *Kleine Schriften*, 1974, 267–323).

pp. 430– *Augustus' legislation on morality, particularly in the field of matrimonial legislation*: Horace on the decline in moral standards: c. 3,6, cf. 3,24,17ff. Scipio Aemilianus on rewards for the fathers of many children (*praemia patrum*): Gell. 5,19,15 (ORF² Malc. 124ff.). Cicero's precepts on marriage: leg. 3,7. The speech made by the censor Metellus Macedonicus *de prole augenda* ('on the increase in progeny'): Suet. Aug. 89,2; Liv. per. 59 (ORF² Malc. 107f.). An account dating from the second half of the third century BC, stating that a man has to take an oath before the censors that he intends to marry for the sake of having children, already shows that to procreate offspring was a duty required by the state (Gell. 4,3,2). Augustus on his refraining from establishing a *cura legum et morum*: Aug. RG 6. The hendiadys *mos et lex* is recorded by Horace c. 4,5,22 and epist. 2,1,2ff. On the refusal of the younger Antonia to remarry after the death of her husband Drusus: Flav. Jos. antiqu. 18,180; Val. Max. 4,3,3. The protest of equestrians in the theatre: Suet. Aug. 34,2. The old man from Faesulae with his sixty-one descendants: Plin. nat. hist. 7,60. The *ius trium liberorum* for Livia: Cass. Dio 55,2,5. Cornelius Sisenna in the Senate: Cass. Dio 54,27,4. On the legislation on marriage in general: Cass. Dio 54,16 (the *lex Iulia*) and 56,1,2–10,3 (the *lex Papia*

*Poppaea*), with the interpolated *suasio* (advocacy) of it by Augustus, which does not exaggerate the total politicization of conduct in marriage, but reflects the tone of the ideas behind it. From modern research on the legislation of marriage see Paul Jörs, 'Die Ehegesetze des Augustus', in *Festschr. Theodor Mommsen zum 50jährigen Doctorjubiläum*, 1893, 1–65 (the older marriage law passed by Augustus that he reads into Prop. 2,7,1–3, dating it to 28 BC, has been rightly rejected, see E. Badian, 'A Phantom Marriage Law', *Philologus* 129, 1985, 82–98, and Mette-Dittmann's work cited below, 16ff.); Paul Jörs/Wolfgang Kunkel, *Römisches Privatrecht*, 1949³, 274ff.; Kaser, *Privatrecht*, 318ff.; Dieter Nörr, 'Planung in der Antike: Über die Ehegesetze des Augustus', in H. Baier (ed.), *Freiheit und Sachzwang, Festschr. für Helmut Schelsky*, 1977, 309–34; Karl Galinsky, 'Augustus' Legislation on Morals and Marriage', *Philologus* 125, 1981, 126–44 (also emphasizing moral values influenced by philosophical ideas of the time as the aim of legislation on marriage); Ernst Baltrusch, *Regimen morum: Die Reglementierung des Privatlebens der Senatoren und Ritter in der römischen Republik und frühen Kaiserzeit*, 1989, 162ff., 153ff.; see also Angelika Mette-Dittmann, *Die Ehegesetze des Augustus: Eine Untersuchung im Rahmen der Gesellschaftspolitik des Princeps*, 1991 (in this work, see also 131ff. on the relationship of the *lex Iulia de maritandis ordinibus* to the *lex Papia Poppaea nuptialis*). On the Julian law on adultery, see Wolfgang Kunkel in RE XXIV, 1963, 770, and Mette-Dittmann, op. cit., 33ff. On the combination of old norms and new law in the legislation of Augustus, see Heinz Bellen, 'Novus status – novae leges: Kaiser Augustus als Gesetzgeber', in Binder, *Saeculum Augustum*, I, 308–48. On the registers of births after the *leges Aelia Sentia* (AD 4) and *Papia Poppaea* (AD 9) see Fritz Schulz, 'Roman Registers of Births and Birth Certificates', *Journ. Rom. Stud.* 32, 1942, 78–91, and 33, 1943, 55–64.

pp. 441–5 *Opposition*: On the concept of opposition in the early imperial period see Syme, *Revolution*, 476ff., and Kurt Raaflaub, 'Grundzüge, Ziele und Ideen der Opposition gegen die Kaiser im 1. Jh. n. Chr.: Versuch einer Standortbestimmung', in *Opposition et résistances à l'Empire d'Auguste à Trajan*, Entretiens sur l'antiquité classique 33, 1987, 1–63. Raaflaub sees the opposition as mainly moral in nature. However, it is difficult to compare opposition to the established empire, the subject of Raaflaub's study, and the beginning of opposition earlier. He and L. J. Samons II have studied the opposition to Augustus after 27 BC in 'Opposition to Augustus', in Raaflaub/Toher, 417–54, and consider it very limited in extent, particularly because of the idealization of monarchy in the principate, and ineffective where it was present at all. Augustus' caution after the year 18: Suet. Aug. 35,2. Dialogue and speech by Livia on the pardon granted to Cornelius Cinna: Cass. Dio 55,14,2–21,4. Cinna's alleged assassination attempt, the last conspiracy against Augustus: Cass. Dio 55,22,2. On historiography and the principate see Dieter Timpe, 'Geschichtsschreibung und Prinzipatsopposition', Entretiens 33 (as above),

65–102. Augustus on Livy: Tac. ann. 4,34,3 (the source of the speech put into the mouth of the historian Aulus Cremutius Cordus). On the passages from Virgil: Aen. 6,826–35 (from the speech of Anchises: the civil war between Caesar and Pompey, esp. 832–5) and 8,670 (from the description of the shield). On the importance of myth to the political consciousness of the time and the self-presentation of Augustus, as well as to the 'outsourcing' in myth of current events, see Tonio Hölscher, 'Mythen als Exempel der Geschichte', in Fritz Graf (ed.), *Mythos in mythenloser Gesellschaft: Das Paradigma Roms*, Colloquium Rauricum 3, 1993, 67–87, esp. 80ff.

pp. 446–8 *The equestrian order in the late Republican period*: See Jochen Bleicken, 'Cicero und die Ritter', *Abhandlg. d. Göttinger Akad. d. Wiss.*, phil.-histor. Kl., III, Folge Nr. 213, 1995; also on the equestrians, studies of the Augustan period by Mommsen, *Staatsrecht*, III, 489ff.; Stein, *Ritterstand*, 54ff.; M. J. Henderson, 'The Establishment of the *Equestor Ordo*', *Journ. Rom. Stud.* 53, 1963, 61–72: T. P. Wiseman, 'The Definition of "eques Romanus" in the Late Republic and Early Empire', *Historia* 19, 1970, 67–83 (the last two, and others, coming to the conclusion that as well as 'knights with a state horse' there were also 'knights on the grounds of the census' alone); Kienast, *Augustus*, I, 151ff.; Werner Eck, 'Die Umgestaltung der politischen Führungsschicht: Senatorenstand und Ritterstand', in idem, *Verwaltung*, 103–58; and Ségolène Demougin, *L'Ordre équestre sous les Julio-Claudiens*, 1988. Those who qualified for membership of the equestrian order by virtue of the census could also sit in the places reserved for equestrians in the theatre: Suet. Aug. 40,1. On the presence at times of 5,000 equestrians in the annual parade on 15 July: Dion. Hal. 6,13,4. Strabo on the equestrians in Patavium and Gades: 3,5,3, 5,1,7. On the *iuventus* see Gertrud Pfister, *Die Erneuerung der römischen iuventus durch Augustus*, 1977 (also on the *collegia iuvenum* of the Roman cities outside Rome). However, I cannot agree with her assumption (39ff.) that the *iuventus* comprised all active equestrians, that is to say all equestrians up to the age of thirty-five, and all sons of senators up to the time of their own entry into the Senate. Senators' sons belonged to the *ordo senatorius*, and 'all equestrians up to the age of thirty-five' is the same thing as the (active) *ordo equester*; see also on the *iuventus* Rigobert W. Fortuin, *Der Sport im augusteischen Rom*, 1996, 72ff. Whether the municipal *magistri iuventutis* were a branch of the *iuventus* of the city of Rome or connected with other youth groups (*collegia*) is a matter of dispute; see Pfister, op. cit., 58ff.

pp. 448–51 *The functions of the equestrians*: The *decuriae* of sworn jurors: Mommsen, *Strafrecht*, 210ff. Mommsen's opinion in *Staatsrecht*, III, 535, to the effect that the senators were entirely free of jury service, was withdrawn in his *Strafrecht*; see Klaus Bringmann, 'Zur Gerichtsreform des Kaisers Augustus', *Chiron* 3, 1973, 235–44. The Julian law covering the entire system of jurisdiction (*lex Iulia iudiciorum publicorum et privatorum*) probably dates from the year 18 BC. On the equestrian officers see below, pp. 497f.; on the opportunities for centurions to rise in the social scale, see Brian Dobson, 'The Centurionate and Social Mobility during the Principate', in Claude Nicolet (ed.), *Recherches sur les structures sociales dans l'antiquité classique*, 1970, 99–116, and idem, *Die primipilares*, 1978, 6–9; on the procurators see p. 361 above. On the prefect of Egypt, whose precise title was *praefectus Alexandreae et Aegypti*, see Oscar William Reinmuth, in RE XXII, 1954, 2353–77, and Hirschfeld, *Verwaltungsbeamte*, 343ff.; on the prefects in general, A. H. M. Jones, 'Procurators and Prefects in the Early Principate', in idem, *Studies in Roman Government and Law*, 1960, 117–25. Werner Eck, 'Die Laufbahn eines Ritters aus Apri in Thrakien', *Chiron* 5, 1975, 379ff., assumes that Augustus, who took a great interest in the road network and traffic of all Italy, had already appointed a 'general postmaster' (*praefectus vehiculorum*).

pp. 452–3 *The municipal nobility and freedmen*: The promotion of municipal officials by recommendation from the cities: Suet. Aug. 46. Laws affecting freedmen: the *lex Fufia Caninia* and the *lex Aelia Sentia*, passed by the consuls of the years 2 BC and AD 4 respectively; on these laws see Kaser, *Privatrecht*, 296ff., and finally Mette-Dittman (see p. 684 above), 187ff. The equestrian ring given to Antonius Musa: Cass. Dio 53,30,3.

## CHAPTER 12
## Explanatory Notes

In the notes I have avoided using the term 'ideology'. It is often used of the Augustan view of the world, but does not seem to me useful, because it is not only typically used of the distance between propaganda and political reality, it is also used against the background of another and equally ideal view of the world. It could conceivably be used in a pre-scholarly sense, but I have preferred to omit it entirely because of the explanations that would subsequently be necessary. Equally, I have avoided here, and elsewhere in this book, the term 'imperialism', which is much used in modern historical writing on Roman expansion in the period following the year 16 BC, but which, through long discussion of it, has become a shifting concept.

pp. 454–7 *Quotation from Augustus' account of his achievements*: Aug. RG 1: 'annos undeviginti natus exercitum privato consilio et privata impensa comparavi, per quem rem publicam a dominatione factionis oppressam in libertatem vindicavi, eo nomine senatus decretis honorificis in ordinem suum me adlegit C. Pansa et A. Hirtio consulibus consularem locum sententiae dicendae tribuens et imperium mihi dedit. Res publica ne quid detrimenti caperet, me pro praetore simul cum consulibus providere iussit, populus autem eodem anno me consulem, cum cos. uterque in bello cecidisset, et triumvirum rei publicae constituendae creavit.' See Wilhelm Hoffmann, 'Der Widerstreit von Tradition und Gegenwart im Tatenbericht des Augustus' (first published 1969), in Binder, *Saeculum Augustum*, I, 92–110, and Horst Braunert, 'Zum Eingangssatz der *res gestae Divi Augusti*', *Chiron* 4, 1974, 343–58. The account by Augustus known as *Res Gestae* ('deeds, achievements') was intended to be made public after his death. He wrote it, or finished writing it, on 3 April AD 13 (Suet. Aug. 101,1), and – probably only lightly edited by Tiberius after the death of Augustus, for instance in the last passage, 35,2, concerning the age of Augustus when he died – it later received four additions, which, like the signature using the term *res gestae*, are not his own. *Res gestae*, in ordinary linguistic use, means achievements, especially the achievements in war by a holder of public office. However, as the account also speaks of gifts and donations, as well as the offices that Augustus held or declined, and the honours awarded to him, none of which comes into the category of *res gestae*, the meaning an 'account of deeds' which was already ascribed to the work in antiquity is inexact. In fact the work eludes any classification in the literary genres of its time; it is not a funerary inscription, nor can it be called a memoir; it is not history or a meditation. In content, it is Augustus representing himself as a monarch, and his connection with the public is a constituent part of the work. Augustus speaks of himself here like a magistrate retiring from his office, and giving an informal account to the people of what he did while he held it (formal accounts by magistrates were not known to the Romans). Theodor Mommsen, 'Der Rechenschaftsbericht des Augustus', *Histor. Zeitschr.* 57, 1887, 385–97, gave the right idea of the genre in calling it, in German, a 'report'. See also Alfred Heuss, 'Zeitgeschichte als Ideologie. Bemerkungen zu Komposition und Gedankenführung der Res Gestae Divi Augusti', in E. Lefèvre (ed.), *Monumentum Chiloniense: Studien zur augusteischen Zeit, Kieler Festschrift für Erich Burck zum 70. Geburtstag*, 1975, 55–95 (= idem, *Ges. Schriften*, II, 1995, 1319–59), and Ramage, *Res Gestae*, esp. 17ff., 111ff.

pp. 457–8 *The idea of peace; closing of the temple of Janus*: See above pp. 262ff. Aug. RG 13: 'Ianum Quirinum, quem claussum esse maiores nostri voluerunt, cum per totum imperium populi Romani terra marique esset parta victoriis pax, cum priusquam nascerer, a condita urbe bis omnino clausum fuisse prodatur memoriae, ter me principe senatus claudendum esse censuit.' See also the last ode of Horace, c. 4,15, the ode to peace, praising Augustus for the peace he has brought on the occasion of his return to Rome in the year 13, and in the last two lines (31f.) referring to the early days of Rome, to Troy, Anchises and his descendants. Funding of statues to Salus Publica, Concordia and Pax: Cass. Dio 54,35,2. The temple of Concordia Augusta in the Forum: Fasti Praenestini for 16 January; its consecration by Tiberius in the year AD 10: Cass. Dio 56,25,1. Horace on the return of Augustus: c. 4,5, esp. 17ff., 25ff.

pp. 458–61 *The ara Pacis Augustae*: Aug. RG 12: 'cum ex Hispania Galliaque rebus in iis provincis prospere gestis Romam redi Ti. Nerone P. Quintilio consulibus, aram Pacis Augustae senatus pro reditu meo consacrandam censuit ad campum Martium, in qua magistratus et sacerdotes virginesque Vestales anniversarium sacrificium facere iussit' ('when I returned from Spain and Gaul after victories won there, in the consulate of Tiberius Nero and Publius Quintilius, the Senate decided, on the occasion of my return, to dedicate an altar to Augustan Peace on the Field of Mars, and also decreed that the magistrates, priests and Vestal Virgins should make an annual sacrifice there'); cf. Ovid. fast. 1,709–22. On the Ara Pacis, see G. Moretti, *Ara Pacis Augustae*, 1948; Nash, *Rom*, I, 63–73; Adolf H. Borbein, 'Die Ara Pacis Augustae: Geschichtliche Wirklichkeit und Programm', *Jahrb. Deutsch. Archäol. Inst.* 90, 1975, 242–66 (on the pan-Athenian procession to the Parthenon as a model for the procession to the altar; the connection assumed here between the Pax Augusta and the Clementia Augusta is difficult to understand); Erika Simon, 'Ara Pacis Augustae', in Binder, *Saeculum Augustum*, III, 234–48 (only the architecture and the reliefs on the front sides); Kolb, *Rom*, 340ff.; and the informative essay by Salvatore Settis, 'Die Ara Pacis', in exhibition catalogue *Kaiser Augustus*, 400–426. The identification of the two female figures on the front reliefs – here described as Tellus (Earth) and Roma – is a matter of controversy; sometimes they are identified as Italia instead of Tellus and Honos instead of Roma. On the sundial, see Edmund Buchner, *Die Sonnenuhr des Augustus*, 1982; Buchner's excavations established the connection of the sundial with the Ara Pacis and the Mausoleum of Augustus. His reconstruction of the sundial, and in particular its relationship with the Ara Pacis, has not gone undisputed; see Michael Schütz, 'Zur Sonnenuhr des Augustus auf dem Marsfeld', *Gymnasium* 97, 1990, 432–57, by whose calculations neither the height of the obelisk (= the gnomon) nor the situation and measurement of the network of lines allow us to assume a connection between the solarium and the altar, and suggest that the relationship of the Augustan complex to Domitian's must be rethought. On the idea of peace in general, see Karl Ernst Laage, 'Der Friedensgedanke in der augusteischen Dichtung', dissertation, Kiel, 1956 (typescript, distinguishing Virgil's positive belief in the hope represented by peace from the initially belligerent warning, and also Horace and his lyric ideas of peace, and then in turn distinguishing Tibullus, Propertius and Ovid from them both, because in the latter three the general political concerns give way to those that are purely personal). See also Greg Woolf, 'Roman Peace', in J. Rich/G. Shipley (eds.), *War and Society in the Roman World*, 1993, 171–94 (with an extensive bibliography).

p. 461 *Augustus' star sign*: Suet. Aug. 94,12, suggesting that the mathematician and astrologer Theogenes interpreted the star sign of Octavian in the year 44, when he was still in Apollonia; also Cass. Dio 56,25,5. According to the passage in Suetonius, Augustus was born under the sign of Capricorn (the goat).

There is a good deal of contentious literature which also inclines to superficial constructions on the date of the birth or conception of Augustus, in which he features as a propagandist manipulating his date of birth to hoodwink the world (Gerhard Radke, 'Augustus und das Göttliche', in *Antike und Universalgeschichte: Festschr. H. E. Stier*, 1972, 258ff.; see also idem, *Fasti Romani. Betrachtungen zur Frühgeschichte des römischen Kalenders*, 1990, 77ff., and on this Jörg Rüpke, *Gnomon* 64, 1992, 141ff.). See finally Michael Schütz, 'Der Capricorn als Sternzeichen des Augustus', *Antike u. Abendland* 37, 1991, 55–67; and Tamsyn Barton, 'Augustus and Capricorn: Astrological Polyvalency and Imperial Rhetoric', *Journ. Rom. Stud.* 85, 1995, 33–51. However, for the attempt to close the gap between 23 September and the end of December with reference to the calendar in the year 63, when it was still in a state of great confusion, hardly any information is available about the three months in question. On the Secular Games, see pp. 322ff. above. On the dictator's reform of the calendar, and its correction by Augustus in the year AD 8 (Macrob. Sat. 1,14,13–15) see Alan E. Samuel, *Greek and Roman Chronology*, 1972, 155ff.; and Jörg Rüpke, *Kalender und Öffentlichkeit*, 1995, 369ff.

pp. 461–4 *On the virtues of the Romans and their ruler*: See C. Joachim Classen, 'Virtutes imperatoriae', *Arctos* 25, 1991, 17–39, according to whom the virtues listed on the shield given to Augustus by the Senate (see p. 292 above) were not compulsory for the emperors who succeeded him and for Roman literature; in addition Martin P. Charlesworth, 'Die Tugenden eines römischen Herrschers: Propaganda und Schaffung von Glaubwürdigkeit', in H. Kloft (ed.), *Ideologie und Herrschaft in der Antike*, Wege d. Forschg 528, 1979, 361–87 (English original 1937); Hans Kloft, 'Aspekte der Prinzipatsideologie im frühen Prinzipat', *Gymnasium* 91, 1984, 306–26, emphasizing the connection of the ideological notions of the early principate and their abstract concepts with the immaturity of the republic; also Galinsky, *Augustan Culture*, 80–90, and Syme, *Revolution*, although the latter, probably influenced by his experience of nationalist totalitarianism in his own time, used the term 'progaganda' in its modern sense, and thus at least tends to see the historical subject in the light of another view of the world, one that rejects propaganda; also Ramage, *Res Gestae*, 73ff. Liv. praef. 10: 'hoc illud est praecipue in cognitione rerum salubre et frugiferum, omnis te exempli documenta in inlustri posita monumento intueri; inde tibi tuaeque rei publicae quod imitere capias, inde foedum inceptu foedum exitu quod vites'. For Livy's awareness of his time, and his relationship to the person and work of Augustus, see Alfred Heuss, 'Zur inneren Zeitform bei Livius', in E. Lefèvre/E. Olshausen (eds.), *Livius, Werk und Rezeption. Festschrift für Erich Burck zum 80. Geburtstag*, 1983, 175–215, esp. 208ff. (= idem, *Ges. Schriften*, 1995, II, 1482–522, esp. 1515ff.). Heuss sees him as a historian with a sense of reality and relatively independent of Augustus, although that is not the majority view. Raban von Haehling, *Zeitbezüge des T. Livius in der ersten Dekade seines Geschichtswerkes: nec vitia nostra nec remedia pati possumus*, 1989, sees Livy in the same way as Heuss (for summary see 184ff., Livy had 'an awareness of conflict'), but Jürgen Deininger, 'Livius und der Prinzipat', *Klio* 67, 1985, 265–72, thinks that Livy was aware only to a limited extent of the political change going on under Augustus, because of the latter's reference to tradition. On Augustus' wish to bear the name of Romulus, see p. 291 above.

p. 465 *Mention of the temple of the Divus Julius, and Augustus' refusal to accept the dictatorship in the Res Gestae*: Aug. RG 19, 21, 5. On his distancing himself from the dictator, see Wolfgang Hoben, 'Caesar-Nachfolge und Caesar-Abkehr in den Res gestae divi Augusti', *Gymnasium* 85, 1978, 1–19.

pp. 465–7 *Virgil's Aeneid*: The speech of Anchises (6,756–853, omitting the attached obituary of young Marcellus): the early history of Rome to Romulus (756–87); Augustus ushering in a Golden Age (792–4) and as ruler of the world (794–807); the other kings and early republican heroes (808–25); interpolation of the civil war between Caesar and Pompey (826–35); more heroes of the third and second centuries (836–46); comparison of the Greeks with the Romans (847–53). The account of the civil war of Caesar and Pompey does not seem to be part of the general composition and has therefore aroused special interest; see also Michael von Albrecht, 'Vergils Geschichtsauffassung in der "Heldenschau"', *Wiener Stud.* n.s. 1, 1967, 156–82; and V. Buchheit, 'Vergilische Geschichtsdeutung', *Grazer Beitr.* 1, 1973, 23–50, who considers that Virgil's interpretation of history (also with reference to Book 6) was already fully formed when he wrote the *Georgics*. The description of the shield (8,626–728): Romulus (630–41); other kings and struggle for freedom against Porsenna (642–51); the Celtic siege of Rome (652–62); two ancient priesthoods, as well as Catiline and Cato (663–70); the battle of Actium (671–713), Cleopatra as Isis (696); the triumph of Octavian (714–28). See Gerhard Binder, *Aeneas und Augustus: Interpretationen zum 8. Buch der Aeneis*, 1971, 150–270; Philip R. Hardie, *Virgil's Aeneid: Cosmos and Imperium*, 1989, esp. 97ff.; and S. J. Harrison, 'The Survival and Supremacy of Rome: The Unity of the Shield of Aeneas', *Journ. Rom. Stud.* 87, 1997, 70–76; on the comparison of a shield description in Virgil and Homer (the *Iliad*), see Carl Becker, 'Der Schild des Aeneas', *Wiener Stud.* 77, 1964, 111–27. Hanns Gabelmann, 'Zur Schlussszene auf dem Schild des Aeneas (Vergil, Aeneis VIII 720–728)', *Röm. Mitt.* 93, 1986, 281–300, relates the scene of Augustus sitting on the threshold of the temple to Apollo on the Palatine to that in Serv. ad. Aen. 8,721 as a *porticus ad nationes* for which there is evidence as a building erected by Augustus, although its location is unknown. The quotation from Book 6 (791–4): 'hic vir, hic est, tibi quem promitti saepius audis / Augustus Caesar, divi genus, aurea condet / saecula qui rursus Latio regnata per arva / Saturno quondam.' The Pisan decree of AD 4: Dessau ILS no. 140.

On the silver goblet from Boscoreale, see Zanker, *Augustus*, 229ff., and Ann L. Kuttner, *Dynasty and Empire in the Age of Augustus: The Case of the Boscoreale Cups*, 1995, who thinks that the figure behind the kneeling barbarian on the Augustus goblet can be identified as the older Drusus, and that the scene on the goblet can thus be dated to 13 or (in her opinion less probably) to 10 BC.

pp. 467–8 *Virgil's references to the republic and its freedom*: The civil war between Caesar and Pompey: Aen. 6,826–35 (the link to the preceding lines is provided by Camillus and Manius Torquatus, two warriors who fought the Celts, but it is a very loose one, since Virgil presents Caesar not as the victor over the Celts but as the commander in the civil war); appearance of Discord at the battle of Actium: Aen. 8,700–703; Cato dispensing justice: Aen. 8,670: 'secretos pios, his dantem iura Catonem': see Eckhard Lefèvre, 'Vergil as a Republican: *Aeneid* 6.815–35', in H.-P. Stahl (ed.), *Vergil's Aeneid: Augustan Epic and Political Context*, 1998, 101–18. The banishment of the last king as a blow struck for freedom: Aen. 6,817–21 and 8,646–51.

pp. 468–70 *The development of the Forum Romanum in the Augustan period*: See Paul Zanker, *Forum Romanum: Die Neugestaltung durch Augustus*, 1972 (with plans showing the different stages of development), and Nicholas Purcell, 'Forum Romanum', in Steinby, *Roma*, I, 336–9; on the Comitium, Filippo Coarelli, in Steinby, *Roma*, I, 309–14. On the fire in the Basilica Aemilia, also affecting other buildings in the central Forum, such as the temple of Castor and Pollux and the sanctuary of the Vestals: Cass. Dio 54,24,2ff. On the beginning of building on the Julian Forum: Cic. Att. 4,16,8 (1 July 54).

pp. 470–74 *On the Forum Augustum*: See Nash, *Rom*, I, 401–10; Valentin Kockel, 'Forum Augustum', in Steinby, *Roma*, II, 289–95; Paul Zanker, *Forum Augustum: Das Bildprogramm*, 1968, and idem, *Augustus*, 196ff.; Kolb, *Rom*, 358ff., as well as Joachim Ganzert, *Der Mars-Ultor-Tempel auf dem Augustusforum in Rom* (with appendices), 1996. On the pictorial programme and its origin see T. J. Luce, 'Livy, Augustus, and the Forum Augustum', in Raaflaub/Toher, 123–38, and José Luis de la Barrera/Walter Trillmich, 'Eine Wiederholung der Aeneas-Gruppe vom Forum Augustum samt ihrer Inschrift in Mérida (Spanien)', *Mitt. des Deutsch. Archäol. Inst. Röm.* 103, 1996, 119–38. The Temple of Mars Ultor and Augustus' vow to build it in 42 BC: Suet. Aug. 29,2; see p. 148 above; the plan for a larger forum prevented: Suet. Aug. 56,2; the senatorial decision on the quadriga in the Forum Augustum: Aug. RG 35; the inscription on the plinth: Vell. Pat. 2,39,2. On the *augurium augustum* see p. 291 above; Augustus as author of the eulogy for Scipio Aemilianus: Plin. nat. hist. 22,13. On the public ceremonies to be performed in the temple of Mars Ultor and its forecourt: Suet. Aug. 29,2; Cass. Dio 55,10,2–6; Aug. RG 29. The financing of the temple of Mars Ultor from plunder taken in war: Aug. RG 21. Quotation on the intention behind the programme of statues: Suet. Aug. 31,5: 'professus est edicto: commentum id se, ut ad illorum ... velut ad exemplar et ipse, dum viveret, et insequentium aetatium principes exigerentur a civibus'.

pp. 474–7 *The historical awareness of the time and the significance of the Roman spring in it*: Greeks and Romans in Virgil: 6,847–53, lines cited 851–3: 'tu regere imperio populos, Romane, memento / (hae tibi erunt artes), pacisque imponere morem, / parcere subiectis et debellare superbos'. Cicero on world rule as an aim of Roman policies: prov. cos. 30–35 (speech of the year 56 in favour of the prolongation of Caesar's governorship of Gaul); on peace as the justification of Roman rule: Cic. Quint. fr. 1,1,33ff. Augustus on the delegations from all over the world: Aug. RG 31. On the minting of coins by Augustan masters of the mint showing feats from their family history, see Kienast, *Augustus*, 324ff., citing further literature. The many kinds of antiquarian studies by Augustan literati also illustrate the growing interest in the early period, for instance Marcus Verrius Flaccus (*Fasti* among other works, on historical and antiquarian memorabilia), Gaius Julius Hyginus (a freedman of Augustus, who wrote among other works a little book about Trojan families, a large mythological work, and a work about Italian cities with a strong mythological element), as well as Dionysios of Halicarnassos (a Roman early history up to the First Punic War, emphasizing the early period). On the presentation of the early period in Augustan literature, see Matthew Fox, *Roman Historical Myths: The Regal Period in Augustan Literature*, 1996, and on the importance of the early Roman period for the political mythology of the Augustan age see Gerhard Binder, 'Vom Mythos zur Ideologie: Rom und seine Geschichte vor und bei Vergil', in G. Binder/B. Effe, *Mythos. Erzählende Weltdeutung im Spannungsfeld von Ritual, Geschichte und Rationalität*, 1990, 137–61, as well as Tonio Hölscher, 'Mythen als Exempel der Geschichte', in F. Graf (ed.), *Mythos in mythenloser Gesellschaft*, Colloquium Rauricum 3, 1993, 67–87, esp. 80ff. The linking of Latin and Roman history to Troy and thus to the early history of Greece through Aeneas preceded Virgil, but in presenting the landing of Aeneas in Latium (by means of a genealogical reference) as a *return*, he was the first to give it an internal necessity; see Werner Suerbaum, 'Aeneas zwischen Troja und Rom', *Poetica* 1, 1967, 176–204. If one removes from Aeneas those traits of character and conviction that Virgil breathed into him, there is not very much left, or anyway not much that is to do with Roman history; see, for instance, Gerhard Binder, 'Der brauchbare Held: Aeneas. Stationen der Funktionalisierung eines Ursprungsmythos', in H.-J. Horn/H. Walter (eds.), *Die Allegorese des antiken Mythos*, 1997, 311–30.

pp. 477–8 *The architecture and art of the Augustan period*: Zanker, *Augustus* (on the buildings, 110ff. and *passim*, on the ornamental vegetation motifs, 184ff.), has put together and interpreted the pictorial world of the Augustan age in a masterly manner. His book represents a new approach that opens the reader's eyes to the political importance of the architecture and ornamentation, the reliefs, the statues, and above all the great pictorial programme through the sum total of the architecture, architectural ornamentation and statues of the time. On certain points of criticism from the archaeological point of view see Angelika Geyer, *Göttingische Gelehrte Anzeige* 241, 1989, 192–8. On the buildings of Augustus in Rome see also Kolb, *Rom*, 330ff.; on the element of form see Galinsky, *Augustan Culture*, esp. 141ff., on the vegetation motifs see David Castriota, *The Ara Pacis Augustae and the Imagery of Abundance in Later Greek and Early Roman Imperial Art*, 1995, citing models for the theme of vegetative abundance in Pergamon and indicating their allusion to the world of the gods. Motifs from the public area on items for private use: see for instance Tonio Hölscher, 'Denkmäler der Schlacht von Actium. Propaganda und Resonanz', *Klio*, 67, 1985, 81–102, and in exhibition catalogue *Kaiser Augustus*, no. 201.

pp. 478–9 *The decline of the old forms of religion and the rise of the mystery cults and other religious cults*: See Latte, *Religionsgeschichte*, 264ff. (on Isis, 282ff.), 327ff.

pp. 479–81 *The trials of Cassius Severus, Titus Labienus and Cremutius Cordus, and the political role of the poets in the Augustan period*: On the trials, see Richard A. Bauman, *Impietas in Principem*, 1974, 28ff., 99ff. On the person and attitude of Labienus: Seneca controv. 10 praef. 4–8, in this passage §5, where the burning of his books is mentioned, the first case of its kind. On his trial, see Dieter Hennig, 'T. Labienus und der erste Majestätsprozess *de famosis libellis*', *Chiron* 3, 1973, 245–54. Augustus on Livy: Tac. ann. 4,34,3. On Marcus Antistius Labeo: Gell. 13,12,1ff.; Tac. ann. 3,75; Pomponius Digest 1,2,2,47. On praise of the murderers of Caesar under Augustus, see the speech in their defence by Cremutius Cordus in the year AD 25, Tac. ann. 4,34,2–35,3; the description of Cassius as the last Roman (*Romanorum ultimum*), in this passage, 34,1. See also Suet. Tib. 61,3 and Cass. Dio 57,24,3. The works of Antony and Brutus still read even in the late Augustan period: Ovid ex Ponto, 1,1,23f. The *Anticato* (*rescripta Bruto de Catone*) of Augustus: Suet. Aug. 85,1. On the poets, see Erich Burck, 'Die Rolle des Dichters und der Gesellschaft in der augusteischen Dichtung', *Antike u. Abendland* 21, 1975, 12–35; Douglas Little, 'Politics in Augustan Poetry' (citing further literature), in ANRW II 30,1, 1982, 254–370; and above all Peter White, *Promised Verse: Poets in the Society of Augustan Rome*, 1993, pointing out the relative independence of poets from Augustus and the men close to him. According to Kienast, *Augustus*, 218ff., the Augustan poets were strongly influenced by Augustus; he claims, probably because of much formal imitation of the Hellenistic panegyrics to rulers, that 'in so far as they were writing political poetry, it was court art' (229), and gets carried away, saying that 'Virgil and Horace were in a way the archegetes of court poetry' (232). His comments on Ovid, 247ff., are much freer of reservations. On the relationship of Augustus to the poets, see also the well-balanced account by Jasper Griffin, 'Augustus and the Poets: "Caesar qui cogere posset"', in Millar/Segal, *Augustus*, 189–218; on the relationship of Augustus to the historians, see Mark Toher, 'Augustus and the Evolution of Roman Historiography', in Raaflaub/Toher, 139–54; on the role of myth among the poets, including myth as covert reference to the present, Tonio Hölscher (as p. 692 above).

p. 482 *The portraiture of Augustus*: I will mention, out of the extensive literature on the subject, Erika Simon, *Augustus. Kunst und Leben in Rom um die Zeitenwende*, 1986, and in particular Paul Zanker, 'Studien zu den Augustus-Porträts I. Der Actium-Typus', *Abhandl. d. Göttinger Akad. d. Wiss.*, phil.-histor. Kl. 3, 85, 1973. See also Klaus Vierneisel/Paul Zanker, *Die Bildnisse des Augustus* (catalogue of exhibition in Munich), 1979; Klaus Fittschen, 'Die Bildnisse des Augustus', in Binder, *Saeculum Augustum*, III, 149–86; and Dietrich Boschung, 'Die Bildnisse des Augustus', *Das römische Herrscherbild* I, 2, 1993. There is considerable controversy, but Zanker and Fittschen put forward convincing arguments for their interpretations. The problem lies in the variety of forms of representation and the fact that we have no portrait of Augustus in the original form as created in Rome, or directly derived from it. The first type is known as the Actium type (Zanker) or, because it can also be shown to have existed before Actium, as the Octavian type (Fittschen); the main type as the Prima Porta type (after the statue of Augustus in armour found in Prima Porta and dating from about 20–17 BC) or as the Principate type (Fittschen); and the last – after the original owner of a copy of it – as the Forbes type. Boschung has set out and distinguished between examples of the early type in particular, but also of the later ones, and has drawn up a catalogue of all portrait busts of Augustus. The Prima Porta type was the most widespread; about two-thirds of all the *c.* 160 portraits of Augustus derive from it.

## CHAPTER 13
## Explanatory Notes

pp. 483–9 *On the Roman army*: There is a great deal of literature on the Roman army. I will mention general works that touch on the Augustan period among others: Kromayer/Veith, *Heerwesen*; Watson, *Soldier*; Campbell, *Army*; Parker, *Legions*; and Saddington, *Auxiliary Forces*, 77ff. On the Augustan army in particular, see Kurt Raaflaub, 'Die Militärreformen des Augustus und die politische Problematik des frühen Prinzipats', in Binder, *Saeculum Augustum*, I, 246–307, and Keppie, *Army*, 132ff., 145ff. On the banners and standards, on religion and on army pay see Alfred von Domaszewski, *Aufsätze zur römischen Heeresgeschichte*, 1972 (a collection of essays from the years 1885, 1895 and 1899); on the everyday life of the soldiers see Roy William Davies, 'The Daily Life of the Roman Soldier under the Principate', in ANRW II 1, 1974, 299–338. On the structural development of the army, particularly in the 200 years between the reformer Marius and the high imperial period, see Werner Dahlheim, 'Die Armee eines Weltreiches: Der römische Soldat und sein Verhältnis zu Staat und Gesellschaft', *Klio* 74, 1992, 197–220.

pp. 489–90 *The soldiers' pay*: See Marquardt, *Verwaltung*, II, 92ff.; Peter A. Brunt, 'Pay and Superannuation in the Roman Army', *Papers of the British School at Rome* 18, 1950, 50–71; Parker, *Legions*, 214ff.; and Watson, *Soldier*, 89ff. The doubling of pay by Caesar: Suet. Div. Jul. 26,3; Augustus: Suet. Aug. 49,2. Bounty paid on Gaius Caesar's first participation in a campaign: Cass. Dio 55,6,4. On the *aerarium militare*, see p. 360 above. The income from Gallia Comata: Suet. Div. Jul. 25,1; from the provinces reorganized by Pompey: Plut. Pomp. 45,4.

pp. 490–91 *Discussions among the soldiers of their problems as long-serving members of the army*: Tac. ann. 1,17. Length of service: Cass. Dio 54,25,5ff., 55,24,8 (*evocati*); Tac. ann., as above. Provision for them: Aug. RG 16; Cass. Dio 55,23,1.

pp. 491–3 *The number of legions in the year 27 BC and their emblems*: After lengthy and controversial arguments, Mommsen's opinion that Augustus had only eighteen legions in 27 BC, and after some changes had twenty-five at the end of his reign, a figure named by Tacitus for the year AD 23, has been generally abandoned today. Cass. Dio 55,23,2 and 55,24,8 speaks of the contradictory nature of his sources, sometime giving figures of twenty-three and sometimes of twenty-five legions. See the discussion in Ritterling, 'Legio', 1216ff., and Parker, *Legions*, 72ff., 78ff. and 281ff. (enumerating the separate legions and their fate in the Augustan period). Ronald Syme, 'Some Notes on the Legions under Augustus', *Journ. Rom. Stud.* 23, 1933, 14–33 (see the list on p. 33) assumes, as his starting point, twenty-eight legions soon after the year 25. As well as the initial and final number of legions in the years from 27 BC to AD 14, the raising of new legions and the discontinuing of old ones are discussed, the only factor agreed upon by all writers being the annihilation of the three legions commanded by Varus (nos. 17, 18 and 19). A Legio Augusta deprived of its epithet by Agrippa: Cass. Dio 54,11,5. Dio on the legions of Augustus still in existence in his time: Cass. Dio 55,23,2–7. The forced recruitment of the Rhaetians: Cass. Dio 54,22,5; on the Breuci see p. 534 below.

pp. 493–5 *The fleet in the Augustan period*: See Chester G. Starr, *The Roman Imperial Navy 31 BC–AD 324*, 1941, and Dietmar Kienast, *Untersuchungen zu den Kriegsflotten der römischen Kaiserzeit*, 1966, esp. 9ff. On the ships built at Actium and brought to the Forum Julii: Tac. ann., 4,5,1. On the Julian Harbour, see p. 184 above.

pp. 495–8 *The recruitment of the legions, auxiliaries, crew for the fleet and the military detachments stationed in Rome*: Extensive literature is available, mainly based on inscriptions. Of this, I will mention: Theodor Mommsen, 'Die Conscriptionsordnung der römischen Kaiserzeit', in idem, *Ges. Schr.*, VI,

20–117 (first published in *Hermes* 19, 1884), which is still a basis for such studies, as are the works of Giovanni Forni, including especially: *Il recluta-mento delle legioni da Augusto a Diocleziano*, 1953, and idem, *Esercito e marina di Roma antica*, 1992. See also Konrad Kraft, *Zur Rekrutierung der Alen und Kohorten an Rhein und Donau*, 1951 (without a summary of the material relevant to the Augustan period in particular). On the *primipilares*, see Brian Dobson, 'The Significance of the Centurion and "Primipilaris" in the Roman Army and Administration', in ANRW II 1, 1974, 395ff., and idem, *Die Primipilares*, 1978, 6ff. Our first evidence for the *numerus primipilarium* is for the year AD 16, from Tac. ann. 2,11,1.

pp. 498–500 *The relationship between princeps and soldier*: See Anton von Pre-merstein, *Vom Werden und Wesen des Prinzipats*, 1937, esp. 13ff. and 36ff., even seeing patronage, through an extension of its significance, as a form of rule that was the institutional basis of the principate; also Volker Fadinger, *Die Begründung des Prinzipats*, 1969, 272ff., and Peter Herrmann, *Der römische Kaisereid*, 1968, 100ff. and *passim*. On the soldiers' veneration of the emperor, especially in pictorial form, see Hans Ankersdorfer, *Studien zur Religion des römischen Heeres von Augustus bis Diokletian*, 1973 (an import-ant but purely systematic presentation, without any summary of the material relevant to the Augustan period). Augustus changes his way of addressing the soldiers: Suet. Aug. 25,1.

pp. 500–502 *The movement of troops in the Augustan period*: See Ronald Syme, 'Some Notes on the Legions under Augustus', *Journ. Rom. Stud.* 23, 1933, 14–33. With his claim that Augustus did not introduce a standing army but that it had been in existence for a long time, R. E. Smith, *Service in the Post-Marian Roman Army*, 1958, 70ff., fails to recognize that the situation under Augustus was entirely changed from what it had been in the late republican period.

pp. 502–3 *The camps*: On Castra Vetera, compare Harald von Petrikovits under 'Vetera', in RE VIII A, 1958, 1815ff., and C. M. Wells, *The German Policy of Augustus: An Examination of the Archaeological Evidence*, 1972, 99ff., to the excavations at Neuss resumed by Harald von Petrikovits, in *Bonner Jahrb.* 161, 1961, 455ff., and Wells, op. cit., 127ff.

## CHAPTER 14

# Explanatory Notes

pp. 505–9 *Theories of the motive for the expansion*: The thesis that Augustus was pursuing a purely defensive policy has probably been most cogently put by Hans D. Meyer, *Die Aussenpolitik des Augustus und die augusteische Dich-tung*, 1961, according to whom 'Augustus . . . firmly placed his foreign policy on a fundamentally defensive basis', but then Meyer has to expend a great deal of (useless) energy on accounting for the tone of the Augustan poets, which firmly contradicts that idea. The opposite position is represented by such scholars as C. M. Wells, *The German Policy of Augustus*, 1972, 3–13, who sees Augustus as a conqueror of the world, backing up his thesis with sources speaking of Roman world domination, and quoting Virg. Aen. 1,278ff. as the political credo of Augustus (p. 13). A decade before Wells, Peter Brunt, in *Journ. Roman. Stud.* 53, 1963, esp. 175, gave us a calculation based on ideas of classical antiquity of the size (or according to him small size) of the world, which might have made Augustus feel a desire to conquer the whole of it; see also R. Moynihan, 'Geographical Mythology and Roman Imperial Ideology', in Winkes, *Augustus*, 149–62. Andreas Mehl, 'Imperium sine fine dedi – die augusteische Vorstellung von der Grenzenlosigkeit des Römischen Reiches', in E. Olshausen/H. Sonnabend (eds.), *Stuttgarter Colloquium zur historischen Geographie des Altertums* 4, 1990, also thinks he can see the geographical conquest of the world as a foreign policy that could have appealed to Augustus as being possible to realize; in old age, he suggests, Augustus then reduced it to the area within the boundaries set by rivers, but still carried out his ambition by upholding the claim to dominion of the world 'in a world of deception ... and self-deception' (p. 464). In contrast to him, while Karl-Wilhelm Welwei, 'Römische Weltherrschaftsideologie und augusteische Germanienpolitik', *Gymnasium* 93, 1986, 118–37, also speaks in terms of Roman domination of the world, to that extent ruling out 'the existence of other powers and centres of power' (p. 120), he does speak accurately of an *ideology* of world rule. Hans Erich Stier, 'Augustusfriede und römische Klassik', in ANRW II 2, 1975, 33ff., among others, suggests that threat was the motive, while Klaus Bringmann, 'Weltherrschaft und innere Krise Roms im Spiegel der Geschichtsschreibung des zweiten und ersten Jahrhunderts v. Chr.', *Antike u. Abendland* 23, 1977, 46ff., ascribes the initiative to Augustus and distinguishes between an ideological 'imperialism' and a practical and 'extensively designed' policy of security. The idea of a river border formed by the Elbe and the Danube, popular with many scholars, is supported by Alfred Heuss, *Römische Geschichte*, 1976[4], 303ff., esp. 306 ('the creation of a river border'). Since the German campaigns in fact made the border shorter, Friedrich Vittinghoff, *Kaiser Augustus*, 1959, 1991[3], 87, thinks: 'The policy of the west was now directed by the basic idea of enclosing the *imperium*, rounding it off geographically, and giving it shorter and, as it were, natural borders', while even so expert a scholar as Harald von Petrikovits, *Rheinische Geschichte*, I, 1: *Altertum*, 1978, 54, thinks that Agrippa and Augustus planned 'to shorten the angle of the Danube and the Rhine, perhaps by using the line of the Elbe as a hypotenuse'. Karlheinz Dietz, in W. Czysz et al. (eds.), *Die Römer in Bayern*, 1995, 37ff., takes a similar line. Dieter Timpe, 'Die politische Wirklichkeit und ihre Folgen', in K. Büchner (ed.), *Latein und Europa*, 1978, 65, in my opinion takes a more sober view and assesses

Augustus' foreign policy in a way more adequate to the political and military situation at the start of expansion, when he sees it as a policy of security against enemy attack and, in connection with that, the creation of a link between the Gallic and Macedonian areas. Karl Christ, 'Zur augusteischen Germanienpolitik', *Chiron* 7, 1977, 183–203 (with a good account of his research work), and idem, *Geschichte der römischen Kaiserzeit*, 1988, 132ff., setting out from the idea of initially rather tentative progress from the Rhine border, prefers to see expansion as a policy of consolidation, and warns readers against assuming that there was a single concept of how it might turn out in the end. The quotation from Virgil: Aen. 1,278ff.: 'his ego nec metas rerum nec tempora pono: / imperium sine fine dedi'. In using the term 'world' we must remember that the Romans, like the Greeks, understood it to mean primarily landscapes inhabited by human beings, the 'inhabited earth' (*oikouméne*), and the Romans also described it as 'the circle of lands' (*orbis terrarum*). They had before their eyes only the historically known parts of the earth, and particularly the Mediterranean world. Pictorially, the 'world' often appears as a globe (sometimes with Victoria on top of it symbolizing Roman rule of the world). Although the Greeks had known that the world was a globe for a long time, and it was also known in Roman times – only a zone in the northern hemisphere was thought to be habitable – this knowledge had the idea of a disc resting on the seas of the world superimposed on it. The globe surmounted by Victoria might be taken as the globe of the earth, but above all the globe also stood for the entire world formed by planets and heavenly bodies (the globe of heaven, the globe of all the world), and, as such, it could symbolize Roman dominion. When the globe of heaven is linked to Augustus, he appears to have moved into the divine world and is associated with Jupiter, the true ruler of heaven. See on the form of the 'world' Johanna Schmidt, 'Oikumene', in RE XVII, 1937, 2123–74, and Joseph Vogt, 'Orbis Romanus: Ein Beitrag zum Sprachgebrauch und zur Vorstellungswelt des römischen Imperialimus', in idem, *Orbis: Ausgewählte Schriften zur Geschichte des Altertums*, 1960, 151–71.

p. 509 *The 'province' of Germania*: When Flor. epit. 2,30,21ff. writes that in honour of Caesar (the dictator), who twice crossed the Rhine, Augustus wished to make Germania a province ('Germaniam ... in illius honorem concupierat facere provinciam'), it is a view after the event, but gives an indication that after the campaigns of Drusus (at the earliest) the idea of such a province had formed.

pp. 509–10 *Unrest on the borders*: Cass. Dio 54,20,1–5. The 'defeat of Lollius': Vell. Pat. 2,97,1; Cass. Dio 54,20,4ff.; Suet. Aug. 23,1; Tac. ann. 1,10,4.

pp. 510–14 *The campaigns of Drusus and Tiberius in the Alpine area*: Vell. Pat. 2,95,1ff.; Cass. Dio 4,22; Strab. 7,1,5 (the battle on the lake; march to the sources of the Danube); 4,6,8 (the places of settlement and ferocity of the Rhaetians and Vindelicians); Flor. epit. 2,22 (on the wildness of their women).

The inscription on the monument in honour of Augustus has come down to us word for word in Plin. nat. hist. 3,137ff., and small remains of the original have been found near the site of the monument itself (CIL V 2,7817); on the remains of the monument and its reconstruction see Jules Formigé, *Le Trophée des Alpes (La Turbie)*, 1949. On the Alpine campaign see Karl Christ, 'Zur römischen Okkupation der Zentralalpen und des nördlichen Alpenvorlandes', *Historia* 6, 1957, 416–28; W. Drack/R. Fellmann (eds.), *Die Römer in der Schweiz*, 1988, 22ff., and also, on various subjects, including the Rhaetians and Vindelicians and the beginnings of Roman rule, Felix Stähelin, *Die Schweiz in römischer Zeit*, 1931², 95ff. and *passim*; Richard Heuberger, *Rätien im Altertum und Frühmittelalter*, 1932; Richard Heuberger, in RE IX A, 1961, 1ff.; Franz Schön, *Der Beginn der römischen Herrschaft in Rätien*, 1986 (on this subject see Hartmut Wolff on the beginning of Roman Rhaetium, in *Journ. Rom. Archaeolog.* 3, 1990, 407–14); and Werner Eck, 'Senatorische Amtsträger und Rätien unter Augustus', *Zeitschr. für Papyrologie und Epigr.* 70, 1987, 203–9. See also Karlheinz Dietz, 'Gründe für Roms Alpenfeldzug', in W. Czysz et al. (eds.), *Die Römer in Bayern*, 1995, 37ff., and Hartmut Wolff, 'Raetia', in CAH² X, 535ff. On the question of the destruction of Manching, see Karl Christ, 'Germanienpolitik' (as p. 698 above), 167–83 (his conclusions are tentative). On the camp of Dangstetten, see Gerhard Fingerlin, in Philipp Filtzinger et al. (eds.), *Die Römer in Baden-Württemberg*, 1976², 253ff. Horace, who had already stopped writing odes, is said to have been inspired or commanded by Augustus to add his fourth book of odes on the victories in the Alpine area, but only two of the odes refer to these victories. Drusus was originally called Decimus Claudius Drusus. His elder brother Tiberius did not change his name of Tiberius Claudius Nero until his adoption by Augustus; after it he used the name of Tiberius Julius Caesar, and as *princeps* (*imperator*) he called himself Tiberius Caesar Augustus. On Noricum: Strab. 5,1,8 tells us of its occupation after the Alpine campaign of Drusus and Tiberius; see Géza Alföldy, *Noricum*, 1974, 52ff.; Gerhard Winkler, 'Noricum und Rom', in ANRW II 6, 1977, 183ff., and Peter Kneissl, 'Zur Entstehung der Provinz Noricum', *Chiron* 9, 1979, 261–73 (it remained independent until the time of the Emperor Claudius). Unrest in the Illyrian area between 14 and 9 BC: Vell. Pat. 2,96,2ff.; Cass. Dio 54,34,3ff., 36,2ff. and 55,2,4.

pp. 516–19 *The German campaigns of Drusus*: Our main source is Vell. Pat. 2,97,2ff. (he disparages the achievements of Drusus compared with those of Tiberius); see also Cass. Dio 54,32–3, 36,3–4 and 55,1; Tac. ann 4,72,1; Suet. Claud. 1,2; Flor. epit. 2,30,23–8. The prophecy to Drusus on the Elbe: Suet. Claud. 1,2; Cass. Dio 55,1,3ff. The camp of Aliso is mentioned again, in connection with the Varus catastrophe, by Vell. Pat. 2,120,4 and Tac. ann. 2,7,3. The camp of Oberaden, on the river Lippe east of Haltern, also belongs to the Drusus period; it was probably a little older than Haltern. The camp mentioned by Cass. Dio 54,33,3 as being established by Drusus in the land of the Chatti directly on the Rhine (and therefore not Rödgen) has not been identified. On the campaigns of Drusus and on the following years up to the catastrophe of Varus and his legions, see in particular, as well as the main authorities, Dieter Timpe's well-balanced account, 'Zur Geschichte und Über-lieferung der Okkupation Germaniens unter Augustus', in *Saeculum* 18, 1967, 278–93; idem, 'Zur Geschichte der Rheingrenze zwischen Caesar und Drusus', in E. Lefèvre (ed.), *Monumentum Chiloniense*, 1975, 124–47; and idem, 'Drusus' Umkehr an der Elbe', *Rhein. Museum* 110, 1967, 289–306, as well as Hans Schönberger, 'The Roman Frontier in Germany: An Archaeologi-cal Survey', *Journ. Rom. Stud.* 59, 1969, 144ff., and Reinhard Wolters, *Römische Eroberung und Herrschaftsorganisation in Gallien und Germ-anien*, 1990, 153ff. (Drusus) and 223 (Varus). On the geographical questions, see again Dieter Timpe, 'Entdeckungsgeschichte des Nordens in der Antike', *Reallexikon der Germanischen Altertumskunde* 7, 1989, esp. 247ff. On the legions' camps on the Rhine at this time see Hans Schönberger, op. cit., and Harald von Petrikovits, 'Die Ausgrabungen in Neuss', *Bonner Jahrb.* 161, 1961, 449–85; on the commanders and troops on the Rhine see Ernst Stein, *Die kaiserlichen Beamten und Truppenkörper im römischen Deutschland unter dem Prinzipat*, 1932, new edn 1965, a book that in spite of many correc-tions to details is still indispensable. On Lugdunum, see P. Wuilleumier, *Lyon métropole des Gaules*, 1953, and Jürgen Deininger, *Die Provinziallandtage der römischen Kaiserzeit*, 1965, 21ff. and 99ff.

p. 520 *The funeral of Drusus and the honours paid to him*: Suet. Claud. 1,3–5 (also for the eulogy and Augustus' biography of him); Cass. Dio 55,2. On the speech of consolation that has come down to us attributed to Ovid, but writ-ten at the earliest in the late Augustan period, and probably rather later, see Henk Schoonhoven, *The Pseudo-Ovidian ad Liviam de morte Drusi (Conso-latio ad Liviam, Epicedium Drusi): A Critical Text with Introduction and Commentary*, 1992. According to Schoonhoven, it was not written until the early Neronian period. On the honorific Germanicus, see Peter Kneissl, *Die Siegestitulatur der römischen Kaiser*, 1969, 27ff.

pp. 520–22 *The detention of the envoys and the conquests of Drusus*: According to Cass. Dio 55,6,3, the envoys were detained on the orders of Augustus. Vell. Pat. 2,97,3ff. on the conquest of Germania by Drusus: 'sed illum [sc. Drusus] magna ex parte domitorem Germaniae ... quod is [sc. Tiberius] ... adminis-travit peragratusque victor omnis partis Germaniae sine ullo detrimento commissi exercitus ... sic perdomuit eam, ut in formam paene stipendiariae redigeret provinciae'. The extension of the *pomerium* by Augustus: Cass. Dio 55,6,6 on the year 8 BC; see also Tac. ann. 12,23,2 (as in Mommsen, *Staats-recht*, II, 1072 note 3). On the withdrawal of Tiberius from public life and his return to it, see pp. 572ff. below.

pp. 523–4 *Domitius on the Elbe*: Tac. ann. 4,44,2; Cass. Dio 55,10a,3. The corduroy roads laid out by Domitius: Tac. ann. 1,63,3ff.; the great revolt towards the end of his governorship: Vell. Pat. 2,104,2 (*immensum bellum*); Cass. Dio 55,10a,3. On the campaigns in Germania after Drusus see, besides the literature mentioned on pp. 699–700 above, in particular Dieter Timpe, 'Geographische Faktoren und politische Entscheidungen in der Geschichte der Varuszeit', in R. Wiegels/W. Woesler (eds.), *Arminius und die Varusschlacht: Geschichte – Mythos – Literatur*, 1995, 13–27; Martin Pietsch/ Dieter Timpe/L. Wamser, 'Das augusteische Truppenlager Marktbreit', *Bericht der Röm.-German. Kommission* 72, 1991, 264–324; and Martin Pietsch, 'Das augusteische Legionslager Marktbreit. Aktuelles zum Forschungsstand', in Wiegels/Woesler (eds.), *Arminius und die Varusschlacht* (op. cit.), 41–66. On the ethnic provenance of the tribes in Germania at this time (Germans and Celts), see Jörg Heiligmann, 'Die Bevölkerung im süddeutschen Raum in augusteischer und frühtiberischer Zeit', in Wiegels/Woesler (eds.), *Arminius und die Varusschlacht* (op. cit.), 29–39.

pp. 525–6 *Tiberius back as commander on the Rhine*: The return of Tiberius to the Rhine: Vell. Pat. 2,104,3ff.; Velleius as cavalry colonel in Tiberius' troops: Vell. Pat. 2,104,3; the campaigns of the year AD 4/5, with the expedition of the fleet, ibid. 2,105ff.; Aug. RG 26; Cass. Dio 55,28,5ff.; Plin. nat. hist. 2,167 (the farthest part of the voyage the *Cimbrorum promontorium*); Tiberius on the banks of the Elbe: Vell. Pat. 2,107 (his time there is regarded by Velleius as the culmination of the campaigns in Germania). Quotation from Velleius after the end of the campaign in the year 4: Vell. Pat. 2,106,1: 'perlustrata armis tota Germania est', after the end of the campaign in the year 5: Vell. Pat. 2,108,1: 'nihil erat iam in Germania, quod vinci posset, praeter gentem Marcomannorum'.

p. 527 *The camps on the Lippe and the Main*: See Schönberger (op. cit.), 147ff., and C. M. Wells, *The German Policy of Augustus*, 1972, 149ff.; on Xanten and the fortified camps on the Lippe in particular, Johann-Sebastian Kühlborn, *Germaniam pacavi – Germanien habe ich befriedet*, 1995, 59ff. (Xanten, Holsterhausen, Haltern, Oberaden, Beckinghausen and Anreppen), as well as Tilmann Bechert/Willem J. H. Willems, *Die römische Reichsgrenze von der Mosel bis zur Nordseeküste*, 1995, 29ff. (Xanten, the fortified camps on the Lippe). On Haltern see also Siegmar von Schnurbein, *Die römischen Militäranlagen bei Haltern*, Bodenaltertümer Westfalens 14, 1974, 1981², and Konrad Kraft, 'Das Enddatum des Legionslagers Haltern', in *Bonner Jahrb.* 155/6, 95–111 (the numismatic evidence suggests that it was vacated after the defeat of Varus); on the newly discovered camp of Marktbreit see Dieter Timpe, op. cit., 'Das augusteische Truppenlager Marktbreit' (p. 318 on the possibility that there was a chain of permanent camps along the Main), and Martin Pietsch, op. cit., 'Das augusteische Legionslager Marktbreit'.

p. 528 *The Germans of the Elbe*: See Rafael v. Uslar, 'Bemerkungen zu einer Karte germanischer Funde der älteren Kaiserzeit', *Germania* 29, 1951, 44–7 (on the density of settlement in the valley of the Elbe and northern Bohemia); idem, 'Archäologische Fundgruppen und germanische Stammesgebiete vornehmlich aus der Zeit um Christi Geburt', *Histor. Jahrb.* 71, 1952, 1–36; Otto Schlüter, *Die Siedlungsräume Mitteleuropas in frühgeschichtlicher Zeit*, part 1 (introduction), 1952, part 2 (on southern and north-western central Europe), 1953, esp. 39ff. and 179ff.; Karl Peschel, *Anfänge germanischer Besiedlung im Mittelgebirgsraum, Sueben – Hermunduren – Markomannen*, 1978, esp. 72ff.; Torsten Capelle, *Studien über elbgermanische Gräberfelder in der ausgehenden Latènezeit und der älteren römischen Kaiserzeit*, 1971; G. Mildenberger, 'Elbgermanen', *Reallexikon der Germanischen Altertumskunde* 7, 1989, 107–13; W. I. Stöckli, 'Römer, Kelten und Germanen. Probleme von Kontinuität und Diskontinuität zur Zeit von Caesar und Augustus zwischen Hochrhein und Rheinmündung', *Bonner Jahrb.* 193, 1993, 121–40, as well as Timpe, 'Zur Geschichte und Überlieferung' (as p. 700 above). There is a map showing the density of settlements between the Rhine and the Elbe in B. Krüger (ed.), *Die Germanen: Ein Handbuch*, I, 1976, 1985[5], p. 384.

p. 528 *Preliminary stages for making a province of Germania*: Cass. Dio 56,18,1–3. According to Welwei, 'Römische Weltherrschaftsideologie' (as p. 697 above), Augustus limited his policy of occupation in Germania 'in essence to the Lippe corridor' (p. 136), in principle following only a policy of 'deterrence or rather terrorization' in the area.

pp. 528–30 *Marbod, the plan for a Marcomanni war; it begins and is then cut short*: Vell. Pat. 2,108–110,2; Cass. Dio 55,30,1; Tac. ann. 2,46,2. Velleius on Marbod and the danger that he presented: Vell. Pat. 2,108–9. The quotation: 2,108.2: 'Maroboduus . . . natione magis quam ratione barbarus'; the size of Marbod's army: Vell. Pat. 2,109,2. The distance between the Alps and Marbod's empire: Vell. Pat. 2,109,4. The march and the cutting short of the Marcomanni campaign: Vell. Pat. 2,109,5–110,1ff.; the plan to unite the two columns of the army at a prearranged place ('in praedicto loco'): Vell. Pat. 2,110,2; the direction of march of Saturninus and Tiberius: Vell. Pat. 2,109,5: 'Sentio Saturnino mandatum, ut per Cattos excisis continentibus Hercyniae silvis legiones Boiohaemum (id regioni, quam incolebat Maroboduus, nomen est), ipse [sc. Tiberius] a Carnunto'; treaty concluded with Marbod: Tac. ann 2,46,2; see on Marbod and his rule of the Bohemian area also Strab. 7,1,3. When Velleius Paterculus, 2,122,2, speaks of three consecutive campaigns in Germania by Tiberius after his adoption, he is counting the one against Marbod.

pp. 530–37 *The Pannonian-Dalmatian rising*: Our main sources are Vell. Pat. 2,110,2–117,1 (110,4 on the aims of the rebels; 111,3 on the attitude of Velleius himself to the army at this time); Cass. Dio 55,29–34, 56,11–17. On particular points: Suet. Aug. 25,2; Cass. Dio 55,31,1 and 4 (the recruitment of freedmen, new taxes); Vell. Pat. 2,111,1 (Augustus in the Senate); Vell. Pat.

2,113,1, see Suet. Tib. 16,1 (the numbers of Tiberius' troops); Vell. Pat. 2.112.4–6; Cass. Dio 55,32,3 (Caecina and Plautius in difficulties); Vell. Pat. 2,114,1–3, 115,4 (Tiberius as a general thoughtful of his men); Suet. Tib. 17,2 (honours for Tiberius); Vell. Pat. 2,117,1 (the reference in his remark 'tantum quod ultimam imposuerat Pannonico ac Delmatico bello Caesar manum, cum intra quinque consummati tanti operis dies funestae ex Germania epistulae nuntium attulere caesi Vari trucidatarumque legionum trium' is certainly not to be related to the last struggle in Pannonia but to the decision of the Senate to honour Tiberius at the end of the war). The man who now took over the Pannonian command, Marcus Aemilius Lepidus, was a grandson of Lucius Aemilius Paullus, consul in the year 50 BC, who was proscribed in the year 43 but whose life was then spared, and thus was a great-nephew of the triumvir. His brother Lucius was married to Julia, Augustus' granddaughter, and was executed at the time of the scandal of the year AD 8. On uprisings in the area and Roman intervention after 13 BC, as well as the general topographical and ethnic context, see Andreas Mócsy, in RE Suppl. IX, 1962, 544–8; J. J. Wilkes, *Dalmatia*, 1969, 46–77; and Ronald Syme, 'Augustus and the South Slav in Lands', in idem, *Danubian Papers*, 1971, 13–25; on the roads in Illyricum see Andreas Mócsy, op. cit., 658ff. On the Gemma Augustea see the information, particularly the naming of the figures discussed, in Megow, *Kameen*, 8ff. and 155ff. (illustrations, plates 3–5); Megow limits its dating to somewhere between AD 4 and 14. See also Heinz Kähler, 'Die Gemma Augustea', in idem, *Rom und seine Welt*, I, 1960, 186–8 (= idem in Binder, *Saeculum Augustum*, III, 303–7), and Zanker, *Augustus*, 232ff. It has been claimed that the scene shown on the gem could be the return of Tiberius from his campaign in Germania in the year 12, but in that case the warrior beside the triumphal chariot cannot be Germanicus, who being consul at the time would have had to be shown in his consular insignia; for the interpretation presented in the text, see finally Helmut Prückner, 'Die Stellung des Tiberius: Vorschlag für eine Ergänzung der Gemma Augustea', in G. Erath et al. (eds.), *Kosmos: Festschr. für Th. Lorenz*, 1997, 718ff.

p. 537 *The altar of the Ubii*: See Fishwick, *Cult*, I, 137ff.; Hermann Schmitz, in RE VIII A, 1955, 539ff., and Otto Doppelfeld, 'Das römische Köln: I. Ubier-Oppidum und Colonia Agrippinensium', in ANRW II 4, 1975, 718ff.

p. 538 *Varus as governor in Germania*: Varus as governor: Cass. Dio 56,18,2 and Vell. Pat. 2,117,2–118 (Velleius is particularly critical of him), as well as Flor. epit. 30,31; see on this subject Dieter Timpe, *Arminius-Studien*, 1970, 81–116; on Varus in general, Walther John, in RE XXIV, 1963, 907–84, as well as the works listed on pp. 696ff. above.

pp. 538–40 *The course of the battle in the Teutoburger Forest*: Vell. Pat. 2,119; Cass. Dio 56,18–22 (the construction of obstacles and fortifications by the Germanic tribesmen: 20,1; storms, rain and slippery ground: 20,3, cf. Tac. ann. 1,61,1; the terrain allowed no proper marching order: 19,4ff., cf. Vell.

Pat. 2,119,2); Flor. epit. 2,32–9. Aliso stormed and at first held: Vell. Pat. 2.120,4; Cass. Dio/Zonaras 56,22,2a.

p. 540–41 *The location of the battle and the latest excavations, still in progress at the time of writing*: The early identification by Mommsen: Theodor Mommsen, 'Die Örtlichkeit der Varus-Schlacht', *Sitz.ber. d. Preuss. Akad. d. Wiss.*, 1885, 63–92 (= idem, *Ges. Schr.*, IV, 1906, 200–246). Previous attempts to identify the site: John (op. cit.), 951ff. There has also been speculation that the Roman troops, whose defeat is well documented by the site of the Kalkriese excavations, were marching from west to east, e.g. recently by Klaus Tausend, 'Wohin wollte Varus?', *Klio* 79, 1997, 372–82 (Varus was moving north-east from the Rhine against the Angrivarii). On the many problems of investigation and excavation in the Kalkriese area, as well as criticism of the sources of antiquity, and of the after-life of the battle fought by Varus, particularly its nationalistic interpretation, see Wolfgang Schlüter (ed., and director of the excavations at Mount Kalkriese), *Kalkriese. Römer im Osnabrücker Land* (contributions and exhibition catalogue), 1993 (on the excavations see, among others, Wolfgang Schlüter, 13ff., and Susanne Wilbers-Rost, 53ff., as well as Frank Berger, 211ff. on the finds of coins, and by the same author, summarizing the latest state of our knowledge, *Kalkriese I: Die römischen Fundmünzen*, 1996). See also Wiegels/Woesler (eds.), *Arminius* (as p. 701 above, esp. Wolfgang Schlüter, 'Neue Erkenntnisse zur Örtlichkeit der Varusschlacht? Die archäologischen Untersuchungen in der Kalkrieser-Niewedder Senke im Vorland des Wiehengebirges', 67–95). The account given by Tacitus ann. 1,61–2: 'ductum inde agmen [sc. the Roman army under Germanicus] ad ultimos Bructerorum, quantumque Amisiam et Lupiam amnes inter vastatum, haud procul Teutoburgiensi saltu, in quo reliquiae Vari legionumque insepultae dicebantur'. Confirmation by Germanicus' army of the identity of the bones of those who fell in the battle: Tac. ann 1,61–2. In assessing the finds we have to remember that the battlefield was thoroughly searched by the Germanic tribesmen, hardly anything was left lying where it was, and the bodies of the dead were stripped. Only items covered up, that is to say those that had sunk or been trodden into the marshy ground during the fighting, can still be brought to light today. The many widely scattered finds of coins, and the metal items – 1,500 found up to 1996, including some 600 large items – then speak for themselves. The finds at Kalkriese have not entirely ended the search for the site of Varus' battle; many classical scholars are still sceptical about the assessment of the excavations. A recent essay by a 'layman' who is not only interested in the subject but familiar with the professional requirements for evaluation is the small book by Manfred Millhoff, *Die Varusschlacht – Anatomie eines Mythos*, 1995; he thinks that the site of the battle is to be sought north of Paderborn and identifies the fortified camp of Aliso with Paderborn itself.

pp. 542–3 *Arminius*: Tacitus on Arminius: ann. 2,88,2: 'liberator haud dubie Germaniae'; cf. Cass. Dio 56,18,4 (according to him, the Germanic tribesmen preferred the usual order of foreign rule) and Strab. 7,1,4 (tribes dependent on the Cherusci; Arminius leader of the Cherusci contingent; his family). On the interpretation of the battle of the Germanic tribesmen against Varus as a mutiny by Germanic auxiliaries against the legions of the Rhine army, mastermindcd by Arminius as leader of the Cherusci auxiliaries rather than as a prince of the Cherusci, see Dieter Timpe, *Arminius-Studien*, 1970 (for a critical view see Gustav Adolf Lehmann, 'Zur historischen-literarischen Überlieferung der Varus-Katastrophe 9 n. Chr.', *Boreas* 13, 1990, 143–64, esp. 16off.). The levying of taxes by Varus: Cass. Dio 56,18,3. The head of Varus sent to Marbod, who later handed it on to Augustus; it was finally buried in the tomb of the Quinctilians: Vell. Pat. 2,119,5; cf. Tac. ann. 1,71,1; Flor. epit. 2,30,38.

pp. 543–5 *Reactions of Augustus to the Varus catastrophe; other German policies*: Suet. Aug. 23 (including the words, §2: 'Quintili Vare, legiones redde!'), 25,2; Cass. Dio 56,23. Tiberius with the Rhine army and in Germania: Suet. Tib. 18ff.; Vell. Pat. 2,120,2 and 121,3. Tac. ann. 1,38, 50,1. Quotation from Aug. RG 26: 'omnium provinciarum populi Romani, quibus finitimae fuerunt gentes, quae non parerent imperio nostro, fines auxi. Gallias et Hispanias provincias item Germaniam, qua includit Oceanus a Gadibus ad ostium Albis fluminis, pacavi'. Vell. Pat. 2,123,1 on the taking over of command on the Rhine: 'quippe Caesar Augustus cum Germanicum nepotem suum reliqua belli patraturum misisset in Germaniam'.

pp. 545–6 *The Danube area*: See the works mentioned on pp. 696ff., and also Christo M. Danov, 'Die Thraker auf dem Ostbalkan von der hellenistischen Zeit bis zur Gründung Konstantinopels', in ANRW II 7,1, 1979, 120ff.

pp. 546–8 *The Parthian question*: Tac. ann. 2,1–4; Flav. Jos. antiqu. 18,2,4; on the expectations of Ovid: ars amat. 1,177–228. On the treaty of the year 20, see pp. 315ff. Kienast, *Augustus*, 286, says, incomprehensibly to my way of thinking, 'that one cannot speak of a fundamentally defensive foreign policy on the part of Augustus in the east'. On the Parthian history of this time, see Neilson C. Debevoise, *A Political History of Parthia*, 1938, new edn 1968, 143ff.; Brian Campbell, 'War and Diplomacy: Rome and Parthia, 31 BC–AD 235', in J. Rich/G. Shipley (eds.), *War and Society in the Roman World*, 1993, 213ff.; and above all Karl-Heinz Ziegler, *Die Beziehungen zwischen Rom und dem Partherreich*, 1964, 45ff.

pp. 548–50 *The Bosphorean empire, Ethiopia and the Saharan border*: Agrippa and the Bosphorean empire: Cass. Dio 54,24,4–8; see Wolfgang Hoben, *Untersuchungen zur Stellung kleinasiatischer Dynasten in den Machtkämpfen der ausgehenden römischen Republik*, 1969, 39ff.; Eckart Olshausen, 'Pontos und Rom (63 v. Chr.–64 n. Chr.)', in ANRW II 7,2, 1980, 910ff.; Michaela Stein-Kramer, *Die Klientelkönigreiche Kleinasiens in der Aussenpolitik der späten Republik und des Augustus*, 1987, 82ff., and V. F. Gajdukevič, *Das bosporanische Reich*, 1971$^2$, esp. 325ff. On the Arabian expedition of Aelius

Gallus see pp. 297f. above, on the expedition of Gaius see pp. 546f. On Juba's account of Arabia see Felix Jacoby, in RE IX, 1916, 2391ff., and on the question of whether Aden was also reached by a fleet in Augustan times see Hermann von Wissmann, 'Die Geschichte des Sabäerreiches', in ANRW II 9,1, 1976, 434ff. Petronius' Ethiopian expedition: Strab. 17,1,53–4; Aug. RG 26 (when he says that Napata 'proxima est Meroe' he is very much mistaken, since Meroe lies between the Fifth Cataract and present-day Khartoum, some 100 kilometres further up the Nile); Plin. nat. hist. 6,181ff. (if, as Pliny claims, Petronius advanced 875 miles from Syene, about 1,300 kilometres, he will still have been some way beyond Napata); Cass. Dio 54,5,4ff. On the expedition of Cornelius Balbus to Garama see Plin. nat. hist. 5,36. On the desert tribes see Charles Daniels, *The Garamantes of Southern Libya*, 1970, and Andreas Gutsfeld, *Römische Herrschaft und einheimischer Widerstand in Nordafrika. Militärische Auseinandersetzungen Roms mit den Nomaden*, 1989, esp. 25–39. On Britannia: Horace epod. 7,7ff. (39 BC); Aug. RG 32; Strab. 4,5,3 (British envoys in Rome). The dark allusion in Livy fr. 64, to the effect that Augustus, on returning from Britain, had subdued the circle of the earth to the *imperium* through war and friendship, can mean, if it means anything, only that Rome and the Britons met with goodwill.

p. 551 *The reference to Tacitus*: Tac. ann. 1,9,5 (from the positive part of his obituary of Augustus): 'mari Oceano aut amnibus longinquis saeptum imperium; legiones provincias classes, cuncta inter se connexa'.

pp. 551–3 *On Illyricum*: Particular emphasis is laid on the importance of the Illyrian area as an indispensable link holding the east and west of the empire together by Ronald Syme; see, for instance, CAH X, 1966, 351–4.

pp. 553–6 *Ideas of world domination*: The reference to Tacitus: ann. 1,11,4: 'addideratque consilium coercendi intra terminos imperii, incertum metu an per invidiam'. The requisite number of legions: Ernst Kornemann, *Gestalten und Reiche*, 1943, 344ff., has described the reduction of the number of legions after Actium to twenty-five as 'leaving the empire defenceless', which, even if we consider the date of his publication, shows little understanding of the political and military situation of the empire. On Augustus' image of himself as ruler of the world see also E. S. Gruen, 'Augustus and the Ideology of War and Peace', in Winkes, *Augustus*, 51–72; on the tension between the semi-official claim to world domination and military policy in fact, see Karl-Wilhelm Welwei, 'Römische Weltherrschaftsideologie und augusteische Germanienpolitik', *Gymnasium* 93, 1986, 118–37. On Virgil, see p. 506. The victory ode by Horace of the year 15: c. 4,14, lines 7ff. on the Vindelicians. Envoys from kings and princes of the Indians, Medes, etc.: Aug. RG 31; Suet. Aug. 21,3. Velleius on the rebellious Pannonians: Vell. Pat. 2,110,2: 'Pannonia insolens longae pacis bonis'. Bato before Tiberius: Cass. Dio 56,16,3.

## CHAPTER 15

## Explanatory Notes

p. 557 *Agrippa's official tribunician and proconsular military powers*: Cass. Dio 54,28,1.

p. 562 *Ode of Horace*: On the return of Augustus: c. 4,15.

pp. 562–3 *Election to the post of pontifex maximus*: Aug. RG 10. Even in antiquity, and more particularly in modern scholarship, Lepidus (on his fall see pp. 197f.) has been branded as weak and incompetent, not just because he lost control of his army twice but for his ignominious quarter of a century of internment. Weigel, *Lepidus*, has tried to correct this image of him to some extent, without going to the opposite extreme.

pp. 563–7 *On the death of Agrippa and his will*: Cass. Dio 54,28,2–5 and 29,4–6. On the fragment of Augustus' eulogy, see Ludwig Koenen, 'Die "laudatio funebris" des Augustus für Agrippa auf einem neuen Papyrus', *Zeitschr. für Papyrologie u. Epigr.* 5, 1970, 217–83, and Walter Ameling, 'Augustus und Agrippa. Bemerkungen zu P.Köln VI 249', *Chiron* 24, 1994, 1–28. On the *novitas* of Agrippa: Vell. Pat. 2,96,1; on his *ignobilitas*: Tac. ann. 1,3,1 and Seneca benef. 3,32,4; on his *rusticitas*: Plin. nat. hist. 35,26; on his loyalty and devotion: Vell. Pat. 2,79,1: 'M. Agrippa, virtutis nobilissimae, labore, vigilia, periculo invictus parendique, sed uni, scientissimus, aliis sane imperandi cupidus et per omnia extra dilationes positus consultisque facta coniungens' ('Marcus Agrippa, a man of most noble virtue, unsurpassed in the efforts he made, his deeds and the dangers he faced being united with watchfulness, extraordinarily experienced in obeying, though obeying only one man, and desirous of commanding others, he carried out everything without delay, combining wisdom with proficiency'), and Cass. Dio 54,29,1–3; on his moderation: Cass. Dio 54,11,6. Agrippa stops reporting to the Senate: Cass. Dio 54,24,7. His abstention (and that of Augustus) from accepting triumphs is seen as *moderatio* in the republican tradition by Klaus Martin Giraudet, '"Traditionalismus" in der Politik des Octavian/Augustus – mentalitätsgeschichtliche Aspekte', *Klio* 75, 1993, 202–18. Agrippa's proposal for works of art to be made accessible to the public: Plin. nat. hist. 35,26; the passage cited: 'quod [i.e. showing them publicly] fieri satius fuisset quam in villarum exilia pelli'. His work on the use of water from public conduits: Frontin. de aquaed. 98ff. On his geographical writings see Alfred Klotz, 'Die geographischen commentarii des Agrippa und ihre Überreste', *Klio* 24, 1931, 38–58 and 386–466 (with a collection of the fragments); Paul Schnabel, 'Die Weltkarte des Agrippa als wissenschaftliches Mittelglied zwischen Hipparch und Ptolemaeus', *Philol.* 90, 1935, 405–40; and Kai Brodersen, *Terra cognita: Studien zur römischen Raumerfassung*, 1995, 268ff. (Brodersen doubts the existence of a map of the

world). On the installation of the map: Plin. nat. hist. 3,17. Agrippa's criticism
of Virgil: Suetonius' life of the poet, which has come down to us in the revision of Donatus, 44: 'M. Vipsanius a Maecenate eum [sc. Virgil] suppositum
appellabat novae cacozeliae repertorem, non tumidae nec exilis, sed ex com-
munibus verbis atque ideo latentis'. Agrippa the 'democrat': Cass. Dio
52,1–13; see on Dio's view Jean-Michel Roddaz, *Marcus Agrippa*, 1984. On
Agrippa, see also Rudolf Hanslik, 'M. Vipsanius Agrippa', in RE IX A, 1961,
1226–75.

pp. 567–8 *The death of friends and relations of Augustus*: The funeral of Octavia:
Cass. Dio 54,35,4. Augustus laments the deaths of his advisers Agrippa and
Maecenas: Seneca benef. 6,32,2. On the mausoleum of Plancus in Gaeta, see
Rudolf Fellmann, *Das Grab des L. Munatius Plancus bei Gaēta*, 1957.

pp. 568–70 *Tiberius as a replacement for Agrippa*: Suet. Tib. 7,2ff.; idem, Aug.
63,2; Cass. Dio 54,31. Tiberius is now (7/6 BC) the most important man after
Augustus: Vell. Pat. 2,99,1.

pp. 570–71 *Honours for the Caesars*: Cass. Dio 55,9,1ff., esp. 9,4; Tac. ann.
1,3,2.

pp. 572–3 *Withdrawal of Tiberius from public life*: Suet. Tib. 10–13; Cass. Dio
55,9,5–8. Birth of a son: Suet. Tib. 7,3. Senator Lucilius Longus: Tac. ann. 4,15,1.

pp. 573–5 *Gaius and Lucius Caesar during the absence of Tiberius*: Suet. Aug.
26,2; Aug. RG 14. On the coins minted in Lugdunum (and Rome), with the
two Caesars shown on the reverse, see CREAM, 148ff.; Kienast, *Augustus*,
323ff. and 329; and Simon, *Selbstdarstellung*, 72ff. The fact that no silver
coins were minted between AD 4 and 13 is also accounted for by the shortage
of silver. On the temple of Nemausus (the Maison Carrée) see R. Amy/P. Gros,
'La Maison Carrée de Nîmes', *Gallia* Suppl. 38, 1979, esp. 177ff.; the dedication inscription: CIL XII 3156. *Pater patriae*: Aug. RG 35; Suet. Aug. 58. The
dedication of the temple of Mars Ultor: Ovid. fast. 5,595–8; Suet. Aug. 43,1;
Cass. Dio/Zonaras 55,10,6–8.

pp. 575–7 *The scandal of Julia (Major)*: Vell. Pat. 2,100,4ff.; Seneca benef. 6,32,1ff.;
Suet. Aug. 65,1–4; Tac. ann.1,53,1ff. and 3,24,2; Cass. Dio/Zonaras 55,10,12–
16 and 13,1 (with the reported remark of Augustus). The planned assassination
of Augustus: Plin. nat. hist. 7,149; the alleged wish of Jullus Antonius to be sole
ruler: Cass. Dio/Zonaras 55,10,15. If, according to Plut. Anton. 87,2, Jullus
Antonius came next in order of succession after Agrippa (and his sons) and the
sons of Livia, this is a far-fetched speculation from his source. See on the entire
complex Peter Sattler, 'Julia und Tiberius', in idem, *Studien aus dem Gebiet der
alten Geschichte*, 1962, esp. 23ff. (restrained in his evaluation of the sources);
Eckhard Meise, *Untersuchungen zur Geschichte der Julisch-Claudischen
Dynastie*, 1969, 3–34 (Meise sees the scandal as the story of a conspiracy that
was supposed to be hushed up by the charges of adultery); and W. K. Lacey, '2
BC and Julia's adultery', *Antichthon*, 14, 1980, 127–42; idem, *Augustus and the
Principate*, 1996, 190–209 (according to Lacey the scandal was linked to

resistance on the part of certain individual noblemen to the idea that the young Caesars would succeed Augustus). On Julia's life in exile, see Jerzy Linderski, 'Julia in Regium', *Zeitschr. für Papyrologie u. Epigr.* 72, 1988, 181–200. The scandal in the ruling house has inspired modern historians, or those who would like to be seen as historians, to flights of fancy into less than serious terrain. The idea that Livia, in the character of wicked witch, brought about Julia's downfall to further the interests of her son Tiberius has been put forward again and again for centuries, although there is no political logic to be found in it (see Sattler, op. cit., 11ff.), and Julia has even been presented as a fighter for the freedom of the republic, in contrast to a conservative Tiberius, who is shown as preferring the stern government of the Senate (Barbara M. Levick, 'Tiberius' Retirement to Rhodes in 6 B.C.', *Latomus* 31, 1972, 798ff.).

pp. 577–9 *Gaius in the east*: Granting of the proconsular *imperium*: Cass. Dio/ Zonaras 55,10,18; see Suet. Tib. 12,1. Designated successor: Dessau ILS No. 140, Z. 13ff.: 'G. Caesarem . . . iam designatum iustissimum ac simillumum parentis sui virtutibus principem' ('Gaius Caesar, already *princeps* designate, justest of men and entirely like his father in his virtues'); Gaius as 'the new Ares': *Inscr. Graecae*, II², 3250. On Gaius and his mission to the east, see F. E. Romer, 'Gaius Caesar's Military Diplomacy in the East', *Transact. Americ. Philol. Assoc.* 109, 1979, 199–214. Lollius as adviser to Gaius Caesar: Suet. Tib. 12,3 ('comes et rector', 'companion and guide'). The return of Tiberius: Suet. Tib. 13,2; Vell. Pat. 2,103,1.

pp. 579–80 *Death of the Caesars*: Vell. Pat. 2,102,3 (Lucius); Vell. Pat. 2,102,2ff.; Cass. Dio 55,10a,6–10 (Gaius); Suet. Aug. 65,1ff.; Cass. Dio/Zonaras 55,12,1 (on both). The elegy of Tiberius for Lucius Caesar: Suet. Tib. 70,2. A cenotaph for Gaius Caesar in Limyra, where he died, has been found by Jürgen Borchhardt, 'Ein Kenotaph für Gaius Caesar', *Jahrb. Deutsch. Archäol. Inst.* 89, 1974, 217–41. The letter from Augustus to Gaius Caesar of 23 September AD 1: Gell. 15,7. On the honours decreed for the Caesars and the mourning of Augustus: two decrees from the *curia* of Pisa honouring Lucius and Gaius have come down to us: Dessau ILS nos. 139 (Lucius) and 140 (Gaius). On the Porticus Iulia: Cass. Dio 56,27,5; see Richardson, *Rome*, 213 and 214. Augustus: Suet. Tib. 23,2: 'quoniam atrox fortuna Gaium et Lucium filios mihi eripuit, Tiberius'; even in the *Res Gestae* he speaks of them in similar terms: Aug. RG 14: 'filios meos, quos iuvenes mihi eripuit fortuna' ('my sons, torn from me by Fate when they were still young').

pp. 580–82 *The adoption of Tiberius by Augustus and arrangements for the rest of the succession*: Suet. Tib. 15,2; Vell. Pat. 103,2ff. and 104,1ff.; Tac. ann. 1,3,1–4, esp. 3; see Hans Ulrich Instinsky, 'Augustus und die Adoption des Tiberius', *Hermes* 94, 324–43. The comment of Augustus on his adoption of Tiberius: Vell. Pat. 2,104,1: 'hoc . . . rei publicae causa facio'; see Suet. Tib. 21,3. Augustus said to have wished that Germanicus could succeed him: Tac. ann. 4,57,3. Parthian envoys referred by Augustus to Tiberius: Suet. Tib. 16,1.

pp. 582–3 *Flood and famine between* AD *5 and 9*: Cass. Dio 55,22,3, 26,1, 27,1–3, 31,2–4, 33,4 and 56,12,1; Suet. Aug. 42,3; Plin. nat. hist. 7,149. The connection between the Pannonian war and famine in Italy: Cass. Dio 56,12,1; see Kienast, *Augustus*, 119.

pp. 583–4 *The banishment of Agrippa Postumus*: Vell. Pat. 2,112,7 (Agrippa described as 'mira pravitate animi atque ingenii in praecipitia conversus', 'unusually eccentric in mind and dispostion, and inclined to swift changes of mood'); Suet. Aug. 51,1, 65,1, 4 (Agrippa described as 'sordidus', 'ferox' and 'amens', i.e. 'base-minded', 'unbridled' and 'deranged'), 101,3; Cass. Dio 55,32,1ff. ('fits of violent rage'). The term *abdicare* used by Suetonius for making a break with Agrippa is the source of controversy (does it signify 'emancipation' or 'disinheritance'? See Barbara M. Levick, 'Abdication and Agrippa Postumus', *Historia* 21, 1972, 674–97), but it is probably used unspecifically here; see Shelagh Jameson, 'Augustus and Agrippa Postumus', *Historia* 24, 1975, 289ff.

pp. 584–6 *On the scandal of Julia (Minor)*: Tac. ann. 4,71,4, 3,24,3ff.; Scholien to Juven. 6,158; Suet. Aug. 19,1ff. (Aemilius Paullus; attempts to free the exiles); 65,1 and 4, 72,3, 101,3. See Meise, *Untersuchungen* (as p. 708 above), 35–50. Ronald Syme, 'The End of L. Aemilius Paullus', in idem, *The Augustan Aristocracy*, 1986, 115–27, suggests, mainly on the basis of Dessau ILS no. 5026, that Aemilius Paullus was sentenced to death before the marital scandal broke, and he survived. Augustus on the two Julias and Agrippa: Suet. Aug. 65,4 ('vomicae' and 'carcinomata').

pp. 586–7 *Ovid*: On the connection of Ovid's wife with Atia, a younger sister of the mother of Augustus, and thus his aunt, and their daughter Marcia, who was the wife of Paullus Fabius Maximus (consul in 11 BC), see ex Pont. 1,2,138ff. On his own offence: trist. 1,5,42, 2,51,207–12, 3,5,47ff.; ex Pont. 2,9,71ff. and frequently thereafter. The *turpe carmen*: trist. 2,211ff.; the accusation of having been a teacher of adultery ('arguor obsceni doctor adul-terii'): trist. 2,212. Romulus and the rape of the Sabine women: ars. amat. 1,101ff. Caesar has no power over his writing of poetry: trist. 3,7,47ff. See on the offence and downfall of Ovid, Walther Kraus, in RE XVIII, 1942, 1916ff.; Syme, *Revolution*, 467ff.; Kienast, *Augustus*, 247ff.; Michael von Albrecht, 'Forschungsbericht Ovid II.', *Anzeiger für d. Altertumswiss.* 26, 1973, 138ff.; Wilfried Stroh, 'Ovids Liebeskunst und die Ehegesetze des Augustus', *Gymnasium* 86, 1979, 323–52 (the 'art of love' was particularly irritating to Augustus in view of his law on adultery); Widu-Wolfgang Ehlers, 'Poet und Exil: Zum Verständnis der Exildichtung Ovids', *Antike u. Abendland* 34, 1988, 144–57 (emphasizing the effect of banishment on Ovid's poetic work; Ovid, says Ehlers, was 'not the innocent victim of imperial autocracy', p. 156, but the concept of 'guilt' itself is in question here); and Siegmar Döpp, *Werke Ovids*, 1992, 21ff. Ulrich Schmitzer, *Zeitgeschichte in Ovids 'Metamorphosen'*, 1990, finds stronger references to contemporary history in the *Metamorphoses* than anyone was previously ready to acknowledge, but one must regard the *Ars Amatoria* as Ovid's *turpe carmen*. See, finally, Niklas Holzberg, *Ovid, Dichter und Werk*, 1997, 184ff.

pp. 578–8 *Germanicus*: See Wilhelm Kroll, in RE X, 1918, 435–64, and Peter Kehne, 'Germanicus', *Reallexikon der germanischen Altertumskunde*, 11, 1998, s.v.; on his military exploits in Pannonia see p. 531 above. Germanicus was originally known, like his father, as Nero Claudius Drusus, but took the name of Germanicus after the death of his father, who was able to pass it on to him as a hereditary title. After his adoption by Tiberius he was officially known as Germanicus Julius, son of Tiberius, grandson of Augustus, great-grandson of Caesar (the dictator).

p. 588 *Claudius*: The saying of his mother Antonia (Minor): Suet. Claud. 3,2: 'portentum eum hominis . . . nec absolutum a natura, sed tantum incohatum'. Claudius with a hood over his head at the games: Suet. Claud. 2,2. The correspondence about him between Augustus and Livia: Suet. Claud. 4,1–4.

pp. 589–91 *Livia*: Livia drank only one kind of wine: Plin. nat. hist. 14,60; ate elecampane salad daily: Plin. nat. hist. 19,91ff.; Livia as Odysseus in skirts: Suet. Calig. 23,2 ('Ulixem stolatum'); *sacrosanctitas* granted to her: Cass. Dio 49,38,1; alleged to be guilty of the deaths of the two Caesars: Tac. ann. 1,3,3 ('Liviae dolus', 'the cunning of Livia', see also 5,1,3); Cass. Dio 55,10a,10. On the 'connection' between Livia and the Claudians, see Syme, *Revolution*, 422ff.; on Livia in general Lotte Ollendorf, in RE XIII, 1926, 900–927, and Perkounig, *Livia*; on the honours conferred on her in the east, Ulrike Hahn, *Die Frauen des römischen Kaiserhauses und ihre Ehrungen im griechischen Osten anhand epigraphischer und numismatischer Zeugnisse von Livia bis Sabina*, 1994, and on her portrait Walter Hatto Gross, *Iulia Augusta*, Abhandlg. d. Göttinger Akad. d.Wiss., phil.-histor. Kl., 1962. Adoption into the Julian family and title of Augusta: Tac. ann. 1,8,1; Cass. Dio 56,46,1; on the question of the constitutional aspect of the title Augusta, see Hans-Werner Ritter, 'Livias Erhebung zur Augusta', *Chiron* 2, 1972, 313–38; and on the significance of the title of Augusta and acceptance into the Julian family: Perkounig, *Livia*, 119ff.

pp. 591–2 *The health of Augustus*: On his illness in the year 23, see pp. 305f. above. The ailments of old age: Gell. 15,7,3 (letter to Gaius Caesar); Suet. Aug. 80 (ailments), 78 (sleep), 76,1 (moderate diet), 77 (drank sparingly), 82,1 (clothes), 82,2 (seldom took a bath), 83 (going for walks, hopping). Increasing weakness: for the senatorial committees, see pp. 351f. above. Germanicus reading speeches for him in front of the Senate, and his preference for dispensing with the *salutatio* and not attending public banquets: Cass. Dio 56,26,2; cf. 56,41,3. Carries out state business lying down: Cass. Dio 56,28,3. Weariness: Suet. Aug. 85,1.

p. 593 *Friends of Augustus in his old age*: Suet. Aug. 71,1–4. Marcia was the daughter of the marriage of Lucius Marcius Philippus, son of Octavian/

Augustus' stepfather of the same name, to Atia Iunior (a younger sister of the mother of Augustus) and thus a cousin of Augustus on the maternal side. Playing games with slave boys: Suet. Aug. 83.

pp. 593–4 *The new men surrounding Tiberius*: See Syme, *Revolution*, 434ff. The triumph of Tiberius: Suet. Tib. 20; Vell. Pat. 2,121,2ff.

pp. 594–5 *The literary style favoured by Augustus; his own literary efforts*: Suet. Aug. 84 (above all on his manner of speech), 85 (his own works), 86 (stylistic criticism), 87ff. (choice of words, orthography). Abandoning Ajax 'to the fungus': Suet. Aug. 85,2; Macrob. Sat. 2,4 (a collection of sayings of Augustus), 12: the parody of the style of Maecenas. Imperfect command of Greek: Suet. Aug. 89,1. On the account by Augustus of his own actions (*res gestae*) see p. 454 above.

pp. 595–6 *Final measures*: Cass. Dio 56,28,1 (extension of military power of proconsular *imperium* of Augustus, the consulate for Drusus). Suet. Tib. 21,1 (military power of proconsular *imperium* for Tiberius). Disagreement with the Senate on inheritance tax: Cass. Dio 56,28,4–6. Alleged visit to Agrippa and Livia's reaction: Tac. ann. 1,5; Cass. Dio 56,30,1ff.

pp. 596–8 *Death of Augustus*: Omens: Suet. Aug. 97,2; Cass. Dio 56,29. Final journey and death: Vell. Pat. 2,123; Suet. Aug. 97,3–100,1; idem, Tib. 21ff.; Tac. ann. 1,5; Cass. Dio 56,30–31. Augustus already dead or still alive on the arrival of Tiberius: still alive, Vell. Pat. 2,123,2; Cass. Dio 56,31,1; dead, Suet. Aug. 98,5; idem, Tib. 21,1 as well as Tac. ann. 1,5,3 (Tacitus is uncertain). Last words to Livia: Suet. Aug. 99,1: 'Livia, nostri coniugii memor vive, ac vale'. The concluding phrase of a comedy: Suet. Aug. 99,1; cf. Cass. Dio 56,30,4. We have no reason to doubt the veracity of the death scene, including the last words of Augustus, particularly as the accounts of them show no kind of tendentious distortion. With the idea that a man has a part like an actor's to play in life, Augustus was following a view widely held in classical antiquity. On criticism of the various and sometimes partly contradictory accounts of the death of Augustus, particularly the alleged role of Livia as the principate passed from him to Tiberius, see Timpe, *Kontinuität*, 27ff., and Perkounig, *Livia*, 82ff. On the last words (*ultima verba*) of the emperor as given by Suetonius, see Helmut Gugel, *Studien zur biographischen Technik Suetons*, 1977, 95ff.

pp. 598–600 *Events following the death of Augustus*: Meeting of the Senate to agree on honours and the funeral: Suet. Aug. 100,2–4; Tac. ann. 1,8,3–6; Cass. Dio 56,31,2–3, 42 (the account of the freeing of the eagle). Will: Suet. Aug. 101,1–3; idem, Tib. 23; Tac. ann. 1,8,1–2; Cass. Dio 56,32. Documents accompanying the will: Suet. Aug. 101,4; Tac. ann. 1,11,3ff.; Cass. Dio 56,33 (only Dio mentions the fourth scroll, for Tiberius). The eulogy by Tiberius, as given in Cassius Dio 56,35–41, is very probably the product of later rhetoric. Advice not to extend the empire further: Tac. ann. 1,11,4: 'addideratque consilium coercendi intra terminos imperii'; Cass. Dio 56,33,5. See on this pp. 553f. above, and on the question of how far Tiberius followed the advice of Augustus, see Josiah Ober, 'Tiberius and the Political Testament of Augustus', *Historia* 31, 1982, 306–28; see also on discussion of this point Karl Christ, 'Zur augusteischen Germanienpolitik', *Chiron* 7, 1977, 198ff. Tiberius said to be a hypocrite: Tac. ann. 1,7,3ff.; see Suet. Tib.24. Consecration of Augustus by the Senate: Cass. Dio 56,46,1–4. On the Augustales see p. 337 above. Death of Agrippa Postumus: on discussion of those who may have given the order for his death see Jameson (as p. 710 above), who clears Augustus and Tiberius, giving Sallustius a more independent role in the affair; on Sallustius see p. 376 above.

## CHAPTER 16
# Explanatory Notes

p. 602 *The birth of Augustus*: Suet. Aug. 94,4; Cass. Dio 45,1,2ff. (Further omens described in Suet. Aug. 94,2–12 and Cass. Dio 45,1–2,6 indicating the future greatness of the newborn child.) The birth legend is obviously borrowed from that of Alexander the Great, whose mother was said to have been visited by a snake in the temple of Zeus Ammon. See Ilse Becher, 'Atia, die Mutter des Augustus – Legende und Politik', in E. G. Schmidt (ed.), *Griechenland und Rom*, 1996, 95–116, giving good arguments to suggest that the dispersal of the birth legend, although effective, was not encouraged by Augustus himself. According to Erika Simon, *Die Portlandvase*, 1957, one of the two scenes on the famous Portland Vase refers to the impregnation of Atia by Apollo. This interpretation (see Hans Möbius, in *Gnomon* 36, 1964, 636ff.) and the many others (see D. E. L. Haynes, *The Portland Vase*, 1975[3]) are disputed; so is the dating (according to Simon, 30 BC; the Claudian period has also been suggested). It is probably more likely that the scenes on the vase are mythical, allowing several possible interpretations; see Zanker, *Augustus*, 254ff. On Augustus on himself, see also Meyer Reinhold, 'Augustus' Conception of Himself', *Thought: Fordham Univ. Quarterly* 55, 1980, 36–50.

p. 603 *The outward appearance of Augustus*: Suet. Aug. 73 and 79ff.; Aur. Vict. epit. 1,20; Plin. nat. hist. 7,211; 11,143; Cass. Dio 48,34,3.

p. 605 *The clemency of Augustus*: On Vedius Pollio see p. 376 above. On the accommodation for slaves (*ergastula*): Suet. Aug. 32,1.

p. 607 *The attitude of Augustus to the supernatural*: On superstitions of Augustus: Suet. Aug. 92,1 (shoes; dew), 90 (fear of thunderstorms), 92,2 (on the nones and nundines); the Ides were the thirteenth or fifteenth day of a month, depending on which month it was.

p. 609 *Justification of caution*: Suet. Aug. 25,4 ('Hasten slowly', *speúde bradéos*, Latin *festina lente*, and the line from Euripides, *The Phoenician Women* 599).

pp. 609–10 *Lifestyle in the house on the Palatine*: See p. 372 above; on the upbringing of his grandchildren: Suet. Aug. 64,2ff. The letter of Augustus to the Senate on his longing for peace and quiet (*otium*): Seneca de brev. vit. 4,2ff.

p. 610 *Fortuna looks favourably on Octavian/Augustus*: See Plin. nat. hist. 7,147–50 (an enumeration of all instances of his escape from perils), as well as pp. 96f. above (spring of the year 43) and pp. 169f. above (spring of the year 40).

p. 000 *The award of the oak wreath (corona civica awarded ob cives servatos) in the year 43*: Cass. Dio 47,13,3; on the award in the year 27, see p. 291 above.

p. 613 *The term statio*: *Statio mea* is the term used by Augustus to give Gaius Caesar, his designated successor, the right politcal and legal position (Gell. 15,7,3), and the word was used with the same significance in connection with the succession of Tiberius to the principate (*statio paterna*, Vell. Pat. 2,124,2).

pp. 615–16 *Augustus as guide of the world and father of mankind*: Dessau ILS no. 112 (from a decision of the city of Narbo, Narbonne): 'VIII k. Octob. [the birthday of Augustus] qua die eum saeculi felicitas orbi terrarum rectorem edidit' ('23 September, on which day a fortunate age bore him as [future] guide of the circle of the earth'). Father of all men, Romans and provincials alike: Strab. 6,4,2: 'It is difficult to rule so great a realm other than by transferring it to one man as to a father. Never have the Romans and their allies enjoyed such peace and abundance of all good things as was granted to them by Caesar Augustus.' Dessau ILS no. 103 (from the inscription on the plinth of the statue of Augustus set up by the province of Baetica): 'quod beneficio eius et perpetua cura provincia pacata est'. See also Ovid metamorph. 15,858–60: (as Jupiter rules the heavenly regions) 'the earth stands under the command of Augustus, who is both father and guide at once' ('terra sub Augusto est; pater est et rector uterque').

p. 617 *Caesar sitting in judgement during his rule*: See Klaus Bringmann, 'Der Diktator Caesar als Richter? Zu Ciceros Reden "Pro Ligario" und "Pro rege Deiotaro"', *Hermes* 114, 1986, 72–88.

p. 618 *Augustus on salutary examples of behaviour*: Suet. Aug. 89,2. In the *Res Gestae* Augustus also emphasizes the good example he has set posterity in many respects (8: 'et ipse multarum rerum imitanda posteris tradidi'). On the historians of the imperial period: Hermann Tränkle, 'Augustus bei Tacitus, Cassius Dio und dem älteren Plinius', *Wiener Studien* n.s. 3, 1969, 108–30, has shown convincingly from the first ten chapters of the *Annals* of Tacitus, particularly the so-called obituary, that the unfavourable picture of Augustus presented by Tacitus 'was in essence the result of historiography in the Julio-Claudian period' (p. 130).

p. 619 *The title 'Caesar' in the early empire*: The ruling position was initially regarded as the possession of the Julio-Claudian family, and so all rulers after

Augustus, even if they did not formally belong to the Julian house by adoption, bore the name 'Caesar'. Only with the confusions of the year AD 68/69 did the principate go out of the Julio-Claudian family, and then the name of Caesar became purely a title. Most ancient accounts have the empire beginning with Augustus, but particularly in collections of the biographies of emperors, for instance in Suetonius, he is preceded by an account of Julius Caesar, not just because of the last five years of his life, when he was in point of fact monarch, but most of all because he was the adoptive father of Augustus, and there were many other connections between his rule and that of Augustus. Since the time of Trajan it has been usual to include Caesar in the series of *imperators*: see Joseph Geiger, 'Zum Bild Julius Caesars in der römischen Kaiserzeit', *Historia* 24, 1975, 444–53.

pp. 619–20 *Augustus on Alexander*: Plut. moral. 270C/D (saying no. 8). The quotation from Dio: Cass. Dio 56,43,4. On the vague concept of freedom: the use of the word 'freedom' (*libertas*) in writers of the imperial Roman period often seems like playing with a term, an allusion to something deliberately glossed over (or more rarely inadvertently glossed over through ignorance). As the imperial period had coined no term of its own for what freedom was still possible under the emperors, among the senators *libertas* referred more to the freedom of the politically sovereign aristocracy of the republic (the nobility), and the word had connotations of a concept that did not and could no longer exist. They might look back with melancholy at the lost freedom of the republic, they could not transport it to their own time, and if they did try to do so, they were living in an unreal world of illusion that clarified nothing in their own reality, but more or less deliberately obscured it.

# Chronology

<table>
<tr><td>133 BC</td><td>Ti. Sempronius Gracchus is tribune of the people. Beginning of the revolutionary period, with the state in internal crisis. Disintegration of the leading aristocratic class of the nobility sets in</td></tr>
<tr><td>82–79</td><td>Dictatorship of Lucius Cornelius Sulla. Attempt at reform by stabilizing the structure of the state</td></tr>
<tr><td>23.9.63</td><td>Augustus born in Rome as Gaius Octavius</td></tr>
<tr><td>59</td><td>Consulate of C. Julius Caesar</td></tr>
<tr><td>59, spring</td><td>Death of the father of C. Octavius</td></tr>
<tr><td>58–50</td><td>C. Julius Caesar governor (proconsul) of Gallia Cisalpina, Gallia Narbonensis and Illyricum. Conquest of the free Celtic land of Gallia Comata, 58–51</td></tr>
<tr><td>53</td><td>Defeat of the Romans under Crassus at Carrhae</td></tr>
<tr><td>51</td><td>C. Octavius delivers the funeral oration (laudatio funebris) for his grandmother Julia</td></tr>
<tr><td>10/11.1.49</td><td>Caesar crosses the river Rubicon, the border between his province and Italy. The civil war begins</td></tr>
<tr><td>49–45</td><td>Civil war. Battles of Ilerda (49), Pharsalos (48), Zela (47), Thapsus (46) and Munda (45). Caesar is master of Rome</td></tr>
<tr><td>45</td><td>Caesar granted the dictatorship for ten years, then for life</td></tr>
<tr><td>48/47</td><td>A. Gabinius defeated in Dalmatia</td></tr>
<tr><td>46</td><td>Forum Julium with temple of Venus Genetrix dedicated</td></tr>
<tr><td>45, autumn</td><td>C. Octavius travels to Apollonia</td></tr>
</table>

## 44 BC

<table>
<tr><td>15.3</td><td>Assassination of the dictator C. Julius Caesar</td></tr>
<tr><td>17.3</td><td>Compromise between the assassins of Caesar and Mark Antony</td></tr>
<tr><td>March/April</td><td>Law passed on the provinces of the consuls Mark Antony (Macedonia) and P. Dolabella (Syria)</td></tr>
</table>

| | |
|---|---|
| 18.4 | C. Octavius, coming from Apollonia by way of Brundisium, arrives in Naples |
| Early May | C. Octavius arrives in Rome and accepts the dictator's will |
| Mid-May | Return of Mark Antony from Campania |
| Early June | Law on the exchange of Mark Antony's provinces passed |
| July | Solemn reconciliation of Mark Antony and Octavian on the Capitol |
| 20–30.7 | Games in honour of the Victoria Caesaris; appearance of the *sidus Iulium* |
| End Aug. | Brutus and Cassius leave Italy |
| 2.9 | Cicero's First Philippic (fourteen speeches made in all by 21.4.43) |
| Oct. | Octavian begins recruiting soldiers |
| *c.*10.11 | Octavian's first march to Rome |
| 9.12 | Cicero returns to Rome |
| After Dec. | Cicero constructs a Republican front |

# 43 BC

| | |
|---|---|
| 1.1 | A. Hirtius and C. Pansa take office as consuls |
| 2.1 | Octavian appointed propraetor and senator (consular) by the Senate |
| 7.1 | Auspices first taken by Octavian (*dies imperii*) |
| Feb. | Senate legalizes the command usurped by M. Brutus in the east (Tenth Philippic) |
| March/Apr. | War of Mutina (*bellum Mutinense*) |
| 14 or 15.4 | Battle of Forum Gallorum; the consul Pansa severely wounded |
| 16.4 | First acclamation of Octavian as *imperator* |
| 21.4 | Battle of Mutina; the consul Hirtius killed |
| 29.5 | Antony and Lepidus unite |
| 27.7 | Cicero's last letter |
| Aug. | Octavian's second march to Rome. |
| 19.8 | Octavian elected consul |
| Sept. | Death of Decimus Brutus |
| End Oct. | Conference of Bononia between Mark Antony, Octavian and M. Lepidus (first treaty). Decision to kill their leading opponents (proscription) |
| 27.11 | Triumvirate set up (*lex Titia*). Antony, Octavian and M. Lepidus become triumvirs 'to restore the state'. The triumvirs decide on war against the murderers of Caesar in the east. |
| 7.12 | Death of Cicero |

## 42 BC

| | |
|---|---|
| Oct./Nov. | First and second battles of Philippi. Death of Cassius and Brutus |
| Dec. | Second treaty between the triumvirs (Octavian to get Spain, Antony Gallia Comata and Gallia Narbonensis, as well as control over the east) |

## 41–36 BC

| | |
|---|---|
| 41 | Antony meets Cleopatra in Tarsos |
| 41/40 Feb. | Perusian War (*bellum Perusinum*) between Octavian and L. Antonius |
| 41/40 | Antony in Alexandria. Parthian raids on Syria and Cilicia |
| 40, autumn | Treaty of Brundisium between Mark Antony and Octavian (Antony to get the east and Octavian the west of the empire; third treaty) |
| 40, autumn | Suicide of Q. Salvidienus Rufus |
| 40, autumn | Fourth Eclogue of Virgil |
| 40 | Birth of the twins Alexandros Helios and Cleopatra Selene, children of Antony and Cleopatra |
| 39 early sum. | Treaty of Misenum between Antony, Octavian and Sextus Pompey (fourth treaty) |
| 39/38 | P. Ventidius Bassus throws the Parthians back over the Euphrates, Antony in Athens |
| 39/38 | Agrippa governor of Gallia Comata. First settlement of a town of the Ubii (later to become Cologne) |
| 17.1.38 | Marriage of Octavian and Livia |
| 38 | First phase of the Sicilian War. Invasion of the island by Octavian and Lepidus fails (Hor. epod. 7 and 16) |
| 37 | Agrippa consul. Building of the *portus Iulius* |
| 37 | Meeting of Antony and Octavian in Tarentum. Extension of the triumvirate to 31.12.33 (fifth treaty) |
| After 37 | Reorganization by Antony of the structure of rule in the east |
| 36 | Birth of Ptolemaios Philadelphos, child of Antony and Cleopatra |
| 36 | Antony's failed Parthian campaign |
| 36 | Building begins on the temple of Apollo on the Palatine |
| 36, Jul.-Sept. | Second phase of the Sicilian War. Naval battles of Mylae (Aug.) and Naulochus (3.9) |
| 36, Sept. | Capitulation of Lepidus |
| 36 | Octavian receives the 'sanctity' of tribune of the people |

## 35–30 BC

| | |
|---|---|
| 35–33 | Octavian's Illyrian war; Siscia is the base for strong troops |
| 35 | Sextus Pompey executed in Miletus |
| 34 | Victory over King Artavasdes of Armenia celebrated in Alexandria |
| 34 | Solemn celebrations of the new structure of rule in the east held in Alexandria. Caesarion as king of kings becomes co-regent with Cleopatra |
| 33 | Octavian is consul II |
| 33/32 | Antony with Cleopatra in Ephesos, then in Samos and Athens. Sends letter of divorce to Octavia |
| 32 | Octavian holds no office as magistrate. Declaration of war on Cleopatra. Antony relieved of his proconsular office. Conduct of the war entrusted to Octavian; Italy and the western provinces take oath of loyalty to him |
| 31 | Octavian is consul III; until 23 (as consul XI) he holds that office without interruption |
| 2.9.31 | Battle of Actium. Horace c. 1,37; epod. 9; Virg. Aen. 8,675ff.; Prop. 3,11, 4,6 |
| 1.8.30 | Last battle outside Alexandria; the city is occupied. Suicide of Antony and Cleopatra |
| 30 | Egypt becomes a province of Rome; C. Cornelius Gallus its first governor (prefect) |
| 30–28 | M. Licinius Crassus, as governor of Macedonia, subdues the land north of his province as far as the Danube |

## 29–17 BC

| | |
|---|---|
| 11.1.29 | Gate of the temple of Janus closed |
| 29 | Octavian reviews the list of senators |
| 29, summer | Arrival of Octavian in Rome. Building of his mausoleum begins |
| 13–15.8.29 | Octavian celebrates triumphs over Dalmatia, for Actium and over Egypt |
| 18.8.29 | Temple of Divus Julius dedicated in the Forum Romanum |
| 28 | Octavian consul VI, Agrippa consul II. Estimate of number of Roman citizens. Re-consecration of temple of Apollo on the Palatine. Octavian becomes *princeps senatus* |
| 27 | Octavian consul VII, Agrippa consul III |
| 13–16.1.27 | Constitutional settlement restoring the *res publica*. Octavian named Augustus (16.1) |
| 27 | Augustus in southern Gaul and Spain. |
| 26 | Suicide of C. Cornelius Gallus |

| | |
|---|---|
| 25 | The Janus gate closed again |
| 25 | Varro Murena defeats the Salassians in the western Alps |
| 25 | M. Claudius Marcellus married to Julia, daughter of Augustus |
| 25 | Arabian campaign of Aelius Gallus |
| 24–22 | C. Petronius, repelling the Ethiopians, reaches Napata |
| 23 | Year of crisis. Trial of M. Primus. Conspiracy of Murena. Illness of Augustus. Marcellus dies. Augustus retires from the consulate (July) and restructures his legal powers in Rome |
| 23, summer | M. Claudius Marcellus dies |
| 23 | Agrippa receives an extraordinary military command for five years; he goes first to the east (23/22), then to Gaul and Spain (20/18) |
| 22 | Rise in prices and famine in Rome; the Tiber floods its banks. Augustus takes over the grain supply office |
| 22 | Augustus travels, by way of Sicily, to the eastern provinces (until 19) |
| 21 | Agrippa marries Augustus' daughter Julia (birth of C. Caesar 20, of L. Caesar summer 17) |
| 21/20 | L. Cornelius Balbus, repelling the Garamantes, reaches their city Garama |
| 20 | Treaty between Augustus and King Phraates IV of Parthia; Armenia becomes a Roman client kingdom; return of Roman prisoners and the captured standards |
| 21.9.19 | Death of Virgil in Brundisium (works on the *Aeneid*, 27–19) |
| 12.10.19 | Augustus returns to Rome. Dedication of altar to Fortuna Redux (15.10) |
| 19 | Electoral intrigues in Rome. Conspiracy of Egnatius Rufus. Final regulations for extension of Augustus' official position (honorary consular rights) |
| 18 | Prolongation of both basic powers for another five years for Augustus and Agrippa, who also receives tribunician power |
| 18 | Julian law on marriage and (probably in the same year) on adultery |
| 17–13 | Agrippa on special mission to the east |
| 17 | Augustus adopts C. and L. Caesar |
| 17, summer | Secular festival |

## 16–7 BC

| | |
|---|---|
| 16 | Unrest on the northern borders |
| 16, summer | Defeat of Lollius in Gaul (*clades Lolliana*) |
| 16–13 | Augustus in Gaul |
| 15 | Campaign of Tiberius and Drusus against the Alpine tribes; Horace c. 4,4 and 4,14 |
| 13, July | Augustus returns to Rome. Vows to build an altar to peace (Ara Pacis) |

| | |
|---|---|
| 13, summer | Five-year prolongation of proconsular power for Augustus and both basic powers for Agrippa |
| 13–11 | Campaign of L. Calpurnius Piso Frugi against the Bessi of Thrace on the Lower Danube |
| 12–9 | Campaigns of Drusus in Germania |
| 6.3.12 | Augustus elected *pontifex maximus* |
| 12, March | Death of Agrippa |
| 12 | Augustus travels to Aquileia |
| 1.8.12 | Dedication of an altar to Roma and Augustus in Lugdunum (Lyon) |
| 11, Feb. | Tiberius marries Augustus' daughter Julia |
| 11, autumn | Death of Octavia |
| 11/10 | Augustus in Gaul (Lugdunum) |
| 30.1.9 | The Ara Pacis dedicated |
| 9, Sept. | Death of Drusus |
| 8 | Death of Horace. The month of Sextilis renamed Augustus. Rome divided into fourteen regions. Last journey of Augustus, to Gaul |
| 8 | Tiberius commands the Rhine army |
| 1.1.7 | Tiberius celebrates his triumph over Germania |

## 6 BC–AD 5

| | |
|---|---|
| 6 | Tiberius is granted tribunician power |
| 6 BC–AD 4 | Tiberius withdraws from politics |
| 4 BC– AD 1 | L. Domitius Ahenobarbus commands the Rhine army |
| 1 BC | C. Caesar goes on a special mission to the east |
| 5.2.2 BC | Augustus receives the title of *pater patriae* from the Senate |
| 12.5.2 BC | Dedication of the temple of Mars Ultor |
| 2 BC | Fufian-Caninian law on the limitation of numbers of freedmen |
| 2 BC | Banishment of Augustus' daughter Julia; Tiberius divorces her |
| AD 1–4 | M. Vinicius commands the Rhine army |
| AD 1 | C. Caesar is consul. Discussions between him and King Phraates IV of Parthia on the Euphrates |
| AD 2, Aug. | Death of L. Caesar |
| AD 4, Feb. | Death of C. Caesar in Limyra |
| AD 4 | Aelian-Sentian law on the limitation of numbers of freedmen |
| AD 4 and 6–7 | C. Sentius Saturninus commands the Rhine army |
| 26.6. AD 4 | Tiberius and Agrippa Postumus adopted by Augustus |
| AD 4 | Tribunician power granted to Tiberius for ten years |
| AD 4–5 | Tiberius commands the Rhine army |
| AD 5 | Cornelian – Valerian law on the committees to decide on consuls and praetors |

## AD 6–14

| | |
|---|---|
| 6 (?) | Dedication of an Ubian altar |
| 6 | Tiberius breaks off his campaign against Marbod when the Pannonian revolt breaks out |
| 6–9 | Pannonian revolt suppressed by Tiberius |
| 7–9 | P. Quinctilius Varus commands the Rhine army |
| 7 | Banishment of Agrippa Postumus |
| 8 | Banishment of Augustus' granddaughter Julia |
| 8 | Banishment of Ovid to Tomis |
| 9 | Papian-Poppaean law on marriage |
| 9 | The army of Varus annihilated in Germania (battle of the Teutoburger Forest) |
| 10–12 | Tiberius commands the Rhine army |
| 12 | Germanicus becomes consul |
| 23.10.12 | Triumph of Tiberius over the Pannonians |
| 13 | Germanicus commands the Rhine army. |
| 13 | Prolongation of Augustus' basic military power and Tiberius' tribunician power, and granting of military power to the latter on equal terms with Augustus |
| 19.8.14 | Death of Augustus in Nola |
| 14, early Sept. | Funeral of Augustus |
| 17.9.14 | Elevation of Augustus to divine status |

# Family and Descendants of C. Julius Caesar

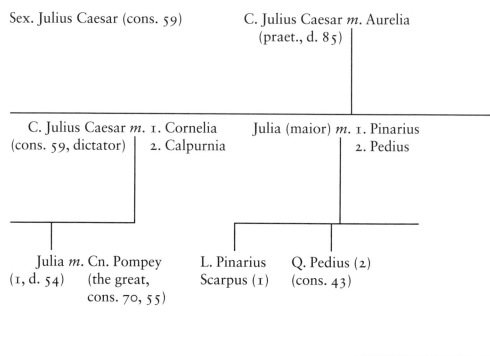

Sex. Julius Caesar (cons. 59)

C. Julius Caesar *m.* Aurelia
(praet., d. 85)

C. Julius Caesar *m.* 1. Cornelia
(cons. 59, dictator) 2. Calpurnia

Julia (maior) *m.* 1. Pinarius
2. Pedius

Julia *m.* Cn. Pompey
(1, d. 54) (the great,
cons. 70, 55)

L. Pinarius
Scarpus (1)

Q. Pedius (2)
(cons. 43)

Octavia (maior)
(daughter of first marriage of
C. Octavius, praet. 61, to
Ancharia)

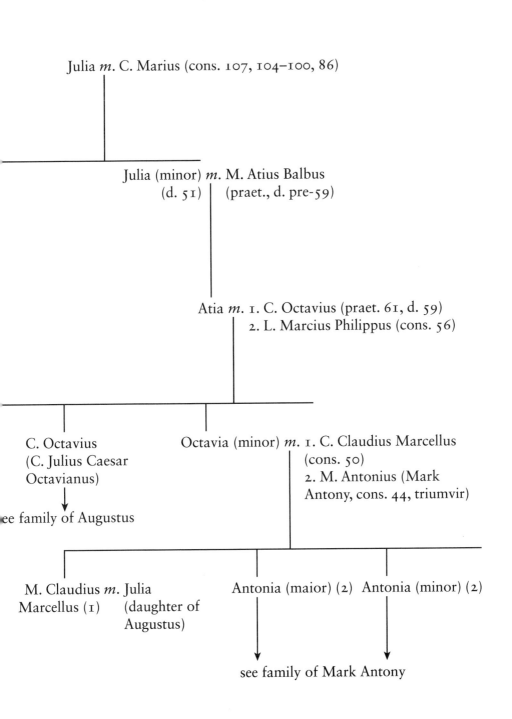

Julia *m.* C. Marius (cons. 107, 104–100, 86)

Julia (minor) *m.* M. Atius Balbus
(d. 51) (praet., d. pre-59)

Atia *m.* 1. C. Octavius (praet. 61, d. 59)
2. L. Marcius Philippus (cons. 56)

C. Octavius
(C. Julius Caesar
Octavianus)

see family of Augustus

Octavia (minor) *m.* 1. C. Claudius Marcellus
(cons. 50)
2. M. Antonius (Mark
Antony, cons. 44, triumvir)

M. Claudius *m.* Julia
Marcellus (1) (daughter of
Augustus)

Antonia (maior) (2)   Antonia (minor) (2)

see family of Mark Antony

# Family and Descendants of Augustus

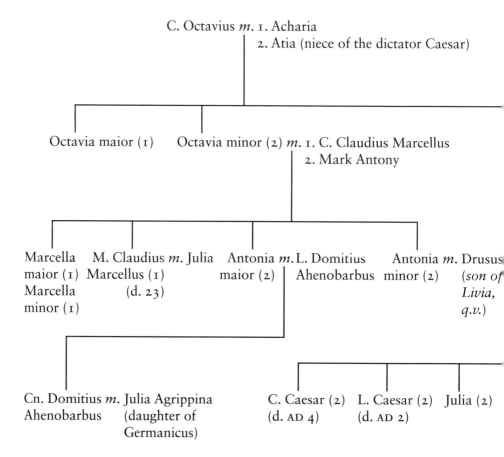

C. Octavius *m.* 1. Acharia
2. Atia (niece of the dictator Caesar)

Octavia maior (1)    Octavia minor (2) *m.* 1. C. Claudius Marcellus
2. Mark Antony

Marcella    M. Claudius *m.* Julia    Antonia *m.* L. Domitius    Antonia *m.* Drusus
maior (1)  Marcellus (1)    maior (2)   Ahenobarbus minor (2)   (*son of*
Marcella    (d. 23)    *Livia*,
minor (1)    *q.v.*)

Cn. Domitius *m.* Julia Agrippina    C. Caesar (2)   L. Caesar (2)   Julia (2)
Ahenobarbus    (daughter of    (d. AD 4)   (d. AD 2)
Germanicus)

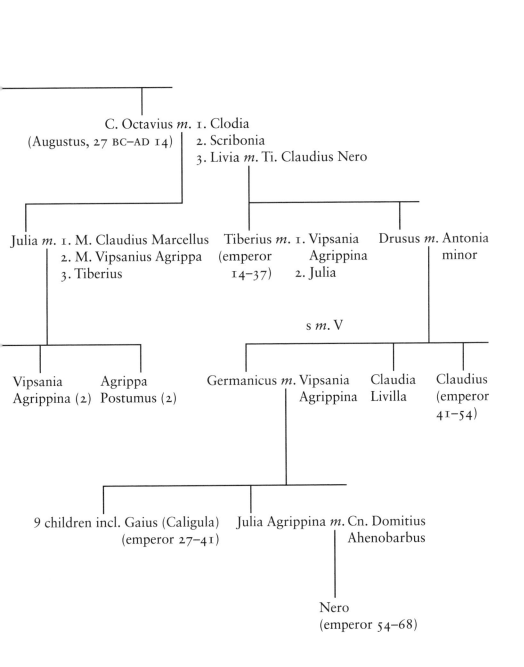

C. Octavius *m.* 1. Clodia
(Augustus, 27 BC–AD 14)    2. Scribonia
                          3. Livia *m.* Ti. Claudius Nero

Julia *m.* 1. M. Claudius Marcellus    Tiberius *m.* 1. Vipsania    Drusus *m.* Antonia
          2. M. Vipsanius Agrippa      (emperor      Agrippina                minor
          3. Tiberius                   14–37)       2. Julia

                                            s *m.* V

Vipsania      Agrippa        Germanicus *m.* Vipsania    Claudia    Claudius
Agrippina (2) Postumus (2)                  Agrippina    Livilla    (emperor
                                                                    41–54)

9 children incl. Gaius (Caligula)    Julia Agrippina *m.* Cn. Domitius
          (emperor 27–41)                                 Ahenobarbus

                                            Nero
                                            (emperor 54–68)

# Family and Descendants of Mark Antony

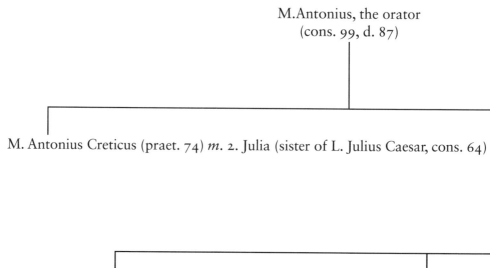

M.Antonius, the orator
(cons. 99, d. 87)

M. Antonius Creticus (praet. 74) *m.* 2. Julia (sister of L. Julius Caesar, cons. 64)

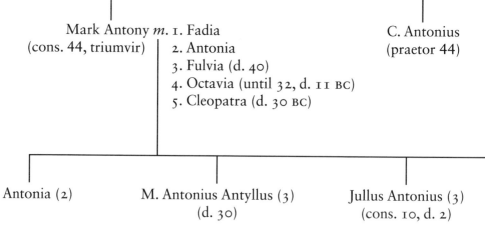

Mark Antony *m.* 1. Fadia
(cons. 44, triumvir)   2. Antonia
3. Fulvia (d. 40)
4. Octavia (until 32, d. 11 BC)
5. Cleopatra (d. 30 BC)

C. Antonius
(praetor 44)

Antonia (2)

M. Antonius Antyllus (3)
(d. 30)

Jullus Antonius (3)
(cons. 10, d. 2)

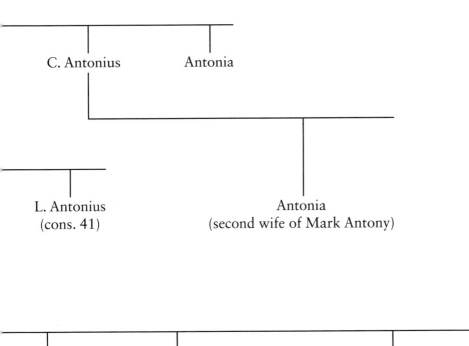

C. Antonius       Antonia

L. Antonius
(cons. 41)

Antonia
(second wife of Mark Antony)

Antonia (maior) (4)   Antonia (minor) (4)      Alexandros Helios (5)
Ptolemaios Philadelphos (5)
Cleopatra Selene (5) *m.* Juba II

see family of Augustus

# Literature on the Augustan Period

(ANRW = Aufstieg und Niedergang der römischen Welt; all other series and journals are abbreviated after first mention; abbreviations of other works in brackets after the title)

## BIBLIOGRAPHIES

*The Cambridge Ancient History* X² , 1996 (= CAH²), 1015–1137 .
Kienast, *Augustus*, 431–52.

## GENERAL LITERATURE ON AUGUSTUS AND HIS TIME

Binder, Gerhard (ed.), *Saeculum Augustum*, I–III, Wege d. Forschg. 266, 512 and 632, 1987–91 (= Binder, *Saeculum Augustum*).
*The Cambridge Ancient History*, IX²: J. A. Crook/A. Lintott/E. Rawson (eds.), *The Last Age of the Roman Republic 146–43 BC*, 1994, and X²: A. K. Bowman/ E. Champlin/A. Lintott (eds.), *The Augustan Empire 43 BC–AD 69*, 1996 (= CAH²).
*The Cambridge Ancient History*, X: S. A. Cook/F. E. Adcock/M. P. Charlesworth (eds.), *The Augustan Empire 44 BC–AD 70*, 1934 (= CAH).
Christ, Karl, *Geschichte der Römischen Kaiserzeit von Augustus bis Konstantin*, 1988, 1995³ (47–177, 'Zeit des Augustus').
Dahlheim, Werner, 'Augustus', in Manfred Clauss (ed.), *Die römischen Kaiser*, 1997, 26–50.
Dessau, Hermann, *Geschichte der römischen Kaiserzeit*, I (up to the first change on the throne), 1924.
Fitzler, Kurt/Seeck, Otto, 'C. Julius Caesar Augustus', in *Paulys Realencyclopädie der classischen Altertumwissenschaft* (RE) X, 1918, 277–381.
Galinsky Karl, *Augustan Culture: An Interpretative Introduction*, 1996 (= Galinsky, *Augustan Culture*).
Gardthausen, Viktor, *Augustus und seine Zeit*, 2 parts in 6 vols., 1891–1904. New edition 1964 (= Gardthausen, *Augustus*).

Halfmann, Helmut, *Itinera principum: Geschichte und Typologie der Kaiser-reisen im römischen Reich*, 1986 (on Augustus: 15–29 and 157–68).

*Kaiser Augustus und die verlorene Republik*, ed. Mathias Hofter (catalogue of the 1988 exhibition in Berlin), 1988 (= exhibition catalogue *Kaiser Augustus*).

Kienast, Dietmar, *Augustus, Prinzeps und Monarch*, 1982, 1992² (= Kienast, *Augustus*).

Kienast, Dietmar, *Römische Kaisertabelle: Grundzüge einer römischen Kaiser-chronologie*, 1990, 1996².

Meier, Christian, 'Augustus. Die Begründung der Monarchie als Wiederherstel-lung der Republik', in idem, *Die Ohnmacht des allmächtigen Dictators Caesar*, 1980, 223–87.

Millar, F./Segal, E. (eds.), *Caesar Augustus. Seven Aspects*, 1984 (= Millar/Segal, *Augustus).*

Raaflaub, K./Toher, M. (eds.), *Between Republic and Empire: Interpretations of Augustus and His Principate*, 1990 (= Raaflaub/Toher).

Rice Holmes, T., *The Architect of the Roman Empire*, 2 vols., 1928–31.

Schmitthenner, Walter (ed.), *Augustus*, Wege d. Forschg. 128, 1969.

Syme, Ronald, *Die römische Revolution*, 1957 and 1992 (with notes and an afterword by Werner Dahlheim); original English edition *The Roman Revolu-tion*, 1939 and 1952³, quotations from the original (= Syme, *Revolution*).

Tarn, William W./Charlesworth, M. P., *Octavian, Antonius und Kleopatra*, 1967 (new edition and translation into German of the first four chapters of vol. X of *The Cambridge Ancient History,* 1934).

Winkes, Rolf (ed.), *The Age of Augustus*, 1985 (= Winkes, *Augustus*).

## SPECIALIZED LITERATURE ON THE LATE REPUBLICAN AND AUGUSTAN PERIODS

Balsdon, J. P. V. D., 'Die Iden des März', in R. Klein (ed.), *Das Staatsdenken der Römer*, 1966, 597–622 (original English version in *Historia* 7, 1958, 80–94).

Bengtson, Hermann, 'Die letzten Monate der römischen Senatsherrschaft', in ANRW I 1, 1972, 967–81.

Bengtson, Hermann, *Marcus Antonius. Triumvir und Herrscher des Orients*, 1977 (= Bengtson, Marcus Antoninus).

Bleicken, Jochen, *Zwischen Republik und Prinzipat: Zum Charakter des Zweiten Triumvirats*, 1990 (= Bleicken, *Prinzipat*).

Bruhns, Hinnerk, *Caesar und die römische Oberschicht in den Jahren 49–44 v. Chr. Untersuchungen zur Herrschaftsetablierung im Bürgerkrieg*, 1978.

Carter, John M., *Die Schlacht bei Aktium: Aufstieg und Triumph des Kaisers Augustus*, 1972 (original English edition 1970).

Dahlheim, Werner, 'Die Iden des März 44 v. Chr.', in A. Demandt (ed.), *Das Attentat in der Geschichte*, 1966, 39–59.

Ehrenwirth, Ursula, *Kritisch-chronologische Untersuchungen für die Zeit vom 1. Juni bis zum 9. Oktober 44 v. Chr.*, 1971 (= Ehrenwirth, *Untersuchungen*).

Frisch, Hartvig, *Cicero's Fight for the Republic: The Historical Background of Cicero's Philippics*, 1946.

Fuhrmann, Manfred, *Cicero und die römische Republik: Eine Biographie*, 1989, 1997[4].

Gelzer, Matthias, 'Marcus Iunius Brutus', in RE X, 1918, 973–1020.

Gelzer, Matthias, *Caesar: Der Politiker und Staatsmann*, 1921, 1960[6].

Gelzer, Matthias, *Cicero: Ein biographischer Versuch*, 1969 (= Gelzer, *Cicero*).

Gesche, Helga, *Caesar*, Erträge der Forschg. 51, 1976 (= Gesche, *Caesar*).

Gotter, Ulrich, *Der Diktator ist tot! Politik in Rom zwischen den Iden des März und der Begründung des Zweiten Triumvirats*, 1996 (= Gotter, *Diktator*).

Gurval, Robert Alan, *Actium and Augustus: The Politics and Emotions of Civil War*, 1995 (= Gurval, *Actium*).

Habicht, Christian, *Cicero der Politiker*, 1990.

Hadas, Moses, *Sextus Pompey*, 1930.

Jehne, Martin, *Der Staat des Dictators Caesar*, 1987 (= Jehne, *Caesar*).

Kraft, Konrad, 'Der goldene Kranz Caesars und der Kampf um die Entlarvung des "Tyrannen"', *Jahrb. für Numismatik und Geldgesch.* 3/4, 1952/3, 7–97; 1969[2] (Libelli 258).

Lacey, W. K., *Cicero and the End of the Roman Republic*, 1978.

Malitz, Jürgen, 'Caesars Partherkrieg', *Historia* 33, 1984, 21–59.

Meier, Christian, *Caesar*, 1982, 1993[3].

Meier, Christian, *Die Ohmacht des allmächtigen Dictators Caesar*, 1978. In an extended version in idem, *Die Ohmacht des allmächtigen Dictators Caesar: Drei biographische Skizzen*, 19–100.

Meyer, Eduard, *Caesars Monarchie und das Principat des Pompejus: Innere Geschichte Roms von 66 bis 44 v. Chr.*, 1918, 1922[3].

Miltner, Franz, 'Sex. Pompeius Magnus', in RE XXI, 1952, 2213–50.

Ortmann, Ursula, 'Cicero, Brutus und Octavian – Republikaner und Caesarianer: Ihr gegenseitiges Verhältnis im Krisenjahr 44/43 v. Chr.', dissertation, Bonn 1987, 1988.

Pelling, Christopher, 'The Triumviral Period', in CAH X[2], 1996, 1–69.

Perkounig, Claudia-Martina, *Livia Drusilla – Iulia Augusta: Das politische Porträt der ersten Kaiserin Roms*, 1995 (= Perkounig, *Livia*).

Roddaz, Jean-Michel, *Marcus Agrippa*, 1984.

Stockton, David, *Cicero: A Political Biography*, 1971 (= Stockton, *Cicero*).

Weigel, Richard D., *Lepidus: The Tarnished Triumvir*, 1992 (= Weigel, *Lepidus*).

Weinstock, Stefan, *Divus Julius*, 1971 (= Weinstock, *Divus Julius*).

Yavetz, Zvi, *Caesar in der öffentlichen Meinung*, 1979.

## MONOGRAPHS

Aigner, Heribert, *Die Soldaten als Machtfaktor in der ausgehenden römischen Republik*, 1974.

Béranger, Jacques, *Recherches sur l'aspect idéologique du Principat*, 1953.

Bleicken, Jochen, *Senatsgericht und Kaisergericht*, 1962 (= Bleicken, *Senatsgericht*).

Botermann, Helga, *Die Soldaten und die römische Politik in der Zeit von Caesars Tod bis zur Begründung des Zweiten Triumvirats*, 1968 (= Botermann, *Soldaten*).

Brunt, Peter A., *Italian Manpower 225 BC–AD 14*, 1971 (= Brunt, *Manpower*).

Campbell, J. B., *The Emperor and the Roman Army 31 BC–AD 235*, 1984 (= Campbell, *Army*).

Coarelli, Filippo, *Il Foro Romano*, II: *Periodo repubblicano e augusteo*, 1985 (= Coarelli, *Foro Romano*).

Coarelli, Filippo, *Rom. Ein archäologischer Führer*, 1975 (translation into German of original Italian edition of 1974) (= Coarelli, *Rom*).

Eck, Werner, *Die staatliche Organisation Italiens in der hohen Kaiserzeit*, 1979 (= Eck, *Italien*).

Eck, Werner, *Die Verwaltung des Römischen Reiches in der Hohen Kaiserzeit. Ausgewählte und erweiterte Beitrage*, I, 1995 (= Eck, *Verwaltung*).

Favro, Diane, *The Urban Image of Augustan Rome*, 1996.

Fishwick, Duncan, *The Imperial Cult in the Latin West*, I–II, 1987–92 (= Fishwick, *Cult*).

Hahn, I., 'Die Legionsorganisation des Zweiten Triumvirats', *Acta Antiqua Academiae Scientiarum Hungaricae* 17, 1969, 199–222 (= Hahn, 'Legionsorganisation').

Hinrichs, Focke Tannen, 'Das legale Landversprechen im bellum civile', *Historia* 18, 1969, 521–44.

Hirschfeld, Otto, *Die kaiserlichen Verwaltungsbeamten bis auf Diocletian*, 1905[2], new edition 1975 (= Hirschfeld, *Verwaltungsbeamte*).

Kaser, Max, *Das römische Privatrecht*, I: *Das altrömische, das vorklassische und klassiche Recht*, 1971[2] (= Kaser, *Privatrecht*).

Keppie, Lawrence, *Colonisation and Veteran Settlement in Italy, 47–14 BC*, 1983 (= Keppie, *Colonisation*).

Keppie, Lawrence, *The Making of the Roman Army: From Republic to Empire*, 1984 (= Keppie, *Army*).

Kolb, Frank, *Rom. Die Geschichte der Stadt in der Antike*, 1995 (= Kolb, *Rom*).

Kromayer, Johannes/Veith, Georg, *Heerwesen und Kriegführung der Griechen und Römer*, 1928, reprinted 1963 (= Kromayer/Veith, *Heerwesen*).

Kromayer, Johannes/Veith, Georg, *Schlachten-Atlas zur antiken Kriegsgeschichte*, 1922 (= Kromayer/Veith, *Schlachten-Atlas*).

Kunkel, Wolfgang, 'Über das Wesen des augusteischen Prinzipats', *Gymnasium* 68, 1961, 353–70 (= W. Schmitthenner, ed., *Augustus*, Wege d. Forschg. 128, 1969, 311–35).

Lacey, W. K., *Augustus and the Principate: The Evolution of the System*, 1996 (= Lacey, *Augustus*).

Latte, Kurt, *Römische Religionsgeschichte*, 1960, 1967² (= Latte, *Religionsgeschichte*).

Le Bohec, Yann, *Die römische Armee von Augustus zu Konstantin d. Gr.*, 1993 (slightly revised translation into German of the original French edition of 1989).

Liebeschuetz, J. H. W. G., *Continuity and Change in Roman Religion*, 1979 ('The Augustan Revival', 55–100).

Lugli, Giuseppe, *Roma antica: Il centro monumentale*, 1946 (= Lugli, *Roma*).

Marquardt, Joachim, *Römische Staatsverwaltung*, 3 vols., 1873–8, 1881–5² (= Marquardt, *Verwaltung*).

Martino, Francesco De, *Storia della costituzione Romana*, IV,1 1974 (= De Martino, *Costituzione Romana*).

Mommsen, Theodor, *Römisches Staatsrecht*, 3 vols., 1887³ (= Mommsen, *Staatsrecht*).

Muth, Robert, 'Vom Wesen römischer "Religio"', in ANRW II 16,1, 1978, 290–354 (= Muth, '"Religio"').

Muth, Robert, *Einführung in die griechische und römische Religion*, 1988, 1998² (= Muth, *Einführung*).

Nash, Ernest, *Bildlexikon zur Topographie des antiken Rom*, 2 vols., 1961–2 (= Nash, *Rom*).

Parker, H. M. D., *The Roman Legions*, 1928, reprinted 1971 (= Parker, *Legions*).

Patterson, John R., 'The City of Rome: From Republic to Empire', *Journ. Rom. Stud.* 82, 1992, 186–215 (= Patterson, 'Rome').

Richardson, L., Jr, *A New Topographical Dictionary of Ancient Rome*, 1992 (= Richardson, *Rome*).

Ritterling, Emil, 'Legio' (Augustan), in RE XII, 1924, 1213–42 (= Ritterling, 'Legio').

Rostovtzeff, Michael, *Gesellschaft und Wirtschaft im römischen Kaiserreich*, 2 vols., 1929 (= Rostovtzeff, *Gesellschaft*). Translation into German of the original English edition of 1926; a second edition appeared in 1957.

Saddington, Denis Bain, *The Development of the Roman Auxiliary Forces from Caesar to Vespasian (49 BC–AD 79)*, 1982 (= Saddington, *Auxiliary Forces*).

Saller, Richard P., *Personal Patronage under the Early Empire*, 1982.

Schneider, Hans-Christian, *Das Problem der Veteranenversorgung in der späteren römischen Republik*, 1977.

Stein, Arthur, *Der römische Ritterstand*, 1927 (= Stein, *Ritterstand*).

Steinby, Eva Margareta (ed.), *Lexicon Topographicum Urbis Romae*, I–III (A–O), 1993–6 (= Steinby, *Roma*).

Syme, Ronald, *Roman Papers*, 7 vols., ed. E. Badian and A. R. Birley, 1979–91 (= Syme, *Papers*).

Syme, Ronald, *The Augustan Aristocracy*, 1986 (collection of essays on individual persons and groups of persons).

Szramkiewicz, R., *Les Gouverneurs de province à l'époque augustéenne. Contribution à l'histoire administrative et sociale du principat*, 2 vols., 1976 (= Szramkiewicz, *Gouverneurs*).

Talbert, Richard J. A., *The Senate of Imperial Rome*, 1984 (= Talbert, *Senate*).

Taylor, Lily Ross, *The Divinity of the Roman Emperor*, 1931 (= Taylor, *Divinity*).

Timpe, Dieter, *Untersuchungen zur Kontinuität des frühen Prinzipats*, 1962 (= Timpe, *Kontinuität*).

Viereck, H. D. L., *Die römische Flotte, Classis Romana*, 1975 (= Viereck, *Flotte*).

Watson, G. R., *The Roman Soldier*, 1969 (= Watson, *Soldier*).

Wickert, Lothar, 'Princeps', in RE XXII, 1954, 1998–2296 (= Wickert, 'Princeps').

Wiseman, Timothy Peter, *New Men in the Roman Senate, 139 BC–AD 14*, 1971 (with a list of all the new senators within the period that he discusses, 209–83) (Wiseman, New Men).

## ON THE PORTRAITS OF AUGUSTUS AND HIS SELF-PRESENTATION

Boschung, Dietrich, 'Die Bildnisse des Augustus', in *Das römische Herrscherbild*, I, 2, 1993.

Fittschen, Klaus, 'Die Bildnisse des Augustus', in Binder, *Saeculum Augustum*, III, 146–86.

Simon, Erika, *Augustus. Kunst und Leben in Rom um die Zeitenwende*, 1986.

Trillmich, Walter, 'Münzpropaganda', in exhibition catalogue *Kaiser Augustus*, 474–528.

Vierneisel, Klaus/Zanker, Paul, 'Die Bildnisse des Augustus', in catalogue to the Munich exhibition, 1979.

Winkler, Lorenz, *Salus: Vom Staatskult zur politischen Idee. Eine archäologische Untersuchung*, 1995 (11–45 on the republic and Augustus).

Zanker, Paul, 'Studien zu den Augustus-Porträts, I. Der Actium-Typus', *Abhandlg. d. Göttinger Akad. d. Wiss.*, phil.-histor. Kl. 3, no. 85, 1973.

Zanker, Paul, *Augustus und die Macht der Bilder*, 1987, 1997³ (= Zanker, *Augustus*).

## ON HISTORIOGRAPHY AND AUGUSTAN POETRY

Binder, Gerhard, '"Augusteische Erneuerung": Kritische Anmerkungen zu einem Schlagwort der Klassischen Altertumswissenschaft im 20. Jahrhundert', in

C. Neumeister (ed.), *Antike Texte in Forschung and Schule. Festschrift Für Willibald Heilmann zum 65. Geburtstag*, 1993, 279–99.

Hose, Martin, *Erneuerung der Vergangenheit: Die Historiker im Imperium Romanum von Florus bis Cassius Dio*, 1994 (esp. Appian and Cassius Dio) (Hose, *Erneuerung*).

Kenney, E. J./Clausen, W. V. (eds.), *The Cambridge History of Classical Literature*, II: *Latin Literature*, 1982; 297–494, 'The Age of Augustus'.

Powell, A. (ed.), *Roman Poetry and Propaganda in the Age of Augustus*, 1992.

White, Peter, *Promised Verse: Poets in the Society of Augustan Rome*, 1993.

Woodman, Tony/West, David (eds.), *Poetry and Politics in the Age of Augustus*, 1984.

## ON INDIVIDUAL WRITERS (COMMENTARIES, TRANSLATIONS, MONOGRAPHS)

## Cicero

*Cicero's Letters to Atticus, Epistulae ad familiares, Epistulae ad Quintum fratrem et M. Brutum*, Latin and English, ed., translated and with a commentary by D. R. Shackleton Bailey, 10 vols, 1965–80.

*Briefe an seine Freunde – Atticus Briefe – Briefe an Bruder Quintus, an Brutus, Brieffragmente und die Denkschrift über die Bewerbung*, 3 vols., Latin and German, ed. H. Kasten, 1990[4] (Sammlung Tusculum).

The Philippics, introduced, translated into German and with notes by Manfred Fuhrmann in, *Cicero, Sämtliche Reden*, vol. VII, 1982.

## Augustus

Heuss, Alfred, 'Zeitgeschichte als Ideologie: Bemerkungen zu Komposition und Gedankenführung des Res Gestae Divi Augusti', in E. Lefèvre (ed.), *Monumentum Chiloniense. Kieler Festschrift für Erich Burck zum 70. Geburtstag*, 1975, 55–95 (= idem, *Ges. Schriften*, II, 1995, 1319–59).

Ramage, Edwin S., *The Nature and Purpose of Augustus' 'Res Gestae'*, 1987 (= Ramage, *Res Gestae*).

*Res Gestae Divi Augusti*, Latin and English, introduced and with a commentary by Peter A. Brunt/J. M. Moore, 1967, 1979[2].

*Res Gestae Divi Augusti*, Latin, Greek and German, with notes, ed. Ekkehard Weber, 1970, 1989[5] (Sammlung Tusculum).

Simon, Barbara, *Die Selbstdarstellung des Augustus in der Münzprägung und in den Res Gestae*, 1993 (= Simon, *Selbstdarstellung*).

# Nicolaus of Damascus

Hall, Clayton Morris, *Nicolaus of Damascus' Life of Augustus*, 1923.
*Life of Augustus* (up to October 44), FgrHistFt.130 JAC.
*Nicolaus of Damascus: Life of Augustus*, Greek and English, with commentary, ed. Jane Bellemore, 1984.
Scardigli, Barbara, *Nicolao di Damasco: Vita di Augusto* (introduction, translation into Italian and historical commentary), 1983.
Toher, Mark, *The 'Bios Kaisaros' of Nicolaus of Damascus: An Historiographical Analysis*, 1985.
Wacholder, Ben Zion, *Nicolaus of Damascus*, 1962.

# Asinius Pollio

Bosworth, A. B., 'Asinius Pollio and Augustus', *Historia* 21, 1972, 441–73.
Haller, Bertram, C. *Asinius Pollio als Politiker und zeitkritischer Historiker*, 1967.

# Livy (59 BC–AD 17)

*Ab urbe condita*, Latin and German, 11 vols. (Artemis), 1st–44th editions 1988/97.
Burck, Erich (ed.), *Wege zu Livius*, Wege d. Forschg. 132, 1967 (collection of essays).
*Commentary* I,1–5 (1965, R. M. Ogilvie), 6–10 (1997, S. P. Oakley), 31–3, 34–7 (1973, 1981, J. Briscoe).
Haehling, Raban von, *Zeitbezüge des T. Livius in der ersten Dekade seines Geschichtswerkes: nec vitia nostra nec remedia pati possumus*, 1989.
Lefèvre, E./Olshausen, E. (eds.), *Livius: Werk und Rezeption. Festschr. für Erich Burck zum 80. Geburtstag*, 1983 (collection of essays).

# Virgil (70–19 BC)

*Aeneis*, Latin and German, ed. M. and J. Götte, 1994[8] (Sammlung Tusculum).
*Eclogues*, commentary by Wendell Clausen, 1994.
*Georgics*, commentary by R. A. B. Mynors, 1990.
Glei, Reinhold F., *Der Vater der Dinge: Interpretationen zur politischen, literarischen und kulturellen Dimension des Krieges bei Vergil*, 1991.
Grimal, Pierre, *Vergil: Biographie*, 1987 (original French edition 1985).

Hardie, Philip R., *Virgil's Aeneid: Cosmos and Imperium*, 1986.

Klingner, Friedrich, *Virgil: Bucolica, Georgica, Aeneis*, 1967.

*Landleben (Catalepton, Bucolica, Georgica, Vergil-Viten)*, Latin and German, ed. M. and J. Götte and K. Bayer, 1995[6] (Sammlung Tusculum).

Pöschl, Viktor, 'Virgil und Augustus', in ANRW II, 31,2, 1981, 709–27.

Rieks, Rudolf, 'Vergils Dichtung als Zeugnis und Deutung der römischen Geschichte', in ANRW II, 31,2, 1981, 728–868 (an important survey of the state of research).

Stahl, Hans-Peter, *Vergil's Aeneid: Augustan Epic and Political Context*, 1998.

Strasburger, Hermann, 'Vergil und Augustus', *Gymnasium* 90, 1983, 41–76.

Suerbaum, Werner, *Hundert Jahre Vergil-Forschung: Eine systematische Arbeits-bibliographie mit besonderer Berücksichtigung der Aeneis*, in ANRW II 31,1, 1980, 3–358.

*The Aeneid of Virgil*, ed., introduction and commentary by R. D. Williams, 1972ff.

## Horace (65–8 BC)

Becker, Carl, *Das Spätwerk des Horaz*, 1963.

Doblhofer, Ernst, *Horaz in der Forschg. nach 1957*, Erträge d. Forschung 279, 1992.

Fraenkel, Eduard, *Horaz*, 1963 (original English edition 1957).

Lefèvre, Eckard, *Horaz: Dichter im augusteischen Rom*, 1993 (= Lefèvre, *Horaz*).

*Oden und Epoden*, commentary by A. Kiessling/R. Heinze, 1960[10].

*Sämtliche Werke*, Latin and German, ed. H. Färber and W. Schöne, 1993[11] (Sammlung Tusculum).

## Propertius

*Gedichte*, Latin and German, with commentary by R. Helm, 1978[2].

Glücklich, Hans-Joachim, 'Zeitkritik bei Properz', *Altspr. Unterr.* 20/4, 1977, 45–62.

Michael von Albrecht, 'Properz als augusteischer Dichter', *Wiener Studien* n.s. 16, 1982, 220–36.

Newman, J. K., *Augustan Propertius: The Recapitulation of a Genre*, 1997.

*Properz und Tibull, Liebeselegien*, Latin and German, ed. G. Luck, 1996 (Sammlung Tusculum).

Stahl, Hans-Peter, *Propertius: 'Love' and 'War'. Individual and State under Augustus*, 1985.

# Ovid

Barchiesi, Alessandro, *Il poeta e il principe. Ovidio e il discorso augusteo*, 1994 (English translation 1997).
Döpp, Siegmar, *Werke Ovids*, 1992.
*Die Fasten*, ed., translation and commentary by Franz Bömer, 2 vols., 1957–8.
Fränkel, Hermann, *Ovid*, 1970.
Herbert-Brown, Geraldine, *Ovid and the Fasti: An Historical Study*, 1994.
M.v. Albrecht/E. Zinn (eds.), *Ovid*, Wege d. Forschg. 92, 1968 (collection of essays).
*Metamorphosen*, commentary by Franz Bömer, 6 vols., 1969–86.
*Metamorphosen*, Latin and German, ed. E. Rösch, new edn N. Holzberg, 1996[14] (Sammlung Tusculum).
*Metamorphosen*, text and commentary by Moritz Haupt and Otto Kern, addenda by Michael von Albrecht, 1969–70 (Weidmann).
Schmitzer, Ulrich, *Zeitgeschichte in Ovids Metamorphosen: Mythologische Dichtung unter politischen Anspruch*, 1990.
Syme, Ronald, *History in Ovid*, 1978.

# Velleius Paterculus

*Roman History*, Latin and English, trans. and ed. Frederick R. Shipley, reprinted 1992.
*Römische Geschichte*, Latin and German, ed. M. Giebel, 1989.
*The Caesarian and Augustan Narrative* (2.41–93), ed. and commentary by A. J. Woodman, 1983.

# Plutarch (*c.* 46 to post AD 120),

*Grosse Griechen und Römer*, introduced and translated by Konrat Ziegler, 6 vols., 1954–65 (1979ff.).
*Life of Antony*, commentary by C. B. R. Pelling, 1988.
Scardigli, Barbara, *Die Römerbiographien Plutarchs: Ein Forschungsbericht*, 1979.
Ziegler, Konrat, 'Plutarchos', in RE XXI, 1951, 895–962.

# Suetonius (*c.* 70 to post AD 121)

*Cäsarenleben*, translated, ed. and with brief comments by M. Heinemann, 1957.

*Kaiserbiographien*, Latin and German, ed. and with comments by O. Wittstock, 1993.

Suetonius, *Divus Augustus*, introduced and with comments by John M. Carter, 1982.

## Appian (*c.* 95–AD 175)

Gabba, Emilio, *Appiano e la storia delle guerre civili*, 1956.

*Römische Geschichte*, II, on the civil wars, translated by O. Veh, introduced and with comments by K. Brodersen, 1988.

Schwartz, Eduard, 'Appianus', in RE II, 1896, 216–37 (= idem, *Griechische Geschichtsschreiber*, 1957, 361–93).

## Cassius Dio (*c.* 150–AD 235)

Gowing, Alain M., *The Triumviral Narratives of Appian and Cassius Dio*, 1992.

Reinhold, Meyer, *From Republic to Principate: An Historical Commentary on Cassius Dio's Roman History, Books 49–52 (56–29 BC)*, 1988.

Reinhold, M./Swan, P. M, 'Cassius Dio's Assessment of Augustus', in Raaflaub/Toher, 155–73.

J. W. Rich, *Cassius Dio: The Augustan Settlement* (Roman history 53–55.9, English translation and commentary), 1994.

*Römische Geschichte*, introduced by Gerhard Wirth, trans. by Otto Veh, 5 vols., 1985–6.

### COLLECTIONS OF TEXTS, COINS AND CARVED STONES

Crawford, Michael H., *Roman Republican Coinage*, 2 vols., 1974, 1995[6] (= Crawford).

Dessau, Hermann, *Inscriptiones Latinae selectae*, 3 vols., 1892–1916 (collection of inscriptions). New edition 1954 (= Dessau ILS no.).

Ehrenberg, V./Jones, A. H. M., *Documents Illustrating the Reigns of Augustus and Tiberius*, 1955[2], new edition (with addenda) 1979.

Grueber, H. A., *Coins of the Roman Republic in the British Museum*, 3 vols., 1923 (= BMCRR).

Mannsperger, Dietrich, 'Die Münzprägung des Augustus', in Binder, *Saeculum Augustum*, III, 348–99.

Mattingly, H./Carson, R. A. G., *Coins of the Roman Empire in the British Museum*, 6 vols., 1923 (= BMCRE).

Megow, Wolf-Rüdiger, *Kameen von Augustus bis Alexander Severus*, 1987 (= Megow, *Kameen*).

Reinhold, M., *The Golden Age of Augustus*, 1978 (collection of sources).

Sutherland, C. H. V./Kraay, C. M., *Catalogue of Coins of the Roman Empire in the Ashmolean Museum*, I, Augustus (*c.* 31 BC–AD 14), 1975 (= CREAM).

Sutherland, C. H. V., *Coinage in Roman Imperial Policy, 31 BC–AD 68*, 1951.

Sutherland, C. H. V., *The Roman Imperial Coinage*, I, 1984² (= RIC²).

Sydenham, Edward A., *The Coinage of the Roman Republic*, 1952 (= Sydenham).

Vollenweider, Marie-Luise, *Die Steinschneidekunst und ihre Künstler in spätrepublikanischer und augusteischer Zeit*, 1966 (= Vollenweider, *Steinschneidekunst*).

# Acknowledgements

When I began work on this book in 1995, I knew that I would be relying on the help of many people, and not only in getting hold of books and looking through the typescript. More important was the advice and, above all, the criticism of several of my students, something that is indispensable for all research, and I was able to draw on it over several years. These men and women followed the progress of the book and, most importantly of all, had a beneficial effect on it, for their criticism was not just of mistakes but touched upon the reconstruction and interpretation of the subject itself. I took great delight in the many stimulating ideas that were put to me, not just because of their diversity and originality, but also because of the way in which they were made; consequently, looking back, my work on this book feels not the slightest bit onerous. I remember with pleasure our many conversations and discussions.

Of the many people to whom I owe thanks, I would like to mention first and foremost Drs Markus Sehlmeyer and Frank Goldmann, the latter studying for his doctoral degree when I was working on this book, both of whom always gave me untiring support. I owe hardly less to Dr Loretana de Libero and Frau Iris Mäckel, as well as Christian Bauerdorf, Mehran Nickbaht and Kai Oltshausen. Without them, I doubt whether I would have brought this work to what I hope is a happy conclusion. Drs Marianne Bergmann and Christof Boehringer gave me advice and help in putting the illustrations together.

Not least, I would like to thank the publisher and his colleagues. Alexander Fest encouraged me to write this biography, contributed ideas in the early phase of its writing and in particular supported it in its final phase with advice and criticism which were very much to its advantage.

Jochen Bleicken, Göttingen, September 1998

# Index